Hidden Southern California

The Adventurer's Guide

Third Edition

"A complete guidebook!"
—*San Diego Tribune*

"A sure-fire clue to a good travel book is if it includes the word 'hidden' in the title and is written by Ray Riegert."
—*Toronto Sun*

"Riegert has a seemingly inexhaustible amount of enthusiasm for set and setting, he is able in a few words to draw pictures of the spirit of a place."
—*The Book Reader*

"A fast-paced, extraordinarily comprehensive, highly readable guidebook to Southern California."
—*Books of the Southwest*

"This exceptionally complete guide discusses in magnificent, alluring detail many points of interest. The chapters make you feel you are in the area as you read, romantically bringing to life the feeling and scenery of Southern California. This book is superb and is recommended for the seasoned or neophyte traveler to the area."
—*St. Louis Post-Dispatch*

Hidden Southern California

The Adventurer's Guide

Third Edition

Ray Riegert

Illustrator Timothy Carroll

Ulysses Press
Berkeley, California

Published by: Ulysses Press
3286 Adeline Street, Suite 1
Berkeley, CA 94703

Library of Congress Catalog Card Number 92-80235
ISBN 0-915233-56-8

Printed in the U.S.A. by the George Banta Company

10 9 8 7 6 5 4

Production Director: Leslie Henriques
Managing Editor: Claire Chun
Editorial Director: Roger Rapoport

Cover Designers: Bonnie Smetts and Leslie Henriques
Editorial Associates: Wendy Ann Logsdon, Laurie Greenleaf, Mark Whitehouse, Khoa Nguyen
Map Design: Rob Harper, Phil Gardner, Lindsay Mugglestone, Claire Chun
Cover Photography: front cover photo by Steve Vidler/SuperStock back cover photos by Ann Purcell and Galen Rowell
Index: Sayre Van Young

Distributed in the United States by Publishers Group West, in Canada by Raincoast Books and in Great Britian and Europe by World Leisure Marketing

Printed on recycled paper

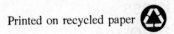

For my mother

Acknowledgments

If publishing a book is comparable to sailing a boat, the vessel I captain is a cross between *The Good Ship Lollipop* and a *Ship of Fools*. Surprisingly, during the two-year voyage, no one mutinied.

My wife and co-publisher Leslie is primarily responsible for keeping the project on course. She worked indefatigably on every phase and shares equally in any credit that may be forthcoming.

Roger Rapoport, displaying a marvelous mix of intelligence and wit, added his talents. Claire Chun also weathered the storms, proving that it's really quite easy to simultaneously research a chapter, type notes, and supervise a production team.

Tim Carroll created a spectacular series of illustrations, to which I can only hope my copy does credit. If not, the cover, designed by Bonnie Smetts and Leslie, will certainly provide a worthy complement. Over in the production department, Phil Gardner served ably as mapmaker.

Wendy Ann Logsdon, Laurie Greeleaf, Mark Whitehouse, and Khoa Nguyen helped with research. Sayre Van Young turned out another in a long line of professionally rendered indexes.

In the original edition Dave Houser ably navigated the San Diego Coast and Jan Butchofsky contributed to the text.

To all of them I want to extend a large, warm, and heartfelt thank you.

Contents

MAPS

SPECIAL FEATURES

Ray Riegert's Best of Southern California

ADVENTURES

Skindiving Santa Catalina *(Santa Catalina, page 163)*
Surfing South Bay *(Pages 183–84)*
Hiking California Coast Trail *(Page 234)*
Sailing the Channel Islands *(Santa Barbara, pages 360–61)*
Horseback Riding in the High Desert *(Page 452)*

BEACHES

Santa Monica State Beach *(Santa Monica, pages 169–70)*
Bolsa Chica State Beach *(Huntington Beach, pages 224–25)*
Crystal Cove State Park *(Corona del Mar, pages 228–29)*
Point Mugu State Park *(Ventura, pages 357–58)*
Point Sal State Beach *(Guadalupe, page 365)*

BED & BREAKFAST INNS

The Venice Beach House *(Venice, page 144)*
The Inn on Mt. Ada *(Avalon, page 148)*
Carriage House *(Laguna Beach, page 210)*
Bed and Breakfast Inn at La Jolla *(La Jolla, page 265)*
Keating House Inn *(San Diego, page 267)*

SOUTHERN CALIFORNIA EXPERIENCES

Touring Paramount Ranch *(Page 105)*
Murals of Venice and Santa Monica *(Pages 156–57)*
Hot Air Ballooning *(Del Mar, page 285)*
Skiing the Southland *(Page 456)*
Exploring Ancient Bristlecone Pine Forest *(White Mountains, page 474)*

COAST AND MOUNTAIN DRIVES

Muholland Drive *(Los Angeles, page 85)*
East End Drive *(Ojai, page 375)*
Scenic Drive *(Santa Barbara, pages 379-81)*
Palms to Pines Tour *(Palm Desert, page 428)*
Artist Drive *(Death Valley, page 481)*

MUSEUMS

PARKS

PLACES TO GO WITH CHILDREN

RESTAURANTS

UNIQUE PLACES

Notes from the Publisher

Throughout the text, hidden locales, remote regions, and little-known spots are marked with a star (★).

* * *

An alert, adventurous reader is as important as a travel writer in keeping a guidebook up-to-date and accurate. So if you happen upon a great restaurant, discover a hidden locale, or (heaven forbid) find an error in the text, we'd appreciate hearing from you. Just write to:

Ulysses Press
3286 Adeline Street, Suite 1
Berkeley, CA 94703

* * *

It is our desire as publishers to create guidebooks that are responsible as well as informative. The danger of exploring hidden locales is that they will no longer be secluded.

We hope that our guidebooks treat the people, country and land we visit with respect. We ask that our readers do the same. The hiker's motto, "Walk softly on the Earth," applies to travelers everywhere . . . in the desert, on the beach, and in town.

CALIFORNIA
DREAMING

CHAPTER ONE

California Dreaming

The Why, When, and How Of Traveling in Southern California

Why

"The lands of the sun," according to an old Spanish proverb, "expand the soul." In the iconography of American life, sunshine is synonymous with Southern California. Life here is lived outdoors. Since the turn of the century the region has been cast as the country's Mediterranean shoreline, picturesque and leisurely.

A land without water resources and lacking natural harbors, it has built its reputation on climate. Warm winters and cool summers, ocean breezes and desert warmth, have created a civilization whose foremost symbol is the palm tree.

Geographically Southern California is a place apart, a domain which historian Carey McWilliams termed "an island on the land." Bounded by the Tehachapis to the north and the Sierra Nevada to the east, it is vast but solitary.

Constituting only half a state, Southern California is broader and more diverse than most nations. Along its western border it nuzzles the Pacific; the interior is a region of piedmont and plain, once given over to cattle ranching and citrus cultivation, but presently being developed into one continuous megalopolis; to the east lies the desert, wind-burnished domain of piñon and palm, Joshua trees and juniper.

Southern California, paradoxically, is a desert facing an ocean. It's a region that has everything—luxurious beaches, dynamic cities, desolate sand dunes, and bald mountains. The highest peak in the contiguous United States rests here just 60 miles from the lowest point.

To capture this diversity in a guidebook, to confine the grandeur of the place within the pages of a single volume, is to square the circle. Los Angeles alone deserves several texts. Here it is covered in two sections—Chapter Two, which extends from Downtown to Hollywood, then out to the San Gabriel and San Fernando valleys; and Chapter Three, which combs the L.A. coastline from Long Beach to Malibu.

Chapter Four is dedicated to Orange County, ranging from the Pacific resorts of Newport Beach and Laguna Beach to theme parks like Disneyland

and Knott's Berry Farm. Then, in a stubborn attempt to find something still "hidden" in this sprawling suburb, it ventures out to the Santa Ana Mountains. San Diego, from city to coast to Mt. Palomar, is the subject of Chapter Five. The Central Coast, Chapter Six, sweeps from Ventura north to Santa Barbara and San Simeon, taking in Ojai and San Luis Obispo along the way.

The California desert is the subject of Chapters Seven and Eight, with the former devoted to the Inland Empire, Palm Springs, and the Sonora desert and the latter covering the central Mojave Desert, Death Valley, and the Sierra Nevada. General information on how, where, when, and why to visit Southern California appears in the chapter you are reading.

Throughout the book I have tried to convey a specific sense of place, providing information on hotels, restaurants, and sightseeing spots, then carrying you several strides further to the beaches, parks, trails, and unknown locales that make adventuring in Southern California high sport. While the region's hidden realms are rapidly falling to the advance of suburbia, the soul of the place prevails.

What remains hidden in Southern California, underlying every aspect of its outward reality, is the mythology of the region. Southern California is a picture in your mind. Envision an orange—plump, round, and spilling over with the promise of good health—and you think of Southern California. Conversely, if you visualize an automobile, L.A.'s smog-shrouded freeways will occur just as naturally. Think of political conservatism—the presidencies of Richard Nixon and Ronald Reagan—and the nation's southwestern corner will flash to the fore. Or conjure a picture of Mexican culture, saturated with romantic imagery, and your daydreams will lead inevitably to the far edge of the Sunbelt.

To tour Southern California is to experience *déjà vu*. Regardless of your place of origin, the area exists, through the medium of film, somewhere in the psyche. More than being inseparable, myth and reality in the Southland feed on one another. Many times during my explorations I felt like I was leading both of us back through our own pasts, to locations not yet real, but already behind us.

The first time I saw Southern California I was 18 years old, hitchhiking down the coast to Mexico. A child of the television age, I had grown up on the East Coast believing that major cities were lined with palm trees, the Wild West began in the Mojave and ended in the Sierra Nevada, and that all oceans resembled the Pacific. To kids like me all across the country, the architecture of Southern California represented the building styles of the world and the people of the Southland portrayed populations everywhere. I was hitchhiking along Memory Lane.

For all of us, Hollywood has elevated Southern California to a metaphor for living. The attributes which initially attracted movie makers to Los Angeles—its Italian climate, diverse geography, and leisurely pace—

are precisely the features that Hollywood projects onto movie screens and television sets around the globe. It is the greatest act of cultural feedback in history. And it continues today.

To provide you with an unclouded picture, I have included historical information and factual details throughout the text. Hopefully you can draw from them substantive ideas for planning and executing a trip. Regardless, you'll find in the end that truth in Southern California is built on a foundation of fiction. The region is living out its own legend. Follow my specific directions to a particular address and you'll discover that the romance rather than the reality of the place sweeps you along. It is the spirit of Southern California that entices and enthralls us all, holding us prisoners in paradise as long as we wish.

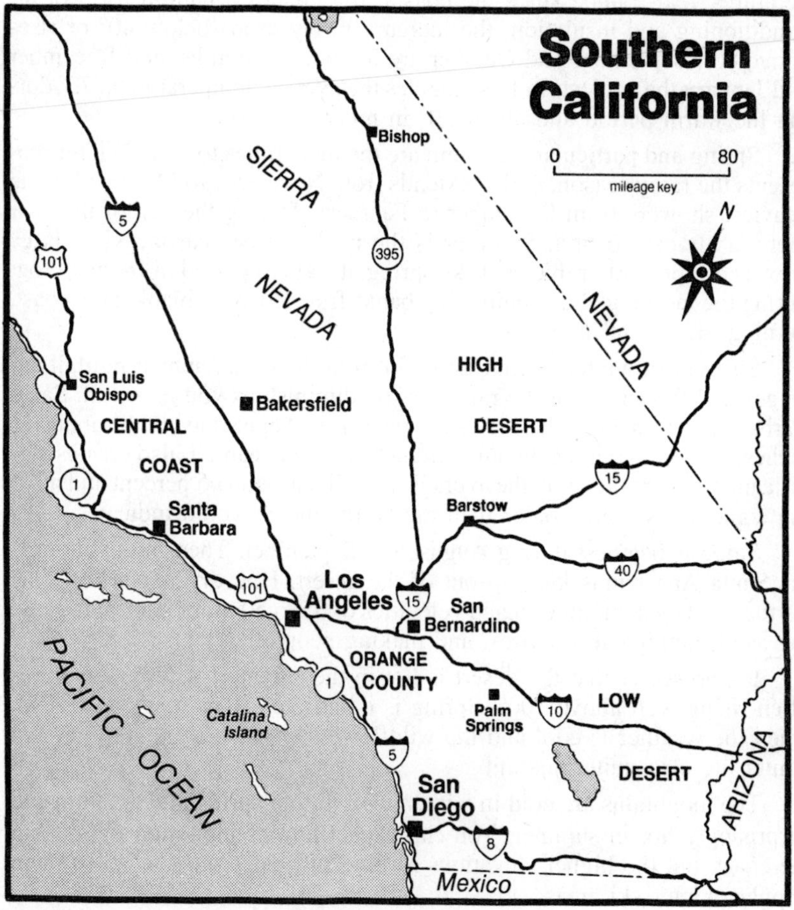

When to Go

SEASONS

Any place the size of Southern California is bound to have several different climates. When it is also a region that ranges from seashore to desert to mountains and climbs from below sea level to over 14,000 feet, the problem is compounded.

In Southern California you can surf and ski in the same day. Temperatures sometimes vary 40° between the beaches and the mountains. In the desert the mercury can fluctuate this drastically in a single location: a balmy 70° day can give way to a 30° night.

Along the Pacific and on the coastal plain, where most visitors concentrate, the weather corresponds to a Mediterranean climate with mild temperatures year-round. Since the coastal fog creates a natural form of air conditioning and insulation, the mercury rarely drops below 40° or rises above 80°. September and October are the hottest months, and December and January the coolest. In Los Angeles the average temperature is 75° during the warm period and about 50° in mid-winter.

Spring and particularly autumn are the ideal times to visit. Winter represents the rainy season, which extends from November to March, with the heaviest showers from December to February. During the rest of the year there is almost no rain. Summer is the peak tourist season, when large crowds can present problems. Like spring, it's also a period of frequent fog; during the morning and evening, fog banks from offshore blanket the coast, burning off around midday.

Since most winter storms sweep in from the north, annual rainfall averages and the length of the rainy season diminish as you go south. Santa Barbara receives 17 inches of rain a year, Los Angeles averages about 15 inches, and San Diego gets only ten inches. The ocean air also creates significant moisture, keeping the average humidity around 65 percent and making some areas seem colder than the thermometer would indicate.

Smog is heaviest during August and September. Then in the autumn, the Santa Ana winds kick up out of the desert. Hot, dry winds from the northeast, they sometimes reach velocities of 35 to 50 miles per hour, blowing sand, fanning forest fires, and making people edgy.

It's no secret that the desert is hot in the summer, with temperatures often rising well above 100°. Spring is a particularly pretty time to visit, when the weather is cool and the wildflowers are in bloom. Autumn and winter are also quite pleasant.

The mountains are cold in winter, cool during spring and autumn, and surprisingly hot in summer. You can expect less precipitation than along the coast, but the higher elevations receive sufficient snow to make them popular winter ski areas.

CALENDAR OF EVENTS

JANUARY

Los Angeles: The **Tournament of Roses Parade** kicks off the **Rose Bowl** game in Pasadena on New Year's Day.

Low Desert: Snow-willing, the **Annual Sled Dog Races**, a cross-country competition in the mountains outside Palm Springs, attracts teams from the United States and Canada. Celebrities and pros gather in Palm Springs for the annual **Bob Hope Desert Chrysler Golf Classic**.

FEBRUARY

Los Angeles: **Chinese New Year** celebrations snake through Chinatown.

Orange County: Arts and crafts displays highlight the **Laguna Beach Winter Festival**.

Low Desert: The **Riverside County National Date Festival** at Indio Fairgrounds features camel races and a diaper derby.

MARCH

Orange County: The **Fiesta de las Golondrinas** commemorates the return of the swallows to Mission San Juan Capistrano. Meanwhile along the coast crowds gather for seasonal **grunion runs**.

San Diego: The **Ocean Beach Kite Festival**, with contests for flying and decorating kites, takes place at Ocean Beach.

Central Coast: Stars and stargazers gather for **Santa Barbara's International Film Festival**.

APRIL

Los Angeles: **Easter Sunrise Services** are marked at the famed Hollywood Bowl. In Little Tokyo **Buddha's Birthday** is celebrated; along nearby Olvera Street the **Blessing of the Animals**, a Mexican tradition, is re-enacted. In Palmdale the Lilac Festival signals the advent of spring.

Los Angeles Coast: Race car buffs train their binoculars on the **Long Beach Grand Prix**.

San Diego: **Lakeside Western Days** features a parade and carnival.

Low Desert: The **Peg Leg Liars Contest**, a tall-tale competition, takes place in Borrego Springs. The **Ramona Pageant** in Hemet depicts Early California history with Indian rituals, music, and dance.

MAY

Los Angeles: Dancers, revelers, and mariachi bands around Olvera Street and East Los Angeles celebrate **Cinco de Mayo**, Mexico's Independence Day. The **UCLA Mardi Gras** offers games, entertainment, and food.

San Diego: In Old Town, mariachis and traditional Mexican folk dancers highlight the **Cinco de Mayo** celebration with Mexican food and displays. The **Wildflower Festival** blossoms in Julian.

Central Coast: The **Ojai Music Festival** includes classical and new music concerts. San Luis Obispo observes **La Fiesta** with a parade, carnival, arts and crafts exhibits, and chili cook-off.

High Desert: A parade, steer roping contest, barbecues, and crafts displays mark **Mule Days** in Bishop.

JUNE

Los Angeles: **Gay Pride Week** is occasioned by a parade through West Hollywood.

San Diego: The **National Shakespeare Festival** starts its summer run at the Old Globe Theater.

Central Coast: A parade and other festivities highlight Santa Barbara's **Summer Solstice Celebration.** Lompoc sponsors an annual **Flower Festival.**

JULY

Los Angeles: The **Hollywood Bowl Summer Festival** explodes with a Fourth of July concert.

Los Angeles Coast: Surfers hang ten at the **International Surf Festival** in Hermosa, Manhattan, Torrance, and Redondo beaches.

Orange County: The **Arts Festival and Pageant of the Masters,** one of Southern California's most notable events, occurs in Laguna Beach.

Central Coast: Santa Barbara is busy with its **Greek Festival.**

Low Desert: Big Bear Lake remembers **Old Miners Day** with week-long festivities featuring burro races, parades, and dances.

AUGUST

Los Angeles: Little Tokyo's **Nisei Week** honors Japanese-American culture with parades, dances, music, and martial arts demonstrations.

San Diego: Crowds sprout up at the Julian **Weed Show** for an artful display of native plants.

Central Coast: Santa Barbara rounds up everyone for the **Old Spanish Days Fiesta, Rodeo, and Stock Show.**

SEPTEMBER

Los Angeles: **Los Angeles County Fair**, the nation's largest county fair, offers music, food, carnival rides, livestock competitions, and just about everything else you can imagine.

San Diego: The **Cabrillo Festival** in Point Loma commemorates the discovery of the California coast by Europeans.

Central Coast: Ojai applauds **Mexican Independence Day** with a grand fiesta. Solvang celebrates **Danish Days** with food, music, and dance.

OCTOBER

San Diego: In the San Diego area, the **La Mesa Oktoberfest** features Bavarian bands, beer gardens, and arts and crafts.

Central Coast: Food, exhibits, and dancing highlight the **Festa Italiana** in Santa Barbara.

Low Desert: An arts and crafts fair, barbecue, and parade mark the Borrego Springs' **Desert Festival**.

High Desert: Parades, parties, and gunfights commemorate **Calico Days** at Calico Ghost Town near Barstow.

NOVEMBER

Los Angeles: Santa arrives early at the **Hollywood Christmas Parade** and is joined by television and movie stars. In Pasadena, the rollicking **Doo Dah Parade** parodies the city's staid Rose Parade.

High Desert: The **Death Valley Annual Encampment** honors desert pioneers with gold panning contests, liars' competitions, and historical programs.

DECEMBER

During December: Several coastal communities, including Marina del Rey, Naples, Huntington Beach, and San Diego, mark the season with **Christmas Boat Parades**. Hispanic communities in Los Angeles, San Luis Obispo, San Diego, and throughout the Southland celebrate the Mexican yuletide with **Las Posadas**.

How to Deal With . . .

VISITOR INFORMATION

Several agencies provide free information to travelers. The **California Office of Tourism** (801 K Street, Sacramento, CA 95814; 916-322-1396) will help guide you to areas throughout the state. The **Los Angeles Visitors and Convention Bureau** (515 South Figueroa Street, 11th floor, Los Angeles, CA 90071; 213-624-7300), the **Anaheim Area Visitor and Convention Bureau** (800 West Katella Avenue, Anaheim, CA 92802; 714-999-8999), the **San Diego Convention and Visitors Bureau** (1200 3rd Avenue, Suite 824, San Diego, CA 92101; 619-232-3101), and the **Palm Springs Desert Resorts Convention and Visitors Bureau** (69-930 Highway 111, Suite 201, Rancho Mirage, CA 92270; 619-770-9000) all have useful information. Also consult local chambers of commerce and information centers, which are mentioned in the various area chapters.

HOTELS

Overnight accommodations in Southern California are as varied as the region itself. They range from highrise hotels and neon motels to hostels and bed and breakfast inns. One guideline to follow with all of them is to reserve well in advance. This is an extremely popular area, particularly in summer, and facilities fill up quickly. Check through the various regional chapters and you're bound to find something to fit your budget and taste.

The neon motels offer bland facilities at low prices and are excellent if you're economizing or don't plan to spend much time in the room. Larger hotels often lack intimacy, but provide such conveniences as restaurants and shops in the lobby. My personal preference is for historic hotels, those slightly faded classics which offer charm and tradition at moderate cost. Bed and breakfast inns present an opportunity to stay in a home-like setting. Like hostels, they are an excellent way to meet fellow travelers; unlike hostels, Southern California's country inns are quite expensive.

To help you decide on a place to stay, I've organized the accommodations not only by area but also according to price. *Budget* hotels generally are less than $50 per night for two people; the rooms are clean and comfortable, but lack luxury. The *moderately* priced hotels run $50 to $90, and provide larger rooms, plusher furniture, and more attractive surroundings. At a *deluxe* hotel you can expect to spend between $90 and $130 double. You'll check into a spacious, well-appointed room with all modern facilities; downstairs the lobby will be a fashionable affair, usually with a restaurant, lounge, and cluster of shops. If you want to spend your time (and money) in the city's very finest hotels, try an *ultra-deluxe* facility, which will include all the amenities and price above $130.

RESTAURANTS

It seems as if Southern California has more restaurants than people, particularly in Los Angeles. To establish a pattern for this parade of dining places, I've organized them according to location and cost.

Within a particular chapter, the restaurants are categorized geographically, with each restaurant entry describing the establishment as budget, moderate, deluxe, or ultra-deluxe in price. Dinner entrées at *budget* restaurants usually cost $8 or less. The ambience is informal café-style and the crowd is often a local one. *Moderately* priced restaurants range between $8 and $16 at dinner and offer pleasant surroundings, a more varied menu, and a slower pace. *Deluxe* establishments tab their entrées above $16, featuring sophisticated cuisines, plush decor, and more personalized service. *Ultra-deluxe* dining rooms, where $24 will only get you started, are gourmet gathering places in which cooking (hopefully) is a fine art form and service is a way of life.

Breakfast and lunch menus vary less in price from restaurant to restaurant. Even deluxe kitchens usually offer light breakfasts and lunch sandwiches, which place them within a few dollars of their budget-minded competitors. These early meals can be a good time to test expensive restaurants.

CAMPING

The state oversees more than 260 camping facilities. Amenities at each campground vary, but there is a standard day-use fee of $5 per vehicle plus $14 per campsite. For a complete listing of all state-run campgrounds, send $2 for the *Guide to California State Parks* to the **California Department of Parks and Recreation** (P.O. Box 942896, Sacramento, CA 94296; 916-653-6995). For campground reservations call 800-444-7275.

For general information on federal campgrounds, contact the **National Park Service** (Western Information Center, Fort Mason, Building 201, San Francisco, CA 94123; 415-556-4122). To reserve campsites call the individual park directly or contact **Ticketmaster** (P.O. Box 617516, Chicago, IL 60661; 800-551-7328).

Reservations for **U.S. Forest Service** (630 Sansome Street, San Francisco, CA 94111; 415-556-0122) campsites must be made through MISTIX (800-283-2267). A fee is charged at these facilities and the length of stay varies from park to park. It's best to reserve in advance, though many parks keep some sites open to be filled daily on a first-come, first-served basis.

Southern California also offers numerous municipal, county, and private facilities. See the "Beaches and Parks" section in each area chapter for the locations of these campgrounds.

WILDERNESS PERMITS

For camping and hiking in the wilderness and primitive areas of national forests, a wilderness permit is required. Permits are free and are issued for a specific period of time, which varies according to the wilderness area. Information is available through the **U.S. Forest Service** (630 Sansome Street, San Francisco, CA 94111; 415-556-0122). You can obtain permits from ranger stations and regional information centers, as described in the "Beaches and Parks" section in each area chapter.

FISHING LICENSES

For current information on the fishing season and state license fees, contact the **Department of Fish and Game** (3211 S Street, Sacramento, CA 95816; 916-739-3380).

TRAVELING WITH CHILDREN

Visiting Southern California with kids can be a real adventure, and if properly planned, a truly enjoyable one. To ensure that your trip will feature the joy, rather than the strain, of parenthood, remember a few important guidelines.

Use a travel agent to help with arrangements; they can reserve spacious bulkhead seats on airlines and determine which flights are least crowded. Also plan to bring everything you need on board—diapers, food, toys, and extra clothes for kids and parents alike. If the trip to Southern California involves a long journey, plan to relax and do very little during the first few days.

Always allow extra time for getting places. Book reservations well in advance and make sure the hotel has the extra crib, cot, or bed you require. It's smart to ask for a room at the end of the hall to cut down on noise. Also, many bed and breakfast inns do not allow children.

Most towns have stores that carry diapers, food, and other essentials; in cities and larger towns, **7-11** stores are sometimes open all night (check the yellow pages for addresses). Hotels often provide access to babysitters, or check the yellow pages for state licensed and bonded babysitting agencies. A first-aid kit is always a good idea. Consult with your pediatrician for special medicines and dosages for colds and diarrhea.

Finding activities to interest children in Southern California couldn't be easier. Especially helpful in deciding on the day's outing is the "Calendar" section of the Sunday *Los Angeles Times*.

BEING AN OLDER TRAVELER

Southern California is an ideal spot for older vacationers. The mild climate makes traveling in the off-season possible, helping to cut down on expenses. Many museums, theaters, restaurants, and hotels offer senior discounts (requiring a driver's license, Medicare card, or other age-identifying card). Be sure to ask your travel agent when booking reservations.

The **American Association of Retired Persons**, or AARP, (3200 East Carson Street, Lakewood, CA 90712; 213-496-2277) offers members travel discounts and provides escorted tours. For those 60 or over, **Elderhostel** (75 Federal Street, Boston, MA 02110; 617-426-7788) provides educational programs in California.

Be extra careful about health matters. Bring along any medications you ordinarily use, together with the prescriptions for obtaining more. Consider carrying a medical record with you—including your medical history and current medical status as well as your doctor's name, phone number, and address. Also be sure to confirm that your insurance covers you away from home.

BEING DISABLED

California stands at the forefront of social reform for the disabled. During the past decade, the state has responded to the needs of the blind, wheelchair-bound, and others with a series of progressive legislative measures.

The **Department of Motor Vehicles** provides special parking permits for the disabled (check the phone book for the nearest location). Many local bus lines and other public transit facilities are wheelchair accessible.

There are also agencies in Southern California assisting disabled persons. For tips and information about the Los Angeles area, contact the **Westside Center for Independent Living** (12901 Venice Boulevard, Los Angeles; 213-390-3611). In the San Diego area, try the **Community Service Center for the Disabled** (1295 University Avenue, San Diego; 619-293-3500).

The **Society for the Advancement of Travel for the Handicapped** (347 5th Avenue, #610, New York, NY 10016; 212-447-7284), **Travel Information Center** (Moss Rehabilitation Hospital, 12th Street and Tabor Road, Philadelphia, PA 19141; 215-329-5715), **Mobility International USA** (P.O. Box 3551, Eugene, OR 97403; 503-343-1284), or **Flying Wheels Travel** (P.O. Box 382, Owatonna, MN 55060; 507-551-7328 offer information. **Travelin' Talk** (P.O. Box 3534, Clarksville, TN 37043; 615-552-6670), a networking organization, also provides assistance.

BEING A WOMAN TRAVELER ALONE

Several Southern California communities offer women's resource centers, referral numbers, and health centers. In the Los Angeles and Orange County area consult the **Women's Yellow Pages** (213-398-5761) or **Family Planning Associates** (213-738-7283). Feminist bookstores are also good sources of information.

BEING A FOREIGN TRAVELER

PASSPORTS AND VISAS Most foreign visitors are required to obtain a passport and tourist visa to enter the United States. Contact your nearest United States Embassy or Consulate well in advance to obtain a visa and to check on any other entry requirements.

CUSTOMS REQUIREMENTS Foreign travelers may carry in the following: 200 cigarettes (or 100 cigars), $400 worth of duty-free gifts, including one liter of alcohol (you must be 21 years of age to bring in the alcohol). You may bring in any amount of currency, but must fill out a form if you bring in over $10,000 (U.S.). Carry any prescription drugs in clearly marked containers. (You may have to produce a written prescription or doctor's statement for the customs officer.) Meat or meat products, seeds, plants, fruits, and narcotics are not allowed to be brought into the United States. Contact the **United States Customs Service** (1301 Constitution Avenue Northwest, Washington, DC 20229; 202-566-8195) for further information.

DRIVING If you plan to rent a car, an international driver's license should be obtained *before* arriving in Southern California. Some rental companies require both a foreign license and an international driver's license. Many car rental agencies require a lessee to be 25 years of age; all require a major credit card.

CURRENCY United States money is based on the dollar. Bills come in six denominations: $1, $5, $10, $20, $50 and $100. Every dollar is divided into 100 cents. Coins are the penny (1 cent), nickel (5 cents), dime (10 cents), quarter (25 cents). Half-dollars and dollar coins are rarely used. You may not use foreign currency to purchase goods and services in the United States. Consider buying traveler's checks in dollar amounts. You may also use credit cards affiliated with an American company such as Interbank, Barclay Card and American Express.

LOS ANGELES

CHAPTER TWO
Los Angeles

Naturally it began as fiction. California, according to the old Spanish novel, was a mythical island populated by Amazons and filled with gold, a place "very near to the terrestrial paradise." The man who set off to pursue this dream was Juan Rodríguez Cabrillo. The year was 1542 and Cabrillo, a Portuguese navigator in the employ of the Spanish crown, sailed north from Mexico, pressing forward the boundaries of empire.

Failing to find either royalty or gilded cities, Cabrillo discovered a land which in the contrary course of its history produced kings of industries not yet invented and cities wealthy beyond the imaginings of even the conquistadors. California, a mythical land indeed, with a cultural capital called Los Angeles.

If California is the land of dreams, L.A. is the dream factory, that worldly workshop where the impossible takes form. Since its founding as a pueblo in 1781, the city has continually recast itself as a promised land, health haven, agricultural paradise, movie capital and world financial center.

Second largest city in the country, it rests in a bowl surrounded by five mountain ranges and an ocean and holds within its ambit sandy beaches, tawny hills, and wind-ruffled deserts. At night from the air Los Angeles is a massive gridwork, an illuminated checkerboard extending from the ink-colored Pacific to the dark fringe of the mountains.

The religious dream of this "city of angels" began way back in 1769 when Padre Junípero Serra and Gaspar de Portolá ventured north from Mexico to establish the first of California's 21 missions. Two years later Mission San Gabriel Archangel was founded several miles from Los Angeles.

The first settlers comprised a mixed bag of Spaniards, Indians, mestizos, and blacks, among them a surprising number of women and children. They planted vines, olives, and grains, and spent 50 years expanding their population to 700.

Today, with a census numbering almost four million urban dwellers and almost nine million throughout Los Angeles County, it remains a multicultural city. In Los Angeles minorities are becoming the majority. Over 80 different languages are spoken in the schools. Neighborhoods are given over to Hispanics, blacks, Chinese, Japanese, Koreans, Jews, Laotians, Filipinos, and Armenians. There are gay communities and nouveau riche neighborhoods, not to mention personality sects such as low riders, Valley girls, punks, and hippies.

One group which never became part of this sun-baked melting pot were the Indians. For Native Americans, Padre Serra's dream of a New World became a nightmare. Before the advent of Westerners, as many as 300,000 indigenous people populated California. Around Los Angeles the Gabrieleños held sway.

Like other groups west of the Sierra Nevada they were hunter-gatherers, exploiting the boundless resources of the ocean, picking wild plants, and stalking local prey. Primitive by comparison with the agricultural tribes of the American Southwest, they fashioned dome-shaped dwellings from woven grasses and wooden poles.

A stone-age civilization, they were clay in the hands of the conquistadors. The Spanish forcibly converted these pagans to Catholicism and pressed them into slavery. Eventually Native Americans built a chain of missions that formed the backbone of the Spanish empire and broke the back of the Indian nation. While their slaves were dying in terrible numbers, the Spanish, dangerously overextended, fell plague to problems throughout the empire. Finally, in 1821 Mexico declared its independence and seized California from Spain.

Then in 1846 American settlers, with assistance from the United States government, fomented the Bear Flag Revolt. That summer Captain John C. Fremont pursued Governor Pío Pico from Los Angeles south to San Juan Capistrano, forcing the Mexican official to flee across the border. Finally in February, 1848, at a home in the San Fernando Valley, a treaty was signed and the Stars and Stripes flew over California.

The Hispanics, who were driven from Los Angeles, now number almost 40 percent of the population and represent the largest concentration of Mexicans outside Mexico. The countryside they departed was a region of ranchos, land grants often measuring 75 square miles, which were used for cattle ranching.

The metropolis they now inhabit will be the world's twelfth largest city by the turn of the century. Once a pastoral realm of caballeros and señoritas, greater metropolitan L.A. now leads the nation in aerospace, boasts the country's largest concentration of high-tech industries and possesses the fastest growing major port in the country. In raw economic terms it is the

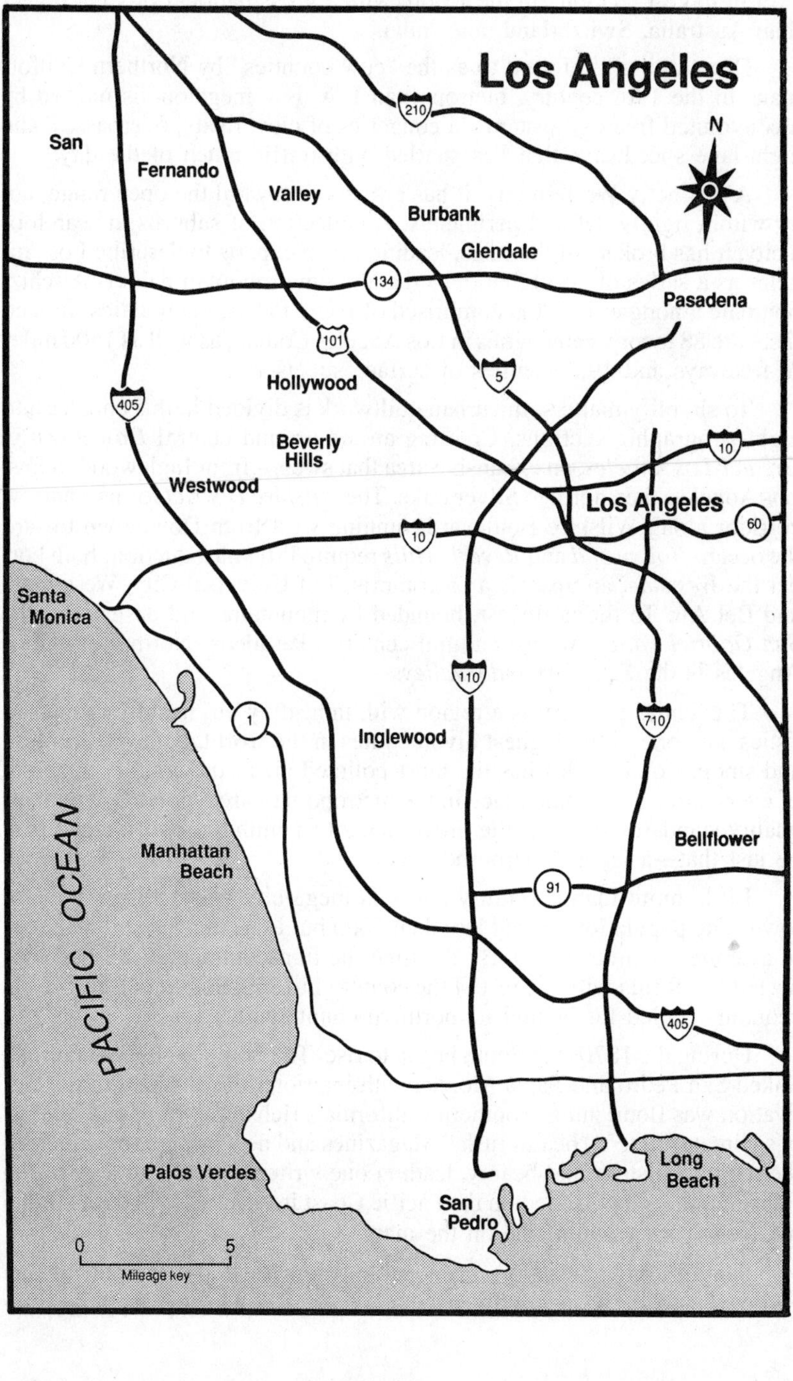
Los Angeles
N
210
San
Fernando
Valley
Burbank
Glendale
134
Pasadena
101
5
Hollywood
405
Beverly
Hills
10
Westwood
Los Angeles
60
10
Santa
Monica
110
1
710
Inglewood
PACIFIC OCEAN
Manhattan
Beach
Bellflower
91
405
Palos Verdes
Long
Beach
San
Pedro
0
5
Mileage key

twelfth largest "nation" in the world, with a gross national product higher than Australia, Switzerland, and India.

Disparagingly referred to as the "cow counties" by Northern Californians in the 19th century, metropolitan L.A. is a megalopolis unified by a convoluted freeway system—a congeries of cloverleafs, overpasses, and eight-lane speedways that lies snarled with traffic much of the day.

A distinctly Western city, it has grown *out* toward the open range, not *up* within tightly defined perimeters. A collection of suburbs in search of a city, it has broken all the rules, leading urban experts to describe Los Angeles as a series of constellations creating a metropolitan galaxy. A schizophrenic among cities, it is comprised of many facets, many cities. In fact, there are 88 incorporated cities in Los Angeles County, as well as 1500 miles of freeways and 19,000 miles of surface streets.

To simplify matters, the urban quiltwork is divided in this chapter into eight geographic sections. Creating an arc around central *Downtown* is *Greater Los Angeles*, an expansive area that sweeps from Inglewood to East Los Angeles, then north to Silver Lake. The *Wilshire District* forms a narrow corridor along Wilshire Boulevard, running west from Downtown toward the ocean. *Hollywood* and *Beverly Hills* require little introduction; both border the *Westside*, an upscale area comprised of Universal City, Westwood, and Bel Air. To the northeast, bounded by mountains and desert, lies the *San Gabriel Valley*, whose cultural center is Pasadena. Northwest of Los Angeles is the *San Fernando Valley*.

This entire territory is a region with unhealthy air, healthy crime statistics, and one of the highest divorce rates in the world. Known for traffic and smog, Los Angeles has the most polluted air in the country. One out of every three days some place in the metropolitan area violates federal air quality standards. In L.A. the proverbial silver lining in every cloud may be just that—a layer of airborne metal.

Little more than a century ago this mega-city was a tough Western town. The population totaled less than 3000 but Los Angeles still managed to average a murder a day. By the time the transcontinental railroad connected California with the rest of the country in 1869, Southern California's economy trailed far behind its northern counterpart.

During the 1870s the South began to rise. The Southern Pacific railroad linked San Pedro and Santa Monica with interior valleys where citrus cultivation was flourishing. Southern California's rich agriculture and salubrious climate led to a "health rush." Magazines and newspapers romanticized the region's history and beauty, leading one writer to proclaim that "if the Pilgrim fathers had landed on the Pacific Coast instead of the Atlantic, little old New York wouldn't be on the map."

Santa Monica became a fashionable resort town and the port of San Pedro expanded exponentially, making Los Angeles a major shipping point.

Around the turn of the century Henry Huntington, nephew of railroad baron Collis P. Huntington, established the Pacific Electric Railway Company and created a series of land booms by extending his red trolley lines in all directions. The city which today has a scandalously deficient transit system then possessed the finest electric trolley network in the world.

When oil was discovered early in the 20th century, Southern California also became a prime drilling region. Oil wells sprang up along Huntington Beach, Long Beach, and San Pedro, adding to coastal coffers while destroying the aesthetics of the shore. The Signal Hill field in Long Beach, tapped by Shell Oil in the 1920s, turned out to be the richest oil deposit in the world and Los Angeles became the largest oil port.

Little wonder that by 1925, flush with petroleum just as the age of the automobile was shifting into gear, Los Angeles became the most motor-conscious city in the world. The Pacific Coast Highway was completed during the 1930s, "auto camps" and "tourist cabins" mushroomed, and motorists began exploring Southern California in unprecedented numbers.

This burgeoning city, with its back to the desert, had already solved its water problems in 1913 when the Los Angeles Aqueduct, bleeding water from the distant Owens Valley, was completed. An engineering marvel, stretching almost 250 miles from the Sierra Nevada, the controversial pipeline supplied enough water to enable Los Angeles to annex the entire San Fernando Valley.

Ironically, the semi-arid Los Angeles Basin was once underwater. Built by volcanic activity, the geologic area is so young that the Palos Verdes Peninsula was a chain of offshore islands just one million years ago. Earthquakes still rattle the region with disturbing frequency. The last colossal quake was back in the 1850s when almost every building in Los Angeles collapsed. As recently as 1971 an earthquake in the San Fernando Valley killed 64 people and caused more than $1 billion damage. A local joke has it that even while awaiting "The Big One," Californians are investing in oceanfront property—in Nevada.

Perhaps with an eye to earthquakes, not to mention Southern California's flaky reputation, architect Frank Lloyd Wright developed a theory of "continental tilt" by which all the loose nuts slid into Hollywood. Its penchant for health, fitness, and glamour have always rendered L.A.'s hold on reality a bit shaky, but it is the city's appeal to religious sects that has particularly added to its aura of unreality.

The first book printed in Los Angeles was a religious tract by a heretical Scotsman. Aimee Semple McPherson preached her Four Square Gospel here in the 1920s and other groups have included everything from the Theosophists and Krishnamurtis to the Mankind United and Mighty I Am movements. Televangelism is now big business throughout the area and Hollywood serves as headquarters for Scientology.

In the end L.A. is a city that one comes to love or scorn. Or perhaps to love *and* scorn. It is either Tinseltown or the Big Orange, Smogville or the City of Angels. To some it is the Rome of the West, a megalopolis whose economic might renders it an imperial power. To others Los Angeles is the American Athens, an international center for cinema, music, and art.

Culturally speaking, the sun rises in the west. L.A., quirky but creative, sets the trends for the entire nation. It has been admired and self-admiring for so long that the city has swallowed its own story, become a reflection of its mythology. Beautifully crazed, pulsing with electric energy, Los Angeles is living its own dream.

Easy Living

Transportation

ARRIVAL

Arriving in Los Angeles by car means entering a maze of freeways. For most Angelenos this is an every day occurrence; they know where they are going and are accustomed to spending a lot of time getting there. It's an intimate affair, a personal relationship between car and driver; they even refer to their freeways by name rather than number.

For the visitor the experience can be very intimidating. The best way to determine a path through this labyrinth is by learning the major highways to and from town.

From the north and west, **Route 101**, the Ventura Freeway, extends from Ventura to Sherman Oaks, then turns southeast to become the Hollywood Freeway.

The Santa Monica Freeway, **Route 10**, cuts through the heart of Los Angeles. It begins in Santa Monica and then becomes the San Bernardino Freeway in downtown Los Angeles.

From Northern California, **Route 5**, the Golden State Freeway, runs south into the center of the city where it changes its name to the Santa Ana Freeway. **Route 405**, better known as the San Diego Freeway, cuts through the San Fernando Valley, the Westside, and then curves east towards Orange County.

BY AIR

Two airports bring visitors to the Los Angeles area: the very big, very busy Los Angeles International Airport and the less crowded Burbank-Glendale-Pasadena Airport. Los Angeles International is convenient if you are headed for the downtown area or out to the coast. Traffic around this major hub is generally ferocious. Those planning to stay around Hollywood and Beverly Hills, in the San Fernando Valley, or out around Pasadena, are better advised to fly in to the Burbank-Glendale-Pasadena Airport.

Los Angeles International Airport, better known as LAX, is served by many domestic and foreign carriers. Currently (and this seems to change daily) the following airlines fly into LAX: Alaska Airlines, American Airlines, America West Airlines, Continental Airlines, Delta Air Lines, Hawaiian Airlines, Northwest Airlines, Southwest Airlines, Trans World Airlines, United Airlines, and USAir.

International carriers are also numerous: All Nippon Airways, Air Canada, Air France, Air New Zealand, British Airways, CAAC, China Airlines, Canadian Airlines International, Japan Airlines, KLM Royal Dutch Airlines, Lufthansa German Airlines, Mexicana Airlines, Philippine Airlines, Qantas Airways, Singapore Airlines, and TACA International Airlines.

Flights to and from **Burbank Airport** are currently provided by Alaska Airlines, Alpha Air, American Airlines, America West Airlines, Delta Air Lines, Skywest Airlines, United Airlines, United Express Airlines, and USAir.

Taxis, limousines, and buses line up to take passengers from LAX and Burbank. **SuperShuttle** (818-244-2700) travels between hotels, businesses, and residences to both Burbank and Los Angeles airports.

NORTH–SOUTH FREEWAYS

405	*San Diego*	
5	*Golden State* *Santa Ana*	*north of Downtown* *south of Downtown*
170	*Hollywood*	
101	*Hollywood*	*south of Hollywood*
210	*Foothill*	
2	*Glendale*	
110	*Pasadena* *Harbor*	*north of Downtown* *south of Downtown*
710	*Long Beach*	
605	*San Gabriel*	
57	*Orange*	

EAST–WEST FREEWAYS

14	*Antelope Valley*	
118	*San Fernando*	
101	*Ventura*	*west of Hollywood*
134	*Ventura*	
210	*Foothill*	
10	*Santa Monica* *San Bernardino*	*west of Downtown* *east of Downtown*
60	*Pomona*	
91	*Redondo Beach* *Artesia* *Riverside*	*west of Route 710* *Rte. 710 to Rte. 5* *east of Route 5*
22	*Garden Grove*	

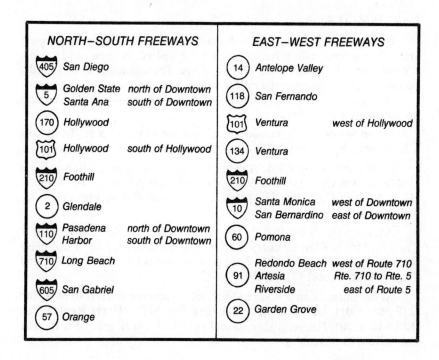

BY BUS

Greyhound/Trailways Bus Lines has service to the Los Angeles area from all around the country. The main Los Angeles terminal is at 1716 East 7th Street (213-629-8400). Other stations are found in Hollywood (1409 Vine Street; 213-466-6381), Pasadena (645 East Walnut Street; 818-792-5116), Glendale (6000 San Fernando Road; 818-244-7295), and North Hollywood (11239 Magnolia Boulevard; 818-761-5119).

Green Tortoise (P.O. Box 24459, San Francisco, CA 94124; 415-821-0803) is an alternative bus company that runs funky (and sometimes unreliable) buses equipped with sleeping platforms. It stops at unusual sightseeing spots and offers an experience in group living. The bus leaves San Francisco for Los Angeles once a week.

BY TRAIN

Amtrak (Union Station, 800 North Alameda Street, Los Angeles; 800-872-7245) will carry you into Los Angeles via the "Coast Starlight" from the Northwest, the "San Diegan" from San Diego, the "Desert Wind" and "Southwest Chief" from Chicago, the "Eagle" from Chicago by way of Texas, and the "Sunset Limited" from New Orleans. There are also stations in Pasadena (222 South Raymond Avenue) and Glendale (400 West Cerritos Avenue).

CAR RENTALS

Having a car in Los Angeles is practically a must. Distances are great and public transportation leaves much to be desired. As you can imagine, it's not difficult to find a car rental agency. The challenge is to find the best deal. Be sure to request a mileage-free rental, or one with at least some free mileage. One thing is certain in the Los Angeles area, you'll be racking up mileage on the odometer.

If you arrive by air, consider renting a car at the airport. These cost a little more but eliminate the hassles of getting to the rental agency.

Looking for a car at Los Angeles International Airport will bring you to **Avis Rent A Car** (310-646-5600), **Budget Rent A Car** (310-645-4500), **Hertz Rent A Car** (310-646-4861), or **National Car Rental** (310-670-4950).

Agencies providing free airport pick-up service include **Avon Rent A Car** (310-568-9990), **Century Car Rental** (310-673-0300), **Enterprise Rent A Car** (310-649-5400), **Snappy Car Rental** (310-937-2172), and **Thrifty Car Rental** (310-645-1880).

At the Burbank airport several companies rent autos: **Avis Rent A Car** (818-566-3001), **Dollar Rent A Car** (818-846-4471), **Hertz Rent A Car** (818-846-8220), **National Car Rental** (818-842-4847), and **USA Rent A Car** (818-840-8816).

Among the used car rentals in the Los Angeles area are **Rent A Wreck** (310-478-0676) and **Ugly Duckling Rent A Car** (310-478-4208).

If there was ever a place to rent a limousine, Los Angeles is it. Dozens of companies specialize in "elegant service for elegant people." Check the Yellow Pages for listings.

PUBLIC TRANSPORTATION

If you arrive in Los Angeles without a car, believe it or not you can still get around. **Southern California Rapid Transit District** (213-626-4455), or RTD, has over 200 bus routes covering more than 2200 square miles. "Rapid" transit may not be quite accurate, but buses do get you where you want to go. Nine customer service centers are located throughout Los Angeles; call for the nearest location.

Before arriving in Los Angeles, write for a free **Rider's Kit** (RTD, Customer Service, 425 South Main Street, Los Angeles 90013). These have information on routes and fares. One brochure, "RTD Self-Guided Tours," covers the traditional sights. When using the bus for an extended period, you can save money by purchasing an RTD Monthly Pass.

For traveling around downtown Los Angeles or Westwood, the **DASH** (213-626-4455) shuttle service is available Monday through Saturday (except holidays). In the Fairfax area, try the **Fairfax Trolley** (213-778-9066).

When going to tourist attractions such as Disneyland, Farmer's Market, Universal Studios, and Magic Mountain, or touring the movie stars' homes, the costlier **Gray Line Tours** (6541 Hollywood Boulevard; 213-856-5900) may be worth the extra fare.

TAXIS

Several cab companies serve Los Angeles International Airport, including **Airport Taxi Service** (310-231-0100), **Celebrity Red Top** (213-934-6700), **L.A. Taxi** (310-412-8000), and **Yellow Cab** (213-627-7000).

From Burbank Airport, **Checker Cab** (818-843-8500), **Red Top Cab** (818-242-3131), and **Universal Cab** (818-845-6712) provide taxi service.

Hotels

Perhaps its fascination for the automobile has resulted in Los Angeles' penchant for motel-style accommodations. Every section of the city contains at least one street that can be called "motel row." Unlike New York and other major cities, L.A. is not a good hotel town. Bed and breakfast inns are practically nonexistent, resort complexes are crowded because of the premium on real estate, and major hotels lie scattered all over the city. Many hotels offer reduced weekend rates or special packages including meals and attractions. Inquire; savings can be considerable.

The hotels below represent the best accommodations available. In terms of cost, they cover the entire economic spectrum, and so far as geography is concerned, they range from the center of town to the far fringes of the Los Angeles Basin.

If central location is your chief criterion, find a place Downtown or in the Wilshire District. Hotels in Hollywood and Beverly Hills are nicely situated in major sightseeing areas. A room on the Westside will place you closer to the ocean. If you choose a San Gabriel Valley or San Fernando Valley locale, plan on lengthy commutes to other parts of town.

DOWNTOWN HOTELS

Hotel Stillwell (838 South Grand Avenue; 213-627-1151), another competitively priced hostelry, offers 232 rooms in a vintage 1920 building. The lobby is decorated with Asian wallhangings, matching the hotel's Indian restaurant. Each guest room has been refurbished with pastel colors, trim carpeting, and modern furniture throughout.

In the moderate price range it's hard to top the **Figueroa Hotel** (939 South Figueroa Street; 213-627-8971). A 1927 Spanish-style building, it offers a beautiful lobby with tile floor and hand-painted ceiling. The palm-fringed courtyard contains a swimming pool, jacuzzi, and lounge. The rooms are very large, adequately furnished, and decorated with wallhangings. Tile baths add a touch of class to this very appealing establishment. Coffee shop and restaurants on the premises.

Chinatown's latest addition to the downtown hotel scene is an 80-room establishment, the **Metro Plaza Hotel** (711 North Main Street; 213-680-0200). Close to Union Station and across the street from the historic Olvera Street complex, this four-story hostelry offers moderate-priced rooms and suites decorated in a blend of contemporary and Oriental styles. Downstairs you'll find a small lobby with two sitting rooms.

Catering largely to an international clientele, the **New Otani Hotel & Garden** (120 South Los Angeles Street; 213-629-1200) is a 440-room extravaganza with restaurants, shops, lounges, spa, and a tranquil half-acre Japanese "garden in the sky." Conveniently located in Little Tokyo, the hotel offers small guest rooms, many decorated in traditional Japanese style with *shoji* screens. The standard accommodations are painted pastel hues and decorated with ultramodern furniture in curvilinear designs. Finest feature of all is the lobby, a vaulted-ceiling affair with a skylight and an eye-catching sculpture. Ultra-deluxe.

What can you say about a place that became a landmark as soon as it was built? To call the **Westin Bonaventure** (404 South Figueroa Street; 213-624-1000) ultramodern would belittle the structure. "Post Future" is a more appropriate tag. Its dark glass silos rise 35 stories from the street like a way station on the road to the 21st century. Within are five levels of shops, 1470 rooms, 20 restaurants, and a revolving cocktail lounge. The

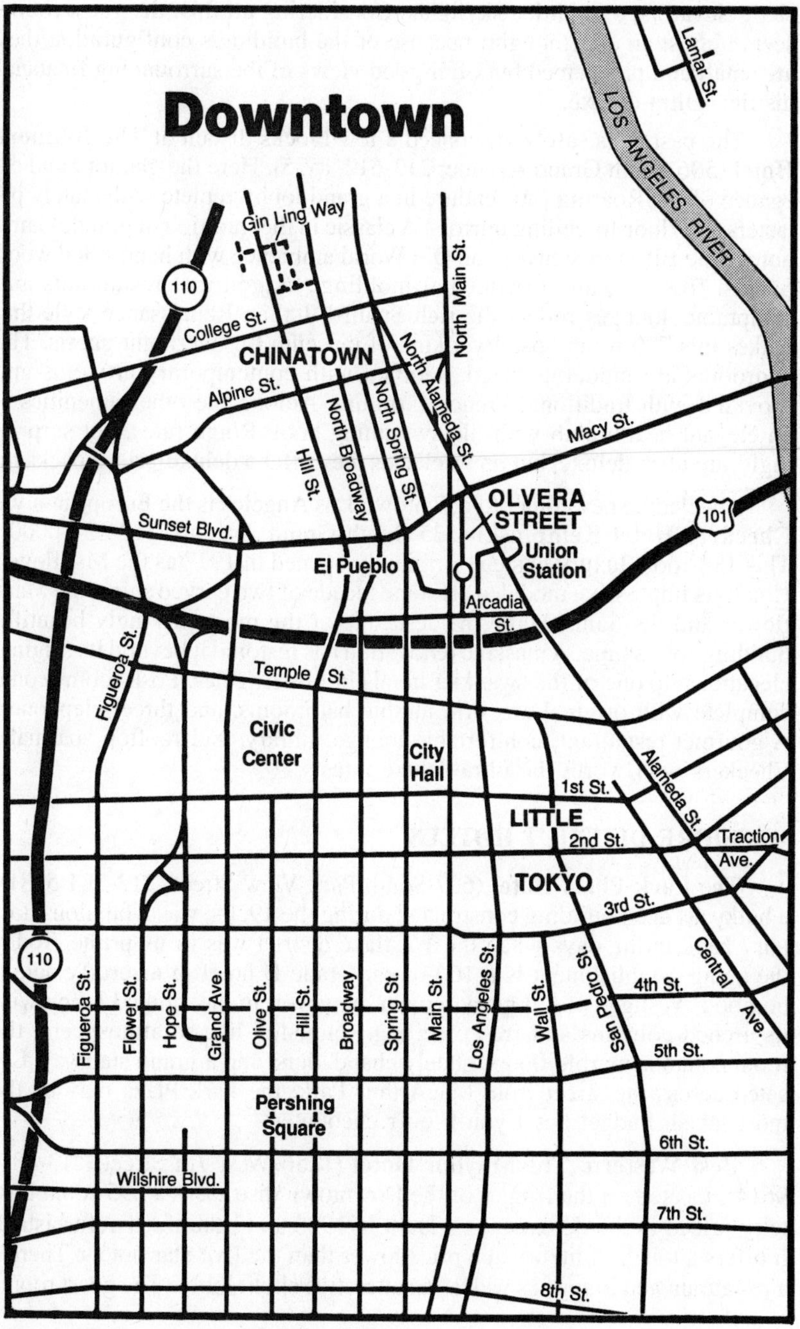
Downtown
Lamar St.
LOS ANGELES RIVER
Gin Ling Way
110
North Main St.
College St.
CHINATOWN
North Alameda St.
Alpine St.
North Spring St.
North Broadway
Hill St.
Macy St.
OLVERA STREET
101
Sunset Blvd.
Union Station
El Pueblo
Arcadia St.
Figueroa St.
Temple St.
Civic Center
City Hall
Alameda St.
1st St.
LITTLE
2nd St.
Traction Ave.
TOKYO
3rd St.
Central Ave.
110
Figueroa St.
Flower St.
Hope St.
Grand Ave.
Olive St.
Hill St.
Broadway
Spring St.
Main St.
Los Angeles St.
Wall St.
San Pedro St.
4th St.
5th St.
Pershing Square
6th St.
Wilshire Blvd.
7th St.
8th St.

atrium lobby furthers the Buck Rogers theme with reflecting pools, glass shaft elevators, and lattice skylights. Considering all this, the guest rooms seem almost an afterthought; because of the building's configuration they are small and pie-shaped but offer good views of the surrounding financial district. Ultra-deluxe.

The past rests safely ensconced a few blocks distant at **The Biltmore Hotel** (506 South Grand Avenue; 213-612-1575). Here the glamour and elegance of the Roaring '20s endure in a grand lobby replete with stately pilasters and floor-to-ceiling mirrors. A classic in the tradition of grande-dame hotels, the Biltmore conveys an Old World ambience with hand-oiled wood panels, frescoes, and ornamental molding. Its gourmet restaurants and sumptuous lounges reflect the rich Spanish-Italian Renaissance style that makes this 700-room hostelry a kind of museum for overnight guests. The bedrooms are moderate-sized, adorned with contemporary artworks and provided with traditional French furniture. Among the other amenities is an elegant health club with tile swimming pool. Room rates, not surprisingly, are ultra-deluxe, but on weekends they offer a deluxe-priced package.

A welcome newcomer to downtown Los Angeles is the European-style **Checkers Hotel Kempinski** (535 South Grand Avenue; 213-624-0000). This 188-room luxury hostelry originally opened in 1927 as the Mayflower Hotel. Its impressive modeled art stone facade of two carved ships, the Mayflower and the Santa Maria, made it one of the most strikingly beautiful buildings of its time. A massive renovation has restored it beyond its original elegance into one of the swankier hotels in Los Angeles. Posh rooms come complete with original artwork, marble bathrooms, and three telephones. A gourmet restaurant, comfortable lounge, library, and rooftop spa make Checkers well worth the ultra-deluxe rates.

WILSHIRE DISTRICT HOTELS

The **Park Plaza Hotel** (607 South Park View Street; 213-384-5281), a bulky art deco building constructed during the 1920s, was a fabulous hostelry back in the days when the Westlake district was in its prime. Today the aging establishment is a 160-room, Grade B hotel in a scruffy neighborhood. Vestiges of old glory remain, however, in the vaulted lobby with its arched columns and fresco ceiling. Cathedral-like in atmosphere, the room contains marble floors, stately chandeliers, and a grand stairway. Located across the street from MacArthur Park, the Park Plaza may be the most lavish budget hotel you'll ever encounter.

Best Western, The Mayfair Hotel (1256 West 7th Street; 213-484-9614), located on the fringes of the Downtown district, is a 295-room hostelry priced in the deluxe range. Built in 1928 and beautifully refurbished, it offers a touch of luxury at a price lower than the five-star hotels. There's a restaurant and lounge as well as an attractive skylit lobby. The guest rooms are average size and feature contemporary furnishings, textured wallpaper, and pastel color schemes.

Another 1920s-era art deco building, the **Wilshire Royale Hotel** (2619 Wilshire Boulevard; 213-387-5311) has been fashionably refurbished and transformed into a contemporary 200-room facility. The lobby is a beamed-ceiling affair with piano, fresh flowers, and upholstered armchairs. Guest rooms, decorated in a peach-colored motif, have tile baths and standard furnishings. Restaurant, lounge, pool, spa; moderate-to-deluxe prices make this historic hotel an excellent choice.

Speaking of antique buildings, the nearby **Sheraton Town House** (2961 Wilshire Boulevard; 213-382-7171) conveys a sense of old-time ease in its 272-room facility. Practically an urban resort, the 1929 complex features a large pool and patio area complete with shade trees, spa, restaurants, lounges, tennis courts, and a restful garden. The rooms upstairs represent some of the largest accommodations in the city. Furnished in hardwood with patterned wallpaper and tile baths, many overlook Lafayette Park. Deluxe.

The **Chancellor Hotel** (3191 West 7th Street; 213-383-1183) is a residence hotel occupied primarily by students and young professionals. This 1924 Romanesque building also accommodates individual travelers, who share the lobby, recreation room, and pool with permanent residents. A five-story complex one block from Wilshire Boulevard, the Chancellor is well maintained. The rates are extraordinary: moderately priced, the room tab includes breakfast and dinner.

If you prefer something more modern, the **Wilshire Towers** (3460 West 7th Street; 213-385-7281) is a contemporary, square-rigged highrise. Also doubling as a residence hotel, it is an all-suite complex. For a moderate-to-deluxe tab you can rent an apartment with bedroom, living room, and kitchen. The establishment is clean and adequately furnished; facilities include a lobby, pool, exercise room, and restaurant.

Wilshire Crest Inn (6301 Orange Street; 213-936-5131) is one of those terribly modern hotels with track lighting, black trim, and fabric wall coverings. The 34 rooms, built around an interior patio, are done in oak and furnished with platform beds. The color scheme, naturally, is pastel. There's a dining room where continental breakfast is served and a sitting area complete with potted plants and trimly upholstered armchairs. Conveniently located near Wilshire Boulevard in the Fairfax district; moderate.

For cut-rate accommodations consider the **Wilshire Orange Hotel** (6060 West 8th Street; 213-931-9533), a funky stucco resting place just off Wilshire Boulevard. Expect plaster walls, spotty carpets, damaged furniture, and some rooms that share baths. But generally the place is clean and neat (some rooms have been repainted and recarpeted); hot plates and refrigerators; budget to moderate.

Salisbury House (2273 West 20th Street; 213-737-7817), one of the city's rare bed and breakfast inns, is a marvelous 1909 Craftsman house with hardwood floors, leaded-glass windows, and dark wood trim. There's a formal dining room as well as a living room with fireplace. The guest quarters include five rooms (two with shared bath), all nicely appointed and furnished with antique pieces. Special attention is given to guests by owners and resident innkeepers Sue and Jay German. The inn is located in the West Adams neighborhood, an historic midtown district. Moderate to deluxe rates include full breakfast.

HOLLYWOOD HOTELS

All those rising stars have to have some place to sleep, so sections of Hollywood have always been low-rent districts. The **Hollywood YMCA** (1553 North Hudson Avenue; 213-467-4161), located off Sunset Boulevard, provides 55 rooms at budget prices. These are clean and share baths. Guests can also use the pools, gymnasium, sauna, and exercise facilities.

The **Hollywood Celebrity Hotel** (1775 North Orchid Avenue; 213-850-6464) occupies a 1930s art deco building just above Hollywood Boulevard. The 40 guest rooms are nicely refurbished, furnished in neo-deco style and decorated in a Hollywood motif. The rooms are quite spacious and include a bottle of wine and continental breakfast. There's a sitting room off the lobby. Moderate to deluxe.

The **Orchid Suites Hotel** (1753 North Orchid Avenue; 213-874-9678) a few doors down is another 40-unit facility. Lacking the character of its neighbor, it substitutes space and amenities for personality. Every room is a suite and includes a kitchenette; there's also a pool. Rooms are fashioned in contemporary style. The building itself is a bland, modern stucco; moderate.

Hollywood Boulevard is one of several strips lined with motels. Representative of the species is the **Hollywood Premiere Motel** (5333 Hollywood Boulevard; 213-466-1691). This L-shaped building contains standard rooms, some with kitchens. Pool; budget.

Astroturf around the pool and time-worn rooms give the **Beverly Sunset Hotel** (8775 Sunset Boulevard; 310-652-0030) the atmosphere of a motel. Obviously, the draw at this 65-unit facility is its location at the heart of Sunset Strip and the price—moderate for a room or suite.

One of Hollywood's best bargains is found at the **Magic Hotel** (7025 Franklin Avenue; 213-851-0800), a 40-unit establishment next to the famed Magic Castle, a private club for magicians. Suites with kitchens are priced moderately, furnished in oak, and decorated (presto!) with magic posters. They are quite spacious and well maintained. Pool and sun deck.

Coral Sands Motel (1730 North Western Avenue; 213-467-5141) is a 58-unit establishment serving the gay community. The guest rooms look out on a central courtyard with pool, jacuzzi, sauna, and exercise area. Each is carpeted wall-to-wall and sentimentally furnished with standard appointments. Continental breakfast; moderate.

It's as much a part of Hollywood as the Academy Awards. In fact, the very first Oscars were presented at the **Hollywood Roosevelt Hotel** (7000 Hollywood Boulevard; 213-466-7000). Built in 1927, the Spanish Revival building has been completely refurbished and now offers 335 rooms, plus restaurants, lounges, and a palm-studded courtyard with pool and sauna. Pricing in the deluxe to ultra-deluxe range, below the city's five-star hotels, this classic caravansary has many features of the finest hostelries. The lobby is a recessed-ceiling affair with colonnades and hand-painted beams. Guest rooms are small but commodiously furnished with plump armchairs and hardwood pieces. Historic and luxurious.

The traditional Hollywood resting place is **Château Marmont** (8221 Sunset Boulevard; 213-656-1010), a Norman-style castle built in 1929. Formerly home to Jean Harlow and Howard Hughes, the hotel still lures Hollywood luminaries such as Robert DeNiro, Dustin Hoffman, and Diane Keaton. They come for the privacy and quirky charm of the place, which offers rooms, suites, and cottages at ultra-deluxe prices. Around its beautifully maintained grounds are flower gardens, shade trees, and a heated swimming pool. More than anything, the Marmont possesses cachet, as if the hotel itself were a celebrity, holding within its cloistered lobby a thousand tales of Hollywood.

L'Ermitage Hotels, a group of several hotels within a ten-block radius, represents one of the most innovative hotel chains in the country. Streamlined and ultra-modern, the hallmark of the Mondrian, Bel Âge, Le Parc, Le Dufy and Le Rêve hotels is the artwork, which hangs seemingly everywhere—in the lobby, public areas, corridors, and guest rooms. You can expect ultra-modern furnishings, creative appointments, and personal service at each address.

The **Mondrian Hotel** (8440 Sunset Boulevard; 213-650-8999) is a stylized tribute to the Dutch painter Piet Mondrian. The exterior of this 12-story highrise has been painted sherbet colors by a contemporary artist, while the interior is filled with works of modern art. Boasting a restaurant, lounge, pool terrace, spa, and fitness center, it provides rooms and suites at ultra-deluxe prices.

Somewhat more offbeat is the **Bel Âge Hotel** (1020 North San Vicente Boulevard; 310-854-1111) in West Hollywood. Offering similar amenities in a complex that is positively laden with artwork, this all-suite hotel rents accommodations at ultra-deluxe prices.

Le Parc (733 West Knoll Street; 310-855-8888) and **Le Dufy** (1000 Westmount Drive; 310-657-7400), both located in quiet residential neighborhoods, offer spacious suites with a kitchen, fireplace, and balcony at ultra-deluxe rates. Among the features are a rooftop garden with pool, spa, city views, and a restaurant open exclusively to hotel guests.

Le Rêve (8822 Cynthia Avenue, West Hollywood; 310-854-1114), last but not least in this lengthy inventory of L'Ermitage properties, offers similar accommodations but manages to bring the room tabs in at deluxe rates by substituting room service for a private restaurant.

The elegant **St. James Club** (8358 Sunset Boulevard, West Hollywood; 213-654-7100) treats guests to an upper-crust club atmosphere. Completed in 1931 as Sunset Towers and now restored to its art deco magnificence, the Club once was home to screen luminaries from nearby studios. To get around its "private club" status yet fill its 63 rooms and suites, it allows $8-per-night temporary memberships. Ultra-deluxe.

Another chic Hollywood resting spot, the **Sunset Marquis Hotel and Villas** (1200 North Alta Loma Road; 310-657-1333) is a Mediterranean-style hotel frequented by beautiful people with big purses. Guest rooms surround a terrace pool, creating a tropical ambience enhanced by pastel colors and potted plants. The rooms are furnished in contemporary style and range from standard facilities to lavish villas, all renting in the ultra-deluxe range. High in snob appeal, the hotel offers complete amenities.

The gay bed and breakfast scene is well served by **San Vicente Inn** (837 North San Vicente Boulevard; 310-854-6915), a conveniently located West Hollywood establishment. Guests stay in two cottages and a converted horse-and-carriage barn that are adjacent to an 1889 historic landmark house. This five-unit complex features an attractive courtyard and offers a room with a kitchenette and shared bath or a cottage with private bath at moderate prices.

BEVERLY HILLS HOTELS

Despite its standing as one of the wealthiest communities in the nation, Beverly Hills offers at least one low-cost lodging facility. The **Beverly Terrace Motor Hotel** (469 North Doheny Drive; 310-274-8141) features moderately priced rooms at its 39-unit facility. The accommodations are typical motel digs and include among the amenities a pool, restaurant, and sun deck, as well as a location one block from Melrose Avenue.

On a knoll overlooking Beverly Hills is the **Beverly Hillcrest Hotel** (1224 Beverwil Drive; 310-277-2800), an 11-story building with 150 rooms. Priced in the deluxe-to-ultra-deluxe range, the hotel offers a lounge, pool, and two restaurants. The rooms are trimly if unimaginatively decorated, carpeted with shag rugs and equipped with patios.

A smaller deluxe-priced facility, the 53-room **Beverly Crest Hotel** (125 South Spalding Drive; 310-274-6801) offers a pool, restaurant, and lounge. Situated on a residential side street off Wilshire Boulevard, the hotel is a plain stucco building reminiscent of the 1950s.

Among these deluxe-priced hostelries my personal favorite is the **Beverly House Hotel** (140 South Lasky Drive; 310-271-2145). A brick Colonial-style structure, it lacks the extra amenities of its competitors but possesses the ambience of a European hotel. Each of the 50 guest rooms is furnished with hardwood pieces and stylishly decorated. Add a friendly staff, comfortable lobby, and free continental breakfast to round out this fine small Beverly Hills hotel.

The **Beverly Rodeo Hotel** (360 North Rodeo Drive; 310-273-0300) possesses one very important feature, location. It sits at the center of Rodeo Drive, a step away from the country's finest shops. Space in this neighborhood is precious and the hotel suffers from lack of it. The lobby is tiny and the rooms are cramped; extra facilities are limited to a sun deck and sidewalk café. The price nonetheless runs ultra-deluxe. With unremarkable washed-pine furniture and a flower decor that is overwhelming, the Beverly Rodeo needs all the location it can muster.

Small and elegant, the all-suite **L'Ermitage** (9291 Burton Way; 310-278-3344) is tucked away on a quiet tree-lined street. Only the discreet sign reveals that it's a hotel. A rooftop garden terrace with a 360° view has a pool and spa filled with mineral water. Although L'Ermitage is ultra-deluxe, you're not dollared to death.

One of Beverly Hill's premier addresses, **The Beverly Hills Hotel** (9641 Sunset Boulevard; 310-278-1487) was built way back in 1912. Today it remains a roosting place for Hollywood notables, who rent the hotel's 21 bungalows and haunt its Polo Lounge restaurant, though not as frequently as during the hotel's celebrity heyday. Surrounded by 12 acres of palm-lined gardens, the hotel boasts over 200 rooms as well as shops, restaurants, pool, spa, and tennis courts. Painted bright pink, tropical in ambience, the Beverly Hills is reminiscent of another "Pink Palace," the Royal Hawaiian Hotel in Waikiki. Guest rooms in this refurbished establishment have been decorated with professional flair. All feature baths of Italian marble and many include patios, fireplaces, and kitchens. The price tag, need one ask, is ultra-deluxe.

The Regent Beverly Wilshire Hotel (9500 Wilshire Boulevard; 310-275-5200), a 1928 Beaux-Arts building, represents Beverly Hills' other grand old hotel. Located at the foot of Rodeo Drive, this freshly renovated landmark features a Wilshire wing with 146 rooms and suites and an adjacent Beverly wing, built during the 1970s. Rooms in the Wilshire wing are quite spacious, designed with flair, and possess the character that makes this a great hotel. The new wing is decorated in a Southern California contemporary style. Both sections draw on a full line of amenities, including shops, restaurants, lounges, and swimming pool. Ultra-deluxe.

WESTSIDE HOTELS

Just one block from the UCLA campus, the **Hotel Claremont** (1044 Tiverton Avenue, Westwood; 310-208-5957) has 60 rooms tabbed in the budget to moderate range. These are plain, clean accommodations that share a large lobby.

The **Royal Palace Westwood** (1052 Tiverton Avenue, Westwood; 310-208-6677) next door offers 35 rooms, many with kitchens, at moderate to deluxe rates. These units are also well maintained and feature private patios.

Nearby **Hilgard House Hotel** (927 Hilgard Avenue, Westwood; 310-208-3945) is a spiffy new brick building with 47 rooms at deluxe prices. Accommodations in this three-story structure are furnished with facsimile antiques, plushly carpeted, and attractively decorated with wallhangings; many come equipped with jacuzzi tubs. Two new suites command an ultra-deluxe rate, complete with private maid service.

Directly across the street, but a big step uptown, stands the **Westwood Marquis Hotel and Garden** (930 Hilgard Avenue, Westwood; 310-208-8765), a 15-floor, all-suite hotel. This liveried-doorman establishment is beautifully appointed with fine furnishings and antique decorations. There are restaurants and lounges steps away from a sumptuous lobby, two pools set in a landscaped garden, plus a complete health spa facility. Ultra-deluxe.

Hotel Del Capri (10587 Wilshire Boulevard, Westwood; 310-474-3511) is a bright, cozy complex complete with two tiers of rooms encircling a pool terrace. The lobby and many of the guest rooms contain modern curvilinear furniture. The tile baths include jacuzzi bathtubs; continental breakfast is served in your room; some accommodations have kitchens. In sum, a very attractive establishment; deluxe.

Los Angeles' most Eden-like address lies in a forested canyon surrounded by peach and apricot trees. A classic country inn, the **Hotel Bel Air** (701 Stone Canyon Road, Bel Air; 310-472-1211) is an exclusive 92-room complex and private haven for show business celebrities and European royalty. The 1920s Mission-style buildings are shaded by a luxuriant garden of silk floss trees and redwoods. A stream tumbles through the property, creating small waterfalls and a pool with swans. All around is a mazework of archways and footbridges, colonnades, and fountains. Numbering among the nation's finest hotels, the Bel Air also provides an oval swimming pool, gourmet restaurant, lounge, and a patio terrace. Ultra-deluxe.

SAN GABRIEL VALLEY HOTELS

Motel row in Pasadena lies along Colorado Boulevard, route of the famous Rose Parade. **Pasadena Central Travelodge** (2131 East Colorado Boulevard; 818-796-3121), a 80-unit stucco complex, is typical of the accommodations. Priced in the budget range, it offers standard rooms with cinderblock walls, stall showers, wall-to-wall carpeting, and other basic amenities.

Over $100 million was poured into the revered **Ritz Carlton Huntington Hotel** (1401 South Oak Knoll Avenue, Pasadena; 818-568-3900), returning the 1907 grande dame to her turn-of-the-century glory. Situated on 20 manicured acres, this 383-room hotel combines modern amenities with the style and charm of another era. The Olympic-size swimming pool (reputed to be the first in California) has been restored, as have the hotel's Japanese and Horseshoe gardens and Georgian dining room. If you are seeking Old World elegance, this is the address. Ultra-deluxe.

SAN FERNANDO VALLEY HOTELS

The **Safari Inn** (1911 West Olive Avenue, Burbank; 818-845-8586) is that rarest of creatures, a motel with soul. In fact this 103-room facility also possesses a pool, jacuzzi, restaurant, lounge, and an adjacent hotel. The film location for several movies, it offers motel rooms at moderate prices and hotel accommodations, some with kitchens, in the moderate-to-deluxe range. The amenities and accouterments are definitely a step above those of a roadside motel.

Set in a quiet North Hollywood residential neighborhood, **La Maida House and Bungalows** (11159 La Maida Street; 818-769-3857) is a gracious Old World villa built in the early 1920s by Italian immigrant Antonio La Maida. The house boasts extensive use of marble, oak, mahogany, tile, and stained glass. Eleven airy rooms and suites, all with private baths, are decorated eclectically and many feature private patios. Personal touches such as cut flowers (from the house's own gardens), a sunny solarium, and gourmet dining make La Maida a rare alternative to the typical hotel. There is also a pool and gymnasium. Deluxe to ultra-deluxe.

Universal City, the center for tours of Universal Studio, is big on high-rise hotels. Among the most luxurious is the **Universal City Hilton and Towers** (555 Universal Terrace Parkway; 818-506-2500), a 24-story steel-and-glass structure overlooking the San Fernando Valley. With a vaulting lobby illuminated through skylights and trimmed in chrome, it's an ultra-modern facility. Guest rooms are contemporary in decor and feature plate-glass views of the surrounding city. Among the amenities are two restaurants, two lounges, shops, pool, jacuzzi, and exercise room. The good life gilded; ultra-deluxe in price.

A recent renovation increases the charm of **Sportsmen's Lodge Hotel** (12825 Ventura Boulevard, Studio City; 818-769-4700). Hidden within this English country-style establishment are gardens with waterfalls and foot-bridges, as well as a swan-filled lagoon. The interior courtyard contains an Olympic-sized swimming pool and the lobby features shops, restaurants, and a pub. Numbering about 200 rooms (each with private patio and room service), the hotel's prices begin in the deluxe range.

Ventura Boulevard, a major thoroughfare in The Valley, is chockablock with motels. Passing through Sherman Oaks, Encino, and Tarzana, you'll find a multitude of possibilities. Among the more upscale motels is **St. George Motor Inn** (19454 Ventura Boulevard, Tarzana; 818-345-6911), a 57-unit, mock-Tudor facility. Rooms with or without kitchens are moderately priced; there is a pool and spa on the premises.

Adding to the Valley's hospitality industry is the 16-story **Warner Center Hilton and Towers** (6360 Canoga Avenue, Woodland Hills; 818-595-1000). The updated art deco look extends from the lobby to the 340 soft pastel guest rooms and suites. The concierge level features a two-story lounge with sweeping mountain views. Suites offer wet bars; other amen ities include a restaurant, gourmet dining room, nightclub and lobby bar. Deluxe to ultra-deluxe.

Restaurants

DOWNTOWN RESTAURANTS

OLVERA STREET

Olvera Street, where the Spanish originally located the pueblo of Los Angeles, is still a prime place for Mexican food. Tiny **taco stands** line this brick-paved alley. Little more than open-air kitchens, they dispense fresh Mexican dishes at budget prices. You'll also find bakeries and candy stands, where old Mexican ladies sell *churros* (Mexican donuts) and candied squash.

La Golondrina (West 17 Olvera Street; 213-628-4349) provides something more formal. Set in the historic Pelanconi House, an 1850-era home built of fired brick, it features an open-air patio and a dining room with stone fireplace and *viga* ceiling. The bill of fare includes a standard selection of tacos, tostadas, and enchiladas as well as specialties such as fajitas, crab meat enchiladas, and grilled jumbo shrimp. Moderate.

Across from Union Station, midway between Olvera Street and Chinatown, stands one of the city's most famous cafeterias. **Philippe The Original** (1001 North Alameda Street; 213-628-3781) has been around since 1908, serving pork, beef, turkey, and lamb sandwiches in a French-dip style. With sawdust on the floors and memories tacked to the walls, this antique eatery still serves ten-cent cups of coffee. Budget.

CHINATOWN

The carved ceilings, ornate posts and elaborate decorations at **Hong Kong Low** (425 Gin Ling Way; 213-628-6217) certainly convey a sense of Chinatown. The menu is as multifaceted as the decor: divided into meat, fowl, seafood, and vegetable sections, it contains over 100 entrées. Both Szechuan and Cantonese dishes are available. Budget to moderate.

Chinese Friends Restaurant (984 North Broadway; 213-626-1837) is a postage-stamp eatery with plastic chairs, formica tables, and a mural-sized photo portraying geese on the wing. In addition to the standard selection of shrimp, pork, and vegetable dishes they offer several unusual specials such as shredded pig stomach, hot and sour chicken, and spicy eggplant. There's little else to note except one salient point: the place is inevitably crowded with Chinese. Budget to moderate.

One of Chinatown's dim sum dining rooms, **Ocean Seafood** (747 North Broadway; 213-687-3088) is a voluminous second-floor establishment. The dim sum service, in which you choose finger foods from passing carts, is only during lunch. At dinner there's a comprehensive Cantonese menu. With its fragile lamps and molded woodwork, Ocean Seafood has established a solid reputation for good food in sumptuous surroundings. Priced in the moderate range.

An anomaly in an Asian neighborhood, **Little Joe's** (900 North Broadway; 213-489-4900) is a throwback to the days when Italians in the area outnumbered Chinese. Long since departed, the southern Europeans left an impressive landmark, a sprawling restaurant with six dining rooms and a spacious lounge. The place is covered with murals of Italia and adorned with knickknacks from the Old Country. The menu, as you might expect, is a mix of cannelloni, ravioli, and fettucine dishes, with specialties such as veal piccata, beef medallions, scampi, *saltimbocca*, and butterflied halibut. Moderate; no breakfast.

Thanh My Restaurant (406 Sunset Boulevard; 213-680-1950), also in Chinatown, is a small Vietnamese plastic-chair-and-linoleum floor eatery. Here the budget dishes include barbecued pork with steamed rice, chicken bamboo rice noodles, and pork tips with steamed noodles. What this café lacks in atmosphere it makes up with good food at great prices.

LITTLE TOKYO

The brick-paved mall at Japanese Village Plaza is the best place in Little Tokyo to shop for restaurants. **Restaurant Plaza** (356 East 1st Street; 213-628-0697) is the local common denominator, a large establishment complete with sushi bar and dining room. The list of dishes resembles a Chinese menu, with nearly 100 items, but the selections are decidedly Japanese. There are pot-style dishes such as *nabe* and sukiyaki, plus tempura, teriyaki, and box-dinner *bento* combinations. The only problem is the ambience, which is that of a busy café. Moderate; no breakfast.

Offering far more atmosphere, **Tokyo Kaikan** (225 South San Pedro Street; 213-489-1333) is a warren of woodframe rooms, each highly stylized and decorated with lanterns and masks. Particularly inviting is one room which has been divided into private bamboo booths. Dinner includes several dishes cooked at your table as well as specialties such as *wafu* steak, tofu broth, and king salmon. Little wonder this is one of the district's most popular restaurants. Moderate to deluxe; no breakfast.

The most elaborate of Little Tokyo's addresses is **Horikawa** (111 South San Pedro Street; 213-680-9355), a restaurant with many faces. This beautifully appointed establishment serves meals in four separate locations—a sushi bar, a dining room, a *teppan* room where meals are prepared at your table and a luxurious teahouse with private rooms. Dining behind *shoji* screens in the teahouse you will experience *kaiseki* cooking, a 14-course meal which represents the pinnacle of Japanese cuisine. The dining room menu is quite varied, mixing staples like tempura with such specials as *isoyaki* (baked seafood combination) and chicken *amiyaki* (grilled with soy-sake sauce); the *teppan* room offers grilled steak, chicken, scallops, and lobster. The dining and *teppan* rooms are deluxe; the teahouse rooms are priced in the ultra-deluxe range and require a seven-day advance reservation; no breakfast.

Suehiro (337 East 1st Street; 213-758-3569) offers a largely Japanese menu in an American-style setting, complete with pink vinyl booths and counter service. Popular after art openings at the Temporary Contemporary. Budget to moderate.

A newcomer on the L.A. scene, **Troy** (418 East 1st Street; 213-617-0790) blurs the line between employee and customer, with a menu of hot beverages, sandwiches, and burgers served by whoever happens to be in the mood. Entertainment ranges from jazz and folk to performance art. Budget in price.

CENTRAL DOWNTOWN

To dine in the true style of Mexico the place to go is not a restaurant at all. **Grand Central Public Market** (317 South Broadway; 213-624-2378), a block-long pro-duce market, features stands selling Mexican finger foods. Tacos, tostadas, and burritos are only part of the fare. Try the *chile rojo* (pork in red chile sauce), *machaca* (shredded beef), and *lengua* (tongue). If you're really daring there's *rellena* (blood sausage), *buche* (hog maws), and *tripas* (intestines). *Mucho gusto!* Budget.

Another funky but fabulous budget eating place is **Clifton's Brookdale Cafeteria** (648 South Broadway; 213-627-1673), a kind of steam-tray vistarama. The second floor of this cavernous place displays illuminated photographs of California's sightseeing spots. The ground floor resembles a redwood forest, with tree trunks bolted to the walls, fake rocks stacked on the floor, and a waterfall tumbling through a cement funnel. A scene you cannot afford to miss.

Casey's Bar and Grill (613 South Grand Avenue; 213-629-2353) is one of those marvelous old dining lounges with dark paneling, trophy cases, and graying photographs. One room displays antique song sheets, another is covered with sports photos; my personal favorite is the back room, where you can request a private booth with curtain. Lunch consists of hamburgers, sandwiches, and entrées such as Dublin broil (steak with mushrooms, spinach, and mashed potatoes). For dinner there are pasta dishes, fish and chips, and barbecued ribs; moderate. Bottoms up!

Gill's Cuisine of India (838 South Grand Avenue; 213-623-1050), set in the lobby of the 1920-era Hotel Stillwell, conveys an air of South Asia. Indian fabrics adorn the walls, complementing a menu of chicken marsala, *tandoori* shrimp, lamb *vindallo*, and curry dishes. Buffet-style lunch; no breakfast; budget to moderate.

The Original Sonora Café (445 South Figueroa Street; 213-624-1800) is a chic Southwestern restaurant with blond wood furnishings, *viga* ceilings, and potted cactus. The patio in front is covered with wrought-iron lattice-work. Lunch and dinner are served from the same menu and include fajitas, duck tamales, chicken tostadas, and blue corn enchiladas. There are also fresh fish and steak dishes. Located in the financial district, the Sonora is popular with the young business crowd; moderate to deluxe.

Incomparable is the perfect adjective to describe **Rex Il Ristorante** (617 South Olive Street; 213-627-2300). Set in a landmark art deco building and modeled after a 1930s Italian luxury liner, it represents one of Los Angeles' loveliest restaurants. This Italian dining room is furnished in burgundy colors and enhanced by a sweeping staircase that curves up to a black marble dancefloor. The decorative glass is Lalique, the silverware Ricci, and the china Ginori, each element adding subtle flair. Not to be upstaged by the appurtenances, the cuisine is exceptional and the wine list is one of the most formidable in the country. The ultimate dining experience is the fixed-price menu, a stunning six-course meal that demonstrates chef Odette Fada's limitless skills. Among the à la carte selections, she prepares fettucini with *tarapanese* pesto, veal *médaillons*, *animellé* (sweet breads), and calamari *al nero di sippia* (in a squid ink sauce). Lunch and dinner only; ultra-deluxe.

It is, quite simply, Everyperson's Eating Place. **The Original Pantry** (877 South Figueroa Street; 213-972-9279), short on looks but long on soul, has been serving meals 24 hours a day since 1924 without missing a beat. When forced to relocate in 1950, they prepared lunch in the old building and served dinner at the new place. It simply consists of a counter with metal stools and a formica dining area decorated with grease-stained paintings. The cuisine is a culinary answer to heavy metal—ham hocks, navy bean soup, standing rib roast, sirloin tips with noodles, and roast pork. Budget-priced and bound to stay that way.

Over in the rough-and-tumble produce district, **Vickman's Restaurant** (1228 East 8th Street; 213-622-3852) has been serving proletarian chow since the 1930s. The food is standard cafeteria style; as an extra draw there's a bakery with homemade goods. Breakfast and lunch only; budget.

Another of downtown Los Angeles' funky but famous restaurants is **Gorky's** (536 East 8th Street; 213-627-4060), a Russian-American café. This plastic-chairs-and-exposed-pipes eatery mixes all-American with all-Russian cuisine. That means bacon and eggs versus cheese blintzes; roast beef sandwiches versus lox plates; and meat loaf versus *piroshkis*. Step in, comrade, and order borscht, *pelmeni* (meat-filled pasta), *shchi* (cabbage soup), or Siberian pasta (with spicy Russian sausage). Budget.

GREATER LOS ANGELES RESTAURANTS

WATTS-INGLEWOOD AREA

Among the many excellent restaurants supported by the black community is a tiny café serving Caribbean and Creole food. **Mika's** (4307 South Vermont Avenue; 213-231-1207) offers little more than a few tables and a take-out counter, but when that tiny kitchen gets cooking it serves up outrageous fish and chicken dishes. If you're daring, try the conch or cow foot soup. Budget.

Another favored spot is **Janet's Original Jerk Chicken Pit** (1541 West Martin Luther King Boulevard; 213-296-4621), a small café serving Jamaican dishes. The chicken, pork, ribs, beef, and fish platters are prepared with special spices in the "jerk" style of Jamaica. A great ethnic restaurant. Prices are budget.

EAST LOS ANGELES

Mexican restaurants are on parade at **El Mercado** (3425 East 1st Street; 213-268-3451), a two-story indoor market adorned with tile floors and colorful murals. Along the mezzanine of this Spanish emporium are chili bars, taco stands, seafood restaurants, and cafés from south of the border. Adding to your dining pleasure, Mexican bands perform love songs and ballads. Budget.

The greatest of all East L.A.'s Mexican restaurants is **El Tepeyac Café** (812 North Evergreen Avenue; 213-268-1960), a hole-in-the-wall with so much soul people migrate across the city to feast on its legendary burritos. Consisting of a small dining room with take-out window and side patio, the place serves everything—*machaca*, tacos, steak *picado*, enchiladas, *chile colorado*, *huevos con chorizo*, and so on. The food is delicious, the portions are overwhelming, and the price is budget. What more can I say?

ECHO PARK-SILVER LAKE AREA

Sunset Boulevard, particularly around Echo Park and Silver Lake, is a veritable restaurant row. Traveling northwest on this famous street you'll come upon restaurants of every ethnic persuasion. **Les Frères Taix** (1911 West Sunset Boulevard; 213-484-1265) is a huge, common-denominator restaurant serving French country cuisine in several dining rooms. The lunch and dinner *cartes* are budget to moderate in price and include sea bass meunière, trout almondine, braised beef, and short ribs Provençal. The interior is attractive, if crowded.

Probably the cheapest place to dine is **Burrito King** (2109 West Sunset Boulevard; 213-413-9444), a take-out stand serving tacos, tostadas, enchiladas, and its namesake. There are also hamburgers at this budget-priced outlet.

Your Colombian connection is **Los Arrieros** (2619 West Sunset Boulevard; 213-483-0074), a fresh, bright café with tile floors and Colombian artwork. Entrées range from shrimp in garlic sauce to *carne asada*. There's oxtail stew, fish soup, ceviche, and paella, all at budget to moderate cost.

Combine dining and art at **L.A. Nicola** (4326 West Sunset Boulevard; 213-660-7217). The cuisine at this exposed-pipe-and-track-light dining room is as contemporary as the canvases adorning the walls. The deluxe-priced menu offers shrimp with tequila, and spinach-wrapped trout with mushroom mousse. A scene at either lunch or dinner.

Seafood Bay (3916 West Sunset Boulevard; 213-664-3902) is the best type of seafood restaurant, one with an adjacent fish market, ensuring freshness. Just a naugahyde café with formica tables, it offers sole, swordfish, trout, calamari, shrimp, and practically everything else that swims. Budget to moderate.

WHITTIER-EL MONTE AREA

You wouldn't expect to find a Chinese seafood restaurant of gourmet caliber in a suburban mall. Granted, the **Dragon Regency** (120 South Atlantic Boulevard; 818-282-1089) is located in the Chinatown section of Monterey Park. But snake soup in a shopping center? Not to mention sea cucumber with straw, braised fish snouts, pan-fried eel, and other adventurous dishes. There are also crab, lobster, oyster, shrimp, conch, clam, and fresh fish entrées, plus selections of duck, beef, and squab. The interior completes the theme of unpredictability, with delicate Chinese paintings and a large aquarium. Outstanding! Lunch and dinner; moderate.

WILSHIRE DISTRICT RESTAURANTS

MID-WILSHIRE DISTRICT

Elegance 24 hours a day? In a restaurant on wheels? Somehow all-night restaurants conjure visions of truck-stop dives, but at **Pacific Dining Car** (1310 West 6th Street; 213-483-6000) 'round-the-clock service is provided in dark wood surroundings. Modeled after an old-style railroad dining car, with plush booths and outsized plate-glass windows, this destination has been a Los Angeles landmark since 1921. The cuisine is well-heeled all-American: breakfast includes eggs Benedict and eggs Sardou, and the dinner menu features seasonal wild game dishes as well as some of the best steaks in the city. Deluxe to ultra-deluxe.

The reason for the balcony at **La Fonda** (2501 Wilshire Boulevard; 213-380-5055) becomes stirringly evident every evening when Los Camperos strikes up a Spanish song. One of the city's best mariachi bands, they lure dinner guests by the dozens to this hacienda-style restaurant. In addition to the sound of Los Camperos, diners enjoy the flavor of Veracruz-style shrimp, steak *picado*, chicken flautas, and *chile verde*. Lunch and dinner; moderately priced.

The interior of **Casa Carnitas** (4067 West Beverly Boulevard; 213-667-9953) is tiny but overwhelming. Colorful as an old mission chapel, the walls are covered with murals portraying Mayan warriors. Naturally, the food is Yucatecan and includes a variety of beef, chicken, and shrimp dishes prepared with tasty *ranchera* sauce. Considering the imaginative decor and budget prices, Casa Carnitas is an excellent find; lunch and dinner.

Tommy's Hamburgers is a Los Angeles landmark. In fact at last count there were 17 such landmarks. But the original Tommy's, dating back to 1946, is at 2575 West Beverly Boulevard (213-389-9060). Here you can enjoy "while you watch" service as they prepare hamburgers, hot dogs, and tamales before your hungry eyes. Open 24 hours, this is the place where they give you paper towels instead of napkins and still charge only budget prices. (Ain't L.A. amazing.)

Well-known for its Siamese cuisine, **Chan Dara** (310 North Larchmont Boulevard; 213-467-1052) is a modern Thai restaurant with mirrored bar and brass-rail dining room. The specialties vary from spicy barbecue to vegetable entrées. Lunch and dinner; patio; moderate.

Also consider **La Fonda Antioqueña** (4903 Melrose Avenue; 213-957-5164), a Columbian restaurant that comes recommended by a former Consul General of Colombia. Here you will discover about 15 different platters, each prepared with South American flair. Situated in the moderate price category, this intriguing ethnic restaurant offers everything from fish, chicken, beef, and pork dishes to liver and tongue. For an adventure in south-of-the-border dining, La Fonda Antioqueña is the place.

FAIRFAX DISTRICT

Angular beam ceiling, bright contemporary paintings, plain white walls, pipe sculpture aquarium, and candles. Sound chic? That's **Muse** (7360 Beverly Boulevard; 213-934-4400), a California-cuisine restaurant with the feel of an offbeat art gallery. At lunch and dinner they serve pasta dishes as well as a changing repertoire of entrées. Examples: salmon with caviar and basmati rice, fusilli pasta with duck, honey-marinated pork with deep-fried won tons, and flame-broiled New York steak with shiitake mushrooms. It's the only menu I've ever seen written in English but still requiring translation. Lunch and dinner; deluxe.

Also out along the edge is the **Nowhere Café** (8009 Beverly Boulevard; 213-655-8895), a vegetarian restaurant decorated in Southwestern fashion. With blond wood furniture, and changing contemporary artwork, it represents one of the city's few upscale vegetarian dining rooms. The bill of fare features baked egg rolls, corn and pinto bean griddle cakes, lentil chili, fresh fish, and organic chicken dishes. Lunch and dinner; moderate.

L.A.'s best known delicatessen lies at the heart of the Jewish neighborhood around Fairfax Avenue. **Canter's** (419 North Fairfax Avenue; 213-651-2030), a casual 24-hour restaurant, doubles as local landmark and ethnic cultural center. As you might have guessed, lox and bagels, hot pastrami, corned beef, and matzo ball soup are the order of the day. When in doubt, go kosher. Budget to moderate.

Farmer's Market (6333 West 3rd Street; 213-933-9211), a sprawling open-air collection of vendor stands, is a good spot to visit and an even better place to eat. The take-out stands lining each corridor dispense burritos, egg rolls, jambalaya, corned beef, hot dogs, fish and chips, and every other type of ethnic food imaginable. Simply order at the counter, then find a table in the sun. Budget.

Also in the Farmer's Market area are two critically acclaimed ethnic restaurants. **Sofi Estiatorion** (8030¾ West 3rd Street; 213-651-0346) is a family-run Greek restaurant with a potful of grandmother's recipes. Open for lunch and dinner, they serve moussaka in the dining room or out on the patio; moderate to deluxe.

Siamese Princess (8048 West 3rd Street; 213-653-2643) is a fashionable Thai bistro oddly decorated with unmatched antiques and pictures of international royalty. There are 160 wines to choose from on the four-star wine list. But remember, you came for the spicy Asian cuisine. Lunch and dinner; moderate to deluxe.

SOUTH OF WILSHIRE

El Izalqueño (1830 West Pico Boulevard; 213-387-2467) is a plain, naugahyde café offering a multitude of Salvadoran dishes. The interior is a strange blend of tacky oil paintings and an overly loud jukebox. But the food—varying from breaded chicken to shredded beef, shrimp with garlic to steamed gizzards—is very inviting. Lunch and dinner; budget.

One of Koreatown's best restaurants is a multiroom complex named **Dong Il Jang** (3455 West 8th Street; 213-383-5757). The place contains several dining rooms as well as a sushi bar, each decorated with bamboo screens and Asian statuary. The Korean dinners include *maewoon tahng* (spicy codfish casserole), *kalbi* (marinated ribs), and *jun bok juk* (abalone porridge). A complete offering of Japanese dishes is also presented. Lunch and dinner; moderate.

Favored among savvy locals, **Rosalind's West African Cuisine** (1044 South Fairfax Avenue; 213-936-2486) serves plantains, yam balls, and *akara* (deep-fried black-eyed peas). Main courses include Niger-style goat (sautéed with African herbs and spices), sautéed beef with onions and herbs, and groundnut stew (with nuts, beef, chicken, and spices). Added to the exotic cuisine is a complete wall mural depicting a waterfall on the Nile river. Dinner only; moderate.

Enjoy *tandoori* chicken and a host of curry dishes prepared in **India's Oven** (5897 West Pico Boulevard; 213-936-1000). It isn't the Taj Mahal. At lunch and dinner you'll dine from plastic plates, but at these budget prices, who can complain?

Another spot which must not be overlooked is **Homer & Edy's Bistro** (2839 South Robertson Boulevard; 213-559-5102), with its "touch of Old New Orleans." Homey as a living room, this Creole/Cajun restaurant is friendly and comfortable. The menu is heavy on seafood—with shrimp jambalaya, scallops *étoufée*, catfish, and baked redfish—but includes lamb, chicken, and beef dishes. A jazz pianist performs weekends; lunch and dinner; deluxe.

HOLLYWOOD RESTAURANTS

The eastern sections of Hollywood constitute the local heartland for good, cheap, informal restaurants. Take **New York George** (4854 Fountain Avenue; 213-666-9100), a homey café where you can dine out on the patio or inside amid photos of the New York skyline. There are omelettes in the morning, hamburgers and deli sandwiches for lunch and dinner, plus an assortment of American entrées; budget.

Jitlada (5233½ Sunset Boulevard; 213-667-9809) is one of those great ethnic restaurants that L.A. likes to tuck away in mini-malls. Just a funky little café, it serves an array of Thai dishes; the most notable are seafood entrées such as squid, mussels, and scallops. Lunch and dinner; moderate.

The Hollywood address for righteous soul food is **Roscoe's House of Chicken & Waffles** (1514 Gower Street; 213-466-7453), a tiny wood-slat café with overhead fans and an easy atmosphere. Ask for an "Oscar" and they'll bring chicken wings and grits; "E-Z Ed's Special" is a chicken liver omelette; and a "Lord Harvey" is a half chicken smothered in gravy and onions. Very hip; moderate.

The fat lady sings at **Sarno's Caffe Dell'Opera** (1714 North Vermont Avenue; 213-662-3403), a dimly lit Italian restaurant that features opera and other music nightly. Amateurs and professionals alike perform; if you're interested, just let the piano player know that you're ready for a Hollywood premiere. Despite the virtuoso performances, dinner is moderately priced. The menu contains standard Italian fare from pizza to pasta to veal plates; lunch and dinner.

Don't be deceived by the budget prices at **India Inn** (1638 Cahuenga Boulevard; 213-461-3774). This *tandoori* restaurant serves good curry and vegetarian dishes as well as chef's specials such as chicken *tikka massaly* (with a tomato and onion sauce). The dining room is tidy but plain.

La Poubelle (5907 Franklin Avenue; 213-465-0807) means "garbage pail," but it is anything but. This small candlelit restaurant serves up delicate French and Italian cuisine with a style (and a local following) all its own. Dinner and Sunday brunch at moderate rates.

Popular with entertainers from nearby studios, **Columbia Bar & Grill** (1448 North Gower Street; 213-461-8800) is the last word in sleek. From the brick patio with topiary trees and peaked skylight to the pullman booths and green-glass shades, the place is designed with a delicate touch. The American regional cuisine menu changes weekly and offers fresh fish, pasta, assorted steaks, chops, and chicken for lunch and dinner. Deluxe.

Hollywood's oldest restaurant, **Musso and Frank Grill** (6667 Hollywood Boulevard; 213-467-7788) is a 1919 original with dark paneling, murals, and red leather booths. A bar and open grill create a clubby atmosphere that reflects the eatery's long tradition. Among the American-style dishes are cracked crab, fresh clams, sea bass, prime rib, roast lamb, plus assorted steaks and chops. A slice of tradition at a moderate-to-deluxe price. They serve a late breakfast, lunch, and dinner.

Hampton's (1342 North Highland Avenue; 213-469-1090) may be the world's only hamburger joint with valet parking. This well-known noshing spot has transformed the art of hamburger-cooking to a science, preparing over two dozen varieties. You can order one with sour plum jam, peanut butter, or creamed horseradish. If you disagree with the when-in-Rome philosophy, there are broiled shrimp, chicken, pasta, and vegetarian platters. Lunch and dinner; moderate.

If Hampton's proves too health-conscious, try **Pink's Famous Chili Dogs** (711 North La Brea Avenue; 213-931-4223). This popular take-out stand has hamburgers and tamales; but at Pink's, not ordering a dog slapped with sauce is like going to Hampton's for waffles.

The fish they serve at **Seafood Village** (5730 Melrose Avenue; 213-463-8090) are not only fresh, they are right there in the display cases of the adjacent market. This nondescript café features several dozen fish dishes plus about a dozen meat entrées. Red snapper, orange roughy, rex sole, sea bass, shark steak, calamari, fried oysters, scallops, shrimp, Alaskan king crab, and Maine lobsters are only some of the offerings. Moderate.

The celebrity photos covering every inch of **Formosa Café** (7156 Santa Monica Boulevard; 213-850-9050) tell a tale of Hollywood that reaches back to the 1940s. This crowded café, originally fashioned from a streetcar, has seen more stars than heaven. Over the years they've poured in from the surrounding studios, leaving autographs and memories. Today you'll find a Chinese-American restaurant serving budget-to-moderate-priced lunches and dinners, a kind of museum with meals.

Hollywood's prettiest restaurant is a re-created Japanese palace called **Yamashiro** (1999 North Sycamore Avenue; 213-466-5125). Set in the hills overlooking Los Angeles, the mansion was built earlier in the century, modeled after an estate in the high mountains of Japan, and trimmed with ornamental gardens. Dine here and you are surrounded by hand-carved columns, *shoji* screens, and Asian statuary. The courtyard garden contains a waterfall, koi pond, and miniature trees. For dinner they serve a complete Japanese menu as well as Western-style entrées; moderate to deluxe.

WEST HOLLYWOOD

Melrose Avenue, where the fashion-conscious can dress to dine and then shop for their next dinner outfit, has vaulted to prominence as one of L.A.'s leading restaurant rows. Among the more savvy gourmets, many squeeze into **Citrus** (6703 Melrose Avenue; 213-939-5354), a white-wall-and-track-lighting dining room where indoor umbrellas protect patrons from the harsh rays of the skylights. Affected as this spot can be, it *is* beautifully highlighted with fresh flowers and *does* serve other-worldly dishes. The theme is California cuisine (what else?) with a focus on fresh fish. Where but Citrus can one go for grilled baby salmon with potato garlic purée, mini goat cheese ravioli, duck breast with couscous and figs, or a tuna burger? Sarcasm aside, it's a great restaurant (with a deluxe tab). Who knows, perhaps the maître d' will kiss your cheek.

Angeli Caffe/Pizzeria (7274 Melrose Avenue; 213-936-9086) is the archetypal Melrose address. Its high-tech interior is a medley of flying buttresses, wood-slat ceilings, exposed ducts, and whitewashed walls. The menu matches this edge design with pizza, calzone, and daily specials like spaghetti *alla carbonara*, linguine with mussels, and mushrooms in garlic. Lunch and dinner; moderate.

Artwork by local artists hangs on the pastel walls of **Border Grill** (7407½ Melrose Avenue; 213-658-7495). The place is packed with the young and the hip eating Tex-Mex food: pork chop *adobado*, Veracruz-style fish, skirt steak with onion relish, soft tacos with cactus, and tongue stew. Lunch and dinner; moderate to deluxe.

Next day the same people are at **Tommy Tang's** (7473 Melrose Avenue; 213-651-1810) munching Thai finger foods. Here the tile is black and pink; it covers the sushi bar, which is draped in canvas. The ever-changing gallery of artwork reflects the trendy crowd. The food is delicious, the portions are small. Happily, everyone is rich. Lunch and dinner; moderate.

Modern art and pastel walls are also standard issue in the neighborhood's best Chinese restaurant. **Genghis Cohen** (740 North Fairfax Avenue; 213-653-0640) serves gourmet dishes to an appreciative crowd at its multiroom complex off Melrose Avenue. Not your ordinary Asian restaurant, specialties here are "scallops on fire," candied shrimp, garlic catfish, soft-shelled shrimp, and "no-name" duck. Lunch and dinner; deluxe.

Anchoring the western reaches of Melrose is **Trumps** (8764 Melrose Avenue; 310-855-1480). Contemporary in decor, nouvelle California in cuisine, the place has received critical acclaim for both. Burlap banquettes, exposed rafters, and square cement tables create an air of nonchalance. For dinner they serve smoked baby back ribs, chicken with mashed potatoes and gravy, Chinese roast duck, and steamed salmon with wild rice pancakes. Lunch, dinner, and late supper menus; Moderate to deluxe.

When you tire of the tinsel along Melrose Avenue you can always retreat to **Noura Café** (8479 Melrose Avenue; 213-651-4581), one of the street's few down-home restaurants. Here the food is Mediterranean and the prices are budget. Just order shish kebab, falafel, grape leaves, or salad at the counter, then enjoy it in a comfortable dining room or out on the patio.

La Toque (8171 Sunset Boulevard; 213-656-7515), a French-Californian restaurant with a bold reputation, is one of the places that put West Hollywood on the culinary map. Nightly the chef prepares venison medallions, saddle of lamb, grilled swordfish, salmon with blood orange sauce, and sliced duck breast with toasted apples. The building is country French in design, with tile floors and wood beam ceilings, giving the dining room a distinctly European feel. Oil paintings and carved wood mirrors add to this sense of natural elegance. Lunch and dinner; deluxe.

Barney's Beanery (8447 Santa Monica Boulevard; 213-654-2287) is the only place around where you can shoot pool while eating chili, burritos, and hamburgers. Or where you can choose from more than 200 varieties of beer. A dive with character, Barney's has rainbow-colored booths, license plates on the ceiling, and a road sign decor. Native funk at budget prices.

An old favorite celebrity-watching restaurant, **Dan Tana's** (9071 Santa Monica Boulevard; 310-275-9444) is small and crowded, making reservations a must. The fare is Italian, pricey but excellent. The New York steak may well be the best served anywhere. Veal, chicken, and pasta dishes round out the fare. Dinner only, deluxe to ultra-deluxe.

Duke's (8909 Sunset Boulevard; 310-652-3100) is another legendary watering hole, especially popular with music industry figures. A crowded coffee shop bedecked with posters, it also attracts West Hollywood's underground population. People with purple hair pile into the communal tables, order meat loaf or Chinese vegetables, and settle down for the day. That's what makes Duke's Duke's: it's a scene, a flash, a slice of unreality. A colorful breakfast stop, with dozens of omelette selections; also hamburgers, sandwiches, diet plates, and a few American dinners. Budget.

With the possible exception of Berkeley's Chez Panisse, **Spago** (1114 Horn Avenue; 310-652-4025) is California's most famous restaurant. Owner Wolfgang Puck helped originate California cuisine, which achieves its pinnacle at his West Hollywood restaurant. Set on a hill overlooking the city, the dining room is dominated by an open-view brick oven. The furnishings are informal, fresh flowers predominate and a back patio is shaded with umbrellas. Everything that can be painted is painted white. The pastas include Sonoma lamb ravioli and angelhair pasta with clams and mussels; there are pizzas with duck sausage, Louisiana shrimp, or prosciutto; among the entrées are roasted Cantonese duck, squab with polenta, and whole black bass roasted in a woodburning oven. Dinner only; reservations required. Deluxe to ultra-deluxe.

The late-night gay crowd heads to **Yukon Mining Co.** (7328 Santa Monica Boulevard; 213-851-8833), an All-American, booth-and-counter-service eatery that's open 24 hours. The motif, in case you couldn't guess, is mining, and the menu is one of those hamburger-sandwich-and-breakfast-all-day affairs that make choosing an entrée simple. Budget.

More upscale but equally popular with West Hollywood's gay population is **Café D'Etoile** (8941½ Santa Monica Boulevard; 310-278-1011). The cuisine here is a Continental mix of pasta, steak, chicken, and roast pork dishes, and the decor is a mix of antique furniture and contemporary artworks (provided by a local art gallery and changing monthly). Moderate.

Over in the Rose Garden Performance Center there's **Erica's Restaurant** (665 Robertson Boulevard; 310-854-4455), which draws both a gay and straight crowd. The dining room is a maze of mirrors separated by art deco sconces, with green chairs against an emerald green background. The nouvelle cuisine varies from squab and chicken to veal chops and rack of lamb. Deluxe.

L'Orangerie (903 North La Cienega Boulevard; 310-652-9770) possesses all the pretensions you would expect from one of Los Angeles' finest, most expensive French restaurants. The building has the look of a château, with imposing arches and finials atop the roof. The dining areas are appointed with oil paintings and outsized wall sconces; fresh flowers and the scent of money proliferate. Food, decor, service, all are the finest. The *foie gras* and seafood are flown in fresh from France. Life, or dinner at least, doesn't get much better than this classic French restaurant. Dinner only; reservations required. Ultra-deluxe.

BEVERLY HILLS RESTAURANTS

The place to nosh in Beverly Hills is **Nate 'n' Al's Deli** (414 North Beverly Boulevard; 310-274-0101), a traditional delicatessen with a complete assortment of kosher dishes. There are bagels, sandwiches on rye and pumpernickel, and a smoked fish plate that includes lox, cod, and whitefish; moderate.

Owned and frequented by celebrities, minimalist in decor, **Maple Drive** (345 North Maple Drive; 310-274-9800) has emerged as one of Beverly Hills' top trysts. Here you can dine on a number of gourmet tidbits while catching the flash and dance of Hollywood on parade. Deluxe to ultra-deluxe.

When you're homesick for New York there's **Carroll O'Connor's Place** (369 North Bedford Drive; 310-273-7585), an upscale eatery owned by Carroll "Archie Bunker" O'Connor. Photos and mementoes from O'Connor's career hang all about the place, creating an East Coast ambience. The menu primarily features seafood, with salads and pasta dishes added for variety. Breakfast, lunch, and dinner; moderate to deluxe.

Most Beverly Hills restaurants are places to be seen; **Kate Mantílini** (9101 Wilshire Boulevard; 310-278-3699) is a place to see. A kind of *Star*

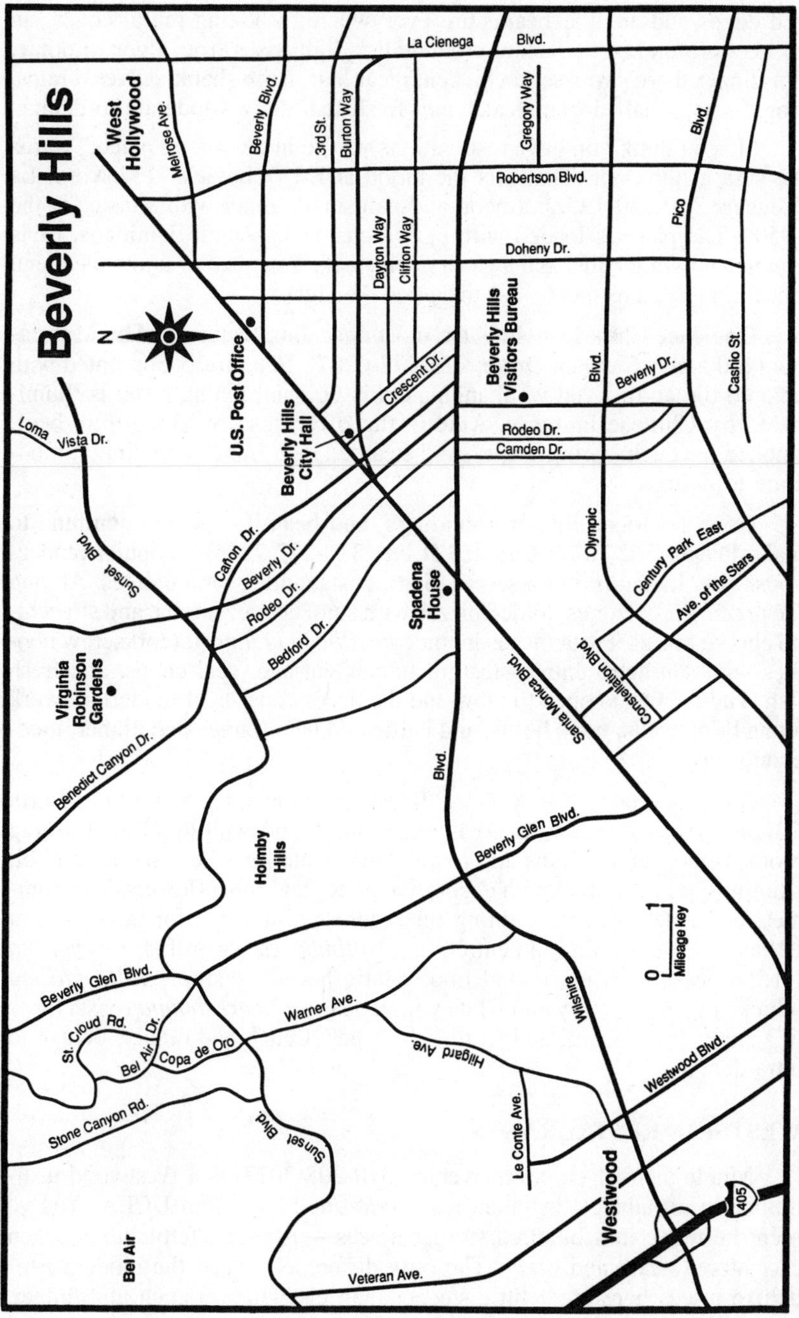
Beverly Hills
West Hollywood
Melrose Ave.
Beverly Blvd.
3rd St.
Burton Way
La Cienega Blvd.
Gregory Way
Robertson Blvd.
Pico Blvd.
Doheny Dr.
Dayton Way
Clifton Way
N
U.S. Post Office
Beverly Hills Visitors Bureau
Crescent Dr.
Beverly Dr.
Cashio St.
Olympic Blvd.
Beverly Hills City Hall
Rodeo Dr.
Camden Dr.
Loma Vista Dr.
Sunset Blvd.
Cañon Dr.
Beverly Dr.
Rodeo Dr.
Bedford Dr.
Spadena House
Century Park East
Ave. of the Stars
Constellation Blvd.
Santa Monica Blvd.
Virginia Robinson Gardens
Benedict Canyon Dr.
Beverly Glen Blvd.
Holmby Hills
0 1
Mileage key
Wilshire Blvd.
Beverly Glen Blvd.
St. Cloud Rd.
Bel Air Dr.
Copa de Oro
Warner Ave.
Hilgard Ave.
Stone Canyon Rd.
Sunset Blvd.
Le Conte Ave.
Westwood Blvd.
Westwood
405
Bel Air
Veteran Ave.

Wars diner, this 21st-century rendezvous is an artwork in steel and tile. Jagged edges and angular beams are everywhere; a boxing mural covers an entire wall; and in the center a sundial/skylight rises from floor to dome. For dinner there's rotisserie chicken, meat loaf, lamb shank, calves' brains, frogs' legs, a half dozen steaks, and fresh fish daily. Moderate to deluxe.

"If you think you have reservations you're in the wrong place," warns the sign at the door. That sets the mood at **Ed Debevic's** (134 North La Cienega; 310-659-1952), a neon-and-naugahyde diner with a taste for the 1950s. The place is loaded with period chatchkas—pink flamingos, Elvis albums, bowling balls, and a Coca Cola clock. You already know the menu (meat, eggs, more meat) and the price—budget.

Opulence Chinese-style is the most appealing feature of **The Mandarin** (430 North Camden Drive; 213-272-0267). Beautifully appointed with colored tile and carved wallhangings, this Oriental dining room is illuminated by Chinese lanterns. Among the offerings are Mongolian beef, smoked tea duck, spring crêpes, and steamed fish. Lunch and dinner; moderate to deluxe.

Gourmet food, chic surroundings, and beautiful people combine to make **Prego** (362 North Camden Drive; 310-277-7346) a popular rendezvous. This Italian trattoria serves pizza, pasta, and several entrées. Among the pizzas are calzones, folded pizzas with smoked mozzarella, and stracchino cheese pizzas. Pasta dishes include *fusilli con luganega* (corkscrew noodles with sausage); entrées feature Italian sausage, veal chops, and fresh fish. The kitchen is open to view and the decor consists of modern artwork along brick walls, track lights, and hardwood trim. Lunch and dinner; moderately priced.

Ranking among Los Angeles' finest restaurants, **La Scala** (410 North Cañon Drive; 310-275-0579) is an intimate and well-appointed dining room. Upholstered booths add to an elegant interior where statues and oil paintings are combined with decorative plates and fresh flowers. The gourmets and celebrities frequenting this address also come for the excellent Italian cuisine. Among the entrées are *saltimbocca*, swordfish *rosemarino* (grilled swordfish marinated in aromatic herbs), scampi, *pollo galleto* (chicken with rosemary and white wine), *penne alla arrabbiata* (pasta tubes in a spicy chili sauce), and fresh fish dishes. Lunch and dinner; deluxe to ultra-deluxe.

WESTSIDE RESTAURANTS

Mario's (1001 Broxton Avenue; 310-208-7077) is a Westwood institution, an oil-tablecloth Italian restaurant one block from UCLA. You've seen the menu in a hundred similar places—spaghetti, fettucine, chicken cacciatore, steak, and pizza. The only difference is that the moderate-to-deluxe prices here are a little steeper than elsewhere. Lunch and dinner.

Another campus hangout, **Stratton's Grill** (1037 Broxton Avenue, Westwood; 310-208-0488) is a turn-of-the-century saloon with a spectacular marble-and-hardwood bar. There are wood-slat booths along the walls for diners. Selections range from sandwiches, pizza, and pasta to mesquite-grilled steak and salmon. Lunch, dinner, and weekend brunch at a budget-to-moderate cost.

Alice's Restaurant (1043 Westwood Boulevard, Westwood; 310-208-3171) has taken an antique building with marble floors and molded ceilings, then added neon signs and a brass rail bar. The effect is an odd mix of old and new—ornamental molding and tube lighting. There's also a patio where you can dine streetside on American cuisine. Among the choices are grilled salmon, crab cakes, chicken dijon, shrimp Mediterranean, steak, and pasta. Moderate.

The cheapest place to eat in the entire Westside district is on the UCLA campus. Here you'll find cafeterias at **Ackerman Student Union** and the **North Campus Student Center** (for visitor information call 310-206-8147). The food will fill your stomach without emptying your purse; beyond that I guarantee nothing.

Farther out on Westwood Boulevard, proceeding south from the UCLA campus, there is a string of ethnic restaurants worth trying. **La Bruschetta** (1621 Westwood Boulevard, Westwood; 310-477-1052) serves high Italian cuisine. This gourmet address is filled along several walls with wine racks. Vibrant artwork of recent vintage decorates the place. Lunch and dinner; moderate to deluxe.

The flavor is Persian at **Shamshiry Restaurant** (1916 Westwood Boulevard, Westwood; 310-474-1410), a pleasant restaurant with latticework booths and hanging plants. The shish kebab and other Middle Eastern dishes, served at lunch and dinner, are moderately priced.

Enjoying a reputation for righteous Cajun food, **Patout's** (2260 Westwood Boulevard, Westwood; 310-475-7100) is a chic café with a knack for Louisiana tradition. The ever-evolving menu might include crawfish pasta, Louisiana Bluepoint crab, or redfish topped with "lump crabmeat and shrimp." The interior features bentwood furniture, a circular skylight, and an open-view kitchen. Dinner only; deluxe.

For standard old American fare, head a little farther out to **The Apple Pan** (10801 West Pico Boulevard, West Los Angeles; 310-475-3585), a clapboard cottage that contains a single U-shaped counter. The food consists of sandwiches (as in ham, swiss cheese, and tuna salad) and pies (as in apple, berry, and pecan). Lunch and dinner; budget.

Fragrant Vegetable Restaurant (11859 Wilshire Boulevard, West Los Angeles; 310-312-1442) is generally considered one of Los Angeles' finest vegetarian restaurants. Here amid placid surroundings you can begin with deep-fried mashed taro or white fungus and sweet corn soup, then choose from over five dozen vegetarian entrées. There are curried vegetables in coconut milk, bean curd in chili, and "Buddha's cushions" (stewed black mushrooms with black moss). The Fragrant Vegetable also offers simulated pork and rib dishes, made with tofu. Lunch and dinner; budget to moderate.

All those two-wheelers suspended from the ceiling give the **Bicycle Shop Café** (12217 Wilshire Boulevard, West Los Angeles; 310-826-7831) its name. This casual bistro offers a pasta and quiche menu which also includes a dozen entrées such as scampi, swordfish, sea bass, salisbury steak, and chicken with béarnaise sauce. A great place for slumming; moderate.

Commercial establishments are rare in residential Bel Air. Finding a restaurant with reasonable prices is an even more challenging feat, especially as you ascend the hills. It seems like the farther you climb, the higher the prices become. At **Four Oaks Restaurant** (2181 North Beverly Glen Boulevard; 310-470-2265) you encounter a French restaurant with deluxe-to-ultra-deluxe prices. Comfortable and understated, this intimate dining room is illuminated through skylights and features a brick patio for dining alfresco. The constantly evolving fare consists of organically-grown ingredients prepared in a contemporary French-Californian style. Lunch, dinner, and Sunday brunch.

The restaurant at the **Hotel Bel-Air** (701 Stone Canyon Road; 310-472-1211) is so low-key it doesn't even have a name. This is no glitzy, glamorous monument to gastronomy. At the end of a graceful arcade in the hotel's mission-style main building, its understated decor soothes diners who settle into comfortable Queen Anne chairs. A menu of topnotch continental/ American food caters to the worldly, well-heeled patron looking for a traditional meal in a comfortable atmosphere. Ultra-deluxe.

SAN GABRIEL VALLEY RESTAURANTS

One of the San Gabriel Valley's best food bargains is the budget-to-moderate-priced **Restaurant Mérida** (20 East Colorado, Pasadena; 818-792-7371). Serving Yucatán-style dishes, this brick-walled eatery offers *birria de chivo* (goat in spicy sauce), *oriental de pavo* (turkey, onions, and garlic in rich broth), and *cochinita pibil* (pork wrapped in banana leaves). For those accustomed to dining closer to Mexico City there are enchiladas, burritos, and tostadas. Serving three meals daily, with a menu numbering over 100 items, it's an exceptional place. Patio courtyard.

For another great buy, try **Burger Continental** (535 South Lake Avenue, Pasadena; 818-792-6634), a congested and crazy café where you order at the counter, then dine indoors or on a patio. Portions are bountiful and the prices ridiculously low. In addition to hamburgers they serve steaks, seafood, sandwiches, and an enticing array of Middle Eastern dishes. Best bargain is the "Armenian feast," a combination of kebab dishes and Mid-Eastern appetizers capable of feeding a large family or small army; budget.

Homesick for mom and apple pie? They'll fix you right up at **Rose City Diner** (45 South Fair Oaks Avenue, Pasadena; 818-793-8282). Open from the wee hours of the morning till the lee hours of the night, this '50s-style dive comes complete with booth jukeboxes, raucous cooks, and celebrity photos from the days of black-and-white television. The menu is heavy on gravy, as in meat loaf with gravy, turkey and gravy, etc. There are hamburgers, omelettes, homemade soups, and "blue-plate" specials like steak smothered in mushrooms and onions. Budget to moderate.

Sammy's Restaurant (24 West Colorado Boulevard, Pasadena; 818-792-9700), features Italian cuisine in a bright, modern setting with live '40s and '50s jazz and rock on the weekends. The menu is a mix of lamb, steak, and fresh fish dishes, with specialties such as lamb filet mignon. Dinner only; moderate.

Tra Fiori Ristorante (9 North Raymond Avenue; 818-796-2233), offers an innovative, contemporary European menu. Decorated with rotating contemporary art, this popular dining room serves everything from *osso buco* (veal marinated in lemon and white wine sauce) to chocolate soup. The service is equal to the cuisine. Moderate to deluxe.

At **Pappagallos** (42 South Pasadena Avenue; 818-578-0224) the taste runs to North Italian. With its dining atrium and open patio Pappagallos prepares duck lasagna and tortellini Sicilian amid an atmosphere of casual elegance. Moderate.

Tucked away in an art deco building on a side street, **Bistro 45** (45 South Mentor Avenue; 818-792-2535) is the newest gathering spot for Pasadena's "elegancia." The airy high-tech atmosphere, pastel walls and contemporary art match the handsomely presented French-Californian cuisine. The menu includes charbroiled free-range chicken, grilled ahi, and pan-roasted beef tenderloin. Deluxe.

Specializing in Mandarin and Szechuan cuisine, **Panda Inn** (3488 East Foothill Boulevard, Pasadena; 818-793-7300) is a dimly lit restaurant with Chinese prints and an atmosphere of intimacy. The spicy Szechuan dishes include hot braised shrimp, sweet and pungent chicken, spicy bean curd, and twice-cooked pork. There are also chow mein, egg foo yung, and noodle entrées, as well as a full inventory of Mandarin-style beef, fowl, seafood, and vegetable dishes. Moderate.

Any town as wealthy and prone to gentrification as Pasadena is bound to have numerous California-cuisine cafés. Foremost is **Parkway Grill** (510 South Arroyo Parkway; 818-795-1001), a brick-wall-and-bare-beam restaurant with track lights and stained glass. The antique bar is hardwood; the kitchen, *naturalement*, sits in the center of the complex, completely open to view. The chefs prepare gourmet pizza and pasta dishes such as calzone with bacon and smoked chicken, pizza with duck, fettucine with lobster, and angelhair primavera. Entrées include catfish in lime-soy sauce, pork marinated in Spanish spices and veal chops with porcini mushrooms in a red wine sauce. Lunch and dinner; moderate to deluxe.

Chez Vous (713 East Green Street; 818-792-4340) is an elegant yet casual French restaurant. The changing menu may include *escargots à l'ail doux* or *crevette escoffier* (large shrimp in a mushroom, sherry, cognac crème sauce) for starters and raspberry crisp duckling or a *mignon de veau du verger* (veal in orange sauce). Lunch and dinner, champagne Sunday brunch. Deluxe.

If you visit San Gabriel it will doubtless be to see the Spanish mission, so the most appropriate place to dine is **Panchito's** (261 South Mission Drive; 818-289-9201), a Mexican restaurant down the street. Housed in an historic building which served as the town's original city hall, it offers an array of south-of-the-border selections as well as steak and shrimp dinners. Lunch and dinner; moderate.

East conquers West at **Chez Sateau** (850 South Baldwin Avenue, Arcadia; 818-446-8806), where a Japanese chef prepares French meals with special flair. The frosted-glass-and-private-booth dining room features a menu that changes seasonally, including specialties such as "rainbow beef" and rack of lamb. Filling out the carte are outlandish desserts like soufflés and crêpes suzettes. Lunch, dinner, Sunday brunch; moderate to deluxe.

Way up in the San Gabriel Mountains, where Angeles National Forest creates an ideal retreat, you'll find **Newcomb's Ranch Inn** (★) (Route 2, one-quarter mile past Chilao Visitor Center, Chilao; 818-440-1001). This remote restaurant, set in a rustic wooden building, specializes in authentic Mexican food but serves an assortment of American dishes, burgers, and sandwiches. Little more than a log diner, it's a welcome sight for anyone wandering the mountains. Budget.

SAN FERNANDO VALLEY RESTAURANTS

GLENDALE AND BURBANK

A tiny Japanese restaurant on a Glendale side street, **Aoba** (201 West Harvard Street; 818-242-7676) contains fewer than a dozen booths laid out in maze-like fashion. The moderate-priced menu offers a standard array of Asian dishes, including sushi.

The most striking feature at **Fresco Ristorante** (514 South Brand Boulevard, Glendale; 818-247-5541) is the interior. The whitewashed stucco, formed into a series of columns, is combined with a skylight and potted plants to create a Mediterranean atmosphere. In addition to a dozen pasta dishes this Italian kitchen features grilled swordfish with pine nuts, veal chops in brandy with shiitake mushrooms, breast of duck, and beef *médaillons*. Lunch and dinner; moderate to deluxe.

VENTURA BOULEVARD

One of Southern California's great restaurant strips, Ventura Boulevard stretches for miles along the southern rim of The Valley, offering fine kitchens all along the route.

The decor at **Teru Sushi** (11940 Ventura Boulevard, Studio City; 818-763-6201) is as inviting as the cuisine. Hand-painted walls and carved figures combine with slat booths and a long dark wood sushi bar. The sushi menu includes several dozen varieties; they also serve a selection of traditional dishes. There is a beautiful garden dining area with a koi pond. Lunch and dinner; moderate to deluxe.

All the critics agree that the food at **Anajak Thai** (14704 Ventura Boulevard, Sherman Oaks; 818-501-4201) is outstanding. The menu features more than four dozen noodle, curry, beef, and chicken dishes, all priced in the budget range. Small and comfortable, the restaurant is painted dark blue and decorated with white latticework and Asian art.

At **Bao Wow** (17209 Ventura Boulevard, Encino; 818-789-9010) the motto is "Dim sum, yum yum." An Asian bistro done in high-tech style with exposed pipes and contemporary canvases, this eatery serves dim sum and other Chinese dishes. Lunch and dinner; moderate.

For French food and charming intimacy try **Mon Grenier** (18040 Ventura Boulevard, Encino; 818-344-8060). With a name which translates as "my attic," this whimsical dining room has a solid reputation for fine cuisine. Open for dinner only, entrées include pheasant with wild mushrooms, crispy duck, and salmon in crust; deluxe to ultra-deluxe.

The **Sagebrush Cantina** (23527 Calabasas Road; 818-222-6062), out in the town of Calabasas, is a sprawling restaurant and bar with a sawdust-floor dining room and ample patio space. In addition to an assortment of Mexican dishes they feature steak, ribs, Texas-style link sausage, barbecued brisket, and seafood; moderate.

Way up in the Santa Monica Mountains, that rocky spine separating the San Fernando Valley from the ocean, you'll uncover a rare find at **Saddle Peak Lodge (★)** (419 Cold Canyon Road, Calabasas; 213-655-9770). A true country lodge, this antique building is constructed of logs lashed together with leather straps. Flintlocks and trophy heads adorn the walls and leather upholstered chairs surround a stone fireplace. Open for dinner and weekend brunch, the restaurant offers quail, buffalo burgers, game hen, duckling, venison, pheasant, veal chops, rack of lamb, and "kick ass chili." If you have the time, it merits the mountain drive; deluxe to ultra-deluxe.

Over at **Delhi Place** (22323 Sherman Way, Canoga Park; 818-992-0913) you can dine on budget priced Indian cuisine. Cloth napkins and Asian decor are part of the bargain at this excellent restaurant. The dishes include lamb curry, chicken *tandoori*, and numerous vegetarian dishes. Lunch and dinner.

If these seem inappropriate just **Follow Your Heart** (21825 Sherman Way, Canoga Park; 818-348-3240) to a vegetarian restaurant popular with folks from miles around. Specialties at this gathering place include tofu plates, deep-dish pizza, nutburgers, black bean and tofu tacos, and steamed organic vegetables; budget.

NORTH SAN FERNANDO VALLEY

Ask anyone in the Valley where to go for downhome cooking and they will tell you **Dr. Hogly Wogly's Tyler Texas Bar-B-Que** (8136 Sepulveda Boulevard, Van Nuys; 818-780-6701). It's just a regular old café which happens to serve delicious brisket of beef and stick-to-the-ribs ribs. Dinner comes with half a loaf of home-baked bread, baked beans, cole slaw, and salad. Chow down! Lunch and dinner; moderate.

Another conversation piece is the **94th Aero Squadron** (16320 Raymer Avenue, Van Nuys; 818-994-7437), a wildly imaginative establishment obliquely modeled after a World War I aviation headquarters in France. The building resembles a provincial French farmhouse, but it's surrounded by charred airplanes and other artifacts of war. The interior is a sandbagged warren with wings and propellers dangling from the ceiling. The cuisine, which somehow seems irrelevant, is American, and combines "farmhouse" chicken with ham and cheese (topped with a mushroom sauce) with prime rib and seafood brochette. The view, naturally, is of Van Nuys Airport. Lunch, dinner, and Sunday brunch; moderate to deluxe.

The Great Outdoors

The Sporting Life

WINDSURFING AND WATERSKIING

Though the beach isn't far away, Los Angeles also contains several lakes which provide ample opportunity for water sports. Try **Frank G. Bonelli Park** (120 Via Verde Park Road, San Dimas; 714-599-8411) or **Castaic Lake Recreation Area** (32132 Ridge Route Road, Castaic; 805-257-4050) if you'd like to ski or windsurf, but remember to bring your own equipment.

BOATING

For those who are happier lolling about in a boat, there are rentals at **Frank G. Bonelli Park** (120 Via Verde Park Road, San Dimas; 714-599-2667), **Whittier Narrows Recreation Area** (Legg Lake) (823 Lexington-Gallatin Road, South El Monte; 818-444-9305), **Santa Fe Dam** (15501 East Arrow Highway, Irwindale; 818-334-1065), and **Castaic Lake Recreation Area** (32132 Ridge Route Road, Castaic; 805-257-2049).

Paddle boating is a big sport at **MacArthur Park** (2230 West 6th Street, Los Angeles).

SWIMMING

From the air, Los Angeles seems to have a swimming pool for every family. For those without access to backyard water holes, there are several public pools. Among the more notable are **Los Angeles Swim Stadium,** just outside Exposition Park (3966 South Menlo Avenue, Los Angeles; 213-485-2844), and **Griffith Park Pool** (4730 Crystal Springs Road, Los Angeles; 213-666-4647).

Those who prefer more natural surroundings can try **Frank G. Bonelli Park** (120 Via Verde Park Road, San Dimas; 714-599-8411), which features a lake as well as an aquatic theme park complete with water slide, or **Castaic Lake Recreation Area** (32132 Ridge Route Road, Castaic; 805-257-4050).

JOGGING

Though driving seems almost an addiction in the city, many Angelenos still manage to exercise. Filling your lungs with smoggy air might not be the healthiest thing to do, but if you're interested in jogging anyway, join the troopers at **Exposition Park and Recreation Center** (3990 South Menlo Avenue, Los Angeles; 213-749-5884), **Elysian Park** (near the intersection of Routes 110 and 5; 213-485-5054), **San Vicente Boulevard** in the Brentwood area, **Lacy Park** (1485 Virginia Road, San Marino), the **arroyo** near the Rose Bowl in Pasadena, or **Griffith Park** (4730 Crystal Springs Road, Los Angeles; 213-665-5188).

GOLF

In Los Angeles it's as easy to tee off at a golf course as it is to get teed off in a traffic jam. Among the more challenging or interesting courses are **Montebello Country Club** (901 Via San Clemente, Montebello; 213-887-4565), **Rancho Park Golf Course** (10460 West Pico Boulevard, West Los Angeles; 310-838-7373), **Brookside Golf Course** (1133 North Rosemont Avenue, Pasadena; 818-796-0177), and **Wilson-Harding Golf Course** (Griffith Park; 213-663-2555).

In the eastern end of the county try **Marshall Canyon Golf Course** (6100 North Stephens Ranch Road, La Verne; 714-593-6914), **Diamond Bar Golf Course** (22751 East Golden Springs Drive, Diamond Bar; 714-861-8282), **San Dimas Golf Course** (2100 Terrebonne Avenue, San Dimas; 818-966-8547), **Mountain Meadows Golf Course** (1875 Fairplex Drive, Pomona; 714-629-1166), or **Whittier Narrows Golf Course** (8640 East Rush Street, Rosemead; 818-280-8225).

In the San Fernando Valley consider **Knollwood Golf Course** (12040 Balboa Boulevard, Granada Hills; 818-363-8161) or **Sepulveda Golf Complex** (16821 Burbank Boulevard, Encino; 818-995-1170).

TENNIS

Most public parks have at least one tennis court; the city's largest facility, **Griffith Park** (4730 Crystal Springs Road, Los Angeles; 213-662-7772 or 213-665-5188) has many. For information on other local parks, contact the nearest Los Angeles City and County Parks and Recreation Department office.

Tennis clubs dot the county; one such club, the **Racquet Center** (10933 Ventura Boulevard, Studio City, 818-760-2303; and 920 Lohman Lane, South Pasadena, 213-258-4178), is open to the public. For further information about clubs and tournaments, contact the **Southern California Tennis Association** (P.O. Box 240015, Los Angeles, CA 90024; 310-208-3838).

HORSEBACK RIDING

With its curving hills and flowering meadows, Griffith Park is a favorite spot among urban equestrians. Several places on the edge of the park provide facilities. Try **Sunset Ranch** (3400 North Beachwood Drive, Hollywood; 213-464-9612), **Circle K Stables** (914 Mariposa Street, Burbank; 818-843-9890), **Griffith Park Livery Stables** (480 Riverside Drive, Burbank; 818-840-8401), or **Bar S Stables** (1850 Riverside Drive, Glendale; 818-242-8443).

HANG GLIDING, BALLOONING, AND BUNGEE-JUMPING

What better way to let yourself go than by coasting or floating on high? The adventurous can try hang gliding at **Windsports International** (16145 Victory Boulevard, Van Nuys; 818-988-0111); or call **Adventures in Paradise** (310-376-7052) for ballooning or bungee-jumping in the Los Angeles area.

BICYCLING

Bikeways in Los Angeles are almost as plentiful as freeways. Unlike the freeways, few of them are normally congested. Many run parallel to parks, rivers, aqueducts, and lakes, offering a different view of this diverse area.

Over 14 miles of bike routes wind through Griffith Park. Two notable excursions skirt many of the park attractions: **Crystal Springs Loop,** which follows Crystal Springs Road and Zoo Drive along the park's eastern edge, passes the merry-go-round and Travel Town; **Mineral Wells Loop,** an arduous uphill climb, passes Harding Golf Course, then coasts downhill to Zoo Drive, taking in Travel Town and the zoo.

For a trip from the mountains to the sea, try the **San Gabriel River Bike Trail**. It begins in Azusa and extends 38 miles to the Pacific near Long Beach.

In the Whittier–El Monte area, bicyclists can choose a long jaunt along the **Upper Rio Hondo Bike Trail** or a leisurely go-round on the **Legg Lake Loop** in Whittier Narrows Recreation Area.

In the Mt. Washington area, the **Arroyo Seco Bike Trail** includes a loop past Heritage Square, the Lummis House, and Casa de Adobe. The trail begins at the Montecito Heights Recreation Center on Homer Street and runs along an arroyo.

The **Kenneth Newell Bikeway** begins on Arroyo Boulevard in Pasadena, then dips down to Arroyo Seco and the famed Rose Bowl. The bikeway follows a flood basin, climbs a steep hill into Linda Vista and continues to Devil's Gate Dam and the world-renowned Jet Propulsion Laboratory.

For a look at the good life, check out the route from **San Gabriel Mission to the Huntington Library**, which winds from San Gabriel through the exclusive town of San Marino.

A strenuous but worthwhile excursion is a bike ride along **Mulholland Drive**. Not recommended during commuter hours, this route traverses the spine of the Santa Monica Mountains and offers fabulous views of the city and ocean.

For more information on bicycle routes contact the **Transportation Commission** (213-626-0370) for a brochure.

Beaches and Parks

Most of the information concerning beaches and parks appears in the "Sightseeing" section of this chapter. You will also find specific parks listed in the index. In addition to the few parks described directly below, those dealt with in "Sightseeing" include Barnsdall Park, Eaton Canyon Nature Center, Echo Park, Elysian Park, Exposition Park, Griffith Park, Los Angeles State and County Arboretum, MacArthur Park, Placerita Canyon State and County Park, Vasquez Rocks County Park, Wattles Park, William S. Hart Park, and Whittier Narrows Nature Center.

Frank G. Bonelli Regional Park—This 2200-acre facility is a combination of tree-covered hills and theme park attractions. For the outdoor-minded there are trails, stables, and a 250-acre lake with boating and fishing facilities. The rest of the crowd beelines to **Raging Waters** (714-592-6453), an aquatic theme park with waterslides and simulated surfing waves. Visitors who can't decide between the natural and artificial head for the golf course and hot tubs.

Facilities: Picnic areas, restrooms, snack bar, grocery; information, 714-599-8411. *Camping:* Permitted in an RV camp, which features a pool and volleyball courts; 714-599-8355.

Getting there: Located at 120 Via Verde in San Dimas.

Angeles National Forest—Nature is rarely reducible to statistics, but numbers are unavoidable in describing this 650,000-acre preserve. Stretching from San Bernardino County across the entire northern tier of Los Angeles County, the park encompasses the San Gabriel Mountains and separates the Los Angeles Basin from the desert. There are four rivers, eight lakes, a 10,000-foot peak, and 189 miles of fishing streams. The forest attracts more than 15 million visitors annually. Most are daytrippers intent on sightseeing and picnicking, but campers and hikers, enjoying over 60 campgrounds and 556 miles of trails, are also prevalent. Flora and fauna range from green-winged teal to black bear to horned toads and rattlesnakes. This is also a prime ski area, with nine winter sports centers.

Facilities: Picnic areas, restrooms; restaurants, except for a few small cafés, are many miles away. The 36,000-acre **San Gabriel Wilderness** is contained within the National Forest. Information, 818-574-5200. *Camping:* Permitted.

Getting there: Route 2 is the main highway through the southern sector of the forest; the northern region is located east of Route 5.

Castaic Lake—Set at the foot of the Tehachapi Mountains, this 2300-acre manmade lake is surrounded by rugged slopes. The countryside—covered with chemise, sage, and chaparral—is stark but beautiful. Along the lake, which carves a V in the hills, are facilities for picnicking, boating, and waterskiing. Castaic is stocked with bass, trout, and bluegill; unlike many of California's reservoirs it permits swimming.

Facilities: Restrooms, picnic areas, playgrounds; restaurants and groceries are nearby in Castaic; there's a Department of Water Resources Museum at the visitor center (805-257-3610).

Getting there: The visitor center is located at 31849 North Lake Hughes Road in Castaic.

Hiking

The idea of natural areas in Los Angeles seems like a contradiction in terms. But the city is so vast—sprawling from the Pacific to the mountains—that even ambitious developers have been unable to pave it all. For backpackers and daytrippers alike, miles of hiking trails still lace the hills and canyons that lie just beyond the housing tracts and shopping malls.

WHITTIER–EL MONTE AREA TRAILS

Located near Roland Heights, in Otterbein Regional County Park, the **Skyline Trail: Otterbein Park to Hacienda Boulevard** (6 miles) traverses the Puente Hills. The hike leads through wild mustard fields to an overlook with views of the San Gabriel Valley.

Miles of hiking trails abound in **Frank G. Bonelli Regional Park** in San Dimas. To get an overview of the park, hike along the southern hills above Puddingston Reservoir. Maps are available at the park headquarters.

SAN GABRIEL MOUNTAINS TRAILS

The San Gabriel Mountains are crisscrossed with hiking trails ripe for exploring.

Several years ago the San Gabriel portion of the **Pacific Crest Trail,** which leads from Canada to Mexico, was completed. One part of that great system, the **Mill Creek Summit to Pacifico Mountain Trail** (4 miles) follows a route through spruce and oak forests to a view overlooking the Mojave Desert.

At the end of Chaney Trail Road in Altadena there's a lovely spot for a family hike through a tree-shrouded canyon. **Lower Millard Canyon Falls Trail** (.5 mile) leads to a 50-foot waterfall surrounded by huge boulders. If you're a little more adventurous, try **Upper Millard Canyon Trail** (2.5 miles).

An even more ambitious hike from the same trailhead is **The Mount Lowe Railway Trail** (3.5 miles). At the end you'll discover an abandoned rail line, the old "Railway to the Clouds," and the ruins of Ye Alpine tavern. It's a moderate trek offering spectacular views of Los Angeles.

From Eaton Canyon Nature Center in Altadena, the **Altadena Crest Trail** (3 miles) explores the foothills of the San Gabriels. A side trip to **Eaton Falls** (.5 mile) follows the stream bed.

Big Santa Anita Canyon north of Sierra Madre is another popular area for hiking. **Sturtevant Falls Trail** (1.8 miles) leads upstream to a 50-foot waterfall. The trailhead is in Chantry Flat. (Don't climb on the rocks at the waterfall; several people have been seriously hurt here.)

There are many ways to scale 5710-foot Mount Wilson. One particularly pleasant route is the **Mount Wilson Trail** (7.5 miles), beginning from Miramonte Avenue in Arcadia. This path leads up Little Santa Anita Canyon past oak and spruce trees to Orchard Camp, a way station offering a perfect place for a picnic. From here the trail ascends through dense chaparral to the ridge and Mount Wilson Road.

Not as well-known as Mount Wilson is a neighboring peak, 5994-foot **Mount Disappointment** (2.8 miles), which offers another opportunity to view Los Angeles from on high. You'll walk through Douglas fir and Coulter pine forests and climb along chaparral-covered ridges. The trailhead is just beyond Red Box off the Mount Wilson Road.

It's all downhill to begin with when you hike **Devil's Canyon Trail** (5.5 miles). This trek through an alder-studded canyon, with a bubbling creek for company, goes from Upper Chilao Campground in the San Gabriel Wilderness to beautiful Devil's Canyon Waterfall.

The **Arroyo Seco Canyon Trail** (9.8 miles), beginning at Switzer's Picnic Area (off Route 2), is a challenging way to explore the serene canyons of the San Gabriels. The trail overlooks Arroyo Seco Falls, joins the **Gabrieleño Trail** (3.5 miles), then descends to the tree-laden floor of the canyon. En route is Oakwilde Trail Camp, an ideal spot for an overnight visit. The trail continues to the mouth of the canyon, which overlooks the massive Jet Propulsion Laboratory.

GRIFFITH PARK TRAILS

Los Angeles' outback is found a few miles from the center of Downtown amid the forested hills of Griffith Park. With over 55 miles of trails to explore, the park rests along the Hollywood Hills at the edge of the Santa Monica Mountains. For information and maps contact the local ranger station (213-665-5188).

Among the best hikes is the **Mt. Hollywood Loop Trail** (6 miles). Beginning near the merry-go-round, the path follows a stream, passes deer and coyote habitats, then leads up out of the canyon onto the chaparral-covered slopes of Mt. Hollywood.

For a combination sightseeing-hiking venture take the **Mineral Wells to Mt. Bell Trail** (4.3 miles). The hike begins on a level bridle trail, ascends Mt. Bell, then wends its way down toward the zoo, and back to Mineral Wells.

The **Pacific Electric Quarry–Bronson Cave Trail** (2.3 miles) snakes through Brush Canyon to an abandoned rock quarry and the Bronson Caves, an area ripe for exploring. If it seems like you've been here before, that's because this was the location for such shows as "Bonanza," "Mod Squad," and "Star Trek."

SAN FERNANDO VALLEY AREA TRAILS

Leading up a 5074-foot peak, the highest within the Los Angeles city limits, **Mount Lukens Trail** (3.8 miles) is a hearty uphill trek. On a clear day the Pacific looms in the distance, beyond a jigsaw puzzle of housing tracts and rolling hills. The trailhead is in Sunland off Doske Road; be sure to bring water.

At the northern edge of the San Fernando Valley, **Placerita Canyon to Sylmar Trail** (9 miles) offers conditioned hikers an opportunity to climb along a chaparral-covered hillside to an oak-studded canyon. The hike begins in Placerita Canyon State and County Park and goes along the Wilson Canyon Saddle. Another challenging trek is the climb up **Manzanita Mountain** (1 mile), with its picturesque views. For the family, there's **Placerita Canyon Loop Hike** (8 miles), an easygoing jaunt through a shady canyon and along a creek.

The old stage road that connected the San Fernando and San Joaquin valleys is now the route of **Beale's Cut Trail** (.3 mile). This short but steep hike cuts through the San Fernando Pass, with its earthquake fault and twisted rock formations.

One of Los Angeles' hidden gems is **O'Melveny Park** (★), a 672-acre preserve in the Santa Susana Mountains at the north end of the San Fernando

Valley. **O'Melveny Park Trail** (2.5 miles) begins in Bee Canyon and follows an old fire road past a stream, then climbs through fields of wildflowers to a series of bluffs. After the steep climb, you are rewarded with a panoramic view of Los Angeles, the Santa Clarita Valley, and the San Gabriel Mountains. The trailhead is near Sesnon Boulevard in Granada Hills.

In Chatsworth, **Devil's Canyon Trail** (1.5 miles) offers a peaceful walk along a streambed through stands of sycamore and oak. Look for the caves which have been etched into the sides of the canyon.

Travelers' Tracks

Sightseeing

DOWNTOWN

Contrary to the opinion of Los Angeles bashers, the city does indeed possess a center. Ever since the town was settled in 1781, the focus of the community has been near Olvera Street and the Civic Center, along the Los Angeles River.

While there's barely enough water in the river these days to cause a ripple, the Downtown district is inundated with people. About 20,000 people live in this vital neighborhood and more than 200,000 commuters arrive daily. Adding to the smog and congestion, they also make Downtown the center for politics, finance, and culture.

For walking tours of the Downtown district contact the **Los Angeles Conservancy** (727 West 7th Street; 213-623-8687).

To help you navigate around this urban core, I've divided the district into several sections: Olvera Street, Chinatown, Little Tokyo, the Civic Center, and Central Downtown (which includes the financial district). In exploring each neighborhood, remember that the DASH shuttle, a purple-striped minibus, serves most of Downtown.

OLVERA STREET

The historic heart of the city is **El Pueblo de Los Angeles**, a 44-acre outdoor museum centered around Olvera Street. In 1781 a few dozen Spanish settlers established hardscrabble farms and buiit adobes here, breaking ground for what eventually became one of the world's largest metropolitan areas. The **visitor center** (622 North Main Street; 213-628-1274), providing maps, brochures, and walking tours, sits in one of the pueblo's vintage buildings, an 1887 brick-faced Victorian called the Sepulveda Block.

Heart of hearts is the **Plaza** (North Main Street and Paseo de la Plaza), a tree-shaded courtyard adorned with statues and highlighted by a wrought-iron bandstand. A colorful gathering place, it's a frequent site for fiestas and open-air concerts.

Anchoring one corner of the plaza is **Firehouse No. 1** (134 Paseo de la Plaza), Los Angeles' original fire station. Built in 1884, the brick structure served the fire department for little more than a decade, after which it became a saloon, boarding house, and store. Today it's a miniature museum filled with horse-drawn fire wagons, old-time helmets, and an ample inventory of memories.

The plaza's most prestigious building, **Pico House** (Paseo de la Plaza and North Main Street) was built in 1870 by Pío Pico, the last Mexican governor of California. Italianate in style, it represented the grandest hotel of its era.

Old Plaza Church (535 North Main Street), first established as a chapel in 1784, also faces the square. The city's oldest Catholic church, it is unassuming from the outside but displays an interior that is a study in wrought iron and gold leaf. Murals cover the ceiling of the diminutive chapel and a collection of religious canvases adorns the altar.

Mexicans with more worldly matters in mind gather in large crowds outside the **Biscailuz Building** (125 Paseo de la Plaza, northeast corner of the plaza), a whitewashed structure decorated with brightly hued murals by Leo Politi, El Pueblo's resident artist for over 30 years.

For the full flavor of Spanish California, wander down **Olvera Street**. Lined with *puestos* (stands) selling Mexican handicrafts, it provides a window on early Los Angeles. The brick-paved alleyway is also one of the West's first pedestrian shopping malls.

Among the antique buildings bordering this narrow corridor is the **Ávila Adobe,** a classic mud-brick house constructed around 1818. The oldest house in Los Angeles, it has undergone numerous incarnations, serving as a private residence, boarding house, and restaurant and surviving numerous earthquakes. Today it's a museum, fully restored and filled with period pieces.

A nearby historical marker points out the vital water source for early Los Angeles. **La Zanja Madre,** the mother ditch, channeled the precious waters of the Los Angeles River to the fledgling community for more than a century.

Just off the plaza is **Masonic Hall** (416½ North Main Street), an 1858 building which houses a museum of Masonic Order memorabilia. With wrought-iron balcony and ornate facade it follows an Italian Renaissance design. Even more elaborate, though of later vintage, the neighboring **Merced Theatre** was constructed in 1870 and represents the city's first theatrical center.

Union Station (800 North Alameda Street), one of the country's great train depots, has been a Los Angeles landmark since 1939. With a Spanish-Mexican exterior, the station is a cavernous structure boasting marble floors, a beam ceiling 52 feet high, arched corridors, and walls of inlaid tile. Embodying the romance and promise of travel, it is a destination with a distinct identity, a point of departure for the far fringes of the imagination.

The **San Antonio Winery** (737 Lamar Street; 213-223-1401) represents the last of a disappearing breed. Years ago vineyards dotted the San Gabriel foothills, but Los Angeles' phenomenal urbanization steadily displaced them. Somehow this family-operated facility remained, situated surprisingly close to the center of the city. Today second- and third-generation members of the Riboli clan lead tasting tours through the vintage 1917 building.

CHINATOWN

Back in 1870, when the Chinese population numbered perhaps 200, "Orientals" were sequestered in a rundown neighborhood southeast of the original plaza. As that area was torn down during the 1930s to build Union Station, they moved in increasing numbers to modern-day **Chinatown**, a multiblock neighborhood which has become the cultural and commercial center for Chinese throughout the city.

For an authentic view, stroll the **600 block of North Spring Street** past the herb shops and fresh fish stores. Here local residents buy goat meat and fresh produce and choose from among the racks of roast ducks that hang forlornly in store windows.

Don't miss **Kong Chow Temple** (★) (931 North Broadway; 213-626-1955), a tiny chapel tucked away on the second floor of an assuming building. Crowded with elderly Chinese, the place is heavy with incense and handwoven tapestries. Gilded altars and bas-relief figures add a touch of the exotic.

The commercial heart of the district lies along Broadway and Hill Street, with stores lining both boulevards for several blocks. Connecting these two thoroughfares is **New Chinatown** (Gin Ling Way), a two-block-long pedestrian mall. Traditional gates with swirling outlines mark the entranceways to this enclave. Figures of animals and ceremonial fish adorn the buildings and dragons breathe fire from the rooftops.

LITTLE TOKYO

The Japanese response to Chinatown is **Little Tokyo**, a discrete neighborhood bounded by Los Angeles Street, Central Avenue, 1st Street and 3rd Street. At the heart of the district is the **Japanese American Cultural and Community Center** (244 South San Pedro Street; 213-628-2725), a stoic plate-glass-and-poured-concrete structure designed by Buckminster Fuller and Isamu Noguchi. The complex, which houses dozens of Asian organizations, faces a spacious brick-paved courtyard. Next door sits the **Japan America Theatre** (244 South San Pedro Street; 213-680-3700), an important showcase for kabuki theater, Asian music, and other performing arts.

Follow the brick paving stones from the cultural center through **Japanese Village Plaza**, a two-block shopping mall adorned with fountains and sculptures. At the end of the plaza stands Little Tokyo's tile-roofed **fire tower**, an ornamental but practical structure which has become a local landmark.

Another cultural gathering place is the lovely **Higashi Buddhist Temple** (505 East 3rd Street; 213-626-4200). With its tile roof, the temple represents Japanese architecture adapted to a Western cityscape.

The **Temporary Contemporary** (152 North Central Avenue; 213-621-2766; admission), a branch of the Museum of Contemporary Art, sits on the outskirts of Little Tokyo. At the cutting edge of the modern art scene, it contains changing exhibits from all over the world. The focus is on the post World War II era with artworks ranging from abstract paintings to wildly imaginative sculptures.

For a taste of the truly avant-garde, be sure to visit the **Museum of Neon Art** (★) (704 Traction Avenue; 213-617-1580; admission). One of the city's most unusual showcases, it specializes in neon, electric, and kinetic art. In addition to a permanent collection of antique neon and electric signs, the museum hosts an ever-evolving series of special displays. Neon-laced exhibits are as imaginative as their titles. "Don't Stand Under the Forklift While Playing the Accordion" mimics an accordion musician strolling under a giant crate. "Nixon's the One" features a bumper-stickered wheelchair. A wonderfully bizarre place.

CIVIC CENTER

Art and politics have always been odd bedfellows, but they make a cozy couple around the Los Angeles Civic Center. Here an impressive group of government buildings combines with an array of museums to create a complex well worth touring.

The centerpiece of the ensemble is **City Hall** (200 North Spring Street; 213-485-4423), a vintage 1928 building. Rendered famous by the old "Dragnet" television show, this pyramid-topped edifice is also a frequent backdrop in many contemporary movies. The tile-and-marble rotunda on the third floor is a study in governmental architecture. But the most impressive feature is the **observation deck** on the 27th floor, from which you can enjoy a 360° view of Los Angeles' smog banks.

Those who report on City Hall reside across the street at the **Los Angeles Times Building** (202 West 1st Street; 213-237-5000). One of the nation's largest and finest newspapers, the *Times* sits in a classic 1934 moderne-style building to which latter day architects, in a fit of ego and insanity, added a glass box monstrosity that appears to be devouring the original. The older structure, housing the newspaper, is open to guided tours; the glass accretion contains corporate offices.

Cultural counterpoint to these centers of power is the nearby **Music Center** (Grand Avenue between 1st and Temple streets; 213-972-7211). Gathered into one stunningly designed complex are the **Dorothy Chandler Pavilion,** a marble-and-black-glass music hall which hosts the opera and symphony; the **Mark Taper Forum,** a world-renowned theater that presents contemporary and experimental drama; and the **Ahmanson Theatre,** a 2000-seat auditorium where traditional plays are staged. Not to be outdone, the visual arts are represented by a pulsating fountain with more than 100 rhythmically timed streams. Guided tours are available.

This last art form reaches flood tide at the **Museum of Contemporary Art** (250 South Grand Avenue, 213-621-2766; admission). Affectionately dubbed "the MOCA," this ultramodern showplace was designed by Japanese architect Arata Isozaki. It's an exotic mix of red sandstone and pyramidal skylights with a sunken courtyard. The galleries consist of expansive open spaces displaying a variety of traveling exhibits and the works of Mark Rothko, Robert Rauschenberg, Jackson Pollock, and others.

It's the noisiest museum in the world. The **Los Angeles Children's Museum** (310 North Main Street; 213-687-8800; admission), with countless hands-on and hands-all-over-everything exhibits, is probably the happiest as well. There's a bus and police motorcycle for kids to ride; make-up rooms for them to paint their faces; a hospital bed, X-ray table, and dentist chair for practicing future professions; plus a recording studio and video cameras for children to tape their own antics.

CENTRAL DOWNTOWN

While social classes may be miles apart culturally, their neighborhoods often stand shoulder to shoulder. Midway between the Los Angeles centers of political and financial power sits **Broadway,** a vibrant Hispanic shopping district. This, not Olvera Street, is where today's Mexican population shops. A cross between New York's 42nd Street and the boulevards of Mexico City, this multiblock strip is crowded with cut-rate clothing stores, swap meets, pawn shops, and stands selling pizza by the slice.

Start at the South 300 block and wander uptown. The first place you'll encounter is **Grand Central Public Market** (317 South Broadway; 213-624-2378), a fresh food bazaar in the tradition of Mexico's *mercados.* Fruit stalls, vegetable stands, butchers, and fresh fish shops line the aisles. There are juice stands dispensing dozens of flavors and vendors selling light meals. More than 30,000 people pass through every day, making it one of the city's most vital scenes.

The **Bradbury Building** (304 South Broadway; 213-626-1893) across the street has undergone a massive restoration. The interior features an extraordinary courtyard illuminated by a skylight, wrought-iron grillwork, and winding stairs surrounding an open cage elevator. Add flourishes of marble and brick to finish off this 1893 masterpiece.

During the 1940s Broadway was the city's Great White Way, where stars mingled and Hollywood premiered its greatest films. Today the boulevard's diminished glory is evident in the old theaters between 3rd and Olympic streets. Once the pride of the studios that built them, they are now in varying stages of disrepair. The **Million Dollar Theater** (310 South Broadway), where movie mogul Sid Grauman began as a showman, has become a Spanish-language movie house which parodies Hollywood's Walk of Fame by setting the names of Chicano stars in the sidewalk.

Also of note are the **Los Angeles Theatre** (615 South Broadway), with its gaudy Versailles-style architecture; the magnificent **Orpheum** (842 South Broadway), a 2000-seat Spanish and French Gothic hybrid built in 1926; and the **United Artists Theatre** (933 South Broadway), a 1926 Spanish Gothic structure with murals depicting Charlie Chaplin and Mary Pickford, now restored for service as Dr. Gene Scott's University Cathedral. Many of these grande dames presently show Spanish films from noon 'til night, but most will allow you to glance inside.

Recapturing part of this past is the nearby **Los Angeles Conservancy** (727 West 7th Street, Suite 955; 213-623-2489), a preservation group that conducts tours of the theaters and other places of historic interest.

Crowds from Broadway in search of greenery inevitably head to **Pershing Square** (bounded by Olive, Hill, 5th, and 6th streets). Despite its palm trees and flower beds, this five-acre park, slated for restoration, is badly run-down.

If Broadway was once The Great White Way, **Spring Street** (between 4th and 7th streets) was the Wall Street of the West. Like its theatrical counterpart, this faded financial district is now the venue of historians and sentimentalists. The former **Pacific Coast Stock Exchange** (618 South Spring Street), a 1930 masterpiece of moderne architecture, has been closed. Among the other hallowed halls of finance are the **Design Center of Los Angeles** (433 South Spring Street), a 1928 building with tile murals and zigzag facade now serving as a temporary home for the Los Angeles Central Library, and **Banco Popular** (354 South Spring Street), a 1903 Beaux-Arts office building.

Today the focus of finance has shifted to a highrise district between Grand Avenue and Figueroa, 3rd, and 8th streets. Here the **First Interstate World Center** (633 West 5th Street) rises 74 stories. Around the corner at the **Wells Fargo History Museum** (333 South Grand Avenue; 213-253-7166) you can view displays re-creating more than a century of Western history. The **World Trade Center** (333 South Flower Street), another architectural extravaganza, looms nearby.

At **ARCO Plaza** (Flower Street between 5th and 6th streets), a twin-tower, 52-story behemoth, you'll encounter the **RTD** (Southern California

Rapid Transit District, Level C; 213-972-7935), where you can obtain route maps of the city's largest transportation agency.

The **Greater Los Angeles Visitors & Convention Bureau** (695 South Figueroa Street; 213-689-8822) is the city's main information center. There you'll find maps, leaflets, and a friendly staff to help point the way through this urban maze.

Amid all these elite and expensive office buildings, one structure stands forth like a visitor from the future. Its five mirror-glass cylinders resembling a space station with legs, the **Westin Bonaventure Hotel** (404 South Figueroa Street; 213-624-1000) is easily the city's most imaginative skyscraper. Because of its unique design, together with an interior of reflecting pools and bubble elevators, the 1978 building is a favorite backdrop for science fiction movies.

Across the street from this symbol of tomorrow stands an emblem of the past. The **Los Angeles Central Library** (5th and Hope streets; 213-612-3200), built in the 1920s, incorporates Egyptian, Roman, and Byzantine elements into a Beaux-Arts design. The most striking feature of all is the pyramid tower inlaid with colorful tile patterns. Unfortunately the interior was gutted by fire in 1986 and the library is not scheduled to reopen until 1993.

For a view of blue-collar Los Angeles, depart Central Downtown for the **Flower Market** (Wall Street between 7th and 8th streets; 213-627-2482), where wholesale flower merchants line an entire block and the air is redolent with fragrant merchandise. Over at the **Produce Markets** (Central Avenue and 7th Street; or San Pedro and 11th streets), the bounty from California's interior valleys goes on the block every morning. The place is a beehive of business, a fascinating area where the farm meets the city.

GREATER LOS ANGELES

In organizing the city geographically, a task tantamount to squaring the circle, I finally decided to cover a multitude of sins (my own, not the city's) with the term "Greater Los Angeles." Forming a concentric circle around the Downtown district, Greater Los Angeles is like a huge urban donut. Immediately to the south sits Exposition Park and further afield are the black communities of Watts and Inglewood. East Los Angeles represents the city's proud Hispanic neighborhood, beyond which lies the middle-class town of Whittier. To the north rests Silver Lake, an upscale neighborhood in an upslope area. Also defined by hills is the Mt. Washington area, an historic district bordering the San Gabriel Valley.

Most of Greater Los Angeles, particularly to the south and east, is flat, predictable, and ugly. Rich in cultural diversity, it lacks architectural character, consisting of unimaginative housing tracts interlarded with industrial quarters. North of Downtown you'll encounter pretty parks and several diversified neighborhoods.

EXPOSITION PARK AREA

Minutes from Los Angeles' ultramodern downtown, where real estate sells by the square foot, sits the spacious, Romanesque campus of the **University of Southern California** (bounded by Jefferson Boulevard, Vermont Avenue, Exposition Boulevard, and Figueroa Street; 213-740-2311). Lined with sycamore and maple trees, this red-brick-and-ivy enclave features a park-like setting filled with historic buildings.

The movie location for everything from *The Hunchback of Notre Dame* to *The Graduate*, it's an ideal spot for a stroll. Among USC's many features are the **Fisher Gallery** (213-740-8229), with an excellent collection of European and New World art from the 15th century to the present, and the **Hancock Memorial Museum** (213-740-0433), containing the furnishings of a 1907 mansion which was modeled after the Villa de Medici.

Of course it is athletics, not academics and architecture, for which USC is famous. More concerned with quarterbacks than quasars, the school has produced four Heisman trophy winners and more than 100 All-Americans while leaving the Nobel prizes to UCLA and Berkeley. O. J. Simpson, not Socrates, is the role model for this 28,000-student university.

The **Skirball Museum** (3077 University Avenue; 213-749-3424), part of Hebrew Union College, sits across the street from USC. Devoted entirely to Judaism, the displays include exhibits on the Torah and the Jewish holy days. The archaeology of the Middle East is also represented in a series of artifacts. One very imaginative exhibit features simulated dig sites as well as a cut-away which shows how different strata of a hill contain remnants from earlier and earlier civilizations.

Exposition Park—a multiblock extravaganza bounded by Exposition Boulevard, Menlo Avenue, Martin Luther King, Jr. Boulevard, and Figueroa Street—is long on exposition and short on park. There *is* an enchanting **sunken garden** with a fountain, gazebos, and almost 20,000 rose bushes representing nearly 200 varieties of roses. Otherwise the park blooms with museums and sports arenas.

The **California Museum of Science and Industry** (Exposition Park; 213-744-7400) is one of those hands-on, great-for-kids-of-all-ages complexes. Rambling between several buildings, it has halls devoted to health and economics and displays demonstrating everything from simple laws of science to the latest advances in high technology.

Over in the **Aerospace Complex** there are exhibits explaining the principles of aerodynamics as well as planes, jets, and space capsules suspended from the ceiling in mock flight. Climbing a catwalk-like series of staircases, you'll have a bird's-eye view of a 1920 glider, Air Force T-38, an F-20 Tiger Shark, and Gemini II spacecraft.

The **Natural History Museum of Los Angeles County** (Exposition Park; 213-744-3466; admission), reputedly the largest and most popular museum in California, is a world (and an afternoon) unto itself. Among the three-dozen galleries are rock and gem displays; dioramas of bears, wolves, and bison; set pieces from the American past, including a cut-away Conestoga wagon demonstrating life on the frontier; and, of course, the dinosaur skeletons required of every self-respecting natural history museum. If this is not enough, the museum contains bird specimens and a "discovery center" where you can play scientist.

Prettiest of all the buildings in this museum park is the **California Afro-American Museum** (Exposition Park; 213-744-7432) with its glass-roofed sculpture court and bright, airy galleries. Devoted to black culture and history, the center displays the work of artists from around the world.

Surprisingly enough, Exposition Park's most notable architectural achievement is not the museum buildings, but rather the **Los Angeles Memorial Coliseum** (Exposition Park; 213-747-7111), a 91,000-seat arena built in 1923. One of the most beautiful stadiums in the country, site of the 1932 and 1984 Olympics, the Coliseum is a classic arena with arched entranceways and rainbow-colored seats. Today it is home to the Los Angeles Raiders and University of Southern California football teams.

WATTS-INGLEWOOD AREA

One of the seven wonders of Los Angeles is located in the industrial town of Vernon, where **Farmer John's Pig Mural (★)** (3049 East Vernon Avenue) covers an entire city block. Probably the biggest mural you'll ever see, it's also one of the funniest, picturing hundreds of pigs running through open fields. This idyllic landscape, in the midst of miles of factories, was begun in 1957 by a movie-industry artist named Les Grimes. For years Grimes gave everything to the project and in the end sacrificed his life, falling from a scaffold while working on the mural. His legacy is a romping, rollicking, technicolor creation.

Another folk-art wonder, also the result of an individual artist with an uncommon vision, is **Watts Towers** (1765 East 107th Street, in Simon Rodia State Historic Park). Fashioned by Simon Rodia over a three-decade period, these delicate, curving towers, inlaid with *objets trouvés*, rise nearly 100 feet above Los Angeles' black ghetto. Encrusted with tile shards, stones, and more than 70,000 sea shells, they form a work of unsettling beauty, a kind of icon to a personal god. After half a lifetime of work Rodia finished the sculpture in 1954, gave the property to a neighbor, and left Los Angeles, never to visit his towers again.

The **Watts Towers Arts Center** (213-569-8181) next door features a rotating series of exhibits by artists in the black community. Watts, you might remember, is the area that exploded in a series of devastating 1965 race riots during which 43 people were killed and over 4000 arrested.

Los Angeles' industrial district also contains some of California's early creations. The **Dominguez Ranch Adobe** (18127 South Alameda Street;

213-631-5981), in the heavy-metal town of Compton, is a 19th-century Spanish rancho which now doubles as a seminary and historic museum. The grounds of this sprawling hacienda are landscaped with lovely flower and cactus gardens. The museum features the original furniture and effects of the Dominguez family, the Spanish dons who first built a home here in 1826.

Hollywood Park (1050 South Prairie Avenue, Inglewood; 213-419-1500; admission), one of the Southland's great tracks, has thoroughbred racing from the end of April to the end of July. Beautifully laid out, the track features a landscape complete with palm trees, lagoon, and children's play area.

EAST LOS ANGELES

The spirit of Mexico is alive and shimmering in the *barrio* of East L.A. With a population that is 90% Latino, this sprawling neighborhood represents the country's largest concentration of Hispanics. Originally settling Los Angeles in the 18th century, Mexicans emigrated en masse following the Mexican Revolution of 1910.

Today they are a rapidly growing minority group flexing political muscle and demonstrating cultural pride. As playwright Luis Valdez explains, "No Statue of Liberty ever greeted our arrival in this country. We did not in fact come to the United States at all. The United States came to us."

Brooklyn Avenue, a major thoroughfare in the Boyle Heights district, represents "Little Mexico," a region rich in Mexican restaurants, candy stores, and family shops. If Brooklyn Avenue is the heart of the *barrio*, **Whittier Boulevard** is the spine, a neon ganglion charged with electric color. It is here that a guy goes to show off his girl, his car, and himself. Lined with discount stores, *tacquerías*, and auto body shops, Whittier is the Sunset Strip of East L.A.

The life of the *barrio* is also evident at **El Mercado** (3425 East 1st Street), an indoor market crowded with shoppers and filled by the strains of Spanish songs. There are clothing shops, fresh food markets, and stores selling everything from cowboy boots to Spanish-language videos. The signs are bilingual and the clientele represents a marvelous multicultural mix.

Of course the full flavor of the Chicano community is found among the murals which decorate the streets of East Los Angeles. Exotic in design, vibrant with color, they are a vital representation of the inner life of the *barrio*, a freeform expression of the Mexican people and their 400-year residence in the United States.

A spectacular series of murals adorn the walls of the **Estrada Courts Housing Project** (★) (Olympic Boulevard between Grande Vista Avenue and Lorena Street). Here dozens of bright-hued images capture the full sweep of Latin history.

Two other buildings also provide a panoramic image of Mexican history. In a succession of panels, the **First Street Store** (3640 East 1st Street) re-creates prehistoric Mexican society, then progresses through the Aztec area to modern times. With a series of surreal tile murals, the nearby **Pan American Bank** (3626 East 1st Street) carries the saga into the future, portraying Latins in the post-atomic age.

"El Corrido de Boyle Heights" ("The Ballad of Boyle Heights"), another color-soaked mural, decorates a building at Brooklyn Avenue and Soto Street. This 1983 painting captures the community at work and play, with the family and on the road. A succession of overlapping scenes, it's an anecdotal expression of the *barrio*, done with a flair unique to Chicano culture.

Many of the muralists decorating these Latin streets started at **Plaza de la Raza** (3540 North Mission Road; 213-223-2475). This Chicano cultural center is intimately involved in the artistic life of the community, sponsoring classes in dance, music, theater, and visual arts. For visitors there are regularly scheduled art exhibits, dramatic performances, concerts, and festivals. Adjacent to the cultural center, **Lincoln Park** features a lake and tree-studded picnic area.

ELYSIAN PARK–SILVER LAKE AREA

Set along sloping hillsides and separated by parks and eucalyptus groves are several suburban neighborhoods. Once a favored spot among Yang-Na Indians, this hill-and-dale district is now inhabited by an intriguing mix of blue- and white-collar workers. While the areas around Elysian and Echo parks have become Hispanic neighborhoods, the heights above Silver Lake are given over to young white professionals, including a significant gay population. In fact, together with West Hollywood, Silver Lake has emerged as one of Los Angeles' major centers of gay culture. With its curving mountain roads, tile-topped houses, jogging paths, and city vistas, this last neighborhood is also popular with artists.

For the outdoor-minded, 575-acre **Elysian Park** (near the intersection of Routes 110 and 5), the city's second largest park, is a forested region of rolling hills and peaceful glens. There are picnic areas, meadows planted with exotic palm trees and numerous nature trails offering views of central Los Angeles and the San Gabriel Valley. For the sports-minded, the park contains 56,000-seat **Dodger Stadium** (213-224-1500), home of the Los Angeles Dodgers.

Nearby **Echo Park** (Glendale Boulevard and Park Avenue; 213-250-3578) features a palm-fringed lake complete with footbridge and ducks. There are rental boats for exploring the fountain and lotus flowers which highlight this 15-acre body of water; playground.

That circular structure with the imposing white columns across the street is **Angelus Temple** (1100 Glendale Boulevard; 213-484-1100). Modeled after Salt Lake City's Mormon Tabernacle, it served the congregation of spiritualist Aimee Semple McPherson during the 1920s and 1930s.

The nearby neighborhood of **Angelino Heights** was the city's first suburb, built during the 1880s on a hill overlooking Downtown and connected to the business district by cable car. Today the once elegant borough, ragged along the edges, still retains vestiges of its glory days. Foremost is the **1300 block of Carroll Avenue**, where a string of gingerbread Victorians have been gussied up in the fashion of the Gay Nineties. Representing Los Angeles' largest concentration of Victorian houses, the street is an outdoor museum lined with turrets, gables, and fanciful woodwork. For further information, call 213-250-5976.

Another noteworthy housing colony surrounds the reservoir at **Silver Lake** (Silver Lake Boulevard). Built after World War II, the homes are generally of stucco construction. Since they cover nearby hills, the best way to tour the neighborhood is by winding through the labyrinth of narrow streets which ascend from the lake.

Of architectural note, though unappealing to my taste, is the row of houses on the **2200 block of East Silver Lake Boulevard**. Designed by Austrian architect Richard Neustra, they are stucco-and-plate-glass structures representative of the International Style.

MT. WASHINGTON AREA

If an entire neighborhood could qualify as an outdoor museum, the Mt. Washington district would probably charge admission. Here within a few blocks are several picture-book expressions of desert culture.

The **Lummis House** (200 East Avenue 43; 213-222-0546), or El Alisal, is the work of one man, Charles Fletcher Lummis, whose life is inextricably bound to the history of the region. Though born in the Northeast, Lummis fell in love with the Southwest, devoting his life to defending the region's Indian tribes and promoting local arts and crafts. A writer and magazine editor, he built this stone house himself, using granite from the nearby arroyo, carving the doors by hand and placing his Indian photos everywhere, even embedding pictures in the windows where the sun still shines through them. Surrounded by a cactus garden, the house is an excellent example of turn-of-the-century Southwestern sensibilities.

Perhaps Charles Lummis' most important role was as founder of the **Southwest Museum** (234 Museum Drive; 213-221-2163; admission). Set in a Mission-style structure overlooking downtown Los Angeles, this important facility contains exquisite jewelry, basketry, weaving, and other handicrafts from Pueblo Indian tribes. California's Indians are represented by their petroglyphs, pottery, weapons, and decorative beadwork. In fact, the museum has so expanded its collection since Lummis' day that the current theme focuses more on Native Americans in general than on the Southwest. There are bead papooses, a tepee, and leather clothing hand-painted by Plains Indians; totem poles and artifacts from the Pacific Northwest tribes; and an excellent research library.

That antique neighborhood on the other side of the Pasadena Freeway is **Heritage Square** (3800 North Homer Street; 818-449-0193; admission), an eclectic collection of historic buildings. Several impressive Victorians, a Methodist church, and the old Palms Railroad Depot rest here. Carted from all over the city, they constitute a kind of architectural graveyard. Open only on weekends and most major holidays.

WHITTIER-EL MONTE AREA

There are hundreds, perhaps thousands of reasons to visit Los Angeles. But could any be as important as a **Richard Nixon pilgrimage (★)**? Think about it, a sacred visit to the hometown of the only president who ever resigned from office, "Tricky Dick" himself, the first national leader ever compelled to assure the American public that "I am not a crook."

Anyone who has ever heard a maudlin Nixon speech knows Whittier, where the 37th President of the United States was raised, schooled, and elected to Congress. The **Whittier Chamber of Commerce** (8158 Painter Avenue; 213-698-9554), still proud of their native son, can provide information on Nixon points of interest.

Among the highlights are **East Whittier Elementary School** (Whittier Boulevard and Gunn Avenue); **Whittier Union High School** (Philadelphia Street and Pierce Avenue), where young Richard graduated in 1930; and the Spanish-style campus of **Whittier College** (Painter Avenue and Philadelphia Street), from which he received his diploma four years later.

The Nixon family store was tragically converted into a gas station, but the **Pat Ryan Nixon House** (13513 Terrace Place), where the future First Lady lived when she met her husband, still stands. The couple married in 1940; after the future President was elected to Congress in 1946, the **Nixon residence** became a modest, low-slung stucco house at 14033 Honeysuckle Lane. Characteristic of the esteem in which Nixon is held these days, none of these places acknowledge the Watergate President. Not to worry, for those of us who remain true believers, each location is an immortal shrine.

Of course the true pilgrimage is to the **Richard Nixon Library** (18001 Yorba Linda Boulevard, Yorba Linda; 714-993-3393; admission). Here you'll find the 900-square-foot home (that "made up in love what it lacked in size") where Nixon was born "on the coldest day of one of the coldest winters in California history." Indeed.

The library itself, with barely a book to be seen, is a marvelous succession of movies, interactive videos and touch-screen presentations that rewrite American history in a fashion that would make even a novelist blush.

Another famous politician, who eventually died in poverty, made his home nearby. **Pío Pico State Historic Park** (6003 Pioneer Boulevard, Whittier; 213-695-1217) contains the 13-room adobe house built by Pío Pico, the last governor of Spanish California. Surrounded today by freeways and railroad tracks, the home was once a vibrant center of Mexican life during the 19th century. The U-shaped adobe, with outlying gardens and pond, is still furnished in period and provides a window on early California life.

A natural island in a sea of commerce, **Whittier Narrows Nature Center** (1000 North Durfee Avenue, South El Monte; 818-444-1872) is a 320-acre preserve near the San Gabriel and Rio Hondo rivers. Over 250 bird species have been sighted within this quiltwork of rivers, lakes, and open fields. To help you get back to the basics, there are nature trails and an interpretive center.

Another point of interest, the **El Monte Historic Museum** (3150 North Tyler Avenue, El Monte; 818-444-3813) resides in a classic Spanish-style building which was actually part of a 1936 WPA project. In addition to a typical 19th-century El Monte home, the facility contains representations of the town's old general store, school, and barber shop. Rich in historic lore, the surrounding area was the terminus of the Santa Fe Trail; as a result, the museum has countless photographs, maps, and diaries from the pioneer era.

Who could have imagined that the City of Industry, located deep in the industrial outlands of Los Angeles, would remember its roots with a tree-lined historic park? **The Workman and Temple Family Homestead Museum** (15415 East Don Julian Road; 818-968-8492), an impressive six-acre site, contains the Workman House (a 19th-century adobe), a Victorian-style gazebo, and the county's oldest private cemetery. The centerpiece of the park is La Casa Nueva, a 1920s-era Spanish Colonial Revival mansion complete with stained-glass windows, hand-carved ornaments, decorative tiles, and intricate iron fittings. Tours of this intriguing complex concentrate primarily on the 1840s, 1870s, and 1920s, when the various buildings were being constructed.

Carrying you forward to the tacky architecture of the 1950s, in the equally tacky town of La Puente, is **The Donut Hole (★)** (15300 East Amar Road; 818-968-2912). This drive-through snack bar consists of two structures in the shape of giant donuts. Though these architectural accretions look more like overinflated truck tires than anything edible, visitors drive through the first donut hole, place their orders, then exit via the second donut.

WILSHIRE DISTRICT

Extending from Downtown all the way to the Pacific, Wilshire Boulevard reaches for 16 miles through the western heart of Los Angeles. In its course the grand avenue passes Jewish, Korean, Southeast Asian, Filipino, Mexican, and Central American neighborhoods. Originally an Indian trail leading from the downtown area to the La Brea tar pits, the boulevard was developed during the 1890s by H. Gaylord Wilshire, a socialist with an ironic knack for making money in real estate.

Not far from Wilshire's street stands an institution which would have offended his socialist sensibilities while piquing his interest in profits. Smaller and more sedate than its New York counterpart, the **Pacific Stock Exchange** (233 South Beaudry Avenue, 12th Floor; 213-977-4500) nevertheless conveys a sense of financial drama. Peering through windows in the visitors' gallery, you can look down on the confetti-strewn floor, banks of computers, and crowds in business suits.

Several stately Victorians, built in the 19th century when the Westlake district was a wealthy neighborhood, remain along the **800 and 1000 blocks of South Bonnie Brae Street**. Particularly dramatic are the Queen Anne confection at 818 and the onion-domed house next door.

MacArthur Park (Alvarado Street between 6th and 7th streets), a 32-acre greensward bisected by Wilshire Boulevard, is one of Los Angeles' oldest parks. Today the place has become a gathering place for local immigrants, who enjoy the shady picnic areas, playground, and snack bar. Home to more than 80 plant species, the park's central feature is a small lake complete with fountain, boat rental, and palm-fringed island inhabited by ducks.

One of Los Angeles' truly exquisite structures, **I. Magnin** (3050 Wilshire Boulevard; 213-382-6161), a 1929 art deco extravaganza, is marked by a solitary tower. Built on several tiers in a series of thin, fluted columns, the building is faced with ornamental copper. The interior, housing a major department store, features wall and ceiling murals.

Another art deco masterpiece, the **Wiltern Center** (3780 Wilshire Boulevard), lies a few blocks away. A towering building with wings flaring from either side, the structure was built in 1931 and is covered in green terra cotta.

Not to be outclassed, the residential architecture of **Hancock Park** (between Wilshire Boulevard and Melrose Avenue, centered around the Wilshire Country Club) includes posh estates once owned by the Crocker, Huntington, and Doheny families. Developed during the 1920s, this well-tended neighborhood contains a variety of architectural styles. With wide boulevards and manicured lawns, it's a perfect place for a Sunday drive (even on a Tuesday).

One of the highlights of the district, politically if not architecturally, is the **Getty House** (605 South Irving Boulevard). A 1921 Tudor home with leaded-glass windows and slate roof, it is the official residence of the mayor of Los Angeles.

St. Elmo Village (★) (4830 St. Elmo Drive; 213-931-3409) marks another breed of neighborhood entirely. Here a complex of cottages has been transformed into a kind of clapboard artist colony. The simple bungalows are painted nursery colors and adorned with murals and sculptures. Containing private residences and art studios, the settlement is luxuriously landscaped.

Back in the 1920s and 1930s the showcase for commercial architecture rested along the **Miracle Mile** (Wilshire Boulevard between La Brea and Fairfax avenues). That was when an enterprising developer turned the area into a classy corridor for shops and businesses. The magnificent art deco towers that lined the strip still survive, particularly between the 5200 and 5500 blocks of Wilshire, but Wilshire's early glory has faded as the area has changed from popular to historic.

Still retaining its luster and heritage is **Carthay Circle**, a cluster of small 1930-era homes. Bounded by Fairfax Avenue and Wilshire and San Vicente boulevards, this antique neighborhood is shaped more like a triangle than a circle. The Spanish stucco and art deco homes create an island surrounded by streets streaming with traffic.

L.A.'s vernacular architecture is alive and well at **Tail O' The Pup** (329 North San Vicente Boulevard; 213-652-4517), a hot dog stand shaped (how else?) like a hot dog. Created in 1946, the hot dog was actually moved to its present location, where it stands in humorous contrast to its well-heeled neighbors.

The West's largest museum is a multibuilding complex with an international art collection. Providing a thumbnail tour of the entire history of art, the **Los Angeles County Museum of Art** (5905 Wilshire Boulevard; 213-857-6111; admission) ranges from pre-Columbian gold objects and African masks to post-World War II minimalist works. Stops along the way include sculpture, paintings, and stained-glass windows from the Middle Ages; a Renaissance gallery featuring Rembrandt and other Masters; Impressionist paintings by Cézanne, Gaughin, and Monet; and early 20th-century creations by Magritte, Chagall, and Miro.

A new addition, the Pavilion for Japanese Art, houses the well-known Shin'enkan collection of paintings as well as Japanese screens, scrolls, ceramics, and sculpture. The entire complex is beautifully laid out around a central courtyard adorned with terra cotta pillars and four-tiered waterfall.

Beauty gives way to the beast at the adjacent **George C. Page Museum** (5801 Wilshire Boulevard; 213-936-2230; admission). This paleontological showplace features displays of mammoths, mastodons, and ground sloths. There are also extinct camels, ancient horses, and ancestral condors.

Together with over 200 varieties of other creatures they fell victim to the **La Brea Tar Pits**, which surround the museum. Dating to the Pleistocene Era, these oozing oil pools trapped birds, mammals, insects, and reptiles, creating fossil deposits which are still being discovered by scientists. Indians once used the tar to caulk boats and roofs. Today you can wander past the pits, which bubble menacingly with methane gas and lie covered in globs of black tar.

The **Craft & Folk Art Museum** (6067 Wilshire Boulevard; 213-937-5544) nearby is a small gallery with a rotating exhibit. Arts and crafts from all over the world are displayed.

Another tiny but intensely powerful exhibit is the **Martyrs Memorial & Museum of the Holocaust** (6505 Wilshire Boulevard; 213-852-1234). Devoted to the tragedy of World War II, it is filled with images from the Nazi extermination camps. The ovens of Buchenwald, the gas chambers of Auschwitz, and skeletal figures from other camps are captured in terrifying detail. The photos portray masses being executed; tiny children, their hands in the air, surrounded by storm troopers; and a mother being shot while clutching a child in her arms. Many of the docents are Holocaust survivors with personal stories to recount as they lead visitors through these harrowing halls.

Nearby **Fairfax Avenue** (between Beverly Boulevard and Melrose Avenue) is the center of the city's Jewish community. Since World War II this middle-class neighborhood has been a local capital for Los Angeles Semites. Filled with delicatessens, bakeries, and kosher grocery stores, it is occupied by Orthodox, Hasidic, and Reform Jews.

Their favorite gathering place is the intersection of Fairfax and Oakwood avenues. Here one corner supports a **mural** depicting Jewish life in Los Angeles and another corner contains **Al's Newsstand**, a 24-hour outdoor vendor reminiscent of the early 20th century when Jews first occupied the area.

Back in 1934 local farmers created a cooperative market where they could congregate and sell their goods. Today **Farmers' Market** (6333 West 3rd Street; 213-933-9211) is an open-air labyrinth of stalls, shops, and vendor stands. There are tables overflowing with vegetables, fruits, meats, cheeses, and baked goods, a total of over 160 outlets. Stop by for groceries, gifts, and finger foods or simply to catch Los Angeles at its relaxed and informal best.

The Asian answer to gentrification is evident in **Koreatown** (centered between Vermont and Pico boulevards, Western Avenue and 4th Street), a burgeoning neighborhood that is rapidly redefining the Wilshire District. Colorful storefronts, refurbished cottages, and Korean calligraphy have transformed the entire area into a unique enclave. In fact, if you take a long drive down Pico Boulevard or Olympic Boulevard from the Harbor Freeway (Route 110) to Fairfax Avenue, you'll pass through a succession of **ethnic neighborhoods** including Indonesian, Japanese, Taiwanese, Vietnamese, and Thai sections.

HOLLYWOOD

It was farm country when Horace and Daeida Wilcox first moved to Cahuenga Valley. Originally part of the Rancho La Brea land grant, the dusty hills lay planted in bell peppers, watermelons, and citrus trees. Then in 1887 Horace had a brainstorm: he subdivided the family farm, Daeida christened the spread "Hollywood," and they put lots on the market for $150 an acre.

By 1910, the cow town's population had grown to 4000 middle-class, god-fearing souls. Like the Wilcoxes, they were staid and sober folk, drawn predominantly from Midwestern stock.

Then came the deluge. The fledgling movie industry—attracted by warm weather and natural locations and conspiring to avoid the royalties levied by Thomas Edison's east coast company for use of his moving picture inventions—began relocating to Hollywood. The first studio arrived in 1911. Two years later the trio of Jesse Lasky, Samuel Goldfish (later Goldwyn), and Cecil B. De Mille set up shop. De Mille soon began shooting *Squaw Man*, the first full-length motion picture, in a barn on the corner of Selma Avenue and Vine Street.

The townsfolk termed these studios "gypsy camps" and posted signs declaring, "No dogs, No actors." Movie people were Easterners, morally suspect and in many cases Jewish, defining characteristics guaranteed to stir unease among the local Protestant majority.

But if there is no stopping progress, it is simply impossible to halt a tidal wave. During the 1920s the movie industry became a billion-dollar business, with Hollywood its capital. Picture palaces mushroomed along Hollywood Boulevard beside glamorous restaurants and majestic hotels and by 1930 the population totaled 150,000.

Hollywood's glory days lasted until the 1960s, when development gave way to decline. The boulevard of dreams became a byway for bikers; Chevys with hydraulic lifters replaced limousines; punks with flaming hair supplanted platinum starlets; and movie studios moved to the San Fernando Valley. Prostitutes worked side streets, leaving the major thoroughfares to hawkers, hustlers, and Hollywood visionaries.

Today the area is in the midst of a renaissance. The sizable Hispanic, Asian, black, and Armenian populations have created ethnic neighborhoods; the commercial districts are being refurbished; and West Hollywood has developed into a center for gay lifestyles. In the flatlands, 1920-era bungalows and Spanish-style apartment houses are undergoing gentrification, and in the Hollywood hills efforts are afoot to preserve both landmark homes and the region's rural ambience.

Regardless of the changes, seemingly in spite of itself, the place remains Hollywood, tawdry and tragic, with all its myth and magic. The town which F. Scott Fitzgerald said "can be understood . . . only dimly and in flashes" is still an odd amalgam of truth and tinsel, promise and impossibility, conjuring images of big studios and bright stars.

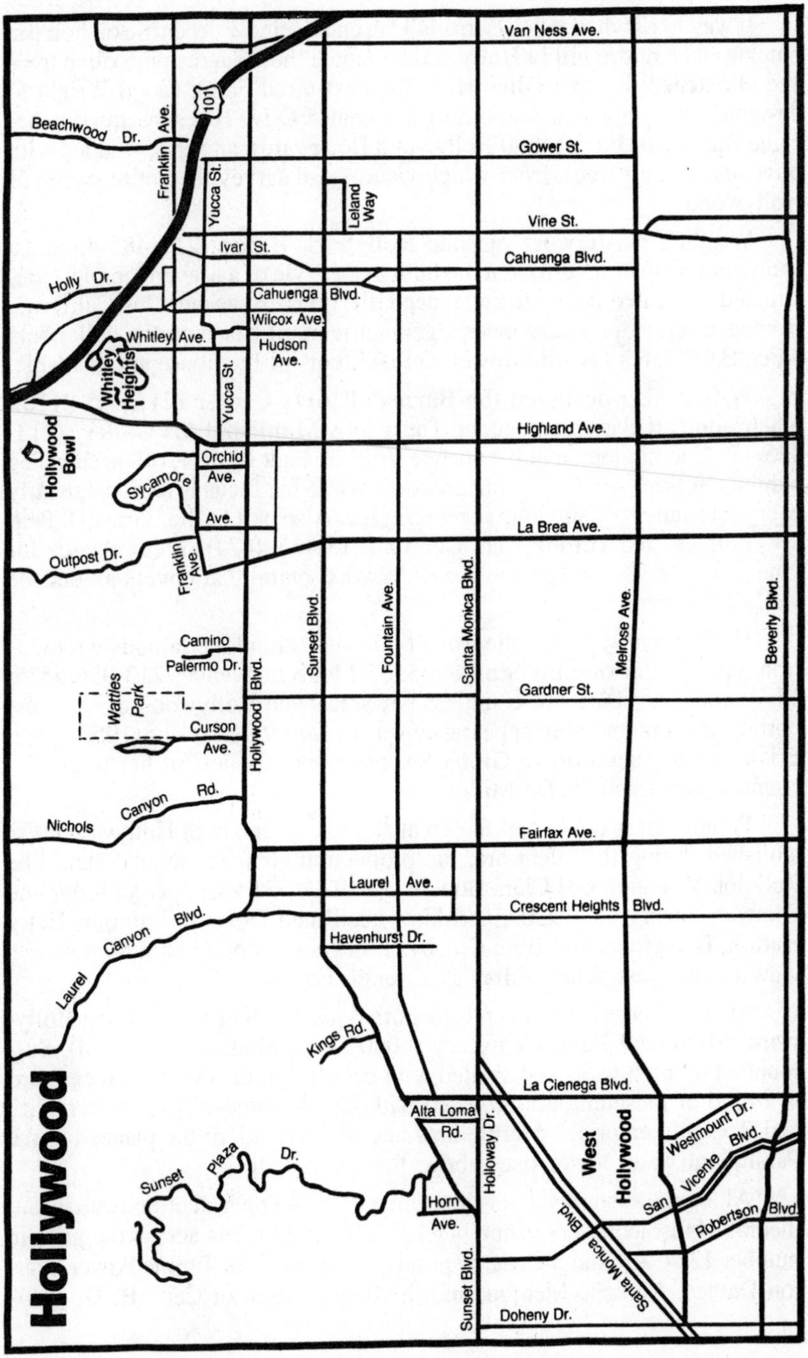
Hollywood
Van Ness Ave.
101
Beachwood Dr.
Franklin Ave.
Gower St.
Yucca St.
Leland Way
Vine St.
Ivar St.
Cahuenga Blvd.
Holly Dr.
Cahuenga Blvd.
Wilcox Ave.
Whitley Ave.
Hudson Ave.
Whitley Heights
Yucca St.
Highland Ave.
Hollywood Bowl
Orchid Ave.
Sycamore Ave.
La Brea Ave.
Outpost Dr.
Franklin Ave.
Sunset Blvd.
Fountain Ave.
Santa Monica Blvd.
Melrose Ave.
Beverly Blvd.
Camino Palermo Dr.
Hollywood Blvd.
Gardner St.
Wattles Park
Curson Ave.
Nichols Canyon Rd.
Fairfax Ave.
Laurel Ave.
Crescent Heights Blvd.
Laurel Canyon Blvd.
Havenhurst Dr.
Kings Rd.
La Cienega Blvd.
Alta Loma Rd.
Westmount Dr.
Holloway Dr.
West Hollywood
San Vicente Blvd.
Sunset Plaza Dr.
Horn Ave.
Robertson Blvd.
Santa Monica Blvd.
Sunset Blvd.
Doheny Dr.

CENTRAL HOLLYWOOD

It was 1918 when Alice Barnsdall, an enchantingly eccentric oil heiress, purchased an entire hill in Hollywood, planted the 36 acres with olive trees and christened the spot Olive Hill. She next hired Frank Lloyd Wright to design a family home and adjoining arts center. Olive Hill subsequently became **Barnsdall Park** (4800 Hollywood Boulevard), an aerie, studded with olive and conifer trees, from which visitors can survey the entire sweep of Hollywood.

Wright's masterwork became **Hollyhock House** (213-485-4580), a sprawling 6200-square-foot home built in the style of a Mayan temple. Constructed of poured concrete and stucco, the house represents his California Romanza style and incorporates a geometric motif based on the hollyhock, Alice Barnsdall's favorite flower. Guided tours of the house are available.

Wright also designed the **Barnsdall Arts Center** (213-485-2116), where adult art classes are taught. The nearby **Municipal Art Gallery** (213-485-4581; admission), a gray concrete structure built in 1971, offers changing exhibits of Southern California artwork. While the focus is regional, nearly every arts and crafts medium is represented. Also part of the Barnsdall Park art complex, the **Junior Arts Center** (213-485-4474) offers classes for young people. Be sure to see the Hollywood mural that covers an outside wall of this building.

Until recently, the public wasn't allowed behind the famous wrought-iron gate, at **Paramount Studios** (5555 Melrose Avenue; 213-956-5575; admission). A subject for countless newsreels and Hollywood movies, the portal's most memorable appearance was in *Sunset Boulevard* (1950) when Erich von Stroheim drove Gloria Swanson onto the lot for her tragic encounter with Cecil B. De Mille.

Paramount is the last of the great studios to remain in Hollywood. Established during the silent era, the production company signed stars like Rudolph Valentino and Clara Bow in the 1920s, Gary Cooper and Marlene Dietrich during the 1930s, and later headlined Dorothy Lamour, Betty Hutton, Bob Hope, and Bing Crosby. Tours consist of a behind-the-scenes view of this vast studio. Monday through Friday.

Many of these same legends lie buried just north of the studio in **Hollywood Memorial Park Cemetery** (6000 Santa Monica Boulevard). Surrounded by high walls and shaded with palm trees, the 60-acre greensward is a kind of museum park crowded with Greek statues, Egyptian temples, and Roman memorials. Marble urns and obelisks adorn the place, and the Paramount water tower rises above the south wall.

Along the eastern side of the cemetery, Rudolph Valentino rests in Cathedral Mausoleum, crypt number 1205; Peter Finch is across the aisle in number 1224. Around the nearby pond are the graves of Tyrone Power, Marion Davies, Adolphe Menjou, and the double tomb of Cecil B. De Mille and his wife, Constance Adam De Mille. Next to the Cathedral Mausoleum, a staircase leads to the reflecting pool and tomb of Douglas Fairbanks.

For a tour of the truly macabre there's **Graveline Tours** (P.O. Box 931694, Hollywood, CA 90093; 213-469-3127). From your resting place in a Cadillac hearse you'll see the hotel where John Belushi died, the spot where George "Superman" Reeves shot himself, and the sites of other infamous Hollywood deaths. Heavy, man.

Despite numerous incarnations, including its most recent as headquarters for A & M Records, the **Charlie Chaplin Studios** (1416 North La Brea Avenue) have weathered the years relatively unchanged. This row of Tudor cottages, built by Chaplin in 1918, housed the star's sound stage, dressing rooms, carpentry shop, and stables.

No one can quite figure how Movieland's most famous address became so prominent. Most of the action occurred elsewhere, but somehow the corner of **Hollywood and Vine** has come to symbolize Hollywood.

Maybe its the many radio studios that lined the thoroughfare during the 1930s, or perhaps because the **Pantages Theater** (6233 Hollywood Boulevard) is just down the street. One of the nation's finest art deco theaters, the Pantages was built in 1930, with a vaulted-ceiling lobby and a monumental auditorium.

Gazing down on all the commotion is the **Capitol Records Tower** (1750 Vine Street), a building you have seen in countless photographs. Resembling a squadron of flying saucers piggy-backed on one another, the 13-story structure was actually designed to look like a stack of records with a stylus protruding from the top.

In a tribute to the great studios once occupying the area, **Home Savings of America** (1500 North Vine Street) adorned its facade with the names of hundreds of stars and added a tile mural depicting the most noteworthy. The interior contains a marvelous stained-glass window with scenes from Hollywood's early movies.

During the halcyon days of the 1920s, as silent movies gave way to talkies, Hollywood Boulevard was door-to-door with mansions. The **Janes House**, one of the last of this long-vanished breed, is a Queen Anne Victorian complete with turret, gable, and stained-glass windows.

The grande belle rests at the end of a plastic shopping mall and houses the **Visitors' Information Center** (6541 Hollywood Boulevard; 213-461-4213). Perhaps they can tell you where to find the lost beauty of Hollywood. Today, Hollywood Boulevard has been taken over by taco vendors, cut-rate video stores, T-shirt shops, and souvenir stands. More like New York's 42nd Street than the Great White Way, it's a cheap strip where photo galleries take tourists' pictures next to cardboard cutouts of stars.

The perfect expression of this high camp neighborhood is **Frederick's of Hollywood** (6608 Hollywood Boulevard; 213-466-8506), a lingerie shop located in an outrageous purple and pink art deco building. With a naughty reputation and a selection of undergarments that leave nothing to the imagination, Frederick's is one of those places we visit in spite of ourselves.

Then there's the **Hollywood Wax Museum** (6767 Hollywood Boulevard; 213-462-8860; admission), a melancholy place where you can "see your favorite stars in living wax." Here they are—Marilyn Monroe and Elvis Presley, Clint Eastwood and Sylvester Stallone—looking just like they would three days after rigor mortis set in, that classic grin or sneer frozen forevermore into a candle with arms.

Two relics from Hollywood's days of yore still cater to the town's movie-hungry populace. The **Egyptian Theater** (6712 Hollywood Boulevard; 213-467-6167) was built by Sid Grauman in 1922, after the discovery of King Tut's tomb. Much of the original architecture has been lost to mindless remodeling, but some Egyptian elements endure. There are murals, statues, and bas-reliefs portraying pharaohs and gods.

Far more famous and better preserved is **Mann's Chinese Theater** (6925 Hollywood Boulevard; 213-464-8111), also built by Sid Grauman in 1927. This fabulous movie palace is fashioned in a kind of Oriental Baroque style with pagoda roof, stone guard dogs, metal towers, Asian masks, and beautiful bas-reliefs. The interior is equally as lavish with its ornate columns, murals, and Oriental vases.

Though the architecture is splendid, the theater is actually known for its sidewalk. Embedded in the cement forecourt are the handprints and footprints of Hollywood's greatest stars. Jean Harlow, Rock Hudson, Cary Grant, and Jimmy Stewart have left their signatures in this grandest of all autograph collections. Not every celebrity simply signed and stepped, however: there are also cement images of Jimmy Durante's nose, Betty Grable's leg, Harpo Marx's harp, Sonja Henie's ice skates, Harold Lloyd's glasses, and the webbed feet of Donald Duck.

Of all the places in Hollywood, one of the best retrospectives on the stars is at the **Max Factor Beauty Museum** (1666 North Highland Avenue; 213-463-6668). The great make-up man's former studio has been converted into a showplace for an important Hollywood art form. There are celebrity make-up rooms, antique tools of the trade, and a gallery of old cosmetic advertisements. They have even managed to dredge up hairpieces worn by George Burns, Jimmy Stewart, and John Wayne. Most impressive is the photograph gallery, with hundreds of autographed stills capturing the celebrities who were once Max Factor's subjects.

Throughout this area—extending for three and a half miles along Hollywood Boulevard from Gower Street to Sycamore Avenue and on Vine Street between Sunset Boulevard and Yucca Street—is the **Walk of Fame**, a star-studded terrazzo commemorating notables from the film, television, radio, theater, and music industries. The names of over 1850 legends appear on brass-rimmed stars embedded in the sidewalk. Pride of Hollywood, it represents the only walkway in Los Angeles to be washed several times weekly.

After completing the grand tour of Hollywood Boulevard, stop by **C. C. Brown's** (7007 Hollywood Boulevard; 213-464-9726) for an ice cream sundae. This traditional malt shop has been around since 1929. Flocked wallpaper, crystal drop chandeliers, and high-backed maple-wood booths are part of the nostalgia. The real business of this soda fountain is not memories but sweets—they're famous for hot fudge sundaes and make their own candy, C. C. Brown originals.

Above Hollywood Boulevard, the **1800 block of North Ivar Street** is lined with apartment buildings reflecting the architecture of the 1920s and 1930s. Nathanael West lived in the mock-Tudor Parua Sed Apartments at #1817 in 1935. Here he wrote screen plays and began work on his great Hollywood novel, *The Day of the Locust.* The Mediterranean-style Alto Nido Apartments up the block (#1851) was the fictional home of the down-and-out screenwriter played by William Holden in *Sunset Boulevard.*

WEST HOLLYWOOD

If a time traveler from the 21st century landed in our era, the voyager would easily feel at home along **Melrose Avenue**. He could go shopping. The chic corridor is door-to-door with designer stores purveying space-age fashions. What Beverly Hills' Rodeo Drive is to classical fashion, Melrose has become to the avant-garde.

Then he could dine. The restaurants lining this strip are tile-and-copper cafés with bare-duct ceilings and Post-Midnight Modern architecture. They serve sushi and whip up recipes on file at the U.S. Patent Office.

Trendy is too lame a term to capture this neighborhood. Melrose Avenue is the cutting edge for L.A.'s young adults, a place to experience and be experienced, the Venice Boardwalk in high heels. The hottest section is from the 6900 to 7700 blocks, though that will probably change by the time this ink dries. Lately the borders of trendiness have been edging south along Beverly Boulevard and West 3rd Street. Stay tuned for future developments.

If you need a landmark to lead you through this tony part of town, consider a whale. The "Blue Whale" to be precise; that's the nickname for the blue-glass monstrosity on Melrose Avenue and San Vicente Boulevard. Formally known as the **Pacific Design Center** (213-657-0800), it's a mammoth mall catering to the interior design industry. Since opening in 1975, it has spawned a Green Whale next door. Rumor has it that Moby Blue is pregnant with a Red Whale, due sometime in the 1990s.

As God no doubt willed, Melrose Avenue ends in **West Hollywood,** the first city in the nation to be governed by avowed homosexuals. Much more than a gay city, West Hollywood is a free-form laboratory for social experiment, a place where the spirit of the '60s is transformed into the art form of a later era. Now that Berkeley has become a haven for revolutionaries-turned-real-estate-speculators, and Madison, Wisconsin is again a quiet campus town, West Hollywood carries on the bohemian ideal of being crazy as a way of life.

Like the Silver Lake neighborhood to the east, Ventura Boulevard in Studio City and Burbank Boulevard near Vineland, West Hollywood is a major gathering place for Los Angeles' gay population. There are countless clubs here, as well as excellent restaurants, good bookstores, and an array of fashionable shops.

The street scene centers along Sunset Boulevard, a flashy avenue studded with nightclubs and fresh cuisine restaurants. During the 1930s and 1940s, the section between Crescent Heights Boulevard and Doheny Drive formed the fabled **Sunset Strip**. Center of Los Angeles night action, it was an avenue of dreams, housing nightclubs like Ciro's, the Trocadero, Mocombo, and the Clover Club. As picture magazines of the times illustrated, starlets bedecked with diamonds emerged from limousines with their leading men. During the 1950s, Ed "Kookie" Byrnes immortalized the street on the television show "77 Sunset Strip."

Today, the two-mile strip is chockablock with the offices of agents, movie producers, personal managers, and music executives. The street's most artistic achievement is the parade of **vanity boards** which captivate the eye with their colors and bold conception. These outsize billboards, advertising the latest movie and record releases, represent the work of the region's finest sign painters and designers. Often done in three dimensions, with lights and *trompe l'oeil* devices, they create an outdoor art gallery.

An artist with equal vision was at work here in 1936. That's when architect Robert Derrah built the **Crossroads of the World** (6671 Sunset Boulevard). Designed as an oceanliner sailing across Sunset Boulevard, the prow of this proud ship is topped by a tower complete with rotating globe.

Château Marmont (8221 Sunset Boulevard; 213-656-1010) stands above the Strip, a brooding presence amid the glitter. It was in this hotel that John Belushi died in 1982. Constructed around 1929 in the pattern of a Norman castle, the place has numbered Boris Karloff, Greta Garbo, and Jean Harlow among its guests. With its petite gardens, imposing colonnade, and arched-window lobby, the hotel is a study in European elegance. Little wonder it is still favored by Hollywood stars as a hometown hideaway.

That streamlined art deco tower nearby is the old Sunset Tower Apartments, refurbished and rechristened the **St. James's Club** (8358 Sunset Boulevard; 213-654-7100). Completed in 1931, this moderne palace contained 46 luxury apartments, leased to luminaries like Errol Flynn, the

Gabor sisters, Zasu Pitts, Clark Gable, and Howard Hughes (who seems to have slept in more places than George Washington).

Hollywood might be noted for its art deco towers, but it also contains architectural works by other schools. The **Schindler House** (835 North Kings Road; 213-651-1510), a house-studio with concrete walls, canvas covers, and sleeping lofts, was designed by Viennese draftsman Rudolph Schindler in 1921. Modeled on a desert camp, the house was a gathering place for avant-garde architects during the 1920s.

F. Scott Fitzgerald fans will want to see the garden court apartments at 1401 North Laurel Avenue where the Roaring '20s novelist spent the final years of his life. Recovering from alcoholism, his career in decline, the author worked here on a film script and his unfinished novel, *The Last Tycoon*.

The **Colonial House** (1416 North Havenhurst Drive) two blocks away was home to celebrities and fictional characters alike. Bette Davis resided in the red brick building, as did Carole Lombard and her husband, William Powell. They were joined, in the imagination of Hollywood novelist Budd Schulberg, by Sammy Glick, the overly ambitious protagonist in *What Makes Sammy Run?*

The **Nelson House** (1822 Camino Palermo Drive), where the entire family lived during the 1950s, was used as the model for their television home on "The Ozzie and Harriet Show." Harriet sold the house several years after Ozzie died in 1975.

HOLLYWOOD HILLS

The lower slopes of the enchanting Santa Monica Mountains contain some of Los Angeles' most fashionable addresses. These rugged foothills, divorced from the glitter of Hollywood by serpentine roads, provide a pricey escape valve from the pressures of Tinseltown. But for those with a car and an afternoon, it costs no more to explore Hollywood's vaunted upcountry than to browse Beverly Hills' Rodeo Drive.

Beachwood Canyon (Beachwood Drive), one of the town's prettiest residential areas, is a V-shaped valley with 1920- and 1930-era homes on either side. First developed as "Hollywoodland" by *Los Angeles Times* publisher Harry Chandler, the neighborhood is now popular with screenwriters. When Chandler broke ground, he hoped to create an urban utopia "above the traffic congestion, smoke, fog, and poisonous gas fumes of the lowlands." (It seems that even in the 1920s, long before Los Angeles had a name for it, the city suffered from smog.)

To advertise "Hollywoodland" the developer erected a huge sign on the hillside. Eventually "land" was removed, the fixture was refurbished, and Chandler's billboard became the **Hollywood Sign**, a 45-foot-tall, 450-foot-long landmark that is now the foremost symbol of Movieland. (Head up Beachwood Drive toward the sign and you'll pass through the stone entrance gates of Hollywoodland at Westshire Drive.)

Los Angeles has little space for idyllic retreats. One of the city's more placid places is **Lake Hollywood** (southern entrance at Weidlake Drive; northern entrance at Lake Hollywood Drive), a forest-framed reservoir created by the Mulholland Dam. Popular with hikers and joggers, the lake is surrounded by a chain-link fence but still offers splendid views.

The reservoir was built in 1925 by Water Commissioner William Mulholland as part of Los Angeles' scandalous water program. Scenes from *Chinatown* (1974), the movie that exposed the civic corruption behind Mulholland's project, were shot around the lake. The dam was also used in *Earthquake*, another 1974 flick in which the dike collapses, inundating the city.

For stars living in **Whitley Heights** (★) during the 1920s, life was much like it is in Beverly Hills today. This hilltop neighborhood, with its tile-roofed Mediterranean homes, was the premier residential area for the silent-movie set. Rudolph Valentino lived here, and later stars included Gloria Swanson, Bette Davis, and Janet Gaynor. Today the realm is as unspoiled as it was when H. J. Whitley, a Los Angeles developer with an eye to Europe, first built his "Italian hilltown." To explore the landmark neighborhood, drive up Whitley Avenue to Whitley Terrace and Wedgewood Place, following all three streets as they spiral around the hilltop.

One of Hollywood's most enduring symbols is the **Hollywood Bowl** (2301 North Highland Avenue; 213-850-2060), a concrete band shell built in 1929. Situated in a sylvan glade called Daisy Dell, the concert hall is an amphitheater within an amphitheater, surrounded by a circle of wooded hills.

The Los Angeles Philharmonic performs here and a regular series of concerts is presented. Many movies have used the shell as a backdrop, including *Anchors Aweigh* and the 1937 version of *A Star Is Born*. The adjacent **Hollywood Bowl Museum** (213-850-2058) features listening rooms and hosts a changing series of exhibits on the culture of music.

A part of Hollywood's history stands just across the street. Back in 1913, a young director named Cecil B. De Mille found a farm town called Hollywood with an empty barn he could convert into a studio. The barn, a kind of woodframe keepsake, moved around with De Mille over the years, seeing use as an office, a set, and even a gymnasium for stars like Gary Cooper and Kirk Douglas. Eventually moved to its present site, the historic building became the **Hollywood Studio Museum** (2100 North Highland Avenue; 213-874-2276; admission), a showplace dedicated to the era of silent films and containing a replica of De Mille's original office.

If that French Renaissance mansion above Hollywood Boulevard begins to levitate, you'll know the residents are busy at work. The **Magic Castle** (7001 Franklin Avenue), built in 1925, is "the only club in the world devoted to magicians and lovers of magic." Home over the years to several movie stars, the private estate now plays host to a secret membership comprised of the town's top tricksters.

Further up the hill lies another dream house, a magnificent replica of a Japanese palace called **Yamashiro** (1999 North Sycamore Avenue; 213-466-5125). Built of cedar and teak in 1913, the former estate is presently a restaurant complete with ceremonial gardens and a 600-year-old pagoda. Of the many films shot here perhaps the most famous was *Sayonara* (1958), in which Yamashiro was cast as the American Officers' Club.

From here it's an easy jaunt up Outpost Drive through **Outpost Estates**. Another of Hollywood's picture-perfect neighborhoods, this residential canyon was developed during the 1920s by a creative contractor who placed the utilities underground and built Mediterranean-style homes. The result is a lovely, tree-shaded community, an unpretentious version of Beverly Hills.

Tucked into a narrow canyon lies **Wattles Park** (1850 North Curson Avenue), part of the old Gurdon Wattles Estate, a 49-acre preserve. While the Wattles Mansion and formal gardens can be viewed by appointment only (213-874-4005), the adjacent park is open on a regular basis. A pond, palm grove, and teahouse occupy the property, together with several walls marred by graffiti.

The real spirit of the Hollywood Hills resides in the deep canyons which climb from Hollywood Boulevard into the Santa Monica Mountains. **Nichols Canyon** (Nichols Canyon Road), a chaparral-coated valley adorned with million-dollar homes, represents one of the toniest parts of town. A narrow two-lane road winds through dense forest to bald heights.

Possessing the same cachet and even greater fame, **Laurel Canyon** (Laurel Canyon Boulevard) became known as a hippie hideaway during the 1960s. With its sinuous side streets and modest bungalows, the wooded vale has a decidedly rustic atmosphere.

Both Nichols and Laurel canyons rise sharply into the mountains, eventually reaching the rim of Los Angeles, a 50-mile-long country road called **Mulholland Drive**, which extends from Hollywood to Malibu. Tracing a course along the ridge of the Santa Monicas, Mulholland is a spectacularly beautiful road, curving through forests and glades, climbing along sharp precipices, and offering magnificent views of the Los Angeles Basin and San Fernando Valley.

BEVERLY HILLS

Back in 1844 a Spanish woman named Maria Rita Valdez acquired controlling interest over 4500 acres of sagebrush and tumbleweed. Luckily she spent only $17.50 on the transaction. The land was of little worth. Even by the turn of the century it consisted only of lima bean fields, sheep meadows, and a few isolated farmhouses. Plans for wheat cultivation, oil drilling, and a community of German immigrants failed.

Finally in 1912 a group of entrepreneurs, struggling to sell this barren real estate, happened on the idea of building a big hotel to publicize their new housing development. Happily, the fledgling movie industry was already attracting people to neighboring Hollywood and the Beverly Hills Hotel became a rendezvous for rising stars.

Then in 1920, when the undisputed King and Queen of Hollywood, Douglas Fairbanks and Mary Pickford, built their palace on a hill above the hotel, the community's future was secure. Within a few years Gloria Swanson, Charlie Chaplin, Rudolph Valentino, Buster Keaton, John Barrymore, and Will Rogers were neighbors. The dusty farmland, now a town named Beverly Hills, had finally blossomed.

It's a rags-to-riches town with a lot of Horatio Alger stories to tell. The world capital of wealth and glamour, Beverly Hills is a place in which driving a BMW makes you a second-class citizen and where the million-dollar houses are in the poorer part of town. The community with more gardeners per capita than any other United States city, Beverly Hills is one of the few spots outside Texas where flaunting your money is still considered good taste. A facelift here is as common as a haircut and many of the residents look like they've been embalmed for the past thirty years.

Still, it's Beverly Hills. The town has style, history, and an indomitable sense of magic. It's a void that became a constellation; a place where everyone—whether in movies, television, clothes design, or business—is a star.

It seems only fitting that the gateway to this posh preserve should be along **Santa Monica Boulevard** (between Doheny Drive and Wilshire Boulevard), a greenbelt with an exotic array of plant life. Each block of this blooming corridor is alive with a variety of vegetation. Trees are closely pruned, shrubs carefully shaped, and the flowers are planted in a succession of colorful beds. Most impressive of all is the landscape of cactus and succulents between Camden and Bedford drives.

Rising near the center of the promenade is **Beverly Hills City Hall** (North Rexford Drive and Santa Monica Boulevard), a newly renovated Spanish Baroque structure capped with a tile cupola. The foyer of this 1932 building has a recessed ceiling with scroll ornaments and hand-painted panels.

A contemporary commentary on City Hall, the adjacent **Beverly Hills Civic Center** features a stepped design in Spanish Deco style. The tile trim and palm landscape further reflect the earlier building.

By contrast the **U.S. Post Office** (9300 Santa Monica Boulevard) is an Italian Renaissance structure of brick and terra cotta. Built in 1933, the interior contains WPA-type murals popular during the Depression.

Cañon Drive, another horticultural corridor, is a parade of palms stretching for four blocks between Santa Monica and Sunset boulevards. The 80-foot trees lining this august street are Mexican and California sand palms.

To help find your way around the winding streets of this hillside community, the **Beverly Hills Visitors Bureau** (239 South Beverly Drive; 310-271-8174) provides printed information.

Regardless of its famous faces and stately residences, Beverly Hills has a single address which symbolizes the entire community. **Rodeo Drive,** where would-be's walk with the wealthy, represents one of the most fashionable strips in the world of shopping. This gilded row extends only from the 200 to 400 block, but within that enclave are shops whose names have become synonymous with style.

Catch the classic-style **Beverly Hills Trolley** (310-271-8174) at Rodeo Drive and Dayton Way, Tuesday through Saturday, for a free guided tour of the posh downtown area.

Surprisingly, little of the architecture is noteworthy. Among the artistic exceptions is the 1928 Beaux-Arts **Regent Beverly Wilshire Hotel** (9500 Wilshire Boulevard), which anchors the avenue. Frank Lloyd Wright's **Anderton Court** (332 North Rodeo Drive), created during the 1950s, projects a fractured effect with each part angling in a different direction, as if the building were about to split in pieces like a child's block pile. Holding it together is a Guggenheim-type circular ramp that curves past multiple levels of shops to a jagged metal tower. Just beyond the commercial district stands the **O'Neill House** (507 North Rodeo Drive), an art nouveau confection reminiscent of the work of Spanish architect Antonio Gaudi.

Like Hollywood, the favorite sport in Beverly Hills is stargazing. Synonymous with glamour, wealth, and fame, the town has been home to actors since the era of silent films. In fact, the best way to discover Hollywood is by driving through Beverly Hills.

That Elizabethan cottage at 508 North Palm Drive was home to **Marilyn Monroe and Joe DiMaggio** in 1954 during their stormy marriage. The couple moved in around April, but by September, when Marilyn was filming *The Seven Year Itch*, the tumultuous tie had already been broken.

The couple who lived on the next street had a happier and far more enduring marriage. If **George Burns and Gracie Allen's** place (720 North Maple Drive) looks familiar, that's because a model of the home was used for their 1950s television show.

Beverly Hills is nothing if not the story of marriages. The bond between **Elizabeth Taylor and Mike Todd** (1330 Schuyler Road) ended tragically in 1958 when Todd's private plane crashed over New Mexico. The couple was occupying this Mediterranean-style mansion when the movie producer died.

Lana Turner and Johnny Stompanato's relationship didn't last long either. It seems that Lana's daughter Cheryl Crane stabbed him to death in their prim Colonial house at 730 North Bedford Drive. Stompanato had threatened Turner's life during a heated argument. The even more heated trial that followed drew tremendous press coverage and exposed secrets of the star's love life.

For over 60 years the winding side streets off Benedict Canyon Drive have housed a who's who of Hollywood celebrities. Today many of movieland's greatest talents still live in this wooded retreat.

Roxbury Drive, a residential street trimmed with trees, has several 1930-era estates which celebrities once called home. **Marlene Dietrich** lived in the squarish, art deco mansion at number 822. **Jimmy Stewart** (918) set up residence in the brick Tudor house one block away, while **Lucille Ball** (1000) and **Jack Benny** (1002) lived next door to one another. Benny's brick Colonial home, like Burns and Allen's house, was sometimes filmed in his television show.

Newspaper baron William Randolph Hearst purchased the mansion at 1700 Lexington Road during the 1920s for his mistress, **Marion Davies**. Later in the decade **Greta Garbo** (1027 Chevy Chase Drive) moved into the neighborhood with a parrot, four cats, and a chow chow.

Pickfair (1143 Summit Drive), the estate of Douglas Fairbanks and Mary Pickford, is the most renowned of all Beverly Hills mansions. Hollywood's greatest stars, the couple lived here from 1920 until they were divorced in 1936, entertaining celebrities and royalty alike. After they parted, Mary Pickford stayed on in the mansion, dying at Pickfair in 1979. (Current owner Pia Zadora has drastically altered the place, however.)

Tower Road around the corner also saw its share of stars. **Juliet Prowse** lived behind the mullioned windows at 1136; **Arthur Rubinstein** occupied 1139; and actor **Spencer Tracy** called 1158 Tower Road home.

Greenacres, the estate of silent film comedian **Harold Lloyd** (1740 Green Acres Place), has been reduced to a mere five acres. When Lloyd moved here in 1928 the grounds included 20 acres and were planted with 12 gardens, each following a different theme. The house he occupied until his death in 1971 has 44 rooms, including 26 bathrooms.

Rudolph Valentino (1436 Bella Drive) chose the distant reaches of Benedict Canyon to escape his adoring fans. In 1925 he moved to Falcon Lair (named for his movie *The Hooded Falcon*), a magnificent mansion appointed with Renaissance art, Oriental carpets, and Medieval armor. Little did the young actor realize when he finally found his retreat that he would die from ulcers the next year.

For years Hollywood's chief gossip factory was the **Beverly Hills Hotel** (9641 Sunset Boulevard; 310-278-1487), a pink Mission Revival building dating to 1912. During the 1930s the hotel's Polo Lounge attracted Darryl Zanuck, Will Rogers, and other polo enthusiasts. Later its private bungalows became trysting places for celebrities. Clark Gable, Carole Lombard, Howard Hughes, Marilyn Monroe, and Sophia Loren rented them. John Lennon and Yoko Ono holed up for a week here, Elizabeth Taylor and Richard Burton made love and war, and Marilyn Monroe reportedly entertained John and Robert Kennedy in a very private bungalow. Today the hotel's manicured grounds are tropically landscaped and well worth visiting, even when the stars are not out.

Beverly Hill's most famous homes may be those of the stars, but its most intriguing residence is the **Spadena House** (516 Walden Drive). Built in 1921 as a movie set and office, this "Witch's House" resembles something out of a fairy tale. Its sharp peaked roof, mullioned windows, and cobweb ambience evoke images of Hansel and Gretel.

By calling in advance you can tour the **Virginia Robinson Gardens** (1008 Elden Way; 310-276-5367; admission), a six-acre estate landscaped with king palm trees and a variety of gardens. The home here (also open by appointment) is the oldest house in Beverly Hills, a 1911 Mediterranean Revival structure.

Greystone Park Mansion (905 Loma Vista Drive; 310-550-4654), a 55-room English Tudor manor, was built during the 1920s by oil tycoon Edward L. Doheny. While the house is closed to the public, visitors can tour the 16-acre grounds, which are landscaped in a succession of balustraded terraces complete with pools and fountains.

WESTSIDE

Like Horace Greeley's proverbial pioneer, wealth in Los Angeles has gone west. With its elite country clubs and walled estates, the Westside has developed during the 20th century into the city's golden ghetto. Cultural diversity is defined here not so much by race and class as by whether one is already rich or simply striving to be. Business mavens from Bel Air whiz along in Maseratis and co-eds buzz by in battered Toyotas.

At UCLA in Westwood, more than 34,000 students are squeezed into one of the most valuable real estate districts in the nation. While this campus town is an odd mix of blocky apartment buildings and mundane office towers, Bel Air and Brentwood are exclusive colonies marked by manicured lawns and lofty mansions.

Nearby Century City, a former film studio, has been transformed into a futuristic city with plazas, greenswards, and vaulting highrises. Culver City, the self-proclaimed "Motion Picture Capital of the World," which produced more than half the movies released in the United States during the 1930s and 1940s, still clings to its aging glory with several studios.

CENTURY CITY

If Beverly Hills is the ultimate in residential communities, **Century City** represents the final word in business centers. Bland as a three-piece suit, this 180-acre highrise heaven is built of office towers and broad boulevards. The only hint of character is the **ABC Entertainment Center** (Avenue of the Stars), a mega-sized complex with theaters and movie houses.

The **Century Plaza Hotel** across the street is a twin-tower city in itself, a 1000-room hotel that vies with Century City's other metal-and-glass palaces for prominence.

What today is a corporate version of Las Vegas was once the fabled backlot of Twentieth Century Fox. While the studio still holds ground in part of the city, it has lost the glamour of its Darryl Zanuck days and is closed to the public.

WESTWOOD

To students everywhere, Westwood is the scholastic capital of California. Home to UCLA, one of the largest universities in the country, the town was little more than ranch land in the early 20th century. Originally developed during the 1920s as a Mediterranean-style complex with shops and restaurants, Westwood boomed when UCLA opened in 1929. Now, with highrises continually springing up along Wilshire Boulevard, it's a major commercial center.

A sense of the old Westwood pervades **Westwood Village** (centered around Westwood Boulevard), near the university. Here you can stroll past a succession of shops, many located in 1920s-era buildings of brick and wood. The Village's true identity, however, is revealed on Friday and Saturday nights when major movies are previewed and the place becomes a world of bumper people, with traffic gridlocked and crowds milling everywhere.

Of Westwood's countless movie houses, the most inventive by far is **Mann's Village Theatre** (961 Broxton Avenue; 310-208-5576), with its lofty tower and Spanish Moderne design. Built in 1931, the landmark features elevated pillars, ornamental scrollwork, and a free-standing box office. The proximity of the 1937 **Mann's Bruin Theatre** (948 Broxton Avenue; 310-208-8998) across the street makes this the city's busiest crosswalk.

Just across Le Conte Avenue from this cinema center lies the **UCLA Campus**, an impressive 419-acre enclave. A true multiversity, UCLA contains 13 colleges and boasts 69 separate departments. The grounds are a labyrinth of grand staircases and brick walkways leading past 85 buildings, which (like on most major campuses) constitute an architectural hodgepodge. Next door to classic structures are blocky metal-and-glass highrises reflective of the Bauhaus movement; modern masterpieces stand cheek-by-jowl with utilitarian monstrosities.

A walking tour of this tree-shaded campus begins at the **Visitor Center** (10945 Le Conte Avenue, #1417 Ueberroth Building; 310-206-8147), where you can obtain information and sign up for guided tours. They can also tell you about the **Campus Express** (310-206-2908), a shuttle service around campus.

Ackerman Student Union represents the center of campus activity. **Kerckhoff Hall** next door is the only Gothic-style building on campus, a brick imitation of King Edward VII's Westminster chapel.

The geographic center of UCLA lies along the quadrangle at the top of **Janss Steps**. Anchoring the corners of the quad are the school's original buildings, magnificent Italian Romanesque structures dating to 1929. **Royce Hall,** a cloister-like building with twin towers and loggia, contains a public auditorium. The **Fowler Museum of Cultural History** (310-825-4361), located next to Royce Hall, offers a changing series of ethnological exhibits.

Powell Hall across the rectangle is an ornate, gargoyled Moorish masterwork housing the **Archive Research and Study Center** (310-206-5388). This important cultural resource, an extension of the Film and Television Archive, has a collection of over 25,000 movies and television shows dating as far back as the silent film era. With at least one week's advance reservation, visitors can view any of the archive films at no change.

Prettiest place on the entire campus is the **Franklin Murphy Sculpture Garden,** a five-acre park planted with jacaranda trees. Among the more than 60 artworks adorning this greensward are pieces by Arp, Calder, Matisse, Moore, and Rodin. Brooding over the garden is the **Wight Art Gallery** (310-825-9345), which features varying exhibits of classic and contemporary art.

In the same building as the Wight Art Gallery you'll find the **Grunwald Center for the Graphic Arts** (310-825-3783). Dedicated to "works on paper," the collection contains more than 35,000 prints, drawings, and photographs.

The **Mildred Mathias Botanical Garden,** an enchanted spot in the southeastern corner of campus, displays nearly 4000 plant species within its eight-acre domain. Focussing on tropical and subtropical vegetation, the glade is filled with lilies and rhododendrons, palms, and cactus. Visits to the **Hannah Carter Japanese Garden,** a Kyoto-style rock garden with teahouse and footbridges, can be arranged through the visitor's center.

Because of its reputation as a university town, Westwood's beautiful residential areas are frequently overlooked. Explore the neighborhood just west of campus and you'll discover the **Tischler House** (175 South Greenfield Avenue), a contemporary home designed by Austrian architect Rudolph Schindler in 1949. With a geometric layout and plate-glass prow, the home is like a ship moored in a hillside port.

The **Strathmore Apartments** (11005 Strathmore Drive), located several blocks away, were built by Schindler's Viennese colleague, Richard Neustra, in 1937. Among the former tenants of this glass-and-stucco court were Orson Welles and Clifford Odets.

In nearby West Los Angeles you'll encounter the **Armand Hammer Museum** (10889 Wilshire Boulevard; 310-443-7000; admission), which features lithographs by Honoré Daumier and a collection of Leonardo Da Vinci's original manuscripts as well as paintings by Rembrandt, Titian, Monet, and Chagall.

BEL AIR AND BRENTWOOD

Seeming extensions of Beverly Hills, the hillside towns of Bel Air and Brentwood are sleek residential communities filled with winding roads that curve past palatial homes. Developed during the 1920s by an entrepreneur with a sense of elegance, Bel Air was originally subdivided into plots of several acres, guaranteeing that only the wealthy would need apply.

At first even movie people, many of whom were Jewish, were excluded from this elite area. Then during the Depression, with other businesses dying while Hollywood flourished, Bel Air's greed proved stronger than its bigotry. Movie stars began moving in en masse and by the 1940s were rapidly becoming the area's most notable residents.

Humphrey Bogart and Lauren Bacall (232 South Mapleton Drive), who met on the set of *To Have and Have Not* in 1944, settled down together in a brick colonial house in Bel Air. Bogey was 25 years older than Bacall, but they became one of America's most legendary couples, starring together in *The Big Sleep* (1946), *Dark Passage* (1947), and *Key Largo* (1948).

The stone mansion at 750 Bel Air Road served for eight seasons as the **"Beverly Hillbillies" House**. This French estate was the prime time home for one of television's oddest families.

A real life family, **Judy Garland** and her mother, lived in the red brick house at 1231 Stone Canyon Road. The childhood star of *The Wizard of Oz* built the place in 1940, equipping it with a badminton court, pinball machines, and her own top-floor suite.

One of Hollywood's most infamous families, **Joan Crawford** and her *Mommie Dearest* daughter Christina, lived in the sprawling Brentwood house at 426 North Bristol Avenue. Crawford moved here in 1929 with her first husband, Douglas Fairbanks, Jr., divorced him in 1934, and went on to marry three more husbands while raising four adopted children. Following the death of her last husband she sold the place in 1959.

A far happier child lived just one block away. During the 1930s **Shirley Temple** and her family moved into the Brentwood mansion at 231 North Rockingham Road. The young actress had already blossomed into the country's archetypal little girl, destined to play the curly-haired beauty in over 20 films and then to become, incongruously, a right-wing politician as an adult.

Cowboys may be buried on Boot Hill, but movie stars are interred in a site overlooking the MGM studios. The celebrities in **Holy Cross Cemetery** (5835 West Slauson Avenue, Culver City) have one thing in common —they were all Catholic. Rosalind Russell of *Auntie Mame* fame is here along with Bing Crosby, Jimmy Durante, and Charles Boyer. Bela Lugosi rests nearby; the most macabre tombstone, however, is that of Sharon Tate Polanski and her unborn son Paul, murdered in 1969 by the Charles Manson gang. (Rosalind Russell's grave is marked by the large crucifix near the center of the park; most of the other resting places are near the "grotto" to the left of the entrance.)

SAN GABRIEL VALLEY

Tucked between the Downtown district and the lofty San Gabriel Mountains lies the San Gabriel Valley. Extending east from the San Fernando Valley toward San Bernardino, this former orange-growing empire has developed into a suburban realm noted for its wealth, botanic gardens, and smog.

Back in 1771, when 14 soldiers, two priests, and several mule drivers founded a mission in San Gabriel, they laid claim to an outpost that controlled the entire countryside, including Los Angeles Pueblo. The priests became land barons as the region was divided into vineyards, cattle ranches, and olive groves. In the mid-19th century American settlers further transformed the valley into an oasis of lemon and orange trees.

PASADENA

By the late-19th century Pasadena was supplanting San Gabriel as the cultural heart of the San Gabriel Valley. Boasting an ideal climate, it billed itself as a health lover's paradise and became a celebrated resort area. Its tree-trimmed boulevards were lined with Beaux-Arts, Mediterranean, Italian Renaissance, and Victorian houses, making the town a kind of open-air architectural museum.

Eventually visitors became residents, hotels were converted to apartments, and by the mid-20th century paradise became suburbia. In the process, Pasadena's overweening wealth and stubborn sense of tradition left the town with a reputation for stodgy conservatism. The Beach Boys captured the sense of the place with their 1964 hit record, "The Little Old Lady from Pasadena." But in recent years the world-famous Rose Parade has been challenged by the annual Doo Dah Parade, a motley gathering of "briefcase drill teams" and "lawnmower marching groups," where the queen of the parade is liable to be in drag.

Meanwhile the decaying downtown district has been transformed into **Old Town,** a ten square block neighborhood of modern galleries and gourmet restaurants (bordered by Holly and Green streets, Pasadena Avenue and Arroyo Parkway). Pasadena, it seems, is rapidly proceeding from the 19th to the 21st century.

Orienting visitors to the old and the new is the **Pasadena Convention and Visitors Bureau** (171 South Los Robles Avenue; 818-795-9311). They will tell you that the best place to begin touring the town is **Pasadena City Hall** (100 North Garfield Avenue), a 1925 Baroque building with a spectacular tile dome. A prime example of the city's classical architecture, the edifice features a colonnaded courtyard with fountain and formal gardens.

The **Pasadena Public Library** (285 East Walnut Street; 818-405-4052), completed two years later, is a Renaissance-style building with sufficient palm trees and red roof tiles to create a quintessentially Southern California setting. Other points of local pride are the **Pasadena Post Office** (281 East Colorado Boulevard), a 1913 Italian Renaissance beauty, and the **Pasadena Civic Auditorium** (300 East Green Street; 818-449-7360), an attractive building that dates to 1932 and hosts television's Emmy awards.

The public sector can never compete with its private counterpart when money is concerned. Pasadena displays its real wealth on the west side of town, where civic gives way to civilian.

First stop at the **Pacific Asia Museum** (46 North Los Robles Avenue; 818-449-2742; admission), a Chinese palace-style building originally owned by a wealthy Pasadena art collector. Dedicated to Oriental art and culture, the museum showcases paintings of Pacific traders and the treasures for which they traded—statuary and stoneware, porcelain and prizes of war. There are anecdotal artworks re-creating the religion and philosophy of the East as well as a courtyard with Chinese garden.

Then drive out Colorado Boulevard, route of the Rose Parade held every New Year's Day, to the **Norton Simon Museum of Art** (411 West Colorado Boulevard; 818-449-6840; admission). Housed in this odd edifice, which looks more like it was planned by a camera maker than an architect, is one of the finest collections of European and Asian art in the country.

Touring the Simon's several galleries is like striding through time and space. The works span 2500 years, traveling from ancient India and Southeast Asia to the world of contemporary art. The Old Masters are represented by Rembrandt, Reubens, and Raphael. There are Goya etchings, 17th-century watercolors, and Impressionist pieces by Cézanne and Van Gogh. Even the gardens are landscaped with 19th- and 20th-century sculptures by Rodin and Henry Moore.

Art on a grander scale is evident at the **Colorado Street Bridge** (Colorado Boulevard west of Orange Grove Boulevard), an antique causeway arching high above an arroyo. Not far from this engineering wonder, the old Wrigley mansion, a splendid Mission-style estate, now serves as the **Tournament House** (391 South Orange Boulevard; 818-449-4100), headquarters of the Rose Parade. Situated on four princely acres, the home's gardens are open daily. For a tour of the house, which contains Rose Bowl memorabilia, you'll have to arrive between 2 and 4 p.m. on a Wednesday afternoon during the months of February through August.

Another mansion with meaning is the imposing 1905 edifice that plays host to the **Pasadena Historical Society Museum** (470 West Walnut Street; 818-577-1660; admission). Containing furnishings and keepsakes from Pasadena's early days, this Neo-Classical house was once home to the Finnish

ish Consul. As a result the museum expresses a second theme—Finland, represented on the grounds by Finnish gardens, a facsimile 16th-century farmhouse, and an exhibit of Finnish folk art.

Humbling all these estates is the **Gamble House** (4 Westmoreland Place; 818-793-3334; admission), jewel of Pasadena, a Craftsman-style bungalow designed by the famous architectural firm of Greene and Greene in 1908. Heavily influenced by such Japanese innovations as overhanging roofs and pagoda flourishes, the wood shingle home is a warm blend of hand-rubbed teak and Tiffany glass. Built for the Cincinnati-based Gamble family (as in Proctor & Gamble), the house displays crafted woodwork and the original furnishings. A veritable neighborhood of these elegantly understated Greene and Greene bungalows lines the **Arroyo Terrace** loop next to the Gamble House.

To continue the architectural tour follow nearby **Prospect Boulevard** and **Prospect Crescent** along their tree-lined courses. The neighborhood entranceway and several local structures were designed by Charles and Henry Greene, the brothers who fashioned the Gamble House. Another architect, one Frank Lloyd Wright, enters the picture at 645 Prospect Crescent. Here Wright designed **La Miniatura** (the Millard House), an unusual assemblage of crosses and concrete blocks resembling a pre-Columbian tower.

Grandest of all the area's architectural achievements is the **Rose Bowl** (1001 Rose Bowl Drive; 818-577-3100). Built in 1922, this 102,000-seat stadium is the home for UCLA's football team and the site of the New Year's Day clash between the Big Ten and the Pacific Athletic Conference. If you don't have tickets for a game, remember that the stadium is open to the public on weekdays.

The future Frank Lloyd Wrights of the world reside up the hill at the **Art Center College of Design** (1700 Lida Street; 818-584-5035). An excellent school of industrial design, the college has galleries displaying work by both students and established artists. It also rests on 175 hillside acres which provide marvelous views of Pasadena and the San Gabriel Mountains.

Students with a more scientific bent are cracking the books at **Cal Tech** (California Institute of Technology, 1201 East California Boulevard; 818-356-6811), an internationally renowned science and engineering school which has won 21 Nobel Prizes and once numbered among its faculty Albert Einstein. These hallowed halls, in case you were wondering, were modeled on a medieval cloister. There are campus tours daily.

While the big kids play with numbers, the little ones are fidgeting with hands-on exhibits at **Kidspace Museum** (390 South El Molino Avenue; 818-449-9144; admission). This innovative facility has a television studio, a disc jockey's booth, fire station, and everything else a futuristic child might desire.

El Molino Viejo (1120 Old Mill Road, San Marino; 818-449-5450), the Old Mill, represents a vital part of the area's Spanish tradition. Built in 1816 by Indians from San Gabriel Mission, it was Southern California's first water-powered grist mill. Only the millstones remain from the actual mill, but the building, an adobe beauty with red tile roof, is still intact. With its courtyard setting and flowering fruit trees, the place is thoroughly enchanting. Down in the basement you'll find a scale model of the mill, complete with miniature Indians and moving parts.

One of the Southland's most spectacular complexes and certainly the premier attraction in the San Gabriel Valley is the **Huntington Library, Art Collections, and Botanical Gardens** (1151 Oxford Road, San Marino; 818-405-2273; admission). This incredible cultural preserve was once presided over by a single individual, Henry E. Huntington (1850–1927), a shrewd tycoon who made a killing in railroads and real estate, then consolidated his fortune by marrying the widow of his equally rich uncle.

The focal point of Huntington's 207-acre aesthetic preserve, the **Huntington Gallery**, was originally his home. Today the mansion is dedicated to 18th- and 19th-century English and French art and houses one of the finest collections of its kind in the country. Gainsborough's "Blue Boy" is here, as well as paintings by Turner and Van Dyck, tapestries, porcelains, and furniture. Another gallery contains Renaissance paintings and French sculpture from the 18th century; the **Virginia Steele Scott Gallery of American Art**, housed in an enchanting building, traces American painting from 1730 to 1930.

Moving from oil to ink, and from mansion to mansion, the **Huntington Library** contains one of the world's finest collections of rare British and American manuscripts and first editions. Representing nine centuries of literature, the exhibit includes a Gutenberg bible, the Ellesmere Chaucer (a hand-painted manuscript dating to 1410), classics like Ovid's *Metamorphosis* and Milton's *Paradise Lost*, and latter-day works by James Joyce and Henry James. The Founding Fathers are present with original manuscripts by Washington, Franklin, and Jefferson; and the American Renaissance is evident in the literary works of such classic authors as Poe, Hawthorne, and Twain.

This describes only the buildings on the property! There are also the grounds, a heavenly labyrinth of **gardens** ranging from a verdant jungle setting to the austerely elegant Desert Garden. Rolling lawns are adorned with Italian statuary and bordered by plots of roses and camellias. The Shakespearean garden is filled with plants mentioned by the playwright and the Japanese garden features an arched bridge, koi pond, and 16th-century teahouse. All are part of the amazing legacy of a philanthropist with a vision equal to his wealth.

EASTERN SAN GABRIEL VALLEY

Fourth in California's historic chain of missions, **Mission San Gabriel Archangel** (537 West Mission Drive, San Gabriel; 818-282-5191) is an oasis in an urban setting. Built in 1771, the church is fashioned from cut stone, brick, and mortar. Its buttressed walls and vaulted roof indicate Moorish influences and lend a fortress-like quality, but inside the sanctuary peace reigns: the grounds are covered in cactus gardens and grape arbors and flanked by a cemetery. The chapel (temporarily closed because of the 1987 earthquake) features an 18th-century altar built in Mexico City as well as colorful statues from Spain. The winery next door (also closed) was once the largest in California.

Rarely does a racecourse represent a work of art, but **Santa Anita Park** (285 West Huntington Drive, Arcadia; 818-574-7223), built in 1934, is one of the country's most beautiful tracks. Surrounded by landscaped gardens and ornamented with wrought-iron fixtures, the clubhouse is a local landmark. Added to the aesthetics is another unique attraction: the park is family oriented, featuring picnic areas and playgrounds and offering free admission to children accompanied by parents. During the morning from 7:30 to 9:30 the public is admitted free to wander the grounds and, during race season, take a guided tour and watch the horses work out. Thoroughbred racing season is from October to mid-November and from Christmas through April.

The **Los Angeles State and County Arboretum** (301 North Baldwin Avenue, Arcadia; 818-821-3222; admission) may be the most photographed location in the world. Everything from Tarzan movies to Bing Crosby's *Road to Singapore* to television's *Fantasy Island* has been filmed in this 127-acre garden. With plants from every corner of the globe, it has portrayed Hawaii, Burma, Africa, Samoa, and Devil's Island. Wander past the duck pond, tropical greenhouse, fountain, and waterfall and you'll be retracing the steps of Humphrey Bogart, Cary Grant, Ingrid Bergman, and Dustin Hoffman.

The history of the surrounding region, captured in several historic structures still standing on the grounds, long precedes the movies. There are *wickiups* similar to those of the original Gabrieleño Indians, who used the local spring-fed pond as a watering hole. Representing the Spanish era is the **Hugo Reid Adobe**, an 1839 structure built with over 3000 mud bricks. Crudely furnished in 19th-century Spanish fashion, the adobe dates to the days when the area was part of a huge Spanish land grant. E. J. "Lucky" Baldwin, the silver-mining magnate who helped introduce horse racing to Southern California, bought the ranch in 1875, and built a **Queen Anne Cottage**. His castle-in-the-sky dream house, painted white with red stripes and topped by a bell tower, is a gingerbread Victorian often featured on the *Fantasy Island* television show. The interior, decorated in period, is a masterwork of hardwoods and crystal, stained glass and marble.

Also part of this never-ending complex is the **Santa Anita Depot**. Built in 1890, it's a classic brick train station filled with equipment and memorabilia from the great age of railroads.

In the trim little town of Claremont, near the foothills of the San Gabriel Mountains, you can tour another idyllic enclave. The **Claremont Colleges**, a collection of six independent colleges, including the famous Harvey Mudd engineering school, form a continuous campus studded with shade trees. There are walking tours of turn-of-the-century buildings and strolls through pretty parks. For information, call 714-621-8000.

Several hundred yards closer to the mountains, **Rancho Santa Ana Botanic Garden** (1500 North College Avenue, Claremont; 714-625-8767) boasts the largest collection of native California plants in the world. This enchanting 85-acre preserve is dedicated to desert plants, coastal vegetation, wildflowers, and woodlands. Wandering its nature trails is like touring a miniature version of natural California. A particularly pretty time to visit is during spring when the California poppies are in bloom.

SAN GABRIEL MOUNTAINS

For an easygoing introduction to the San Gabriel Mountains, which rise from the San Gabriel Valley to over 6000 feet in elevation, tour **Eaton Canyon Nature Center** (1750 North Altadena Drive, Pasadena; 818-398-5420). Set in the foothills, this 164-acre park is laced with hiking trails which traverse an arroyo and four different plant communities. Sufficiently close to the ocean and mountains to support flora from both regions, the park is a mix of coastal sage scrub, chaparral, oak woodland, and riparian vegetation. There's also a museum, interpretive center, and a nexus of trails leading deep into the adjacent Angeles National Forest.

Another of the region's botanic preserves, **Descanso Gardens** (1418 Descanso Drive, La Cañada; 818-952-4400; admission), stretches across 165 acres at the foot of the San Gabriel Mountains. This former estate has the largest camellia garden in the world, numbering 100,000 plants, as well as a rose garden which follows the development of the species from the pre-Christian era to the present. There is also a Japanese teahouse and garden and a section devoted to native California plants. Unifying this restful hideaway is a tumbling stream that meanders through an oak forest past bird preserves and duck ponds.

To fully explore the **San Gabriel Mountains**, follow the Angeles Crest Highway (Route 2) in its sinuous course upward from La Cañada. With their sharp-faced cliffs and granite outcroppings, the San Gabriels form a natural barrier between the Los Angeles Basin and the Mojave Desert. Embodied in the 691,000-acre Angeles National Forest, these dry, semi-barren mountains are a mix of high chaparral, pine forest, and rocky terrain. Hiking trails crisscross the heights and wildflowers bloom in spring.

A side road from Route 2 leads to 5710-foot Mount Wilson, from which you can gaze across the entire expanse of Los Angeles to the Pacific. **Mount Wilson Observatory**, the region's most famous landmark, supports a 100-inch reflecting telescope credited years ago with the discovery that the universe consists of more than a single galaxy. Today the sleek white structure is closed to the public, but you can walk around a mountaintop park, observing the surrounding peaks, if not the stars.

For complete information on the mountains and the Angeles National Forest, there is an **information booth** near the turnoff to Mount Wilson. The **Chilao Visitor Center** (818-796-5541), a small facility complete with nature museum, is located on Route 2 about 12 miles past the turnoff.

SAN FERNANDO VALLEY

Sprawling across 220 square miles and containing a population of more than 1.3 million suburbanites, the San Fernando Valley is an inland version of Los Angeles. This mirror image across the mountains, known simply as "The Valley," is a smog-shrouded gridwork of tract homes and shopping malls, a kind of stucco version of the American Dream.

Bounded by the Santa Monica Mountains to the south and the San Gabriels on the east, The Valley first entered the history books in 1796 when Spanish padres established the San Fernando Mission, an isolated outpost which became a cultural center for the sprawling *ranchos* that soon sprang up between the mountains.

During the 1870s, when the Spanish land grants were subdivided and the railroad entered the area, the San Fernando region enjoyed its first boom. But the major escalation in population and real estate prices came early the next century during one of the biggest scandals in Los Angeles history.

When Los Angeles voters passed a $1.5 million bond issue in 1905 to buy water-rich land in the distant Owens Valley, they believed they were bringing water to their own parched city. In fact much of this liquid gold poured into the San Fernando Valley, filling the coffers of a cabal of civic leaders who bought up surrounding orange groves and transformed them into housing developments.

In 1914, when Universal turned a 230-acre chicken ranch into a world-acclaimed movie studio, The Valley found a home industry. With its stark mountains and open spaces, the place proved an ideal location for filming Westerns. Columbia, Warner Brothers, and other television and movie studios eventually arrived, as the San Fernando Valley began rivaling that celluloid center on the far side of the Hollywood Hills.

By the post-World War II era, the aerospace industry had landed in The Valley, adding money and glamour to an area fast becoming a kind of promised land for the middle class. With its checkerboard lawns, prefab houses, and predominantly white population, the place is now the West Coast answer

(Text continued on page 102.)

Hollywood in Action

The tram is filled with innocent people, a random collection of folks from all walks, some with little kids in tow. Suddenly it is blasted by aliens and highjacked onto a giant spaceship. As the Cyclons prepare to destroy the tram, a laser battle of galactic proportions breaks out.

Escaping one peril, the passengers cross a collapsing wooden bridge, dodge a flash flood and are swept up in an avalanche. This is all child's play compared to the next adventure, when the tram crosses the Brooklyn Bridge with flames erupting, sirens screaming, and King Kong clinging to the trembling girders.

Sound like Hollywood? Actually it's **Hollywood Universal Studios** (100 Universal City Plaza, Universal City; 818-508-9600; admission), a Disneyesque introduction to one of the nation's biggest motion picture and television facilities. Founded in 1912 when Carl Laemmle, a Bavarian immigrant, converted a chicken farm into a production lot for silent films, Universal is a mammoth 420-acre complex complete with 36 sound stages, a 15-story administration building, and a staff of over 10,000 filmmakers.

More like an amusement park than an authentic studio tour, Universal offers visitors an ersatz introduction to Hollywood. The tram passes the locations for classic films like *My Little Chickadee* (1940) and *The Sting* (1973) and explores the backlot with its street sets of Europe, Texas, New York, and Mexico. If Hollywood is one step away from reality, the Universal Tour is two steps. It's a staging of a staging, a Hollywood version of Hollywood.

Among the newest and most exciting rides at this movie-studio-cum-theme-park are "Back to the Future" and "E.T.'s Adventure," based on the 1980s-era movies. But be prepared for long lines!

The **NBC Studio Tour** (3000 West Alameda Avenue, Burbank; 818-840-3537; admission) provides a similar view of the television industry. Though only 75 minutes long (in contrast to Universal's half-day extravaganza), it takes in a special-effects center and visits a mini-studio where visitors participate in a mock game show. The wardrobe area, set-construction shop, and make-up room are also on the itinerary. Here and at **CBS Ticket Information** (7800 Beverly Boulevard, Los Angeles; 213-852-2624), free tickets to television shows are available.

The **Warner Brothers** (4000 Warner Boulevard, Burbank; 818-954-1744; admission), by contrast, takes you behind the scenes to see the day-to-day activities of a multimedia complex. The studio accepts only small groups; tours are mostly technical and educational and change daily.

Paramount Studios (5555 Melrose Avenue, 213-956-5575; admission) operates weekday tours in a behind-the-scenes fashion with an historical overview.

KCET (4401 Sunset Boulevard, Hollywood; 213-667-9242), the Los Angeles public television station, also conducts technical tours of its studio.

For a personal introduction to the practices and personalities of Hollywood, there's nothing like being there. If you're interested in finding out where movies and television shows are being filmed around town, the **Motion Picture Coordination Office** (6922 Hollywood Boulevard, Hollywood; 213-485-5324) issues a daily shoot sheet for a nominal fee.

That's Hollywood!

to middle America, with parents who commute to Los Angeles and kids who commute to the nearest shopping mall.

GLENDALE AND BURBANK

The portal to the land of the living, some say, is through the gates of death. In the San Fernando Valley that would be **Forest Lawn** (1712 South Glendale Avenue, Glendale; 818-241-4151), one of the most spectacular cemeteries in the world.

Within the courtyards of this hillside retreat are replicas of Michelangelo's "David," Ghiberti's "Baptism of Jesus," and John Trumbull's painting "The Signing of the Declaration of Independence." There are also re-creations of a 10th-century English church and another from 14th-century Scotland. The museum houses a collection with every coin mentioned in the Bible. "The Crucifixion," the nation's largest religious painting, a tableau 195 feet long and 45 feet high, is also on display.

Death has never been prouder or had more for which to be prideful. On the one hand Forest Lawn is quite beautiful, a parkland of the dead with grassy slopes and forested knolls, a garden planted with tombstones. On the other hand it is tasteless, a theme park of the dead where the rich are buried amid all the pomp their heirs can muster.

Every great city boasts a great park. Consider New York's Central Park, Golden Gate Park in San Francisco, and in Los Angeles, **Griffith Park** (entrances near Western Canyon Road, Vermont Avenue, Riverside Drive, and Route 5). Set astride the Hollywood Hills between the Westside and the San Fernando Valley, this 4000-acre facility offers a flatlands area complete with golf courses, playgrounds, and picnic areas, plus a vast hillside section featuring meadows, forests, and miles of mountain roads.

Along Crystal Springs Drive, traversing the eastern edge of the park, you'll pass the **Griffith Park & Southern Railroad** (213-664-6788), a miniature train ride; nearby is a track offering **pony rides** (213-664-3266). The **ranger station** (213-665-5188) will provide maps and information while directing you across the street to the **merry-go-round**, a beautiful 1926-vintage carousel.

Featuring real life versions of these whirling animals, the **L.A. Zoo** (5333 Zoo Drive; 213-666-4650; admission) is among the highlights of the park. Over 2000 animals inhabit this 113-acre facility, many in environments simulating their natural habitats. The African exhibit houses elephants, rhinos, zebras, and monkeys; Eurasia is represented by Siberian tigers and black leopards; there are jaguars and anteaters from South America as well as wombats and Tasmanian devils from Australia. The adjacent **Children's Zoo** contains a baby animal nursery, where newborn mammals are bottle-fed, and an exhibition area filled with every baby animal from squirrel to grizzly bear.

Travel Town (5200 Zoo Drive; 213-662-9678; admission) is a transportation museum featuring a train yard full of cabooses, steam engines, and passenger cars from the glory days of the railroad. The exhibit also includes a fleet of 1920-era fire trucks, old milk wagons, and several retired and rusting military jets. For the kids there are narrow-gauge train rides here and at **Live Steamers** next door.

For Hollywood's version of American history, there's the **Gene Autry Western Heritage Museum** (4700 Zoo Drive; 213-667-2000; admission). The focus here is more on Westerns than the West. There are displays of saloons and stagecoaches, silver saddles and ivory-handled six-shooters, plus photos and film-clips of all your favorite stars, kids.

Standing above the urban fray at the southern end of the park is the **Griffith Observatory and Planetarium** (Observatory Drive; 213-664-1191), a copper-domed beauty that perfectly represents the public-monument architecture of the 1930s. With its bas-reliefs and interior murals, this eerie site also resembles a kind of interplanetary temple. In fact it has been the setting for numerous science fiction films such as *When Worlds Collide* (1951). The Observatory's most famous appearance, however, was in *Rebel Without A Cause* (1955) when James Dean and Sal Mineo confronted the police here.

Apart from a movie setting, the Observatory features a Planetarium Theatre and a space-age Laserium (admission) complete with high-tech light shows. The Hall of Sciences offers museum displays on astronomy and meteorology. A lot of people come simply for the view, which on clear days (in Los Angeles?) extends from the Hollywood Hills to the Pacific.

Local bird species nest in **Fern Dell** (Western Canyon Road), a shady glade with a spring-fed stream. The picnic tables lining the dell create an inviting spot to while away an afternoon.

High on a slope overlooking Los Angeles stands the **Ennis-Brown House** (2607 Glendower Avenue, Los Feliz; 213-660-0607; admission), a squarerigged, Mayan Temple-style home. Designed by Frank Lloyd Wright in 1924, the mansion resides in the same neighborhood as the **Lovell House** (4616 Dundee Drive, Los Feliz), a prime example of Richard Neutra's International Style of architecture (1929).

Another of Frank Lloyd Wright's pre-Columbian block houses is located in Glendale at 2535 East Chevy Chase Drive. The **Derby House**, dating to 1926, was fashioned from pre-cast concrete. One of the master architect's more traditional designs, a Mediterranean-style house, lies up the street at 3021 East Chevy Chase Drive.

Far simpler in effect is the **Casa Adobe de San Rafael** (1330 Dorothy Drive, Glendale), a single-story, mud-brick home built in the 19th century. Once occupied by the Los Angeles County Sheriff, the hacienda's chief feature is the grounds, which are trimly landscaped and covered with shade trees. The house itself is furnished in early-California style.

Rising above them all, situated in the foothills overlooking Glendale, is the **Brand Library & Art Center** (1601 West Mountain Street; 818-548-2051). While neither the library nor the galleries are exceptional, both are set in **El Miradero**, a unique 1904 mansion modeled after the East Indian Pavilion of the 1893 Columbian World Exposition. With bulbous towers, crenelated archways, and minarets, the building is Saracenic in concept, combining Spanish, Moorish, and Indian motifs. The grounds also include a spacious park with nature trails and picnic areas as well as "The Doctor's House," a heavily ornamented 1890 Queen Anne Eastlake Victorian.

VENTURA BOULEVARD

Only in the San Fernando Valley could a single street define an entire geographic area. Running from east to west along the southern edge of The Valley, Ventura Boulevard parallels the Santa Monica Mountains as it passes through Universal City, Studio City, Sherman Oaks, and Encino, then continues to the distant towns of Calabasas and Agoura.

Along the way you'll encounter a house called **Campo de Cahuenga** (3919 Lankershim Boulevard, Universal City; 818-763-7651), a 1923 recreation of a building constructed in 1845. Of little architectural interest, the place is noteworthy because the treaty ending the Mexican War was signed here by Lt. Col. John C. Fremont and General Andreas Pico in 1848.

Several phases of San Fernando Valley life are preserved at **Rancho de los Encinos State Historical Park** (16756 Moorpark Street, Encino; 818-784-4849). This five-acre facility is studded with orange trees, which covered the valley at the turn of the century. The De La Ossa Adobe, built in 1850 and utilized as a resting place along El Camino Real, is a squat eight-room ranch house. Nearby stands the Garnier Building, a two-story limestone residence constructed in 1873 after the fashion of a French farmhouse. With its duck pond and shaded lawns the park is also a choice spot for a picnic.

Making these old houses seem like youngsters is the **Encino Oak Tree** (Ventura Boulevard and Louise Avenue, Encino). With branches spreading 150 feet and a trunk eight feet thick this magnificent specimen dates back about 1000 years.

Farther out in The Valley lies the town of Calabasas, which prides itself on a Wild West heritage but looks suspiciously like surrounding suburban towns. It does possess a few remnants from its romantic past, including the **Leonis Adobe** (23537 Calabasas Road; 818-712-0734), an 1844 mud-brick house which was expanded around 1879 into a stately two-story home with porches on both levels. This Monterey-style beauty stands beside the **Plummer House,** an antique Victorian home.

An ersatz but enchanting version of the Old West awaits at **Paramount Ranch** (in Santa Monica Mountains National Recreation Area; 818-597-9192), a 335-acre park which once served as the film location for Westerns. Paramount owned the spread for two decades beginning in the 1920s, using it as a set for *Broken Lullaby* (1932) with Lionel Barrymore, *Thunder Below* (1932) with Tallulah Bankhead, and *Adventures of Marco Polo* (1937), the Samuel Goldwyn extravaganza which included a fortress, elephants, and 2000 horses. During the heyday of television Westerns in the 1950s, the property was a location for "The Cisco Kid," "Bat Masterson," and "Have Gun, Will Travel."

Today you can hike around the ranch, past the rolling meadows, willow-lined streams, grassy hillsides, and rocky heights that made it such an ideal set. "Western Town" still stands, a collection of falsefront buildings that change their signs depending on what's being filmed. If you're lucky a film crew will be shooting a commercial or even producing the last of that dying breed of movie, a Western.

Orcutt Ranch Horticultural Center (23600 Roscoe Boulevard, West Hills; 818-883-6641), once a private estate, is now an outdoor museum in full bloom. In addition to farm equipment, horticultural displays, and a ranch house, this 25-acre reserve is landscaped with rose gardens and citrus orchards. Nature trails wind through the oak groves, providing a vision of the San Fernando Valley before the advent of suburbia.

NORTH SAN FERNANDO VALLEY

The **Tujunga Wash Mural** (★) (on Coldwater Canyon Boulevard between Burbank Boulevard and Oxnard Street, North Hollywood), one of the Southland's local wonders, is reputedly the world's longest mural. Extending for one-half mile along the wall of a flood control channel, it portrays the history of California from prehistoric times to the present. Bright-hued panels capture the era of Native Americans and early Spanish explorers, the advent of movies, and the terrors of World War II.

Among the finest of California's missions, **Mission San Fernando Rey de España** (15151 San Fernando Mission Boulevard, Mission Hills; 818-361-0186; admission) has been beautifully restored and reconstructed. Exploring the gardens and courtyards of this 1796 institution, visitors encounter the workshops of resident weavers, blacksmiths, and carpenters, as well as an excellent collection of altar furnishings and religious oil paintings.

The wine cellar—deep, cool, and dark—has ironically been placed next to the convent. One of the chapels, rebuilt after an earthquake, is decorated with *trompe l'oeil* murals while another is literally covered with gilded appointments, as if God were somehow more receptive to baroque icons. At the rear of this complex lies the site which best symbolizes the experience of the neophyte Indians who struggled and suffered here—the cemetery.

Nearby stands Los Angeles' second oldest house. Built before 1834 by mission Indians, the **Andrés Pico Adobe** (10940 Sepulveda Boulevard, Mission Hills; 818-365-7810) is a prime example of Spanish architecture. Possessing both beauty and strength, it's a simple rectangular structure with a luxurious courtyard.

Just in case you thought Los Angeles County was entirely urban, there are 314 acres of oak forest and native chaparral at **Placerita Canyon State and County Park** (19152 Placerita Canyon Road, Newhall; 805-259-7721). A stream runs through the property and there are hiking trails and a nature center.

Over at **William S. Hart Park** (24151 San Fernando Road, Newhall; 805-259-0855) there's another 246-acre spread once owned by a great star of silent Westerns. A Shakespearean actor who turned to cinema—starring in his last feature, *Tumbleweeds*, in 1925—William S. Hart left his mansion and estate to the movie-going public.

While much of the property is wild, open to hikers and explorers, the most alluring features are the buildings. The old ranch house, once Hart's office, contains photos of friends and mementoes from his career. The central feature is Hart's home, a 22-room Spanish hacienda filled with guns, cowboy paintings, and collectibles from the early West.

California's haunting history of earthquakes is evident at **Vasquez Rocks County Park** (Escondido Road, northeast of Newhall off Route 14; 805-268-0840), where faulting action has compressed, folded, and twisted giant slabs of sandstone. Tilted to 50° angles and rising 150 feet, these angular blocks create a setting that has been used for countless Westerns as well as science fiction films such as *Star Trek* (1979) and *Star Wars* (1977).

Shoshone Indians first lived among these natural rock formations over 2000 years ago. During the 1870s the infamous bandito Tiburcio Vasquez hid amid the caves and outcroppings to elude sheriff's deputies. A kind of Mexican Robin Hood, Vasquez gave his name to the rocks when he shot it out with lawmen here and escaped, only to be captured and hanged later.

To explore this parched and rocky terrain further, head up into **Bouquet Canyon** (Bouquet Canyon Road), a curving, lightly wooded valley with hiking trails and picnic areas. **San Francisquito Canyon** (San Francisquito Canyon Road) is a river-carved valley that parallels Bouquet Canyon. Back in 1928 the Saint Francis Dam collapsed, inundating this quiet canyon and killing more than 400 people in one of the worst natural disasters in United States history. Today it's a placid mountain valley providing ample opportunities to wander. Like Bouquet Canyon it lies outside Saugus near a region appropriately tagged Canyon Country.

Shifting from the natural to the unnatural, **Six Flags Magic Mountain** (26101 Magic Mountain Parkway, Valencia; 818-367-5965; admission) is the kind of colossal amusement park only Southern California could produce. Spreading across 260 acres and featuring more than 100 rides, shows, and attractions, it's an entertainment center with everything from picnic areas to dance club to a Coney Island-style boardwalk village.

Of course the *raison d'être* (and the reason for paying the stiff admission charge) is the array of rides. Take for instance the Viper, a 188-foot-high megacoaster, reputedly the highest looping roller coaster in the world. We're talking three vertical loops, plus a boomerang and corkscrew, all taken at 70 miles per hour. Z-Force is a pendulum rocket that pulls the force of 3 Gs; and the Sky Tower is a 380-foot space needle. The latest addition is the Psyclone, a wooden replica of the classic Coney Island roller coaster. There are also gentler rides for small children (like the classic 1912 carousel) as well as a dolphin and sea lion show.

Shopping

Trendsetting Los Angeles has evolved into an international shopping mecca, catering to every whim and style. A myriad of shopping districts lie ready to be discovered. Some encompass entire neighborhoods, like Chinatown and Little Tokyo, or line major boulevards, like Wilshire and Melrose. Still others are concentrated in Los Angeles' new mega-malls. Locally produced goods as well as imports from around the world make the metropolis a Shangri La for shoppers.

DOWNTOWN SHOPPING

OLVERA STREET, CHINATOWN, AND LITTLE TOKYO

Historic **Olvera Street**, the site of Los Angeles' original pueblo, is the setting for a traditional Mexican marketplace. Its brick-paved walkways are lined with shops and stalls selling Mexican artworks and handicrafts. You can shop at **Casa de Sousa** (19 Olvera Street; 213-626-7076) for Mexican Indian folk art, then stroll the plaza where food vendors serve homemade *maza* (cornmeal) tortillas, fresh tropical fruits, and tempting *nopales* (fresh diced cactus candies).

The heart of Chinatown, where local Chinese shop at food emporiums, markets, and cookware stores, rests nearby along North Spring Street.

Ornate Chinese-style roofs in reds and greens adorn **Chinatown Plaza** (900 block of North Broadway), the focal point of Chinatown. Along this promenade, well-stocked gift shops offer everything from imported trinkets to very fine, very ancient antiques and artworks.

Walk through the Plaza, then cross Hill Street, and you'll discover a treasure trove of antique stores dotting Chung King Road. **Fong's** (943 Chung King Road; 213-626-5904) and **The Jade Tree** (957 Chung King Road; 213-624-3521) are two of the finest.

The smell alone will lure you into the **Phoenix Bakery** (969 North Broadway; 213-628-4642). A Chinatown institution since 1938, this Asian-style bakery prepares whimsical confections that seem inevitably to attract a long line to its door.

Mandarin Plaza (970 North Broadway) is a "modern" pedestrian mall housing stores like **Kay's Asiatic Imports** (213-625-7597), which carries the largest selection of kimonos and silks in Chinatown, and **Asian Craft Imports** (213-626-5386), an imaginative shop filled with a large selection of import gift items.

The Japanese answer to Chinatown is Little Tokyo, a busy shopping district centered along 1st Street between Main Street and Alameda Boulevard. **Japanese Village Plaza** (327 East 2nd Street), in the heart of the neighborhood, is a commercial expression of the sights, sounds, smells, and flavors of Japan. Enter at the site of the Fire Tower, a traditional fireman's lookout that faces 1st Street, and walk the Plaza's winding brick pathways while browsing its tile-roofed shops. One such store, **Mikawaya Sweet Shop** (213-624-1681), tempts you with subtle Japanese candies.

Just beyond the Plaza, **Bun-ka Do** (340 East 1st Street; 213-625-1122) offers an interesting collection of Japanese art objects, records, and magazines. The oak trees at **Little Tokyo Bonsai Nursery** (622 East 1st Street; 213-626-4079) might be 200 years old, but they measure only a few inches in height. A beautifully groomed selection of these amazing miniatures is displayed outside the shop.

Weller Court (South Onizuka and 3rd streets), a modern tri-level shopping arcade, boasts among its tenants **Matsuzakaya America, Inc.** (213-626-2112), a branch of Japan's oldest and largest department store. Also featured is **Kinokuniya Book Store of America** (213-687-4447), with a complete selection of books on Japan. Conveniently, the mall is connected via walking bridges to the **New Otani Hotel Shopping Arcade** (110 South Los Angeles Street), where a series of specialty shops showcase everything from fine jewelry to tourist trinkets.

CENTRAL DOWNTOWN

Los Angeles' downtown business district is experiencing a major renaissance which has elevated the area to its former status. The shopping scene has blazed back to life with the development of malls like the **Atlantic Richfield Shopping Center** (ARCO Plaza, 5th and Flower streets), where 55 shops and restaurants create one of the largest subterranean shopping centers in the country.

In a space age linkup, this mall connects via glass footbridge with the **Westin Bonaventure Shopping Gallery** (404 South Figueroa Street), where numerous other stores, located on three levels, surround the Bonaventure's vaulting atrium lobby. Among these elegant shops are **August Moon** (213-626-4395), with a beautiful selection of Oriental arts and jewelry, and **Arias**

International Boutique (213-687-4406), which boasts an intriguing array of men's and women's accessories.

Broadway Plaza (700 South Flower Street) lies at the heart of the downtown shopping hub and features **The Broadway** (213-628-9311) department store as well as a galleria of specialty shops.

A charming European-style center, **Seventh Market Place** (Citicorp Plaza, 735 South Figueroa Street; 213-955-7150) contains dozens of shops and restaurants in an open-air setting. With an emphasis on fashion, the mall is highlighted by stores like as **G. B. Harb** (213-624-4785), **Ann Taylor** (213-629-2818), and **Johnston & Murphy** (213-614-1068).

The city's old jewelry district (Hill Street between 5th and 7th streets) still houses a variety of shops selling goods at competitive prices. Historic **St. Vincent Jewelry Center** (650 South Hill Street; 213-629-2124) is reputed to be the world's largest jewelry outlet, covering an entire square block. Here and at the **International Jewelry Center** (550 South Hill Street), another mammoth complex, you'll find items in every price range, from ten dollars to ten thousand.

As in many urban areas, warehouses and industrial districts around Los Angeles have become home to young artists seeking low rents. Among the small galleries which have resulted is **Cirrus Gallery** (542 South Alameda Street; 213-680-3473), where contemporary works by Los Angeles artists are displayed. **Los Angeles Artcore** (652 South Mateo Street; 213-617-3274) is a nonprofit artists' organization where you'll find outstanding modern works. Another nonprofit gallery, the **Los Angeles Contemporary Exhibitions** (LACE) (1804 Industrial Street; 213-624-5650) also provides space for performance art, video productions, and film forums.

The former Theater District (Broadway between 3rd and 10th streets), which served as Los Angeles' Great White Way during the 1930s, is now the main shopping district for the Hispanic community. Today, discount clothing, luggage, and electronic stores line this crowded boulevard. Latino sounds and the spicy aroma of Mexican food fills the air. The **Old Globe Theater** (744 South Broadway), once a legitimate theater, has been converted into a swap meet.

Grand Central Public Market (317 South Broadway), a huge indoor public market dating back to 1917, is filled with Spanish-speaking crowds shopping for fresh produce, ethnic goods, and Mexican specialties. Here you can sample a glass of *jamica* (flower drink) at the juice bar, taste tripe soup, or indulge in Mexican sweet candies. Stroll the aisles of this classic old market and you'll swear you've been transported to Mexico City.

You can literally shop until you drop in Los Angeles' bustling **Garment District**. Known as a major manufacturing center since the 1930s, the district today lies concentrated along Los Angeles Street between 4th and 10th streets. The **Cooper Building** (860 South Los Angeles Street) offers eight floors of name brand clothes and accessories, with prices as much as 70 percent below retail.

Some of the best shops are **My Style** (213-612-0332), for ladies' designer and contemporary wear, and the **Fantastic Designer Room** (213-627-4536).

Across the street at **Academy Award Clothes** (811 South Los Angeles Street; 213-622-9125), they stock thousands of quality men's suits at very reasonable prices.

The Garment District does not begin and end on Los Angeles Street, but rather extends along side streets and down alleyways. A bargain hunter's delight, **The Alley** (between Santee Street and Maple Avenue) is part and parcel of this busy neighborhood. Boxes, bins, and mannequins line the two-block-long alleyway where hawkers and vendors vie for your attention.

Also consider **Bronson's LA Action** (1101-A South Maple Avenue; 213-749-3320), a manufacturer's outlet with prices 50 percent below retail, and **Bell of California** (1018 South Santee Street; 213-748-5716), which displays a beautiful selection of silks and cottons for ladies and juniors. Happy hunting!

At the **Produce Markets** (Central Avenue and 7th Street; or San Pedro and 11th streets), you can purchase produce by the lug or bushel. Even if a box of lettuce doesn't sound like the perfect souvenir from your Los Angeles' sojourn, plan to visit these early-morning markets. Burly truckers, out-of-town farmers, and Hispanic workers are all part of this urban tableau.

You can also watch the city work through its paces in the **Flower District** (Wall Street between 7th and 8th streets). Huge warehouses are filled with flowers and potted plants in one of the region's most amazing floral displays. There are proteas from Southern California, New Zealand calla lilies, lilacs from Holland, Columbian roses, and French tulips, all fresh and blooming with pride.

Nearby **Basket World & Supply** (741 South Maple Avenue; 213-622-8640) is floor to ceiling with baskets (sold at wholesale, even to retail buyers). **Nuts To You** (644 San Pedro Street; 213-627-8855) has been selling nuts to the public (also at wholesale) in the same location since early in the century.

GREATER LOS ANGELES SHOPPING

For neighborhood shopping in an ethnic environment, just traverse the Macy Street Bridge over the Los Angeles River and enter East Los Angeles. Affectionately known as "Little Mexico," the area around Brooklyn Avenue is chockablock with restaurants, markets, bridal shops, and toy stores. **El Mercado** (3425 East 1st Street) is an enclosed marketplace filled with shops and stalls. Vendors sell cowboy boots and Mexican blankets, restaurants serve up tacos *de cabeza* and strolling mariachis create an atmosphere of Old Mexico.

Elsewhere in Greater Los Angeles, you can browse the stacks or snuggle up in a reading chair at **Chatterton's Bookshop** (1818 North Vermont Avenue; 213-664-3882) in Los Feliz. This marvelous facility has an extensive selection of foreign and American literature as well as literary periodicals. Over in the Silver Lake neighborhood, **Studio Sixteen-Seventeen** (1617 Silver Lake Boulevard; 213-660-7991) carries an intriguing collection of contemporary paintings, prints, drawings and sculptures by Los Angeles artists.

The Silver Lake neighborhood is home to **A Different Light** (4014 Santa Monica Boulevard; 213-668-0629), sister store to the well-known gay bookstore in West Hollywood.

WILSHIRE DISTRICT SHOPPING

A spate of new art galleries, and restaurants has attracted a flood of shoppers along **La Brea Avenue**. The La Brea corridor, as the area between Wilshire Boulevard and Melrose Avenue has come to be called, is home to a collection of innovative galleries. Among those featuring unique art exhibits are **Jan Baum** (170 South La Brea Avenue; 213-932-0170) and **Garth Clark** (170 South La Brea Avenue; 213-939-2189), **Ovsay** (126 North La Brea Avenue), **Wenger** (828 North La Brea Avenue; 213-464-4431) and **Jack Rutberg Fine Arts** (357 North La Brea Avenue; 213-938-5222).

Along Wilshire Boulevard, stop in at the gift shop at the **Los Angeles County Museum of Art** (5905 Wilshire Boulevard; 213-857-6146), where you'll find art books, photographic items, and graphic reproductions. Or visit the **Craft and Folk Art Museum** (6067 Wilshire Boulevard, 4th floor; 213-937-5544) where contemporary folk art is the theme. In addition to arts and crafts items, this gallery-cum-museum stocks books and unusual gift items.

Farmers Market (6333 West 3rd Street; 213-933-9211), an informal, open-air market which originated during the Depression to help farmers sell eggs and produce, has evolved into a giant shopping complex. Frequented by Angelenos and tourists alike, Farmers Market is a European boulevard, Oriental bazaar, and Mexican market all in one. In addition to fruit and vegetable stands, there are crafts shops, clothing outlets, and sundry shops lining the corridors of this urban marketplace.

Nearby Fairfax Avenue, the center of Los Angeles' Jewish community, is a neighborhood steeped in religious tradition and filled with delis, bakeries, and kosher grocery stores. **Canter's** (419 North Fairfax Avenue; 213-651-2030), with its sumptuous baked goods and delicious sandwiches, is by far the most popular deli in the district. **Al's Newsstand** (370 North Fairfax Avenue; 213-935-8525), another Fairfax landmark, sells periodicals from around the world.

Journeying from the ethnic to the futuristic, you'll arrive at the **Beverly Center** (8500 Beverly Boulevard; 310-854-0070), a neon-laced shopping mall with signature clothing stores, world-class restaurants, and a multiplex entertainment center. Exterior glass-enclosed elevators move shoppers quickly through this eight-acre complex.

Among the center's 200 international shops and restaurants are the **Irvine Ranch Farmers Market** (310-657-1931), an expansive gourmet marketplace with some of the prettiest produce in town, and **Following Sea** (213-659-0592), a gift shop selling many items you didn't know you wanted and a few that you didn't know existed.

The city's burgeoning Koreatown (bounded by 4th Street and Western Avenue, Vermont Avenue, and Pico Boulevard) is a warren of small shops and markets, each brightly painted in the calligraphy of the East. While many sell Korean foodstuffs and cater to local clientele, each provides a small glimpse into the life of this energetic community.

The **Korean Shopping Center** (3300 West 8th Street), a small shopping arcade housing quality shops, features an exceptional boutique, **Marie France** (213-480-0013). Also stop at **Betsy's Korean Bakery** (3332 West 8th Street; 213-385-8091) for tasty Korean bakery goods and *papunsu* (shaved ice topped with fresh berries).

HOLLYWOOD SHOPPING

Nowhere is the nostalgic heartbeat of Hollywood more evident than along Hollywood Boulevard's Walk of Fame. Although the past couple of decades have witnessed the street's decline, the neighborhood is currently being revitalized and signs of rebirth are everywhere.

Most tourist attractions revolve around **Mann's Chinese Theater** (6925 Hollywood Boulevard), where the souvenir shops, poster studios, T-shirt stores, and postcard vendors are packed tight as a crowd on opening night.

Enter the art deco **Cosmetic Outlet** (1666 North Highland Avenue; 213-463-6164), adjacent to the Max Factor Beauty Museum and you'll find a full stock of cosmetics in an historical landmark location. Even if you're not interested in painting your face, you can tour this intriguing museum. Then head over to **Supply Sergeant** (6664 Hollywood Boulevard; 213-463-4730) and stock up on military gear. A favorite among survivalists, bargain hunters, and pink-coifed punks, this civilian commissary has everything from the subtle to the bizarre.

Hollywood Boulevard probably has more bookstores than movie theaters. **Larry Edmonds Bookshop** (6644 Hollywood Boulevard; 213-463-3273) claims to have the world's largest collection of books and memorabilia on cinema and theater. If any place can challenge their claim, it is **Collectors Bookstore** (1708 North Vine Street; 213-467-3296) with its museum-quality inventory of stills, posters, books, and scripts from the movies and television. **Universal News Agency** (1655 North Las Palmas Avenue; 213-467-3850), reputedly the oldest outdoor newsstand in the country, has newspapers and magazines from around the world.

Frederick Mellinger started a tiny mail order company in 1946 based on the philosophy that "fashion may change but sex appeal is always in style." Today, **Frederick's of Hollywood** (6608 Hollywood Boulevard; 213-466-8506), strikingly set in a purple art deco building, continues to entice and enrage onlookers with its fantasy lingerie.

A bigger-than-life mural of Marilyn Monroe marks **Cinema Collectors** (1507 Wilcox Avenue; 213-461-6516). Selling film and television collectibles from every period, they have over 18,000 movie posters and two million photos.

WEST HOLLYWOOD

The section of Sunset Boulevard between Crescent Heights Boulevard and Doheny Drive, commonly known as Sunset Strip, is marked by creatively designed billboards announcing the latest Hollywood releases. Amid this skein of signs is a series of star-studded cartoon characters signaling the way to **Dudley Do-Right's Emporium** (8200 Sunset Boulevard; 213-656-6550). Jay Ward's cartoon characters come to life at this Bullwinkle enthusiast's mecca.

Hollywood's chic leather crowd frequents **North Beach Leather** (8500 West Sunset Boulevard; 310-652-3224), where original designs attract a celebrity clientele.

Sunset Plaza (Sunset Boulevard between Sunset Plaza Drive and Sherbourne Drive), a two-block cluster of shops, offers some of the most luxurious shopping on the Strip. Among the nearby stores, **Eleanor Keeshan** (8625 West Sunset Boulevard; 310-657-2443) has a wonderful selection of designer women's wear. Climb **The Staircase** (8645 Sunset Boulevard; 310-854-0176) and you'll discover a treasure trove of gifts, many imported from afar.

Book Soup (8818 West Sunset Boulevard; 310-659-3110), a small but special bookstore, offers a top-notch selection of art books, classic literature, current fiction, and international magazines. Step over to **Aahs!** (8878 West Sunset Boulevard; 310-657-4221) for greeting cards, informal gifts, and crazy toys.

The unique architecture of **Esprit** (8491 Santa Monica Boulevard; 310-659-9797), a former roller rink, is as strong a draw as the colorful clothing inside. Filled with vibrant fashions, this chic establishment is so irresistible they furnish visitors with shopping carts.

Not only is **A Different Light** (8853 Santa Monica Boulevard; 310-854-6601) a "full service gay and lesbian bookstore," it also serves as a focal point for West Hollywood's gay population, complete with community bulletin board and an ongoing schedule of events.

Specializing in erotica, **The Pleasure Chest** (7733 Santa Monica Boulevard; 213-650-1022) offers an unparalleled array of leather goods, lingerie, latex clothing, novelties, and gay literature.

At **Out Of The Closet Thrift Store** (9813 North La Brea; 213-937-2727) customers can simultaneously shop and contribute to a worthy cause. Proceeds from sales go to AIDS-related programs. Near the Silver Lake neighborhood there is a similar shop at 3160 Glendale Boulevard (213-664-4394).

Don't worry, you won't miss **Arturo's Flowers** (1261 North La Brea Avenue; 213-876-6482). If the festive mural doesn't catch your eye, the character on the corner (dressed as Santa, the Easter Bunny, or Uncle Sam) will flag you down. Once inside, if you dare to enter, you'll find flowers, cards, produce and piano music in an exotic setting.

Ultramodern shoppers make a beeline for **Melrose Avenue** (between Sycamore Avenue and Ogden Drive). West Hollywood's proving ground for innovative style, Melrose is the smartest street in all L.A., a multiblock mélange of signature boutiques, fresh cuisine restaurants, and heartthrob nightspots. Peopled by visionaries and voluptuaries, it's sleek, fast, and very, very chic. Shops and galleries, with names as trendy as their concepts, come and go with tidal regularity in this super-heated environment.

Of course the most futuristic element of all is the past. At **Chic-A-Boom** (6905 Melrose Avenue; 213-931-7441), the "Mother Lode" of vintage retail, you'll find such shards of American history as a Davy Crockett lamp, a Howdy Doody cookie jar, a drugstore display from the '50s, vintage *T.V. Guides*, plus movie memorabilia. If it's rock-and-roll memorabilia you're after, a few doors away the same owners opened **The Rock Store** (6817 Melrose Avenue; 213-930-2980), with an endless collection of Beatles posters, guitars, and one-of-a-kind collectibles.

Off The Wall (7325 Melrose Avenue; 213-930-1185) is known for "weird stuff" and unusual antiques.

Ever wonder what it'd be like to stand in John Travolta's shoes or Cher's boots? At **A Star Is Worn** (7303 Melrose Avenue; 213-939-4922), you can browse through the wardrobes of celebrities, who sell their old clothes by consignment through this shop. Victoria Principal, Joni Mitchell, Farrah Fawcett, and Ryan O'Neal are among the notables contributing, and you can also find wardrobes from such films as *Taps*, *Rainman*, and *Chances Are*.

Boutiques specializing in late-modern and early-future fashions are ubiquitous. Displaying in-house designs and one-of-a-kind creations are **Tiziana** (7369 Melrose Avenue; 213-653-5203) and **No Name** (7429 Melrose Avenue; 213-653-0590); Olivia Newton-John's **Koala Blue** (7366 Melrose Avenue; 213-655-3596) showcases Australian-inspired designs.

The bold exterior of **Soap Plant/Zulu** (7400-7402 Melrose Avenue; Soap Plant, 213-651-5587; Zulu, 213-651-4857) hints at the crazy collection of gift items and clothes within this duplex store. The wild space of **Wacko** (7416 Melrose Avenue; 213-651-3811) is jam-packed with crazy toys and keepsakes, L.A. style. **Joys and Toys** (7375 Melrose Avenue; 213-658-8697), with its intriguing collection of unusual playthings, is a delight for children of every age.

Occupying an entire block, **Fred Segal** (8100 Melrose Avenue; 213-651-3342) is a series of stores within stores. Seeming to specialize in everything, this consumer labyrinth has clothes for men, women, and children, plus lingerie, luggage, shoes, electronic gear, and cosmetics. There's even a café at hand when you tire of browsing or simply become lost.

The Bodhi Tree (8585 Melrose Avenue; 310-659-1733) is the place for books on mysticism, metaphysics, nature, health, and religion. Behind the main store, **The Used Book Ranch** displays used books as well as herbs, teas, and homeopathic remedies.

A section of West Hollywood within whistling distance of the glass-encased Pacific Design Center, **Designer's Row** consists of classy interior design shops and high-ticket antique stores.

Clustered nearby around Robertson Boulevard are several prestigious art galleries. At **Margo Leavin** (812 North Robertson Boulevard and 817 North Hilldale Avenue; 310-273-0603), two large buildings house an impressive collection of work by painters of regional and national renown. Artworks in ceramic and bronze are displayed in a delightful outdoor sculpture garden at **Asher/Fauré** (612 North Almont Drive; 310-271-3665), an important gallery which handles both established and emerging talents.

Another constellation of galleries lies along the 600-to-800-block stretch of North La Cienega Boulevard. Most venerable of all these art centers is the **Southern California Contemporary Art Galleries** (825 North La Cienega Boulevard; 310-652-8272), which showcases talents from the Los Angeles Art Association. A great place to discover the up and coming while they are still down and out.

Hunsaker/Schlesinger (812 North La Cienega Boulevard; 310-657-2557) specializes in California artists, presenting regional work in a broad range of media. **Gemini GEL** (8365 Melrose Avenue; 213-651-0513), a few blocks away, is one of the country's top art publishers. Producing limited-edition prints and sculptures, it features two display galleries.

BEVERLY HILLS SHOPPING

Without doubt, the capital of consumerism is Beverly Hills. In the mythic order of things, this gilded neighborhood is a kind of shopper's heaven, where everything sparkles just out of reach.

At the heart of the capital lies the "golden triangle," an exclusive shopping district bounded by Wilshire Boulevard, Rexford Drive, and Santa Monica Boulevard. The heart within the heart is, you guessed it, **Rodeo Drive**. World-famous designer showcases like Gucci, Van Cleef, Cartier, Vitton, Giorgio, Ralph Lauren, and Arpel are part of the scenery on Rodeo Drive. Some are soooo exclusive they open only by appointment.

The **Rodeo Collection** (421 North Rodeo Drive; 310-276-6064), a pink marble shopping complex, houses an array of designer boutiques, including **Jantan**, which carries Stephanie Anais and Thalian designs, and **Sonia Rykeil** (310-273-0753).

The **Barakat** (429 North Rodeo Drive; 310-859-8408) collection of jewelry features an amazing combination of Old World antiquities, like 5th-century B.C. Greek coins. This magnificent shop also holds an extensive pre-Columbian art collection. Even the catalog is a collectors' item.

Often the fun of shopping in Beverly Hills (especially if you're on a budget) is in the people watching. Among the town's chic spots is **Fred Hayman Beverly Hills** (273 North Rodeo Drive; 310-271-3000). Owned by the gentleman who launched Giorgio, it features European men's and women's fashions.

Or consider **Giorgio Beverly Hills** (327 North Rodeo Drive; 310-274-0200) itself, boasting a wide array of haûte couture and perfume.

Francis Klein Antique & Estate Jewelry (310 North Rodeo Drive; 310-276-1839) could be the world's most exclusive mom-and-pop store. Mr. and Mrs. Klein still work here, surrounded by enough antique jewelry to make their shop seem more like a museum.

Beverly Hills supports several dozen art galleries, many located along Rodeo Drive. Most galleries stay open until 10 p.m.

Hanson Art Galleries (323 North Rodeo Drive; 310-205-3922) spotlights Erté, as well as more contemporary figures such as Peter Max and Robert Rauschenberg. The breathtaking etchings of Rembrandt are among the rare selections at **Galerie Michael** (430 North Rodeo Drive; 310-273-3377). American and international artists are represented at **Dyansen Gallery** (339 North Rodeo Drive; 310-275-0165).

A recent addition to this vaunted neighborhood, **Two Rodeo Drive**, is a $200-million cobblestone mall featuring about two dozen shops. Built along three levels, it's a brass-door-and-antique-street-lamp promenade reminiscent of a European boulevard.

"Little" Santa Monica Boulevard has less formal, less expensive shops, such as **Camp Beverly Hills** (9640 Little Santa Monica Boulevard; 310-274-8317), which stocks T-shirts, sweats, and other California styles. **Banana Republic** (9669 Little Santa Monica Boulevard; 310-858-7900), an ever-popular emporium, sells fashionable safari clothing.

Some of the country's most famous department stores line Wilshire Boulevard between the 9600 and 9900 blocks. **Neiman-Marcus** (310-550-5900), **I. Magnin** (310-271-2131), and **Saks Fifth Avenue** (310-275-4211) are only part of this elite company. **Tiffany's** (210 North Rodeo Drive; 310-273-8880), in the stately Regent Beverly Wilshire Hotel, continues to awe and inspire. South Robertson Boulevard, by contrast, is home to dozens of small boutiques.

WESTSIDE SHOPPING

Over in Century City, where broad boulevards and highrise buildings rest on the former lot of 20th Century Fox, there's a 100-store mall complete with boutiques, markets, crafts shops, and international food pavilions. **Century City Shopping Center** (10250 Little Santa Monica Boulevard) sprawls across 18 acres, counting among its most inviting addresses **Cottura** (310-277-3828), with a beautiful line of imported ceramics from southern Europe; **Lolita's** (310-277-7148), an emporium filled with crystal and porcelain; and **Imaginarium** (310-785-0227), a toy store for kids with creativity and imagination. Also here is **Westminster Lace** (310-201-0855), a haven for Victorian lovers specializing in clothing and dining and bed ware; this immacluate store also sells reproductions of antique jewelry and exclusive lace patterns.

There is also a shopping section in the nearby **ABC Entertainment Center** (2020 Avenue of the Stars). Contained within this sky-tower setting are numerous specialty shops.

Westwood might house UCLA, but this highrise city is a far cry from the typical campus town. Among its cosmopolitan attributes is a shopping district large enough to wear a hole in any shopper's shoes (and purse). **Westwood Village,** located along Westwood Boulevard adjacent to UCLA, is the Westside's premier shopping and entertainment district. Designed with the pedestrian in mind, "the village" is frequented by college crowds and fashionable Westside residents alike. Student-oriented shops devoted to books, clothes, and accessories combine with cafés and first-run theaters to keep the district hopping day and night.

One of the most noteworthy shops, **Contempo Casuals** (1081 Westwood Boulevard; 310-208-8503), happens to be located in the oldest building in Westwood, a 1929 Mediterranean-style beauty. In an ironic commentary on its surroundings, this up-beat emporium specializes in ultra-contemporary clothing for women.

Bookstores, of course, are a Westwood specialty. Large chain stores and small specialty shops proliferate throughout the neighborhood. Among the finest is **Butler/Gabriel Books** (310-208-4424), a dual-location store with photography, architecture, art, gardening, and cookbooks at 901 Westwood Boulevard, and fiction, poetry, cinema, travel, reference, and children's books in its 919 Westwood Boulevard store. If you can't find the title at either address, browse the 2000 to 2300 blocks of Westwood Boulevard, affectionately known as "Booksellers Row."

Westside Pavilion (10800 West Pico Boulevard, West Los Angeles), an urban mall designed by the architects of the 1984 Olympics, is a glass atrium affair that spans Westwood Boulevard and contains nearly 200 shops. Department stores anchor this triple-tiered mall. Among the independent shops is **Future Tronics** (310-470-7827), with every gadget from dancing

Coke cans to phones shaped like juke boxes. **Shaunzo's Hat City** (310-475-2085) designs its own line of headgear and claims to be the largest hat store in the country.

Boys and girls with dreams of the great outdoors can chart a course to **Adventure 16, Inc.** (11161 West Pico Boulevard, West Los Angeles; 310-473-4574). Catering to the wilderness enthusiast, this shop can outfit you for rock climbing and backpacking. The inventory for adventurers includes clothing, luggage, and travel gear.

For specialty foods there's no place quite like **Trader Joe's** (10850 National Boulevard, West Los Angeles; 310-474-9289), with its endless array of nuts, cheeses, wines, and gourmet items.

Not far from Westwood, in a hillside setting complete with country estates, lies the town of Brentwood. Commercial establishments in this well-heeled community center around San Vicente Boulevard, a beautiful tree-lined street. **P. J. London** (11661 San Vicente Boulevard; 310-826-4649 is Brentwood's ultimate resale shop, offering designer clothes handed down from wealthy Westside and Malibu residents. **Brentwood Country Mart** (26th Street and San Vicente Boulevard), a village-style shopping complex, features several dozen stores. Located in another small shopping center, **Martin Lawrence Galleries** (11701 Wilshire Boulevard; 310-479-5566) features limited editions and original works by major 20th-century artists.

Shopping in Culver City, on the other hand, centers around **Fox Hills Mall** (Slauson Avenue and Sepulveda Boulevard), a modern, 140-store center anchored by large department stores. The old Helms Bakery building, another Culver City institution, was converted into The **Antique Guild** (8800 Venice Boulevard; 310-838-3131), an entire warehouse filled with period furniture and antiques. Each section of this sprawling building is a different style. You can stroll through the Oriental area and shop for original artwork at the **Fine Art Gallery**.

There are more dads than lads at **Allied Model Trains** (4411 South Sepulveda Boulevard; 310-313-9353), a toy wonderland and replica of the Los Angeles Union Station that's filled with every type of model train imaginable.

Westchester Faire Antique Mall (8655 South Sepulveda Boulevard, Westchester; 310-670-4000), a massive marketplace, houses about 70 shops selling antiques, collectibles, and jewelry. **The Place and Company** (8820 South Sepulveda Boulevard, Westchester; 310-645-1539), one of the best resale stores in the city, carries a large selection of top-designer fashions.

SAN GABRIEL VALLEY SHOPPING

Shopping in the San Gabriel Valley centers around Pasadena. **South Lake Avenue**, the oldest and most prestigious shopping district in town, had its origins in 1947 when Bullocks department store opened for business.

Today the venerable establishment has been joined by other department stores as well as a host of small, sophisticated shops.

Among the high points of Pasadena's smartest street are **The Chocolate Giraffe** (516 South Lake Avenue; 818-796-5437), a delightful children's boutique and **Harold Grant** (238 South Lake Avenue; 818-405-8940), an elegant address specializing in top-designer clothes for women.

Also stop by **The Colonnade** (350 South Lake Avenue; 818-796-8737), a small arcade which houses **Kokila's Boutique** (818-584-1157), where you'll find natural fiber fashions for women, and **Dirk Cable, Bookseller** (818-449-7001), specializing in rare books on California and the West. **Burlington Arcade** (380 South Lake Avenue), modeled after The Burlington in London, is another elegant gallery of specialty shops.

Just west of South Lake Avenue, visit **Haskett Court** (824 East California Boulevard), a charming group of English-style cottages. Here at the **Rose Tree Cottages**, you can browse for fine British imports or enjoy afternoon tea in a traditional setting. Reservations required for tea (818-793-3337).

Another major Pasadena shopping district lies along **Colorado Boulevard**, the town's main artery and the route of the annual Rose Parade. **Vroman's Bookstore** (695 East Colorado Boulevard; 818-449-5320), one of the area's oldest and finest bookstores, is among the revered shops along this boulevard. Just doors away, the **House of Fiction** (663 East Colorado Boulevard; 818-449-9861) projects an atmosphere of the '60s with its disheveled book stacks.

Nearby, there's also **Page One Bookstore** (966 North Lake Avenue, Pasadena; 818-798-8694), a women's bookstore that features scheduled readings and a community bulletin board.

Anchoring the entire street is **Plaza Pasadena** (between Marengo and Los Robles avenues), a mega-mall with over 100 stores. About 17 fine jewelers are represented across the street at **Pasadena Jewelry Mart** (440 East Colorado Boulevard; 818-449-9096).

Watch for changing exhibits at **White's Old Town Gallery and Frame Shop** (85 West Colorado Boulevard; 818-795-8383), where the displays alternate between photography, painting, sculpture, and mixed media.

Pasadena's current beautification and redevelopment program reaches its apogee in **Old Town** (bordered by Holly and Green streets, Pasadena Avenue and Arroyo Parkway), a lively historic district that is fast becoming the pride of the city. Particularly prevalent in this gentrified ghetto are antique stores. **Jan's Fine Art Collection** (62 North Raymond Avenue; 818-793-6637) includes an extensive and unusual collection of paintings. Exquisite museum-quality antiques are elaborately displayed at **Design Center Antiques** (70 North Raymond Avenue; 213-681-6230), which also contains a fabric showroom with over 100,000 designs.

del Mano (33 East Colorado Boulevard; 818-793-6648) displays three-dimensional artwork and fine crafts by American artists. Here you'll find a beautiful collection of ceramics, blown glass, hand-painted silks, and jewelry.

Matinee (10 East Holly Street; 818-578-1288) features vintage jewelry, including wonderful art deco pieces.

Pasadena Antique Center (480 South Fair Oaks Avenue; 818-449-7706), the city's largest gallery of shops, houses more than 60 antique dealers. Among them is **Djanet**, with a collection of antique glassware, and **Things of Interest**, specializing in Mission furniture.

The colorful exterior of **The Folk Tree** (217 South Fair Oaks Avenue; 818-795-8733) will inevitably draw you in to see the shop's amazing collection of folk art. Originating from Mexico and South America, the inventory includes a fascinating collection of dolls.

Touted as the world's largest swap meet, the **Rose Bowl Flea Market** (1001 Rose Bowl Drive; 213-588-4411; admission) is held on the second Sunday of each month. This bargain hunter's heaven contains everything from collectibles to contemptibles.

Elsewhere in the San Gabriel Valley, there's **Santa Anita Fashion Park** (Baldwin Avenue and Huntington Drive, Arcadia), a colossal 150-store mall adjacent to Santa Anita Racetrack.

Behind the rustic Northwoods Inn (Rosemead Boulevard and Huntington Drive) in San Gabriel, a small group of merchants has opened a cluster of imaginative shops. If it's baseball cards you're after, consider a trip to **Kenrich Co.** (9418 East Las Tunas Drive, Temple City; 818-286-3888), where you'll find everything in paper collectibles, from maps to autographs.

SAN FERNANDO VALLEY SHOPPING

Out in "The Valley," shopping is such popular sport that the area has bred a new species—"mallies"—who inhabit the shopping malls from the moment the stores open until the second they close.

GLENDALE AND BURBANK

Shopping in Glendale centers around the **Glendale Galleria** (Central Avenue and Broadway), a mammoth 240-store complex anchored by such heavies as **The Broadway** (818-240-8411) and **Nordstrom** (818-502-9922). A host of apparel stores, specialty shops, knickknack stores, and restaurants offer variety, if not imagination.

Glendale's more personalized businesses still reside around Brand Boulevard (between California Avenue and Colorado Street). **Novotny's Antiques** (228 North Orange Street; 818-246-9800) has a grandma's attic worth of memorabilia, antiques, and old records. Another promised land for browsers is **The Costume Shoppe** (315 North Brand Street, in the Glendale Center Theater; 818-244-1161), with masks, magic tricks, pixie ears, fake cigars, and period costumes for every character imaginable.

If it happens to be the first Sunday of the month, add the **Glendale Civic Auditorium** (1401 North Verdugo Road; 818-548-2147) to your list of must-see addresses. That's when more than 80 antique dealers gather to sell their wares.

Burbank is not really geared to shopping, with the exception of San Fernando Boulevard between San Jose and Tujunga avenues. Home to several used bookstores, the area includes **Movie World** (212 North San Fernando Boulevard; 818-846-0459), which adds movie memorabilia to its inventory of books.

For New Age titles consider the **Psychic Eye Book Store** (1011 West Olive Avenue, Burbank; 818-845-8831). Decorated with crystals and Asian statuary, it sells volumes on metaphysics, palmistry, numerology, and the occult.

Good Neighbors Thrift Store (2700 West Magnolia Boulevard, Burbank; 818-566-7701) has a variety of clothing items and sundries, the proceeds from which go to AIDS programs.

VENTURA BOULEVARD

Cities blend into one another on Ventura Boulevard, the busy east–west corridor that stretches across the entire southern rim of the San Fernando Valley. Shops line every point along the thoroughfare, with only subtle distinctions marking changes in locale. Start in Studio City and you'll find your credit cards still working in Sherman Oaks, Encino, Tarzana, and points west.

Traders of Studio City (12238 Ventura Boulevard, Studio City; 818-985-6136) may not look like a pawnshop, but a hock shop it is. You'll find everything from bangles to bongos at this secondhand store.

Bread & Roses (13812 Ventura Boulevard, Sherman Oaks; 818-986-5376) is "a full line bookstore for women." In addition to feminist theory and spirituality titles, it features lesbian fiction and non-fiction plus an array of general titles.

Stacked to the rafters with vintage Walt Disney mementoes, **Nickelodeon** (13826 Ventura Boulevard, Sherman Oaks; 818-981-5325) is a surprising and welcome discovery.

The Valley's answer to Melrose Avenue is a three-block stretch of Ventura Boulevard (centered around the 14500 block in Sherman Oaks) where Valley girls (and guys) hang out, hook up, and put down their bucks. Clothing stores here are even equipped with live disc jockeys. The shops pop every night 'til 10 or 11, with the largest clothiers drawing the biggest crowds.

The **Sherman Oaks Galleria** (15301 Ventura Boulevard, Sherman Oaks) is an atrium-style mall with a host of high-class shops and big department stores.

Strange as it may sound here in Shopperland, there are no department stores at **Town and Country Shopping Center** and **Plaza de Oro** (17200 Ventura Boulevard, Encino). These beautifully landscaped, multitiered plazas provide for more relaxed shopping. Within these open-air facilities are several novel stores offering everything from clothing to chocolate. Or shop in a salon atmosphere at **The Shoe and Clothing Connections** (17404 Ventura Boulevard, Encino; 818-784-2810), a highly touted store with clothing and shoes for men and women.

Specializing in 19th-century works, **Catchpenny Art Gallery** (18555 Ventura Boulevard, Tarzana; 818-881-3218) offers a museum-quality selection of Impressionist paintings. This exemplary gallery also features work by other artistic schools.

Out in the Western-style town of Calabasas, a two-block shopping area offers a chance to browse in a sedate environment. Wander Calabasas Road and you'll discover a variety of small, one-of-a-kind shops. Among them, in an adobe complex is **Connie B's Exclusives** (23564 Calabasas Road; 818-222-4438), a small gift shop in the country craft genre.

Over at **Old Town Canoga Park's Antique Row** (Topanga Canyon Boulevard and Sherman Way, Canoga Park), you'll find a door-to-door procession of thrift shops, discount centers, and antique stores. **Ye Olde Curiosity Shoppe** (21602 Sherman Way; 818-347-6883), **Auntie M's Antiques** (21529 Sherman Way; 818-992-0094), **Sadie's Antiques** (21515 Sherman Way; 818-704-7600), and **The Antique Company** (21513 Sherman Way; 818-347-8778) are among the best and most unusual.

NORTH SAN FERNANDO VALLEY

A life-size model horse stands at the entrance to **Nudie's Rodeo Tailors** (5015 Lankershim Boulevard, North Hollywood; 818-762-3105). Much more than a Western-wear outlet, this store was once a showcase for Nudie, the internationally renowned rodeo tailor. Even today the walls are filled with photos of celebrities like Roy Rogers and Gene Autry strutting about in Nudie's elaborate designs. For you, pardner, they have patterned boots, cowboy hats, and embroidered suits, all designed with the well-heeled cowboy in mind.

Nearby **Valley Book City** (5249 Lankershim Boulevard, North Hollywood; 818-985-6911) stocks over 100,000 new and used books.

Nightlife

Its dual role as music center of the United States and film capital of the world makes Los Angeles one very hot entertainment destination. There are nightclubs frequented by Hollywood stars, movie theaters premiering major films, and dancehalls headlining top musicians from local recording studios. With so much talent concentrated in one city, the performing arts also flourish. Attending the theater in Los Angeles often means seeing a famous movie star playing the lead in a new drama.

The top nightspots are in the Downtown district, Hollywood, and the Westside. To find out what's happening all over town, check out the *Los Angeles Times* "Calendar" section, the "Style" section of the *Los Angeles Herald Examiner*, the *L.A. Reader*, the *L.A. Weekly*, and *Los Angeles* and *California* magazines.

DOWNTOWN NIGHTLIFE

THE BEST BARS

Traditionally, downtown bars cater to an after-work, wait-out-the-traffic clientele. Much of that is changing these days. Some bars still close around 10 p.m. on weeknights, but the trend is towards later nights and more live entertainment.

Mariachi music and margaritas draw Angelenos and outlanders alike to **La Golondrina** (213-628-4349) on Olvera Street. You can sit by the fireplace or out on the patio of this historic adobe building.

The Genji Bar (120 South Los Angeles Street; 213-629-1200) at the New Otani Hotel is a restful piano bar in the heart of Little Tokyo.

Al's Bar (305 South Hewitt Street; 213-687-3558) is a favorite loft district hangout. Entertainment here varies from a jukebox and live bands to Al's in-house **National Theater** providing cabaret-style entertainment. Cover, most nights.

An upbeat dinner theater located several blocks from the Music Center, **Itchey Foot Ristorante** (801 West Temple Street; 213-680-0007) boasts its own Itchey Foot Cabaret performing lively theater. Cover.

Located next to the Dorothy Chandler Pavilion, **Otto Rothschild's Bar & Grill** (135 North Grand Avenue; 213-972-7322) is *the* place to meet before and after the theater. Sixty years of theatrical photos, taken by the club's namesake, cover the walls.

A lovely place for evening cocktails, **Bonavista** (404 South Figueroa Street; 213-624-1000) offers a revolving 360° panorama of the city from the 34th floor of the Westin Bonaventure Hotel. One floor up, the lounge at the **Top of Five** restaurant also sports a tremendous although nonrevolving view and live piano entertainment. There is also music in the **Lobby Court** downstairs and dancing at the **Fantasia** (213-623-8438). Cover.

The **Grand Avenue Bar** (506 South Grand Avenue; 213-624-1532) offers an all-star jazz lineup weeknights until 9 p.m. in the stately Biltmore Hotel. For piano music Friday and Saturday nights, check the hotel's **Rendezvous Court**.

Located below street level, **Casey's Bar and Grill** (613 South Grand Avenue; 213-629-2353) may well be the most popular downtown bar. A comfortable pub filled with sports memorabilia, it draws business people on weekdays until 10 p.m.

NIGHTCLUBS AND CABARETS

Brightly-painted terra cotta warrior priests welcome guests to **The Mayan Nightclub** (1038 South Hill Street; 213-746-4287). Here a young and fashionable crowd dances to deejay tunes and occasional live bands in a grandiose Mayan tomb.

At **Vertigo** (333 South Boylston Street; 213-747-4849), another upscale downtown late-night restaurant and nightclub, the doorman decides who is sufficiently chic to enter. A giant dancefloor pulsates with top-of-the-chart tapes and live bands nightly. Cover, reservations a must for dinner.

THEATER, OPERA, SYMPHONY AND DANCE

The most prestigious performing arts complex on the West Coast, the **Music Center** (135 North Grand Avenue; 213-972-7211) consists of three major theaters located within a massive, white marble plaza.

The elegant **Dorothy Chandler Pavilion**, home to the Los Angeles Philharmonic Orchestra, is a spectacular 3000-seat facility. The concert hall also hosts performances by the Joffrey Ballet, Los Angeles Master Chorale, and Los Angeles Music Center Opera.

The 2000-seat **Ahmanson Theatre** presents classic dramas and comedies as well as West Coast premieres like *Phantom of the Opera*.

The more intimate, 700-seat **Mark Taper Forum** is ideal for contemporary dramatic and musical performances. The resident Center Theater Group is committed to the development of new works and artists and has produced such award-winning plays as *Zoot Suit*, *Children of a Lesser God*, and *The Shadow Box*.

Tickets for Dorothy Chandler Pavilion performances are available through Ticketmaster (213-486-3232). Ticketron (213-410-1062) handles reservations at the Ahmanson Theatre and the Mark Taper Forum.

Housed in the Japanese American Cultural and Community Center in Little Tokyo, the **Japan America Theatre** (244 South San Pedro Street; 213-680-3700) presents traditional and contemporary Japanese productions. Performances include Grand Kabuki, Bugaku, and Noh dramas as well as Japanese puppet theater. In addition, Western dance troupes and chamber orchestras are sometimes featured.

Chamber Music in Historic Sites (10 Chester Place; 213-747-9085) is a marvelous series of world-class performances presented in unique historical settings.

The American Ballet Theatre performs during March and December at the 6200-seat **Shrine Civic Auditorium** (665 West Jefferson Boulevard; 213-749-5123), which also hosts major music events, including classical opera, jazz, pop, rock, and ethnic folk music presentations.

GREATER LOS ANGELES NIGHTLIFE

EAST AND SOUTH LOS ANGELES

The **Margo Albert Theatre** (3540 North Mission Road; 213-223-2475), part of the Plaza de la Raza arts center, hosts drama, music, and dance programs which are often related to Mexican holidays.

The East L.A. theater scene is dominated by the **Bilingual Foundation of the Arts** (421 North Avenue 19; 213-225-4044), which presents plays in English and Spanish.

Marla's Jazz Supper Club (2323 Martin Luther King Jr. Boulevard; 213-294-8430) hosts top-name jazz and rhythm-and-blues performers. Cover.

A perfect place for a "girls night out," **Chippendale's** (310-396-4045) features exotic male dancers and a ladies-only crowd. The scene gets wild as the dancers strut about while the women stuff greenbacks into their G-strings. Cover.

LOS FELIZ AND SILVER LAKE

The **Dresden** (1760 North Vermont Avenue; 213-665-4294), a stately brick-and-stained-glass restaurant, hosts an elegant piano bar.

They'll serenade you tableside with operas and show tunes at **La Strada** (3000 Los Feliz Boulevard; 213-664-2955), a northern Italian dinner club.

The Bavarian-style **Red Lion Tavern** (2366 Glendale Boulevard; 213-662-5337), a friendly German rathskeller, serves lagers in two-liter boots. The German bartenders occasionally initiate impromptu sing-alongs, especially after games at nearby Dodger Stadium.

There are two small theaters of note in the Silver Lake area. **Colony Studio Theatre Playhouse** (1944 Riverside Drive; 213-665-3011), originally built in 1927 as a movie palace, hosts classic dramas, musicals, and new plays. The **Celebration Theatre** (7051-B Santa Monica Boulevard; 213-957-1884) presents gay and lesbian productions.

It's levis and leather at **The Bunk House** (4519 Santa Monica Boulevard, Silver Lake; 213-667-9766), a country-and-western-style gay bar. Featured are a video deejay, pool table, and pinball machines.

Speaking of gay nightlife in Silver Lake, there's **Detour** (5209 Santa Monica Boulevard; 213-669-1090), a neighborhood cruise bar complete with pool tables and neighbors.

The Hyperion (2810 Hyperion Avenue; 213-660-1503), known locally as Woody's, is a casual levis bar with deejay music spinning.

WILSHIRE DISTRICT NIGHTLIFE

The Mexican food may be good at **El Cholo** (1121 South Western Avenue; 213-734-2773), but the famed margaritas really draw the crowds to this lively bar scene.

City Restaurant (180 South La Brea Boulevard; 213-938-2155), a high-tech warehouse, features a dynamic bar with a streetfront patio. The angled designs and white-and-red interior match the style of the clientele.

Tom Bergin's (840 South Fairfax Avenue; 213-936-7151), a traditional Irish pub dating to the 1930s, was voted one of the top 100 bars in the United States by *Esquire* magazine. Judging from the 5000 patron-inscribed shamrocks mounted on the wood-paneled walls, the regular crowd confirms *Esquire's* vote.

Actors, musicians, and writers meet in the small **Coronet Bar** (370 North La Cienega Boulevard; 213-659-4583), a comfortable and unpretentious spot to carouse.

The Hard Rock Café (8600 Beverly Boulevard; 213-276-7605), a wildly popular gathering place in the Beverly Center, features the loud music and rock memorabilia decor for which this nightclub chain is renowned. A Cadillac protruding from the roof and walls covered with Beatles artifacts and Madonna icons add to the ambience.

Here in the land of celluloid, where movies began, what could be more appropriate than the **Silent Movie** (611 North Fairfax Avenue; 213-653-2389). This imaginative movie house shows old silent films complete with organ accompaniment.

THEATER, OPERA AND DANCE

The **Wiltern Theater** (3790 Wilshire Boulevard; 213-380-5005) opened its doors in 1931 as a Warner Brothers movie house. Now restored to its art deco splendor, the terra cotta structure is a center for the performing arts. Rock and classical music, drama, and opera programs are regularly scheduled.

A beautiful 1927 Renaissance-style building, the **Wilshire Ebell Theatre** (4401 West 8th Street; 213-939-1128) is the setting for television specials and live theater, opera, and dance presentations.

The **Coronet Theatre** (366 North La Cienega Boulevard; 213-652-9199) houses the Serendipity Theatre Company, which performs family and youth-oriented theater.

HOLLYWOOD NIGHTLIFE

Reminiscent of the 1930s, the Hollywood Roosevelt Hotel's deco-style **Cinegrill** (7000 Hollywood Boulevard; 213-466-7000) is putting glamour back into Hollywood nightlife. Crème de la crème cabaret entertainers perform here in an intimate, sophisticated atmosphere. Cover.

The Palace (1735 North Vine Street; 213-462-3000) also has a colorful history dating back to 1927. Today the luxurious complex showcases popular names in rock and jazz. Several bars, dancefloors, a restaurant, and an open courtyard add to the luxury. Cover.

Following a $6 million remodel, **Pacific's El Capitan Theatre** (6838 Hollywood Boulevard; 213-467-7674) has been returned to its early glory as one of Hollywood's classic theaters. Opened in 1926, the El Capitan is part of the newly conceived "Cinema District," an eight-block section along Hollywood Boulevard filled with historic landmarks, including several vintage theaters. If you're going to the movies, this is the place!

Famous jazz, blues, and swing artists appear regularly at **Vine Street Bar and Grill** (1610 North Vine Street; 213-463-4375), an art deco dinner club with a solid reputation. Cover. Reservations strongly recommended.

For sunset panoramas, nothing quite matches **Yamashiro** (1999 North Sycamore Avenue; 213-466-5125). Set in a Japanese palace, the lounge overlooks gracious Oriental gardens from a perch in the Hollywood Hills.

Club Lingerie (6507 Sunset Boulevard; 213-466-8557) is a bare-walls dance club packed to the rafters with trendy Hollywood crowds. A prime place for hot, live rock-and-roll, reggae, and blues. Cover.

Sparkle Productions (310-278-7712) offers audience-participation whodunits at both the **Cat and the Fiddle Pub and Restaurant** (6530 Sunset Boulevard) and **Les Freres Taix** (1911 Sunset Boulevard).

The lounge at **The Roxbury** (8225 Sunset Boulevard; 213-656-1750) is a rendezvous for record company executives and show business figures.

Another popular entertainment industry club, **Carlos and Charlies** (8240 Sunset Boulevard; 213-656-8830) offers comedy routines and variety shows. Cover.

The level of talent at the **Comedy Store** (8433 West Sunset Boulevard; 213-656-6225) is evident from the celebrity signatures covering the building's black exterior and photo-lined interior. The Main Room features established comedians, the Original Room showcases new talent, and the Belly Room presents female comics. Cover.

What's hot and what's not depends on a very fickle Hollywood crowd. **Nicky Blair's** (8730 Sunset Boulevard; 310-659-0929) was hot the minute it opened to a star-studded crowd and still hasn't cooled off. The bar is packed shoulder-to-shoulder every night with beautiful people dressed to kill.

The Central (8852 Sunset Boulevard; 310-652-5937) a small, casual, understated club is known for live rhythm-and-blues. Many celebrity musicians sit in on Tuesday night jam sessions. Cover.

Three long-standing rock clubs dominate Sunset Strip. **Whiskey A Go Go** (8901 Sunset Boulevard; 310-652-4202) had its heyday in the '60s and is still popular with younger dance crowds. **The Roxy** (9009 Sunset Boulevard; 310-276-2222) headlines known rock and jazz performers in an art deco-style room. **Gazzarris** (9039 Sunset Boulevard; 310-273-6606), the oldest rock club on the Strip, offers a stage for dancing. Cover charge at all three clubs.

Doug Weston's Troubador (9081 Santa Monica Boulevard; 310-276-6168), another of Hollywood's many rock-and-roll clubs, headlines heavy metal bands. No age requirement. Cover.

La Cage Aux Folles (643 North La Cienega Boulevard; 310-657-1091), an outrageous cabaret, is overrun by female impersonators who would have you believe that show biz's biggest stars—Dolly Parton, Diana Ross, Marilyn Monroe—are men. Great entertainment. Cover.

Nucleus Nuance (7267 Melrose Avenue; 213-939-8666) is an art deco nightclub with pizzazz. Well-dressed singles stand three-deep at the bar; quiet tables on the patio offer romantic privacy; live jazz is on tap nightly. Cover.

One of the hottest trends in Hollywood nightlife is the coffeehouse. With plump armchairs, weatherbeaten tables and walls covered by contemporary art, places like **Java** (7286 Beverly Boulevard; 213-931-4943), **The Living Room** (110 South La Brea Avenue; 213-933-2933) and **Bourgeois Pig** (5931 Franklin Avenue; 213-962-6366) serve cappuccino and light meals until 4 a.m. Poetry readings, performance art, music and an edge clientele are also on the menu.

A cozy view lounge, **Café Mondrian** (8440 Sunset Boulevard; 213-650-8999) features live jazz in a comfortable setting.

Another of Hollywood's jazz clubs, **Catalina Bar & Grill** (1640 North Cahuenga Boulevard; 213-466-2210) draws a relaxed crowd. This intimate room features name performers. Cover.

There are often as many comedians in the bar as on stage at the **Improvisation** (8162 Melrose Avenue; 213-651-2583). This spacious brick-walled club, patterned after the New York original, draws top-name comics as well as local talent. Cover.

Who would imagine that a neighborhood saloon could survive the gentrification of Melrose Avenue? **J. Sloan's** (8623 Melrose Avenue; 310-659-0250), with its sawdust floor and old movie props, has not only survived but flourished in the shadow of Melrose's chrome-and-tile nightspots.

THEATER

Theater in Hollywood varies from tiny storefront establishments to famous stages. In a city filled with actors, the playhouses inevitably are loaded with talent. Professionals from local television and movie studios continually hone their skills on stage, and the area's "equity-waiver" theaters provide an opportunity to see these veterans perform at affordable prices.

The **Hollywood Arts Council** (P.O. Box 931056, Hollywood, CA 90093; 213-462-2355) offers seasonal calendar listings of all Hollywood theaters.

To secure tickets for productions, call ticket agencies to charge by phone. Major ticket agencies include **Ticketmaster** (213-480-3232), **Goodtime Tickets** (213-464-7383), and **Murray's Tickets** (213-234-0123). Or contact the theater directly; oftentimes day-of-the-event tickets are available for as much as 50 percent off.

Pantages Theatre (6233 Hollywood Boulevard; 213-480-3232), one of Hollywood's largest playhouses, offers major productions, including Broadway musicals.

The refurbished **James DoLittle Theatre** (1615 North Vine Street; 213-462-6666), built in 1926, features top shows from Broadway and London. **The John Anson Ford Theatre** (2580 Cahuenga Boulevard; 213-480-3232), an outdoor amphitheater, produces Shakespearean and experimental dramas as well as dance and jazz concerts. One of Hollywood's oldest legitimate theaters, the **Henry Fonda Theatre** (6126 Hollywood Boulevard; 213-480-3232) also hosts dramatic and musical performances.

But it's really the smaller theaters and local playwrights that make sections of Hollywood the Off-Broadway of the West. Dozens of talented companies perform regularly on these less-known stages.

One of Hollywood's oldest playhouses, **Cast Theatre** (804 North El Centro Avenue; 213-462-0265) presents a varied bill of musicals, comedies, and dramas. **The Coast Playhouse** (8325 Santa Monica Boulevard; 213-650-8507) specializes in original musicals and new dramas. A replica of the British original, the **Globe Playhouse** (1107 North Kings Road; 213-654-5623) stages Shakespearean plays and other dramas of historical significance.

The **Matrix Theatre** (7657 Melrose Avenue; 213-653-3279) is home to Joseph Stern's award-winning troupe, Actors for Themselves. Comedy and improvisation top the bill at the **Groundling Theatre** (7307 Melrose Avenue; 213-934-9700).

Il Vittoriale (2035 North Highland Avenue; 213-480-3232), an old American Legion headquarters converted into an elaborate three-story villa, is the setting for *Tamara*. This "living movie" is staged in various parts of the house and involves audience participation.

One of the world's largest natural amphitheaters, seating 17,620, the **Hollywood Bowl** (2301 North Highland Avenue; 213-850-2000) dates back to the 1920s. The concert shell hosts the Los Angeles Philharmonic and features top-bill pop, jazz, and dance concerts. Bring a cushion, sweater, and picnic, and come join the festivities in this park-like setting.

The **Hollywood Palladium** (6215 Sunset Boulevard; 213-466-4311), which once headlined the swing bands of the '40s, now features new wave, rock, and Latin groups.

THE GAY SCENE

Grecian columns are incongruously combined with high-tech appointments at **Studio One** (652 North La Peer; 213-659-0472), a popular gay disco. In the adjoining **Backlot Theater** (657 North Robertson Boulevard), the club's cabaret and live male acts range from the sublime to the raucous. Cover.

The **Rose Garden Performance Center** (665 North Robertson Boulevard; 310-854-4455) attracts a gay and straight crowd to its pink-and-white cabaret. Cover.

Rage (8911 Santa Monica Boulevard; 310-652-7055) is a spacious dance club that spills onto the sidewalk; inside there are outrageous videos plus sounds ranging from rap to rock. Cover on weekends.

The "videotainment" program at **Revolver** (8851 Santa Monica Boulevard; 310-550-8851) means color monitors on every wall. With two bars, an espresso bar, and a lively crowd, the place is hot. Cover on weekends.

It is primarily gay men who frequent **Micky's** (8857 Santa Monica Boulevard; 310-657-1176), a West Hollywood nightspot that offers dancing to a deejay video.

On different nights some of the same people may be found at **The Eagle** (7864 Santa Monica Boulevard; 213-654-3252). This stand-up bar features a platter-spinning deejay.

Palms (8572 Santa Monica Boulevard; 310-652-6188) is the oldest women's bar in Los Angeles. It features pool playing, a dancefloor, music videos, a deejay, and (occasionally) a live band.

BEVERLY HILLS NIGHTLIFE

Refined decor and sophisticated cabaret entertainment make **435 North** (435 North Beverly Drive; 310-273-2292) a popular Beverly Hills nightspot. Guest appearances by celebrities, as well as a lineup of regular jazz and blues performers, are the drawing cards.

Christies Bar and Grill (8442 Wilshire Boulevard; 213-655-8113), a comfortable art deco lounge located next door to the Wilshire Theatre, is the perfect before- and after-theater stop.

Another ritzy spot for celebrity voyeurs is **Jimmy's** (201 Moreno Drive; 213-879-2394), a lively art deco piano bar.

The **Polo Lounge** (9641 Sunset Boulevard; 310-276-2251) at the swank Beverly Hills Hotel has been a celebrity meeting place for decades. Sip a glass of chardonnay in this pretty pink lounge and watch the action. The piano man performs every evening.

For a New York-style piano bar, consider **Carroll O'Connor's Place** (369 North Bedford Drive; 213-273-7585). Owned by actor Carroll "Archie Bunker" O'Connor, the lounge is an East Coast answer to staid Beverly Hills, with O'Connor himself sometimes in residence.

The surroundings are cool and sleek at **Asylum** (182 North Robertson Boulevard; 213-657-8484) and the sound ranges from live jazz to recorded disco.

Sleeker still is the crowd at **Stringfellows** (206 Via Rodeo; 310-285-9909), a chrome-and-neon watering hole where high fashion is on display at an upstairs disco and downstairs patio bar.

The **Wilshire Theatre** (8440 Wilshire Boulevard; 213-480-3232), a 1929 movie house, has been restored and currently stages musicals and dramas.

WESTSIDE NIGHTLIFE

In Century City, the expansive **ABC Entertainment Center** (2020 Avenue of the Stars) offers a variety of entertainment options. The **Schubert Theatre** (800-233-3123) can pack 1746 people into its cavernous facility for Broadway plays with top-bill casts. **Harry's Bar and American Grill** (310-277-2333), a replica of Harry's Bar in Florence complete with wood paneling and brass detailing, caters to the after-theater crowd (not all 1746 of them at once). Also located in the ABC Entertainment Center, the New York-style **Harper's** (310-553-1855) features an open-air patio with views of the city lights. **Twenty/20 The Club** (213-933-2020), an exciting and modern club, is modeled after a photographer's studio, with black and white decor, umbrella lightstands, and a large mirrored dancefloor. Deejay and live entertainment. Cover.

Westwood Village, located at the heart of Westwood a few strides from the UCLA campus, bubbles with nighttime activity. Students and moviegoers crowd the sidewalks and spill into the streets. While many are headed to the first-run movie theaters for which this college town is known, some frequent the local clubs.

The Mediterranean-style **Alice's Restaurant** (1043 Westwood Boulevard, Westwood; 310-208-3171), popular with students and moviegoers, features live jazz in its cozy upstairs bar.

Stratton's Grill (1037 Broxton Avenue, Westwood; 310-208-0488) is an old-time saloon complete with marble bar, mahogany railings, and people-watching mezzanine. A popular campus hangout.

For escaping the college crowds, there's **Westwood Lounge** (930 Hilgard Avenue, Westwood; 310-208-8765), a restful piano bar in the gracious Westwood Marquis Hotel.

San Francisco Saloon and Grill (11501 West Pico Boulevard, West Los Angeles; 310-478-0152) is a small, intimate fern bar. Wood paneling, historic photos of San Francisco, and comfortable surroundings create a sense of intimacy.

Igby's Comedy Cabaret (11637 Tennessee Place, at West Pico Boulevard and Barrington Avenue), West Los Angeles; 310-477-3553) headlines known and unknown comedians in a cozy, contemporary club. Cover.

Hidden in a forested Bel Air canyon, **The Bar** (701 Stone Canyon Road; 310-472-1211) at the Bel Air Hotel is the perfect place for an intimate cocktail. Piano music from this wood-paneled den wafts onto the patio and out across the garden, waterfall, and pond.

THEATER, OPERA, SYMPHONY AND DANCE

Westwood Playhouse (10866 Le Conte Avenue, Westwood; 310-208-5454), a 500-seat Egyptian-style "event theater," often showcases new plays.

The "equity-waiver" **Odyssey Theatre** (2055 South Sepulveda Boulevard, West Los Angeles; 213-477-2055) offers avant-garde productions by local playwrights.

The **UCLA Center for the Performing Arts** (405 Hilgard Avenue, Westwood; 213-825-9261) holds performances on campus.

SAN GABRIEL VALLEY NIGHTLIFE

Like most everything else in the San Gabriel Valley, the entertainment scene centers around Pasadena.

A woodsy decor and cozy fireplace set the stage at the **Sawmill** (340 South Lake Avenue, Pasadena; 818-796-8388), where Top-40 and country-and-western entertainers perform nightly.

Monahan's (110 South Lake Avenue, Pasadena; 818-449-4151), the quintessential Irish pub, is known for its green-and-red plaid carpet, friendly bartenders, and Saint Patrick's Day extravaganza. They also feature cabaret-style entertainment and karaoke.

The Ice House (24 North Mentor Avenue, Pasadena; 818-577-1894) presents new and established comedians nightly. Another section of the 1920-era ice house, **The Ice House Annex**, features comedians and live music. Cover.

A cabaret-style dinner club, **Maldonados** (1202 East Green Street, Pasadena; 818-796-1126) entertains diners with Broadway musical medleys and light opera. Some of the performers at this sophisticated little dining room are stage veterans. Reservations recommended for dinner, but you can see the show from the small bar.

Barney's Ltd. (93 West Colorado Boulevard, Pasadena; 818-577-2739), an old-style saloon with village charm and friendly spirit, pours over 50 brands of beer from all over the world.

At **Dodsworth** (2 West Colorado Boulevard, Pasadena; 818-578-1344), a New York-style restaurant and lounge, you'll find a tony crowd at the marble bar listening to live jazz.

During the thoroughbred horse-racing season, beautiful Santa Anita Park attracts huge crowds every day. At night the bawdy track crowd goes to sing along karaoke-style at the **100 to 1 Club** (100 West Huntington Drive, Arcadia; 818-445-3520).

For more refined evenings, Pasadena provides the palatial **Ambassador Auditorium** (300 West Green Street; 818-304-6161), an excellent 1262-seat facility that has presented musical programs by such luminaries as Vladimir Horowitz, Luciano Pavarotti, and the Julliard String Quartet.

Or consider the **Pasadena Playhouse** (39 South El Molino Avenue, Pasadena; 818-356-7529), an historic theater which has been the birthplace for numerous stars of stage and screen. Dramatic performances are produced on the 700-seat central stage and in a 121-seat space.

SAN FERNANDO VALLEY NIGHTLIFE

BURBANK AND GLENDALE

The giant 6000-seat **Greek Theatre** (2700 North Vermont Avenue; 213-480-3232), nestled in the rolling hills of Griffith Park, is patterned after a classical Greek amphitheater. The entertainment in this enchanting spot ranges from stellar jazz, classical, pop, and rock music to dance and dramatic performances. Bring a sweater and picnic.

Jax Bar & Grill (339 North Brand Boulevard, Glendale; 818-500-1604), with its brass elephants and local clientele, is a supper club that headlines notable jazz musicians.

For sophisticated entertainment there's the **Glendale Center Theatre** (324 North Orange Street, Glendale; 818-244-8481), which presents musicals, comedies, and dramas and **The Third Stage** (2811 West Magnolia Boulevard, Burbank; 818-842-4755), with its comedy programs.

Stop by for a drink at **The Castaway** (1250 Harvard Road, Burbank; 818-848-6691) and enjoy the view from the patio. Then you can step inside this comfortable fern bar for a little musical entertainment.

Chadney's (3000 West Olive Avenue, Burbank; 818-843-5333), popular with entertainment people from nearby NBC Studio, offers live jazz, rock, and pop.

Named after Shirley Temple, **Dimple's** (3413 West Olive Avenue, Burbank; 818-842-2336) is a showcase for fledgling singers. Dance music alternates every half hour with musical auditions. Sing for your drinks while pursuing those dreams of stardom!

The after-work crowd pedals over to **Bombay Bicycle Club** (321 South 1st Street, Burbank; 818-846-8711), where antique bikes decorate a large cocktail lounge.

Just up the block, the **Lobby Lounge** (555 Universal Terrace Parkway; 818-506-2500) at the Universal Hilton and Towers represents another choice piano bar.

VENTURA BOULEVARD

Telly's A Sporting Bar (333 Universal Terrace Parkway, Universal City; 818-980-1212) is named in honor of Sheraton Universal Hotel's in-house resident, Telly Savalas, who can often be seen controlling the television sports channels. The bar is decorated in sports memorabilia.

The Baked Potato (3787 Cahuenga West Boulevard, Studio City; 818-980-1615) serves up contemporary jazz every night. If you want to rub shoulders with L.A. music heavies, this is the place. Cover.

Representative of the gay scene in The Valley are three Studio City clubs: **Apache** (11608 Ventura Boulevard; 818-506-0404), the area's most popular disco; **Venture Inn** (11938 Ventura Boulevard; 818-769-5400), a stylish lounge popular with a well-heeled clientele; and **Queen Mary's** (12449 Ventura Boulevard; 818-506-5619), a pretty pastel club with a camp floor show that features a parade of queens dressed in their finest regalia; cover; reservations recommended.

Oil Can Harry's (11502 Ventura Boulevard, Studio City; 818-760-9749), with its live music and theatrical shows, is another gay gathering place.

Club 22 (4882 Lankershim Boulevard, North Hollywood; 818-760-9792) is a women's bar complete with pool room and dancefloor. The music is provided by a video deejay.

The "Room Upstairs" at **Le Café** (14633 Ventura Boulevard, Sherman Oaks; 818-986-2662) is a delightful retreat with a hot lineup of jazz groups. Cover.

The L.A. Connection (13442 Ventura Boulevard, Sherman Oaks; 818-784-1868) developed a unique comedy concept several years back. They show camp film classics with house comedians ad-libbing the dialogue. Other shows include regular audience participation improvisation. Cover.

The **L.A. Cabaret Comedy Club** (17271 Ventura Boulevard, Encino; 818-501-3737) also features stand-up comedy. Showcased on the lounge's two stages are top entertainers ranging from Milton Berle to Robin Williams. Cover.

The Country Club (18415 Sherman Way, Reseda; 818-881-5601), a massive 1000-seat nightclub, brings in headline entertainers. Cover.

The outdoor patio and country atmosphere at **Sagebrush Cantina** (23527 Calabasas Road, Calabasas; 818-222-6062) draw steady crowds. Here you can sip margaritas, linger after sunset and workout on the sawdust floors to the sound of rock bands.

For something more subdued, the lounge at **Calabasas Inn** (23500 Park Sorrento Drive, Calabasas; 818-222-8870) overlooks woods and waterfalls.

NORTH SAN FERNANDO VALLEY

The Valley is a prime place for jazz. For live jazz performances try **The Money Tree** (10149 Riverside Drive; 818-769-8800).

Norah's Place (5667 Lankershim Boulevard, North Hollywood; 818-980-6900) is an altogether different experience. This lively Bolivian supper club serves up tango music. In between sets by the resident band the dancefloor fills with dancers moving to merengue, cumbia, and salsa tunes. Cover.

The Palomino (6907 Lankershim Boulevard, North Hollywood; 818-764-4010), a top showcase for country and rock talents, is a Texas-style honky tonk. Jerry Lee Lewis, Leon Russell, and Delbert McClinton are among the good old boys who have performed here. Cover.

LOS ANGELES COAST

CHAPTER THREE

Los Angeles Coast

L.A., according to a popular song, is a great big freeway. Actually this sprawling metropolis by the sea is a great big beach. From Long Beach north to Malibu is a 74-mile stretch of sand that attracts visitors in the tens of millions every year. Life here reflects the culture of the beach, a freewheeling, pleasure-seeking philosophy that combines hedonism with healthfulness.

Perfectly fitted to this philosophy is the weather. The coastal climatic zone, called a maritime fringe, is characterized by cooler summers, warmer winters, and higher humidity than elsewhere in California. Sea breezes and salt air keep the beaches relatively free from smog. During summer months the thermometer hovers around 75° or 80° and water temperatures average 67°. Winter carries intermittent rain and brings the ocean down to a chilly 55°.

Add a broadly ranging coastal topography and Los Angeles has an urban escape valve just minutes from downtown. The shoreline lies along the lip of the Los Angeles basin, a flat expanse interrupted by the sharp cliffs of the Palos Verdes Peninsula and the rocky heights of the Santa Monica Mountains. There are broad strands lapped by gentle waves and pocket beaches exploding with surf. Though most of the coast is built up, some sections remain raw and undeveloped.

Route 1, the Pacific Coast Highway, parallels the coast the entire length of Los Angeles County, tying its beach communities together. To the south lie Long Beach and San Pedro, industrial enclaves which form the port of Los Angeles, a world center for commerce and shipping. Embodying 50 miles of heavily developed waterfront, the port is a maze of inlets, islets, and channels protected by a six-mile breakwater. It is one of the world's largest manmade harbors; over $55 billion in cargo crosses its docks every year, making it the country's most profitable port. Despite all this hubbub, the waterfront supports over 125 fish species and over 90 types of birds, including several endangered species.

The great port dates to 1835 when a small landing was built on the shore. Following the Civil War an imaginative entrepreneur named Phineas Banning developed the area, brought in the railroad, and launched Los Angeles into the 20th century. Now Long Beach wears several hats. In addition to being a major port and manufacturing center, it is the site of a naval base and a revitalized tourist center. Home to the retired ocean liner *Queen Mary* and financier Howard Hughes' dream plane, the *Spruce Goose*, Long Beach also contains the neighborhood of Naples, a system of islands, canals, and footbridges reminiscent of Italy's gondola cities.

Once an amusement center complete with airship, carousel, and sword swallowers, the city became one big oil field during the 1920s. That's when wildcat wells struck rich deposits and the region was transformed into a two-square-mile maze of derricks. Even today the offshore "islands" hide hundreds of oil wells.

Commercial fishing, another vital industry in Long Beach and San Pedro, supports an international collection of sailors. Mariners from Portugal, Yugoslavia, Greece, and elsewhere work the waterfront and add to the ethnic ambience.

Just a few miles north, along the Palos Verdes Peninsula, blue collar gives way to white collar and the urban surrenders to the exotic. A region of exclusive neighborhoods and striking geologic contrasts, Palos Verdes possesses Los Angeles' prettiest seascapes. A series of 13 marine terraces, interrupted by sheer cliffs, descend to a rocky shoreline. For 15 miles the roadway rides high above the surf past tidepools, rocky points, a lighthouse, and secluded coves.

This wealthy suburban environment is replaced in turn by another type of culture, typified by blond-haired surfers. Santa Monica Bay, the predominant feature of the Los Angeles Coast, is a single broad crescent of sand extending 30 miles from Redondo Beach through Venice and Santa Monica to Point Dume. South Bay—comprising the towns of Redondo Beach, Hermosa Beach, and Manhattan Beach—is the surfing center of Southern California, where the sport was first imported from Hawaii. This strip of coast is also home to Los Angeles International Airport and is considered the world's top aerospace research center.

Like most of the coastal communities, South Bay didn't take off as a beach resort until the turn of the century, after railroad lines were extended from the city center to the shore and several decades after downtown Los Angeles experienced its 1880s population boom.

It was well into the 20th century, 1962 to be exact, that neighboring Marina del Rey, the largest manmade small boat harbor in the world, was developed. Nearby Venice, on the other hand, was an early 1900s attempt to re-create its Italian namesake. Built around plazas and grand canals, Venice originally was a fashionable resort town with oceanfront hotels and an

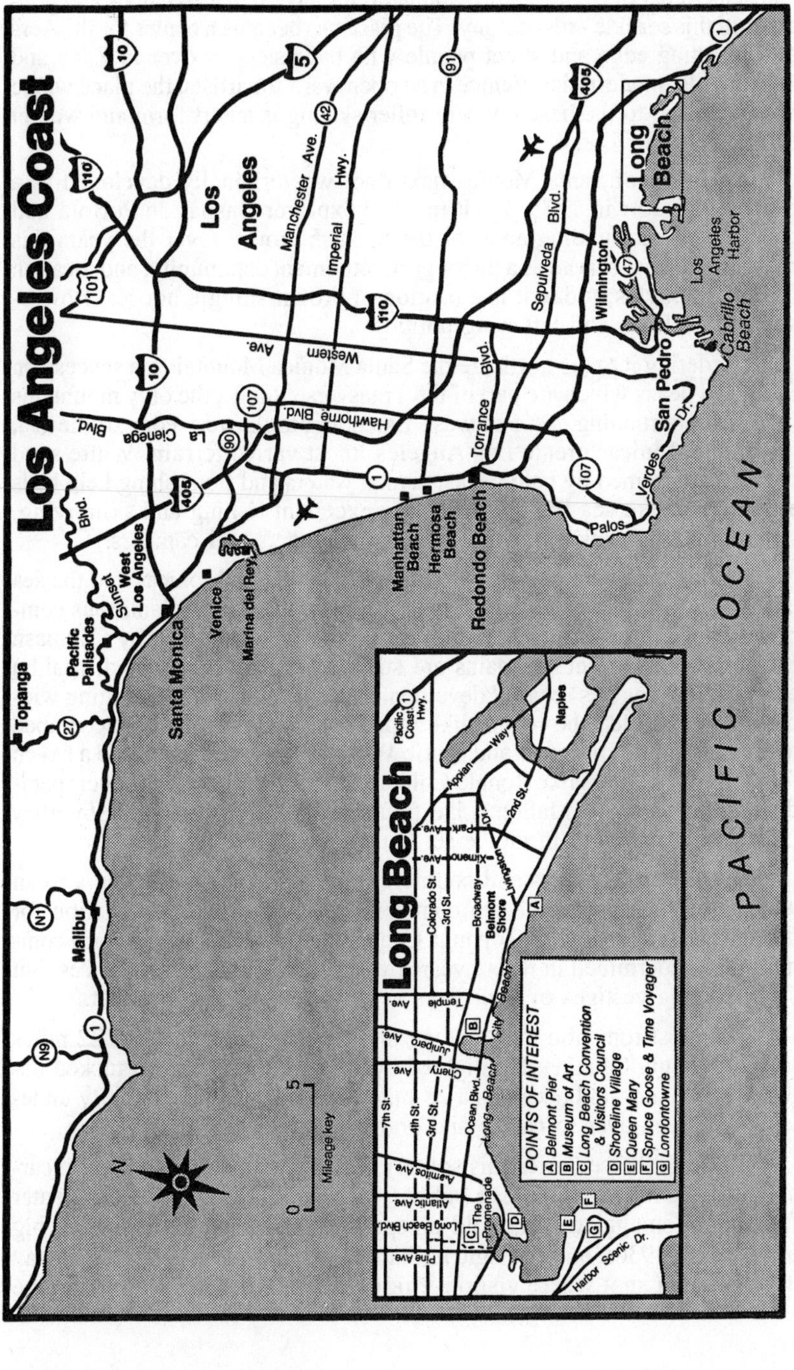
Los Angeles Coast
Topanga
Pacific Palisades
Sunset Blvd.
West Los Angeles
Santa Monica
Venice
Marina del Rey
La Cienega Blvd.
Los Angeles
Manchester Ave.
Imperial Hwy.
Western Ave.
Hawthorne Blvd.
Manhattan Beach
Hermosa Beach
Redondo Beach
Torrance Blvd.
Sepulveda Blvd.
Palos Verdes Dr.
San Pedro
Cabrillo Beach
Los Angeles Harbor
Wilmington
Long Beach
Malibu
Mileage key
0
5
N
PACIFIC OCEAN
Long Beach
Pacific Coast Hwy.
Pine Ave.
Long Beach Blvd.
Atlantic Ave.
Alamitos Ave.
Junipero Ave.
Cherry Ave.
Temple Ave.
7th St.
4th St.
3rd St.
Ocean Blvd.
Colorado St.
Broadway
Belmont Shore
Ximeno Ave.
Park Ave.
Livingston Dr.
2nd St.
Appian Way
Naples
The Promenade
Long Beach City Beach
Harbor Scenic Dr.
POINTS OF INTEREST
A Belmont Pier
B Museum of Art
C Long Beach Convention & Visitors Council
D Shoreline Village
E Queen Mary
F Spruce Goose & Time Voyager
G Londontowne

amusement park. Today studios and galleries have replaced canals and gondolas in this seaside artist colony. The place has become a center for thinkers at the cutting edge and street people who have stepped over it. Zany and unchartable, modern-day Venice is an open ward for artists, the place where bohemians go to the beach, where roller skating is an art form and weight lifting a way of life.

The town of Santa Monica next door was originally developed as a beachside resort in 1875. Back in 1769 explorer Gaspar de Portolá had claimed the surrounding area for the Spanish crown. Over the years this royal domain has served as a major port, retirement community, and location for silent movies; today it is a bastion of brown-shingle houses, flower-covered trellises, and left-wing politics.

Bordering it to the north are the Santa Monica Mountains, a succession of rugged peaks which are part of the Transverse Range, the only mountains in California running east and west. Extending to the very edge of the sea, the Santa Monicas create Los Angeles' most varied terrain. White sand beaches are framed by bald peaks, crystal waters and flourishing kelp beds attract abundant sea life and make for excellent fishing and skindiving, while the mountains provide a getaway for hikers and campers.

Lying along a narrow corridor between the Santa Monicas and the sea is Malibu, that quintessential symbol of California, a rich, glamorous community known for its movie stars and surfers. Once inhabited by Chumash Indians, whose skeletal remains are still occasionally uncovered, Malibu escaped Los Angeles' coastal development until 1928, when the aging widow who controlled the region like a personal fiefdom finally succumbed to the pressures of progress and profit. Within a few years it became a haven for Hollywood. Stars like Ronald Colman and John Gilbert found their paradise on the sands of Malibu. Like figures out of *The Great Gatsby*, they lived insouciant lives in movie-set houses.

By the 1960s artists and counterculturalists, seeking to flee a town which in turn had become too commercial and crowded, left Malibu for the outlying mountains. In Topanga Canyon they established freeform communities, undermined in recent years by breathtaking real estate prices, but still retaining vestiges of their days as a flower children's retreat.

The most romantic locale along the Los Angeles Coast lies 22 miles offshore. Santa Catalina, highlighted by Avalon, a resort town tucked between mountains and ocean, is a 28-mile-long island almost entirely undeveloped, given over to cactus and grazing buffalo.

Through the centuries this solitary island has undergone many incarnations—habitat for Stone Age Indians; base for Russian fur hunters; center for pirates, smugglers, and gold prospectors; gathering place for the big bands of the 1930s; and strategic military base during World War II. Today it's a singular spot where visitors enjoy the amenities of Avalon and the seclusion of the island's outback. If Avalon, with its art deco waterfront, provides a picture of Los Angeles circa 1933, the rest of the island is a window on Los Angeles in its natural state, wild and alluring, long before freighters embarked from Long Beach, surfers worked the South Bay, and movie moguls uncovered Malibu.

Easy Living

Transportation

ARRIVAL

Route 1, which parallels the coast throughout Los Angeles County, undergoing several name changes during its course, is the main coastal route. **Route 101** shadows the coast further inland, while **Route 405** provides access to the Los Angeles basin from San Diego and **Route 10** arrives from the east.

BY AIR

Two airports bring visitors to the Los Angeles coast area: the small **Long Beach Airport** and the very big, very busy **Los Angeles International Airport** (LAX). (See Chapter Two for information pertaining to Los Angeles International Airport.)

Presently, carriers into Long Beach are American Airlines, Alaska Airlines, America West, and United Airlines.

The Airport in the Sky (310-510-0143), set at 1600-foot elevation in the mountains of Santa Catalina, may be the prettiest landing strip anywhere. The small terminal building conveys a mountain lodge atmosphere with a stone fireplace adorned by a trophy bison head. **Allied Air Charter** (310-510-1163) and **National Air**, also called **Catalina Vegas Airlines** (619-292-7311), service the airport from the mainland.

Another means of transportation to Catalina is **Island Express** (310-491-5550), a helicopter service from Long Beach and San Pedro. (They also offer around-the-island tours.) Or try **Helitrans** (310-548-1314), a commuter jet helicopter service from San Pedro, John Wayne Airport, Los Angeles International, and Long Beach to Avalon.

BY BOAT

Several companies provide regular transportation to Catalina by boat. The island is just "26 miles across the sea," but it's still necessary to make advance reservations. **Catalina Express** (P.O. Box 1391, San Pedro; 310-519-1212) has service to Avalon and Two Harbors from the Catalina Terminal in San Pedro, from Long Beach next to the *Queen Mary* and from Redondo Beach Marina; **Catalina Cruises** (P.O. Box 1948, San Pedro; 800-888-5939) travels from the Catalina Landing in Long Beach to Two Harbors and Avalon; and **Catalina Passenger Service** (400 Main Street, Newport Beach; 714-673-5245) has service from Orange County. (Catalina Passenger Service provides transportation only from Easter through October with weekend service December 26 to Easter.)

BY BUS

Greyhound/Trailways Bus Lines has service to the Los Angeles area from all around the country. The Long Beach terminals are located at 6601 Atlantic Avenue (310-428-7777) and 464 West 3rd Street (213-432-1842); the Santa Monica terminal is at 1433 5th Street (310-394-5433).

CAR RENTALS

At the Long Beach Airport you'll find **Avis Rent A Car** (310-988-3255), **Budget Rent A Car** (310-421-0143), **Dollar Rent A Car** (310-421-8841), **Hertz Rent A Car** (310-420-2322), and **National Car Rental** (310-421-8877).

Located outside the Long Beach Airport, **Enterprise Rent A Car** (310-494-3532) will pick up the tab for a taxi from the airport.

To save even more money, try agencies that rent used cars. In the Long Beach area these include **Robin Hood Rent A Car** (310-518-9807) and **ABC U Save Rent A Car** (310-597-2232).

In Catalina, golf carts are the only vehicles permitted for sightseeing Avalon. Check with **Cartopia Cart Rentals** (615 Crescent Avenue; 310-510-2493) or **Island Rentals** (125 Pebbly Beach Road; 310-510-1456). For further information on vehicle rentals on Santa Catalina Island see the "Sightseeing" section in this chapter.

PUBLIC TRANSPORTATION

Long Beach Transit (1300 Gardenia Avenue, Long Beach; 310-591-2301) transports riders throughout the Long Beach area. Among their services is the Long Beach Runabout Shuttle Van, which carries visitors between major points of interest.

RTD Bus Line (425 South Main Street, Los Angeles; 800-252-7433) serves the Los Angeles area from Topanga Beach south; disabled riders can call a hotline for information, 800-621-7828.

In Santa Monica, call the **Big Blue Bus** (Santa Monica Municipal Bus Lines, 1660 7th Street; 310-451-5444).

In Catalina, **Catalina Safari Bus** (310-510-2800) provides daily buses from Avalon to Two Harbors and all campgrounds. This shuttle service also takes passengers from Avalon to the Airport in the Sky.

TAXIS

From Long Beach Airport **Long Beach Yellow Cab** (310-435-6111) provides taxi service.

In Catalina you will find the **Catalina Cab Company** (310-510-0025).

Hotels

LONG BEACH AND SAN PEDRO HOTELS

Beach Terrace Manor Motel (1700 East Ocean Boulevard, Long Beach; 310-436-8204) is a 43-unit complex which occupies both sides of a side street off Long Beach's main drag. Mock-Tudor in design, the facility has some units fronting the beach; many others are equipped with kitchen facilities. Guest rooms are comfortable if undistinguished. At moderate price for a room with a kitchen, the Beach Terrace provides a fair bargain.

The **Surf Motel** (2010 East Ocean Boulevard, Long Beach; 310-437-0771), a similar layout, has 39 units, some with ocean views, many offering kitchens and all with easy access to the beach. Each room is furnished in contemporary fashion. There's a pool and jacuzzi. Prices are moderate, deluxe for ocean front.

Granted I'm a fool for gimmicks, but somehow the opportunity to stay aboard an historic ocean liner seems overwhelming. Where else but at the **Hotel Queen Mary** (Pier J, Long Beach; 310-432-6964) can you recapture the magic of British gentility before World War II? What other hotel offers guests a "sunning deck?" Staying in the original state rooms of this grand old ship, permanently docked on the Long Beach waterfront, you are surrounded by the art deco designs for which the *Queen Mary* is famous. Some guest rooms are small (this *is* a ship!) and dimly illuminated through portholes, but the decor is classic. There are also restaurants, lounges, and shops on board. Prices begin in the deluxe range.

The **Los Angeles International Hostel** (3601 South Gaffey Street, Building 613, San Pedro; 310-831-2836) is located in the army barracks of old Fort MacArthur. Set in Angel's Gate Park on a hilltop overlooking the ocean, it's a pretty site with easy access to beaches. Men and women are housed separately in dorms; kitchen facilities are provided; guests cannot occupy rooms during the day; budget.

SOUTH BAY HOTELS

Route 1 barrels through Los Angeles' beach towns and serves as the commercial strip for generic motels. As elsewhere, these facilities are characterized by clean, sterile rooms and comfortable, if unimaginative surroundings. **Starlite Motel** (716 South Pacific Coast Highway, Redondo Beach; 310-540-2406) and **East West Motel** (625 South Pacific Coast Highway, Redondo Beach; 310-316-1184), for instance, each with about two dozen units, have accommodations at budget prices. Or try the **Hi View Motel** (100 South Sepulveda Boulevard, Manhattan Beach; 310-374-4608).

The Portofino Inn (260 Portofino Way, Redondo Beach; 310-379-8481) is a big, brassy hotel set on King Harbor. The 165 units are decorated in contemporary fashion and look out either on the ocean or the adjoining marina. There is a decorous lobby as well as a waterside swimming pool; restaurants and other facilities are nearby in the marina. Ultra-deluxe.

The best bargain on lodging in South Bay is found at **Sea Sprite Apartment Motel** (1016 Strand, Hermosa Beach; 310-376-6933). Located right on Hermosa Beach, this multibuilding complex offers oceanview rooms with kitchenettes at moderate to deluxe price. The accommodations are tidy, well furnished, and fairly attractive. There is a swimming pool and sun deck overlooking the beach. The central shopping district is just one block away, making the location hard to match. You can also rent suites at deluxe prices or a turn-of-the-century, two-bedroom beach cottage (ultra-deluxe). Be sure to ask for an oceanview room in one of the beachfront buildings.

The Sea View Inn At the Beach (3400 Highland Avenue, Manhattan Beach; 310-545-1504) is an eight-unit stucco hotel a block up from the beach. There's a swimming pool, plus two floors of guest rooms, recently remodeled. You'll find comfortable furniture, wall-to-wall carpeting, refrigerator, and cable television in accommodations that are tidy. In addition, it is close to the surf and lodging is rare in these parts, so . . . . Moderate.

Far from the South Bay beach scene, though only a mile inland, is **Barnabey's Hotel** (3501 North Sepulveda Boulevard, Manhattan Beach; 310-545-8466), a sprawling 128-room Edwardian-style hostelry. Re-creating turn-of-the-century England, Barnabey's provides stylish guest rooms with antique furnishings, floral-patterned carpets, and vintage wallpaper. The lobby is finished in dark woods and appointed with gilded clocks and crystal light fixtures. There's a restaurant and British pub and guests also enjoy a pool and jacuzzi. Deluxe.

VENICE, SANTA MONICA, AND MALIBU HOTELS

There's nothing quite like **The Venice Beach House** (15 30th Avenue, Venice; 310-823-1966). That may well be because there are so few bed and breakfast inns in the Los Angeles area. But it's also that this is such a charming house, an elegant and spacious California bungalow-style home built early in the century. The living room, with its beam ceiling, dark wood paneling, and brick fireplace, is a masterwork. Guests also enjoy a sunny alcove, patio, and yard. The stroll to the Venice boardwalk and beach is only one-half block. The nine guest rooms are beautifully appointed and furnished with antiques; each features patterned wallpaper and period artwork. Add to this the fact that rooms with shared bath are moderate in price (deluxe for private bath) and I can't recommend the place highly enough.

Also consider the **Marina Pacific Hotel** (1697 Pacific Avenue, Venice; 310-452-1111). Located in the commercial center of Venice only 100 yards from the sand, this three-story hostelry has a small lobby and café downstairs. The guest rooms are spacious, nicely furnished, and well maintained; very large one-bedroom suites, complete with kitchen and fireplace, are also available. Most rooms have small patios; standard accommodations are deluxe in price, suites are ultra-deluxe.

Ocean Avenue, which runs the length of Santa Monica, paralleling the ocean one block above the beach, boasts the most hotels and the best location in town. Among its varied facilities are several generic motels. These are all-American type places furnished in veneer, carpeted wall-to-wall, and equipped with telephones and color televisions. If you book a room in one, ask for quiet accommodations since Ocean Avenue is a busy, noisy street.

One such establishment, the **Pacific Sands Motel** (1515 Ocean Avenue, Santa Monica; 310-395-6133), a 50-unit facility, features a small swimming pool. Rooms are moderately priced.

A better bargain by far is the **Bayside Hotel** (2001 Ocean Avenue, Santa Monica; 310-396-6000). Laid out in motel fashion, this two-story complex offers plusher carpets and plumper furniture than motels hereabouts and is decorated with patterned wallpaper. More important, it's just 50 yards from the beach across a palm-studded park. Some rooms have ocean views; no pool; moderate.

Of course the ultimate bargain is found at the **Santa Monica International AYH Hostel** (1436 2nd Street, Santa Monica; 310-393-9913). This four-story, dorm-like structure boasts 30,000 square feet, room for 200 beds. There are several living rooms, a central courtyard, library, and kitchen. In addition to facilities for independent travelers, the hostel has set aside rooms for couples and families. Budget.

Despite its location on a busy street, **Channel Road Inn** (219 West Channel Road, Santa Monica; 310-459-1920) conveys a cozy sense of home. Colonial Revival in style, built in 1910, this sprawling 14-room bed and breakfast offers guests a living room, library, and dining room as well as a jacuzzi and hillside garden. The guest rooms vary widely in decor—some traditional, others contemporary; some florid, others demure. Deluxe to ultra-deluxe.

The **Pacific Shore Hotel** (1819 Ocean Avenue, Santa Monica; 310-451-8711) looks the part of a contemporary Southern California hotel. One block from the beach, this sprawling 168-room facility boasts a pool, sauna, jacuzzi, and sun deck. There's a restaurant off the lobby as well as a lounge and gift shop. Guests are whisked to their rooms in a glass elevator. The accommodations are furnished with modular pieces painted in brilliant enamels; the appointments are art deco and the wallpaper has been roughed to resemble raw fabric; some rooms have ocean views. Slightly plastic, but what the hell. Deluxe to ultra-deluxe.

The Sovereign (205 Washington Avenue, Santa Monica; 310-395-9921) on the other hand is the classic Southern California hostelry. Constructed during the 1920s, it's a massive whitewashed building. The style is Mediterranean and the sheer size of the structure lends grandeur to the place. The lobby is filled with antiques and designed with a series of archways leading in all directions. Each guest room is furnished differently—some in art deco fashion, others with Oriental pieces or antiques. Despite the remodeling you're liable to find a carpet stain here or a paint nick there, but the rooms are very large and attractively appointed. Matter of fact, the moderate price on standard rooms, and deluxe tab on the huge "superior" rooms with kitchens and terraces, make this somewhat funky hotel a fair bargain; three blocks from the beach.

The much-needed **Loews Santa Monica Beach Hotel** (1700 Ocean Avenue; 310-458-6700) is the first hotel to be built in Santa Monica in 20 years (it opened in 1989) and the first L.A. luxury hotel with direct beach access. The peach, blue, and seafoam green "contemporary Victorian" features a mock turn-of-the-century design. Its spectacular five-story glass atrium lobby and most of the 352 rooms provide views of the famed Santa Monica Pier. Rooms are furnished in rattan and wicker and offer special amenities. Non-beachies love the oceanview indoor/outdoor pool. Ultra-deluxe in price.

Now forget everything I've said. Never mind the variety and quality of accommodations here, there's only one place to stay in Santa Monica. Just ask Cybil Shepherd, Diane Keaton, Bill Murray, or Gene Hackman. They all stay at the **Hotel Shangri-La** (1301 Ocean Avenue, Santa Monica; 310-394-2791). The place is private, stylish, and nothing short of beautiful. A 1939 art deco building with a facade like the prow of a steamship, the 55-room home-away-from-paparazzi is entirely remodeled. The art moderne-era furniture has been laminated and lacquered and each appointment is a perfect expression of the period. Randy Newman filmed his "I Love L.A." rock video here, but it seems more likely that you'll see detective Philip Marlowe saunter in with liquor on his lips and a bulge beneath his jacket. Located on the palisades one block above Santa Monica Beach, many rooms sport an ocean view. Rooms (with kitchens) price in the deluxe range; with views they're ultra-deluxe. There's no pool or restaurant, but the hotel has a sun deck, serves continental breakfast and afternoon tea, and is close to the beach, shops, and pier.

There are several motels scattered along the coastal highway in Malibu, two of which I can recommend. **Topanga Ranch Motel** (18711 Pacific Coast Highway, Malibu; 310-456-5486) is a 30-unit complex that dates back to the 1920s. Here are cute little cottages painted white with red trim and clustered around a circular drive. Granted they're somewhat timeworn, but each is kept neat and trim with plain furnishings and little decoration. A few have kitchens; some are two-room suites. A good deal for a location right across the highway from the beach. Moderate.

At **Casa Malibu Motel** (22752 Pacific Coast Highway, Malibu; 310-456-2219) you'll be in a 21-room facility that actually overhangs the sand. Located smack in the center of Malibu, the building features a central courtyard with lawn furniture and ocean view plus a balcony dripping with flowering plants. The moderate-to-deluxe-priced rooms are decorated in an attractive but casual fashion; some have private balconies, kitchens, and/or ocean views.

The **Malibu Beach Inn** (22878 Pacific Coast Highway, Malibu; 310-456-6444) is posh and ultra-deluxe, and each of its 47 rooms offers spectacular ocean views from private balconies. Fireplaces and minibars round out the amenities. The location on the beach, one block from the Malibu Pier, make this an ideal getaway.

SANTA CATALINA ISLAND HOTELS

One fact about lodging in Catalina everyone seems to agree upon is that it is overpriced. Particularly during summer months, when Avalon's population swells from under 3000 to over 10,000, hotels charge stiff rates for rooms. But what's a traveler to do? The island is both pretty and popular, so you have no recourse but to pay the piper.

It's also a fact that rates jump seasonally more than on the mainland. Summer is the most expensive period, winter the cheapest, with spring and fall somewhere in between. Weekend rates are also sometimes higher than weekday room tabs and usually require a two-night minimum.

The last fact of life for lodgers to remember is that since most of the island is a nature preserve, the hotels, with one lone exception, are located in Avalon.

Low-price lodgings are as rare as snow in Avalon. But at the **Hotel Atwater** (125 Sumner Street; 310-510-1788) you'll find accommodations priced in the moderate-to-deluxe category (budget during winter months). What that buys is a room with a veneer dresser, nicked night tables, soft mattress, spotty carpet, postage stamp bathroom, and, if it's like the room I saw, a hole in the wall. But, hey, the place *is* clean and this *is* Catalina. Besides it has a friendly lobby with oak trim and naugahyde furniture plus dozens of rooms to choose from. Good luck.

One of Santa Catalina's most popular hotels is the **Pavilion Lodge** (513 Crescent Avenue; 310-510-1788), a 72-room facility on Avalon's waterfront street. Designed around a central courtyard, it offers guests a lawn and patio for sunbathing. The rooms contain modern furniture, wall-to-wall carpeting, and stall showers. For decoration there are vintage Catalina prints. If you want to be at the heart of downtown in a comfortable if undistinguished establishment, this is the place. Rates are moderate in winter, deluxe to ultra-deluxe during the rest of the year.

Plainly put, the **Hotel Vista del Mar** (417 Crescent Avenue; 310-510-1452) is a gem. Each of the 15 spacious Mediterranean-style rooms is decorated in soft pastels and features a wet bar, fireplace, and full tiled bath. All surround an open-air atrium courtyard lobby, where guests enjoy ocean breezes and views from comfortable wicker rockers. One smaller room is priced moderate to deluxe, while courtyard rooms command deluxe to ultra-deluxe rates.

Farther along the same street is **Hotel Villa Portofino** (111 Crescent Avenue; 310-510-0555) with 34 rooms situated around a split-level brick patio. The accommodations are small but have been stylishly decorated with modern furniture, dressing tables, and wallpaper in pastel shades. There are tile baths with stall showers. A small lobby downstairs has been finished with potted plants and marble. Deluxe rates are in effect year-round on weekends and during the week from May through October; on weekdays during the rest of the year moderate rates apply.

It's a big, bold, blue and white structure rising for five levels above the hillside. **Hotel Catalina** (129 Whittley Avenue; 310-510-0027) has been a fixture on the Avalon skyline since 1892. The 32-unit facility features a comfortable lobby complete with overhead fans, plus a sun deck and jacuzzi. The sleeping rooms are small but comfy with standard furnishings; many offer ocean views. There are also trim little cottages that are warmly decorated. A bright, summer atmosphere pervades the place. Deluxe in summer; moderate in winter.

La Paloma Cottages (326 Sunny Lane; 310-510-0737), a rambling complex consisting of several buildings, features a string of contiguous cottages at deluxe prices (budget to moderate during winter months). These are cozy units with original decor and comfortable furnishings. There are also larger family units (with kitchens) available in a nearby building at deluxe to ultra-deluxe rates (moderate to deluxe in winter). Set on a terraced street in a quiet part of town, La Paloma is attractively landscaped. No daily maid service or phones in the rooms.

Catalina Canyon Hotel (888 Country Club Drive; 310-510-0325) is a chic, modern 80-room complex complete with pool, jacuzzi, sauna, weight room, restaurant, and bar. This Mediterranean-style hotel sits on a hillside in Avalon Canyon. The grounds are nicely landscaped with banana plants and palm trees. Each guest room is furnished in white oak, adorned with art prints, and decorated in a motif of soft hues. Moderate to deluxe.

The romantic **Hotel St. Lauren** (Metropole and Beacon streets; 310-510-2299) rises with a pink blush a block from the sand above Catalina's famed harbor. The Victorian-style hotel is a honeymoon paradise, with spacious rooms and jacuzzi tubs in minisuites. Continental breakfast in the lobby can be brought back to your room or enjoyed on the sixth-floor view patio. Moderate to deluxe.

Rare and incredible is the only way to describe **The Inn on Mt. Ada** (P.O. Box 2560, Avalon, CA 90704; 310-510-2030). Nothing on the island, and few places along the California coast, compare. Perched on a hillside overlooking Avalon and its emerald shoreline, this stately hostelry resides in the old Wrigley mansion (398 Wrigley Road), a 7000-square-foot Georgian Colonial home built by the chewing gum baron in 1921. A masterwork of french doors and elegant columns, curved ceilings, and ornamental molding, the grande dame is beautifully appointed with antiques and plush furnishings. The entire ground floor—with rattan sitting room, oceanfront veranda, formal dining room, and spacious living room—is for the benefit of visitors. Wine and hors d'oeuvres are served in the afternoon and there's a full breakfast, deli lunch, and dinner served to guests and a limited number of visitors. The wonder of the place is that all this luxury serves just six guest rooms, guaranteeing personal service and an atmosphere of intimacy. The private rooms are stylishly furnished in period pieces and adorned with a creative selection of artwork. Ultra-deluxe, with all meals included. Reserve in advance.

Banning House Lodge (Two Harbors; 310-510-0303), the only hotel on the island located outside Avalon, is a turn-of-the-century hunting lodge. Set in the isthmus that connects the two sections of Santa Catalina, it's a low-slung shingle building with a dining room, bar, and a mountain lodge atmosphere. The living room boasts a brick fireplace and is adorned with a dozen trophy heads. Staring out dolefully from the wood-paneled walls are deer, bison, fox, wild turkey, boar, and mountain goats. The guest rooms are trimly decorated with throw rugs and rustic wood furniture. The lodge provides an excellent opportunity to experience the island's outback. Continental breakfast is served in the lodge's dining room. Deluxe.

Restaurants

LONG BEACH AND SAN PEDRO RESTAURANTS

If you don't like hamburgers, you are fated never to set foot in **Hamburger Henry** (4700 East 2nd Street, Long Beach; 310-433-7070). It's a cosmic center for burger lovers everywhere, a diner decorated in neon and painted with murals of '50s-era convertibles. The counter has swivel stools and there are individual jukeboxes in the booths. Get the picture? We're talking vintage cuisine in a local hotspot that's open until midnight weekdays and until 3 a.m. on weekends. There are hamburgers served with pineapple or peanut butter, blue cheese or deep-fried bananas, asparagus or ice cream, eggs or apples. They also serve breakfast dishes, salads, chili, and special dinner platters. Definitely a scene; patio dining; budget to moderate. Hamburgers with ice cream?

Southern cooking at the **Shenandoah Café** (4722 East 2nd Street, Long Beach; 310-434-3469) is becoming a tradition among savvy shore residents. The quilts and baskets decorating this understated establishment lend a country air to the place. Add waitresses in aprons dishing out hot apple fritters and it gets downright homey. Dinner is all she wrote here, but it's a special event occasioned with "riverwalk steak" (sirloin steak in mustard caper sauce), shrimp in beer batter, country-style sausage, gumbo, "granny's fried chicken," and Texas-style beef brisket. Moderate to deluxe. Try it!

In downtown Long Beach the **Pine Avenue Fish House** (100 West Broadway; 213-432-7463) is a prime spot for seafood. The private booths and dark wood trim lend an antique atmosphere to this open-kitchen establishment. The seafood platters are too numerous to recite (besides, the menu changes daily); suffice it to say that you can have them baked, broiled, sautéed, or grilled. Moderate to deluxe.

Birds of Paradise Café (1800 East Broadway, Long Beach; 310-590-8773), drawing a largely gay clientele, serves three square meals a day. Tabbed in the moderate price range is an assortment of steak, chicken, and seafood dishes. Posters of old movie stars adorn the walls.

For Italian fare, there's **L'Opera** (101 Pine Avenue, Long Beach; 310-491-0066), a plate-glass dining room with views of the Blue Line train. The chef is from Rome and the menu represents a mixture of classical and modern dishes. There's a seafood, chicken, rice, and pasta dish of the day, everyday. Deluxe.

Back in the world of budget-priced establishments, **Acapulco Mexican Restaurant & Cantina** (733 East Broadway, Long Beach; 310-435-2487) offers standard as well as innovative dishes. Tacos, burritos, and enchiladas are only the beginning; this comfortable eatery also serves several Mexican-style seafood dishes.

Shoreline Village, the shopping mall cum fishing village on the Long Beach waterfront, has several restaurants including **Mardi Gras** (401 Shoreline Village Drive; 213-423-2900). Balloons and waitresses with painted faces add to the festive atmosphere. Despite the name, Mardi Gras serves Mexican cuisine. A good bet for fajitas and south-of-the-border seafood. Moderate.

The Reef (880 Harbor Scenic Drive, Long Beach; 310-435-8013) is rambling, ramshackle, and wonderful. Built of rough-sawn cedar, it sits along the waterfront on a dizzying series of levels. The walls may be decorated with rusty signs and old farm implements, but the cuisine in this deluxe-priced restaurant includes such contemporary choices as blackened prime rib and beer batter shrimp. For the traditionalists, there are steaks, swordfish, and rack of lamb. Lunch and dinner only.

What more elegant a setting in which to dine than aboard the *Queen Mary* (Pier J, Long Beach; 310-435-3511). There you will find everything from snack kiosks to coffee shops to first-class dining rooms. The **Promenade Café** offers a moderately priced menu of chicken teriyaki, steak, seafood, and vegetarian dishes. They also have salads, sandwiches, and hamburgers. The coffee shop is a lovely art deco room featuring wicker furnishings and period lamps.

For a true taste of regal life aboard the old ship, cast anchor at **Sir Winston's**. The continental cuisine in this ultra-deluxe-priced dining emporium includes rack of lamb, breast of capon, beef medallions, roast duckling with raspberry sauce, sautéed scallops, and broiled swordfish with caviar. Open for dinner only, Sir Winston's is a wood-paneled dining room with copper-rimmed mirrors, white tablecloths, and upholstered armchairs. The walls are adorned with photos of the great Prime Minister and every window opens onto a full view of Long Beach.

The vintage shopping mall at **Ports O' Call Village** (entrance at the foot of 6th Street, San Pedro; 310-831-0287) is Los Angeles Harbor's prime tourist center. It's situated right on the San Pedro waterfront and houses numerous restaurants. Try to avoid the high-ticket dining rooms, as they are overpriced and serve mediocre food to out-of-town hordes. But there are a number of take-out stands and ethnic eateries, priced in the budget and moderate ranges, which provide an opportunity to dine inexpensively on the water.

Of course local fishermen rarely frequent Ports O' Call. The old salts are over at **Canetti's Seafood Grotto** (309 22nd Street, San Pedro; 310-831-4036). It ain't on the waterfront, but it is within casting distance of the fishing fleet. Which means it's the right spot for fresh fish platters at moderate prices. Dinner Friday and Saturday; breakfast and lunch all week.

There are shrimp on the barbie at **Wallaby Darned** (617 South Centre Street, San Pedro; 310-833-3629), an Australian café. This is the place for "sundowner chicken" and "dinky di Aussie pie," not to mention an assortment of curry dishes. Adding to the ambience is the memorabilia on the walls—cricket bats, boomerangs, even a kangaroo skin.

Trade the Pacific for the Aegean and set anchor at **Papadakis Taverna** (301 West 6th Street, San Pedro; 310-548-1186). It's dinner only, with a menu that features moussaka, Greek-style cheese dishes, and daily specials like stuffed eggplant, fresh seafood, and regional delicacies. Moderate to deluxe in price.

PALOS VERDES PENINSULA RESTAURANTS

Restaurants are a rare commodity along the Palos Verdes Peninsula. You'll find a cluster of them, however, in the Golden Cove Shopping Center. Granted, a mall is not the most appetizing spot to dine, but in this case who's complaining?

There's **Francesco's Italian Gourmet** (31218 Palos Verdes Drive West, Rancho Palos Verdes; 310-541-3350), a homey little café with congenial staff. Here you can order pizza, sandwiches, and a variety of pasta dishes at budget prices; lunch and dinner.

Then there's **The Admiral Risty** (31250 Palos Verdes Drive West, Rancho Palos Verdes; 310-377-0050). It's one of those nautical cliché restaurants decorated along the outside with ropes and pilings and on the interior with brass fixtures. Know the type? Normally I wouldn't mention it, but the place has a full bar, a knockout view of the ocean, and happens to be the only member of its species in the entire area. My advice is to play it safe and order fresh fish (or never leave the bar). The menu is a surf-and-turf inventory of local fish (prepared four ways), steaks, chicken dishes, and so on. Dinner and Sunday brunch. Deluxe.

For genuine elegance, make lunch, or dinner reservations at **La Rive Gauche** (320 Tejon Place, Palos Verdes Estates; 310-378-0267), an attractively appointed French restaurant. With its upholstered chairs, brass wall sconces, and vintage travel posters, this cozy candlelit dining room is unique to the peninsula. The dinner menu is a study in classic French cooking including veal chop with *foie gras* and truffles, boneless duck in Grand Marnier sauce, venison in brandy crème sauce, rack of lamb in garlic, and a selection of fresh seafood like Norway salmon and Dover sole. A harpist adds to the romance. The lunch offerings, while more modest, follow a similar theme. In sum, excellent gourmet cuisine, warm ambience, a world-class wine list, and deluxe tabs.

SOUTH BAY RESTAURANTS

In downtown Redondo Beach, just a couple blocks from the water, are several small restaurants serving ethnic cuisines. **Golden Siam Restaurant** (247 Avenida del Norte; 310-316-9451) specializes in Thai dishes and seafood. Open for lunch and dinner; budget to moderate. **Petit Casino** (1767 South Elena Avenue; 310-543-5585), a French bakery, serves quiche, *croque monsieur*, soups, salads, and sandwiches. At **Kikusui** (1809 South Catalina Avenue; 310-375-1244) there is a sushi bar as well as a menu featuring other Japanese dishes.

In addition to serving good Asian food, **Thai Thani** (1109 South Pacific Coast Highway, Redondo Beach; 310-316-1580) is an extremely attractive restaurant. Black trim and pastel shades set off the blond wood furniture and etched glass. There are fresh flowers all around plus a few well placed wall prints. The lunch and dinner selections include dozens of pork, beef, vegetable, poultry, and seafood dishes. Unusual choices like spicy shrimp coconut soup, whole pompano smothered in pork, and whole baby hen make this a dining adventure. Budget to moderate.

One wall of **Millie Riera's Seafood Grotto** (1700 Esplanade, Redondo Beach; 310-375-1483) is entirely filled with a plate-glass view of the ocean. The rest of this family-run restaurant is decorated with flowers and traditional wallhangings. Open for lunch and dinner (dinner only on weekends), the "grotto," true to its title, specializes in seafood. Expect to find bouillabaisse, cracked crab, lobster Newburg, sea bass, and a few steak entrées at moderate to deluxe prices.

The capital of "in" dining around the South Bay is **Chez Mélange** (1716 Pacific Coast Highway, Redondo Beach; 310-540-1222). As the name suggests, and as current trends demand, the cuisine is eclectic. You'll find a hip crowd ordering everything from Cajun to Japanese. Moderate to deluxe in price.

The Strand, a pedestrian byway paralleling the waterfront in Hermosa Beach, is lined with small restaurants. **La Playita By The Sea** (37 14th Street, Hermosa Beach; 310-376-2148) has a complete Mexican menu at budget prices. They offer a take-out stand if you're headed for the beach or an oceanview patio for leisurely dining. **Good Stuff On The Strand** (1286 The Strand, Hermosa Beach; 310-374-2334) serves a standard fare for breakfast; hamburgers, turkey burgers, pita-bread sandwiches, and salads at lunch; and, in the evening, entrées like ratatouille, teriyaki steak, calamari, and quiche; budget.

There is excellent thin-crust pizza at **Pedone's** (1501 Hermosa Avenue; 310-376-0949) in Hermosa Beach. Popular with the beach crowd, it's a good spot for a quick, budget-tabbed meal in a convenient locale.

Albanian cuisine? Albania, in case you've forgotten, is that tiny Balkan country that went communist after World War II and hasn't been heard from since. But its culinary tradition lives on at **Ajeti's Restaurant** (425 Pier Avenue, Hermosa Beach; 310-379-9012). Open for dinner only, this small dining room with oversized chandeliers serves lamb dishes, excellent salads, and a host of Balkan-style platters. Priced moderate.

Café Pierre (317 Manhattan Beach Boulevard, Manhattan Beach; 310-545-5252) is another excellent choice for budget-minded gourmets. This fashionable French bistro—with pastel walls, art prints, and skylight—offers the same moderate-priced menu at lunch and dinner. You can feast on veal sweetbreads cognac, boneless saddle of lamb, marinated chicken on a bed of spinach, roast duckling, and homemade pasta. There are different daily specials at lunch and dinner, which in the evening may include stuffed swordfish, or venison.

No restaurants line the strand in Manhattan Beach, so you'll have to make do with the pier's snack shop or trot a half-block uphill to **Hibachi** (120 Manhattan Beach Boulevard, Manhattan Beach; 310-374-9493). Here is a take-out stand and a patio crowded with sawed-off picnic tables. Beachgoers chow down on hamburgers and hot dogs while table diners feast on stir-fry, seafood platters, teriyaki dishes, and other Japanese entrées. Lunch and dinner only; budget to moderate.

From the outside it's certainly unassuming. A diminutive dining room in a suburban shopping mall. The furniture is blond wood. The decor consists of changing contemporary artwork. But behind the simple surfaces lies one of the region's finest, most innovative restaurants. **St. Estephe** (2640 North Sepulveda Boulevard, Manhattan Beach; 310-545-1334) is a pioneer in modern Southwestern cuisine. Blending American Indian foods with Southwestern herbs and spices, then preparing them in a French nouvelle style, the restaurant has created a series of unique dishes. Lamb, veal, poultry, fish, and scallops are part of the fare. Sauces are painted onto the plate, creating swirling, multihued designs reminiscent of New Mexico landscapes. Highly recommended by friends and critics alike, it is open for lunch and dinner, priced ultra-deluxe, and well worth a visit.

VENICE RESTAURANTS

The best place for finger food and junk food in all Southern California might well be the **boardwalk** in Venice. Along Ocean Front Walk are vendor stands galore serving pizza, yogurt, hamburgers, falafels, submarine sandwiches, corn dogs, etc., etc.

Regardless, there's really only one spot in Venice to consider for dining. It simply *is* Venice, an oceanfront café right on the boardwalk, **The Sidewalk Café** (1401 Ocean Front Walk; 310-399-5547). Skaters whiz past, drummers beat rhythms in the distance, and the sun stands like a big orange wafer above the ocean. Food is really a second thought here, but eventually they're going to want you to spend some money. So, on to the menu. . . Breakfast, lunch, and dinner are what you'd expect—omelettes, sandwiches, hamburgers, pizza, and pasta. There are also fresh fish dishes plus platters of wok-fried vegetables, steak, spicy chicken, and fried shrimp. Budget to moderate in price.

Take a walk down the boardwalk to **Venice Bistro** (323 Ocean Front Walk; 310-392-7472). This beachfront establishment is a casual dining room with a tile floor and brick walls. Cozy and comfortable, it features a menu including burgers, salads, and pasta. There's a full bar and Sunday brunch. Moderate.

Or check out **Jody Maroni's Sausage Kingdom** (2011 Ocean Front Walk; 310-306-1995), a beach stand with over a dozen types of sausage, all natural. There's sweet Italian, Yucatán chicken, Louisiana boudin, and, of course, Polish. Budget.

The landing ground for Venetians is a warehouse dining place called **The Rose Café** (220 Rose Avenue; 310-399-0711). There's a full-scale deli, bakery counter, and a restaurant offering indoor and patio service. The last serves three meals daily, including moderately priced dinners from an ever-changing menu that may include entrées like lemon linguine with flaked salmon, bay scallops salad, roast duck in plum sauce, and a couple of vegetarian dishes. A good spot for pasta and salad, The Rose Café, with its wall murals and paintings, is also a place to appreciate the vital culture of Venice.

In the mood for Asian cuisine? **Hama** (213 Windward Avenue; 310-396-8783) is a well-respected Japanese restaurant in the center of Venice. The place features an angular sushi bar, a long, narrow dining room, and a patio out back. The crowd is young and the place is decorated to reflect Venice's vibrant culture. There are paintings on display representing many of the area's artists. In addition to scrumptious sushi, Hama offers a complete selection of Japanese dishes including tempura, teriyaki, and sashimi. Lunch and dinner; moderate.

For a gourmet restaurant tabbed in the moderate-to-deluxe price range, **West Beach Café** (60 North Venice Boulevard; 310-823-5396) is quite understated. The walls are cinderblock, adorned by changing contemporary artworks, and the chairs are metal-and-plastic. But track lighting and skylights add flourish while the menu demolishes any doubts about the standing of this trendy eating place. Open for lunch and dinner, the restaurant offers a seasonal menu that always includes a variety of fresh seafood like salmon, swordfish, or sea bass, New York steaks, and chicken and turkey dishes, all prepared with a host of delicious sauces. The lunch menu is equally creative and in the evening after 11:30 they serve gourmet pizza. *Très chic, très* California.

72 Market Street (72 Market Street; 310-392-8720) could be the last word in modern art restaurants. The place is a warren of brick, mirrors, opaque glass, and studio lights. It's adorned with striking art pieces and equipped with a sound system that seems to be vibrating from the inner ear. Moderne to the max, the restaurant serves Cajun-style catfish, grilled Louisiana sausages, and other regional dishes. Open for lunch, dinner, and Sunday brunch, it also hosts an oyster bar; deluxe to ultra-deluxe.

SANTA MONICA RESTAURANTS

Santa Monica is a restaurant town. Its long tradition of seafood establishments has been expanded in recent years by a wave of ethnic and California cuisine restaurants. While some of the most fashionable and expensive dining rooms in Los Angeles are right here, there are also many excellent and inexpensive cafés. Generally you'll find everything from the sublime to the reasonable located within several commercial clusters—near the beach along Ocean Avenue, downtown on Wilshire and Santa Monica boulevards, and in the chic, gentrified corridors of Main Street and Montana Avenue.

One of the best places in Southern California for stuffing yourself with junk food while soaking up sun and having a whale of a good time is the **Santa Monica Pier** (foot of Colorado Avenue). There are taco stands, fish and chips shops, hot dog vendors, oyster bars, snack shops, pizzerias, and all those good things guaranteed to leave you clutching your stomach. The prices are low to modest and the food is amusement park quality.

There's a sense of the Mediterranean at the sidewalk cafés lining Santa Monica's Ocean Avenue: palm trees along the boulevard, ocean views in the distance, and (usually) a warm breeze blowing. Any of these bistros will do (since it's atmosphere we're seeking), so try **Ivy at the Shore** (1541 Ocean Avenue; 310-393-3113). It features a full bar, serves espresso, and,

(Text continued on page 158.)

The Murals of Venice and Santa Monica

Nowhere is the spirit of Venice and Santa Monica more evident than in the murals adorning their walls. Both seaside cities house major art colonies and the numerous galleries and studios make them important centers for contemporary art.

The region's freewheeling, individualistic lifestyle has long been a magnet for painters and sculptors. Over the years, as more and more artists made their homes here, they began decorating the twin towns with their art. The product of this creative energy lives along street corners and alleyways, on storefronts and roadways.

Crowded with contemporary and historic images, these murals express the inner life of the city. Some are officially commissioned and appear on major thoroughfares, others represent guerrilla art and are found in out-of-the-way spots.

Murals adorn nooks and crannies all over Venice. You'll find a cluster of them around Windward Avenue between Main Street and Ocean Front Walk. The interior of the **Post Office** (Main Street and Windward Avenue) is adorned with public art. There's a *trompe l'oeil* mural nearby that beautifully reflects the street (Windward Avenue and Speedway) along which you are gazing.

On the other side of the building (the old St. Marks Hotel) stands a large mural facing the ocean. **Venus Reconstituted** (Windward Avenue and Speedway) depicts the unique culture of Venice Beach as it is today.

At last count Santa Monica boasted about two dozen outdoor murals. Route 1, or Lincoln Boulevard, is a corridor decorated with local artworks. **John Muir Woods** (Lincoln and Ocean Park boulevards) portrays a redwood forest; **Early Ocean Park and Venice Scenes** (two blocks west of Lincoln Boulevard along Kensington Road in Joslyn Park) captures the seaside at the turn of the century. Nearby Marine Park (Marine and Frederick streets) features **Birthday Party**, with a Noah's ark full of celebratory animals.

Ocean Park Boulevard is another locus of creativity. At its intersection with the 4th Street underpass you'll encounter **Whale Mural**, illustrating whales and underwater life common to California waters, and **Unbridled**, which pictures a herd of horses fleeing from the Santa Monica Pier carousel. One of the area's most famous murals awaits you at Ocean Park Boulevard and Main street, where **Early Ocean Park** vividly re-creates scenes from the past.

If you'd like a tour of these and other murals around the city, contact the **Social and Public Art Resource Center** (685 Venice Boulevard; 310-822-9560). Los Angeles has earned a reputation as the mural capital of the United States, making this tour a highpoint for admirers of public art.

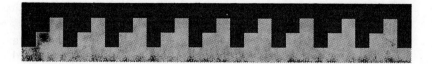

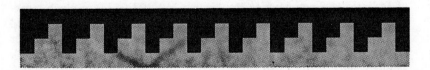

if you want to get serious about it, has a full lunch and dinner menu with pizza, pasta, Cajun dishes, and sandwiches. Deluxe.

Every type of cuisine imaginable is found on the bottom level of **Santa Monica Place** (Broadway between 2nd and 4th streets). This multitiered shopping mall has an entire floor of take-out food stands. It's like the United Nations of dining, where everything is budget-priced.

Wolfgang Puck, the California cuisine chef who gave the world Spago, gave Santa Monica the **Eureka Restaurant & Brewery** (1845 South Bundy Drive; 310-447-8000). Expect homemade sausages, cheeses, pastas, and breads as well as meat and fish that have been smoked on the premises. You can also expect ear-splitting noise and a casually chic crowd. Moderate to deluxe.

Along the Third Street Promenade there is **Benita's Frites** (1437 3rd Street; 310-458-2889), a Belgian french-fry stand. This diminutive entry in Santa Monica's rough-and-tumble restaurant race does not just serve plain old fries, however. They feature 16 different dips, including spicy barbecue, peanut sauce, and garlic mayonnaise. Budget.

Benita's, however, is only one of many excellent eateries along Santa Monica's vaunted Third Street Promenade. This three-block-long walkway, filled with movie theaters and located in the downtown district, boasts some of the best coffeehouses and restaurants in the area.

For a Berkeley-style café, complete with funky furniture and creative clientele, there's **Congo Square** (1238 3rd Street; 310-395-5606), where you can order espresso and cappuccino, hunker down over a sandwich, and listen to live music and a lively crowd. Moderate.

Nearby, **Broadway Bar and Grill** (1460 3rd Street; 310-393-4211), a California cuisine dining room, features spacious booths indoors and curbside tables outside. A perfect spot for checking out the scene, this classic bar and grill serves steaks, fresh fish, and grilled chicken at moderate prices.

If steak-and-kidney pie, bangers and mash, or shepherds pie sound appetizing, head over to **Ye Olde King's Head** (116 Santa Monica Boulevard; 310-451-1402). You won't see a king's head on the wall of this British pub, but there are several trophy animals adorning the place. You'll find them beside photographs of the celebrities who inhabit the place. Like you, they are drawn here by the cozy ambience, lively crowd, and budget to moderate prices. Open for lunch and dinner.

For Indian cuisine the best-known restaurant is **British Raaj Cuisine of India** (504 Santa Monica Boulevard; 310-393-9472), a plush, pink-tablecloth dining room. Trimly decorated with Asian chandeliers and carved wood screens, the place is small enough to convey intimacy. The dinner menu includes *tandoori* chicken, lamb *tikka* (marinated in herbs and lemon), Bombay *machli* (fresh fish with ginger in curry sauce), and curry lobster.

At lunch there is a similar selection of dishes from the subcontinent. Priced in the moderate range.

Zucky's (431 Wilshire Boulevard; 310-393-0551) is the place for late-night munchies. Open 24 hours on weekends, this popular delicatessen has an endless assortment of hot platters, kosher sandwiches, and delicious pastries. It's a sprawling formica-counter-and-plastic-booth establishment that has been around since 1946. Budget-priced to boot!

Tampico Tilly's (1025 Wilshire Boulevard; 310-451-1769) is long on atmosphere. Laid out in courtyard style, the dining room is surrounded by a wrought-iron balcony and illuminated through a skylight. Potted ferns and palms decorate the place and the floor is inlaid with brick. The menu is similarly inspired. Rather than simply serving the standard Mexican dishes, Tampico Tilly's offers specialties like *burritos ornelas* (shredded beef with chile peppers), skewered meat dishes, ranchero-style chicken, and seafood flautas. Open for lunch, dinner, and Sunday brunch and featuring a full bar, it's well worth the moderate meal tab.

Pioneer Boulangerie (2012 Main Street; 310-399-7771) is a sprawling, multiroom establishment with a patio and a full-fledged bakery. Out on the patio they serve cafeteria-style meals at budget to moderate prices. The bakery features all kinds of breads and yummy sweets.

In the world of high chic, **Chinois on Main** (2709 Main Street; 310-392-9025) stands taller than most. Owned by famous restauranteur Wolfgang Puck, the fashionable dining room is done in nouveau art deco-style with track lights, pastel colors, and a central skylight. The curved bar is hand-painted; contemporary artworks adorn the walls. Once you drink in the glamorous surroundings, move on to the menu, which includes Shanghai lobster risotto, whole sizzling catfish, grilled Szechuan beef, barbecued quail, and wok-charred salmon. The appetizers and other entrées are equal in originality, a medley of French, Chinese, and California cuisine. Open for lunch Wednesday through Friday and dinner nightly, this is an excellent restaurant, deluxe to ultra-deluxe in price, with high standards of quality.

The spot for breakfast in Santa Monica is **Rae's Restaurant** (2901 Pico Boulevard; 310-828-7937), a diner on the edge of town several miles from the beach. With its formica counter and naugahyde booths, Rae's is a local institution, always packed. The breakfasts are hearty American-style feasts complete with buttermilk biscuits and country-style gravy. At lunch they serve the usual selection of sandwiches and side orders. Come dinner time they have fried shrimp, pork chops, veal, liver, fried chicken, steaks, and other hot platters at prices that seem like they haven't changed since the place opened in 1958. Budget.

There are many who believe the dining experience at **Michael's** (1147 3rd Street; 310-451-0843) to be the finest in all Los Angeles. Set in a restored stucco structure and decorated with original artworks by David Hockney and Jasper Johns, it is certainly one of the region's prettiest dining rooms. The menu is a nouvelle cuisine affair with original entrées like squab on duck liver, duck with Grand Marnier sauce, and scallops on watercress purée. At lunch there is charbroiled salmon, chicken on watercress, and several elaborate salads. Haute cuisine is the order of the evening here. The artistry that has gone into the restaurant's cuisine and design have permanently established Michael's stellar reputation. Open for lunch, dinner, and Sunday brunch; there is a cozy lounge and a garden terrace; deluxe to ultra-deluxe.

MALIBU RESTAURANTS

Malibu's best-known eating spot sits at the foot of Malibu Pier. **Alice's Restaurant** (23000 Pacific Coast Highway; 310-456-6646) is a trim, glass-encased dining room with views extending across the beach and out over the ocean. A gathering place for locals in the know and visitors on the make, it serves a lunch and dinner menu of seafood and pasta dishes. Salads—including roasted goat cheese and warm duck—are another specialty. The good food, friendly bar, and lively crowd make it a great place for carousing. Lunch and dinner; moderate to deluxe.

The **Reel Inn** (18661 Pacific Coast Highway; 310-456-8221) is my idea of heaven—a moderately priced seafood restaurant. Located across the highway from the beach, it's an oilcloth restaurant with an outdoor patio and a flair for serving good, healthful food at low prices. Among the fresh fish lunches and dinners are salmon, snapper, lobster, and swordfish.

There's nothing fancy about **Malibu Fish & Seafood** (25653 Pacific Coast Highway; 310-456-3430). It's just a fish and chips stand with a few picnic tables outside, but the menu includes such tantalizing specialties as ahi tuna burgers and steamed lobster. The budget price is hard to beat when you add the ocean view.

When you're out at the beaches around Point Dume or elsewhere in northern Malibu, there are two adjacent roadside restaurants worth checking out. **Coral Beach Cantina** (29350 Pacific Coast Highway; 310-457-5503) is a simple Mexican restaurant with a small patio. The menu contains standard south-of-the-border fare and prices in the budget category.

Over at **Zuma Sushi** (29350 Pacific Coast Highway; 310-457-4131) they have a sushi bar and table service. In addition to the house specialty there are tempura and teriyaki dishes, all at moderate prices. Like its neighbor, this is a small, unassuming café. Dinner only.

The quintessential Malibu dining experience is **Geoffrey's** (27400 Pacific Coast Highway; 310-457-1519), a clifftop restaurant overlooking the ocean. The marble bar, whitewashed stucco walls, and flowering plants exude wealth and elegance. The entire hillside has been landscaped and beautifully terraced, creating a Mediterranean atmosphere. The menu features a variation on California cuisine, and includes swordfish with onion-cucumber-raddichio salsa, and salmon with angelhair pasta. The lunch and dinner menus are almost identical and on Sunday they serve brunch. The setting, cuisine, and deluxe to ultra-deluxe prices make Geoffrey's a prime place for celebrity gazing.

Beaurivage Mediterranean Restaurant (26025 Pacific Coast Highway; 310-456-5733), another gourmet gathering place, located across the highway from the ocean, is a cozy dining room. With exposed-beam ceiling, brick trim, and copper pots along the wall, it has the feel of a French country inn. But the dinner menu is strictly Mediterranean. In addition to several fettucine and linguine dishes there is white fish in meunière sauce, baby lamb chops, Norwegian salmon, and daily specials that range from grilled shark with persimmon sauce to ragoût of wild boar. Deluxe to ultra-deluxe.

Up in the Santa Monica Mountains, high above the clamor of Los Angeles, rests the **Inn of the Seventh Ray** (128 Old Topanga Canyon Road; 310-455-1311). A throwback to the days when Topanga Canyon was a hippie enclave, this mellow dining spot serves "energized" foods to "raise your body's light vibrations." These auricly charged entrées include "artichoke queen of light" (artichokes stuffed with tofu) and "five secret rays" (steamed veggies with organic brown rice and five sauces). There is also a selection of fresh seafood, duckling, and lamb dishes. Open for lunch and dinner, the restaurant features dining indoors or outside on a pretty, tree-shaded patio, where coyotes can often be seen from your table. Far out (and priced moderate to deluxe).

SANTA CATALINA ISLAND RESTAURANTS

As with Catalina hotels, there are a few points to remember when shopping for a restaurant. Prices are higher than on the mainland. With very few exceptions the dining spots are concentrated in Avalon; services around the rest of the island are minimal. Also, business is seasonal, so restaurants may vary their schedules, serving three meals daily during summer and weekends but dinner only during winter. The wisest course is to check beforehand.

Antonio's Pizzeria (114 Sumner Avenue; 310-510-0060) is a hole-in-the-wall, but a hole-in-the-wall with panache. It's chockablock with junk—old pin-up pictures, record covers, dolls, trophies, fish nets. There's sawdust on the floor and a vague '50s theme to the place. The food—pizza, pasta, and hot sandwiches—is good, filling, and served daily at lunch and dinner. "Come on in," as the sign suggests, "and bask in the ambience of the decaying 1950s." Budget to moderate.

The Busy Bee (306-B Crescent Avenue; 310-510-1983), established in 1923, is a local gathering place located right on the beach. It's hard to match the views from the patio of this simple café. This is one place in Catalina that's open for breakfast, lunch, and dinner year-round. For lunch you can dine on vegetable platters, tacos, tostadas, salads, and sandwiches while gazing out at the pier and harbor. The dinner menu offers lamb chops, fried shrimp, teriyaki chicken, and steak. Moderate.

The other half of the vintage stucco-and-red-tile building housing the Busy Bee is the site of **Armstrong's Seafood Restaurant** (306-A Crescent Avenue; 310-510-0113). The interior is trimly finished in knotty pine and white tile with mounted gamefish on the walls. Since the establishment doubles as a fish market you can count on fresh seafood. The menu is the same at lunch and dinner with only the portions and prices changing. Mesquite-grilled dishes include mahimahi, scallops, swordfish, skewered shrimp, and steak. They also feature lobster, abalone, and orange roughy. You can dine indoors or on the patio right along the waterfront, making Armstrong's moderate prices a bargain.

Café Prego (609 Crescent Avenue; 310-510-1218), a small Italian bistro complete with oilcloth tables and stucco arches, comes highly recommended. The specialties are seafood and pasta; you'll find a menu offering fresh swordfish, sea bass, halibut, snapper, and sand dabs, plus manicotti, rigatoni, lasagna, and fettucine. There are also steak and veal dishes at this waterfront nook. Open for dinner only, it features good food at moderate to deluxe prices.

For a step upscale head down the street to **Ristorante Villa Portofino** (111 Crescent Avenue; 310-510-0508). Here a baby grand piano is set off by pink stucco walls and the candlelit tables are decorated with flowers. With art deco curves and colorful art prints the place has an easy Mediterranean feel about it. The northern Italian cuisine includes several veal dishes, scampi, cioppino chicken *à lemone*, New Zealand lamb chops, grilled filet mignon, swordfish, and a selection of pasta dishes. Romance in the moderate to deluxe league.

The **Runway Café** (310-510-2196), situated up in the mountains at 1600 feet, is part of Catalina's Airport in the Sky complex. This breakfast-and-lunch facility serves egg dishes, hot cakes, buffalo burgers, and a variety of sandwiches. There's not much to the self-service restaurant itself, but it adjoins a lobby with stone fireplace and a tile patio that overlooks the surrounding mountains. Budget.

Catalina's remotest dining place is **Doug's Harbor Reef Restaurant** (Two Harbors, 310-510-0303), located way out in the Two Harbors area. This rambling establishment has a dining room done in nautical motif with fish nets, shell lamps, and woven *lauhala* mats. There's also an adjoining patio for enjoying the soft breezes that blow through this isthmus area. Doug's offers pork ribs, shrimp tempura, and chicken teriyaki. Prime rib and swordfish are local favorites and at lunch in the summer there are buffalo burgers. Moderate to deluxe. There's also an adjoining **snack bar** serving three meals daily; breakfast and lunch in winter months. Budget priced, it offers egg dishes, sandwiches, burgers, and burritos.

The Great Outdoors

The Sporting Life

SPORTFISHING

Fish the waters around Los Angeles and you can try your hand at landing a barracuda, white croaker, halibut, calico bass, or maybe even a relative of Jaws. For sportfishing outfits call, **Annie B. Barge, Inc.** (Berth 79, San Pedro, 310-832-2274), **Belmont Pier Sportfishing** (Ocean and Termino avenues, Belmont Shore; 310-434-6781), **L.A. Harbor Sportfishing** (Berth 79, San Pedro; 310-547-9916), **Queen's Wharf Sportfishing** (555 Pico Avenue, Long Beach; 310-432-8993), **Redondo Sportfishing** (233 North Harbor Drive, Redondo Beach; 310-372-2111), and **Marina del Rey Sportfishing** (13759 Fiji Way, Marina del Rey; 310-822-3625).

In Catalina you can contact the **Santa Catalina Island Chamber of Commerce and Visitors Bureau** (310-510-1520) for listings of private boat owners who outfit sportfishing expeditions.

SCUBA DIVING

To explore Los Angeles' submerged depths, call **Pacific Sporting Goods** (11 39th Place, Long Beach, 310-434-1604), **Pacific Wilderness Ocean Sports** (1719 South Pacific Avenue, San Pedro, 310-833-2422), **Marina del Rey Divers** (2539 Lincoln Boulevard, Marina del Rey; 310-827-1131), **Dive 'n Surf** (504 North Broadway, Redondo Beach; 310-372-8423), **Sea D Sea** (1911 South Catalina Avenue, Redondo Beach; 310-373-6355), **Blue Cheer Ocean Water Sports** (1110 Wilshire Boulevard, Santa Monica; 310-828-4289), **Scuba Haus** (2501 Wilshire Boulevard, Santa Monica; 310-828-2916), or **Malibu Divers** (21231 Pacific Coast Highway, Malibu; 310-456-2396) to rent gear and/or take a dive trip.

Without doubt Santa Catalina Island offers some of the finest scuba diving anywhere in the world. Perfectly positioned to attract fish from both the northern and southern Pacific, it teems with sea life. Large fish ascend from the deep waters surrounding the island while small colorful species inhabit rich kelp forests along the coast. There are caves and caverns to explore as well as the wrecks of rusting ships.

Several outfits rent skindiving and scuba equipment and/or sponsor dive trips. In Avalon call **Catalina Divers Supply** (310-510-0330), **Island Charters, Inc.** (310-510-0600), or **Argo Diving Service** (310-510-2208). In Two Harbors try the **Dive Shop** (310-510-2800).

WHALE WATCHING

During the annual migration the following outfits offer whale-watching trips: **Mickey's Belmont, Inc.** (Belmont Pier, Long Beach; 310-434-6781), **Queen's Wharf Sportfishing** (555 Pico Avenue, Long Beach; 310-432-8993), **Los Angeles Harbor Cruise** (Berth 77, San Pedro; 310-831-0996), **Pilgrim Sailing Cruise** (Berth 76, San Pedro; 310-547-0941), **Spirit Adventures** (Berth 75, San Pedro; 310-831-1073), **L.A. Harbor Sportfishing** (Berth 79, San Pedro; 310-547-9916), **Billy V.** (Berth 79, San Pedro; 310-431-6837), and **Catalina Cruises** (320 Golden Shore, Long Beach; 310-514-3838).

WINDSURFING, SURFING, AND KAYAKING

"Surfing is the only life," so grab a board from **Fun Bunns** (1116 Manhattan Avenue, Manhattan Beach; 310-545-3300), **Jeffers** (39 14th Street, Hermosa Beach; 310-372-9492), **Zuma Jay Surfboards** (22775 Pacific Coast Highway, Malibu; 310-456-8044), or **Catalina Adventure Tours** (The Mole, Avalon; 310-510-2888).

Long Beach Water Sports (730 East 4th Street, Long Beach; 310-432-0187) offers kayak rentals and adventures.

SKATING AND SKATE BOARDING

Los Angeles may well be the roller skating capital of California. To rent skates or maybe even a skate board call, **Fun Bunns** (1116 Manhattan Avenue, Manhattan Beach; 310-545-3300), **Rollerskates of America** (1312 Hermosa Avenue, Hermosa Beach; 310-372-8812), **Spokes 'n Stuff** (parking lot on Admiralty Way at Jamaica Bay Inn Hotel, Marina del Rey; 36 Washington Street, 310-306-3332; and near the Santa Monica Pier in Loews Santa Monica, 310-306-1763), or **Sea Mist Skate Rentals** (1619 Ocean Front Walk, Santa Monica Pier, Santa Monica; 310-395-7076).

GOLF

For the golfers in the crowd, try **El Dorado Park Municipal Golf Course** (2400 Studebaker Road, Long Beach; 310-430-5411), **Skylink Golf Course** (4800 East Wardlow Road, Long Beach; 310-421-3388), **Recreation Park** (5000 East Anaheim Street, Long Beach; 310-494-5000), **Los Verdes Golf Course** (7000 West Los Verdes Drive, Rancho Palos Verdes; 310-377-7370), **Penmar Golf Course** (1233 Rose Avenue, Venice; 310-396-6228), or **Westchester Golf Course** (6900 West Manchester Boulevard, Los Angeles; 310-670-5110). In Catalina call **Catalina Visitors Golf Club** (1 Country Club Drive, Avalon; 310-510-0530).

TENNIS

There are public tennis courts available in **El Dorado Park** (2800 Studebaker Road, Long Beach; 310-425-0553), **Billie Jean King Tennis Center** (1040 Park Avenue, Long Beach; 310-438-8509), **Alta Vista Tennis Courts** (715 Julia Avenue, Redondo Beach; 310-318-0670), **The Sport Center at King Harbor** (819 North Harbor Drive, Redondo Beach; 310-

372-8868), **Marina Tennis World** (13199 Mindanao Way, Marina del Rey; 310-822-2255), **Lincoln Park** (1155 7th Street, Santa Monica; 310-394-6011), **Memorial Park** (Colorado Boulevard at 14th Street; 310-394-6011), and **Ocean View Park** (Barnard Way south of Ocean Park Boulevard; 310-394-6011).

BICYCLING

Though Los Angeles might seem like one giant freeway, there are scores of shoreline bike trails and routes for scenic excursions. Foremost is the **South Bay Bike Trail**, with over 19 miles of coastal vistas. The trail, an easy ride, extends from King Harbor in Redondo Beach to the Santa Monica Pier and is extremely popular and crowded. It passes the Venice Boardwalk, as well as piers and marinas along the way.

Naples, a Venice-like neighborhood in Long Beach, provides a charming area for freeform bike rides. There are no designated paths but you can cycle with ease past beautiful homes, parks, and canals.

Of moderate difficulty is the **Palos Verdes Peninsula** coastline trail. Offering wonderful scenery, the 14-mile round trip ride goes from Malaga Cove Plaza in Palos Verdes Estates to the Wayfarers Chapel. (Part of the trail is a bike path, the rest follows city streets.)

The **Santa Monica Loop** is an easy ride starting at Ocean Avenue and going up San Vicente Boulevard, past Palisades Park and the Santa Monica Pier. Most of the trail is on bike lanes and paths; ten miles round trip.

In Catalina, free use of bikes is allowed only in Avalon. Elsewhere permits are required: they may be obtained free of charge from the **Catalina Conservancy** (P.O. Box 2739, Avalon, CA 90704; 310-510-1421). Cross-channel carriers have special requirements for transporting bicycles and must be contacted in advance for complete details.

For maps, brochures, and additional information on bike routes in Los Angeles contact the **Department of Transportation** (205 South Broadway; 310-485-3051).

BIKE RENTALS To rent bikes in coastal Los Angeles try **Fun Bunns** (1116 Manhattan Avenue, Manhattan Beach; 310-545-3300), **Jeffers** (39 14th Street, Hermosa Beach; 310-372-9492), **Spokes N Blades** (2100 and 3100 Ocean Front Walk, Marina Del Rey; 310-574-2848), **Spokes 'n Stuff** (parking lot on Admiralty Way at Jamaica Bay Inn Hotel, Marina del Rey; 36 Washington Street, 310-306-3332; and near the Santa Monica Pier in Loews Santa Monica, 310-306-1763), and **Sea Mist Skate Rentals** (1619 Ocean Front Walk, Santa Monica; 310-395-7076).

In Catalina try **Brown's Bikes** (107 Pebbly Beach Road, Avalon; 310-510-0986).

Beaches and Parks

LONG BEACH AND SAN PEDRO BEACHES AND PARKS

Alamitos Peninsula—The ocean side of this slender salient offers a pretty sand beach looking out on a tiny island. Paralleling the beach is an endless string of woodframe houses. The sand corridor extends all the way to the entrance of Alamitos Bay where a stone jetty provides recreation for anglers, surfers, and strollers.

Facilities: Restrooms, lifeguards, volleyball courts; restaurants and groceries nearby. *Fishing:* Try your luck from the jetty. *Swimming:* Good. *Surfing:* Best bet is the jetty.

Getting there: Located along Ocean Boulevard between 54th Place and 72nd Place in Long Beach; park at the end of the road.

Alamitos Bay Beach—This hook-shaped strand curves along the eastern and southern shores of a narrow inlet. Houses line the beach along most of its length. Protected from the ocean by a peninsula and breakwater, the beach faces the lovely waterfront community of Naples.

Facilities: Restrooms; restaurants and groceries nearby; information, 310-432-4496. *Fishing:* Good. *Swimming:* Protected from surf and tide, this is a safe, outstanding spot. *Surfing:* There's no surf, but the bay presents perfect conditions for windsurfing.

Getting there: Located along Bayshore Avenue and Ocean Boulevard in Long Beach.

Long Beach City Beach—They don't call it Long Beach for nothing. This strand is broad and boundless, a silvery swath traveling much the length of the town. There are several islets parked offshore. Along the miles of beachfront you'll find numerous facilities and good size crowds. **Belmont Pier**, a 1300-foot-long, hammerhead-shaped walkway, bisects the beach and offers boat tours and fishing services.

Facilities: Restrooms, lifeguards, snack bar, playground, volleyball; information, 310-432-4496. *Fishing:* Good from Belmont Pier. *Swimming:* The beach is protected by the harbor breakwater, making for safe swimming.

Getting there: Located along Ocean Boulevard between 1st and 72nd places in Long Beach. Belmont Pier is at Ocean Boulevard and 39th Place.

Cabrillo Beach—The edge of Los Angeles harbor is an unappealing locale for a beach, but here it is, a two-part strand, covered with heavy-grain sand and bisected by a fishing pier. One half faces the shipping facility; the other looks out on the glorious Pacific and abuts on the **Point Fermin Marine Life Refuge**, a rocky corridor filled with outstanding tidepools and backdropped by dramatic cliffs. If you like tidepooling, beeline to Cabrillo, if not—there are hundreds of other beaches in the Golden State.

Facilities: Restrooms, picnic areas, lifeguards, snack bar on pier, museum, playground, volleyball courts; fires permitted; restaurants and groceries nearby in San Pedro; information, 310-832-1179. *Fishing:* From pier. *Swimming:* People do it, but I saw a lot of refuse from the nearby shipping harbor. *Surfing:* Try in front of the beach and near the jetty. Great for windsurfing.

Getting there: Located at 3720 Stephen M. White Drive in San Pedro.

Royal Palms State Beach—Situated at the base of a sedimentary cliff, this boulder-strewn beach gains its name from a grove of elegant palm trees. Before it was swallowed by a 1920s storm, the Royal Palms Hotel was located here. Today the guests of honor are surfers and tidepoolers. While the location is quite extraordinary, I prefer another beach, Point Fermin Park's **Wilder Annex,** located to the south. This little gem also lacks sand, but is built on three tiers of a cliff. The upper level is decorated with palm trees, the middle tier has a grassy plot studded with shady magnolias, and the bottom floor is a rocky beach with promising tidepools and camera-eye views of Point Fermin.

Facilities: Restrooms, lifeguards at Royal Palms; restaurants and groceries nearby in San Pedro; information, 310-832-1179. *Fishing:* Very good at both parks. *Swimming:* Try Royal Palms since there are lifeguards. *Surfing:* Very popular at Royal Palms and off White Point, a peninsula separating the two parks.

Getting there: Both parks are located along Paseo del Mar in San Pedro. Royal Palms is near the intersection with Western Avenue and Wilder Annex is around the intersection with Meyler Street.

PALOS VERDES PENINSULA BEACHES AND PARKS

Abalone Cove County Beach—The Palos Verdes Peninsula is so rugged and inaccessible that any beach by definition will be secluded. This gray sand hideaway is no exception. It sits in a natural amphitheater guarded by sedimentary rock formations and looks out on Catalina Island. There are tidepools to ponder and a marine ecological reserve to explore.

Facilities: Picnic areas, restrooms, part-time lifeguards; restaurants and groceries several miles away in San Pedro; information, 310-372-2166. *Fishing:* Good. *Swimming:* Good. *Surfing:* Try the east end of the cove.

Getting there: Located off Palos Verdes Drive South in Rancho Palos Verdes. From the parking lot a path leads down to the beach.

Torrance County Beach—This is a lengthy stretch of bleach-blond sand guarded on one flank by the stately Palos Verdes Peninsula and on the other by an industrial complex and colony of smokestacks. Just your average middle class beach, it's not one of my favorites, but it has the only white sand hereabouts. Also consider adjacent **Malaga Cove** (nicknamed "RAT" beach because it's "right after Torrance"), a continuation of the strand, noted for tidepools, shells, and rock-hounding. Prettier than its pedestrian partner, Malaga Cove is framed by rocky bluffs.

Facilities: At Torrance there are restrooms, some concession stands, and lifeguards; restaurants and groceries are located downtown. Around Malaga Cove you're on your own; information, 310-372-2166. *Fishing:* Good at both beaches. *Swimming:* Recommended at Torrance where lifeguards are on duty. *Surfing:* Very good at Malaga Cove.

Getting there: Paseo de la Playa in Torrance parallels the beach. To reach Malaga Cove, walk south from Torrance toward the cliffs.

SOUTH BAY BEACHES AND PARKS

Redondo State Beach—Surfers know this strand and so should you. Together with neighboring Hermosa and Manhattan beaches, it symbolizes the Southern California beach scene. You'll find a long strip of white sand bordered by a hillside carpeted with ice plants. In addition to surfers, the area is populated by bicyclists and joggers, while anglers cast from the nearby piers.

Facilities: Restrooms, lifeguards, volleyball courts; restaurants on the pier and groceries nearby; information, 310-372-2166. *Fishing:* Good from nearby Fisherman's Wharf. *Swimming:* Good. *Surfing:* Very good.

Getting there: Located along the Esplanade in Redondo Beach.

Hermosa City Beach—One of the great beaches of Southern California, this is a very, very wide (and very, very white) sand beach extending the entire length of Hermosa Beach. Two miles of pearly sand is only part of the attraction. There's also The Strand, a pedestrian lane that runs the length of the beach; Pier Avenue, an adjacent street lined with interesting shops; a quarter-mile fishing pier; and a local community know for its artistic creativity. Personally, if I were headed to the beach, I would head in this direction.

Facilities: Restrooms, lifeguards, volleyball courts, pier, playground; restaurants and groceries nearby; information, 310-372-2166. *Fishing:* Good from the Municipal Pier. *Swimming:* Good. *Surfing:* Very good around the pier and all along the beach.

Getting there: Located at the foot of Pier Avenue in Hermosa Beach.

Manhattan State Beach—Back in those halcyon days when their first songs were climbing the charts, the Beach Boys were regular fixtures at this silvery strand. They came to surf, swim, and check out the scene along The Strand, the walkway that extends the length of Manhattan Beach. What can you say, the gentlemen had good taste. This sand corridor is wide as a desert, fronted by an aquamarine ocean and backed by the beautiful homes of the very lucky. If that's not enough, there's a fishing pier and an adjacent commercial area door-to-door with excellent restaurants.

Facilities: Restrooms, lifeguards, volleyball courts; restaurants and groceries nearby; information, 310-372-2166. *Fishing:* Try Manhattan Beach Pier. *Swimming:* Good. *Surfing:* Good, especially around the pier.

Getting there: Located at the foot of Manhattan Beach Boulevard in Manhattan Beach.

Dockweiler State Beach—It's long, wide, and has fluffy white sand—what more could you ask? Rather, it's what less can you request. Dockweiler suffers a minor problem. It's right next to Los Angeles International Airport, one of the world's busiest terminals. Every minute planes are taking off, thundering, reverberating, right over the beach. To add insult to infamy, there is a sewage treatment plant nearby.

Facilities: Picnic areas, restrooms, playground; fires permitted; restaurants and groceries nearby in Playa del Rey; information, 310-372-2166. *Fishing:* Good from jetties. *Swimming:* Good. *Surfing:* Good.

Getting there: Located at the foot of Imperial Highway, along Vista del Mar Boulevard in Playa del Rey.

VENICE AND SANTA MONICA BEACHES AND PARKS

Venice Beach—If you visit only a single Southern California beach, this should be the one. It's a broad white sand corridor that runs the entire length of Venice and features Venice Pier (which is temporarily closed). But the real attraction—and the reason you'll find the beach described in the "Restaurants," "Sightseeing," and "Shopping" sections—is the boardwalk. A center of culture, street artistry, and excitement, the boardwalk parallels Venice Beach for two miles.

Facilities: Picnic areas, restrooms, showers, lifeguards, playgrounds, basketball courts, and paddle ball courts; restaurants, groceries, and vendors line the boardwalk; information, 310-399-2775. *Swimming:* Good. *Surfing:* Good.

Getting there: Ocean Front Walk in Venice parallels the beach.

Santa Monica State Beach—If the pop song is right and "L.A. is a great big freeway," then truly Santa Monica is a great big beach. Face it, the sand is very white, the water is very blue, the beach is very broad, and they all continue for miles. From Venice to Pacific Palisades, it's a sandbox gone wild. Skaters, strollers, and bicyclists pass along the promenade, sunbathers lie moribund in the sand, and volleyball players perform acrobatic shots. At the center of all this stands the Santa Monica Pier with its amusement park atmosphere. If it wasn't right next door to Venice this would be the hottest beach around.

Facilities: Picnic areas, restrooms, lifeguards, snackbars, volleyball courts, pier; restaurants and groceries nearby; information, 310-458-8311. *Fishing:* From Santa Monica Pier. *Swimming:* Good. *Surfing:* Good.

Getting there: Along Route 1, at the foot of Colorado Avenue in Santa Monica.

Will Rogers State Beach—Simple and homespun he might have been, but humorist Will Rogers was also a canny businessman with a passion for real estate. He bought up two miles of beachfront property which eventually became his namesake park. It's a wide, sandy strand with an equally expansive parking lot running the length of the beach. Route 1 parallels the parking area and beyond that rise the sharp cliffs that lend Pacific Palisades its name.

Facilities: Restrooms, lifeguard; restaurants and groceries nearby; information, 310-451-2906. *Swimming:* Good. *Surfing:* Good where Sunset Boulevard meets the ocean.

Getting there: Located south along Route 1 from Sunset Boulevard in Pacific Palisades.

Will Rogers State Historic Park—The former ranch of humorist Will Rogers, this 186-acre spread sits in the hills of Pacific Palisades. The late cowboy's home is open to visitors and there are hiking trails leading around the property and out into adjacent Topanga Canyon State Park.

Facilities: Picnic areas, museum, restrooms; restaurants and groceries nearby in Pacific Palisades; information, 310-454-8212.

Getting there: Located at 14253 Sunset Boulevard in Pacific Palisades.

Santa Monica Mountains National Recreation Area—One of the few mountain ranges in the United States to run transversely (from east to west), the Santa Monicas reach for fifty miles to form the northwestern boundary of the Los Angeles basin. This federal preserve, which covers part of the mountain range, encompasses about 150,000 acres between Routes 1 and 101; in addition to high country, it includes a coastal stretch from Santa Monica to Point Mugu. Considered a "botanical island," the mountains support chaparral, coastal sage, and oak forests; mountain lions, golden eagles, and many of California's early animal species still survive here.

Facilities: Hiking trails; information center located at 22900 Ventura Boulevard, Woodland Hills, CA 91364 (818-597-9192). *Camping:* Permitted; primitive campgrounds.

Getting there: Several access roads lead into the area; Mulholland Drive and Mulholland Highway follow the crest of the Santa Monica Mountains for about 50 miles from Hollywood to Malibu.

MALIBU BEACHES AND PARKS

Topanga Canyon State Park—Not much sand here, but you will find forests of oak and fields of rye. This 10,000-acre hideaway nestles in the Santa Monica Mountains above Malibu. Along the 35 miles of hiking trails and fire roads are views of the ocean, San Gabriel Mountains, and San Fer-

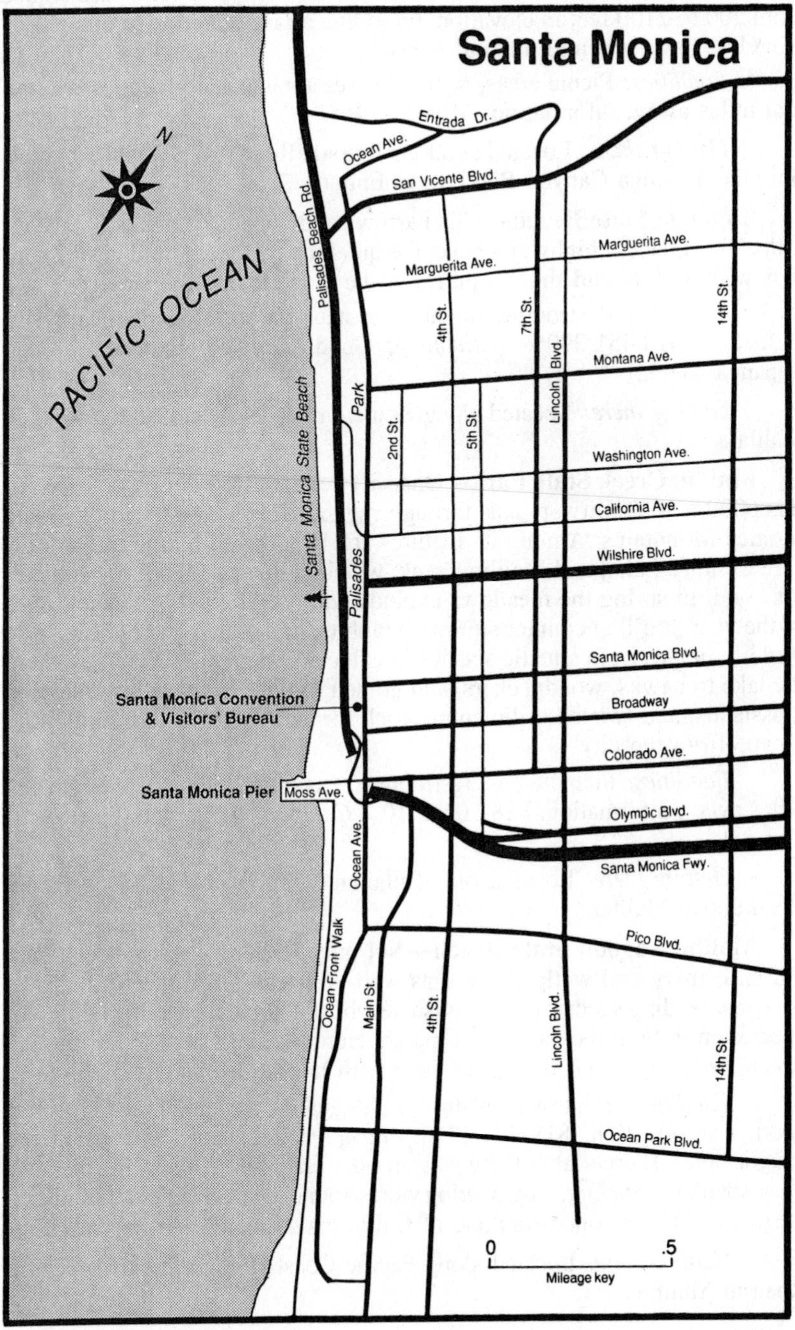
Santa Monica
PACIFIC OCEAN
N
Entrada Dr.
Ocean Ave.
San Vicente Blvd.
Palisades Beach Rd.
Marguerita Ave.
Marguerita Ave.
4th St.
7th St.
14th St.
Montana Ave.
Lincoln Blvd.
Park
2nd St.
5th St.
Santa Monica State Beach
Washington Ave.
California Ave.
Wilshire Blvd.
Palisades
Santa Monica Blvd.
Santa Monica Convention
& Visitors' Bureau
Broadway
Colorado Ave.
Santa Monica Pier
Moss Ave.
Olympic Blvd.
Ocean Ave.
Santa Monica Fwy.
Pico Blvd.
Ocean Front Walk
Main St.
4th St.
Lincoln Blvd.
14th St.
Ocean Park Blvd.
0
.5
Mileage key

nando Valley. There are meadows and a stream to explore. The park climbs from 200 to 2100 feet in elevation, providing an introduction to one of Los Angeles' few remaining natural areas.

Facilities: Picnic areas, restrooms; restaurants and groceries are several miles away; information, 310-455-2465.

Getting there: Located at 20825 Entrada Road; from Route 1 in Malibu take Topanga Canyon Road up to Entrada Road.

Topanga State Beach—This narrow sand corridor extends for over a mile. The adjacent highway breaks the quietude, but the strand is still popular with surfers and those wanting to be close to Malibu services.

Facilities: Restrooms, lifeguards; restaurants and groceries nearby; information, 310-451-2906. *Swimming:* Good. *Surfing:* Excellent around Topanga Creek.

Getting there: Located along Route 1 near Topanga Canyon Road in Malibu.

Malibu Creek State Park—Once a Twentieth Century Fox movie set, this 6000-acre facility spreads through rugged, virgin country in the Santa Monica Mountains. Among its features are 15 miles of hiking trails, four-acre Century Lake, and Malibu Creek, which is lined with willow and cottonwood. In spring the meadows explode with wildflowers; at other times of the year you'll encounter squirrels, rabbits, mule deer, and bobcats. The bird life ranges from aquatic species like ducks and great blue herons along the lake to hawks, woodpeckers, and golden eagles. The lava hills, sloping grasslands, and twisted sedimentary rock formations make it an intriguing escape from the city.

Facilities: Picnic areas, restrooms; restaurants and groceries several miles away; information, 818-706-1310. *Camping:* Permitted; no fires allowed.

Getting there: Located off Mulholland Highway and Las Vírgenes Road above Malibu.

Malibu Lagoon State Beach—Not only is there a pretty beach here but an estuary and wetlands area as well. You can stroll the white sands past an unending succession of lavish beachfront homes, or study a different species entirely in the park's salt marsh. Here Malibu Creek feeds into the ocean, creating a rich tidal area busy with marine life and shorebirds.

Facilities: Picnic area, restrooms, lifeguards; restaurants and groceries nearby; information, 818-706-1310. *Fishing:* Excellent. Surf perch are caught here. There's also fishing from adjacent Malibu Pier. *Swimming:* Very popular. *Surfing:* Engineering work around the channel has diminished the waves at what once was one of California's greatest surfing beaches.

Getting there: Located along Pacific Coast Highway at Cross Creek Road in Malibu.

Robert H. Meyer Memorial State Beaches—This unusual facility consists of three separate pocket beaches—**El Pescador, La Piedra,** and **El Matador**. Each is a pretty strand with sandy beach and eroded bluffs. Together they are among the nicest beaches in Malibu. My favorite is El Matador with its rock formations, sea stacks, and adjacent Malibu mansions.

Facilities: Toilet; restaurants and groceries several miles away; information, 818-706-1310. *Swimming:* Use caution since there are no lifeguards.

Getting there: Located on Route 1 about 11 miles west of Malibu.

Westward Beach Point Dume State Park—This long narrow stretch is really a southerly continuation of Zuma Beach. Unlike its neighbor, it is conveniently located away from the highway and bordered by lofty sandstone cliffs. There are tidepools here and trails leading up along the bluffs. For white sand serenity this is a choice spot. Matter of fact, on the far side of Point Dume you'll encounter what was once a popular nude beach in **Pirate's Cove (★)**.

Facilities: Restrooms, lifeguards; restaurants and groceries nearby; information, 310-457-9891. *Swimming:* Good. *Surfing:* Good along Westward Beach and off Point Dume.

Getting there: The park entrance is adjacent to the southern entrance to Zuma Beach County Park, just off Route 1 about six miles west of Malibu. To reach the beach at Pirate's Cove, park at Paradise Cove, on Route 1 two miles further east, and hike back toward Point Dume; or you can take the trail over the Point Dume Headlands and down to Pirate's Cove.

Zuma Beach County Park—This long, broad beach is a study in the territorial instincts of the species. Los Angeles County's largest beach park, it is frequented in one area by Chicanos; "Vals," young residents of the San Fernando Valley, have staked claim to another section, while families and students inhabit another stretch (Zuma 3 and 4). Not as pretty as other Malibu beaches, it offers more space and better facilities, making Zuma a popular spot.

Facilities: Restrooms, lifeguards, playgrounds, volleyball; restaurants and groceries nearby; information, 310-457-9891. *Swimming:* Good. *Surfing:* Good; information on surf conditions, 310-457-9701.

Getting there: Located along Route 1 approximately six miles west of Malibu.

Leo Carrillo State Beach—Extending more than a mile, this white sand corridor rests directly below Route 1. Named after Leo Carrillo, the television actor who played sidekick Pancho in *The Cisco Kid*, the beach offers sea caves, tidepools, interesting rock formations, and a natural tunnel. Nicer still is **Leo Carrillo Beach North**, a sandy swath located just beyond Sequit Point and backdropped by a sharp bluff. This entire area is a prime whale-watching site. At the south end of this 1600-acre park you can bathe in the buff: but beware, if caught you will be cited.

Facilities: Limited picnic areas, restrooms, showers, lifeguards; restaurants and groceries several miles away; information, 818-706-1310. *Camping:* Permitted. *Swimming:* Good. *Surfing:* Good, especially around Sequit Point. There's also excellent surfing a few miles north at **County Line Beach**.

Getting there: Located on Route 1 about 14 miles west of Malibu. There is access to Leo Carrillo Beach North from the parking lot at 35000 Pacific Coast Highway.

SANTA CATALINA ISLAND BEACHES AND PARKS

If you are planning to camp on Catalina, there are a few things to know. First, there is a fee for camping and reservations are a must (reservation numbers are listed under the particular park).

In addition to designated beaches, camping is permitted in many of the island's coves. These are undeveloped sites with no facilities and are most readily accessible by boat. Patrolling rangers collect the fees here.

For more information on camping, contact the **Los Angeles County Department of Parks and Recreation** (213 Catalina Street, Avalon; 310-510-0688) or the **Catalina Cove and Camp Agency** (P.O. Box 5044, Two Harbors; 310-510-0303).

For information on transportation to campgrounds and on hiking permits (which are required of everyone venturing beyond Avalon) see the "Sightseeing" section in this chapter.

Crescent Beach—About as relaxing as Coney Island, this beach is at the center of the action. Avalon's main drag parallels the beach and a pier divides it into two separate strips of sand. Facing Avalon Harbor, the strand is flanked on one side with a ferry dock and along the other by the famous Avalon Casino.

Facilities: Full service facilities (including restrooms, showers, and beach rentals) are available on the street adjacent to the beach; lifeguards. *Fishing:* Good from the pier. *Swimming:* The harbor provides protection from the surf, making it an excellent swimming area.

Getting there: Located along Crescent Avenue in Avalon.

Descanso Beach—Somehow the appeal of this private enclave escapes me. A rock-strewn beach on the far side of the Avalon Casino, it seconds as a mooring facility for sailboats. Granted, there is a rolling lawn dotted with palm trees and the complex is nicely surrounded by hills. But with all the commotion at the snack bar and volleyball courts it's more like being on an amusement pier than a beach. Besides that, you have to pay to get onto the beach.

Facilities: Restrooms, playground, showers; information, 310-510-2780. *Swimming:* Good.

Getting there: Located off Crescent Avenue past the Avalon Casino.

Hermit Gulch Campground—Once the site of the Wrigley Bird Park, this grassy field is dotted with palm and pine trees. Located up in Avalon Canyon inland from the beach, it provides a convenient and inexpensive way to visit Avalon and utilize its many services. There are pretty views of the surrounding hills.

Facilities: Picnic areas, restrooms, showers; restaurants and groceries nearby in Avalon; information, 310-510-8368. *Camping:* Permitted.

Getting there: Located on Avalon Canyon Road about one mile from downtown Avalon.

Black Jack Campground—Situated at 1500 feet elevation, this facility sits on a plateau below Mt. Black Jack, the island's second highest peak. It's a lovely spot shaded by pine and eucalyptus trees and affording views across the rolling hills and out along the ocean. The old Black Jack silver mine is nearby. Among backcountry facilities this is about the most popular on the island.

Facilities: Picnic areas, toilets; restaurants and groceries are way back in Avalon; information, 310-510-0688. *Camping:* Permitted.

Getting there: Located south of The Airport in the Sky off Airport Road.

Ben Weston Beach—A favorite among locals, this pewter-colored beach is surrounded by rocky hills. Located at the end of a long canyon road, it is serene and secluded. Avalon residents come here to flee the tourists, so you might consider making it your hideaway.

Facilities: Toilet. *Camping:* Permitted, but there is no water. *Fishing:* Good. *Swimming:* Good when the surf is low. *Surfing:* One of the island's best spots.

Getting there: Located about two miles south of Little Harbor off Middle Ranch Road.

Little Harbor Campground—On the Pacific side of the island, this camp sits near a sandy beach between rocky headlands. It's studded with palm trees and often filled with grazing bison. A good base camp for hikers, it is one of the island's prettiest facilities. In addition, **Shark Harbor**, an adjacent strand, is excellent for shell collecting and bodysurfing.

Facilities: Picnic areas, toilets, showers; restaurants and groceries about six miles away in Two Harbors; information, 310-510-0688. *Camping:* Permitted. *Fishing:* Good. *Swimming:* Good. *Skindiving:* Good.

Getting there: Located about six miles south of Two Harbors along Little Harbor Road.

Two Harbors Campground—Set along a series of terraces above a brown sand beach, this facility is adjacent to the services at Two Harbors. It's also a convenient base camp from which to hike out along the island's west end.

Facilities: Picnic areas, restrooms, showers, lockers, laundry, volleyball; restaurants and groceries nearby; information, 310-510-0303. *Camping:* Permitted. *Fishing:* Good. *Swimming:* Good. *Skindiving:* Very good; the waters here are particularly colorful.

Getting there: Located next to Two Harbors.

Parson's Landing—The most remote of Catalina's campgrounds, this isolated facility sits along a small brown sand beach with heavily eroded hills in the background.

Facilities: Picnic areas, toilets; restaurants and groceries are several miles away in Two Harbors; information 310-510-0303. *Camping:* Permitted. *Fishing:* Good. *Swimming:* Good. *Skindiving:* Good.

Getting there: Located 6.8 miles west of Two Harbors along West End Road.

Hiking

COASTAL TRAILS

The **Los Angeles portion of the California Coastal Trail** begins on Naples Island in Long Beach. From here the trail is a varied journey across open bluffs, boat basins, rocky outcroppings accessible only at low tide, along beachwalks filled with roller skaters, jugglers, and skate boarders, and up goat trails with stunning views of the Pacific Ocean.

Set beneath wave-carved bluffs, the **Palos Verdes Peninsula Trail** (5 miles) takes you along a rocky beachside trail past coves and teeming tidepools. The trail begins at Malaga Cove and ends at Point Vicente Lighthouse.

If you're interested in exploring a shipwreck, head out to Palos Verdes Estate Shoreline Preserve, near Malaga Cove, and hike along the **Seashore–Shipwreck Trail** (2.25 miles). The trail hugs the shoreline (and requires an ability to jump boulders), skirting tidepools and coves, until it arrives at what is left of an old Greek ship, the *Dominator*.

Zuma-Dume Trail (1 mile) in Malibu takes you from Zuma Beach County Park, along Pirate's Cove (which used to be a nude beach) to the Point Dume headlands and Paradise Cove, a popular diving spot.

SANTA MONICA MOUNTAINS TRAILS

It is difficult to imagine, but Los Angeles does have undeveloped mountain wilderness areas prime for trekking. The Santa Monica Mountains offer chaparral-covered landscapes, grassy knolls, mountain streams, and dark canyons.

When visiting Will Rogers State Historic Park, take a walk down **Inspiration Point Trail** (2 miles) for a view overlooking the Westside.

Topanga Canyon State Park has over 32 miles of trails. The **Musch Ranch Loop Trail** (4 miles) passes through five different types of plant communities. Or try the **Santa Ynez Canyon Trail** (6.6 miles), which guides you along the Palisades Highlands with views of the ocean and Santa Ynez Canyon. In spring wildflowers add to the already spectacular scenery.

Several trails trace the "backbone" of the Santa Monica Mountains. In fact, conservationists are trying to secure a trail that extends from Will Rogers State Historic Park to Point Mugu State Park. Presently, you will have to be happy with routes that hop, skip, and jump through the area.

Eagle Rock to Eagle Springs Loop Trail (4 miles), for instance, begins in Topanga State Park and traverses oak and chaparral countryside on its way to Eagle Spring. Another section of the "Backbone Trail," **Tapia Park–Malibu Creek State Park Loop** (12 miles) begins near Tapia Park, just off of Malibu Canyon Road. The trail follows fire roads and offers choice views of the ocean and Channel Islands before it winds into Malibu Creek Canyon.

For a nostalgic visit to the location of many movie and television shows, including *MASH* and *Love Is A Many Splendored Thing*, check out the **Century Ranch Trail** (2.3 miles) in Malibu Creek State Park. The trail travels along Malibu Creek to Rock Pool, the Gorge, and Century Lake.

An easy climb up **Zuma Ridge Trail** (6.3 miles) brings you to the center of the Santa Monica Mountains and affords otherworldly views of the Pacific. The trail begins off Encinal Canyon Road, 1.5 miles from Mulholland Highway.

SANTA CATALINA ISLAND TRAILS

For a true adventure in hiking, gather your gear and head for Santa Catalina. A network of spectacular trails crisscrosses this largely undeveloped island. Bring plenty of water and beware of rattlesnakes and poison oak. You'll also need a hiking permit (see the "Sightseeing" section in this chapter).

Catalina Trail (8 miles) begins at Black Jack Junction and ends up at Two Harbors. The path passes a lot of interesting terrain and provides glimpses of island wildlife, especially buffalo. (You can arrange with the ferry service to ride back to the mainland from Two Harbors.)

If you are an experienced hiker and ready for a good workout, hike **Silver Peak Trail** (10.1 miles). There are wonderful views of mountains and ocean along the way.

Other routes you might consider are **Sheep Chute Trail** (3.3 miles), a moderate hike between Little Harbor and Empire Landing; **Empire Landing Road Trail** (6.2 miles), another moderate hike from Two Harbors; and **Boushay Road** (2.1 miles), a strenuous trek between Silver Peak Trail and Parsons Landing.

Travelers' Tracks

Sightseeing

LONG BEACH

Anchoring the southern end of Los Angeles County is Long Beach, one of California's largest cities. Back in the Roaring Twenties, after oil was discovered and the area experienced a tremendous building boom, Long Beach became known as "The Coney Island of the West." Boasting five miles of beachfront and a grand amusement park, it was a favorite spot for daytripping Angelenos.

Several decades of decline followed, but recently the metropolis began a $1.5 billion redevelopment plan. Today it ranks together with neighboring San Pedro as one of the largest manmade harbors in the world and is becoming an increasingly popular tourist destination. Ignoring the Chamber of Commerce hoopla about the city's refurbishment, you should find Long Beach a revealing place, a kind of social studies lesson in modern American life. Travel Ocean Boulevard as it parallels the sea and you'll pass from quaint homes to downtown skyscrapers to fire-breathing smokestacks.

For a dynamic example of what I mean, visit the enclave of **Naples** near the south end of town. Conceived early in the century, modeled on Italy's fabled canal towns, it's a tiny community of three islands separated by canals and linked with walkways. Waterfront greenswards gaze out on Alamitos Bay and its fleet of sloops and motorboats. You can wander along bayside paths past comfortable homes, contemporary condos, and humble cottages. Fountains and miniature traffic circles, alleyways and boulevards, all form an incredible labyrinth along which you undoubtedly will become lost.

Adding to the sense of old Italia is the **Gondola Getaway** (5437 East Ocean Boulevard, Long Beach; 310-433-9595), a romantic hour-long cruise through the canals of Naples. For a hefty price (less, however, than a ticket to Italy), you can climb aboard a gondola, dine on hors d'oeuvres, and be serenaded with Italian music.

The **Long Beach Museum of Art** (2300 East Ocean Boulevard; 310-439-2119) is a must. Dedicated to 20th-century art, this avant-garde museum has ever-changing exhibitions ranging from German Expressionism to contemporary Southern California work. Particularly noted for its video presentations, the museum is a window on modern culture.

For a touch of early Spanish culture, plan on visiting the region's old adobes. **Rancho Los Alamitos** (6400 Bixby Hill Road; 310-431-3541), built in 1806 with walls four feet thick, is Southern California's oldest remaining house. Among its gardens, brick walkways, and majestic magnolias, you can tour old barns, a blacksmith shop, and feed shed. There's also a restored chuck wagon with a coffee pot still resting on the wood-burning stove.

Rancho Los Cerritos (4600 Virginia Road; 310-424-9423), a two-story Spanish colonial home, once served as headquarters for a 28,000-acre ranch. Now the 19th-century adobe is filled with Victorian furniture and surrounded by gardens.

The Pacific Ocean may be Long Beach's biggest natural attraction, but many birds in the area prefer the **El Dorado Nature Center** (7550 East Spring Street; 310-421-9431, ext. 3415). Part of the 420-acre El Dorado Park complex, this wildlife sanctuary offers one- and two-mile hikes past a lake and creek. About 150 bird species as well as numerous land animals can be sighted. Though located in a heavily urbanized area, the facility encompasses several ecological zones.

Chapter Two in the Long Beach civics lesson is the steel-and-glass downtown area, where highrise hotels vie for dominance. The best way to tour this crowded commercial district is to stroll **The Promenade**, a six-block brick walkway leading from 3rd Street to the waterfront. There's a **tile mosaic** (Promenade and 3rd Street) at the near end portraying an idyllic day at the beach complete with sailboats, sunbathers, and lifeguards. Midway along the landscaped thoroughfare sits the **Long Beach Area Convention & Visitors' Council** (1 World Trade Center, #300; 310-436-9982), home to maps, brochures, and other bits of information. Then you'll arrive at a park shaded with palm trees and adjacent to Shoreline Village (407 Shoreline Village Drive), a marina and shopping center disguised as a 19th-century fishing village.

Long Beach Part III rises in the form of oil derricks and industrial complexes just across the water. To view the freighters, tankers, and warships lining the city's piers, gaze out from the northern fringes of Shoreline Village.

Fittingly, the climax of a Long Beach tour comes at the very end, after you have experienced the three phases of urban existence. Just across the Los Angeles River, along Harbor Scenic Drive ("scenic" in this case meaning construction cranes and cargo containers), lies one of the strangest sights I've ever encountered. The first time I saw it, peering through the steel filigree of a suspension bridge, with harbor lights emblazoning the scene, I thought something had gone colossally wrong with the world. An old-style ocean liner, gleaming eerily in the false light, appeared to be parked on the ground. Next to it an overgrown geodesic dome, a kind of giant aluminum breast, was swelling up out of the earth.

Unwittingly I had happened upon Long Beach's two top tourist attractions, the *Queen Mary* and the *Spruce Goose*, respectively the world's largest ocean liner and airplane. Making her maiden voyage in 1936, the **Queen Mary** (Pier J; 310-435-3511) was the pride of Great Britain. Winston Churchill, the Duke and Duchess of Windsor, Greta Garbo, and Fred Astaire sailed on her, and during World War II, converted to military service, she carried so many troops across the Atlantic Ocean that Adolf Hitler offered $250,000 and the Iron Cross to the U-boat captain who sank her.

Today she is the pride of Long Beach, a 1000-foot-long "city at sea" transformed into a floating museum which brilliantly re-creates shipboard life. An elaborate walking tour carries you down into the engine room (a world of pumps and propellers), out along the decks, and up to each level of this multistage behemoth. Or try a "ghost tour" for an introduction to the ship's most haunting inhabitants.

The grand lady is a masterpiece of art deco architecture. Dioramas throughout the ship realistically portray every aspect of sailing life during the great age of ocean liners.

The *Queen Mary* is expertly refurbished and wonderfully laid out, an important addition to the Long Beach seafront. Her neighbor in the geodesic dome, on the other hand, is an absurdity capped by an absurdity. The **Spruce Goose** (Pier J; 310-435-3511), the largest plane ever built, resides in the world's biggest clear-span aluminum dome.

In case you've forgotten, the *Spruce Goose* was built by Howard Hughes, the bizarre billionaire who ended his life hiding in a hotel room, addicted to drugs, imprisoned by his own employees. His plane, with a 320-foot wing span and a tail section eight stories high, is the biggest white elephant in history.

Built to ferry World War II troops and material across the Atlantic, the 200-ton behemoth was deemed "a half-baked" idea by critics. It was. The monster cost millions to build, wasn't completed until after the war, and then flew only once, for one mile. Why anyone would memorialize this monument to waste and excess is a question to ponder. Happily, the admission you pay to see this eighth wonder includes tours of the *Queen Mary* and **Londontowne**, an ersatz-shopping-mall-cum-19th-century-English-village.

SAN PEDRO

San Pedro is home to **Los Angeles Harbor**, a region of creosote and rust, marked by 28 miles of busy waterfront. This landscape of oil tanks and cargo containers services thousands of ships every year and houses one of the country's largest commercial fishing fleets.

Head over to the **22nd Street Landing** (foot of 22nd Street) and watch sportfishing boats embark on high sea adventures. Then wander the waterfront and survey this frontier of steel and oil. Here awkward, unattractive ships glide as gracefully as figure skaters and the machinery of civilization goes about the world's work with a clatter and boom. The most common shorebirds are cargo cranes.

Ports O' Call Village (entrance at foot of 6th Street; 310-831-0287) a shopping mall in the form of a 19th-century port town, houses several outfits conducting harbor cruises. The boats sail around the San Pedro waterfront and venture out for glimpses of the surrounding shoreline; for information, contact **Buccaneer/Mardi Gras Cruises** (Ports O' Call Village, San Pedro; 310-548-1085).

Extending along 6th Street between Mesa Street and Harbor Boulevard is the **Sportswalk**. San Pedro's answer to Hollywood's Walk of Fame, it features plaques dedicated to Olympic medalists as well as great collegiate and professional athletes.

For a view of how it used to be, stop by the **Los Angeles Maritime Museum** (Berth 84; 310-548-7618). This dockside showplace displays models of ships ranging from fully rigged brigs to 19th-century steam sloops to World War II battleships. There's even an 18-foot re-creation of the ill-starred *Titanic* and the ocean liner model used to film *The Poseidon Adventure*.

Another piece in the port's historic puzzle is placed several miles inland at the **Phineas Banning Residence Museum** (401 East M Street, Wilmington; 310-548-7777; admission). This imposing Greek Revival house, built in 1864, was home to the man who dreamed, dredged, and developed Los Angeles harbor. Today Phineas Banning's Mansion, complete with a cupola from which he watched ships navigate his port, is furnished in period pieces and open for guided tours.

By definition any shipping center is of strategic importance. Head up to **Fort MacArthur** (Angel's Gate Park, 3601 South Gaffey Street; 310-519-0936) and discover the batteries with which World War II generals planned to protect Los Angeles Harbor. From this cement-and-steel compound you can inspect the bunkers and a small museum, then survey the coast. Once a site of gun turrets and grisly prospects, today it is a testimonial to the invasion that never came.

Another war, the Korean, will be commemorated in a monument being built nearby, but until it's completed you can visit the **Bell of Friendship**, which the people of South Korea presented to the United States during its 1976 bicentennial. Housed in a multicolor pagoda and cast with floral and symbolic images, it rests on a hilltop looking out on Los Angeles Harbor and the region's sharply profiled coastline.

Down the hill at the **Cabrillo Marine Museum** (3720 Stephen M. White Drive; 310-548-7562) there is a modest collection of display cases with samples of shells, coral, and shorebirds. Several dozen aquariums demonstrate local fish and marine plants. Nearby stretches 1200-foot **Cabrillo Fishing Pier**.

Of greater interest is **Point Fermin Park** (807 Paseo del Mar; 310-548-7756), a 37-acre blufftop facility resting above spectacular tidepools and a marine preserve. The tidepools are accessible from the Cabrillo Marine Museum, which sponsors exploratory tours, and via steep trails from the park. Also of note is the **Point Fermin Lighthouse**, a unique 19th-century clapboard house with a beacon set in a rooftop crow's nest. From the park plateau, like lighthouse keepers of old, you'll have open vistas of the cliff-fringed coastline and a perfect perch for sighting whales during their winter migration.

Then drive along Paseo del Mar, through arcades of stately palm trees and along sharp sea cliffs, until it meets 25th Street. The sedimentary rocks throughout this region have been twisted and contorted into grotesque shapes by tremendous geologic pressures.

PALOS VERDES PENINSULA

The forces of nature seem to dominate as you proceed out along the **Palos Verdes Peninsula** from San Pedro. Follow 25th Street, then Palos Verdes Drive South and encounter a tumbling region where terraced hills fall away to sharp coastal bluffs.

As you turn **Portuguese Bend**, the geology of this tumultuous area becomes startlingly evident when the road begins undulating through landslide zones. The earthquake faults which underlie the Los Angeles basin periodically fold and collapse the ground here. To one side you'll see the old road, fractured and useless. Even the present highway, with more patches than your favorite dungarees, is in a state of constant repair.

Of course the terrible power of nature has not dissuaded people from building here. Along the ridgetops and curving hills below are colonies of stately homes. With its rocky headlands, tidepool beaches and sun-spangled views, the place is simply so magnificent no one can resist.

Most lordly of all these structures is **The Wayfarer's Chapel** (5755 Palos Verdes Drive South, Rancho Palos Verdes; 310-377-1650), a simple but extraordinary center designed by the son of Frank Lloyd Wright. Nestled neatly into the surrounding landscape, the sunlit chapel is built entirely of glass and commands broad views of the terrain and ocean. With its stone altar and easy repose the temple was built to honor Emanuel Swedenborg, the 18th-century Swedish philosopher and mystic.

The **Point Vicente Lighthouse** rises further down the coast, casting an antique aura upon the area. While the beacon is not open to the public, the nearby **Point Vicente Interpretive Center** (31501 Palos Verdes Drive West, Rancho Palos Verdes; 310-377-5370; admission) offers a small regional museum. This is a prime whale-watching spot in the winter when onlookers gather in the adjacent park to catch glimpses of migrating gray whales.

For a vision of how truly beautiful this region is, turn off Palos Verdes Drive West in Palos Verdes Estates and follow Paseo Lunado until it meets the sea at **Lunada Bay**. This half-moon inlet, backdropped by the jagged face of a rocky cliff, looks out upon an unending expanse of ocean. Steep paths lead down to a rocky shoreline rich in tidepools.

The road changes names to Paseo del Mar but continues past equally extraordinary coastline. There is a series of open fields and vista points along this **shoreline preserve** where you can gaze down from the blufftop to beaches and tidepools. Below, surfers ride the curl of frothing breaks and a few hardy hikers pick their way goat-like along precipitous slopes.

The setting is decidedly more demure at the **South Coast Botanic Gardens** (26300 South Crenshaw Boulevard, Palos Verdes; 310-544-6815; admission). This 87-acre garden is planted with exotic vegetation from Africa and New Zealand as well as species from other parts of the world.

SOUTH BAY

The birthplace of California's beach culture lies in a string of towns on the southern skirt of Santa Monica Bay—Redondo Beach, Hermosa Beach, and Manhattan Beach. It all began here in the South Bay with George Freeth, "the man who can walk on water." It seems that while growing up

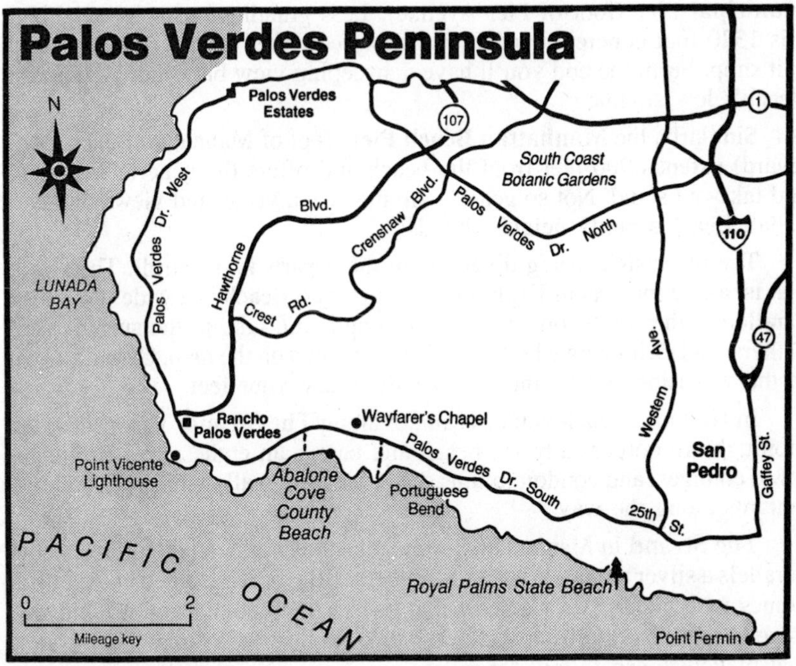

in Hawaii, Freeth resurrected the ancient Polynesian sport of surfing and transplanted it to California. Equipped with a 200-pound, solid wood board, he introduced surfing to fascinated onlookers at a 1907 event in Redondo Beach.

It wasn't until the 1950s that the surfing wave crested. That's when a group of local kids called The Beach Boys spent their days catching waves at Manhattan Beach and their nights recording classic surfing songs. The surrounding towns became synonymous with the sport and a new culture was born, symbolized by blond-haired, blue-eyed surfers committed to sun, sand, and the personal freedom to ride the last wave.

Sightseeing spots are rather scarce in these beach towns. As you can imagine, the interesting places are inevitably along the waterfront. Each town sports a municipal pier, with rows of knickknack shops, cafés, and oceanview lounges, either along the pier or on the nearby waterfront.

In Redondo Beach, **Fisherman's Wharf** (Municipal Pier) is home to surfcasters and hungry seagulls. Walk out past the shops, salt breeze in your face, and you can gaze along the waterfront to open ocean. Waves wash against the pilings. Beneath the wood plank walkway, sea birds dive for fish. These sights and sounds are repeated again and again on the countless piers that line the California coast.

In fact you'll find them recurring right up in Hermosa Beach at the **Municipal Pier** (foot of Pier Avenue). Less grandiose than its neighbor, this 1320-foot concrete corridor is simply equipped with a snack bar and bait shop. From the end you'll have a sweeping view back along Hermosa Beach's low skyline.

Similarly, the **Manhattan Beach Pier** (foot of Manhattan Beach Boulevard) extends 900 feet from the beach and offers the generic bait store and take-out stand. Not so generic are the ocean vistas and views of Manhattan Beach's pretty neighborhoods.

The other sightseeing diversion in these parts is the stroll. The stroll, that is, along the beach. **Esplanade** in Redondo Beach is a wide boulevard paralleling the waterfront. Wander its length and take in the surfers, sunbathers, and swimmers who keep this resort town on the map. Or walk down to the waterline and let the cool Pacific bathe your feet.

In Hermosa Beach you can saunter along **The Strand**. This pedestrian thoroughfare borders a broad beach and passes an endless row of bungalows, cottages, and condominiums. It's a pleasant walk with shops and restaurants along the way.

The Strand in Manhattan Beach lacks the commercial storefronts but parallels a silver strand. Wide and wonderful, the beach is lined by beautiful homes with plate-glass windows that reflect the blue hues of sea and sky. Together, these oceanfront walkways link the South Bay towns in a course that bicyclists can follow for miles.

VENICE

Venice, California was the dream of one man, a tobacco magnate named Albert Kinney. He envisioned a "Venice of America," a Renaissance town of gondoliers and single-lane bridges, connected by 16 miles of canals.

After convincing railroad barons and city fathers, Kinney dredged swampland along Santa Monica Bay, carved a network of canals, and founded this dream city in 1905. The place was an early 20th-century answer to Disneyland with gondola rides and amusement parks. The canals were lined with vaulted arches and rococo-style hotels.

Oil spelled the doom of Kinney's dream. Once black gold was discovered beneath the sands of Venice, the region became a landscape of drilling rigs and oil derricks. Spills polluted the canals and blackened the beaches. In 1929 the city of Los Angeles filled in the canals and during the subsequent decades Venice more resembled a tar pit than a cultural center.

But by the 1950s latter-day visionaries—artists and bohemians—rediscovered "Kinney's Folly" and transformed it into an avant-garde community. It became a magnet for Beats in the 1950s and hippies during the next decade. Musician Jim Morrison of The Doors lived here and Venice developed a reputation as a center for the cultural renaissance that Albert Kinney once envisioned.

Today Venice retains much of the old flavor. Palatial hotels have given way to beach cottages and funky wood houses, but the narrow streets and countless alleyways remain. More significant, the town is filled with galleries and covered by murals, making it one of the region's most important art centers.

The revolution might have sputtered elsewhere, but in Venice artists have seized control. City Hall has become the **Beyond Baroque Literary Arts Center** (681 Venice Boulevard; 310-822-3006), housing a library and bookstore devoted to small presses.

Next door, the Venice City Jail is home to **SPARC**, or the **Social and Public Art Resource Center** (685 Venice Boulevard; 310-822-9560). The prison is an imposing 1923 art deco-style building with a cell block converted into an art gallery. Many of the cells are intact and you'll walk through an iron door to view contemporary artwork by alternative, cutting-edge artists. The center also sponsors lectures, mural tours, and mural projects around Los Angeles.

Both the Venice City Hall and Jail are great places to learn about what's going on in the community. Also consider the **Venice Chamber of Commerce** (13470 Washington Boulevard; 310-827-2366). If you can find someone in (which is not always easy), they will provide maps, brochures, and answers.

The commercial center of Venice rests at the intersection of Windward Avenue and Main street. Windward was the central boulevard of Kinney's dream city and the Traffic Circle, marked today by a small sculpture, was to be an equally grand lagoon. Continue along Windward Avenue to the **arcades**, a series of Italian-style colonnades which represent one of the few surviving elements of old Venice.

The heart of modern-day Venice pulses along the **boardwalk**, a two-mile strip that follows Ocean Front Walk from Washington Street to Ozone Avenue. **Venice Pier** (Ocean Front Walk and Washington Street), an 1100-foot fishing pier, anchors one end. (The pier is temporarily closed to the public.) Between Washington Street and Windward Avenue, the promenade is bordered by a palisade of beachfront homes, two- and three-story houses with plate-glass facades.

Walking north, the real action begins around 18th Avenue, at **Muscle Beach**, where rope-armed heavies work out in the weight pen, smacking punching bags and flexing their pecs, while gawking onlookers dream of oiling their bodies and walking with a muscle-bound strut.

The rest of the boardwalk is a grand open-air carnival which you should try to visit on the weekend. It is a world of artists and anarchists, derelicts and dreamers, a vision of what life would be if heaven was an insane asylum. Guitarists, jugglers, conga drummers, and clowns perform for the crowds. Kids on roller skates and bicycles whiz past rickshaws and unicycles. Street hawkers and panhandlers work the unwary while singers with scratchy voices pass the hat. Vendors dispense everything from corn dogs to cotton candy, T-shirts to wind-up toys. Venice, to quote Bob Dylan, represents "life and life only," but a rarefied form of life, slightly, beautifully askew.

Up the coast, **Marina del Rey** represents the largest manmade small boat harbor in the world. Over 6000 pleasure boats and yachts dock here. Harbor cruises are provided aboard a mock Mississippi riverboat by the **Hornblower Yachts** (13755 Fiji Way; 310-301-9900).

The entire region was once a marsh inhabited by a variety of waterfowl. Personally I think they should have left it to the birds. Marina del Rey is an ersatz community, a completely fabricated place where the main shopping area, **Fisherman's Village** (13755 Fiji Way; 310-823-5411), resembles a New England whaling town, and everything else attempts to portray something it's not. With its endless condominiums, pretentious homes, and overpriced restaurants, Marina del Rey is an artificial limb appended to the coast of Los Angeles.

SANTA MONICA

Pass from Venice into Santa Monica and you'll trade the boardwalk for a **promenade**. It's possible to walk for miles along Santa Monica's fluffy beach, past pastel-colored condominiums and funky woodframe houses. Roller skaters and bicyclists galore crowd the byways and chess players congregate at the picnic tables.

A middle-class answer to mod Malibu, Santa Monica started as a seaside resort in the 1870s when visitors bumped over long, dusty roads by stagecoach from Los Angeles. After flirting with the film industry in the age of silent movies, Santa Monica reverted in the 1930s to a quiet beach town which nevertheless was notorious for the gambling ships moored offshore. It was during this period that detective writer Raymond Chandler immortalized the place as "Bay City" in his brilliant Philip Marlowe novels.

Today Santa Monica is *in*. Its clean air, pretty beaches, and attractive homes have made it one of the most popular places to live in Los Angeles. As real estate prices have skyrocketed, liberal politics have ascended. Former Chicago Seven activist Tom Hayden is the state assemblyman here, working on local causes. Santa Monica, it seems, has become Southern California's answer to Berkeley.

Highlight of the beach promenade (and perhaps all Santa Monica) is the **Santa Monica Pier** (foot of Colorado Avenue). No doubt about it, the place is a scene. Acrobats work out on the playground below, surfers catch waves offshore, and street musicians strum guitars. And I haven't even mentioned the official attractions. There's a turn-of-the-century carousel with hand-painted horses that was featured in that cinematic classic, *The Sting*. There are shooting galleries, peep shows, video parlors, pinball machines, skee ball, bumper cars, and a restaurant.

From here it's a jaunt up to the **Santa Monica Convention & Visitors' Bureau** information kiosk (1400 Ocean Avenue; 310-392-9631). Here are maps, brochures, and helpful workers.

The booth is located in **Palisades Park**, a pretty, palm-lined greensward that extends north from Colorado Avenue more than a mile along the sandstone cliffs fronting Santa Monica beach. One of the park's stranger attractions here is the **Camera Obscura** (located in the Senior Recreation Center, 1450 Ocean Avenue), a periscope of sorts through which you can view the pier, beach, and surrounding streets.

For a glimpse into Santa Monica's past, take in the **Santa Monica Heritage Museum** (2612 Main Street; 310-392-8537). Heirlooms and antiques are housed in a grand American Colonial Revival home. The mansion dates to 1894 and is furnished entirely in period pieces. There are photo archives and historic artifacts galore.

Angels' Attic (516 Colorado Avenue; 310-394-8331; admission) is more than a great name. Contained in this 1894 Victorian is a unique museum of antique playthings for children. There's a Noah's ark worth of miniature animals plus a gallery of precious dolls. In keeping with the spirit of the museum, they serve tea on the front porch (by reservation).

The **Museum of Flying** (Santa Monica Airport, 2772 Donald Douglas Loop North; 310-392-8822; admission) is a miniature Smithsonian. Tracing the history of aviation in a single, brightly painted hangar, the museum houses everything from a 1924 Douglas World Cruiser (built in Santa Monica, it was the first plane to circle the globe) to a Douglas A-4 Skyhawk flown by the Blue Angels.

Sympathetic as it is to liberal politics, Santa Monica is nonetheless an extremely wealthy town. In fact it's a fusion of two very different neighbors, mixing the bohemian strains of Venice with the monied elements of Malibu. For a look at the latter influence, take a drive from Ocean Avenue out along **San Vicente Boulevard**. This fashionable avenue, with its arcade of magnolias, is lined on either side with lovely homes. But they pale by comparison with the estates you will see by turning left on **La Mesa Drive**. This quiet suburban street boasts a series of marvelous Spanish Colonial, Tudor, and contemporary-style houses.

At first glance, the **Self Realization Fellowship Lake Shrine** (17190 Sunset Boulevard; 310-454-4114) in nearby Pacific Palisades is an odd amalgam of pretty things. Gathered along the shore of a placid pond are a Dutch windmill, a houseboat, and a shrine topped with something resembling a giant artichoke. In fact, the windmill is a chapel, the houseboat is a former stopping place of yogi and Self Realization Fellowship founder Paramahansa Yogananda, and the oversized artichoke is a golden lotus archway near which some of Indian leader Mahatma Gandhi's ashes are enshrined. A strange but potent collection of icons in an evocative setting.

Several miles inland at **Will Rogers State Historic Park** (14253 Sunset Boulevard, Pacific Palisades; 310-454-8212; admission), on a hillside overlooking the Pacific, you can tour the ranch and home of America's greatest cowboy philosopher. Will Rogers, who started as a trick roper in traveling rodeos, hit the big time in Hollywood during the 1920s as a kind of cerebral comedian whose humorous wisdom plucked a chord in the American psyche.

From 1928 until his tragic death in 1935, the lariat laureate occupied this 31-room home with his family. The house is deceptively large but not grand; the woodframe design is basic and unassuming, true to Will Rogers' Oklahoma roots. Similarly the interior is decorated with Indian rugs and ranch tools. Western knickknacks adorn the tables and one room is dominated by a full-sized stuffed calf which Rogers utilized for roping practice. Well worth visiting, the "house that jokes built" is a simple expression of a vital personality.

MALIBU

Continuing north, Los Angeles County's final fling is **Malibu**, a 27-mile long ribbon lined on one side with pearly beaches and on the other by the Santa Monica Mountains. Famed as a movie star retreat and surfer's heaven, Malibu is one of America's mythic communities.

It has been a favored spot among Hollywood celebrities since the 1920s when a new highway opened the region and film stars like Clara Bow and

John Gilbert publicized the idyllic community. By the 1950s Malibu was rapidly developing and becoming nationally known for its rolling surf and freewheeling lifestyle. The 1959 movie *Gidget* cast Sandra Dee and James Darren as Malibu beach bums and the seaside community was on its way to surfing immortality.

Today blond-mopped surfers still line the shore and celebrities continue to congregate in beachfront bungalows. Matter of fact, the most popular sightseeing in Malibu consists of ogling the homes of the very rich. **Malibu Road**, which parallels the waterfront, is a prime strip. To make it as difficult as possible for common riffraff to reach the beach, the homes are built townhouse-style with no space between them. It's possible to drive for miles along the water without seeing the beach, only the backsides of baronial estates. Happily there are a few accessways to the beach, so it's possible to wander along the sand enjoying views of both the ocean and the picture-window palaces. Among the accessways is one which local wags named after "Doonesbury" character Zonker Harris.

What's amazing about these beachfront colonies is not the houses, which really can't compare to the estates in Beverly Hills, but the fact that people insist on building them so close to the ocean that every few years several are demolished by high surf while others sink into the sand.

One of Malibu's loveliest houses is open to the public. The **Adamson Home**, located at Malibu Lagoon State Beach (23200 Pacific Coast Highway; 310-456-8432; admission), is a stately Moorish-Spanish-Colonial Revival-style structure adorned with ceramic tiles. With its bare-beam ceilings and inlaid floors, the house is a study in early 20th-century elegance. Outstanding as it is, the building is upstaged by the landscaped grounds, which border the beach at Malibu and overlook a lagoon alive with waterfowl.

The town's most prestigious address is that of the **J. Paul Getty Museum** (17985 Pacific Coast Highway; 310-458-2003; advance reservation required for parking), one of the wealthiest art museums in the world. Set on a hillside overlooking the sea, the building re-creates a 2000-year old Roman villa in the most splendid manner imaginable.

The colonnaded entranceway, which greets the visitor with a reflecting pool and fountains, is nothing short of magnificent. This grand passage is adorned by bronze sculptures and lined with hedgerows. The floors are inlaid with tile, the walls are painted fresco style.

The galleries are equally as beautiful. Focusing on Greek and Roman antiquities, Renaissance and Baroque art, and French furniture, the museum reflects the taste of founder J. Paul Getty. Some of the world's finest artworks are displayed here and the relatively young museum has already established an awesome reputation in the art world.

Another seafront attraction is **Malibu Pier** (23000 Pacific Coast Highway) where you can walk out over the water, cast for fish, or gaze back along Malibu's heavily developed coastline. If you're in a sporting mood, they rent fishing tackle here; if you prefer less strenuous sports, there's a bar at the foot of the pier.

When you tire of Malibu's sand and surf, take a drive along one of the canyon roads which lead from Route 1 up into the Santa Monica Mountains. This chaparral country is filled with oak and sycamore forests and offers sweeping views back along the coast. Topanga Canyon Boulevard, perhaps the best known of these mountain roads, curves up to the rustic town of **Topanga**. Back in the '60s it was a fabled retreat for flower children. Even today vestiges of the hip era remain in the form of health food stores, New Age shops, and natural restaurants. Many of the woodframe houses are handcrafted and the community still vibrates to a slower rhythm than coastal Malibu and cosmopolitan Los Angeles.

To reach the top of the world (while making a mountain loop of this uphill jaunt), take Old Topanga Canyon Road from town and turn left out on **Mulholland Highway**. With its panoramic views of the ocean, Los Angeles Basin, and San Fernando Valley, Mulholland is justifiably famous. The road rides the ridgetop of the Santa Monica Mountains for almost fifty miles from Hollywood down to the Malibu shore. Late on weekend nights it's a rendezvous for lovers and a drag strip for daredevil drivers, but the rest of the time you'll find it a sinuous country road far from the madding mobs. (To complete the circle follow Kanan–Dume Road back down to the ocean.)

SANTA CATALINA ISLAND

Twenty-six miles across the sea,
You know the song.
Santa Catalina is a waitin' for me,
Everyone has heard it.
Santa Catalina, the island of
Romance, romance, romance, romance.

Actually this Mediterranean hideaway is parked just 22 miles off the Los Angeles coastline. But for romance, the song portrays it perfectly. Along its 54 miles of shoreline Catalina offers sheer cliffs, pocket beaches, hidden coves, and some of the finest skindiving anywhere. To the interior mountains rise sharply to over 2000 feet elevation. Island fox, black antelope, mountain goats, and over 400 bison range the island while its waters teem with marlin, swordfish, and barracuda.

Happily, this unique habitat is preserved for posterity and adventurous travelers by an arrangement under which 86 percent of the island lies undeveloped, protected by the Santa Catalina Conservancy. Avalon, the famous coastal resort enclave, is the only town on the island. The rest is given over to mountain wilderness and pristine shoreline.

As romantic as its setting is the history of the island. Originally part of the Baja coastline, it broke off from the mainland eons ago and drifted 100 miles to the northwest. Its earliest inhabitants arrived perhaps 4000 or 5000 years ago, leaving scattered evidence of their presence before being supplanted by the Gabrieleño Indians around 500 B.C. A society of sun worshippers, the Gabrieleños constructed a sacrificial temple, fished island waters, and traded ceramics and soapstone carvings with mainland tribes, crossing the channel in canoes.

Juan Rodríguez Cabrillo discovered Catalina in 1542, but the place proved of such little interest to the Spanish that other than Sebastian Vizcaíno's exploration in 1602 they virtually ignored it.

By the 19th century Russian fur traders, attracted by the rich colonies of sea otters, succeeded in exterminating both the otters and the indigenous natives. Cattle and sheep herders took over the Gabrieleños' land while pirates and smugglers, hiding in Catalina's secluded coves, menaced the coast.

Later in the century Chinese coolies were secretly landed on the island before being illegally carried to the mainland. Even during Prohibition it proved a favorite place among rumrunners and bootleggers. Gold fever swept Santa Catalina in 1863 as miners swept onto the island, but the rush never panned out.

Other visionaries, seeing in Catalina a major resort area, took control. After changing hands several times the island was purchased in 1919 by William Wrigley, Jr. The Wrigley family—better known for their ownership of a chewing gum company and the Chicago Cubs baseball team—developed Avalon for tourism and left the rest of the island to nature.

Attracting big-name entertainers and providing an escape from urban Los Angeles, Avalon soon captured the fancy of movie stars and wealthy Californians. Today **Avalon** is the port of entry for the island. Set in a luxurious amphitheater of green mountains, the town is like a time warp of Southern California early in the century. The architecture is a blend of Mediterranean and Victorian homes as well as vernacular structures designed by creative locals who captured both the beautiful and whimsical.

From the ferry dock you can wander **Crescent Avenue**, Avalon's oceanfront boulevard. Stroll out along the **Avalon Pleasure Pier** (Crescent Avenue and Catalina Street) for a view of the entire town and its surrounding crescent of mountains. Along this wood plank promenade are food stands, the harbormaster's office, and bait-and-tackle shops. The **Santa Catalina Island Chamber of Commerce and Visitors Bureau** (310-510-1520) has an information center here that will help orient you to Avalon and the island.

Among the pier kiosks are some offering **glass bottom boat tours** out to a nearby cove filled with colorful fish and marine plant life. Known as Catalina's "undersea gardens," the area is crowded with rich kelp beds and is a favorite haunt of brilliant red goby, golden adult Garibaldi, and leopard sharks. **Santa Catalina Island Company** (Avalon Harbor Pier; 310-510-2000) features tours during the day and also at night when huge floodlights are used to attract sea life. During summer months they seek out the spectacular phosphorescent flying fish which seasonally inhabit these waters.

Further along the waterfront, dominating the skyline, sits the **Avalon Casino** (end of Crescent Avenue). A massive circular building painted white and capped with a red tile roof, it was built in 1929 after a Spanish Moderne design. What can you say other than that the place is famous: it has appeared on countless post cards and travel posters. The ballroom has heard the big band sounds of Glenn Miller and Tommy Dorsey and the entire complex is a study in art deco with fabulous murals and tile paintings. (For information on tours call 310-510-2000.) Downstairs is the **Catalina Island Museum** (310-510-2414) with a small collection of local artifacts. Of particular interest is the contour relief map of the island which provides an excellent perspective for anyone venturing into the interior.

Another point of particular interest, located about two miles inland in Avalon Canyon, is the **Wrigley Memorial and Botanical Garden** (1400 Avalon Canyon Road; 310-510-2288; admission), a tribute to William Wrigley, Jr. The monument, an imposing 130-foot structure fashioned with glazed tiles and Georgia marble, features a spiral staircase in a solitary tower. The gardens, a showplace for native island plants, display an array of succulents and cactus.

The most exhilarating sightseeing excursion in Avalon lies in the hills around town. Head out Pebbly Beach Road along the water, turn right on Wrigley Terrace Road, and you'll be on one of the many terraces that rise above Avalon. The old Wrigley Mansion (currently the Inn on Mt. Ada, Wrigley Road), an elegant estate with sweeping views, was once the (ho hum) summer residence of the Wrigley family. Other scenic drives on the opposite side of town lie along Stage and Chimes Tower roads. Here you'll pass the **Zane Grey home** (199 Chimes Tower Road; 310-510-0966). The Western novel writer's pueblo adobe is also now a hotel.

Both routes snake into the hills past rocky outcroppings and patches of cactus. The slopes are steep and unrelenting. Below you blocks of houses run in rows out to a fringe of palm trees and undergrowth. Gaze around from this precarious perch and you'll see that Avalon rests in a green bowl surrounded by mountains.

When it comes time to venture further afield, you'll find that traveling around Santa Catalina Island is more complicated than it first seems. You can hike or bicycle to most places on the island. **Brown's Bikes** (107 Pebbly Beach Road; 310-510-0986) rents bicycles, tandems, and mountain bikes. In Avalon proper it's possible to rent golf carts from outfits like **Cartopia Cars** (615 Crescent Avenue; 310-510-2493) or **Catalina Auto Rental** (301 Crescent Avenue; 310-510-0111). There are also taxis in town.

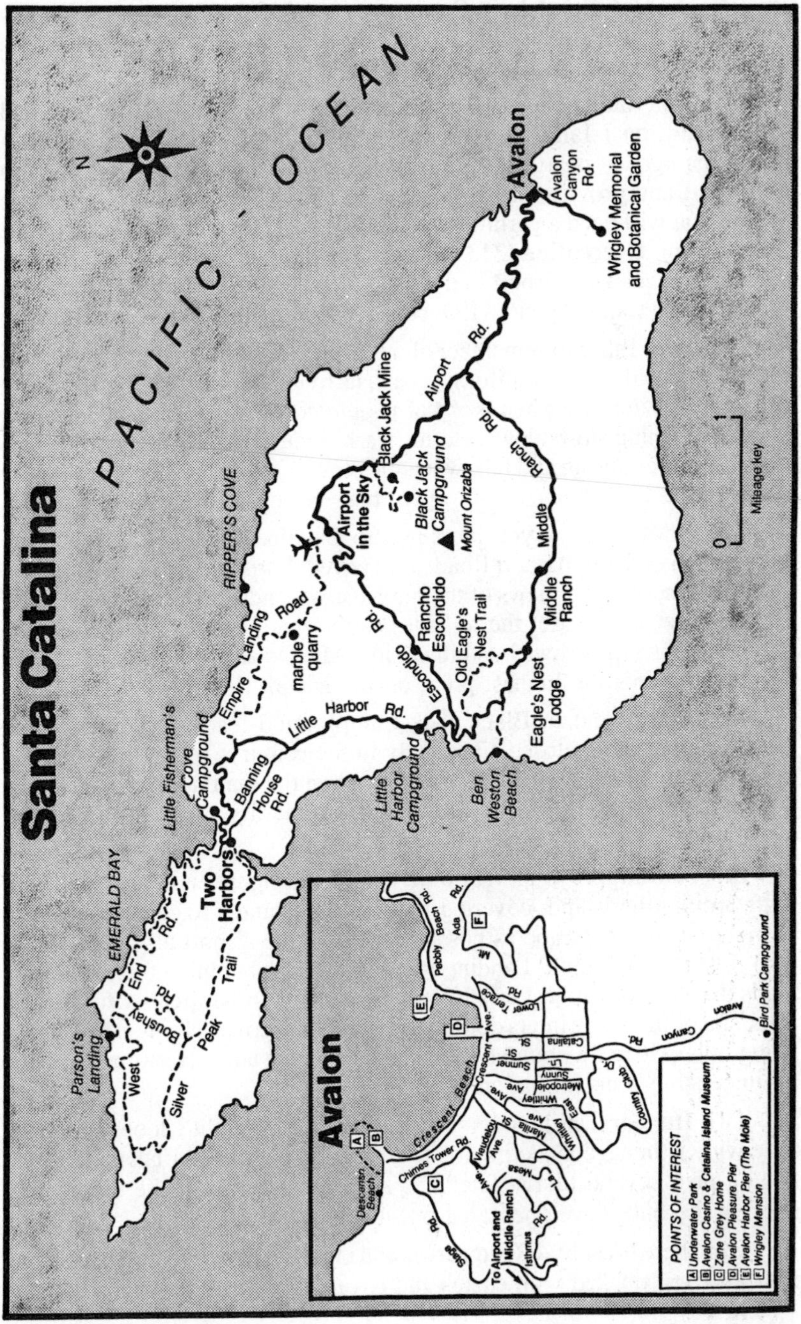
Santa Catalina
PACIFIC OCEAN
N
Parson's Landing
EMERALD BAY
West End Rd.
Boushay Rd.
Silver Peak Trail
Two Harbors
Little Fisherman's Cove Campground
Banning House Rd.
Empire Landing Road
marble quarry
RIPPER'S COVE
Little Harbor Rd.
Little Harbor Campground
Ben Weston Beach
Escondido Rd.
Rancho Escondido
Old Eagle's Nest Trail
Eagle's Nest Lodge
Middle Ranch
Middle Ranch Rd.
Airport in the Sky
Black Jack Campground
Mount Orizaba
Black Jack Mine
Airport Rd.
Avalon
Avalon Canyon Rd.
Wrigley Memorial and Botanical Garden
0
1
Mileage key
Avalon
Descanso Beach
Crescent Beach
Chimes Tower Rd.
Crescent Ave.
Pebbly Beach Rd.
Ada
Mt.
Lower Terrace Rd.
Catalina St.
Sumner St.
Sunny Ln.
Metropole Ave.
Whitley Ave.
East Whitley Ave.
Marilla St.
Vieudelou Ave.
La Mesa
Country Club Dr.
Avalon Canyon Rd.
Bird Park Campground
Stage Rd.
Isthmus Rd.
To Airport and Middle Ranch
POINTS OF INTEREST
A Underwater Park
B Avalon Casino & Catalina Island Museum
C Zane Grey Home
D Avalon Pleasure Pier
E Avalon Harbor Pier (The Mole)
F Wrigley Mansion

No rental cars operate on the island and visitors are not permitted to drive. **Santa Catalina Island Company** (310-510-2000), which has a visitor information center at 420 Crescent Avenue, conducts tours around the island. They offer coastal cruises and inland motor tours.

Catalina Safari Bus (310-510-2800) provides tours and drop-offs and **Santa Catalina Island Conservancy** (206 Metropole Avenue; 310-510-1421), the agency charged with overseeing the island, shuttles visitors to the airport and provides drop-off services. To hike independently outside Avalon you will need a permit from the **Los Angeles County Department of Parks and Recreation** (213 Catalina Street; 310-510-0688). Permits are also available at The Airport in the Sky (310-510-0143) and from the Catalina Cove and Camp Agency (P.O. Box 5044, Two Harbors; 310-510-0303).

The other thing to remember about Catalina is that perhaps more than any other spot along the California coast, its tourism is seasonal. The season, of course, is summer, when mobs of people descend on the island. During winter everything slows down, storms wash through intermittently, and some facilities close. Spring and fall, when the crowds have subsided, the weather is good, and everything is still open, may be the best seasons of all.

Regardless of how you journey into Catalina's outback, there's only one way to get there, Airport Road. This paved thoroughfare climbs steadily from Avalon, offering views of the rugged coast and surrounding hills. Oak, pine, and eucalyptus dot the hillsides as the road follows a ridgetop with steep canyons falling away on either side. **Mt. Orizaba**, a flat-topped peak which represents the highest point on the island, rises in the distance.

A side road out to Black Jack Campground leads past **Black Jack Mine**, a silver mine closed since early in the century. Today little remains except tailing piles and a 520-foot shaft. Then the main road climbs to Catalina's **Airport in the Sky**, a small landing facility located at 1600-foot elevation.

From the airport you might want to follow a figure eight course in your route around the island, covering most of the island's roads and taking in as much of the landscape as possible (beyond the airport all the roads are dirt). Just follow Empire Landing Road, a curving, bumping track with side roads that lead down past an **old marble quarry** to **Ripper's Cove**. Characteristic of the many inlets dotting the island, the cove is framed by sharply rising hills. There's a boulder-and-sand beach here and a coastline bordered by interesting rock formations.

Two Harbors, at the intersection of the figure-eight's loops, is a half-mile wide isthmus connecting the two sections of Catalina Island. A small fishing pier, several tourist facilities, and a boat harbor make this modest enclave the only developed area outside Avalon.

From here West End Road curves and climbs, bends and descends along a rocky coast pocked with cactus and covered by scrub growth. There are

Catalina cherry trees along the route and numerous coves at the bottom of steep cliffs. Not for the faint-hearted, West End Road is a narrow, bumpy course that winds high above the shore.

Anchored off **Emerald Bay** are several rock islets crowded with sea birds. From **Parson's Landing,** a small inlet with a gray sand beach, dirt roads continue in a long loop out to the west end of the island, then back to Two Harbors.

Catalina possesses about 400 species of flora, some unique to the island, and is rich in wildlife. Anywhere along its slopes you are likely to spy quail, wild turkey, mountain goats, island fox, mule deer, and wild boar. Bison, placed on the island by a movie company filming a Western way back in the 1920s, graze seemingly everywhere. En route back toward Avalon, Little Harbor Road climbs into the mountains. From the hilltops around **Little Harbor** you can see a series of ridges which drop along sheer rockfaces to the frothing surf below.

Take a detour up to **Rancho Escondido**, a working ranch that breeds champion Arabian horses. There's an arena here where trainers work these exquisite animals through their paces, and a "saddle and trophy room" filled with handcrafted riding gear as well as prizes from major horse shows.

Back at Little Harbor, Middle Ranch Road cuts through a mountain canyon past **Middle Ranch**, a small spread with livestock and oat fields. En route lies **Eagles' Nest Lodge**, a stagecoach stop dating to 1890. Numbered among the antique effects of this simple woodframe house are wagon wheels and a split-rail fence. Carry on to Airport Road then back to Avalon, completing this easy-eight route around an extraordinary island.

Shopping

LONG BEACH AND SAN PEDRO SHOPPING

The best street shopping in Long Beach is near the Naples neighborhood along **East 2nd Street**. This 15-block strip between Livingston Drive and Bayshore Avenue is a gentrified row. Either side is lined with art galleries, book shops, boutiques, jewelers, and import stores.

Shoreline Village (407 Shoreline Village Drive, Long Beach; 310-590-8427) is one of those waterfront malls Southern California specializes in. With a marina on one side, the buildings are New England-style shingle and clapboard structures designed to re-create an Atlantic Coast port town. My favorite spot here is not a shop at all but the carousel, a vintage turn-of-the-century beauty awhirl with colorful animals.

There are more than a dozen stores onboard the **Queen Mary** (Pier J, Long Beach; 310-435-3511). There is a fee charged to board the ship. Concentrated in the Piccadilly Circus section of the old ship are several souvenir shops as well as stores specializing in articles and artifacts from Great

Britain. Perhaps the prettiest shopping arcade you'll ever enter, it is an art deco masterpiece with etched glass, dentil molding, and brass appointments.

Adjacent to the *Queen Mary* and *Spruce Goose*, **Londontowne Village** is a shopping plaza styled after a 19th-century British village and offering a variety of specialty and souvenir shops.

Los Angeles Harbor's answer to the theme shopping mall craze is **Ports O' Call Village** (entrance at the foot of 6th Street, San Pedro; 310-831-0287), a mock 19th-century fishing village. There are clapboard stores with shuttered windows, New England-style structures with gabled roofs, and storehouses of corrugated metal. Dozens of shops here are located right on the water, giving you a chance to view the harbor while browsing the stores. It's one of those hokey but inevitable places that I swear to avoid but always seem to end up visiting.

SOUTH BAY SHOPPING

If they weren't famous Pacific beach communities, the South Bay enclaves of Redondo, Hermosa, and Manhattan beaches would seem like small-town America. Their central shopping districts are filled with pharmacies, supply shops, and shoe stores.

There are a few places of interest to folks from out of town. In Redondo Beach, scout out Catalina Avenue, particularly along its southern stretches. Shops in Hermosa Beach concentrate along Pier and Hermosa avenues, especially where they intersect. Likewise in Manhattan Beach, Manhattan Beach Boulevard is traversed by Highland and Manhattan avenues.

Be sure to stop in at the **Either/Or Bookstore** (124 Pier Avenue, Hermosa Beach; 310-374-2060). Situated on a hillside above the ocean, it's a multilevel affair built in a series of terraces. With an outstanding inventory of books and magazines, the store is also endowed with an intriguing history. It seems that years ago Thomas Pynchon—the brilliant, reclusive, rarely photographed author of *V* and *Gravity's Rainbow*—stopped in regularly to buy books and talk contemporary literature.

VENICE SHOPPING

To combine slumming with shopping, be sure to wander the **boardwalk** in Venice. Ocean Front Walk between Windward and Ozone avenues is lined with low-rent stalls selling beach hats, cheap jewelry, sunglasses, beach bags, and souvenirs. You'll also encounter **Small World Books and the Mystery Annex** (1407 Ocean Front Walk, Venice; 310-399-2360), a marvelous beachside shop with books and magazines.

L.A. Louver (55 North Venice Boulevard and 77 Market Street; 310-822-4955), with two locations, is one of Venice's many vital and original galleries. It represents David Hockney and other contemporary American

and European artists. There is also a covey of **art galleries** and **antique shops** along the 1200 to 1500 blocks of West Washington Boulevard.

The **Native American Art Gallery** (215 Windward Avenue; 310-392-8465) offers a fascinating collection of pottery, rugs, woven baskets, turquoise jewelry, and Kachina dolls.

The **Beyond Baroque Literary Arts Center** (681 Venice Boulevard; 310-822-3006), a clearinghouse for local talent, sponsors poetry readings, dramatic revues, lectures, and concerts. It's located in the old Venice City Hall. Next door, in the town's erstwhile jail, the **Social and Public Art Resource Center** (685 Venice Boulevard; 310-822-9560), or **SPARC**, has a store offering Latin American and Southwestern folk art.

SANTA MONICA SHOPPING

Montana Avenue is Santa Monica's version of designer heaven, making it an interesting, if inflationary, strip to shop. From 7th to 17th Street chic shops and upscale establishments line either side of the thoroughfare.

There's **Weathervane For Men** (1132 Montana Avenue; 310-395-0397) when shopping for men's clothing.

Sara (1324 Montana Avenue; 310-394-2900) up the street is like a miniature department store with fashions, jewelry, art pieces, and distinctive gifts. At **Sara for Kids** (800 14th Street; 310-451-1494) there is everything from toys to batik dresses to Panama hats. The **Quilt Gallery** (1611 Montana Avenue; 310-393-1148) has folk art, handwoven quilts, and other items of Americana.

The **Brenda Cain Store** (1617 Montana Avenue; 310-393-3298) features vintage duds for ladies and gentlemen alike. Among the array of styles is a collection of Hawaiian aloha shirts.

At **Federico** (1522 Main Street; 310-458-4134) the merchandise ranges from textiles to jewelry to antiques in a variety of Native American and Mexican styles.

Browse Main Street and you'll realize that Montana Avenue is only a practice round in the gentrification of Santa Monica. Block after block of this thoroughfare has been made over in trendy fashion and filled with stylish shops. Main Street was even the focus of a civic campaign which highlighted its upscale amenities.

On the 2400 block of Main Street, the Frank Geary-designed Edgemar Building houses the **Santa Monica Museum of Art** (2437 Main Street; 310-399-0433) and the **Gallery of Functional Art** (2429 Main Street; 310-576-0883), specializing in non-traditional sculptured furniture.

The shopper's parade stretches most of the length of Main Street, but the center of action resides around the 2700 block. **Galleria Di Maio** (2525 Main Street) is an art deco mall with several spiffy shops. The **Gallery of**

Eskimo Art (2665 Main Street; 310-392-8741), set in a beautifully refurbished brick building, has wonderful examples of Alaskan carving.

The **B-1 Gallery** (2730 Main Street; 310-392-9625) displays strikingly original paintings by contemporary California artists; and **Keely's Kites** (2900 Main Street; 310-396-5483) flies colorful kites and wind socks.

Venture out Wilshire Boulevard and you'll uncover several specialty locations. **I. M. Chait Gallery** (2409 Wilshire Boulevard; 310-828-8537) features a very exclusive selection of Oriental artworks. Next door at **Wounded Knee** (2413 Wilshire Boulevard; 310-394-0159) there is an assortment of Native American crafts including sand paintings, jewelry, Kachina dolls, and Southwestern pottery.

Tortue Gallery (2917 Santa Monica Boulevard; 310-828-8878) could be better described as a museum of contemporary California art than a shop selling art. The canvases hanging here are brilliant and the gallery provides a singular insight into the local art scene.

The last of Santa Monica's several shopping enclaves is in the center of town. Here you'll find **Santa Monica Place** (Broadway between 2nd and 4th streets; 310-394-5451), a mammoth triple-tiered complex with about 160 shops. This flashy atrium mall has everything from clothes to books to sporting goods to luggage to leather work, jewelry, toys, hats, and shoes.

Step out from this glittery gathering place and you'll immediately encounter the **Third Street Promenade** (between Broadway and Wilshire Boulevard), a three-block walkway lined on either side with shops, upscale cafés, and movie theaters. There is one shop in particular that exemplifies Santa Monica's liberal politics. **Midnight Special Bookstore** (1318 3rd Street Promenade; 310-393-2923) specializes in politics and social sciences. Rather than current best sellers, the window displays will feature books on Latin America, world hunger, Africa, or disarmament.

Close to museum status is the array of crystals, shells, and fossils at **Nature's Own** (1334 3rd Street Promenade; 310-576-0883).

Muskrat Clothing (1434 3rd Street Promenade; 310-394-1713) specializes in vintage items like aloha shirts, bowling shirts, velour jackets, and silk coats with maps of Japan embroidered on the backs. (Thought you'd never find one, eh?)

Also consider **Na Na** (1228–30 3rd Street Promenade; 310-394-9690) where the future is happening in the form of alternative accouterments like skull-and-crossbone earrings and leather biker hats.

For the outward bound, **California Map & Travel Center** (3211 Pico Boulevard; 310-829-6277) has it all—maps, directories, and guidebooks. Or, if you're planning a little armchair traveling at home, there are globes and travelogues.

MALIBU SHOPPING

Somehow the name **Malibu Country Mart** (3835 Cross Creek Road; 310-456-2047) doesn't quite describe this plaza shopping mall. There's not much of the "country" about the pricey boutiques and galleries here. The parking lot numbers more Porsches than pickup trucks. But these two dozen stores will provide a sense of the Malibu lifestyle and give you a chance to shop (or window shop) for quality.

Zuma Canyon Orchids (5949 Bonsall Drive; 310-457-9771) offers elegant and exquisite prize-winning orchids that can be shipped anywhere in the world. If you call for a reservation, they will even provide a tour of the greenhouses.

Up in the secluded reaches of Topanga Canyon there are numerous artists and craftspeople who have traded the chaos of the city for the serenity of the Santa Monica Mountains. Craft shops come and go with frustrating regularity here, but it's worth a drive into the hills to see who is currently selling their wares.

SANTA CATALINA ISLAND SHOPPING

No one sails to Santa Catalina Island searching for bargains. Everything here has been shipped from the mainland and is that much more expensive as a result. The town of Avalon has a row of shops lining its main thoroughfare, Crescent Avenue, and other stores along the streets running up from the waterfront. Within this commercial checkerboard are also several minimalls, one of which, **Metropole Market Place** (Crescent and Sumner avenues), is a nicely designed, modern complex. Half the stores in town are either souvenir or curio shops. I'd wait until you return to that shopping metropolis 26 miles across the sea.

Nightlife

LONG BEACH AND SAN PEDRO NIGHTLIFE

Panama Joe's (5100 East 2nd Street, Long Beach; 310-434-7417) cooks seven nights a week. The bands are jazz ensembles, rock groups, and assorted others, which create an eclectic blend of music. Your average Tiffany-lamp-and-hanging-plant nightspot, the place is lined with sports photos and proudly displays an old oak bar.

Over at **The Reef** (880 Harbor Scenic Drive, Long Beach; 310-435-8013), a sprawling waterfront establishment, there's live jazz every weekend.

No matter how grand, regardless of how much money went into its design, despite the care taken to assure quality, any Long Beach nightspot is hard pressed to match the elegance of the **Observation Bar** aboard the *Queen Mary* (Pier J, Long Beach; 310-435-3511). Once the first-class bar for this grand old ship, the room commands a 180° view across the bow and out to the Long Beach skyline. The walls are lined with fine woods, a mural decorates the bar, and art deco appointments appear everywhere. Besides that, they feature live jazz and '30s and '40s music nightly. For softer sounds you can always adjourn aft to **Sir Winston's Piano Bar,** a cozy and elegant setting decorated with memorabilia of the World War II British leader.

Long Beach's gay community frequents the piano bar at the **Birds of Paradise Café** (1800 East Broadway, Long Beach; 310-590-8773).

Another gathering place is **Ripples** (5101 East Ocean Boulevard; 310-433-0357), which has a male dance club upstairs and a karaoke stage downstairs. There's also a game room, pool table, and patio. Cover on weekends.

Mineshaft (1720 East Broadway; 310-436-2433)is a levis-and-leather cruise bar with pool tables, pinball machines, and deejay music.

Le Chat (1435 East Broadway; 310-432-4146) is a women's bar complete with pool table and CD player.

Buccaneer/Mardi Gras Cruises (Ports O' Call Village, San Pedro; 310-548-1085) hosts sunset dinner cruises around Los Angeles Harbor. These feature dining and dancing. Cover.

Landlubbers can enjoy a quiet drink on the waterfront at **Ports O' Call Restaurant** (Ports O' Call Village, San Pedro; 310-833-3553). In addition to a spiffy oak bar, they have a dockside patio. Better yet, **Hornblower Yachts** (Catalina Landing, Long Beach; 310-519-9400) runs dinner cruises with live music and dancing aboard a turn-of-the-century steamboat.

SOUTH BAY NIGHTLIFE

The Comedy & Magic Club (1018 Hermosa Avenue, Hermosa Beach; 310-372-1193) features name acts nightly. Many of the comedians are television personalities with a regional, if not national, following. The supper club atmosphere is upscale and appealing. Cover.

The Lighthouse Café (30 Pier Avenue, Hermosa Beach; 310-372-6911) spotlights blues, reggae, rock-and-roll, and '60s-style surfing groups.

Orville & Wilbur's Restaurant (401 Rosecrans Boulevard, Manhattan Beach; 310-545-6639) is a lush, wood-paneled establishment with an upstairs bar that looks out over the ocean. The music, usually Top-40 or vintage rock, is live every night.

For dance music to a rock-and-roll band consider **Reactor** (3600 Highland Avenue, Manhattan Beach; 310-545-4444).

VENICE, SANTA MONICA, AND MALIBU NIGHTLIFE

The Townhouse (52 Windward Avenue, Venice; 310-392-4040), set in a '20s-era speakeasy, has live music as well as deejays spinning Top-40 platters. Cover.

Merlin McFly's (2702 Main Street, Santa Monica; 310-392-8468) is a must. Magic is the password here: every evening magicians wander from table to table performing sleight-of-hand tricks. Even more unique is the wildly baroque interior. There's an elaborate carved wood bar guarded on either end by menacing griffins and highlighted by a stained-glass image of the great Merlin himself. Even the bar stools are decorated with molded figures while the walls are adorned with old show biz posters.

At My Place (1026 Wilshire Boulevard, Santa Monica; 310-451-8596), a spacious dinner club with live acts nightly, offers an eclectic blend of jazz, rhythm-and-blues, pop music, and comedy; cover. Reservations required.

Ye Olde King's Head (116 Santa Monica Boulevard, Santa Monica; 310-451-1402) might be the most popular British pub this side of the Thames. From dart boards to dark wood walls, trophy heads to draft beer, it's a classic English watering hole. Known throughout the area, it draws crowds of local folks and expatriate Britishers.

McCabe's Guitar Shop (3101 Pico Boulevard, Santa Monica; 310-828-4497) is a folksy spot with live entertainment on weekends. The sounds are almost all acoustic and range from Scottish folk bands to jazz to blues to country. The concert hall is a room in back lined with guitars. Get down. Cover.

For a raucous good time try **The Oar House** and **Buffalo Chips** (2941 Main Street, Santa Monica; 310-396-4725). These adjoining bars are loud, brash places that draw hearty crowds. The music is recorded and the decor is Early Insanity—sawdust floors, mannequins and wagon wheels on the ceiling, alligator skins on the wall.

For blues, try **Harvelle's** (1432 4th Street, Santa Monica; 310-395-1676); if it's reggae you're after then **Kingston 12** (814 Broadway, Santa Monica; 310-451-4423) is the spot. Cover at both clubs.

Tranca's (30765 Pacific Coast Highway; 310-457-5516), Malibu's lone nightclub, features live music Wednesday to Saturday. Cover.

SANTA CATALINA ISLAND NIGHTLIFE

Like all other Catalina amenities, nightspots are concentrated in Avalon. During summer months the **Santa Catalina Island Company** (420 Crescent Avenue; 310-510-2000) conducts buffet cruises along the coastline in an old paddlewheeler. There are splendid sunsets, pretty views of the shore, music, and dancing.

The **Chi Chi Club** (107 Sumner Avenue; 310-510-2828) is one of the hottest dance clubs on the island with deejay music and a lively crowd.

There's also dancing to deejay records at **Solomon's Landing** (101 Marilla Avenue; 310-510-1474). The bar here is outdoors and the motif decidedly Mexican. Check the schedule for **Avalon Casino** (end of Crescent Avenue; 310-510-2000). This fabulous vintage ballroom still hosts big bands and most of the island's major events.

ORANGE COUNTY

CHAPTER FOUR

Orange County

Places are known through their nicknames. More than official titles or proper names, sobriquets reveal the real identity of a region. "Orange Coast" can never describe the 42 miles of cobalt blue ocean and whitewashed sand from Seal Beach to San Clemente. That moniker derives from the days when Orange County was row on row with orchards of plump citrus. Today prestigious homes and marinas sprout from the shoreline. This is the "Gold Coast," habitat of beachboys, yachtsmen, and tennis buffs, the "American Riviera."

The theme which ties the territory together, and gives rise to these nicknames, is money. Money and the trappings that attend it—glamor, celebrity, elegance, power. Orange County is a sun-blessed realm of beautiful people, where politics is right wing and real estate sells by the square foot.

Some half-dozen freeways crisscross the broad coastal plane where Spain's Gaspar de Portolá led the first overland expedition into present-day Orange County in 1769. Today, more than two million people live, work, and play where during the mid-19th century a few hundred Mexican ranchers tended herds of livestock on a handful of extensive land grants.

Ever since Walt Disney founded his fantasy empire here in the 1950s, Orange County has exploded with population and profits. In Disney's wake came the crowds, and as they arrived they developed—housing projects and condominium complexes, mini-malls and business centers. To the interior, towns now look alike and Orange County, once an empire of orange groves, has become a cookie-cutter civilization. Only in the distant mountain areas to the south and east does any wilderness remain. Here the granite escarpments, oak-studded valleys, and chaparral-covered hillsides of the Santa Ana Mountains continue to hold out against the encroachment of suburban blight.

Along the coast progress also levied a tremendous toll but has left intact some of the natural beauty, the deep canyons and curving hills, soft sand beaches and sharp escarpments. The towns too have retained their separate styles, each projecting its own identifying image.

Seal Beach, Orange County's answer to small-town America, is a pretty community with a sense of serenity. To the south lies Huntington Beach, a place that claims the nickname "Surfing Capital of the World." The social capital of this beachside society is Newport Beach, a fashion conscious center for celebrities, business mavens, and those to whom God granted little patience and a lot of money.

Corona del Mar is a model community with quiet streets and a placid waterfront. Laguna Beach is an artist colony so *in* that real estate prices have driven the artists *out.* Dana Point represents a marina development in search of a soul. San Juan Capistrano, a small town surrounding an old mission, is closer to its roots than any place in this futuristic area. San Clemente, which served as President Nixon's Western White House, is a trim, strait-laced residential community. Linking this string of beach towns together is Route 1, the Pacific Coast Highway, which runs south from Los Angeles to Capistrano Beach.

The geography throughout Orange County is varied and unpredictable. Around Newport Beach and Huntington Beach, rugged heights give way to low-lying terrain cut by rivers and opening into estuaries. These northerly towns, together with Dana Point, are manmade harbors carved from swamps and surrounded by landfill islands and peninsulas. Huntington Harbor, the first of its kind, consists of eight islands weighted down with luxury homes and bordered by a mazework of marinas. To the south, particularly around Laguna Beach, a series of uplifted marine terraces create bold headlands, coastal bluffs, and pocket coves.

Land here is so highly prized that it's not surprising the city fathers chose to create more by dredging it from river bottoms. The Gabrieleño and Juañero Indians who originally inhabited the area considered the ground sacred, while the Spanish who conquered them divided it into two immense land grants, the San Joaquin and Niguel ranchos.

Establishing themselves at the San Juan Capistrano mission in 1776, the Spanish padres held sway until the 19th century. By the 1830s American merchants from the East Coast were sending tall-masted trading ships up from Cape Horn. Richard Henry Dana, who sailed the shoreline, giving his name to Dana Point, described the area in *Two Years Before the Mast* as "the most romantic spot along the coast."

Orange County's first real spurt of growth came in the late 1850s when European immigrants, inspired by the agricultural successes of Franciscan missionaries, left the worked-out gold fields of the north to try their luck farming the fertile soil of the Santa Ana River Valley. German immigrants formed a successful winegrowing colony at Anaheim in 1857 and soon began planting the citrus trees which would eventually give the county its name.

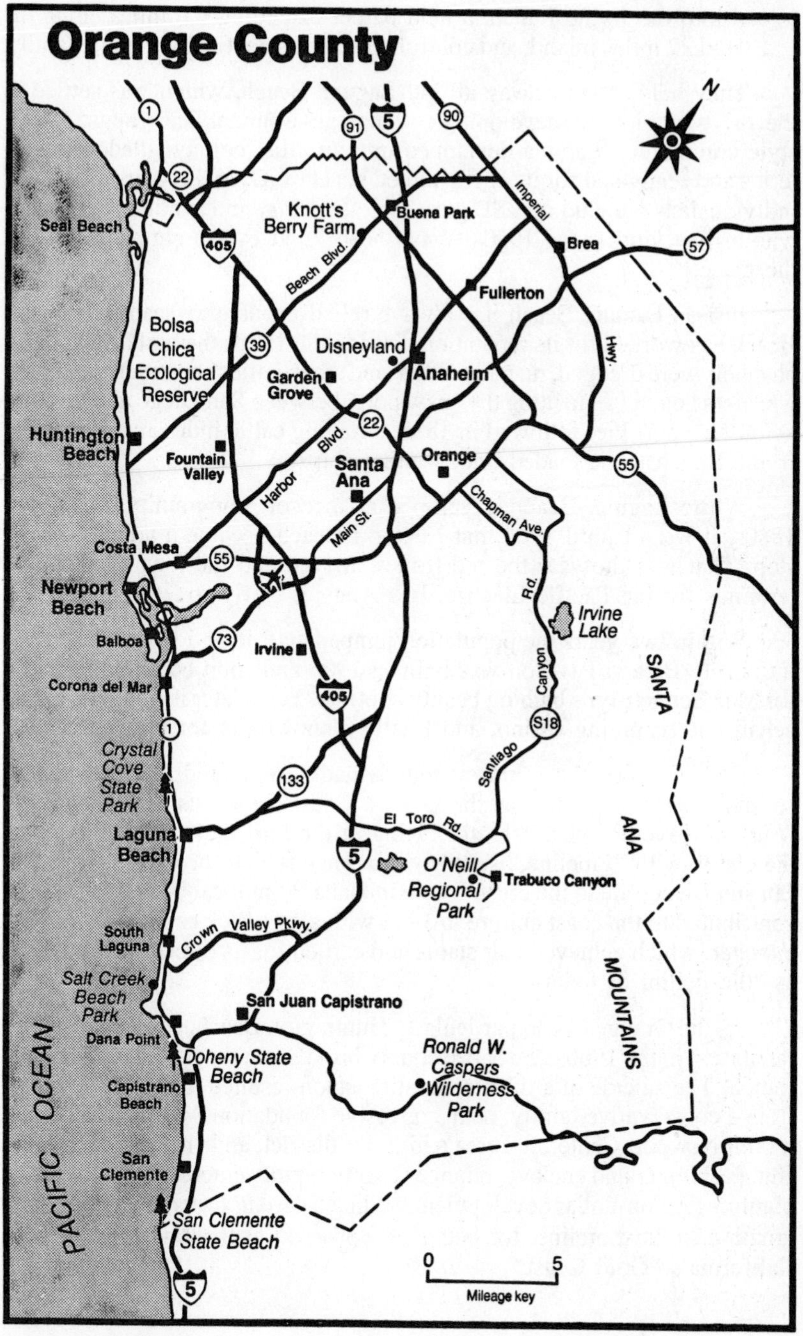
Orange County
Seal Beach
Knott's Berry Farm
Buena Park
Brea
Fullerton
Imperial
Hwy.
Beach Blvd.
Bolsa Chica Ecological Reserve
Disneyland
Anaheim
Garden Grove
Huntington Beach
Fountain Valley
Harbor Blvd.
Santa Ana
Orange
Chapman Ave.
Main St.
Costa Mesa
Newport Beach
Balboa
Irvine
Irvine Lake
Corona del Mar
Canyon Rd.
Santiago
Crystal Cove State Park
Laguna Beach
El Toro Rd.
O'Neill Regional Park
Trabuco Canyon
SANTA ANA MOUNTAINS
South Laguna
Crown Valley Pkwy.
Salt Creek Beach Park
San Juan Capistrano
Dana Point
Doheny State Beach
Ronald W. Caspers Wilderness Park
Capistrano Beach
San Clemente
San Clemente State Beach
PACIFIC OCEAN
N
0
5
Mileage key
1
22
405
39
91
5
90
57
55
73
133
S18

By the 1860s, after California became a state, the Spanish ranchos were joined into the Irvine Ranch, a land parcel extending ten miles along the coast and 22 miles inland, and controlled with a steel fist by a single family.

They held in their sway all but Laguna Beach, which was settled in the 1870s by pioneers developing 160-acre government land grants. A free-style community, Laguna developed into an artist colony filled with galleries and renowned for its cliff-rimmed beaches. Over the years artists and individualists—including LSD guru Timothy Leary and a retinue of hippies, who arrived during the 1960s—have been lured by the simple beauty of the place.

Just as Laguna Beach has always relied on natural beauty, Newport Beach has worked for its reputation. During the 1870s the harbor was built; channels were dredged, marshes filled, and stone jetties constructed as sternwheelers began frequenting the "new port" between San Diego and Los Angeles. Newport Pier followed in 1888, allowing cattle hides and grain from Irvine Ranch to be loaded onto waiting ships.

While Laguna Beach developed as a resort community during the 1880s, it wasn't until 1904 that Newport Beach became a noted pleasure stop. That was the year the red trolley arrived and the town became the terminus for the Pacific Electric, Los Angeles' early streetcar line.

Within two years the population jumped sixfold and land values went into orbit. Balboa Pavilion was built in 1905 and soon became the center for Max Sennett-type bathing beauty contests. Years later it would be a dancehall and gambling casino, and finally a showroom for the Big Bands.

By the 1960s those brassy sounds had surrendered to the twanging strains of electric guitars as the Orange Coast earned its final nickname, "Surfer Heaven." Dick Dale, the "King of the Surf Guitar," hit the top of the charts with "Pipeline," setting off a wave which the Beach Boys and Jan and Dean rode to the crest. Down in Dana Point local boy Bruce Brown contributed to the coast culture in 1964 with a surf flick called *The Endless Summer*, which achieved cult status and earned for its director a reputation as "the Fellini of foam."

As the Orange Coast, particularly Huntington Beach, earned its surfing reputation in the 1960s, the entire county broke from the power of the Irvine Ranch. The suicide of a third-generation scion resulted in the land passing from a conservative family to an aggressive foundation. Within a few years it built Newport Center, the area's highrise district, and crowned it with the chic Fashion Island enclave. Orange County rapidly entered the modern age of multi-million-dollar development, adding a certain luster to its image and granting to its shoreline, for better or worse, an everlasting reputation as California's "Gold Coast."

Easy Living

Transportation

ARRIVAL

Several major highways crisscross Orange County. **Route 1**, known in this area as the Pacific Coast Highway, ends its long journey down the California Coast in Capistrano Beach. A few miles further inland, **Route 405** runs from Long Beach to Irvine, with feeder roads leading to the main coastal towns. Connecting Los Angeles and San Diego, **Route 5** follows an inland course through the heart of Orange County passing Anaheim and Santa Ana, then heads south to Dana Point and San Clemente.

BY AIR

John Wayne International Airport, located in Irvine, is the main terminal in these parts. Major carriers presently serving it include Alaska Airlines, American Airlines, America West, Continental Airlines, Delta Airlines, Northwest Airlines, States West, Trans World Airlines, United Airlines, and USAir.

BY BUS

Greyhound/Trailways Bus Lines serves Orange County, stopping in Anaheim, Santa Ana, Seal Beach, Huntington Beach, Newport Beach, Corona del Mar, Dana Point, Laguna Beach, and San Clemente. Most stops are flag stops; depots are located in Anaheim (2080 South Harbor Boulevard; 714-635-5060), Santa Ana (1000 East Santa Ana Boulevard; 714-542-2215), and San Clemente (510 North Avenida de la Estrella; 714-492-1187).

BY TRAIN

Amtrak's (800-872-7245) "San Diegan" travels between Los Angeles and San Diego, with Orange County stops at Fullerton, Anaheim Stadium, Santa Ana, San Juan Capistrano, and San Clemente.

CAR RENTALS

Arriving at John Wayne International Airport, you'll find the following car rental agencies: **Avis Rent A Car** (714-852-8608), **Budget Rent A Car** (714-252-6240), **Dollar Rent A Car** (714-756-6100), **Hertz Rent A Car** (714-756-8161), and **National Car Rental** (714-852-1284). For less expensive (and less convenient) service, try the outfits providing free airport pick-up: **Alamo Rent A Car** (714-852-0403), **Cal American Rent A Car** (714-756-8313), **Enterprise Rent A Car** (714-851-7701), and **Thrifty Car Rental** (714-549-9151).

PUBLIC TRANSPORTATION

Orange County Transit District (714-636-7433), or OCTD, has bus service throughout Orange County, including most inland areas. Along the coast it stops at beach fronts including Seal Beach, Huntington Beach, Newport Beach, Corona del Mar, Laguna Beach, San Juan Capistrano, and San Clemente.

In addition, **Southern California Rapid Transit District** (213-626-4455), or RTD, serves some areas of Orange County including Fullerton, Disneyland, and Knott's Berry Farm.

Hotels

NORTH ORANGE COUNTY HOTELS

It's only fitting that Seal Beach, Orange County's answer to a small town, houses the area's most appealing bed and breakfast. With its wrought-iron balcony, ornate fence, and garden ambience, the **Seal Beach Inn and Gardens** (212 5th Street; 213-493-2416) has garnered a reputation for style and seclusion. Its 23 rooms, pricing from deluxe to ultra-deluxe, are furnished in hardwood antiques and appointed with period wallhangings. Guests breakfast in a cozy "tea room," then adjourn to the parlor with its upholstered armchairs and tile fireplace. The guest rooms are named for flowers, many of which grow on the grounds. Indeed the landscaping, which includes wrought-iron lawn furniture and early 20th-century lampposts, may be the most appealing feature of this fine old inn.

The **Colonial Inn Youth Hostel** (421 8th Street, Huntington Beach; 714-536-3315) is a cavernous three-story house located four blocks from the beach. Capable of accommodating couples and families as well as individual travelers, its many rooms each contain two to eight beds. The house is in a residential neighborhood and offers a kitchen, dining room, television room, and yard. Chores are required and the hostel is closed during the day; budget.

Sunset Bed and Breakfast (16401 Coast Highway; 213-592-1666) is a tiny six-room hostelry right on the highway in Huntington Beach. Decorated in bed and breakfast fashion, it has individual rooms as well as accommodations with bedroom-sitting room combinations. Features like overhead fans, oak armoires, and handwrought headboards add to the ambience. Budget to moderate.

NEWPORT BEACH HOTELS

You'd have a hell of a time docking your boat at the **Sail Inn Motel** (2627 Newport Boulevard; 714-675-1841). Actually it's on an island, but the island is a median strip dividing the two busiest streets on the Balboa Peninsula. Offering standard motel accommodations at moderate to deluxe prices, the Sail Inn is a block from the beach and walking distance from many restaurants.

The **Balboa Inn** (105 Main Street; 714-675-3412), next to the beach at Balboa Pier, is a Spanish-style hotel built in 1930. With its cream-colored walls and tile-roofed tower this 34-room hostelry is vintage Southern California. Adding to the ambience is a swimming pool that looks out on the water. The rooms, some of which have ocean views, are furnished in knotty pine, decorated with colorful prints, and adorned with tile baths and brass fixtures. A Mediterranean atmosphere at a deluxe price.

Portofino Beach Hotel (2306 West Ocean Front; 714-673-7030), a 15-room bed and breakfast inn, rests on the beach in an early 20th-century building. Richly appointed with brass beds, armoires, and antique fixtures, the Portofino has a wine bar downstairs and two oceanfront parlors overlooking Newport Pier. Each room is decorated with antiques and equipped with a private bath; many have jacuzzis, skylights, fireplaces, and ocean views. Room rates are deluxe to ultra-deluxe in the off-season, ultra-deluxe during summer months.

The *only* hotel on tiny Balboa Island is the **Balboa Island Hotel** (127 Agate Avenue; 714-675-3613), a family-operated, three-bedroom, bed-and-breakfast affair. Set in a 1925 house, it's about one block from the water (of course on Balboa Island everything is one block from the water). Each room of this bed and breakfast inn has been decorated in period and furnished with antiques. The place has a small, intimate, homey feel. Guests share bathrooms and there are two porches which serve as sitting rooms; moderate.

By way of full-facility destinations, Southern California-style, few places match the **Hyatt Newporter Resort** (1107 Jamboree Road; 714-644-1700). Situated on a hillside above Upper Newport Bay, it sprawls across 26 acres and sports three swimming pools, three jacuzzis, a nine-hole pitch-and-putt course, and a tennis club. There are restaurants and lounges, a lavishly decorated lobby, and a series of terraced patios. Guest rooms are modern in design, comfortably furnished, and tastefully appointed. An inviting combination of elegance and amenities; ultra-deluxe.

LAGUNA BEACH HOTELS

Boasting 70 rooms, a pool, sauna, and sun deck overlooking the sea, the **Inn At Laguna** (211 North Coast Highway; 714-497-9722) offers great ocean views from its blufftop perch. Rooms are small, the construction uneven, and the furnishings modern at this newly renovated property. Room rates jump from the deluxe category in the off-season to ultra-deluxe during the summer months.

Even if you never stay there, you won't miss the **Hotel Laguna** (425 South Coast Highway; 714-494-1151). With its octagonal tower and Spanish motif, this huge whitewashed building dominates downtown Laguna

Beach. The oldest hotel in Laguna, it sits in the center of town, adjacent to Main Beach. In addition to 65 guest rooms there is a restaurant, lounge, and a casual lobby terrace. The place shows signs of age and suffers some of the ills characteristic of large old hotels. But for a place on the water *and* at the center of the action, it cannot be matched. Moderate to deluxe.

The premier resting place in Laguna Beach is a sprawling 161-room establishment overhanging the sand. The **Surf & Sand Hotel** (1555 South Coast Highway; 714-497-4477) is a blocky 1950s-era complex, an architectural mélange of five buildings and a shopping mall. The accent here is on the ocean: nearly every room has a sea view and private balcony, the pool sits just above the sand, and the beach is a short step away. A full-service hotel, the Surf & Sand has two restaurants and an art deco lounge. Guest rooms are understated but attractive with raw-silk furnishings, unfinished woods, and sand-hued walls. Ultra-deluxe.

Casa Laguna Inn (2510 South Coast Highway; 714-494-2996), a hillside hacienda, has a dreamlike quality about it. The cottages and rooms are nestled in a garden setting complete with stone terraces and winding paths. Built in the 1930s, the Spanish-style complex features a courtyard, bell tower, and a swimming pool with an ocean view. The rooms are small, equipped with overhead fans, and furnished in antiques; many offer ocean views, though they also pick up noise from the highway. Continental breakfast and afternoon tea are served in the library. Rooms price deluxe; suites and cottages with kitchens are ultra-deluxe.

It's not just the residential neighborhood that makes **The Carriage House** (1322 Catalina Street; 714-494-8945) unique. The colonial architecture of the "New Orleans style" bed and breakfast inn also sets it apart. Within this historic landmark structure are six suites, renting at deluxe to ultra-deluxe prices, each with a sitting room and separate bedroom. All face a luxurious brick courtyard filled with flowering plants and adorned with a tiered fountain. Certainly the Carriage House is one of the prettiest and most peaceful inns along the entire Orange Coast.

Accommodations with kitchen facilities are hard to come by in Laguna Beach. You'll find them at **Capri Laguna** (1441 South Coast Highway; 714-494-6533), a multilevel motel situated on the beach. This 43-unit resting place provides contemporary motel-style furnishings, plus a pool, sauna, and sun deck with barbecue facilities. Moderate to deluxe.

Hotel San Maartén (696 South Coast Highway; 714-494-1001) is one of those places destined to gain increasing renown. Fashioned in the style of the French Caribbean, it creates a luxurious atmosphere. The lobby is a breezy affair with provincial furnishings and hand-painted ceiling. The 54 guest rooms surround a lushly landscaped courtyard complete with swimming pool and patio restaurant. For a touch of the tropics right here in Laguna Beach, you can't go astray at this deluxe-priced hotel.

SOUTH ORANGE COUNTY HOTELS

Tucked into a secluded canyon is **Aliso Creek Resort** (31106 South Coast Highway, South Laguna; 714-499-2271), an appealing 87-acre resort complete with swimming pools, jacuzzi, restaurant, lounge, and nine-hole golf course. Particularly attractive for families, every unit includes a sitting area, patio, and kitchen. Removed from the highway but within 400 yards of a beach, the resort is surrounded by steep hillsides which are populated by deer and raccoon. Tying this easy rusticity together is a small creek that tumbles through the resort. Studios and one-bedroom suites are moderate to deluxe, two-bedroom complexes are ultra-deluxe.

The **Ritz Carlton Laguna Niguel** (33533 Ritz Carlton Drive, Dana Point; 714-240-2000), set on a cliff above the Pacific, is simply the finest resort hotel along the California coast. Built in the fashion of a Mediterranean villa, it dominates a broad sweep of coastline, a 393-room mansion replete with gourmet restaurants and dark wood lounges. An Old World interior of arched windows and Italian marble is decorated with one of the finest hotel collections of 19th-century American and English art anywhere. The grounds are landscaped with willows, sycamores, and a spectrum of flowering plants. Tile courtyards lead to two swimming pools, a pair of jacuzzis, four tennis courts, and a fitness center. The guest rooms, equal in luxury to the rest of the resort, are priced at the etherial end of the ultra-deluxe range.

Most motels have a stream of traffic whizzing past outside, but the **Dana Marina Inn Motel** (34111 Coast Highway, Dana Point; 714-496-1300), situated on an island where the highway divides, manages to have traffic on both sides! The reason I'm mentioning it is not because I'm sadistic but because rooms in this 29-unit facility are priced on the cusp between budget and moderate. The accommodations are roadside-motel style.

Four Sisters Inns, a bed-and-breakfast "chain" with several properties along the coast, has a 29-room property, **Blue Lantern Inn** (34343 Street of the Blue Lantern; 714-661-1304), situated on an oceanside bluff in Dana Point. A contemporary building designed in classic Cape Cod style, the bed and breakfast combines an ultramodern glass elevator with antique decor. Each room features a fireplace and jacuzzi as well as a four-poster bed, hardwood armoire, and shuttered windows. The sitting rooms are spacious and comfortable and the inn provides a well-done, though self-conscious, re-creation of a classic era.

Algodon Motel (135 Avenida Algodon, San Clemente; 714-492-3382), a standard type 18-unit facility several blocks from the beach, has rooms at budget prices. Accommodations with a kitchen rent in the moderate range. Not much to write home about, but it is clean and trim (and cheap!).

Cheaper still is the **San Clemente Beach Hostel** (233 Avenida Granada, San Clemente; 714-492-2848), an AYH facility located in a stucco building on a residential street. The accommodations consist of bunk beds in dormitory rooms; one family room is also available. Visitors share a television room, kitchen, and small patio. Budget.

INLAND ORANGE COUNTY HOTELS

A bit off the mainstream but still only a few blocks from Knott's Berry Farm is **Fullerton "A" Inn** (2601 West Orangethorpe Avenue, Fullerton; 714-773-4900). This 43-room motel may be the best budget-priced lodging in close proximity to Knott's. Rooms are clean, air-conditioned, and nicely furnished in a contemporary mode. Pool, sauna, whirlpool, and exercise room.

Best of the old-time motels and "tourist courts" that line Beach Boulevard near Knott's Berry Farm is the **Silver Moon Motel** (212 South Beach Boulevard, Anaheim; 714-527-1102). It's been around since 1955; but nostalgia aside, the place is clean, carefully maintained, and offers 44 rooms, some with kitchens. Located one mile from Knott's Berry Farm, five from Disneyland. Budget.

Most of Orange County's 19th-century homes have fallen before the developer's wrecking ball. One thankfully spared is the roomy 1910 Queen Anne now housing **Anaheim Country Inn** (856 South Walnut Street, Anaheim; 714-778-0150). Built by a former mayor, it's a lovely home, surrounded by porches and blessed with a tree-shaded, acre-sized lot. Victorian furnishings prevail and there's a comfortable living room as well as a small retreat upstairs for reading. Eight rooms provide a variety of accommodations. Guests gather in the sunny, country-style dining room for a complete breakfast, graced with the owner's home-baked goodies. Located only minutes from Disneyland. Moderate.

Designed specifically for the needs of visitors bound for Disneyland (just three blocks away), **Days Inn** (1030 West Ball Road, Anaheim; 714-520-0101) offers "family suites" that can accommodate up to five adults, plus complimentary continental breakfast. It has a heated pool and spa as well as a large guest laundry. For honeymooners or other fun-seekers there are several suites with in-room spas and wet bars. Budget to deluxe depending on the season.

Covering 60 acres and containing 1131 rooms, 11 restaurants and lounges, 20 shops, and almost as many gimmicks as the Magic Kingdom itself, **Disneyland Hotel** (1150 West Cerritos Avenue, Anaheim; 714-778-6600) is a self-contained world. Situated anywhere else it would rank as a full-blown destination. You can swim, play tennis, sun on a sandy "beach," feed koi fish, watch a light show, shop, dine, drink, dance—or even sleep here. And if that isn't enough, step out front to the monorail station and three minutes later you are at the real thing! Deluxe to ultra-deluxe.

Two blocks from Disneyland stands the cavernous, 1576-room **Anaheim Hilton** (777 Convention Way, Anaheim; 714-750-4321), a glass-enclosed monolith. The airy atrium lobby, set off by brass railings and blue and mauve tones, holds four restaurants, three lounges, a nightclub, and assorted shops, along with a pond and fountain. The modern guest rooms are individually decorated and priced ultra-deluxe.

Like the little alpine lass who curtsies from her signboard perch above the entrance, the **Heidi Motel** (815 West Katella Avenue, Anaheim; 714-533-1979) is kind of cute. This 30-unit court was here even before Disneyland and occupies an ideal location nearby. The owners collect budget rates for rooms that are small but clean, well maintained, and trimly furnished. There's also a pool.

One of the nicest of the hundreds of hotels and motels encircling the perimeter of Disneyland is **Best Western Park Place Inn** (1544 South Harbor Boulevard, Anaheim; 714-776-4800). Crisp, contemporary styling set it apart from many of its neighbors. Accommodations are fresh and colorful. There's a pool, sauna, and jacuzzi. You can walk to Disneyland, a block away. Budget to moderate.

Raffles Inn (2040 South Harbor Boulevard, Anaheim; 714-750-6100) offers a compromise between the huge highrise hotels and roadside motels in central Orange County. Just three stories high and sensibly sized (122 rooms), it actually conveys a bit of the "inn" feeling. It looks like one, too, with its tree-shrouded manor house facade. Inside it has all the modern amenities: pool with jacuzzi, laundry facilities, and complimentary continental breakfast. Rooms feature Early American furnishings and some contain kitchenettes. Free shuttle to Disneyland; moderate.

Farm de Ville Motel (7800 Crescent Avenue; Buena Park; 714-527-2201) is a rambling 128-room complex located across the street from Knott's Berry Farm. It's clean, well maintained, and has a pair of pools and saunas in addition to efficiency units and suites. A good value at a moderate rate.

For visitors planning to bike Santiago Canyon Road, explore O'Neill Regional Park, or fish the Santa Ana River lakes, the nicest motel is **Sky Palm International Lodge** (210 North Tustin Avenue, Orange; 714-639-6602). It has 27 clean, spacious, moderate-priced rooms, plus a pool with cabaña.

Restaurants

NORTH ORANGE COUNTY RESTAURANTS

Dating back to 1930, the **Glide 'er Inn** (1400 Coast Highway, Seal Beach; 213-431-3022) is an unusual landmark indeed. The motif is aviation, as in model airplanes dangling from the ceiling and aeronautical pictures covering every inch of available wall space. The menu is covered with biplanes and, almost as an afterthought, includes an extensive list of seafood selections as well as European dishes like wienerschnitzel and veal *smetana* (sautéed in light cream and mushrooms). Lunch and dinner; moderate.

For a quick budget meal near the water, try **Maxie's** (317 Pacific Coast Highway, Huntington Beach; 714-536-5127). This easygoing eatery is an all-American establishment serving omelettes in the morning, then hamburgers, hot dogs, sandwiches, and pizza the rest of the day.

In a connected building at the same address, **Maxwell's** (714-536-2555) is a choice spot for a more elaborate oceanside meal. This vintage 1924 building is done entirely in art deco fashion, a motif which nicely fits its beachfront locale. Specialty of the house is seafood; at dinner there are well over a dozen selections varying from fresh Hawaiian fish to halibut, lobster, and Cajun-style shrimp. There are pasta dishes, vegetarian plates, plus steak entrées. Also offering breakfast and lunch, Maxwell's is a choice spot for an oceanfront meal; in the budget to moderate range; reservations recommended; deluxe.

Harbor House Café (16341 Coast Highway, Huntington Beach; 213-592-5404) is one of those hole-in-the-wall places packed with local folks. In this case it's "open 24 hours, 365 days a year" and has been around since 1939. Add knotty-pine walls covered with black-and-whites of your favorite movies stars and you've got a coastal classic. The menu, as you have surmised, includes hamburgers and sandwiches. Actually, it's pretty varied—in addition to croissant and pita bread sandwiches there are Mexican dishes, seafood platters, chicken entrées, and omelettes. Budget to moderate.

NEWPORT BEACH RESTAURANTS

Everything in Newport Beach was built last week. Everything, that is, except **The Cannery** (3010 Lafayette Avenue; 714-675-5777). This 1921 fish cannery is today much as it was way back when. The conveyor belts and pulleys are still here, their gears exposed; and there are fire wagons, a fierce-looking boiler, and more tin cans than you can imagine. All part of a waterfront seafood restaurant that serves lunch, dinner, and weekend brunch at moderate to deluxe prices. Dinner cruises (in summer months) and weekend brunch cruises aboard a 58-foot boat are also offered; deluxe to ultra-deluxe.

Don't worry, you won't miss **The Crab Cooker** (2200 Newport Boulevard; 714-673-0100). First, it's painted bright red; secondly, it's located at a busy intersection near Newport Pier; lastly, the place has been a local institution since the 1950s. Actually, you don't *want* to miss The Crab Cooker. This informal eatery, where lunch and dinner are served on paper plates, has fish, scallops, shrimp, crab, and oysters at a moderate price. There's a fish market attached to the restaurant, so freshness and quality are assured.

21 Ocean Front (2100 West Ocean Front; 714-675-2566) is a gourmet seafood dining place that known for fine cuisine. Located on the beach overlooking Newport Pier, the interior is done (or rather, overdone) in a kind of shiny Victorian style with black trim and brass chandeliers. The secret is to close your eyes and surrender to the senses of taste and smell. At dinner the chef prepares ono, opakapaka, and other Hawaiian fish specials as well as abalone, Maine lobster, bouillabaisse, and halibut. For those who miss the point there is rack of lamb, veal piccata, and filet mignon. Dinner only; ultra-deluxe.

Around **Balboa Pavilion** you'll find snack bars and amusement park food stands.

A place nearby that's worth recommending is **Newport Landing** (503 East Edgewater Avenue; 714-675-2373), a double-decker affair where you can lounge downstairs in a wood-paneled dining room or upstairs on a deck overlooking the harbor. Serving lunch, dinner, and Sunday brunch, it specializes in fresh fish selections and also features hickory-smoked prime rib, chicken cordon bleu, and opakapaka with Hawaiian papaya salsa. Lunch is budget to moderate in price, dinner is deluxe.

Who could imagine that at the end of Balboa Pier there would be a vintage 1940s-era diner complete with art deco curves and red plastic booths. **Ruby's Diner** (1 Balboa Pier; 714-675-7829) is a classic. Besides that it provides 180° views of the ocean at budget prices. Of course the menu, whether breakfast, lunch, or dinner, contains little more than omelettes, hamburgers, sandwiches, chili, and salads. But who's hungry anyway with all that history and scenery to consider?

The top Thai restaurant hereabouts is **Bangkok 3** (101 Palm Street; 714-673-6521), a sparkling dining room painted in pastel hues and adorned with fabric paintings. The surroundings are ultramodern but the cuisine is traditional, a tasteful mix of curry and ginger dishes. Start off with chicken coconut soup or vegetable vermicelli, add a spicy beef salad, then move to the main courses. There is *ped op* (marinated baked duck), beef *satay*, *kai phad keng* (chicken with ginger), shrimp and scallop curry, and *pla nam lard prig* (fish in spice sauce). Be sure to try the avocado or coconut ice cream (sweetened with corn). A fine restaurant with a friendly staff; moderate.

The fact of the matter is that there are very few restaurants on Balboa Island. As a result, one place stands out. **Amelia's** (311 Marine Avenue; 714-673-6580), a family-run restaurant serving Italian dishes and seafood, is a local institution. At lunch you'll find them serving a half-dozen pasta dishes, fresh fish entrées, sandwiches, and salads. Then in the evening the chef prepares calamari stuffed with crab, scallops, Icelandic cod, bouillabaisse, veal piccata, and another round of pasta platters; moderate; no breakfast, but they serve Sunday brunch.

If you were hoping to spend a little less money, **Wilma's Patio** (225 Marine Avenue; 714-675-5542) is just down the street. It's a family-style restaurant—open morning, noon, and night—that serves multicourse American and Mexican meals at budget prices.

For a multicourse feast, Moroccan-style, reserve a tent at **Marrakesh** (1100 West Coast Highway; 714-645-8384). Decorated in the fashion of North Africa with tile floor and cloth drapes, this well-known dining room conveys a sense of Morocco. There are belly dancers Thursdays through Sundays and any night of the week you can experience *harira* (an aromatic soup), *jine fassi* (chicken with marinated lemon rinds), couscous, and a host of rabbit, lamb, quail, duck, and chicken dishes. Deluxe.

Ironically enough, one of Newport Beach's top dining bargains lies at the heart of the region's priciest shopping malls. Encircling the lower level of **Fashion Island** (Newport Center, 600 Newport Center Drive; 714-721-2000) is a collection of stands dispensing sushi, soup and sandwiches, Mexican food, pasta salads, hamburgers, and other light fare. Budget to moderate in price.

At **Antoine** (Hotel Le Méridien, 4500 MacArthur Boulevard; 714-476-2001) romantic intimacy, fine cuisine, and personal service are *de rigeur.* Gallic through and through, the *flan de foie gras* (a melt-in-your-mouth goose liver custard served warm with poached oysters and fresh asparagus tips), *escalope de turbot*, and saddle of lamb au jus represent the finest in nouvelle cuisine. Dinner served Tuesday through Saturday; deluxe to ultra-deluxe.

A local favorite in Corona del Mar, the small town adjacent to Newport Beach, is **The Quiet Woman** (3224 East Coast Highway; 714-640-7440), a small, dark, friendly place serving mesquite-grilled food. Lunch and dinner are served, both featuring steak and seafood menus at deluxe prices.

The atmosphere is markedly different across the street at **Studio Café** (3201 East Coast Highway, Corona del Mar; 714-675-7575). Sprawling, noisy and trendy, this restaurant cum gathering place offers everything from winetasting to champagne brunch to a pasta bar. A popular lounge dominates one room and in the other diners choose from an eclectic American menu. A good spot for slumming. Moderate.

LAGUNA BEACH RESTAURANTS

Laguna Beach is never at a loss for oceanfront restaurants. But somehow the sea seems closer and more intimate at **Laguna Village Café** (577 South Coast Highway; 714-494-6344), probably because this informal eatery is entirely outdoors, with tables placed at the very edge of the coastal bluff. The menu is simple and budget-to-moderate-priced: egg dishes in the morning, and a single menu with salads, sandwiches, and smoothies during the rest of the day. There are also house specialties like calamari, scallops amandine, teriyaki chicken, skewered shrimp, and Chinese-style chicken dumplings.

The **Penguin Malt Shop** (981 South Coast Highway; 714-494-1353) is from another era entirely. The 1930s to be exact. A tiny café featuring counter juke boxes, swivel stools, and period posters, it's a time capsule with a kitchen. Breakfast and lunch are all-American affairs from ham and eggs to hamburgers to pork chops. It's budget-priced, so what have you got to lose? Step on in and order a chocolate malt with a side of fries.

The White House (340 South Coast Highway; 714-494-8088) seems nearly as permanent a Laguna Beach fixture as the ocean. Dating to early in the century this simple wooden structure serves as bar, restaurant, and local landmark. Paneled in dark wood and trimmed with wallpaper, The White House is lined with historic photos of Laguna Beach. You can drop by from early morning until late evening to partake of a moderate-priced menu that includes pasta, steak, chicken, and seafood dishes.

Choose one place to symbolize the easy elegance of Laguna and it inevitably will be **Las Brisas** (361 Cliff Drive; 714-497-5434). Something about this whitewashed Spanish building with arched windows captures the natural-living-but-class-conscious style of the Southland. Its cliffside locale on the water is part of this ambience. Then there are the beautiful people who frequent the place. Plus a dual kitchen arrangement that permits formal dining in a white-tablecloth room or bistro dining on an outdoor patio. The moderate-to-deluxe-priced menu consists of continental Mexican seafood dishes and other specialties from south of the border. Out on the patio there are sandwiches, salads, and fajitas; moderate.

Five Feet Restaurant (328 Glenneyre Street; 714-497-4955) prepares "Chinese cuisine European style." This "interpretation of modern Chinese cuisine" carries you from catfish to veal loin sautéed with sweet pepper. Also on the ever-changing and always unique bill of fare is blackened ahi, spring lamb in curry-cilantro sauce, and steak chinoise. Applying the principles of California cuisine to Chinese cooking and adding a few French flourishes, Five Feet has gained an impressive reputation. The decor is as avant garde as the food. Dinner only Saturday through Thursday, with lunch on Friday; deluxe.

Dizz's As Is (2794 South Coast Highway; 714-494-5250) represents one of those singular dining spots that should not be overlooked. Funk is elevated to an art form in this woodframe house. The tiny dining room is decorated with art deco pieces and 1930s-era tunes play throughout dinner. This studied informality ends at the kitchen door where a continental cuisine that includes veal piccata, Cornish game hen, chicken stuffed with cheese and shallots, pasta with prawns, and cioppino is prepared by talented chefs. Moderate to deluxe; dinner only.

The most remarkable aspect of the **Cottage Restaurant** (308 North Coast Highway; 714-494-3023) is the cottage itself, an early 20th-century California bungalow. The place has been neatly decorated with turn-of-the-century antiques, oil paintings, and stained glass. Meal time in this historic house is a traditional American affair. Lunch consists of salads and sandwiches plus specials like top sirloin, fresh fish, and steamed vegetables. For dinner there is chicken fettuccine, top sirloin, broiled lamb, fresh shrimp and swordfish as well as daily fresh fish specials at moderate prices.

SOUTH ORANGE COUNTY RESTAURANTS

Monique French Restaurant (31727 Coast Highway, South Laguna; 714-499-5359) is a little jewel set on a coastal bluff. Situated in a former home it offers intimate dining indoors or outside on the patio. The restaurant is contemporary in decor. In addition to ocean views it offers lunch, Tuesday through Friday, and a dinner menu that changes daily. On a typical evening you can anticipate such entrées as filet of pork à l'orange, tournedos, bouillabaisse, and fresh seafood. Highly recommended by local residents, Monique is deluxe in price.

The **Harbor Grill** (34499 Golden Lantern Street, Dana Point; 714-240-1416), located in spiffy Dana Point Harbor, lacks the view and polish of its splashy neighbors. But this understated restaurant serves excellent seafood dishes at moderate to deluxe rates. The menu includes brochettes of swordfish and prawns, fried calamari, steak, prime rib, and grilled chicken, but the real attraction is the list of daily specials. This might include Cajun selections such as blackened sea bass, gumbo, and other fresh fish dishes. Lunch, dinner, and Sunday brunch are served in a light, bright dining room with contemporary artwork.

If you'd prefer to dine alfresco overlooking the harbor, there's **Proud Mary's** (34689 Golden Lantern Street, Dana Point; 714-493-5853), a little hole in the wall where you can order sandwiches, hot dogs, hamburgers, and a few platters, then dine on picnic tables outside. Budget.

Japanese food in these parts is spelled **Gen Kai** (34143 Coast Highway, Dana Point; 714-240-2004). In addition to a trimly appointed dining room this chain restaurant features a sushi bar. The menu is comprehensive and moderately priced. When I ate here the food was quite good. Dinner only.

One of San Juan Capistrano's many historic points, a 19th-century building, **El Adobe de Capistrano** (31891 Camino Capistrano; 714-493-1163) has been converted into a restaurant. The interior is a warren of whitewashed rooms, supported by *vigas* and displaying the flourishes of Spanish California. Stop by for a drink next to the old jail (today a wine cellar) or tour the building. (Counterpoint to all this dusty history is a display of Nixon memorabilia.) If you decide to dine, the menu includes breakfast, lunch, dinner, and Sunday brunch. Naturally the cuisine is Mexican, prices in the moderate to deluxe range.

Just up the street, the 1895 railroad station has been reincarnated as the **Rio Grande Bar & Grill** (26701 Verdugo Street; 714-496-8181). Brick archways lead from the old waiting room and station master's office to the freight and pullman cars, all neatly transformed into a restaurant and lounge. The dining room features regional Southwestern cuisine like herb chicken, pollo cilantro, carnitas, and shrimp enchiladas. Moderate.

Who can match the combination of intimacy and French-Belgian cuisine at **L'Hirondelle** (31631 Camino Capistrano, San Juan Capistrano; 714-

661-0425)? Add a moderate to deluxe price tag and you have a rare dining room indeed. It's quite small, about a dozen tables and banquettes, and conveys a French country atmosphere. Serving dinner and Sunday brunch, the restaurant offers a varied menu beginning with escargots, garlic toast, and crab crêpes. Entrées include roast duckling, rabbit in wine sauce, veal cordon bleu, bouillabaisse, sautéed sweetbreads, and daily fresh fish specials.

Center of the casual dining scene in San Clemente is along the beach at the foot of the municipal pier (end of Avenida del Mar). Several take-out stands and cafés are here. **The Fisherman's Restaurant** (714-498-6390), a knotty-pine-and-plate-glass establishment, sits right on the pier, affording views all along the beach. With a waterfront patio it's a good spot for seafood dishes at moderate prices. There is also breakfast and Sunday brunch.

INLAND ORANGE COUNTY RESTAURANTS

As the name suggests, **Charlie's Hideaway** (15470 Magnolia Street, Westminster; 714-895-3244) is well hidden, tucked into a nondescript shopping center far from Orange County's culinary center. Word-of-mouth is how you learn about it. Charlie's is nothing fancy in terms of decor, just a neighborhood beer bar atmosphere that's both friendly and comfortable. But the food's sensational, prepared as only native Thais know how. Favorites are spring rolls with pork, barbecued pork with peanut sauce, spicy beef steak salad, and chicken cooked in coconut milk. Best enjoyed with a bottle of Boon Rawd beer direct from Bangkok. Dinner only; moderate.

Restaurants of every description surround Disneyland, most offering moderately priced but mediocre food. An exception, one of the area's best values for atmosphere and satisfying dining, is **Mr. Stox** (1105 East Katella, Anaheim; 714-634-2994), which boasts a versatile menu of rabbit, rack of lamb, veal, pasta, and mesquite-broiled fresh seafood. Special touches include savory herbs and spices grown in a garden out back, plus homemade breads and desserts. Lunch and dinner; moderate to deluxe.

The top restaurant in these parts can be found at the Anaheim Marriott Hotel. **JW's** (700 West Convention Way, Anaheim; 714-750-0900) offers an outstanding continental cuisine menu. The candlelit ambience, attentive service and contemporary flourishes add to the experience. Ultra-deluxe.

Painted bright pink, **Belisle's Restaurant** (12001 Harbor Boulevard, Garden Grove; 714-750-6560) is hard to miss. Once inside this converted house you'll find truck drivers, radically coifed coeds, and neat-as-a-pin Orange County families all shoveling away good old-fashioned country-style chow. There's a two-pound steak, "poke" chops, catfish 'n hushpuppies, and baked meat loaf. Belisle's is open 24 hours a day and most everything on its voluminous menu is moderately priced.

Somewhat distant from metropolitan Orange County is **La Vie En Rose** (240 South State College Boulevard, Brea; 714-529-8333). Portraying a Norman farmhouse, complete with eight-sided steeple, it's an intimate dining room with French country appointments. The theme of rural Normandy is carried to completion by costumed waitresses who stream forth with hearty and authentic provincial dishes like *escalope de veau* and *poulet du bon Normand* (a baked boneless chicken stuffed with veal and pork). Be sure to make reservations; moderate to deluxe.

Orange County's most unique dining adventure is found at **The Hobbit** (2932 East Chapman Avenue, Orange; 714-997-1972). Here you'll be ushered into a gracious old 1930s hacienda for a magical evening of food and wine. Dinner begins with a tour of the wine cellar where guests select their favorite wines. For two or three hours you are tempted with a parade of hot and cold hors d'oeuvres, soup, salad, fowl, beef, and fish courses followed by sorbet and dessert. During "intermission" you can visit the chef in his immaculate kitchen or stroll in the art gallery and gardens. Ultra-deluxe; reserve weeks in advance.

Antonello Ristorante (1611 Sunflower Avenue, Santa Ana; 714-751-7153), Orange County's best-decorated and most highly rated Italian eatery, is a re-creation of an actual Italian street setting. Quaint shutters and window flower boxes give the place a genuine Old-Country feel. When it comes to cuisine, the nouvelle treatments of traditional Northern Italian dishes are outstanding. Pasta is made fresh daily and is quite good, but try something you won't find in run-of-the-mill Italian restaurants, like scampi *al anice* or veal *à la forestiera*. Very highly recommended; lunch and dinner; deluxe to ultra-deluxe.

For curry lovers there's **Gandhi** (3820 South Plaza Drive, Santa Ana; 714-556-7273), an Indian restaurant with a decidedly British decor. Earth tones, wood panelling, English china, and heavy silver-plated tableware create a colonial atmosphere. The rich, exotic combination of herbs and spices that flavor the curried lamb, Muglai chicken, or *tandoori* treats make this award-winning restaurant a wise choice. Lunch and dinner; moderate to deluxe.

Flagship of a family fleet of popular Chinese restaurants is **Mandarin Gourmet** (1500 Adams Avenue, Costa Mesa; 714-540-1937), a modern, sophisticated, and exciting restaurant. As the name implies, most dishes are from the northern provinces though there are samplings of Hunan, Peking, and Szechwan cooking. The signature dish and almost everyone's favorite is aromatic shrimp. Moderate to deluxe.

To savvy diners, **Chanteclair** (18912 MacArthur Boulevard, Irvine; 714-752-8001) spells "enchantment." Entering the château along a brick walkway flanked by Italian terra cotta planters, you'll encounter a dining room furnished with antiques. Pure continental elegance, backed by fine food and consummate service, is almost taken for granted here. Filet Wellington with truffle sauce, veal Orloff, and a fabulous fresh lobster served over fettucine lead the list of favorite dishes. Magnificent to the eye and palate, Chanteclair is one of Orange County's best (and most expensive) dining spots. Dressy by its very nature. Ultra-deluxe.

A high-tech Chinese restaurant? Lipstick reds and glossy blacks combine with lots of neon at **Chinatown Restaurant and Bar** (4139 Campus Drive, Irvine; 714-856-2211). The list of entrées includes 20 original house specialties such as gunpowder scallops and veal Marco Polo. Exciting and different (how many Chinese restaurants have an outdoor dining patio?), Chinatown should not be overlooked. Lunch and dinner; budget to moderate in price.

Upscale, contemporary **Prego** (18420 Von Karman Avenue, Irvine; 714-553-1333) packs 'em in both for tasty, authentic Italian food and a breathtaking interior scheme. Arched ceilings and a sizzling open-fire rotisserie greet the eye. Hardwood floors are accented by marbletop tables and black lacquered chairs. Aromas of saffron, oregano, and steaming pasta will quickly turn your attention to eating, however, and that's a real pleasure at Prego. The big surprise is Prego's pizza, superb pies baked in a huge woodburning oven. *Buon appetito!* Lunch and dinner; moderate.

Mandarin Taste Restaurant (23600 Rockfield Boulevard, Lake Forest; 714-830-9984) prepares traditional Mandarin fare. The oyster sauce, used to top a number of dishes, is especially good, as is the Chinese chicken salad. Lunch and dinner; moderate.

Some of the best Greek food this side of Athens can be found down El Toro way at **Mene's Terrace** (23532 El Toro Road in Orange Tree Plaza; 714-830-3228). Charmingly decorated to resemble a small terrace tucked between two whitewashed Greek houses, Mene's serves up renditions of such traditional favorites as spanakopita, moussaka, roast leg of lamb, and seafood *souvlaki*. Gyro sandwiches are a lunchtime favorite. Open for lunch and dinner, it offers a casual atmosphere at a moderate price.

A lovely hideaway can be found at **La Ferme** (28451 Marguerite Parkway, Mission Viejo; 714-364-6664), an intimate restaurant in the European country cottage tradition. Not surprisingly, its hallmark is French country cuisine like crisp roasted duckling, fresh poached salmon in tarragon cream sauce, and rack of lamb served on a bed of bordelaise sauce. Everything at La Ferme seems to taste better before a crackling fireplace, beside richly textured walls, and on tables dressed in forest green linens and set with fine china and fresh flowers. Lunch and dinner; moderate to deluxe.

Trabuco Oaks Steak House (20782 Trabuco Oaks Road, Trabuco Canyon; 714-586-0722) is popularly known as "the home of the two-pound cowboy steak." Don't be put off by its rundown facade or funky-rustic decor; nobody in Orange County turns out a bigger, tastier steak or better french fries (they're hand-cut daily). The dog-eared menu lists ribs, chicken, fish, and spaghetti as well, but you should stick to steak here. Leave your tie at home (they cut 'em) but be sure to bring a business card to add to the thousands plastered around the place. Dinner only; priced in the moderate to deluxe category.

The Great Outdoors

The Sporting Life

FISHING AND WHALE WATCHING

Among the Orange County outfits offering sportfishing charters are: **Davey's Locker** (400 Main Street, Balboa; 714-673-1434) and **Dana Wharf Sportfishing** (34675 Golden Lantern Street, Dana Point; 714-496-5794). For those more interested in gazing at California's big grays, these companies also sponsor whale-watching cruises during the migratory season.

Inland you can fish at **Irvine Lake** (714-649-2560), possibly landing a "super trout," bass, bluegill, or white sturgeon.

SCUBA DIVING

The coastal waters abound in interesting kelp beds rich with sea life. To explore them contact **Aquatic Center** (4537 West Pacific Coast Highway, Newport Beach; 714-650-5440), **Mr. Scuba** (14151 Red Hill Avenue, Tustin; 714-838-6483), **Laguna Sea Sports** (925 North Coast Highway, Laguna Beach; 714-494-6965), and **Black Bart's Aquatics** (34145 Coast Highway, Dana Point; 714-496-5891).

SURFING AND WINDSURFING

Orange County is surfer heaven. So grab a board from **The Fog House** (6908 West Coast Highway, Newport Beach; 714-642-5690), **Hobie Sports** (34195 Coast Highway, Dana Point; 714-496-1251), **Jack's Surf Ski and Sport** (34318 Coast Highway, Dana Point; 714-493-6100), or **Steward Sports** (2102 South El Camino Real, San Clemente; 714-492-1085) and head for the waves. For surf reports call 714-673-3371.

GOLF

The climate and terrain make for excellent golfing. Tee up at **Newport Beach Golf Course** (3100 Irvine Avenue, Newport Beach; 714-852-8681), **Aliso Creek Golf Course** (31106 Coast Highway, South Laguna; 714-499-1919), **The Links at Monarch Beach** (33080 Niguel Road, Laguna Niguel; 714-240-8247), **San Clemente Municipal Golf Course** (150 East Avenida Magdalena, San Clemente; 714-492-3943), or **Shorecliffs Golf Course** (501 Avenida Vaquero, San Clemente; 714-492-1177).

The inland sections of Orange County feature numerous golf links. Among them are **Anaheim Municipal (H. G. "Dad" Miller) Golf Course** (430 North Gilbert Street, Anaheim; 714-774-8055), **Anaheim Hills Golf Course** (6501 East Nohl Ranch Road, Anaheim; 714-637-7311), **Fullerton Golf Course** (2700 North Harbor Boulevard, Fullerton; 714-871-7411), or **Mile Square Golf Course** (10401 Warner Avenue, Fountain Valley; 714-968-4556).

TENNIS

Public courts are hard to find, except in San Clemente. Try the **Hotel Tennis Club** (Marriott Hotel, 900 Newport Center Drive, Newport Beach; 714-729-3566), **Moulton Meadows Park** (Del Mar and Balboa avenues, Laguna Beach; 714-497-0716), **Laguna Niguel Regional Park** (28421 La Paz Road, Laguna Niguel; 714-831-2791), **Dana Hills Tennis Center** (24911 Calle de Tennis, Dana Point; 714-240-2104), **Bonito Canyon Park** (El Camino Real and Calle Valle, San Clemente; 714-361-8264), **San Luis Rey Park** (Avenida San Luis Rey, San Clemente; 714-361-8264), and **San Gorgonio Park** (Via San Gorgonio, San Clemente; 714-361-8264).

For courts around Anaheim and Buena Park try **Anaheim Tennis Center** (975 South State College Boulevard, Anaheim; 714-991-9090), **Disney's Tennisland** (1330 Walnut Street, Anaheim; 714-535-4851), or **Ralph B. Clark Regional Park** (8800 Rosecrans Avenue, Buena Park; 714-670-8045).

SAILING

With elaborate marina complexes at Huntington Beach, Newport Beach, and Dana Point, this is a great area for boating. Sailboats and powerboats are available for rent at **Davey's Locker** (400 Main Street, Newport Beach; 714-673-1434), **Marina Sailing** (600 East Bay Avenue, Suite B6, Newport Beach; 714-673-7763), **Balboa Boat Rentals** (510 Edgewater Avenue, Newport Beach; 714-673-1320), and **Embarcadero Marina** (Embarcadero Place, public launch ramp, Dana Point; 714-496-6177).

JOGGING

Mecca for Orange County runners is the Santa Ana Riverbed Trail, a smooth asphalt ribbon stretching 20.6 miles from Anaheim to Huntington Beach State Park. There are par courses and excellent running trails at both Laguna Niguel Regional and Mile Square Regional parks (see "Beaches and Parks" section in this chapter). In Mission Viejo there's a beautiful two-and-a-half-mile trail around Lake Mission Viejo. And then there are the miles and miles of beaches for which Orange County is renowned.

BICYCLING

Route 1, the Pacific Coast Highway, offers cyclists an opportunity to explore the Orange County coastline. The problem, of course, is the traffic. Along **Bolsa Chica State Beach**, however, a special pathway runs the length of the beach. Other interesting areas to explore are **Balboa Island** and the **Balboa Peninsula** in Newport Beach. Both offer quiet residential streets and are connected by a ferry which permits bicycles. A popular inland ride is along **Santiago Canyon Road**; leaving from Orange the route skirts Irvine Lake and Cleveland National Forest.

BIKE RENTALS To rent bikes in Orange County try **Jack's Beach Concession** (on Huntington Beach; 714-536-8328), **Bolsa Chica Schwinn**

(4911 Warner Avenue, Suite 101, Huntington Beach; 714-846-6646), **Baldy's Tackle** (100 McFadden Place, Newport Beach; 714-673-4150), and **Rainbow Bicycle Company** (485 North Coast Highway, Laguna Beach; 714-494-5806).

Beaches and Parks

NORTH ORANGE COUNTY BEACHES AND PARKS

Seal Beach—Rare find indeed, this is a local beach tucked between Huntington Beach and Long Beach. In addition to a swath of fine-grain sand, there is a fishing pier from which you can take a **barge ride** (213-598-8677) to Long Beach. Oil derricks loom offshore and Long Beach rises in the misty distance.

Facilities: Restrooms, lifeguards; restaurants and groceries are nearby. *Fishing:* Very popular from the pier. *Swimming:* Good. *Surfing:* Good breaks at the pier and around 13th Street.

Getting there: Located along Ocean Avenue in Seal Beach; the pier is at the intersection with Main Street.

Surfside Beach and **Sunset Beach**—These contiguous strands extend over three miles along the ocean side of Huntington Harbor. Broad carpets of cushioning sand, they are lined with beach houses and lifeguard stands. Both are popular with local people, but Surfside is still a great beach to get away from the crowds.

Facilities: Surfside fronts a private community and lacks facilities; Sunset Beach has restrooms, lifeguards; restaurants and groceries are nearby. *Fishing:* Good at Sunset. *Swimming:* Good. *Surfing:* There are reliable sandbar peaks along both beaches; spectacular winter breaks near the jetty at the end of Surfside Beach.

Getting there: Surfside runs north from Anderson Street, which provides the only public access to the beach; Sunset is off the Pacific Coast Highway, extending from Warner Avenue to Anderson Street in Huntington Beach.

Bolsa Chica State Beach—With six miles of fluffy sand, this is another in a series of broad, beautiful beaches. There are regular grunion runs and rich clam beds here; the beach is backdropped by the **Bolsa Chica Ecological Reserve**, an important wetlands area. Since the summer surf is gentler here than at Huntington Beach, Bolsa Chica is ideal for swimmers and families.

Facilities: Picnic areas, restrooms, lifeguards, showers, snack bars, beach rentals; restaurants and groceries are nearby in Huntington Beach; information, 714-848-1566. *Camping:* Permitted for self-contained vehicles only. *Fishing:* Good. *Swimming:* Good in summer. *Surfing:* Small waves in summer, big breaks in winter.

Getting there: Located along Coast Highway in Huntington Beach between Warner Avenue and Huntington Pier.

Huntington City Beach—An urban continuation of the state beach to the south, this strand runs for several miles. This is one of the most famous surfing spots in the world. The Huntington Pier, closed due to extensive storm damage, silently sits awaiting renovation funding. The surrounding waters are crowded with surfers in wet suits. A great place for water sports and people-watching. This surfer heaven gives way to an industrial inferno north of the pier where the oil derricks that plague offshore waters climb right up onto the beach, making it look more like the Texas coast than the blue Pacific.

Facilities: Picnic areas, restrooms, lifeguards, showers, volleyball courts, beach rentals; restaurants and fishing tackle shops are nearby in Huntington Beach; information, 714-536-5281. *Camping:* Self-contained camping is permitted at Sunset Vista (714-536-5280). *Swimming:* Good when the surf is flat. *Surfing:* It pumps year-round. There are international competitions in September.

Getting there: Located along Coast Highway in Huntington Beach with numerous accesses.

Huntington State Beach—One of Southern California's broadest beaches, this strand extends for three miles. In addition to a desert of soft sand it has those curling waves that surfer dreams (and movies) are made from. Pismo clams lie buried in the sand, a bike path parallels the water, and there is a five-acre preserve for endangered least terns. Before you decide to move here permanently, take heed: these natural wonders are sandwiched between industrial plants and offshore oil derricks.

Facilities: Restrooms, picnic areas, lifeguards, showers, dressing rooms, snack bars, volleyball, beach rentals; restaurants and groceries are about two miles away in Huntington Beach; information, 714-848-1566. *Fishing:* Good. *Swimming:* Excellent when the surf is low. *Surfing:* Excellent along most of the beachfront.

Getting there: Located along Coast Highway in Huntington Beach; entrances are at Beach Boulevard, Newland Street, and Magnolia Street.

NEWPORT BEACH AREA BEACHES AND PARKS

Newport Beach—Narrow at the northern end and widening to the south, this sandy strip extends for several miles along the base of the Balboa Peninsula. Newport Pier (also known as McFadden's Pier) and the surrounding facilities serve as the center of the strand. Here fishermen from the Newport Dory Fishing Fleet beach their boats and sell their daily catches. A wonderful beach, with entrances along its entire length, this is an important gathering place for the crowds that pour into town.

Facilities: Restrooms, lifeguards, beach rentals; restaurants, groceries, and all amenities imaginable are at the foot of the pier. *Fishing:* Good from the pier. *Swimming:* Good. *Surfing:* Good in the morning around Newport (McFadden's) Pier and then in the afternoon at the 30th Street section of the beach. There are year-round breaks near the Santa Ana River mouth at the far north end of the beach.

Getting there: The beach parallels Balboa Boulevard in Newport Beach. Newport Pier is between 20th and 21st streets.

Balboa Beach—This broad sandy strip forms the ocean side of Balboa Peninsula and extends along its entire length. There are entrances to the beach from numerous side streets, but the center of the facility is around Balboa Pier, a wooden fishing pier. With a palm-shaded lawn and many nearby amenities, this beach, together with neighboring Newport Beach, is the most popular spot in town.

Facilities: Restrooms, showers, lifeguards, playground, beach rentals; restaurants, groceries, etc. are near the pier. *Fishing:* Good from the pier. *Swimming:* Good. *Surfing:* Good in different spots at different times.

Getting there: The beach parallels Balboa Boulevard. Balboa Pier is at the end of Main Street.

Jetty View Park—Set at the very end of the Balboa Peninsula, this triangle of sand is perfectly placed. From the tip extends a rock jetty that borders Newport Harbor. You can climb the rocks and watch boats in the bay, or turn your back on these trifles and wander across the broad sand carpet that rolls down to the ocean. There are wonderful views of Newport Beach and the coast. If you're daring enough you can challenge the waves at **The Wedge**. Known to bodysurfers around the world, the area between the jetty and beach is one of the finest and most dangerous shore breaks anywhere, the "Mount Everest of bodysurfing."

Facilities: Lifeguards; restaurants and groceries are about a half mile away. *Fishing:* Good from the jetty. *Swimming:* Very dangerous; the shore break here is fierce. *Surfing:* Bodysurfing is the main sport; surfing is permitted further down the beach. But take heed, these breaks are only for veteran bodysurfers.

Getting there: Located at the end of Balboa and Ocean boulevards at the tip of the Balboa Peninsula.

Newport Dunes RV Resort—This private facility is a broad, horseshoe-shaped beach about one-half mile in length. It curves around the lake-like waters of Upper Newport Bay, one mile inland from the ocean. Very popular with families and campers, it offers a wide range of activities, including volleyball, playground activities, and boat rentals. There's ample opportunity for swimming, with lifeguards on duty. The park is very popular, so plan to come for the attractions, not peace and quiet.

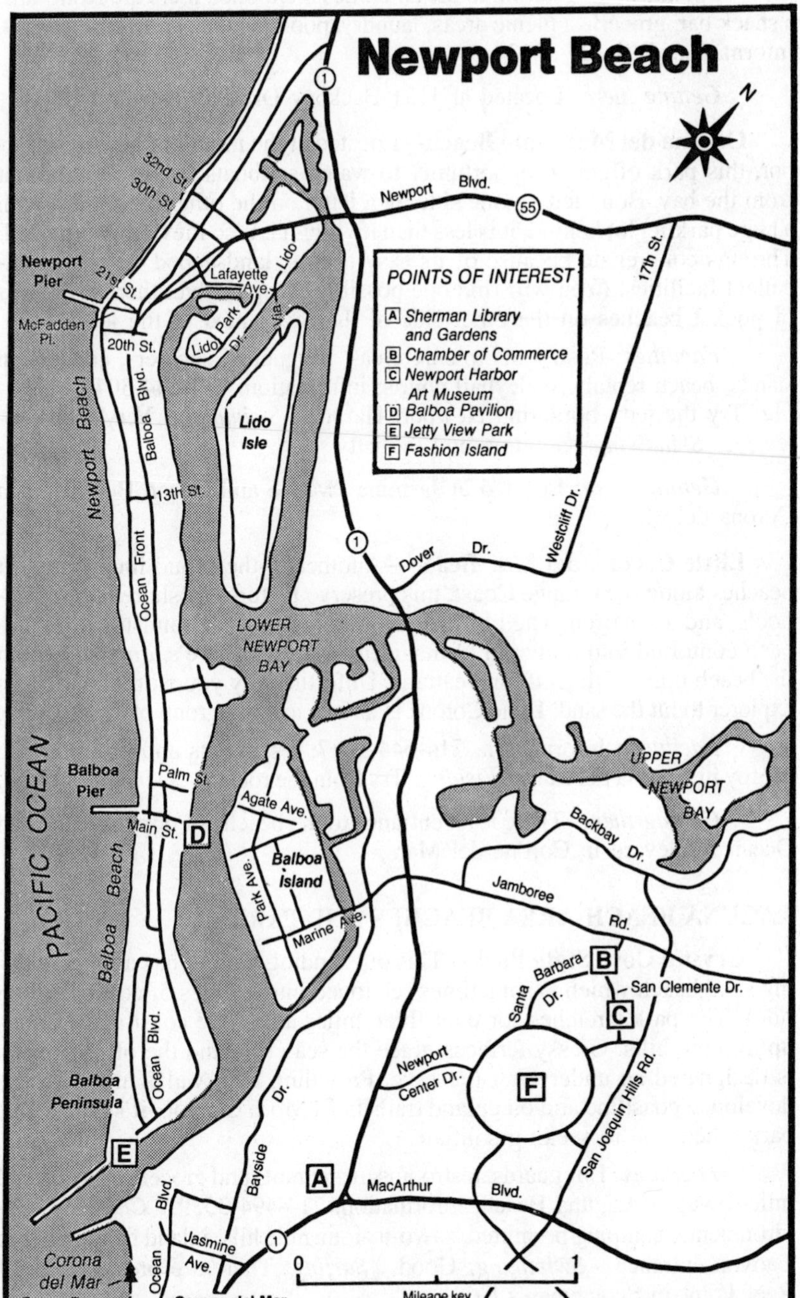
Newport Beach
POINTS OF INTEREST
A Sherman Library and Gardens
B Chamber of Commerce
C Newport Harbor Art Museum
D Balboa Pavilion
E Jetty View Park
F Fashion Island
N
1
55
Newport Blvd.
32nd St.
30th St.
21st St.
20th St.
13th St.
17th St.
Newport Pier
McFadden Pl.
Lafayette Ave.
Via Lido
Lido Park Dr.
Lido Isle
Balboa Blvd.
Ocean Front
Newport Beach
Westcliff Dr.
Dover Dr.
LOWER NEWPORT BAY
UPPER NEWPORT BAY
Backbay Dr.
PACIFIC OCEAN
Balboa Pier
Palm St.
Main St.
Agate Ave.
Park Ave.
Balboa Island
Marine Ave.
Jamboree Rd.
Santa Barbara Dr.
San Clemente Dr.
San Joaquin Hills Rd.
Newport Center Dr.
Bayside Dr.
Balboa Beach
Ocean Blvd.
Balboa Peninsula
MacArthur Blvd.
Jasmine Ave.
Corona del Mar State Beach
Corona del Mar
0
1
Mileage key

Facilities: In addition to the amenities mentioned there are restrooms, a snack bar, groceries, picnic areas, laundry, pool, jacuzzi, and beach rentals. Information, 714-729-3863.

Getting there: Located at 1131 Backbay Drive in Newport Beach.

Corona del Mar State Beach—Located at the mouth of Newport Harbor, this park offers an opportunity to watch sailboats tacking in and out from the bay. Bounded on one side by a jetty, on the other by homes, with a huge parking lot behind, it is less than idyllic. It is also inevitably crowded. Throngs congregate because of its easy access, landscaped lawn, and excellent facilities. (You will find one possible escape valve: there are a pair of pocket beaches on the other side of the rocks next to the jetty.)

Facilities: Restrooms, picnic areas, lifeguards, showers, concession stands, beach rentals, volleyball courts; information, 714-644-3047. *Fishing:* Try the jetty bordering Newport Harbor. *Swimming:* Very well protected. *Skindiving:* Good around the jetty.

Getting there: Located at Jasmine Avenue and Ocean Boulevard in Corona del Mar.

Little Corona del Mar Beach—Another in the proud line of pocket beaches along the Orange Coast, this preserve features offshore rocks, tidepools, and a sea arch. The bluff to the north consists of sandstone that has been contorted into a myriad of magnificent lines. There's a marsh behind the beach thick with reeds and cattails. Unfortunately you won't be the first explorer to hit the sand; Little Corona is known to a big group of local people.

Facilities: Information, 714-644-3047; restaurants and groceries are nearby in Corona del Mar. *Fishing:* Try from the rocks. *Swimming:* Good.

Getting there: There is an entrance to the beach at Poppy Avenue and Ocean Boulevard in Corona del Mar.

LAGUNA BEACH AREA BEACHES AND PARKS

Crystal Cove State Park—This outstanding facility has a long, winding sand beach which is sometimes sectioned into a series of coves by high tides. The park stretches for over three miles along the coast and extends up into the hills. Grassy terraces grace the sea cliffs and the offshore area is designated an underwater preserve. Providing long walks along an undeveloped coastline and on upland trails in El Moro Canyon, it's the perfect park when you're seeking solitude.

Facilities: Lifeguards, restrooms; restaurants and groceries are several miles away in Laguna Beach; information, 714-494-3539. *Camping:* Environmental camping permitted, a two-to-four-mile hike inland from El Moro Canyon entrance. *Swimming:* Good. *Surfing:* There are breaks north of Reef Point in Scotchman's Cove.

Getting there: Located along the Coast Highway between Corona del Mar and Laguna Beach. There are entrances at Pelican Point, Los Trancos, Reef Point, and El Moro Canyon.

Crescent Bay—This half-moon inlet is flanked by a curving cliff upon which the fortunate few have parked their palatial homes. Down on the beach, the sand is as soft and thick as the carpets in those houses. Offshore stands Seal Rock with barking denizens whose cries echo off the surrounding cliffs. This, to say the least, is a pretty place. You can swim, skindive, sunbathe, explore the rocks and tidepools, or venture up to the vista point that overlooks this natural setting.

Facilities: Restrooms, lifeguards; restaurants and groceries are nearby. *Fishing:* Good. *Swimming:* A great place to take the plunge. *Surfing:* Very good bodysurfing; occasionally good surfing. *Skindiving:* Excellent.

Getting there: Entrances to the beach are located near the intersection of Cliff Drive and Circle Way.

Shaw's Cove, **Fisherman's Cove**, and **Diver's Cove**—These three miniature inlets sit adjacent to one another, creating one of Laguna Beach's most scenic and popular sections of shoreline. Each features a white sand beach backdropped by a sharp bluff. Rock formations at either end are covered in spuming surf and honeycombed with tidepool pockets (particularly at the south end of Shaw's Cove). Well known to local residents, the beaches are sometimes crowded.

Facilities: Lifeguards; restaurants and groceries are nearby. *Fishing:* Good. *Swimming:* Generally good but can be hazardous at Fisherman's Cove because of rocks. *Skindiving:* Excellent along this entire shoreline. Diver's Cove is often awash with scuba divers.

Getting there: All three rest along Cliff Drive. The walkway to Shaw's Cove is at the end of Fairview Street; the entrances to Fisherman's and Diver's are within 50 feet of each other in the 600 block of Cliff Drive.

Heisler Park, **Picnic Beach**, and **Rock Pile Beach**—One of Laguna's prettiest stretches of shoreline lies along the clifftop in Heisler Park and below on the boulder-strewn sands of Picnic and Rock Pile beaches. The park provides a promenade with grassy areas and shade trees. You can scan the coastline from Laguna Beach south for miles, then meander down to the beach where sedimentary formations shatter the wave patterns and create marvelous tidepools. Picnic and Rock Pile form adjacent coves, both worthy of exploration.

Facilities: Picnic areas, restrooms, lifeguards, shuffleboard; restaurants and groceries are nearby. *Fishing:* Excellent here and along most of the Laguna coast. Perch, cod, bass, and halibut inhabit these waters. *Swimming:* Good at both beaches. *Skindiving:* The rocks offer great places to explore. *Surfing:* There is no surfing at Picnic, but Rock Pile has some of the biggest waves in Laguna Beach. The best spots are at the south end.

Getting there: Heisler Park is located along Cliff Drive. Picnic Beach lies to the north at the end of Myrtle Street; Rock Pile Beach is at the end of Jasmine Street.

Main Beach—You'll have to venture north to Muscle Beach in Venice to find a scene equal to this one. It's located at the very center of Laguna Beach, with shopping streets radiating in several directions. A sinuous boardwalk winds along the waterfront, past basketball players, sunbathers, volleyball aficionados, little kids on swings, and aging kids on roller skates. Here and there an adventuresome soul has even dipped a toe in the wa-wa-water. In the midst of this humanity on holiday stands the lifeguard tower, an imposing glass-encased structure that looks more like a conning tower and has become a Laguna Beach icon.

Facilities: Unless someone has gotten to them first, the amenities I mentioned are all available to you. There are also restrooms, showers, picnic areas, a playground, and a grassy area. *Fishing:* Try the rocks near the north end of the beach. *Swimming:* Very good; well guarded. *Skindiving:* The Laguna Beach Marine Life Refuge lies just offshore, making this a popular place for diving.

Getting there: Located at Coast Highway and Broadway.

Street Beaches—Paralleling downtown Laguna for nearly a mile is a single slender strand known to locals by the streets that intersect it. Lined with luxury homes, it provides little privacy but affords easy access to the town's amenities.

Facilities: Lifeguards; everything you want, need, or couldn't care less about is within a couple blocks. *Swimming:* Good. *Surfing:* Excellent peaks are created by a submerged reef off Brooks Street, which is also a prime bodysurfing locale. The surf is also usually up around Thalia Street.

Getting there: Off Coast Highway there are beach entrances at the ends of Sleepy Hollow Lane, and Cleo, St. Ann's, Thalia, Anita, Oak, and Brooks streets.

Arch Cove—Stretching for more than a half mile, bordered by a palisade of luxury homes and resort hotels, this sandy swath is ideal for sunbathers. A sea arch and blowhole rise along the south end of the beach; the northern stretch is more populated and not as pretty.

Facilities: Lifeguards; restaurants and groceries are nearby. *Swimming:* Not as protected as the pocket beaches but still okay. *Surfing:* There are sizeable breaks around Agate Street.

Getting there: Entrances to the beach are at the ends of Cress Street, Mountain Road, Bluebird Canyon Drive, Agate Street, and Pearl Street. As a result, you will hear sections of the strand referred to as "Agate Beach," "Pearl Beach," etc.

Wood's Cove (★)—An S-shaped strand backed by Laguna's ever-loving shore bluff, this is another in the town's string of hidden wonders. Three rock peninsulas give the area its topography, creating a pair of sandy pocket beaches. The sea works in, around, and over the rocks, creating a tumultuous presence in an otherwise placid scene.

Facilities: Lifeguards; restaurants and groceries are nearby. *Swimming:* Well protected by rock outcroppings. *Skindiving:* Good off the rocks.

Getting there: Steps from Diamond Street and Ocean Way lead down to the water.

Moss Point (★)—This tiny gem is little more than 50 yards long, but for serenity and simple beauty it challenges the giant strands. Rocky points border both sides and sharp hills overlook the entire scene. The sea streams in through the mouth of a cove and debouches onto a fan-shaped beach.

Facilities: Lifeguard; restaurants and groceries are nearby. *Swimming:* The cove is well protected. *Skindiving:* Surrounding rocks provide interesting areas.

Getting there: Located at the end of Moss Street.

Victoria Beach (★)—Known primarily to locals, this quarter-mile sand corridor is flanked by homes and hills. The rocks on either side of the beach make for good exploring and provide excellent tidepooling opportunities. Amenities are few, but that is the price to pay for getting away from Laguna's crowds.

Facilities: Lifeguard, volleyball; restaurants and groceries are nearby. *Swimming:* Okay, but watch for the strong shore break and offshore rocks. *Surfing:* Good bodysurfing.

Getting there: From Coast Highway take Victoria Drive, then turn right on Dumond Street.

SOUTH ORANGE COUNTY BEACHES AND PARKS

Aliso Creek Beach Park—Set in a wide cove and bounded by low coastal bluffs, this park is popular with local folks. The nearby highway buzzes past and the surrounding hills are adorned with houses. A sand scimitar with rocks guarding both ends, the beach is bisected by a fishing pier. To escape the crowds head over to the park's **southern cove (★)**, a pretty beach with fluffy sand.

Facilities: Picnic areas, restrooms, showers, lifeguard, volleyball, snack bar. Restaurants and groceries are nearby. *Fishing:* Good from the pier. *Swimming:* Beware of strong shore breaks. *Surfing:* Better for bodysurfing.

Getting there: Located along Coast Highway in South Laguna; there is a public accessway to the southern cove along the 31300 block of Coast Highway.

South Laguna coves (★)—Hidden by the hillsides that flank South Laguna's waterfront are a series of pocket beaches. Each is a crescent of white sand bounded by sharp cliffs of conglomerate rock. These in turn are crowned with plate-glass homes. Two particularly pretty inlets can be reached via accessways called **1000 Steps and West Street**.

Facilities: Both beaches have lifeguards and restrooms. Restaurants and groceries are nearby. *Swimming:* Good. *Surfing:* The bodysurfing is excellent in both coves.

Getting there: Both accessways are on Coast Highway in South Laguna. 1000 Steps is at 9th Avenue; West Street is (surprise!) at West Street.

Salt Creek Beach Park—This marvelous locale consists of two half-mile sections of beach divided by a lofty point on which the Ritz Carlton Laguna Niguel Hotel stands. Each beach is a broad strip of white sand, backdropped by bluffs and looking out on Santa Catalina Island. The hotel above dominates the region like a palatial fortress on the Mediterranean. Though both beaches are part of Salt Creek, the strand to the south is also known as **Laguna Niguel Beach Park**. It's possible to walk from one beach to the other.

Facilities: Both beaches have restrooms and lifeguards; at Salt Creek (north) there is also a snack bar. *Fishing:* Better at Laguna Niguel. *Swimming:* Good. *Surfing:* From Laguna Niguel you can surf "Dana Strand," located a short distance south. Salt Creek has two well-known breaks, "The Beach," just north of the outcropping that separates the two beaches, and at "The Point" itself.

Getting there: Laguna Niguel Beach Park is reached via a long stairway at the end of Selva Road. The staircase to Salt Creek is on Ritz Carlton Drive. Both lie off Coast Highway in Laguna Niguel.

Doheny State Beach—This park wrote the book on oceanside facilities. In addition to a broad swath of sandy beach there is a five-acre lawn complete with private picnic areas, beach rentals, and food concessions. The grassy area offers plenty of shade trees. Surfers work the north end of the beach and divers explore an underwater park just offshore. Dana Point Harbor, with complete marina facilities, borders the beach.

Facilities: In addition to the services above there are restrooms with changing areas, lifeguards, volleyball courts; restaurants and groceries are nearby; information, 714-496-6171. *Camping:* Permitted. *Fishing:* Try the jetty in Dana Point Harbor. *Swimming:* Good. *Surfing:* Comfortable for beginners, particularly on a south swell.

Getting there: Located off Dana Point Harbor Drive in Dana Point.

Capistrano Beach Park—This is a big rectangular sandbox facing the open ocean. Like many beaches in the area it offers ample facilities and is often quite crowded. Bounded by sedimentary cliffs and offering views of Dana Point Harbor, the beach is landscaped with palm and deciduous trees. The park is particularly popular with families and surfers.

Facilities: Picnic areas, restrooms, showers, lifeguards, volleyball, basketball court; restaurants and groceries are nearby. *Swimming:* Good.

Surfing: "Killer Capo" breaks are about 400 yards offshore along the northern fringes of the beach (near Doheny State Park). "Dody's Reef" breaks are about one half mile to the south but are not predictable.

Getting there: Located along Coast Highway in Capistrano Beach.

San Clemente City Beach—Running nearly the length of town this silver strand is the pride of San Clemente. Landlubbers congregate near the municipal pier, anglers work its waters, and surfers blanket the beachfront. There are railroad tracks and coastal bluffs paralleling the entire beach. Eden this ain't: San Clemente is heavily developed, but the beach is a pleasant place to spend a day.

Facilities: There are restaurants and other amenities at the municipal pier; picnic areas, restrooms, lifeguard, playground. The **Ole Hanson Beach Club** (105 Avenida Pico; 714-361-8207; admission), at the north end of the beach, is a public pool with dressing rooms. *Fishing:* Try the pier. *Swimming:* Good. *Surfing:* Good on one side of the pier.

Getting there: The pier is located at the foot of Avenida del Mar in San Clemente.

San Clemente State Beach—Walk down the deeply eroded cliffs guarding this coastline and you'll discover a long narrow strip of sand that curves north from San Diego County up to San Clemente City Beach. There are camping areas and picnic plots on top of the bluff. Down below a railroad track parallels the beach and surfers paddle offshore. You can stroll north toward downtown San Clemente or south to former President Nixon's old home (see the "Sightseeing" section in this chapter).

Facilities: Lifeguards, picnic areas, restrooms; restaurants and groceries are nearby in San Clemente; information, 714-492-3156. *Camping:* Permitted. *Swimming:* Beware of rip currents. *Surfing:* Year-round breaks at the north end of the beach.

Getting there: Located off Avenida Calafia in San Clemente.

INLAND ORANGE COUNTY BEACHES AND PARKS

Featherly Regional Park—Unique among Orange County parks, this one's only for camping. There's no day use. Situated in the heart of Santa Ana Canyon, it covers 700 acres, a fraction of which has been developed for campgrounds. The balance is a natural streamside wilderness which includes a nature trail flanked by cottonwood, oak, and willow trees.

Facilities: Restrooms, showers, nature and bike trails; visitor center; restaurants and groceries are several miles away; information, 714-637-0210. *Camping:* Permitted.

Getting there: Located at 24001 Santa Ana Canyon Road, Anaheim.

Irvine Regional Park—This 477-acre park offers more than ten miles of biking, hiking, and equestrian trails. There's a boating lagoon, petting zoo, and pony stables with rides for the kids.

Facilities: Picnic areas, bike and paddleboat rentals, restrooms, snack bar; restaurants and groceries are nearby; information, 714-633-8072.

Getting there: Located at 21501 Chapman Avenue, Orange.

O'Neill Regional Park—Originally part of an 1841 Mexican land grant, this 1700-acre county park straddles Trabuco and Live Oak canyons in a delightfully undeveloped region of the Santa Ana Mountains. Topography varies from oak-lined canyon bottomlands and grassy meadows to chaparral-covered hillsides. There's a surprising variety of wildlife: opossum, raccoon, rabbit, and coyote are frequently seen, as are hawk, quail, dove, and roadrunner. Far more elusive, but ever present in the park, are mountain lion.

Facilities: Picnic areas, restrooms, showers; restaurants and groceries are nearby; information, 714-858-9366. *Camping:* Permitted.

Getting there: Located in southeastern Orange County at 30892 Trabuco Canyon Road, 18 miles east of Route 405 via El Toro Road exit.

Ronald W. Caspers Wilderness Park—A gem of a park, this is Orange County's largest preserve, covering 7600 acres of rugged mountain and canyonland bordering Cleveland National Forest. Within this vast domain are more than 30 miles of marked trails for hiking and horseback riding. The key feature here is San Juan Hot Springs, where nature's own hot mineral water is piped into a pool and 25 smaller hot tubs.

Facilities: Small museum, picnic areas, restrooms, showers; groceries are several miles away; information, 714-728-0235. For hot springs information, call 714-728-0400. *Camping:* Permitted.

Getting there: Located at 35501 Ortega Highway (Route 74), San Juan Capistrano.

Hiking

COASTAL ORANGE COUNTY TRAILS

Though heavily developed, the Orange Coast still provides several outstanding trails. All are located near the beaches and offer views of private homes and open ocean.

The **California Coastal Trail** extends over 40 miles from the San Gabriel River in Seal Beach to San Mateo Point in San Clemente. Much of the route follows sandy beachfront and sedimentary bluffs. There are lagoons and tidepools, fishing piers, and marinas en route.

At **Bolsa Chica Lagoon Loop Trail** (3 miles) you can say hello to birds traveling along the Pacific Flyway. A migratory rest stop, this lagoon features a loop trail which runs atop a levee past fields of cord grass and pickleweed.

Huntington Beach Trail (4 miles) parallels the Pacific from Bolsa Chica Lagoon to Beach Boulevard in Huntington Beach. Along the way it takes in Huntington Pier, a haven for surfers, and passes an army of unspeakably ugly oil derricks.

Newport Trail (2.5 miles) traces the ocean side of Balboa Peninsula from Newport Pier south to Balboa Pier, then proceeds to the peninsula's end at Jetty View Park. Private homes run the length of this pretty beach walk.

Back Bay Trail (1.8 miles) follows Backbay Drive in Newport Beach along the shores of Upper Newport Bay. This fragile wetland, an important stop on the Pacific Flyway, is an ideal birdwatching area.

Crystal Cove Trail (3.2 miles) provides a pleasant seaside stroll. Starting from Pelican Point at the western boundary of Crystal Cove State Park, the paved path leads to the beach. The trail continues another mile to a cluster of cottages at Crystal Cove, then follows an undeveloped beach to Abalone Point, a 200-foot high promontory.

Aliso Creek Canyon Hiking Trail (1 mile) begins near the fishing pier at Aliso Beach County Park in South Laguna, leads north through a natural arch, and passes the ruins of an old boat landing.

INLAND ORANGE COUNTY TRAILS

Rising along the entire length of Orange County's eastern perimeter, the Santa Ana Mountains offer several challenging and surprisingly uncrowded trails.

Holy Jim Trail (10 miles) is a good Santa Ana sampler, with a creek, waterfall, oak woodland, and chaparral-covered slopes. It leads to Bear Springs where hikers can take a three-mile optional climb on **Main Divide Truck Trail** to the crest of 5687-foot Santiago Peak. The trail begins on Holy Jim Road, six miles from O'Neill Regional Park.

Bear Canyon Trail (5.5 miles) is a broad, well-graded and rather pleasant hike climbing through brush and meadow country to refreshing Pigeon Springs. Arrive at the spring early in the morning and you'll likely see deer, coyote, or even bobcat drinking from the cool waters. From Pigeon Springs there's an optional five-mile hike to Sitton Peak via **Verdugo and Sitton Peak Trail**. The trail is on Route 74, 20 miles east of Route 5.

Nearby **Chiquito Basin Trail** (10.5 miles) switchbacks past a sparkling waterfall and over oak-studded slopes to shady Lion Canyon. Don't be confused: the trailhead (just east of Bear Canyon trailhead) is signed San Juan Loop Trail, but Chiquito Basin Trail branches off a mile up.

Should you be city-bound during your visit to Orange County you can still get out and stretch the legs, thanks to the **Santa Ana Riverbed Trail** (20.6 miles). True to the name, it follows the Santa Ana River on a smooth asphalt surface from Imperial Highway in Anaheim south to Route 1 at Huntington Beach State Park. A great way to hike to the beach, it's also popular with joggers and bikers.

Traveler's Tracks

Sightseeing

HUNTINGTON BEACH

As Route 1 buzzes south from Los Angeles it is bordered on one side by broad beaches and on the other by **Bolsa Chica Ecological Reserve** (accessways across from the entrance to Bolsa Chica State Beach and at Warner Avenue). An important wetlands area dotted with islands and overgrown in cord grass and pickleweed, this 530-acre preserve features a mile-long loop trail. Among the hundreds of animal species inhabiting the marsh are egrets, herons, and five endangered species. There are raucous seagulls as well as rare Belding's savannah sparrows and California least terns.

Leave this natural world behind and you will enter the surf capital of California. In the mythology of surfing, Huntington Beach rides with Hawaii's Waimea Bay and the great breaks of Australia. Since the 1920s boys with boards have been as much a part of the seascape as blue skies and billowing clouds. They paddle around what is left of storm-damaged **Huntington Pier** (end of Main Street), poised to catch the next wave that pounds the pilings. At night Huntington's 500 fire rings blaze with light, making it one of Southern California's great party beaches.

NEWPORT BEACH

Newport Beach is a mélange of manmade islands and peninsulas surrounding a small bay. For help finding your bearings around this labyrinth of waterways, contact the **Newport Harbor Area Chamber of Commerce** (1470 Jamboree Road; 714-644-8211) or the **Newport Beach Conference & Visitors Bureau** (366 San Miguel, Suite 200; 714-644-1190).

While it cannot compete with Laguna Beach as an art center, the town does offer the **Newport Harbor Art Museum** (850 San Clemente Drive; 714-759-1122; admission). Specializing in contemporary art, this facility possesses perhaps the finest collection of post-World War II California art in existence.

Further evidence of Newport's creativity can be found at the **Lovell Beach House** (13th Street and West Ocean Front). This private residence, set on the beach, is a modern masterpiece. Designed by Rudolf Schindler in 1926, it features a Bauhaus-like design with columns and cantilevers of poured concrete creating a series of striking geometric forms.

One of Newport Beach's prettiest neighborhoods is **Balboa Island**, comprised of two manmade islets in the middle of Newport Bay. It can be reached by bridge along Marine Avenue or via a short ferry ride from Balboa Peninsula. Walk the pathways that circumnavigate both islands and you will pass clapboard cottages, Cape Cod homes, and modern block-design houses that seem made entirely of glass. While sailboats sit moored along the waterfront, streets that are little more than alleys lead into the center of the island.

Another landfill island, **Lido Isle**, sits just off Balboa Peninsula. Surrounded by Newport Bay, lined with sprawling homes and pocket beaches, it is another of Newport Beach's wealthy residential enclaves.

Nearby **Lido Peninsula** seems like yet one more upscale neighborhood. But wait a minute, doesn't that house have a corrugated roofline? And the one next to it is made entirely of metal. Far from an ordinary suburban neighborhood, Lido Peninsula is a trailer park. In Newport Beach? Granted they call them "mobile homes" here, and many are hardly mobile with their brick foundations, flower boxes, and shrubs. But a trailer park it is, probably one of the fanciest in the country, with tin homes disguised by elaborate landscape designs, awnings, and wooden additions. Surreal to say the least.

The central piece in this jigsaw puzzle of manmade plots is **Balboa Peninsula,** a long, narrow finger of land bounded by Newport Bay and the open ocean. High point of the peninsula is **Balboa Pavilion** (end of Main Street), a Victorian landmark that dates back to 1905, when it was a bathhouse for swimmers in ankle-length outfits. Marked by its well-known cupola, the bayfront building hosted the nation's first surfing tournament in 1932 and gave birth to its own dance sensation, the "Balboa." Today it's a miniature amusement park with carousel, ferris wheel, photograph booths, skee ball, video games, and pinball machines.

Cruise ships to Catalina Island debark from the dock here and there are harbor cruises offered by **Catalina Passenger Service** (714-673-5245; admission) aboard the *Pavilion Queen*, a mock riverboat which motors around the mazeway that is Newport Bay.

This is also home to the **Balboa Island Ferry** (714-673-1070), a kind of floating landmark that has shuttled between Balboa Peninsula and Balboa Island since 1919. A simple, single-deck ferry that carries three cars (for about 50 cents each) and sports a pilot house the size of a phone booth, it crosses the narrow waterway every few minutes.

The beach scene in this seaside city extends for over five miles along the Pacific side of Balboa Peninsula. Here a broad white sand beach, lined with lifeguard stands and houses, reaches along the entire length. The centers of attention and amenities are **Newport Pier** (Balboa Boulevard and McFadden Place) and **Balboa Pier** (Ocean Front Boulevard and Main Street). At Newport Pier, also known as McFadden's pier, the skiffs of the **Newport Dory Fishing Fleet** are beached every day while local fishermen sell their catches. This flotilla of small wooden boats has been here so long it has achieved historic landmark status. At dawn the fishermen sail ten miles offshore, set trawl lines, and haul in the mackerel, flounder, rock fish, and halibut sold at the afternoon market.

To capture a sense of the beauty which still inheres in Newport Beach, take a walk out to **Jetty View Park** (end of Ocean Boulevard) at the tip of Balboa Peninsula. Here civilization meets the sea. To the left extend the rock jetties forming the mouth of Newport Harbor. Behind you are the plate-glass houses of the city. A wide beach, tufted with ice plants and occasional palm trees, forms another border. Before you, changing its hue with the phases of the sun and clouds, is the Pacific, a single sweep of water that makes those million-dollar homes seem fragile and tenuous.

Not all the wealth of Newport Beach is measured in finances. The richness of the natural environment is evident as well when you venture through **Upper Newport Bay Ecological Reserve** (Backbay Drive). The road passes limestone bluffs and sandstone hills. Reeds and cattails line the shore. Southern California's largest estuary, the bay is a vital stopping place for migrating birds on the Pacific Flyway. Over 200 species can be seen here; and two endangered species, Belding's savannah sparrow and the light-footed clapper rail, live along the bay.

Back on Route 1, head south through Corona del Mar en route to Laguna Beach. A wealthy enclave with trim lawns and spacious homes, Corona del Mar offers a pretty **coastal drive** along residential Ocean Boulevard.

Also drop by the **Sherman Library and Gardens** (2647 East Coast Highway, Corona del Mar; 714-673-2261). Devoted to the culture and recent history of the "Pacific Southwest," this complex features a specialized library set in Early California-style buildings. Also inviting is the botanical garden, a kind of desert museum alive with cacti, succulents, and other plant species.

LAGUNA BEACH

Next stop on this cavalcade of coastal cities is Laguna Beach. Framed by the San Joaquin hills, the place is an intaglio of coves and bluffs, sand beaches and rock outcroppings. It conjures images of the Mediterranean with deep bays and greenery running to the sea's edge.

Little wonder that Laguna, with its wealthy residents and leisurely beachfront, has become synonymous with the chic but informal style of Southern California. Its long tradition as an artist colony adds to this sense of beauty and bounty, aesthetics and aggrandizement.

Adding to its artistic tradition is the **Festival of the Arts & Pageant of the Masters** (Irvine Bowl, 650 Laguna Canyon Road; 714-494-1145; admission), staged every year during July and August. While the festival displays the work of several dozen local artists and craftspeople, the Pageant of the Masters is the high point, an event which you *absolutely must not miss*. It presents a series of *tableaux vivants* in which local residents, dressed to resemble figures from famous paintings, remain motionless against a frieze that re-creates the painting. Elaborate make-up and lighting techniques flatten the figures and create a sense of two-dimensionality.

During the 1960s freelance artists, excluded from the more formal Festival of the Arts, founded the **Sawdust Festival** (935 Laguna Canyon Road; 714-494-3030; admission) across the street. Over the years this fair too has become pretty established, but it still provides an opportunity to wander along sawdust-covered paths past hundreds of arts and crafts displays accompanied by musicians, clowns, and mimes. It also runs during July and August.

Laguna Beach's artistic heritage is evident in the many galleries and studios around town. The **Laguna Beach Chamber of Commerce** (357 Glenneyre Street; 714-494-1018), with its maps and brochures, can help direct you. The **Laguna Art Museum** (307 Cliff Drive; 714-494-6531; admission) has a wonderfully chosen collection of historic and contemporary California paintings. Complementing the Chamber of Commerce, it will help you find your way through the local art world.

Beauty in Laguna is not only found on canvases. The coastline too is particularly pretty and well worth exploring (see the "Beaches and Parks" section in this chapter). One of the most enchanting areas is along **Heisler Park** (Cliff Drive), a winding promenade set on the cliffs above the ocean. Here you can relax on the lawn, sit beneath a palm tree, and gaze out on the horizon. There are broad vistas out along the coast and down to the wave-whitened shoreline. Paths from the park descend to a series of coves with tidepools and sandy beaches. The surrounding rocks, twisted by geologic pressure into curving designs, rise in a series of protective bluffs.

Cliff Drive streams along Heisler Park and then past a series of entranceways to sparkling coves and pocket beaches. At the north end of this shoreline street take a left onto Coast Highway, then another quick left onto Crescent Bay Drive, which leads to **Crescent Bay Point Park**. Seated high upon a coastal cliff, this landscaped facility offers magnificent views for miles along the Laguna shore.

When you're ready to leave the beach behind and head for the hills, take Park Avenue up from the center of Laguna Beach, turn right at the end onto Alta Laguna Boulevard, and right again to head back down on Temple Hills Drive and Thalia Street. This climbing course will carry you high into the **Laguna Hills** with spectacular vistas along the entire coastline and into the interior valleys.

DANA POINT

South on Route 1, called the Pacific Coast Highway in these parts, you will pass through **Dana Point**. This ultramodern enclave, with its manmade port and 2500-boat marina, has a history dating back to the 1830s when

Richard Henry Dana immortalized the place. Writing in *Two Years Before the Mast*, the Boston gentleman-turned-sailor described the surrounding countryside: "There was a grandeur in everything around."

Today much of the grandeur has been replaced with condominiums, leaving little for the sightseer. There is the **Orange County Marine Institute** (24200 Dana Point Harbor Drive; 714-496-2274) with a small sea life museum and a 121-foot replica of Dana's brig, *The Pilgrim* (Saturday and Sunday only; admission).

The **Dana Point Lighthouse** (24532 Del Prado Avenue; 714-661-1001), a facsimile of an old beacon, serves as a nautical museum. Here you can view a collection of model sailing ships and other miniatures. Then, for a lighthouse keeper's view of the harbor and outlying coastline, take in either of the **lookout parks** at the ends of Old Golden Lantern and Blue Lantern streets.

SAN JUAN CAPISTRANO

When you're ready to flee Southern California's ultramodern coastline, Camino Capistrano is the perfect escape valve. Just north of San Clemente it leads from the Coast Highway up to **Mission San Juan Capistrano** (Camino Capistrano and Ortega Highway; 714-493-1424; admission). Seventh in the state's chain of 21 missions, the church was founded in 1776 by Father Junípero Serra. Considered "the jewel of the missions" it is a hauntingly beautiful site, placid and magical.

There are ponds and gardens here, archaeological sites, and the ruins of the original 1797 stone church, destroyed by an earthquake in 1812. The museum displays Native American crafts, early ecclesiastical artifacts, and Spanish weaponry, while an Indian cemetery memorializes the enslaved people who built this magnificent structure.

The highlight of the mission is not the swallows, which are vastly outnumbered by pigeons, but the chapel, a 1777 structure decorated with Indian designs and baroque reredos. The oldest building in California, it is the only remaining church used by Father Serra.

Of course the mission's claim to notoriety is a 1939 ditty, "When the Swallows Return to Capistrano," a tune which, like many schmaltzy songs about California, seems to remain eternally lodged in the memory whether you want it there or not. The melody describes the return of flocks of swallows every March 19. And return they do, though in ever-decreasing numbers and not always on March 19, only to depart in October for Argentina.

At the **O'Neill Museum** (31831 Los Rios Street; 714-493-8444), housed in a tiny 1870s Victorian, there are walking-tour maps of the town's old adobes. Within a few blocks you'll discover about a dozen 19th-century structures.

The **Capistrano Depot** (26701 Verdugo Street) appeared a little later in the century but is an equally vital part of the town's history. Still operating as a train station, the 1895 depot has been beautifully preserved. Built of brick in a series of Spanish-style arches, the old structure houses railroad memorabilia. An antique pullman, a brightly colored freight car, and other vintage cars line the tracks.

Jolting you back to contemporary times are two nearby buildings, both constructed in the 1980s. The **New Church of Mission San Juan Capistrano** (31522 Camino Capistrano), a towering edifice next to the town's historic chapel, is a replica of the original structure. Spanish Renaissance in design, the new church even re-creates the brilliantly painted interior of the old mission.

Across the street rises the **San Juan Capistrano Regional Library** (31495 El Camino Real; 714-493-1752), an oddly eclectic building. Drawing heavily from the Moorish-style Alhambra in Spain, the architect also incorporated ideas from ancient Egypt and classical Greece.

SAN CLEMENTE

If any place is the capital of Republican politics, it is San Clemente, a seaside town which sets the standard for Southern California's notorious conservatism because of one man. Richard Milhous Nixon, President of the United States from 1969 until his ignominious resignation during the Watergate scandal in 1974, established the Western White House on a 25-acre site overlooking the ocean. **La Casa Pacífica**, a magnificent Spanish-style home, was famous not only during Nixon's presidency, but afterwards when he retreated to San Clemente to lick his wounds. There are stories of Nixon, ever the brooding, socially awkward man, pacing the beach in a business suit and leather shoes.

The Nixon house is located off Avenida del Presidente in a private enclave called Cypress Shore. You can see it, a grand white stucco home with red tile roof, on the cliffs above San Clemente State Beach. Just walk south from the beach entrance about one half mile toward a point of land obscured by palms; the house is set back in the trees.

Another point of interest (quite literally) is **San Clemente Municipal Pier** (foot of Avenida del Mar), a popular fishing spot and centerpiece of the city beach. There are food concessions, bait and tackle shops, and local crowds galore.

For more information on the area, contact the **San Clemente Chamber of Commerce** (1100 North El Camino Real; 714-492-1131).

INLAND ORANGE COUNTY

Like much of inland Orange County, Anaheim appears as a vast and bewildering plane of urbanization, an uninspiring amalgam of housing tracts and shopping centers. But within this thickly populated and frenetic city lies the virtual epicenter of visitor appeal—**Disneyland** (1313 South Harbor Bou-

(Text continued on page 244.)

Orange County's Outback

To explore the last vestiges of Orange County's open country, plan to spend a day wandering the area's southeastern fringes. Along the ridges and valleys of the **Santa Ana Mountains** you'll find all that remains of the county's undeveloped countryside. It's your final chance to catch a glimpse of Orange County as it looked back in 1769 when the Spanish first probed the region's rugged, chaparral-covered mountains. But at the rate new housing tracts are pushing into the region, you'd better hurry!

Simply point your steed south along Route 5, then turn east on El Toro Road (Route S18) toward those lovely mountains. Ride on to Live Oak Canyon Road, then turn right and you'll slip beneath a canopy of live oaks. This leafy tunnel into Orange County's distant past is also the way to **O'Neill Regional Park** (714-858-9366). A perfect spot for a picnic lunch, the 1700-acre preserve is highlighted by Trabuco Creek Trail, which follows a bubbling stream well shaded by oak and cottonwood.

Returning to El Toro Road, which becomes Santiago Canyon Road, the route curves up what locals call Modjeska Grade, leaving in its wake a spate of subdivision projects that promise to spoil the view for solace seekers someday. Turn right on Modjeska Valley Road, another winding lane, then left at the junction of Modjeska Canyon and Foothill roads (there's a large tree forming an island between the two streets).

As you enter the rustic town of Modjeska, watch for the fire station on your left; across from it lies a small bridge leading to Hill Road. Once over the bridge, the first gate on the left belongs to one of Orange County's most important historic treasures, the **Modjeska House** (★). Formerly the retreat of the renowned Polish actress Madame Helena Modjeska, this white frame mansion, designed in the late 1880s by famed New York architect Stanford White, sits in disrepair. Surrounded by a forest of olive trees, the secluded home is officially closed to the public, but caretakers usually permit visitors to walk around the grounds.

A talented tragedienne, Madame Modjeska left the European stage to move to California with her venturesome husband, Count Karol Chlapowski. While the count tried unsuccessfully to develop a vineyard, Madame Modjeska began acting in the United States, achieving stardom in such roles as Mary Queen of Scots, Cleopatra, and Lady Macbeth. When the couple retired to Newport Beach, the estate was sold, becoming first a country club and later a private home. One can only hope that it will someday be restored to its original magnificence and opened to the public.

A mile further along Modjeska Canyon Road lies **Tucker Wildlife Sanctuary** (714-649-2760). This 12-acre refuge is home to more than 170 species of birds and animals, which can be viewed along a series of short loop trails. Tucker is best known for its hummingbirds; all seven varieties known to exist in California can be seen here. An island of conservation in a sea of development, the preserve is also home to hawks and woodpeckers. Guided tours are available.

Back on Santiago Canyon Road continue northwest to **Irvine Lake** (714-649-2560), an 800-acre private lake. Stocked and maintained with the serious angler in mind, these waters have produced a state record 59-pound catfish as well as trophy-sized "super trout" (triploid rainbow) in the 20-pound range. Bass up to nearly 15 pounds have been caught and there are bluegill and white sturgeon as well.

To wrap up this backcountry adventure, continue for four miles on Santiago Canyon Road to Chapman Avenue, turn left and go three miles to the Newport Freeway (Route 55), then proceed south to Route 5 or 405. Either will carry you back to the civilization from which you so recently departed.

levard; 714-999-4565). Almost everyone, no matter how reclusive, regardless of age, race, creed, or religion, inevitably visits this colossal theme park.

Cynics—who snicker at its fantasy formula, orderliness, ultra-cleanliness, cornball humor, and conservative overtones—nevertheless often seem to be swept away by the pure joy of Uncle Walt's fertile imagination. While absolutely nothing about it is "hidden," Disneyland can provide one of life's great escapes.

When Walt Disney cleared away orange groves to open his dream park back in 1955, he provided 18 attractions and promised that Disneyland would never stop growing. Today the park features over 50 attractions, with plans afoot to add even more rides.

If at all possible, plan your Disneyland visit to avoid the peak summer months. Huge crowds mean long waiting lines. In any case, it's a good idea to arrive as the park opens and to go directly down Main Street (the park's entry corridor) to be among the first wave of visitors fanning out into the park's many theme lands.

The Magic Kingdom is divided into seven areas. *Main Street*, portrays an all-American town at the turn of the century. *Adventureland* is a region of jungle rivers filled with hippos and crocodiles. In *Frontierland* you encounter blazing forts, Indians, and Western saloons.

Wrought-iron balconies and Mardi Gras parades create a sense of the South at *New Orleans Square*, while in *Critter Country* you can listen to a jamboree performed by mechanical bears or venture down the harrowing Splash Mountain log ride. Sleeping Beauty's castle, Pinocchio's village, and the white-knuckle Matterhorn ride are only some of the highlights of *Fantasyland*.

With ultramodern high-tech attractions, *Tomorrowland* draws the biggest crowds of all. A big hit is "Captain EO," a 3-D space adventure created by George Lucas, directed by Francis Coppola, and starring Michael Jackson.

The wizardry of George Lucas is also an ingredient in Disneyland's most sensational ride, "Star Tour." Entering Tomorrowland's realistic Spaceport, visitors are ushered aboard 40-passenger StarSpeeders which blast off on a madcap flight to the Moon of Endor. Employing the same flight simulator technology used to train military and commercial pilots, this ride synchronizes realistic motion with a stunning film, creating the sensation of intergalactic travel.

The list of things to see and do in Disneyland is staggering: take a jungle cruise, ride a Mississippi paddlewheeler, soar over the 76-acre park in a gondola, commute on a monorail, watch parades and live entertainment, eat at a mind-boggling array of restaurants, shop for just about anything, and have your picture taken with Mickey Mouse.

During off-peak periods, most adults can tour the park in a day. If you take children or visit during peak periods when lines are long, plan on a couple of days. Disneyland now employs the "Passport" type ticket, which includes park admission and unlimited use of rides and attractions. Two- and three-day passports are discounted but a family of four can figure on spending at least $100 a day, including meals, snacks, and souvenirs. Even at that, not many will argue the value of a day or two at the "Happiest Place on Earth."

California's second biggest tourist attraction, **Knott's Berry Farm** (8039 Beach Boulevard; 714-827-1776; admission), lies just five miles away in Buena Park. While some have alluded to it as a country cousin to Disneyland, this 150-acre theme park with more than 165 rides and attractions is both larger and some 15 years older than its sophisticated neighbor. "The Farm," as it is known locally, actually began life back in 1920 when Walter and Cornelia Knott planted a ten-acre berry and rhubarb patch and opened a roadside stand. Eventually the stand evolved into a "Chicken Dinner Restaurant" to which Walter Knott added a mock California Gold Rush town, complete with narrow gauge railroad.

The original restaurant still serves up Mrs. Knott's chicken dinners—at the rate of 1.5 million a year—and Walter's old *Ghost Town*, though rickety with age, looks much as it did in the beginning. To be sure, the park has grown right along with Disneyland, in a sort of symbiotic surge, meeting the demands of ever-increasing attendance. Today, more than five million people visit The Farm each year.

Beyond the Ghost Town is *Fiesta Village*, a south-of-the-border entertainment center complete with California mission replicas, open markets, strolling mariachis, and a wild ride called "Montezooma's Revenge," an upside-down-and-backwards thriller that reaches speeds of 55 miles per hour in less than five seconds.

Camp Snoopy is the official home of Charles Schultz's beloved "Peanuts" pals—Snoopy, Linus, Lucy, and Charlie Brown. Life-size versions of the popular cartoon characters roam the six-acre area hugging guests and posing for pictures. Modeled after the Sierra Nevada mountains, Camp Snoopy features a lake, waterfalls, petting zoo, animal show, and kiddie rides.

A fourth theme area, the *Roaring '20s* has thrill rides, a penny arcade, and an aquatic show, as well as the "Kingdom of the Dinosaurs." Here guests embark on an indoor boat ride, encountering 21 animated dinosaurs poised in a variety of stances amid what purports to be their natural habitat.

Knott's *Wild Water Wilderness* resembles a 1900s California river wilderness park highlighted by "Bigfoot Rapids," a wet and wild ride down California's longest manmade white water river.

Theme parks aren't the only visitor attractions in the inland reaches of Orange County. Their very existence, in fact, has spawned the growth of other travel destinations. The **Movieland Wax Museum** (7711 Beach Boulevard, Buena Park; 714-522-1154; admission), with its collection of more than 200 wax figures of movie and television stars, has grown up right in the shadow of Knott's Berry Farm. Movie buffs and stargazers will either like or loath this wax mausoleum, which presents stars frozen in realistic scenes from their most famous movies and television programs.

Collectors and students of military history often visit the **Museum of World Wars** (7884 East La Palma Avenue, Buena Park; 714-952-1776). The exhibit of uniforms, weapons, posters, and flags here is reputedly the largest of its kind in the country.

Museums catering to broader interests include the **Anaheim Museum** (241 South Anaheim Boulevard; 714-778-3301), with exhibits depicting the city's meteoric growth from a 19th-century farm society; and the excellent **Bower's Museum** (2036 North Main Street, Santa Ana; 714-972-1900), whose cultural art exhibits include Native American and Hispanic collections as well as displays from the Pacific Rim and Africa. The museum in closed for renovations until October 1992.

Located on a prehistoric fossil field that may be as extensive as the famed La Brea Tar Pits, **Ralph B. Clark Regional Park** (8800 Rosecrans Avenue, Buena Park; 714-670-8045) permits visitors to dig through centuries-old fossil beds. This unique facility also offers an interpretive center with fossil displays and a working paleontology lab. Providing marvelous educational opportunities, the digs and lab activities are structured as part of an organized tour program.

One of urban Orange County's most unusual edifices is the **Crystal Cathedral** (12141 Lewis Street, Garden Grove; 714-971-4000), a spectacular glass cathedral which rises in the shape of a star to a height of 124 feet. The pipe organ, amplified by banks of speakers that would be the envy of any rock concert promoter, is one of the largest in the world. Through the cathedral's 10,661 panes of glass you can see both the steel tubing that forms the structure's skeleton and the cars that assemble every Sunday to attend "drive-in services" in the parking lot.

Unorthodox though it may seem, even for Southern California, drive-in religion was developed by the church's pastor, Reverend Robert Shuller, when his hard-sell evangelism grew so rapidly during the 1950s that he had to conduct services at a local drive-in movie theater. Even today many of Shuller's penitents continue to prefer bucket seats to wooden pews. A massive glass door slides open during services so auto-bound worshippers can receive the word. Nor are they overlooked by ushers who glide like carhops from window to window with collection plates.

For a sense of Orange County's cultural life, head down Costa Mesa way to the South Coast Plaza Town Center, across Bristol Street from South Coast Plaza Shopping Center. Here Japanese-American sculptor Isamu Noguchi has created **California Scenario** (714-241-1700), a sculpture garden surrounded by office towers. An abstract expression of the Golden State, this stone-and-steel creation reflects the many faces of California.

The state's majestic redwoods are represented along Forest Walk, a curving path lined with granite. At the Energy Fountain, a stainless steel cone, resembling the nose of a rocket, symbolizes the space-age vitality of the state. The Desert Land section features an array of plants and cacti including the native tricereus, golden barrel cactus, and agave. The featured piece, Noguchi's tribute to the lima bean farmers who once worked this region, is a collection of 15 bronze-colored granite boulders, precisely cut and fit together to resemble a mound of the noble beans.

Shopping

NEWPORT BEACH SHOPPING

The streets radiating out from **Balboa Pavilion** (end of Main Street) are lined with beachwear stores, sundries shops, and souvenir stands. While there's little of value here, it is a good place to shop for knickknacks. The scene is much the same around **Newport Pier** (Balboa Avenue and McFadden Place).

For more upscale shopping, cast anchor at **Lido Marina Village** (Via Oporto; 714-675-8662). This well-heeled complex features a host of shops lining a brick courtyard and adjacent boardwalk.

Another Newport Beach shopping enclave lies along Marine Avenue on Balboa Island. This consumer strip is door-to-door with card shops, gift shops, and sundries stores. Without exaggerating, I would estimate that more than half the outlets here sell beachwear.

After all is said and done, but hopefully before the money is all spent, the center for Newport Beach shopping is **Fashion Island** (Newport Center Drive; 714-721-2000). Situated at the heart of Newport Center, the town's highrise financial district, it is also the best place for beautiful-people watching. Every self-respecting department store is here. **Neiman Marcus**, **I. Magnin**, **Bullock's Wilshire**, **Robinson's**, and **The Broadway** are all represented.

There's an outdoor plaza filled with fashion outlets and an atrium displaying three floors of designer dreams. If you don't believe Newport Beach is a match for Beverly Hills in flash and cash, take a tour of the parking lot. It's a showplace for Rolls Royces, Jaguars, and Mercedes, as well as plebeian models like Volvos and Audis.

LAGUNA BEACH SHOPPING

Given its long tradition as an artist colony, it's little wonder that Laguna Beach is crowded with galleries and studios. In addition to painters and sculptors the town claims to support more goldsmiths and jewelers than any place in the country. Add a few designer clothing shops plus antique stores and you have one very promising shopping spot. The center of all this action lies along Route 1 (Coast Highway) between Bluebird Canyon Drive and Laguna Canyon Road.

There are several art galleries clustered together which I found particularly interesting. Foremost is **Redfern Gallery** (1540 South Coast Highway; 714-497-3356); the others include **Vladimir Sokolov Studio Gallery** (1540 South Coast Highway; 714-494-3633), and **The Esther Wells Collection** (1390 South Coast Highway; 714-494-2497). All feature carefully chosen selections of contemporary California art.

At **Sherwood Gallery** (460 South Coast Highway; 714-497-2668), on the other hand, they have a hilarious collection of soft sculptures portraying an odd assortment of frumpy people.

Fine fashion is taken for granted at **Shebue** (540 South Coast Highway; 714-494-3148). This plush shop houses beautiful designer clothing for women. *Très chic* (and *très cher*).

Chicken Little's (574 South Coast Highway; 714-497-4818) bills itself as "The Museum of Modern Retail." Translation: they stock New Wave knickknacks like inflatable dinosaurs, ceramic fish, and Betty Boop cups. Similar in spirit, though not in age, is **Tippecanoes** (648 South Coast Highway; 714-494-1200), a vintage clothing store with a collection of antique knickknacks.

Bookstores are as rare as radicals in Orange County. One notable exception is **Fahrenheit 451** (509 South Coast Highway; 714-494-9013), a pocket-sized pocketbook store. You won't miss it, that's for sure: the outside wall is decorated with a huge whale mural. Unfortunately, the store is much smaller than the artwork, but within its limited space is a connoisseur's selection of newspapers, magazines, and used books. If that doesn't suit you, there is *yet another* **Fahrenheit 451** (540 South Coast Highway; 714-494-5151) across the street. This one sells new books and features a coffeehouse as well.

Laguna Beach's other shopping strip is Forest Avenue, a three-block promenade wall-to-wall with specialty stores. **From Laguna** (241 Forest Avenue; 714-494-4300) is here, a clothing store specializing in upscale sportswear, in-house suede designs, and women's cowboy boots, as well as jewelry by local designers.

For imported goods there's **Khyber Pass** (305 Forest Avenue, Suite 101; 714-494-5021), dealing in rugs, statuary, and lapis lazuli pieces from Afghanistan, and **A Touch of Latin** (265 Forest Avenue; 714-497-3090), which carries clothing and handcrafts from Latin and South America. **Thee Foxes Trot** (264 Forest Avenue; 714-497-3047) has an unpredictable inventory, a kind of cultural hodgepodge ranging from ethnic jewelry to African art. For contemporary painting I particularly recommend **Diane**

Nelson Gallery (278 Forest Avenue; 714-494-2440), which displays the work of modern-day impressionist Marco Sassone and other artists.

There are also two rustic, raw wood malls, **Forest Avenue Mall** (332 Forest Avenue) and **Lumberyard Plaza** (384 Forest Avenue), which blend neatly into the background. The former features the intriguing **Kristalle Natural History Gallery** (714-494-7695), specializing in fine minerals and natural crystals.

Nearby, **Aqua Classics** (14000 Coast Highway, Laguna Beach; 714-494-0138) carries ceramics, paintings, and sculpture, all with an aquatic theme.

SAN JUAN CAPISTRANO SHOPPING

The mission town of San Juan Capistrano has many shops clustered along its main thoroughfare, Camino Capistrano. Not surprisingly, the most common establishment in this two-century-old town is the antique store. In line with contemporary times, there are also pocket malls featuring boutiques, jewelers, and other outlets.

Particularly noteworthy are **The Old Barn** (31792 Camino Capistrano; 714-493-9144), a warehouse-size store filled to the rafters with antiques, and **El Peón** (26832 Ortega Highway; 714-493-3133), a modern emporium crowded with ironwood carvings, folk art, Southwestern jewelry, Peruvian wallhangings, Mexican tiles, and other Latin American imports.

INLAND ORANGE COUNTY SHOPPING

Inland Orange County is a maze of suburban shopping centers large and small. Which is all right if you're really intent on buying but rather unappealing when you simply want to browse. For those charming little boutiques and artisan shops, stick to the beach area.

In spite of its discount-store facade, the **Crystal Factory** (8010 Beach Boulevard, Buena Park; 714-952-4135) is a treasure trove of crystal and glassware. It's possible to spend from two bucks to two grand on everything from stemware to handblown crystal lamps. While browsing you can watch craftsmen hand-blow and engrave crystal items.

Fill a 16,000-square-foot building with 110 separate cubicles and you've got the **Old Chicago Antique Mall** (8960 Knott Avenue, Buena Park; 714-527-0275). Independent vendors sell wares ranging from fine old furniture to '50s memorabilia. One fellow displays more than 5000 model electric trains and some 4000 toys!

Hobby City (1238 South Beach Boulevard, Anaheim; 714-527-2323) looks like a miniature Knott's Berry Farm, anchored by a "perfect half-scale replica" of the White House and encircled by the wee tracks of the "Hobby City Choo Choo," a mini-train for kids. It also features an intriguing array of 24 specialized shops, each devoted entirely to the hobbyist and collector. Among them are stamp, coin, gem, antique, stitchery, and doll dealers.

Biggest and best of the Orange County malls is **South Coast Plaza Shopping Center** (3333 South Bristol Street, Costa Mesa; 714-241-1700). Some say this is the most distinguished retail address on the West Coast, loaded with showcase stores, sleek signature shops, and a host of lesser-known establishments.

Orange County Market Place (Orange County Fairgrounds, 88 Fair Drive, Costa Mesa; 714-723-6616) is the area's biggest flea market with some 1500 vendors displaying their wares each weekend. Saturday and Sunday, 7 a.m. to 4 p.m.

A true "find" for bargain hunters is the **Cooper Building** (1928 South Grand Avenue, Santa Ana), a collection of about 20 shops proffering designer label fashions at 25 to 75 percent off. Although aimed at the ladies, there are some men's and children's outlets.

Serious antique shoppers always head over to Orange where there's a gaggle of great shops. Considered the "antique capital of Southern California," **Orange Circle Antique Mall** (118 South Glassell Street; 714-538-8160) is the biggest and one of the best. Housed in a refurbished 1909 brick building are some 120 independently operated booths, each offering something different. Tiffany lamps, toy soldiers, barber poles, mahogany armoires . . . you name it.

Sounds foreboding, but **The Mole Hole** (4237 Campus Drive, Irvine; 714-854-8510) is a colorful and inviting gift shop specializing in limited-edition collectibles from around the world. David Winter cottages, hand-painted Limoges, Swarovshi crystal, and original Tiffany shades are part of the unusual selection.

Nightlife

NORTH ORANGE COUNTY NIGHTLIFE

The after-dark scene in Huntington Beach centers around the pier, where beach fires and parties rage long into the night. At the foot of the pier, **Maxwell's** (317 Pacific Coast Highway; 714-536-2555), an art deco lounge, offers live Top-40 music Friday and Saturday, Dixieland jazz on Sunday.

NEWPORT BEACH NIGHTLIFE

For an evening on Newport Bay, climb aboard the *Pavilion Queen*, a double-deck boat which departs from the Balboa Pavilion on a **harbor cruise** (end of Main Street; 714-673-5245).

There's live jazz nightly at the **Studio Café** (100 Main Street; 714-675-7760), a waterfront watering hole near Balboa Pier.

Even if you don't care for '30s-era sounds, stop by **Bubbles Balboa Club** (111 Palm Street; 714-675-9093). This art deco club is trimly decorated with vintage accouterments and highpointed by a translucent "bubble column." The music fits the period motif, ranging from the Ink Spots to a 14-piece band; live nightly.

Rumpelstiltskin's (114 McFadden Place; 714-673-5025) has rock music and dancing seven nights a week in the summer; on weekends the rest of the year. The rhythms range from hard rock to New Wave to jazz; very popular with locals; a good party bar. Cover.

The Cannery (3010 Lafayette Avenue; 714-675-5777), an old fish cannery that's been converted into a restaurant-cum-museum (and a fascinating one at that), has entertainment nightly. Live rock and Top-40 music is performed Friday and Saturday.

LAGUNA BEACH NIGHTLIFE

Admirers of art deco are bound to fall in love with the **Towers Lounge** in the Surf & Sand Hotel (1555 South Coast Highway; 714-497-4477). This softly lit piano bar combines the ambience of the 1930s with wide-angle views of the ocean.

The White House (340 South Coast Highway; 714-494-8088) is a landmark 1918 building in downtown Laguna Beach. A long, narrow lounge with mirrored walls, it turns tradition upside down every night with live rock, reggae, and Motown; cover.

One of Laguna Beach's hottest nightspots is also its most funky. **The Sandpiper** (1183 South Coast Highway; 714-494-4694) is a run-down club filled with dart boards and pinball machines. Often it is also filled with some of the finest sounds around. Rock, reggae, oldies, and other music is live nightly, sometimes preformed by well-known groups. Cover.

Las Brisas (361 Cliff Drive; 714-497-5434), a sleek, clifftop restaurant overlooking the ocean, is a gathering place for the fast and fashionable. A wonderful place to enjoy a quiet cocktail, it features a tile bar as well as an open-air patio.

Laguna Beach's gay scene centers around the **Boom Boom Room** (1401 South Coast Highway; 714-494-7588) at the Coast Inn. A three-tiered discotheque one half block from the beach, it contains a dancefloor, pinball machines, and two bars. Weekend cover.

There's a quieter gay scene at **Main Street** (1460 South Coast Highway; 714-494-0056), a piano bar with a predominantly male clientele.

SOUTH ORANGE COUNTY NIGHTLIFE

The ultimate evening destinations are at the ultra-posh Ritz Carlton Laguna Niguel (Ritz Carlton Drive, Laguna Niguel; 714-240-2000). Here, along corridors of polished stone, is the **Club Grill and Bar,** a wood-paneled rendezvous decorated with 19th-century paintings of equestrian scenes. Also located in the Ritz Carlton is **The Bar**, an elegant two-tiered, glass-walled lounge with sweeping ocean views. The first offers a combo nightly and the latter features a solo pianist. Dinner jackets, gentlemen.

The **Wind and Sea Restaurant** (34699 Golden Lantern, Dana Point; 714-496-6500), on the waterfront in Dana Point Harbor, features sparkling views and solo entertainers nightly.

Swallows Inn (31786 Camino Capistrano, San Juan Capistrano; 714-493-3188) is a hellbent Western bar with sawdust on the floors and ranch tools tacked to the walls. As you've already guessed, the music is country-and-western. A band kicks into action every evening.

More appealing is the **Capistrano Depot Restaurant** (26701 Verdugo Street, San Juan Capistrano; 714-496-8181), a converted station house where you can lounge in an old pullman car while listening to a duo perform nightly. They also feature jazz on Sunday afternoon.

INLAND ORANGE COUNTY NIGHTLIFE

It seems hokey at first: dining with your fingers in an imitation 12th-century castle while knights ride into battle. Actually, **Medieval Times** (7662 Beach Boulevard, Buena Park; 714-521-4740) is a brilliant concept, a re-creation of a medieval tournament, complete with games of skill and jousting matches. It can get pretty wild when the knights—highly trained horsemen and stuntmen—perform dangerous jousting and sword-fighting routines.

While original and creative forms of nightlife may be lacking in Orange County, it's through no fault of a couple local residents who were just crazy enough to string together a laundromat, barbecue joint, and beer bar. Although regulars begin by tossing in the wash, you may want to start out at **Brian's Beer & Billiards** (1944 North Placentia Avenue, Fullerton; 714-993-1401). No worries about the wash, in case you brought yours—the bar has lights connected to the washers and driers telling you exactly when your load is finished.

Sgt. Preston's Yukon Saloon (1150 West Cerritos, Anaheim; 714-778-6600) in the Disneyland Hotel is modeled on an old sourdough watering hole straight from Whitehorse or Dawson. It features an 1890s follies-type review plus dancing and other goings-on.

Cowboy Boogie (1721 South Manchester Avenue, Anaheim; 714-956-1410) is a nightclub where you can dance. Live country-and-western bands are featured Tuesday through Sunday. Otherwise it's deejay time to rock and Top-40. Cover.

While fading elsewhere, the fine art of dinner theater remains live and well received in Orange County. The **Grand Dinner Theater** (Grand Hotel, 7 Freedman Way, Anaheim; 714-772-7777) offers Broadway plays and musicals with your meal.

It's a bit wacky and sometimes corny, but **Crackers** (710 East Katella Avenue, Anaheim; 714-978-1828) provides nonstop entertainment. You'll be regaled by singing bartenders, waitresses, magicians, and jugglers. And, for better or worse, by your own peers. Audience participation is the big thing here.

Peppers (12361 Chapman Avenue, Garden Grove; 714-740-1333) is a colorful Mexican-theme restaurant that owes most of its popularity to its dancefloor rather than its food. Young singles dig the scene as deejays spin Top-40 hits nightly; cover.

Happy Hour (12081 Garden Grove Boulevard, Garden Grove; 714-537-9079) is a women's bar that features pool tables, video games, deejay music; on weekends the music is live and there's a cover charge.

You can two-step to live country-and-western music at **Crazy Horse Steak House & Saloon** (1580 Brookhollow Drive, Santa Ana; 714-549-1512), Orange County's most popular and long-lived nightspot. Cover.

Owned by the Righteous Brothers, **The Hop** (18774 Brookhurst Street, Fountain Valley; 714-963-2366) is hot. Do your hopping here on a regulation high-school gym dancefloor (hoops included) to the nostalgic strains of '50s and '60s hits. Cover, except Thursdays.

CLASSIC ENTERTAINMENT

Featuring a 2500-seat "theater in the round," the **Celebrity Theatre** (201 East Broadway, Anaheim; 714-535-2000) highlights top-name pop entertainers plus various concerts, musicals, magic shows, and comedy acts.

Grove Shakespeare (12852 Main Street, Garden Grove; 714-636-7213) presents Shakespeare in the summer and other classical dramas, comedies, and musicals year-round.

Orange County Performing Arts Center (600 Town Center Drive, Costa Mesa; 714-556-2787) is one of Southern California's great cultural assets, a 3000-seat theater which regularly features the New York City Ballet and Joffrey Ballet, plus a host of visiting dance, opera, and musical companies.

Offering the best in classic and contemporary plays, **South Coast Repertory Theatre** (655 Town Center Drive, Costa Mesa; 714-957-4033) has established itself as a major theatrical presence in California and nationwide.

Pacific Amphitheatre (Orange County Fairgrounds, 100 Fair Drive, Costa Mesa; 714-740-2000) presents concerts by name performers in the largest outdoor concert setting on the West Coast. Closed during the winter.

Irvine Meadows Amphitheatre (8808 Irvine Center Drive, Irvine/ Laguna Hills; 714-855-4515) features leading musical acts in a lovely outdoor amphitheatre. Closed during the winter.

SAN DIEGO

CHAPTER FIVE
San Diego

San Diego County's 4261 square miles occupy a Connecticut-size chunk of real estate that forms the southwestern corner of the continental United States. Geographically, it is as varied a parcel of landscape as any in the world. Surely this spot is one of the few places on the planet where, in a matter of hours, you can journey from bluff-lined beaches up and over craggy mountain peaks and down again to sun-scorched desert sands.

Moving east from the Pacific to the county's interior, travelers discover lush valleys and irrigated hillsides. Planted with citrus orchards, vineyards, and rows of vegetables, this curving countryside eventually gives way to the Palomar and Laguna mountains—cool, pine-crested ranges that rise over 6500 feet.

But it is the coast—some 76 sparkling miles stretching from San Mateo Point near San Clemente to the Mexican border—that always has held the fascination of residents and visitors alike.

When Portuguese explorer Juan Rodríguez Cabrillo laid eyes on these shores in 1542, he discovered a prospering settlement of Kumeyaay Indians. For hundreds of years, these native peoples had been living in quiet contentment on lands overlooking the Pacific; they had harvested the rich estuaries and ventured only occasionally into the scrubby hills and canyons for firewood and game.

Sixty years passed before the next visitor, Spanish explorer Sebastian Vizcaíno, came seeking a hideout for royal galleons beset by pirates. It was Vizcaíno who named the bay for San Diego de Alcala.

In 1769, the Spanish came to stay. The doughty Franciscan missionary Junípero Serra marched north from Mexico with a company of other priests and soldiers and built Mission San Diego de Alcala. It was the first of a chain of 21 missions and the earliest site in California to be settled by Europeans. Father Serra's mission, relocated a few miles inland in 1774, now sits incongruously amid the shopping centers and housing developments of Mission Valley.

California's earliest civilian settlement evolved in the 1820s on a dusty mesa beneath the hilltop presidio that protected the original mission. Pueblo San Diego quickly developed into a thriving trade and cattle ranching center after the ruling Spanish colonial regime was overthrown and replaced by the Republic of Mexico.

By the end of the century, new residents, spurred partly by land speculators, had taken root and developed the harbor and downtown business district. After the rails finally reached San Diego in 1885, the city flourished. Grand Victorian buildings lined 5th Avenue all the way from the harbor to Broadway and 1400 barren acres were set aside uptown for a city park.

After its turn-of-the-century spurt of activity, the city languished until World War II, when the U.S. Navy invaded the town en masse to establish the 11th Naval District headquarters and one of the world's largest Navy bases. San Diego's reputation as "Navytown USA" persisted well after the war-weary sailors went home. Some 140,000 Navy and Marine personnel are still based in San Diego and at Camp Pendleton to the north, but civilians now outnumber service types twenty to one and military influence has diminished accordingly.

The military has not been the only force to foster San Diego's growth. In the early 1960s, construction began on an important university that was to spawn a completely new industry. Many peg the emergence of the "new" San Diego to the opening of the University of California's La Jolla campus. Not only did the influx of 15,000 students help revive a floundering economy, it tended to liberalize an otherwise insular and conservative city.

Truth is, San Diego is no longer the sleepy, semitransparent little resort city it once was. Nowhere is the fact more evident than in the downtown district, where a building boom has brought new offices, condominiums, and hotels as well as a spectacular business and entertainment complex at Horton Plaza.

But for all the city's manmade appeal, it is nature's handiwork and an ideal Mediterranean climate that most delights San Diego visitors. With bays and beaches bathed in sunshine 75 percent of the time, less than ten inches of rainfall per year and average temperatures that mirror a proverbial day in June, San Diego offers the casual outdoor lifestyle that fulfills vacation dreams. There's a beach for every taste, ranging from broad sweeps of white sand to slender scimitars beneath eroded sandstone bluffs.

Situated a smug 120 miles south of Los Angeles on Route 5, San Diego is not so much a city as a collection of communities hiding in canyons and gathered on small shoulders of land that shrug down to the sea. As a result, it hardly seems big enough (just over 1.1 million) to rank as America's sixth

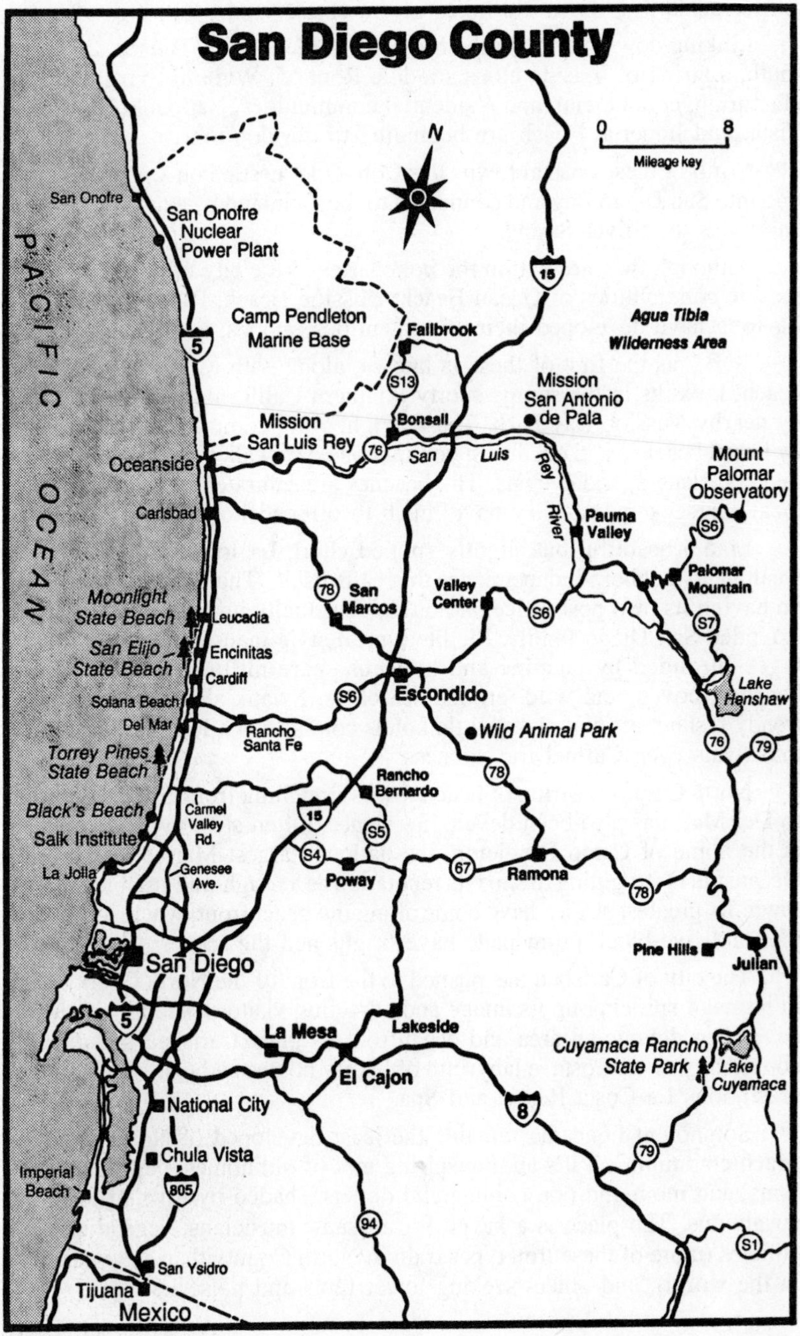
San Diego County
N
0 8
Mileage key
PACIFIC OCEAN
San Onofre
San Onofre Nuclear Power Plant
Camp Pendleton Marine Base
Fallbrook
Agua Tibia Wilderness Area
Mission San Antonio de Pala
Bonsall
Mission San Luis Rey
San Luis Rey River
Oceanside
Mount Palomar Observatory
Carlsbad
Pauma Valley
Palomar Mountain
San Marcos
Valley Center
Moonlight State Beach
Leucadia
San Elijo State Beach
Encinitas
Cardiff
Lake Henshaw
Solana Beach
Escondido
Del Mar
Rancho Santa Fe
Wild Animal Park
Torrey Pines State Beach
Rancho Bernardo
Black's Beach
Carmel Valley Rd.
Salk Institute
La Jolla
Genesee Ave.
Poway
Ramona
Pine Hills
Julian
San Diego
Lakeside
La Mesa
El Cajon
Cuyamaca Rancho State Park
Lake Cuyamaca
National City
Chula Vista
Imperial Beach
San Ysidro
Tijuana
Mexico
5
15
8
805
S13
76
S6
78
S7
79
S5
S4
67
94
S1

largest city. Total county population is two and a half million, and nine of ten residents live within 30 miles of the coast.

Linking downtown with the Mexican border city of Tijuana, 20 miles south, a string of seaside cities straddle Route 5. While thriving as manufacturing, commercial, and residential communities, National City, Chula Vista, and Imperial Beach are beginning to develop tourist industries.

North of these coastal towns lies Coronado, nestled on a peninsula jutting into San Diego Bay and connected to the mainland by a narrow sandbar known as the Silver Strand.

Although they are within the boundaries of the city of San Diego, the seaside communities of Ocean Beach, Mission Beach, Pacific Beach, and La Jolla have developed their own identities, moods, and styles.

"OB," as the first of these is known, along with Mission and Pacific beaches, exults in the sunny, sporty Southern California lifestyle fostered by nearby Mission Bay Park. These neighboring communities are fronted by broad beaches and an almost continuous boardwalk that is jammed with joggers, skaters, and cyclists. The beaches are saturated in the summer by local sun-seekers, but they have much to offer visitors.

Like a beautiful but slightly spoiled child, La Jolla is an enclave of wealth and stubborn independence that calls itself "The Village" and insists on having its own post office, although it's actually just another part of the extended San Diego family. Mediterranean-style mansions and small cottages shrouded by jasmine and hibiscus share million-dollar views of beaches, coves, and wild, eroded sea cliffs. Swank shops and galleries, trendy restaurants and classy little hotels combine in a Riviera-like setting that rivals even Carmel for chicness.

North County, a string of beach towns stretching from Oceanside south to Del Mar, has also been developing apace. Often stereotyped because it is the home of Camp Pendleton, the nation's largest Marine Corps base, Oceanside is struggling to shed its reputation as a rough-and-tumble military town. Its greatest strides have come along the beachfront, where a concrete pier and five-block promenade have brightened the scene.

The city of Carlsbad has pushed to the front of the North County pack in terms of sprucing up its image and attracting visitors. Along with its redeveloped downtown area and oceanfront lodging, Carlsbad includes the community of La Costa, a labyrinth of luxury homes and parks built around prestigious La Costa Resort and Spa.

Somnolent Leucadia remains the least developed of North County's beach communities. It's an uninspiring mix of old homes, new condominiums, and mom-and-pop commercial outlets, shaded by rows of towering eucalyptus. The place is a haven for artisans, musicians, vegetarians, triathletes (more of these iron types train in North County than anywhere else in the world), and others seeking lower rents and noise levels.

Encinitas, known as the "Flower Capital of the World," is home to some of the nation's largest growers. While they are slowly disappearing under pressure from housing developers, giant greenhouses, and fields of flowers still dot the area.

Cardiff-by-the-Sea appears from Route 101 to be little more than a row of chain restaurants strung along an otherwise lovely beach.

That could also be said about Cardiff's southern neighbor, Solana Beach. There's no town center—no real focus—to this coastal community and that has always been Solana Beach's problem and charm. Visitors whiz through on Route 5 or Route 101 (the coastal highway that threads North County beaches from Oceanside to Del Mar) without even noticing the place or its excellent beaches, hidden from view by a string of condominiums and a dramatic sandstone bluff.

One gets the feeling that North County neighbor Del Mar would love to become another La Jolla. While it lacks the natural attributes of cliff and cove, it does attract the rich, famous, and hopeful to its thoroughbred racetrack.

It is safe to say that San Diego is not as eccentric and sophisticated as San Francisco, nor as glamorous and fast-paced as Los Angeles. But those who still perceive it as a laid-back mecca for beach bums—or as a lunch stop en route to Mexico—are in for a huge surprise.

Easy Living

Transportation

ARRIVAL

Even though it is located in California's extreme southwest corner, San Diego is the hub of an elaborate highway network. The city is easily reached from north or south via **Route 5**; **Route 8** serves drivers from the east; and **Route 15** is the major inland freeway for travelers arriving from the mountain west. **Route 76** runs inland from Oceanside to the Palomar Mountains, then becomes **Route 79**, which leads to Julian. From Carlsbad, **Route 78**, connects the coast with inland communities like Escondido.

BY AIR

San Diego International Airport (Lindbergh Field) lies just three miles northwest of downtown San Diego and is easily accessible from either Route 5 or Route 8. The airport is served by most major airlines, including Alaska Airlines, American Airlines, American West Airlines, Continental Airlines, Delta Airlines, Northwest Airlines, Skywest Western Express, Southwest Airlines, States West Airlines, Trans World Airlines, United Airlines, USAir, and Wardair Canada.

Taxis, limousines, and buses provide service from the airport. **San Diego Transit System** bus #2 (619-233-3004) carries passengers to downtown destinations. Or try the **Coast Shuttle** (619-231-1123) which travels to major points in the city as well as to Orange County and Los Angeles.

BY BUS

Greyhound/Trailways Bus Lines (619-239-9171) services San Diego from around the country. The terminal is located in the downtown area at 120 West Broadway and 1st Avenue. Greyhound also carries passengers inland from San Diego to Escondido (700 West Valley Parkway; 619-745-6522) and El Cajon (250 South Marshall Avenue; 619-444-1591).

BY TRAIN

Chugging to a stop at historic Santa Fe Depot, at Kettner Boulevard and Broadway downtown, is a nice and convenient way to arrive in San Diego. **Amtrak** (800-872-7245) offers several coast-hugging roundtrips daily between Los Angeles and San Diego, with stops at Oceanside and Del Mar.

CAR RENTALS

Much like the rest of Southern California, San Diego is spread out over a wide area and is best seen by car. Car rental companies abound. Most major rental agencies have franchises at the airport. These include **Avis Rent A Car** (619-231-7171), **Budget Rent A Car** (619-297-3360), **Dollar Rent A Car** (619-234-3388), **Hertz Rent A Car** (619-231-7023), and **National Car Rental** (619-231-7103).

For better rates (but less convenient service) try agencies located near the airport that provide pick-up service: **Avon Rent A Car** (619-291-7368), **Aztec Rent A Car** (619-232-6117), **Fuller Auto Rental** (619-232-3444), **Ladki International Rent A Car** (619-233-9333), and **Rent A Wreck** (619-224-8235).

PUBLIC TRANSPORTATION

North County Transit District (619-743-6283), or NCTD, covers the general area from Camp Pendleton to Del Mar along the coast. NCTD operates numerous North County bus routes that service the communities of Oceanside, Carlsbad, Encinitas, Leucadia, Cardiff, Rancho Santa Fe, Solana Beach, and Del Mar.

Several modern and efficient public transportation systems operate throughout San Diego. Information and schedules are available for all systems by calling **San Diego Transit** (619-233-3004).

The San Diego Transit bus system is the city's largest public transportation network, with lines linking all major points. All San Diego Transit stops are marked with a blue triangle.

The city's newest and most venturesome mode of public transportation is the **San Diego Trolley** (619-233-3004). The light rail system's line operates daily from the Santa Fe Depot to the Mexican border. Understandably, this line is known as the "Tijuana Trolley," but it also serves the south bay cities of National City, Chula Vista, and Imperial Beach. The East Line, also departing from the Santa Fe Depot, serves southeastern San Diego and inland communities to El Cajon.

National City Transit (619-474-7505) serves National City and **Chula Vista Transit** (619-691-5260), or SCOOT, serves Bonita and the city of Chula Vista. **Southwest Coaches** (619-232-8505) runs from downtown San Diego to National City and Chula Vista and on to the San Ysidro international border. In addition, Southwest runs from Coronado along the Silver Strand to Imperial Beach.

For Inland San Diego, NCTD provides bus service from Escondido to Ramona. **Northeast Rural Bus System** (619-765-0145) takes passengers from El Cajon to Julian, Santa Ysabel, and Cuyamaca Rancho.

TAXIS

In North County (La Jolla to Carlsbad), you can call **Bill's Cab** (619-755-6737) or **Oceanside Yellow Cab** (619-722-4217).

San Diego is not a taxi town in the usual big city sense, but there's a cab if you need it—just a telephone call away. Leading companies include **Checker Cab** (619-234-4477), **Silver Cabs** (619-280-5555), and **Yellow Cab** (619-234-6211). In Coronado there's **Coronado Cab** (619-435-6211).

Hotels

San Diego has a vast resource of accommodations, ranging from exclusive luxury suites to budget rooms, with a broad range in between. Even so, San Diego offers few beachfront hotels. What there are tend to be moderately priced, rather ordinary chain-variety hotels and motels.

Nonetheless, I have scoured city and shore in an effort to provide a listing of the best and most interesting accommodations, covering a range of prices, always with the principle of good value as a guide. Unless you plan ahead, you will have difficulty finding a room anywhere on the water during the summer months, when many beachfront properties rent only by the week or month. Room rates at the beaches vary, usually going up at least ten percent or so during the peak summer season.

NORTH SAN DIEGO COUNTY HOTELS

Many of San Diego's best beaches lie to the north, between Oceanside and Del Mar. Sadly, most of the good hotels do not. But don't worry, among those listed below all but two are either oceanfront or oceanview properties.

The **Southern California Beach Club** (121 South Pacific, Oceanside; 619-722-6666) is a 44-suite Mediterranean-style time-share facility situated on the beach near Oceanside Pier. Each suite is graciously appointed with quality furnishings in contemporary hues of peach, heather, and blue. Kitchens are standard; other extras include a mini-gym, rooftop jacuzzis, and laundry facilities; deluxe to ultra-deluxe.

You are literally surrounded by water at **Villa Marina** (2008 Harbor Drive North, Oceanside; 619-722-1561), a 67-room resort motel situated on a jettylike peninsula at the mouth of Oceanside Harbor. Villa Marina's exterior is not inspiring, but its rooms belie the roadside-motel appearance. For starters, they are mostly large, moderate-to-deluxe-priced, family-sized, one-, and two-bedroom suites smartly decorated and replete with fireplaces, full kitchens, and private balconies. There are swimming and therapy pools on the property. Best of all are the marvelous views of harbor and ocean.

Carlsbad offers several nice oceanfront facilities, including **Tamarack Beach Resort** (3200 Carlsbad Boulevard, Carlsbad; 619-729-3500), a Spanish contemporary-style condominium. Finished in peach and aqua hues, the Tamarack rents standard rooms as well as suites of all sizes. Most are smashingly decorated in upbeat tones and textures and incorporate sensitive touches like fresh flowers and photographic prints. Suites, though priced in the ultra-deluxe range, may be the best value on the North Coast. They have kitchens and private balconies. Rooms are deluxe-priced. All guests can make use of the oceanfront restaurant, clubhouse, fitness center, jacuzzis, and activities program as well as enjoying the adjacent beach.

Advertised as "a very special bed and breakfast," the **Pelican Cove Inn** (320 Walnut Avenue, Carlsbad; 619-434-5995) is a lovely Cape Cod-style house with eight guest rooms. Each features a fireplace and is well furnished with antique pieces, including feather beds while some rooms have jacuzzis. Visitors share a sun deck and patio with gazebo. Located two blocks from the beach, the inn is priced deluxe to ultra-deluxe.

Affordability and quietude are the order of the day at **Ocean Manor Motel** (2950 Ocean Street, Carlsbad; 619-729-2493). This tidy, 47-room mom-and-pop complex is so near the sea you can hear it, but a row of expensive beach houses blocks the view. Some sections of the rambling Ocean Manor date back to 1939, and "new" additions are 1950s vintage, so the general decor could best be described as Early-American Motel. An oldie but goodie in this case, however. The furniture may be oddly matched and a bit stodgy, but the place is clean and lovingly maintained and features a pretty garden. All rooms have fully equipped kitchens. Budget to moderate in price.

There's not much to say about the **Beach Terrace Inn** (2775 Ocean Street, Carlsbad; 619-729-5951). A 49-unit establishment with stucco facade and the feel of a motel, it is part of the Best Western chain. There's a pool, sauna, and jacuzzi, plus a single feature that differentiates the Beach Terrace from most other places hereabouts—it is located right on the beach. A broad swath of white sand borders the property, making the moderate-to-deluxe price for a room with kitchen a worthwhile investment.

Sporting a fresh look, the fabled **La Costa Hotel & Spa** (Costa del Mar Road, Carlsbad; 619-438-9111) can justly claim to be one of the world's great "total" resorts. This luxurious 400-acre complex boasts 482 rooms plus villas and châteaus, its own movie theater, two 18-hole championship golf courses, 23 tennis courts (hard court, clay, *and* grass), seven restaurants, and one of the country's largest and most respected spa and fitness centers. Simply put, the place is awesome. With rooms *starting* well up in the ultra-deluxe range, La Costa's appeal to the well-monied few is apparent.

Located on a lofty knoll above the Pacific, **Radisson Inn Encinitas** (85 Encinitas Boulevard, Encinitas; 619-942-7455) is one of the largest and best moderate-priced hotels in North County. Built on three levels, the 96-room complex looks like a condominium. With a pool and jacuzzi, it has many of the same features. The rooms are stylishly decorated in light pastel tones, with contemporary oak and bentwood furniture, and include private balconies overlooking the ocean. Continental breakfast is served at the pool-side cabaña.

The best budget-to-moderate-priced lodging around the beach in Encinitas is **Moonlight Beach Motel** (233 2nd Street, Encinitas; 619-753-0623). This three-story, 24-unit family-run motel is tucked away in a residential neighborhood overlooking Moonlight Beach State Park. Rooms are threadbare but clean, and contain everything you'll need, including kitchenettes. Some of the accommodations on the upper two floors command ocean views.

It's all in the name when it comes to locating **Del Mar Motel On The Beach** (1702 Coast Boulevard, Del Mar; 619-755-1534), the only motel between Carlsbad and La Jolla on the beach. All 45 rooms in this plain stucco building are steps from the sand. That's undoubtedly where you'll spend your time because there is little about the rooms to enchant you. They are basic in design, equipped with stick furniture, refrigerators, color televisions, and air-conditioning. Because the hotel is at a right angle to the beach, only a few rooms have full views of the water. Nevertheless, summer rates begin at deluxe prices. Winter rates are moderate.

Built on the site of a once-famous Del Mar Beach getaway, **The Inn/L'Auberge at Del Mar** (1540 Camino del Mar; 619-259-1515) replicates the old hotel's nostalgic past of the '20s, '30s, and '40s. The Tudor/Craftsman inn was frequented by Hollywood greats such as Bing Crosby, Jimmy Durante, and Rudolph Valentino. Its rich lobby is dominated by a replica of the huge original brick fireplace. Along with 123 guest rooms and suites, the inn features a restaurant with patio dining, bar, full-service European spa, tennis courts, leisure and lap pools, shops, a park amphitheater, and ocean views. Each room has its own patio. Ultra-deluxe.

On a hill overlooking Del Mar's village center and coastline is the romantic little **Rock Haus Inn** (410 15th Street, Del Mar; 619-481-3764). One of the region's finest bed and breakfasts, it would be hard to top this sprawling Craftsman-style bungalow for location, charm, or quality. Built in 1910 and located two blocks from the beach, it saw action during Prohibition as a speakeasy and gambling den. Today its ten rooms, four with private baths, are thematically decorated and reflect considerable taste and talent. Rates range from deluxe for the little "Wren's Nest" with its ocean view and old-time iron twin beds to the ultra-deluxe "Huntsman's" suite, which features a fireplace. Guests assemble on a sunny veranda for light breakfast and sunset snacks.

For an elegant country inn consider **The Inn at Rancho Santa Fe** (Paseo Delicias and Linea del Cielo, Rancho Santa Fe; 619-756-1131). Widely known among the world's genteel, it is a country inn comprised of Early California-style casitas on a wooded 20-acre site. Situated five miles inland from Solana Beach, the inn offers individually decorated guest rooms as well as two- and three-bedroom cottages. The latter generally feature private sun terraces, fireplaces, and kitchenettes. Furnishings, true to the understated theme, are old but durable, built from sturdy woods like chestnut and maple. Displayed in the homespun lobby is a priceless collection of antique hand-carved model ships. There are tennis courts, swimming pool, croquet, and two restaurants. Rooms are deluxe, suites and cottages ultra-deluxe.

LA JOLLA HOTELS

Like a Monopoly master, La Jolla possesses the lion's share of excellent accommodations in the San Diego area. Understandably, there are no budget hotels in this fashionable village by the sea; only a few, in fact, offer rooms in the moderate range. Among that scarce number, two stand out as the best values. **Sands of La Jolla** (5417 La Jolla Boulevard; 619-459-3336) is a small 38-room motel on a busy thoroughfare. Rooms are not exactly designer showcases, but they are tastefully appointed and neatly maintained. Budget to moderate.

Tucked away on the north fringe of the village is **Andrea Villa Inn** (2402 Torrey Pines Road; 619-459-3311), a classy-looking 49-unit motel that packs more amenities than some resorts. There is a pool, spa, valet, concierge, and continental breakfast service. The rooms are spacious and professionally decorated with quality furniture. Andrea Villa is one of La Jolla's best hotel buys; moderate to deluxe.

Small European-style hotels have always been popular in La Jolla, and the granddaddy of them all is the **Colonial Inn** (910 Prospect Street; 619-454-2181). Established in 1913, the 75-room establishment features lavishly redecorated rooms that beautifully blend antique and contemporary furnishings. Oceanfront rooms provide matchless views. Deluxe to ultra-deluxe.

More than just a hotel, **La Valencia** (1132 Prospect Street; 619-454-0771) is a La Jolla institution and one of the loveliest hotels in San Diego. Resplendent in pink stucco and Spanish tile, it is perched on a breezy promontory overlooking the coves and sea cliffs of La Jolla. From the moment guests enter via a trellis-covered tile loggia into a lobby that could pass for King Juan Carlos' living room, they are enveloped in elegance. The private accommodations, however, don't always measure up to the hotel's image. Some of the 100 rooms are rather small and furnished in reproduction antiques. Ah, but out back there's a beautiful garden terrace opening onto the sea and tumbling down to a free-form swimming pool edged with lawn. Facilities include a gym, sauna, and three distinctive restaurants. Ultra-deluxe in price.

The **Sheraton Grande Torrey Pines** (10950 North Torrey Pines; 619-558-1500), adorned with marble and polished wood, is an equally spectacular white-glove establishment. Here art deco visits the 21st century in a series of terraces that lead past plush dining rooms, multi-tiered fountains and a luxurious swimming pool. Ultra-deluxe.

Just as the village boasts San Diego's finest selection of small hotels, it can also claim a well-known bed and breakfast. **The Bed and Breakfast Inn at La Jolla** (7753 Draper Avenue; 619-456-2066), listed as an historical site, was designed as a private home in 1913 by the renowned architect Irving Gill. The John Phillip Sousa family resided here in 1921. Faithfully restored by its present owners as a 16-room inn, it stands today as Gill's finest example of salt box-style architecture. Impeccably decorated and ideally situated a block from the ocean, this inn is the essence of La Jolla. Each room features an individual decorative theme carried out in period furnishings. Some have fireplaces and ocean views. All but one tiny sleeping room have private baths. Deluxe to ultra-deluxe.

La Jolla's only true beachfront hotel is **Sea Lodge** (8110 Camino del Oro; 619-459-8271). Designed and landscaped to resemble an old California hacienda, this 128-room retreat overlooks the Pacific on a mile-long beach. With its stuccoed arches, terra-cotta roofs, ceramic tilework, fountains, and flowers, Sea Lodge offers a relaxing south-of-the-border setting. Rooms are large and fittingly appointed with "rustic-Hispanic" furnishings. All feature balconies and the usual amenities; pool and tennis courts. Deluxe to ultra-deluxe.

MISSION BAY AND THE BEACHES HOTELS

Pacific Beach boasts the San Diego County motel with the most character of all. **Crystal Pier Motel** (4500 Ocean Boulevard; 619-483-6983) is a throwback to the 1930s. Fittingly so, because that's when this quaint-looking assemblage of 25 cottages on Crystal Pier was built. This blue-and-white woodframe complex, perched over the waves, features little cottages that are hardly more than huts. Each comes with a kitchen and patio-over-the-sea, not to mention your own parking place on the pier. A unique discovery indeed. Deluxe.

There aren't many beachfront facilities along Pacific Beach, Mission Beach, and Ocean Beach, except for condominiums. One particularly pretty eight-unit condominium, **Ventanas al Mar** (3631 Ocean Front Walk; 619-459-7125), overlooks the ocean in Mission Beach. Its contemporary two- and three-bedroom units feature fireplaces, jacuzzi tubs, kitchens, and washer-dryers. They sleep as many as eight people and rent in the deluxe to ultra-deluxe range.

Just a few doors away is **Far Horizons** (3643-45 Ocean Front Walk; 619-459-7125), a rustic, two-story gray frame fourplex. Here two-bedroom apartments with views are deluxe-priced. Summer rentals by the week only.

Most of the hotels within sprawling Mission Bay Park are upscale resorts in the deluxe to ultra-deluxe price range. But there's budget-priced relief at the **Western Shores Motel** (4345 East Mission Bay Drive; 619-273-1121), located just across the street from Mission Bay Golf Course. This is a quiet, newly refurbished 40-unit court that simply can't be matched for value anywhere in the area.

Only one Mission Bay resort stands out as unique—the **San Diego Princess** (1404 West Vacation Road; 619-274-4630). Over 40 acres of lush gardens, lagoons, and white sand beach surround the villas and cottages of this 450-room resort. Except for some fancy suites, room decor is motel-modern, with quality furnishings. But guests don't spend much time in their rooms anyway. At the Princess there's more than a mile of beach, a children's playground, boat rentals, eight tennis courts, five pools, three restaurants, and lounges. A self-contained island paradise. Deluxe.

DOWNTOWN SAN DIEGO HOTELS

Among the few decent downtown budget overnight spots, **Churchill's Castle** (827 C Street; 619-236-1673) is about the cleanest and most livable. Billed as "small, quaint, and unique," this venerable seven-story, 92-room hotel is mostly quaint. Built in 1915, it was somewhat tastelessly remodeled to "depict an authentic medieval English castle." In an equally schmaltzy decorative scheme, 30 of the Churchill's better rooms are done up in different thematic motifs such as "Hawaiian Sunset" and "American Indian." Bedspreads and wall murals are the only difference. To really save money during a downtown stay, ask for one of the rooms with a shared bathroom.

If you are driving, you might try one of downtown's handiest budget to moderate priced accommodations, **Clarke's Flamingo Lodge** (1765 Union Street; 619-234-6787). Conveniently situated, this 70-unit motel offers small, plainly furnished rooms plus a pool and coffee shop.

Chain hotels are normally not included in these listings, but because of the lack of good, low-cost lodgings downtown, I'm compelled to tell you about **Budget Hotels of America** (1835 Columbia Street; 619-544-0164). One of a chain including six other San Diego area motels, this 101-room property offers the nicest and newest rooms downtown in the budget range. Queen-sized beds complement a bright, functional, and contemporary environment.

The best value for your dollar among moderately priced downtown hotels is the 67-room **Comfort Inn** (719 Ash Street; 619-232-2525). A million-dollar renovation has left the rooms looking very slick. They feature wood furniture, designer color schemes, and high-grade carpeting. The inn has a pool-sized jacuzzi and serves a continental breakfast. Conveniently located next to Balboa Park just a few blocks from the city center.

Highest marks for a midtown hotel in the moderate category go to **Best Western Bayside Inn** (555 West Ash Street; 619-233-7500). Small enough (122 rooms) to offer some degree of personalized service, this modern high-rise promises nearly all the niceties you would pay extra for at more prestigious downtown hotels, including a harbor view. Furnishings and amenities are virtually at par with those found in the typical Hilton or Sheraton. There is a pool and spa, plus a restaurant and cocktail lounge.

On the more charming side are San Diego's guesthouses, bed and breakfasts, and historic hotels. **Harbor Hill Guest House** (2330 Albatross Street; 619-233-0638) overlooks the harbor in a centrally located area known as "Banker's Hill." This elegant 1920 home once belonged to the city's mayor. Five smartly decorated rooms and suites in the moderate price range are arranged on three levels, each with a kitchen-dining area, and sitting room. There is also a lovely garden and redwood deck where continental breakfast is served.

My vote for the prettiest and most hospitable of San Diego's bed and breakfasts goes to the **Keating House Inn** (2331 2nd Avenue; 619-239-8585). This historically designated 1888 Victorian home in a sunny hillside residential neighborhood between Balboa Park and downtown offers eight comfy-cozy rooms in the moderate category. With its gabled roof, octagonal window turret, and conical peak, this beautifully restored Queen Anne is every bit as nice inside, where quality period furnishings and accessories round out the decor. A nice patio and garden and a friendly resident family of Irish setters complete the homey scene.

Looking much as it did when it was built in 1887, the majestic **Britt House** (406 Maple Street; 619-234-2926) stands three stories high and has space aplenty for ten rooms, all priced in the deluxe category. This immaculate Victorian, just steps from Balboa Park, is old lace and walnut and afternoon teas in the parlor. Just like staying at a rich aunt's. The innkeepers provide great care and attention, even preparing full breakfasts. San Diego's oldest and most popular bed and breakfast; deluxe.

No downtown hotel has a more colorful past than the **Horton Grand Hotel** (311 Island Avenue; 619-544-1886). This 132-room Victorian gem is actually two old hotels that were disassembled piece by piece and resurrected a few blocks away. The two were lavishly reconstructed and linked by an atrium-lobby and courtyard. The 1880s theme is faithfully executed, from the hotel's antique-furnished rooms (each with a fireplace) to its period-costumed staff. Room rates hover in deluxe territory, but such amenities as a concierge and afternoon tea combine with friendly service and perfect location to make it one of the city's best hotel values.

Built in 1910 in honor of the 18th president by his son Ulysses S. Grant, Jr., the **U. S. Grant Hotel** (326 Broadway; 619-232-3121) reigned as downtown San Diego's premier hotel for decades. Now, after an extensive refurbishing, the U.S. Grant is once again a showcase boasting 280 rooms, a restaurant, and a lounge. It is quite possibly the most elegant and certainly the most beautifully restored historic building in the city. There's a marble-floored lobby with cathedral-height ceilings and enormous crystal chandeliers. Rooms are richly furnished with mahogany poster beds, Queen Anne-style armoires, and wing-back chairs. Ultra-deluxe.

Attracting an exclusively gay clientele, **Dmitri's Guesthouse** (931 21st Street; 619-238-5547) has six rooms, with shared or private baths, priced moderately. Among the amenities is a yard, jacuzzi, and swimsuit-optional pool. Situated in a century-old house, Dmitri's serves a continental breakfast poolside every morning.

Balboa Park Inn (3402 Park Boulevard; 619-298-0823), also very popular with gays, sits in four buildings near Balboa Park. Like the park itself, they were built in 1915 for the Panama-California Exposition. In addition to 25 rooms and suites the complex features a courtyard and sun terrace. Continental breakfast is served in the rooms. Moderate.

CORONADO HOTELS

Coronado has long been a playground of the rich and famous and the city's hotel rates reflect its ritzy heritage. The best deal on a nice, moderately priced room in the heart of Coronado seems to be at **El Cordova Hotel** (1351 Orange Avenue; 619-435-4131). Originally built as a private mansion in 1902, El Cordova's moderate size (40 rooms) and lovely Spanish-hacienda architecture make it a relaxing getaway spot. A pool and patio restaurant are added niceties.

Nothing can detract from the glamour of the **Hotel del Coronado** (1500 Orange Avenue; 619-522-8000). With its turrets, cupolas, and gingerbread facade, it is one of the great hotels of California. The last in a proud line of extravagant seaside resorts, the Hotel del Coronado has long been the resting place of United States presidents and Hollywood stars. Remember, however, this celebrated 100-year-old Victorian landmark is a major tourist attraction, so in addition to guests, who usually fill its 691 rooms to capacity, thousands of visitors crowd the lobby, grounds, and shops every day. Be aware, too, that many rooms are in a highrise wing adjacent to the original building and though more comfortable are not the real thing. "Hotel Del" has two pools, a long stretch of beach, tennis courts, a first-class health club, and a gallery of shops. Ultra-deluxe.

Across the street rises the **Glorietta Bay Inn** (1630 Glorietta Boulevard; 619-435-3101), the 1908 Edwardian mansion of sugar king John D.

Spreckels which has been transformed into an elegant 98-room hotel. Suites here reflect the grandeur of Spreckels' time, but ordinary rooms are, in fact, rather ordinary. Continental breakfast, ladies and gentlemen is served on the mansion terrace. Deluxe.

POINT LOMA, SHELTER AND HARBOR ISLANDS HOTELS

Ensconced in a plain vanilla, two-story former church building, the **Elliot International** (3790 Udall Street; 619-223-4778) is filled with 60 to 76 budget-minded guests almost every night in the summer. Comfortable bunk beds are grouped in 18 rooms housing from two to ten people in youth-hostel fashion. Family rooms are also available and there is a common kitchen and dining area. Bring your own bedding.

A rare beachfront find in residential Point Loma is the **Ocean Manor Hotel** (1370 Sunset Cliffs Boulevard; 619-222-7901). This trim, white, two-story, 25-room apartment hotel sits right on the seaside cliffs. Rooms are neat and clean but very basic. Rates for bachelor and studio apartments, including kitchen facilities, are budget to moderate.

Manmade Shelter and Harbor Islands jut out into San Diego Bay, providing space for several large resorts. For a relaxing, offbeat alternative to these mammoth hotels try **Humphrey's Half Moon Inn** (2303 Shelter Island Drive; 619-224-3411). Surrounded by subtropical plants, this nautical-rustic 182-room complex overlooks the yacht harbor and gives the feeling of staying on an island. The rooms are tastefully but simply decorated using top-quality wood and rattan furnishings. There is a pool, spa, putting green, and restaurant. A good value at a moderate to deluxe price.

OLD TOWN HOTELS

Best bet in the budget to moderate category is the appropriately named **Old Town Inn** (4444 Pacific Highway; 619-260-8024). Strolling distance from Old Town, this spiffy little 83-room family-owned motel has small rooms but adds amenities like a guest laundry. You couldn't expect much more for a budget price.

For the romantic, **Heritage Park Bed & Breakfast Inn** (2470 Heritage Park Row; 619-295-7088), a storybook 1889 Queen Anne mansion with a striking turret, is an enchanting bed and breakfast. Set on a grassy hillside, it provides a tranquil escape. Choose from nine distinctive chambers (five with private baths), each furnished with museum-quality antiques. Most feature ornate brass or four-poster canopy beds and old-fashioned quilts. Deluxe in price.

SOUTH SAN DIEGO COUNTY HOTELS

Among all those identical motels grouped around the freeway exits in Chula Vista, **The Traveler Motel** (235 Woodlawn Avenue; 619-427-9170) is your best bet. Conveniently located just a block from the highway, this family-owned 84-unit motel is early Holiday Inn throughout, but its rates hark back to 1960s. Not that you would really expect them, but extras include two pools, laundry facilities, and color cable television. Budget.

Beds at the **Imperial Beach Hostel** (170 Palm Avenue, Imperial Beach; 619-423-8039), tabbed in the low budget range, are the least expensive anywhere in San Diego County. Located in a former firehouse, the hostel features 36 bunk beds arranged none too privately in men's and women's dorms. There is a community kitchen and common room plus a rear courtyard with picnic tables.

The **Seacoast Inn** (800 Seacoast Drive; 619-424-5183) is the only hostelry located directly on the sands of Imperial Beach. Recently modernized and decked out with a heated outdoor pool and hot tub, this 38-room complex looks good inside and out. Beachside units are especially nice and have full kitchens. Summer reservations should be made a year in advance; moderate in price.

INLAND SAN DIEGO COUNTY HOTELS

San Luis Rey Downs (31474 Golf Club Drive, Bonsall; 619-758-3762) is a casual little resort nestled along the San Luis Rey River. There are only 26 rooms, neat, clean, and basic, in a two-story woodframe lodge overlooking the golf course. But this inviting hideaway also offers a restaurant, lounge, pool, spa, and tennis courts. Moderate.

Pine Tree Lodge (425 West Mission Avenue; 619-745-7613) is clearly the nicest of the reasonably priced motels in Escondido. Family owned and operated, it is sparkling clean and well maintained. Some of the 38 rooms have kitchens and fireplaces; pool and sun deck; budget to moderate.

One of the county's leading resorts is **Rancho Bernardo Inn** (17550 Bernardo Oaks Drive, Rancho Bernardo; 619-487-1611). World-class golf and tennis aside, this handsome hacienda-style complex is a gracious country retreat. Rooms here, however, are rather ordinary considering the deluxe to ultra-deluxe rates.

Overnighting in the Mount Palomar area is limited to camping, except for the **Lazy H Ranch** (Route 76, Pauma Valley; 619-742-3669). When the proprietor said the place "dates back to the '40s," I wondered which '40s—it has the look and feel of an early California homestead. The 12 rooms include amenities you'd expect from a budget to moderate-priced establishment. But here you can adjourn to the Spanish-style patio, stroll among the lemon trees in the garden, or take a dip in the pool.

One of Southern California's oldest hostelries, the 1897 **Julian Hotel** (Main and B streets, Julian; 619-765-0201) is a Victorian charmer. Even though most of its 18 rooms share European-style baths, the place is often full, particularly on weekends, so reserve in advance. Two charming cottages and the rooms are done in period fashion with plenty of brass, lace, porcelain, and mahogany. In addition to an historic building, guests share

a lovely sitting room furnished with
to deluxe.

The 23-room **Julian Lodge** (4th an
designed after a 19th-century hotel, is a ne
recaptures the original. The rooms are sı
riod-style furnishings. The breakfast parlo
tables and an inviting fireplace. Moderate.

Shadow Mountain Ranch (2771 Frisiu
0323), a large, attractive country house near Ju ... ost
unique lodging in its "enchanted cottage," comp ... ed stove,
and the "grandma's attic cottage," containing all ... s antiques. For
the adventurous, they even have a tiny treehouse ... h built-in commode.
And there is one room in the main house as well. Full breakfast; moderate to deluxe.

Also consider **Pine Hills Lodge** (2960 La Posada Way, Pine Hills; 619-765-1100), a wonderfully rustic complex with a lodge and cabins that date back to 1912. Surrounded by pines and cedars, this cozy retreat features six European-style rooms (with shared bath) in the lodge. The 12 equally countrified cabins are woodframe structures complete with clawfoot tubs. Located at 4500 feet elevation, Pine Hills is a mini-resort featuring a restaurant, bar, and dinner theater. Moderate to deluxe.

Can't get a room in Julian? Don't despair, go to the **Ramona Valley Inn** (4th and Main streets, Ramona; 619-789-6433). It's a roadside motel, clean and comfortable, located 22 miles west of Julian. Pool; kitchenettes in some rooms; budget to moderate.

Magnolia Travel Lodge (471 North Magnolia Avenue, El Cajon; 619-447-3999) is the nicest of a gaggle of budget to moderate-priced motels lining Route 8. You won't confuse its Spanish stucco styling with the Alhambra, but you will find the attractively furnished rooms quite comfortable. Pool.

It's not listed or advertised anywhere, but if you need clean, cozy, budget-rate lodgings, check out the **St. Francis Motel** (1368 East Main Street, El Cajon; 619-444-8147). This trim 37-room court offers small, simply decorated rooms, some with kitchens. Pool.

Restaurants

Although panned by food critics since pioneer times, San Diego area restaurants have made great strides in recent years. The county is shackled with more than its share of fast food outlets and identical Mexican eateries, but there are dozens of excellent restaurants, too. Spurred by a wave of talented chefs from all over the world, San Diego is beginning to close the gourmet gap on San Francisco and Los Angeles.

O COUNTY RESTAURANTS

the end of the historic Oceanside Pier, **The Fisherman's** (1 Oceanside Pier; 619-722-2314) boasts the most prominent ews in North County. Heavy wood, floor-to-ceiling glass, and patio g make this a comfortable lunch or dinner stop. Mesquite-broiled seaood entrées are my favorites, but there is a pasta and salad selection. An upstairs bar and a 25-cent golf cart ride back down the pier add to this perfect sunset stop. Sunday brunch. Moderate to deluxe.

Painted white and blue like an Aegean taverna, **Mykonos** (258 Harbor Drive South, Oceanside; 619-757-8757) adds dining diversity to Oceanside's marina. Greek owned and operated, it features traditional dishes like moussaka, *souvlaki*, and chicken *salonika*, plus a variety of seafood specialties. Favorites are *kalamari Mykonos* (squid sautéed with bell peppers and wine) and scampi baked in tomato sauce and feta cheese. Complete with a patio dining area overlooking the harbor, live entertainment, and Greek dancing, Mykonos serves lunch and dinner at moderate prices.

La Costa Hotel and Spa (Costa del Mar Road; Carlsbad; 619-438-9111) features six restaurants, including the stylish **Champagne Dining Room** (jackets please, gentlemen) and **Ristorante Figaro**, specializing in Northern Italian cuisine. Of the six, **The Spa Dining Room** offers the best and most interesting dishes. Low-calorie, low-cholesterol meals, designed to dovetail with La Costa's excellent spa programs, are superbly prepared and colorfully presented. Prices at the various restaurants range from moderate to ultra-deluxe.

Neiman's (2978 Carlsbad Boulevard, Carlsbad; 619-729-4131), an eye-catching Victorian landmark, houses both a dining room and café/bar. My favorite for lunch or dinner is the café, where LeRoy Neiman lithographs hang on the walls and the menu includes trendy dishes such as rack of lamb, chicken dijonaise, and smoked chicken with cheese quesadillas. It also has burgers, pasta, and salads at budget to moderate prices. The Sunday brunch in the sprawling turn-of-the-century Sea Grill Restaurant is a definite "must," featuring a tremendous buffet assortment of breakfast and lunch items. Moderate.

For light, inexpensive fare there's the **Daily News Café** (3001-A Carlsbad Boulevard, Carlsbad; 619-729-1023). Breakfast features eggs, pancakes, and french toast while the heartier lunch fare includes an array of soups, salads, sandwiches, and burgers. No dinner. Budget.

I'm always tempted to call it a vegetarian restaurant, but the **Gordon's Basil St. Café** (576 North Route 101, Leucadia; 619-942-5145) is more than that. It offers everything from seafood and chicken dishes to calzone and gourmet pizza. All the vegetables and herbs are lovingly grown in the owners' organic garden. The cooking is imaginative, sprightly, and healthful. Dinner only; moderate.

Pasta lovers should be sure to try the *penne* or *fusilli* in vodka-tomato sauce at **When In Rome** (828 North Route 101, Leucadia; 619-944-1771). High ceiling, arched windows, and an art-filled Roman decor provide the proper atmosphere, and the Italian owners certainly know their trade. All the breads and pastas are made fresh daily. Entrées include a variety of veal and seafood items. Lunch; dinner only on weekends; moderate to deluxe.

Most visitors to Encinitas never lay eyes on the **Potato Shack Café** (120 West I Street; 619-436-1282), hidden away on a side street. But locals start packing its pine-paneled walls at dawn to tackle North County's best and biggest breakfast for the buck. There are great three-egg omelettes, including a tasty cheese-and-tuna creation; but best of all are the home-style taters and the old-fashioned biscuits and gravy. Lunch is also served, but the Potato Shack is really a breakfast institution. Budget.

Another popular feeding spot is **Sakura Bana Sushi Bar** (1031 1st Street, Encinitas; 619-942-6414). The sushi here is heavenly, especially the *sakura* roll, crafted by Japanese masters from shrimp, crab, scallop, smelt egg, and avocado. The bar serves only sushi and sashimi, but table service will bring you such treats as teriyaki, tempura, and shrimp *shumai*. Lunch and dinner; budget to moderate.

Encinita's contribution to the Thai food craze is an intimate café called **Siamese Basil** (527 1st Street; 619-753-3940) set along the town's main drag. At lunch and dinner this white-washed eatery serves up about six dozen dishes. You can start with the spicy shrimp soup and satay, then graduate to an entrée menu that includes noodle, curry, seafood, and vegetable selections. House specialties include roast duck with soy bean and ginger sauce, honey-marinated spare ribs, and barbecued chicken. Prices range from budget to moderate.

Best of the beachfront dining spots in Cardiff is **Charlie's Grill and Bar** (2526 South Route 101; 619-942-1300), where the surf rolls right up to the glass. Here you can choose from an innovative selection of fresh seafood items or an all-American menu of hickory-smoked ribs and chicken, steak, and prime rib. Charlie's has a smartly decorated contemporary setting with a full bar, but still creates an easy and informal atmosphere. Dinner and Sunday brunch only; moderate to deluxe.

For Tex Mex cuisine try **Taco Auctioneers** (1951 San Elijo Road, Cardiff; 619-942-8226), a roadside café with a deck overlooking the ocean. In addition to homemade tortillas and chips, you can feast on *arroz cabezon*, a barbecued chicken and pork dish. Budget to moderate.

Mille Fleurs (6009 Paseo Delicias, Rancho Santa Fe; 619-756-3085) tops everyone's list as San Diego's best French restaurant. The à la carte menu, which changes daily, provides exquisite appetizers, soup, and such entrées as rack of veal in garlic and rosemary, Norwegian salmon in pink grapefruit sauce, and whole Dover sole. A sophisticated interior features fireside dining, Portuguese tiles, and stunning *trompe l'oeil* paintings. There is also a Spanish courtyard for lunch as well as a piano bar. Lunch; dinner only on weekends; ultra-deluxe.

Mention the words "Mexican food" in Solana Beach and the reply is sure to be **Fidel's** (607 Valley Avenue; 619-755-5292). This favored spot has as many rooms and patios as a rambling hacienda. Given the good food and budget prices, all of them inevitably are crowded. Fidel's serves the best *tostada suprema* anywhere and the burritos, enchiladas, and *chimichangas* are always good. Lunch and dinner only.

Celebrity chef Wolfgang Puck has made **Delicias** (6106 Paseo Delicias, Rancho Santa Fe; 619-756-8000) an instant, and well-deserved, success. The comfortable and spacious restaurant with adjoining bar is decorated in a mixture of antiques and wicker, accented by woven tapestries and flowers. The chefs in the open view kitchen whip up pizza with smoked salmon, Chinese duck with ginger and orange essence, and roasted veal chop with mushroom-potato purée. Delicious food, personable service; deluxe to ultra-deluxe.

North County's favorite newcomer, hands down, is **Il Fornaio** (1555 Camino del Mar, Del Mar Plaza, Del Mar; 619-755-8876). This Italian restaurant/bakery boasts magnificent ocean views, outside dining terraces, elegant Italian marble floors and bar, trompe l'oeil murals, and an enormous exhibition kitchen. The place is packed with eager patrons ready to sample the pastas, pizzas, rotisserie, meats, and *dolci* (desserts); Saturday and Sunday brunch. Moderate to deluxe.

Since life is lived outdoors in Southern California, **Pacifica Del Mar** (Del Mar Plaza, 1555 Camino del Mar, Del Mar; 619-792-0476), latest link in a restaurant mini-chain, features a terrace overlooking the ocean as well as a white tablecloth dining room. The accent here is on seafood, as in barbecued salmon with spice mustard, ahi with shiitake mushrooms and ginger, and wok-charred catfish. Moderate to deluxe.

The place is mobbed all summer long, but **The Fish Market** (640 Via de la Valle; 619-755-2277) remains one of my favorite Del Mar restaurants. I like the noise, nautical atmosphere, oyster bar, budget-to-moderate prices, on-the-run service, and the dozen or so fresh fish items. Among the best dishes are the sea bass, yellowtail, orange roughy, and salmon, either sautéed or mesquite charbroiled.

Scalini (3790 Via de la Valle, Del Mar; 619-259-9944), housed in a classy new contemporary-style building with arched windows overlooking a polo field, is strictly star quality. The place has been decorated in a mix of modern and antique furnishings and wrapped in all the latest Southern California colors. But the brightest star of all is the menu. The Caesar salad and mesquite-broiled veal chops are exceptional, as is the duck à l'orange. There are many good homemade pasta dishes including lobster fettucine, lasagna, linguine, and tortellini. Dinner only; deluxe to ultra-deluxe.

LA JOLLA RESTAURANTS

Just as it is blessed with many fine hotels, La Jolla is a restaurant paradise. **George's at the Cove** (1250 Prospect Street; 619-454-4244), which based its climb to success on a knockout view of the water, a casual, contemporary environment, fine service, and a trendsetting regional menu. Daily menus incorporate the freshest seafood, veal, beef, lamb, poultry, and pasta available. Spicy Jamaican chicken quesadilla and rock shrimp with snow peas are two of my favorites. The food presentation alone is a work of art. Open for lunch, dinner, and Sunday brunch; there is also a café menu in the upstairs bar. Deluxe to ultra-deluxe.

Another important La Jolla dining place is **Cindy Black's** (5721 La Jolla Boulevard; 619-456-6299). Illuminated with tiny bulbs along an informal grey interior, this well-known establishment features new Continental cooking. There's Provençal chicken stew, steamed clams with cilantro, and veal with prosciutto. Deluxe to ultra-deluxe.

Manhattan (7766 Fay Avenue; 619-554-1444), which successfully replicates a New York City family-style Italian restaurant (despite the palms and pink stucco), features Neopolitan waiters who sing as they toss your salad. The most popular dishes include zesty scampi *fra diavalo* over pasta, veal marsala, and rack of lamb. Wonderful Caesar salads and *cannoli* desserts. Lunch, dinner, and Sunday brunch; moderate to deluxe.

Jose's Court Room (1037 Prospect Street; 619-454-7655), a noisy, down-to-earth Mexican pub, is the best place in town for quick, casual snacks. They offer all the typical taco, tostada, and enchilada plates plus tasty sautéed shrimp and steak ranchero dinners. Budget to moderate.

John's Waffle Shop (7906 Girard Avenue; 619-454-7371) is a traditional La Jolla stopping place for old-fashioned, budget-priced, counter-style breakfasts or lunches. Locals start their day here with Belgian waffles and eggs Benedict. The best lunches are the country-fried steak and grilled tuna melt on sourdough.

La Jolla's so-called "restaurant row" lies along La Jolla Boulevard south of the village. One Italian dining room here ranks among the city's best in that category. **Issimo** (5634 La Jolla Boulevard; 619-454-7004) is a tiny gourmet shop with a stone facade and devoted following. Sophisticated Northern Italian and French dishes are painstakingly prepared and beautifully presented. Favorites include canelloni, lasagna, gnocchi Parisienne, *agnolotti*, and antipasti as well as the wonderful desserts. Wall murals by internationally known Wing Howard create an artsy atmosphere. Lunch and dinner only. Moderate to deluxe in the café; ultra-deluxe in the restaurant.

MISSION BAY AND THE BEACHES RESTAURANTS

A good breakfast is hard to find in the Pacific Beach area. So rather than punishing yourself with formula flapjacks, go straight to the Rack. The **Spice Rack** (4315 Mission Boulevard; 619-483-7666), that is. Locals know about it, so there is usually a crowd, and you'll also have the aroma of muffins fresh from the oven to keep you awake. Bakery items are the best buy here, but the herb-and-cheese omelettes are great, too. Wicker and garden greenery make for a relaxing atmosphere, and there is alfresco dining on the patio. They also serve lunch and dinner daily to mixed reviews. Budget.

The most creative restaurant in Pacific Beach is **Château Orleans** (926 Turquoise Street; 619-488-6744), one of the city's finest Cajun restaurants. Cajun, that is, with a delightfully different, delicate nouvelle twist. Tasty appetizers fresh from the bayous include Louisiana frogs' legs and Southern-fried 'gator bites. Yes, indeed, they eat alligators down in Cajun country, and you should be brave enough to find out why. Seafood gumbo chocked with crawfish, pan-blackened prime rib, chicken sauce piquant, and gorgeous tiger-tail scampi fresh from the Gulf are typical menu choices. Everything is authentic except the decor, which thankfully shuns board floors and bare bulbs in favor of carpets, classy furnishings, and a contemporary color scheme. Quality at a moderate to deluxe price; dinner only.

Hidden away in Ocean Beach is a cottage restaurant called **The Belgian Lion (★)** (2265 Bacon Street; 619-223-2700). Nobody in San Diego provides lustier, tastier European provincial fare than the folks here, who prepare French onion soup, braised rabbit, crispy confit of duck, veal sweetbreads, turnip soufflé, and steaming cassoulets in the classic manner. Home-grown herbs and spices delight both the sauces and the senses. But go easy when you order; the portions are meant to satisfy a Flemish farmer. Service here is especially personalized. Dinner only; moderate-to-deluxe-priced, and worth every franc.

DOWNTOWN SAN DIEGO RESTAURANTS

A couple of San Diego's better restaurant finds lie "uptown" just east of Route 5. **Fifth and Hawthorn** (5th Avenue and Hawthorn Street; 619-544-0940) is a neighborhood sensation, but not many tourists find their way to this chic little dining room. The owners present an array of tasty dishes, specializing in fresh seafood ranging from sea bass with ginger to sautéed fresh salmon. Usually available is filet mignon with green peppers and cabernet sauce. Moderate.

A comfortable little bistro, **The French Side of the West** (2202 4th Avenue; 619-234-5540) has been heralded as one of the city's best values. The prix fixe dinner is an intriguing four-course meal at a deluxe price. The menu varies and may include filet mignon with roquefort and peppercorn, fresh sea bass with sorrel sauce, or a variety of veal, lamb, and chicken dishes. This is the place to enjoy a French dining experience with the relaxed influence of the Caribbean. Lunch and dinner; dinner only on weekends. Reservations recommended.

Attracting attention has never been a problem for the **Corvette Diner, Bar and Grill** (3946 5th Avenue; 619-542-1001). Cool 1950s music, a soda fountain (complete with resident jerks), rock-and-roll memorabilia, video replays of "Ozzie and Harriet," and a classy Corvette have proven a magnetic formula for this Hillcrest hotspot. The place is jammed for breakfast, lunch, and dinner. Simple, budget-priced "blue-plate" diner fare features meat loaf, chicken-fried steak, and hefty burgers named for 1950s notables like Annette, Eddie, and Kookie.

Everyone likes the warm, friendly atmosphere of a real family restaurant like **Hob Nob Hill** (2271 1st Avenue; 619-239-8176). Here's a place where the waitresses call you "hon" and remind you to finish your veggies. The owners have been serving breakfast, lunch, and dinner since 1946, and a gang of grandmas couldn't do it better. Favorites are waffles, homemade breads, chicken and dumplings, potatoes *avec* gravy, and corned beef cured in the restaurant's own vats. Wholesome, tasty food at budget prices.

Following a visit to Balboa Park or the zoo, there is nothing better than a plate of *poo ja* followed by a spicy serving of *gang ped*. Enjoy these and other wonderful Thai favorites at **Celedon** (3628 5th Avenue; 619-295-8800). Mild or spicy, Celedon's curried and stir-fried specialties are delicious. The stylish art nouveau surroundings, nicely appointed with original Thai brassworks and tapestries, add to the graceful flair of this excellent eatery. Budget to moderate prices.

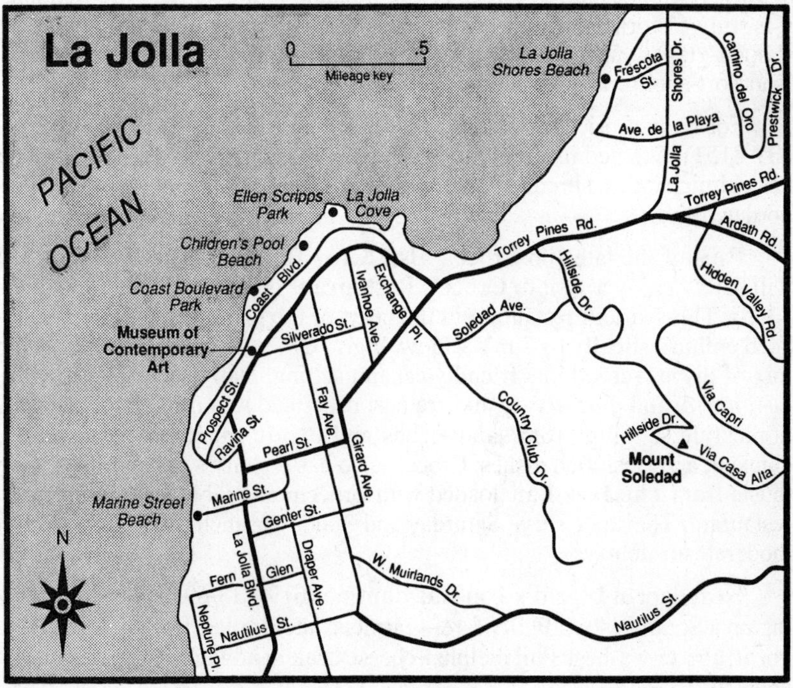

History, atmosphere, and great cooking combine to make dining at **Ida Bailey's Restaurant** (311 Island Avenue; 619-544-6888) a memorable experience. Located in the Horton Grand Hotel, Ida's was once a brothel, operated back in the 1890s by a madam of the same name. Things are tamer now, but the rich Victorian furnishings serve as a reminder of San Diego's opulent past. The chef serves a varied menu highlighted by old fashioned American fare, including Victorian pot roast, lamb chops, and tenderloin. Lunch and dinner during the week; dinner only on weekends. Prices are tabbed in the moderate range.

Visitors to Horton Plaza are bombarded with dining opportunities. But for those who can resist the temptation to chow down on pizza, french fries, and enchiladas at nearby fast-food shops, there is a special culinary reward. On the plaza's top level sits **Panda Inn** (506 Horton Plaza; 619-233-7800), one of the city's finest Chinese restaurants. Here the plush, contemporary design alludes only subtly to the Orient with a scattering of classic artwork. But the menu is all-Asian. Three dishes stand out: orange-flavored beef with asparagus, lemon scallops, and chicken with garlic sauce. Lunch and dinner menus together present more than 100 dishes. Dine on the glassed-in veranda for a great view of the harbor. Moderate to deluxe.

A newly established restaurant in the Gaslamp Quarter is **Johnny M's 801** (801 4th Avenue; 619-233-1131). Situated in a historic 1907 building, it is truly a work of art with its handsome crown molding and magnificent stained-glass dome. The menu features burgers and steaks as well as Maryland soft-shell crab. Moderate.

For budget-priced Mexican food head to **El Indio** (409 F Street; 619-239-8151). Dressed in a pink-and-white color scheme, this self-service café has chimichangas, shredded beef burritos, and a host of other south-of-the-border dishes.

Fans of the late Jim Croce ("Bad Leroy Brown," "Time in a Bottle") will surely enjoy a visit to **Croce's Restaurant** (802 5th Avenue; 619-233-4355). This bar and restaurant in the heart of the Gaslamp Quarter is managed enthusiastically by Jim's widow, Ingrid Croce, and features an eclectic mix of dishes served in a friendly cabaret setting. Daily specials for breakfast, lunch, and dinner vary and are best described as a mixed international homestyle ranging from sandwiches and exotic salads to pastas, beef, chicken, and fresh fish dishes. Croce's also has the city's best blintzes. Live music from **The Jazz Bar**, loaded with Croce memorabilia, filters in to the restaurant. They also serve Saturday and Sunday brunch. Prices range from moderate to deluxe.

Next door at **Ingrid's Top Hat Cantina** (619-233-6945) Ingrid is serving up a Southwestern Philly fare—carnitas, quesadillas, fish tacos, and you got it, the city's best Philadelphia cheesesteak sandwich. Budget to moderate in price.

You'd be remiss to visit San Diego without enjoying a fresh seafood feast at a spot overlooking the harbor. Why not go first class at **Anthony's Star of the Sea Room** (1360 North Harbor Drive; 619-232-7408)? This place wears more awards than a Navy admiral. Dramatically set over the water and elegantly decorated, Anthony's presents a remarkable menu including abalone, broad-bill swordfish, and Florida pompano. Prices range from deluxe to ultra-deluxe. Reservations and coat and tie are essential. If your budget can't handle the "Star," check out the other Anthony's next door—the **Fish Grotto** (619-232-5103). It's more moderately priced.

For decades, San Diegans have enjoyed the authentic Mexican dishes at **Chuey's** (1894 Main Street; 619-234-6937). Nestled in the shadow of Coronado Bridge, it draws crowds with its great tacos, made the authentic way, crammed with juicy string beef and heaped with grated Mexican cheese. Budget.

When you're visiting Balboa Park consider **Café Del Rey Moro** (1549 El Prado; 619-234-8511). Located just across from the museums, it features simple but intriguing dishes like quesadillas with sun-dried tomatoes and pine nuts as well as spicy crab salad with avocado. Moderate.

CORONADO RESTAURANTS

Visitors crossing over to Coronado invariably tour the famous Hotel del Coronado, and many are lured into the **Crown-Coronet Room** (1500 Orange Avenue; 619-435-6611). Its grand Victorian architecture and enormous domed ceiling set a tone of elegance and style unmatched anywhere on the Pacific Coast. The place is so magnificent the food seems unimportant. Most critics, in fact, assert that dinner in the hotel's **Prince of Wales Room** is better, but breakfast, lunch, dinner, or Sunday brunch at the Crown Room will never disappoint; deluxe.

Locals looking to avoid the crowds at "Hotel Del" usually head for **Chez Loma** (1132 Loma Avenue; 619-435-0661). Located in a charming 1889 Victorian house, it serves lovely French lunches and dinner—excellent *canard roti façon Chez Loma* (traditional roast duckling with Montorency cherry port wine sauce and lingon berries)—plus Sunday brunch. Dine inside or out. A cozy salon *du vin* upstairs features appetizers, light meals, desserts, beer, and wine. Moderate to deluxe.

Peohe's (1201 1st Street; 619-437-4474), located at the Old Ferry Landing, is primarily praised for its panoramic views of San Diego Bay and for its tropical decor. The aqua-accented dining room features green palms and rushing cascades of water flowing into ponds of live fish. The moderate-to-deluxe dinner menu is mostly fresh fish plus lobster, shrimp, scallops, and a daily featured "catch." There is also prime rib and lamb. I prefer the lunch, with a tasty soup/salad/sandwich combo at moderate price. Sunday brunch.

POINT LOMA, HARBOR AND SHELTER ISLANDS RESTAURANTS

A marine view and whirling ceiling fans at **Humphrey's** (adjacent to the Half Moon Inn, 2241 Shelter Island Drive; 619-224-3411) suggest Casablanca. Italian fish specialties and Eastern-style "shore dinners" are popular at moderate to deluxe prices. Breakfast, lunch, and dinner.

At Fisherman's Village in Point Loma you'll find **The Blue Crab Restaurant** (4922 North Harbor Drive; 619-224-3000). Appealing Cape Cod decor and terrific bay views set the mood for fresh seafood, including Maryland blue and soft-shell crabs. There's great mesquite-broiled swordfish. No breakfast; deluxe.

Critic's choice for the area's best omelettes is **Café Broken Yoke** (3350 Sports Arena Boulevard; 619-226-0442). Choose from nearly 30 of these eggy creations or invent your own. If you can eat it all within an hour, the ironman/woman special—including a dozen eggs, mushrooms, onions, cheese, etc.—it costs only $1.98. Faint or fail and you pay much more. Soups, sandwiches, and salads, too. Breakfast and lunch only; budget.

The same Point Loma neighborhood boasts San Diego's best soup-and-salad bar and my personal favorite for healthy budget dining. **Souplantation** (3960 West Point Loma Boulevard; 619-222-7404) features two bars loaded with the prettiest produce this side of the farmer's market. Included are over 60 items to heap on your plate. Six tasty soups are made from scratch daily, and a variety of muffins are served hot from the oven. Fresh fruit rounds out this wholesome fare. It's a comfortable wood-paneled environment. Lunch and dinner only; budget.

OLD TOWN AND MISSION VALLEY RESTAURANTS

Mexican food and atmosphere abound in Old Town, especially in the popular Bazaar del Mundo. Here two restaurants lure a steady stream of diners into festive, flowered courtyards. **Casa de Pico** (2754 Calhoun Street; 619-296-3267) is my favorite place to sit and munch cheese nachos and sip margaritas. Budget-priced Mexican entrées are served outside or in one of the hacienda-style dining rooms. Next door, in a magnificent 1829 hacienda, **Casa de Bandini** (619-297-8211), you will find the cuisine a bit more refined. Seafood is good here, especially the crab enchiladas. Mariachis often play at both restaurants. Lunch and dinner; prices are budget to moderate.

Two Old Town charmers provide satisfying diversions from a Mexican diet. **Berta's** (3928 Twigg Street; 619-295-2343) is new to the area and specializes in Latin American cuisine. *Vatapa* (coconut sauce over mahimahi) and chicken in an olive oil and chile sauce are wonderfully prepared and offered at a moderate price. Lunch and dinner.

Café Pacífica (2414 San Diego Avenue; 619-291-6666) rates equally high marks for a creative menu of fresh fish specialties. Stylish but comfortable environs include a patio under a removable roof and a friendly bar. Lunch and dinner only; moderate to deluxe prices.

Less than a mile from Old Town lies a pair of excellent ethnic take-out shops that few visitors ever find. **El Indio (★)** (3695 India Street; 619-299-0333) opened in 1940 as a family-operated *tortillería*, then added an informal restaurant serving quesadillas, enchiladas, tostadas, burritos, tacos, and taquitos (or "little tacos"). Quality homemade Mexican food at Taco Bell prices; you can sit indoors, out on the patio, or order to go.

Another one-of-a-kind fast-food operation with an equally fervent following, **Saffron** (3731-B India Street; 619-574-0177) turns out zesty Thai-grilled chicken on a special rotisserie. The aroma is positively exquisite and so is the chicken served with jasmine rice, Cambodian salad, and the five tangy sauces. Eat on an adjacent patio or take a picnic to the beach. Prices are budget.

SOUTH SAN DIEGO COUNTY RESTAURANTS

La Bella Pizza Garden (373 3rd Avenue, Chula Vista; 619-426-8820) is like an annex to Chula Vista's town hall, and owner Kitty Raso is known as the "Mayor of Third Avenue." But the food will interest you far more than the latest political gossip. Besides pizza, there's great lasagna, rigatoni, and ravioli. La Bella features tender veal dishes, too, from a menu that amazingly rarely strays beyond budget prices. Best Italian food for the money in San Diego.

Another good bet for low-cost dining with an international twist lies just up the *strasse* at **House of Munich** (230 3rd Avenue, Chula Vista; 619-426-5172). Here the Austrian chef prepares such traditional German dishes as wienerschnitzel, potato pancakes, *frikadellen*, and brats 'n kraut. Try the homemade traditional apple strudel! Moderate.

INLAND SAN DIEGO COUNTY RESTAURANTS

Aunt Emma's Restaurant (1495 East Valley Parkway, Escondido; 619-746-2131) is the hot ticket for tasty breakfasts. You can order bacon and eggs all day. Auntie also serves five kinds of waffles and 20 types of pancakes as well as sandwiches, salads, and complete dinners. Budget.

Whatever you do during your North County visit, don't pass up the chance to dine at **El Bizcocho** (17550 Bernardo Oaks Drive, Rancho Bernardo; 619-487-1611). Tucked away in the upscale Rancho Bernardo Inn, an Early California-style resort, this award-winning restaurant rates among greater San Diego's best. The French haute cuisine includes a nice balance of beef, veal, fish, and fowl dishes. Deluxe to ultra-deluxe.

Peg Henry's (16220 Route 76, Pauma Valley; 619-742-8986) is a favorite among smart locals and savvy travelers. The tasty Mexican-American fare includes huge servings of enchiladas, tostadas, tacos, and quesadillas. On the gringo side of the menu, there's a less interesting roster of steak, chicken, and seafood dishes. The rustic interior is paneled with pine, and the prices are moderate.

The **Lazy H Ranch** (Route 76, Pauma Valley; 619-742-3669) serves up steaks, prime rib, chicken, and fish dishes in a family-style dining room set in the leafy environs of a six-acre orchard. Lunch and dinner; moderate.

Hikers will appreciate **Palomar Mountain General Store** (Routes S6 and S7, Palomar Mountain; 619-742-3496), whose adjacent vegetarian café serves hearty soups, salads, sandwiches, and hot entrées at lunch and dinner. Budget.

The Julian Grill (2224 Main Street, Julian; 619-765-0173), situated in a 1920-vintage house, is cozy and folksy, especially around the living room fireplace. The menu emphasizes such hearty mountain fare as steaks, prime rib, scampi, and broasted chicken. They also feature sophisticated chef's specials like chicken Jerusalem. Moderate.

At **Romano's Dodge House** (2718 B Street, Julian; 619-765-1003) you will feel like a Romano family guest. This intimate Italian restaurant, with its homespun ambience, dishes out delicious chicken cacciatore, veal parmigiana, lasagna, and authentic Sicilian pizza. At budget to moderate prices, Romano's is hard to beat.

At least a dozen places in Julian prepare the local specialty, apple pie. But buyer beware: all pies are not created equal: some are definitely better than others. The pies at the **Julian Pie Company** (2225 Main Street; 619-765-2449), for instance, always have flaky crusts and just the right mix of apples, cinnamon, and sugar.

For buffalo burgers and local gossip, the townsfolk all head over to **Kendall's Korner** (2603-B Street, Julian; 619-765-1560). This friendly café, with its all-American cuisine and Early American decor serves up a standard-fare breakfast and lunch menu weekdays, with special dinner plates like steak and potatoes on the weekend. Budget.

Ask anyone in El Cajon where to find a good restaurant, and two out of three times they'll tell you **Kozak's** (401 West Main Street; 619-442-7768). The city's all-purpose eatery, it offers a 24-hour coffee shop up front and a classy dining room in back. The food is good, all-American fare, with budget prices at the coffee shop and moderate to deluxe tabs out back.

For a touch of Europe at budget prices, consider **Dansk** (8425 La Mesa Boulevard, La Mesa; 619-463-0640). Here both the food and the mood are Scandinavian. Belgian waffles, Swedish pancakes, and Danish sausage are favorites at breakfast, while Swedish meatballs top the lunch menu. Breakfast and lunch only.

The Great Outdoors

The Sporting Life

SPORTFISHING

The lure of sport and bottom fishing attracts thousands of enthusiasts to San Diego every year. Albacore and snapper are the close-in favorites, with marlin and tuna the prime objectives for longer charters. For deep-sea charters, see **Helgren's Sportfishing** (315 Harbor Drive, Oceanside; 619-722-2133), **Seaforth Sportfishing** (1717 Quivira Road, Mission Bay; 619-224-3383), **Islandia Sportfishing** (1551 West Mission Bay Drive, Mission Bay; 619-222-1164), **Coronado Boat Rental** (1715 Strand Way, Coronado; 619-437-1514), **H & M Sportfishing Landing** (2803 Emerson Street, Point Loma; 619-222-1144), **Fish N' Cruise** (1231 Shafter Street, Point Loma; 619-224-2464), or **Point Loma Sportfishing Association** (1403 Scott Street, Point Loma; 619-223-1627).

Spearfishing is very popular off La Jolla beaches, especially south of La Jolla Cove. Contact **San Diego Divers Supply** (7522 La Jolla Boulevard, La Jolla; 619-459-2691) for supplies, tours, and information. Note: Spearfishing is not allowed in protected reserves from La Jolla Cove north.

WHALE WATCHING

For whale-watching tours contact **Helgren's Sportfishing** (315 Harbor Drive, Oceanside; 619-722-2133), **Islandia Sportfishing** (1551 West Mission Bay Drive; 619-222-1164), **H & M Sportsfishing Landing** (2803 Emerson Street, Point Loma; 619-222-1144), **Point Loma Sportfishing Association** (1403 Scott Street, Point Loma; 619-223-1627), or **Fisherman's Landing** (Harbor and Scott streets, Point Loma; 619-222-0391).

Also, a free whale-watching station at Cabrillo National Monument on Point Loma offers a glassed-in observatory from which to spot whales.

SCUBA DIVING

San Diego offers countless spots for skindiving. The rocky La Jolla coves boast some of the best diving in San Diego. Bird Rock, La Jolla Underwater Park, and the underwater Scripp's Canyon are ideal havens for scuba and skindivers. In Point Loma try the colorful tidepools at Cabrillo Underwater Reserve; at "No Surf Beach" (Sunset Cliff Boulevard) pools and reefs are for experienced divers only.

For diving rentals, sales, instruction, and dive tips contact **Underwater Schools of America** (707 Oceanside Boulevard, Oceanside; 619-722-7826), **Ocean Enterprises** (191 North El Camino Real, Encinitas; 619-942-3661), **Diving Locker** (405 North Route 101, Solana Beach; 619-755-6822), **San**

Diego Diver's Supply (7522 La Jolla Boulevard, La Jolla; 619-459-2691, and 4004 Sports Arena Boulevard, San Diego; 619-224-3439), **Diving Locker** (1020 Grand Avenue, Pacific Beach; 619-272-1120), and **Buhrow Into Surf and Dive** (1536 Sweetwater Road, Suite B, National City; 619-477-5946).

SURFING AND WINDSURFING

Surf's up in the San Diego area. Pacific, Mission, and Ocean beaches, Tourmaline Surfing Park, and Windansea, La Jolla Shores, Swami, and Moonlight beaches are well-known hangouts for surfers. Sailboarding is concentrated within Mission Bay. Oceanside is home to annual world-class boogie-board and surfing competitions.

For surfboard rentals try **Mitch's** (631 Pearl Street, La Jolla; 619-459-5933), **Nector** (2571 Route 101, Cardiff-By-The-Sea; 619-753-6649), **Hanson's** (1105 First Street, Encinitas; 619-753-6595), or **Hobie Oceanside** (1909 South Hill Street, Oceanside; 619-433-4020).

BOATING AND SAILING

You can sail under the Coronado Bridge, skirt the gorgeous downtown skyline, and even get a taste of open ocean in this Southern California sailing mecca. Several sailing companies operate out of Harbor Island West in San Diego, including **Harbor Sailboats** (2040 Harbor Island Drive, Suite 118; 619-291-9568), **San Diego Yacht Charters** (1880 Harbor Island Drive, 619-297-4555) and **San Diego Sailing Club and School** (1880 Harbor Island Drive; 619-298-6623).

Other motor boat and sail rentals in the area can be found at **C. P. Sailing Sports** (2211 Pacific Beach Drive, Mission Bay; 619-276-4010), **Mission Bay Sportscenter** (1010 Santa Clara Place, Mission Bay; 619-488-1004), **Coronado Boat Rental** (1715 Strand Way, Coronado; 619-437-1514), and **Seaforth Mission Bay Boat Rental** (1641 Quivira Road, Mission Bay; 619-223-1681).

Yacht charters are available through **Hornblower Dining Yachts** (1202 Kettner Boulevard, Suite 3300, Coronado; 619-238-1686). **Bagheera Sailing Adventures** (H & M Landing, 2803 Emerson Street, San Diego; 619-222-1144) charters a beautiful schooner.

HANG GLIDING

Torrey Pines Flight Park, Inc. (2800 Torrey Pines Scenic Drive, La Jolla; 619-452-3202) is an expert-rated hang gliding site, located atop a towering sandstone bluff overlooking Black's Beach. If you're not yet an expert, there is a great vantage point to watch from. Contact **The Hang Gliding Center** (4206 Sorrento Valley Center, Suite K, San Diego; 619-450-9008) for rentals, sales, and instruction.

BALLOONING

Hot-air ballooning is a romantic pursuit that has soared in popularity in the Del Mar area. A growing number of ballooning companies offer spectacular dawn and sunset flights, most concluding with a traditional champagne toast. Some of the ballooning companies flying in the Del Mar Valley are: **A Beautiful Morning** (619-481-6225), **A Skysurfer Balloon Company** (619-481-6800), and **Del Mar Balloons** (619-259-3115).

GOLF

For the golfing set there's **Emerald Isle Golf Course** (660 El Camino Real, Oceanside; 619-721-4700), **Oceanside Golf Course** (825 Douglas Drive, Oceanside; 619-433-1360), **Rancho Carlsbad Golf Course** (5200 El Camino Real, Carlsbad; 619-438-1772), **Whispering Palms Golf Course** (4000 Cancha de Golf, Rancho Santa Fe; 619-756-2471), **Torrey Pines Municipal Golf Course** (11480 North Torrey Pines Road, La Jolla; 619-570-1234), **Balboa Park Municipal Golf Course** (Golf Course Drive, Balboa Park; 619-235-1184), **Coronado Golf Course** (2000 Visalia Row, Coronado; 619-435-3121), **River Valley Golf Course** (2440 Hotel Circle North, Mission Valley; 619-297-3391), and **Mission Bay Golf Center** (2702 North Mission Bay Drive, Mission Bay; 619-490-3370).

For Inland San Diego County, consider **Fallbrook Golf and Country Club** (2757 Gird Road, Fallbrook; 619-728-8334), **San Luis Rey Downs Golf Resort & Country Club** (31474 Golf Club Drive, Bonsall; 619-758-3762), **Lake San Marcos Executive Course** (1556 Camino del Arroyo, San Marcos; 619-744-9092), **Lawrence Welk Resort Village Golf Courses** (8860 Lawrence Welk Drive, Escondido; 619-749-3000), **Rancho Bernardo Inn Golf Course** (17550 Bernardo Oaks Drive, Rancho Bernardo; 619-487-0700), and **Singing Hills Golf Courses** (3007 Dehesa Road, El Cajon; 619-442-3425).

TENNIS

North County suffers from a lack of public tennis courts; however, Del Mar has free courts located off 22nd Street between Camino del Mar and Jimmy Durante Boulevard.

San Diego has many private and public courts open to traveling tennis buffs. For information call **Balboa Tennis Club** (2221 Morley Field Drive, San Diego; 619-295-9278), **Cabrillo Recreation Center** (3051 Cañon Street, Point Loma; 619-531-1534), **Mission Valley YMCA** (5505 Friars Road, Mission Valley; 619-298-3576), **Peninsula Tennis Club** (2525 Bacon Street, Ocean Beach; 619-226-3407), and **La Jolla Recreation Center** (615 Prospect Street, La Jolla; 619-552-1658).

In Coronado call the **Tennis Pro Shop** (1501 Glorietta Boulevard; 619-435-1616) for information on courts.

For Inland San Diego County, try **Pala Mesa Resort** (2001 Old Route 395, Fallbrook; 619-728-5881), **San Luis Rey Downs Resort** (31474 Golf Club Drive, Bonsall; 619-758-3762), **Kit Carson Park** (3333 Bear Valley Parkway, Escondido; 619-741-4691), **Rancho Bernardo Inn Tennis Club & College** (17550 Bernardo Oaks Drive, Rancho Bernardo; 619-487-2413), **Lindo Lake Park** (Lindo Lane, Lakeside; 619-565-5928), and **Parkway Tennis Club** (444 Broadway, El Cajon; 619-442-9623).

HORSEBACK RIDING

An area just outside Imperial Beach is one of the few places in the county where you can ride on the beach. **Hilltop Stable** (2671 Monument Road, San Diego; 619-428-5441) rents mounts for rides at Border Field State Beach.

San Diego's backcountry, on the other hand, boasts hundreds of miles of riding trails. Cleveland National Forest, Palomar Mountain Park, William Heise Park, and Cuyamaca Rancho State Park all feature fine mountain riding. **Holidays on Horseback** (24928 Viejas Boulevard, Descanso; 619-445-3997) offers a variety of day and multiday rides around Cuyamaca Rancho State Park; reservations required.

BICYCLING

North County's **Old Route 101** provides almost 40 miles of scintillating cycling along the coast from Oceanside to La Jolla. Traffic is heavy but bikes are almost as numerous as autos along this stretch. Bike lanes are designated along most of the route.

Cycling has skyrocketed in popularity throughout San Diego County, especially in coastal areas. **Balboa Park** and **Mission Bay Park** both have excellent bike routes (see the "Sightseeing" section of this chapter).

BIKE RENTALS To rent a bicycle in San Diego, contact **Pennyfarthings** (520 5th Avenue in the Gaslamp Quarter; 619-233-7696) and in the Mission Bay area, go to **Rent A Bike** (First and Harbor streets, across from the Marriott Hotel; 619-275-2644). Other bike outlets include **Holland's Bicycles** (977 Orange Avenue at 10th Street, Coronado; 619-435-3153) and **Cycles By The Sea** (2185 San Elijo Avenue, Cardiff; 619-753-0737).

WALKING TOURS

Several San Diego organizations and tour operators offer organized walks: **Gaslamp Foundation** (410 Island Avenue; 619-233-5227) conducts walking tours of the restored downtown historic district. Walking tours of Old Town State Historic Park are offered through **Old Town Walking Tours** (3977 Twiggs Street; 619-296-1004). Join **Coronado Touring** (1110 Isabella Avenue, Coronado; 619-435-5993) for a leisurely guided stroll through quaint Coronado.

Beaches and Parks

NORTH SAN DIEGO COUNTY BEACHES AND PARKS

San Onofre State Beach—San Diego County's northernmost beach is about 16 miles north of Oceanside, uneasily sandwiched between Camp Pendleton and the San Onofre nuclear power plant. It's well worth a visit if you're not put off by the nearby presence of atomic energy. Technically, San Onofre is two parks, North and South, separated by the power plant and connected via a public walkway along the seawall. The southern beach features a superb campground with trailer spaces and primitive tent sites, the only primitive campsite anywhere on San Diego County beaches. Eroded bluffs rumple down to the beach creating a variety of sandy coves and pockets. Gentle surf, which picks up considerably to the north, makes this a good swimming and bodysurfing spot. It is more than a rumor that some discreet nude sunbathing takes place at the end of beach path #6. The north side of the park is a favorite with surfers who flock to "Surf Beach," not far from famous "Trestles Beach," which is just beyond the park boundary.

Facilities: Picnic areas, restrooms, lifeguards; hiking trails; restaurants and groceries are about five miles away in San Clemente; information, 714-492-4872. The campground has showers. *Camping:* Permitted. *Fishing:* Good from the surf; also good clamming. *Swimming:* Good.

Getting there: From Route 5, take Basilone Road exit and follow the signs.

Oceanside Beaches—Over three miles of clean, rock-free beaches front North County's largest city, stretching from Buena Vista Lagoon in the south to Oceanside Harbor in the north. Along the entire length the water is calm and shallow, ideal for swimming and bodysurfing. Lots of Marines from nearby Camp Pendleton favor this beach. The nicest section of all is around Oceanside Pier, a 1900-foot-long fishing pier. Nearby, palm trees line a grassy promenade dotted with picnickers; the sand is as clean as a pin. Added to the attractions is **Buena Vista Lagoon**, a bird sanctuary and nature reserve.

Facilities: Picnic areas, restrooms, lifeguards, basketball and volleyball courts; restaurants and groceries are nearby; information, 619-722-8000. *Fishing:* Try from the pier, rocks, or beach. *Swimming:* Good. *Surfing:* Reliable year-round.

Getting there: Located along The Strand in Oceanside; the pier is at the foot of 3rd Street.

Carlsbad State Beach—Conditions here are about the same as at South Carlsbad (see below), a sand and rock beach bordered by bluffs. Rock and surf-fishing are quite good at this beach and even better at the adjoining Encinas Fishing Area (at the San Diego Gas and Electric power plant), where Agua Hedionda Lagoon opens to the sea. **Carlsbad City Beach** connects to the north, extending another mile or so to the mouth of the Buena Vista Lagoon.

Facilities: Restrooms, lifeguards; restaurants and groceries are nearby; information, 619-729-8947. *Swimming:* Good. *Surfing:* Good. *Skindiving:* Good.

Getting there: Park entrance is at Tamarack Avenue, west of Carlsbad Boulevard, in Carlsbad.

South Carlsbad State Beach—This is a big, bustling beachfront rimmed by bluffs. The pebbles strewn everywhere put towel space at a premium, but the water is gentle and super for swimming.

Facilities: Restrooms, lifeguards, showers, grocery, beach rentals; restaurants nearby; information 619-438-3143. *Camping:* Permitted. *Fishing:* Good. *Swimming:* Good. *Surfing:* Good. *Skindiving:* Good.

Getting there: Located west of Carlsbad Boulevard near Ponto Drive in Carlsbad.

Leucadia State Beach—A broad sand corridor backdropped by coastal bluffs, this beach has appeal, though it's certainly not North County's finest. The strand is widest at the north end, but the breakers are bigger at the south end, an area local surfers call "Beacon's Beach."

Facilities: None; information, 619-944-3398. *Fishing:* Good. *Swimming:* Good. Skindiving: Good.

Getting there: There is a trail off the parking lot at Leucadia Boulevard and Neptune Avenue in Leucadia.

Stone Steps Beach—Locals go there to hide away from the tourists. It is indeed stony and narrow to boot, but secluded and hard to find. Much like Moonlight to the south, its surf conditions are good for several types of water sports.

Facilities: None. *Fishing:* Good from the surf. *Swimming:* Good. *Surfing:* Good.

Getting there: The staircase to the beach is located at South El Portal Street, off Neptune Avenue, in Leucadia.

Moonlight State Beach—A very popular beach, Moonlight boasts a big sandy cove flanked by sandstone bluffs. Surf is relatively tame at the center, entertaining swimmers and bodysurfers. Volleyball and tennis courts are added attractions. Surfers like the wave action to the south, particularly at the foot of D Street.

Facilities: Picnic areas, restrooms, lifeguards, snack bar, equipment rentals; information, 619-944-3398. *Fishing:* Good from the surf. *Swimming:* Good.

Getting there: Located in Encinitas near 4th Street and the end of C Street.

Swami's Park—North County's most famous surfing beach derives its name from an Indian guru who founded the Self-Realization Fellowship Temple here in the 1940s. The gold-domed compound is located on the cliff-top just to the north of the park. A small, grassy picnic area gives way to stairs leading to a narrow, rocky beach favored almost exclusively by surfers, though divers and anglers like the spot as well. The reef point break here makes for spectacular waves.

Facilities: Restrooms, picnic areas, lifeguards, and a funky outdoor shower.

Getting there: Located at 1298 Old Route 101 in Encinitas about one mile south of Encinitas Boulevard.

San Elijo State Beach—Although the beach is wide and sandy, low tide reveals a mantle of rocks just offshore and there are reefs, too, making this one of North County's most popular surf-fishing and skindiving spots. Surfers brave big breakers at "Turtles" and "Pipes" reefs at the north end of the park. There is a campground atop the bluff overlooking the beach.

Facilities: Most amenities are located at the campground and include restrooms, showers, beach rentals, and grocery. Lifeguards; restaurants found nearby; information, 619-729-8947. *Camping:* Permitted; information, 619-753-5091. *Swimming:* Good.

Getting there: Located off Old Route 101 north of Chesterfield Drive in Cardiff.

Cardiff State Beach—This strand begins where the cliffs of Solana Beach end and where the town's most intriguing feature, a network of tide-pools, begins. Popular with surfers because of the interesting pitches off its reef break, this wide, sandy beach is part of a two-mile swath of state beaches.

Facilities: Restrooms, lifeguards; restaurants and groceries are nearby; information, 619-729-8947. *Fishing:* Good from the surf. *Swimming:* Good.

Getting there: Located off Old Route 101 in Cardiff directly west of San Elijo Lagoon.

Fletcher Cove—Lined by cliffs and carpeted with sand, this is a popular spot for water sports. There's a natural break in the cliffs where the beach widens and the surf eases up to allow comfortable swimming. Surfers gather to the north and south of Plaza Street where the beach is narrow and the surf much bigger. It's also a prime area for grunion runs.

Facilities: Restrooms, lifeguards, basketball, shuffleboard; restaurants and groceries are nearby; information, 619-755-1560.

Getting there: Located at the end of Plaza Street in Solana Beach.

Del Mar Beach—Though rather narrow from Torrey Pines to about 15th Street, the beach widens further north. **Seagrove Park,** at the foot of

15th Street, is action central, with teens playing volleyball and frisbee while the elders read magazines beneath their umbrellas. Surfers congregate at the foot of 13th Street. Quintessential North County!

Facilities: Restrooms, showers, lifeguards; restaurants and groceries are nearby; information, 619-755-1556. *Fishing:* Good from the surf; regular grunion runs. *Swimming:* Good. *Surfing:* Typical beach surf with smooth peaks, year-round.

Getting there: Easiest beach access is at street ends from 15th to 29th streets off Coast Boulevard, one block below Old Route 101 in Del Mar.

LA JOLLA BEACHES AND PARKS

Torrey Pines State Beach—A long, wide, sandy stretch adjacent to Los Peñasquitos Lagoon and Torrey Pines State Reserve, this beach is highly visible from the highway and therefore heavily used. It is popular for sunning, swimming, surf-fishing, volleyball, and sunset barbecues. Nearby trails lead through the reserves with their lagoons, rare trees, and abundant birdlife. The beach is unpatrolled so exercise caution in and out of the surf.

Facilities: Restrooms; restaurants and groceries are two miles away in Del Mar; information, 619-729-8947. *Fishing:* Good. *Surfing:* Powerful peaks; exercise caution.

Getting there: Located just north of Carmel Valley Road in Del Mar.

Black's Beach—One of the world's most famous nude beaches, on hot summer days it attracts bathers by the thousands, many in the buff. The sand is lovely and soft and the 300-foot cliffs rising up behind make for a spectacular setting. Hang-gliders soar from the glider port above to add even more enchantment.

Facilities: None. *Fishing:* Good from the surf. *Swimming:* Very dangerous; beware of the currents and exercise caution as the beach is unpatrolled. *Surfing:* Excellent. One of the most awesome beach breaks in California.

Getting there: From Route 5 in La Jolla follow Genesee Avenue west; turn left on North Torrey Pines Road, then right at Torrey Pines Scenic Drive. There's a parking lot at the Torrey Pines Glider Port, but trails to the beach from here are very steep and often dangerous. If you're in doubt just park at the Torrey Pines State Reserve lot one mile north and walk back along the shore to Black's.

Scripps Beach—With coastal bluffs above, narrow sand beach below, and rich tidepools offshore, this is a great strand for beachcombers. Two underwater reserves as well as museum displays at the Scripps Institute of Oceanography are among the attractions (see the "Sightseeing" section in this chapter).

Facilities: There are museum facilities at Scripps Institute.

Getting there: Scripps Institute is located at the 8600 block of La Jolla Shores Drive in La Jolla.

Kellogg Park–La Jolla Shores Beach—The sand is wide and the swimming is easy at La Jolla Shores; so, naturally, the beach is covered with bodies whenever the sun appears. Just to the east is Kellogg Park, an ideal place for a picnic.

Facilities: Restrooms, lifeguards; restaurants and groceries are located nearby. *Swimming:* Good. *Surfing:* Reliable beach surf. *Skindiving:* Native American artifacts have been discovered off the north end of the beach.

Getting there: Located off Camino del Oro and Costa Boulevard in La Jolla.

Ellen Scripps Park and **La Jolla Cove**—This grassy park sits on a bluff overlooking the cove and is the scenic focal point of La Jolla. The naturally formed cove is almost always free of breakers, has a small but sandy beach, and is a popular spot for swimmers and divers.

Facilities: Picnic areas, restrooms, shuffleboard, lifeguards; restaurants and groceries are nearby. *Skindiving:* Good. *Surfing:* La Jolla's big wave action lies outside the cove; exercise caution.

Getting there: Located near Coast Boulevard and Girard Avenue in La Jolla.

Children's Pool Beach—At the north end of Coast Beach (see below) a concrete breakwater loops around a small lagoon to provide relatively calm waters for the kids. Seasonal rip tides can be a hazard, however, so check with lifeguards on duty year-round at the site.

Facilities: Lifeguards, restrooms; restaurants and groceries are nearby. *Fishing:* Good from the surf.

Getting there: Located off Coast Boulevard in La Jolla.

Coast Boulevard Park—After about a half-mile of wide sandy beach, the bluffs and tiny pocket beaches that characterize Windansea (see below) reappear at what locals call "Coast Beach." The pounding waves make watersports unsafe, but savvy locals find the smooth sandstone boulders and sandy coves perfect for reading, sunbathing, and picnicking.

Facilities: Picnic area.

Getting there: Paths lead to the beach at several points along Coast Boulevard in La Jolla.

Marine Street Beach—Separated from Windansea to the south by towering sandstone bluffs, this is a much wider and more sandy strand, favored by sunbathers, swimmers, and frisbee-tossing youths. The rock-free shoreline is ideal for walking or jogging.

Facilities: None. Restaurants and groceries are nearby. *Skindiving:* Good. *Surfing:* Good for board and bodysurfing; watch for rip currents.

Getting there: Turn west off La Jolla Boulevard on Marine Street.

Windansea Beach—This is surely one of the most picturesque beaches in the country. It has been portrayed in the movies and was immortalized in Tom Wolfe's 1968 nonfiction classic, *The Pumphouse Gang*, about the surfers who still hang around the old pumphouse (part of the city's sewer system), zealously protecting their famous surf from outsiders. Windansea is rated by experts as one of the best surfing locales on the West Coast. In the evenings, crowds line the Neptune Place sidewalk, which runs along the top of the cliffs, to watch the sunset. North of the pumphouse are several sandy nooks sandwiched between sandstone outcroppings. Romantic spot!

Facilities: None. Restaurants and groceries are nearby.

Getting there: Located at the end of Nautilus Street in La Jolla.

Hermosa Terrace Park—This beach is said to be "seasonally sandy," which is another way of saying its rocky at times. Best chance for sand is in the summer when this is a pretty good sunning beach.

Facilities: None; restaurants and groceries nearby. *Surfing:* Good.

Getting there: Off Winamar Avenue in La Jolla; a paved path leads to the beach.

Bird Rock—Named for a large sandstone boulder about 50 yards off the coast, this beach is rocky and thus favored by surfers and divers.

Facilities: None. Restaurants and groceries are nearby. *Fishing:* Good. *Surfing:* Rarely breaks but when it does this spot is primo; exercise caution.

Getting there: Located at the end of Bird Rock Avenue in La Jolla.

South Bird Rock—Tidepools and good fishing are the attractions along this rocky, cliff-lined beach.

Facilities: None. Restaurants and groceries are nearby. *Surfing:* Best in summer.

Getting there: From Midway or Forward streets in La Jolla follow paths down to the beach.

Tourmaline Surfing Park—A year-round reef break and consistently big waves make La Jolla one of the best surfing areas on the West Coast. Because of its narrow, rocky strand, Tourmaline has been designated a surfing-only beach. Skindiving is permitted, too, but no swimming.

Facilities: Picnic areas, restrooms; restaurants and groceries are nearby in Pacific Beach.

Getting there: Located at the end of Tourmaline Street in La Jolla.

MISSION BAY BEACHES AND PARKS

Pacific Beach Park—At its south end, "PB" is a major gathering place, its boardwalk crowded with teens and assorted rowdies, but a few blocks north, just before Crystal Pier, the boardwalk becomes a quieter concrete promenade that follows scenic, sloping cliffs. The beach widens here and the crowd becomes more family oriented. The surf is moderate and fine for swimming and bodysurfing. North of the pier Ocean Boulevard becomes a pedestrian-only mall with a bike path, benches, and picnic tables.

Facilities: Restrooms, lifeguards, restaurants.

Getting there: Located near Grand Avenue and Pacific Beach Drive.

Mission Bay Park—As one of the nation's largest and most diverse city-owned aquatic parks, Mission Bay has something to suit just about everyone's recreational interest. Key areas and facilities are as follows: **Dana Landing** and **Quivira Basin** make up the southwest portion of this 4600-acre park. Most boating activities begin here, where port headquarters and a large marina are located. Adjacent is **Bonita Cove**, used for swimming, picnicking, softball, and volleyball. Mission Boulevard shops, restaurants, and recreational equipment rentals are within easy walking distance. **Ventura Cove** houses a large hotel complex but its sandy beach is open to the public. Calm waters make it a popular swimming spot for small children.

Vacation Isle and **Ski Beach** are easily reached via the bridge on Ingraham Street, which bisects the island. The west side contains public swimming areas, boat rentals, and a model yacht basin. Ski Beach is on the east side and is the favorite spot in the bay for waterskiing. **Fiesta Island** is situated on the southwest side of the park. It's ringed with soft sand swimming beaches and laced with jogging, cycling, and skating paths. A favorite spot for fishing from the quieter coves and for kite flying.

Over on the **East Shore** you'll find landscaped picnic areas, playgrounds, a physical fitness course, a sandy beach for swimming, and the park information center. **De Anza Cove**, at the extreme northeast corner of the park, has a sandy beach for swimming plus a large private campground. **Crown Point Shores** provides a sandy beach, picnic area, nature study area, physical fitness course, and a waterski landing.

Sail Bay and **Riviera Shores** make up the northwest portion of Mission Bay and back up against the apartments and condominiums of Pacific Beach. Sail Bay's beaches aren't the best in the park and are usually submerged during high tides. Riviera Shores has a better beach with waterski areas.

Santa Clara and **El Carmel Points** jut out into the westernmost side of the bay. Santa Clara Point is of interest to the visitor with its recreation center, tennis courts, and softball field. A sandy beach fronts San Juan Cove between the two points.

Facilities: Just about every facility imaginable can be found somewhere in the park. Catamaran and windsurfer rentals; playgrounds and parks; frisbee and golf; restaurant and grocery. For further information contact the Mission Bay Aquatic Center (619-488-1036). *Camping:* The finest and largest of San Diego's commercial campgrounds is **Campland On The Bay**

(2211 Pacific Beach Drive; 619-274-6260), featuring hook-up sites for RVs, vans, tents, and boats.

Getting there: Located along Mission Boulevard between West Mission Bay Drive and East Mission Bay Drive.

Mission Beach Park—The wide, sandy beach at the southern end is a favorite haunt of high schoolers and college students. The hot spot is at the foot of Capistrano Court. A paved boardwalk runs along the beach and is busy with bicyclists, joggers, and roller skaters. Farther north, up around the old Belmont Park roller coaster, the beach grows narrower and the surf rougher. The crowd tends to get that way, too, with heavy-metal teens, sailors, and bikers hanging out along the sea wall, ogling and sometimes harassing the bikini set. This is the closest San Diego comes to Los Angeles' colorful but funky Venice Beach.

Facilities: Restrooms, lifeguards; boardwalk lined with restaurants and beach rentals. *Surfing:* Good along jetty.

Getting there: Located along Mission Boulevard north of West Mission Bay Drive.

DOWNTOWN AND CORONADO BEACHES AND PARKS

Coronado Shores Beach—It's the widest beach in the county but hardly atmospheric, backed up as it is by a row of towering condominiums. Still, crowds flock to this roomy expanse of clean, soft sand where gentle waves make for good swimming. The younger crowd gathers at the north end, just past the Hotel del Coronado.

Facilities: None. Restaurants and groceries nearby. *Fishing:* Good from the surf. *Surfing:* Good.

Getting there: Located off Ocean Boulevard in Coronado.

Coronado City Beach—That same wide sandy beach prevails to the north. Here the city has a large, grassy picnic area known as **Sunset Park** where frisbees and the aroma of fried chicken fill the air.

Facilities: Restrooms, lifeguards; restaurants and groceries nearby. *Fishing:* Good. *Swimming:* Good. *Surfing:* Safe but unpredictable breaks.

Getting there: Located on Ocean Boulevard north of Avenue G in Coronado.

Embarcadero Marina Park—The center city's only real waterfront park is a breezy promenade situated on the bay and divided into two sections. The northern part has a nicely landscaped lawn and garden, picnic tables, and benches. The southern half features a fishing pier, basketball courts, and an athletic course.

Facilities: Restrooms; restaurants and groceries are nearby. *Fishing:* Try the pier.

Getting there: Enter at the southern end at Harbor Drive and 8th Street; at the northern end, from Seaport Village Shopping Center.

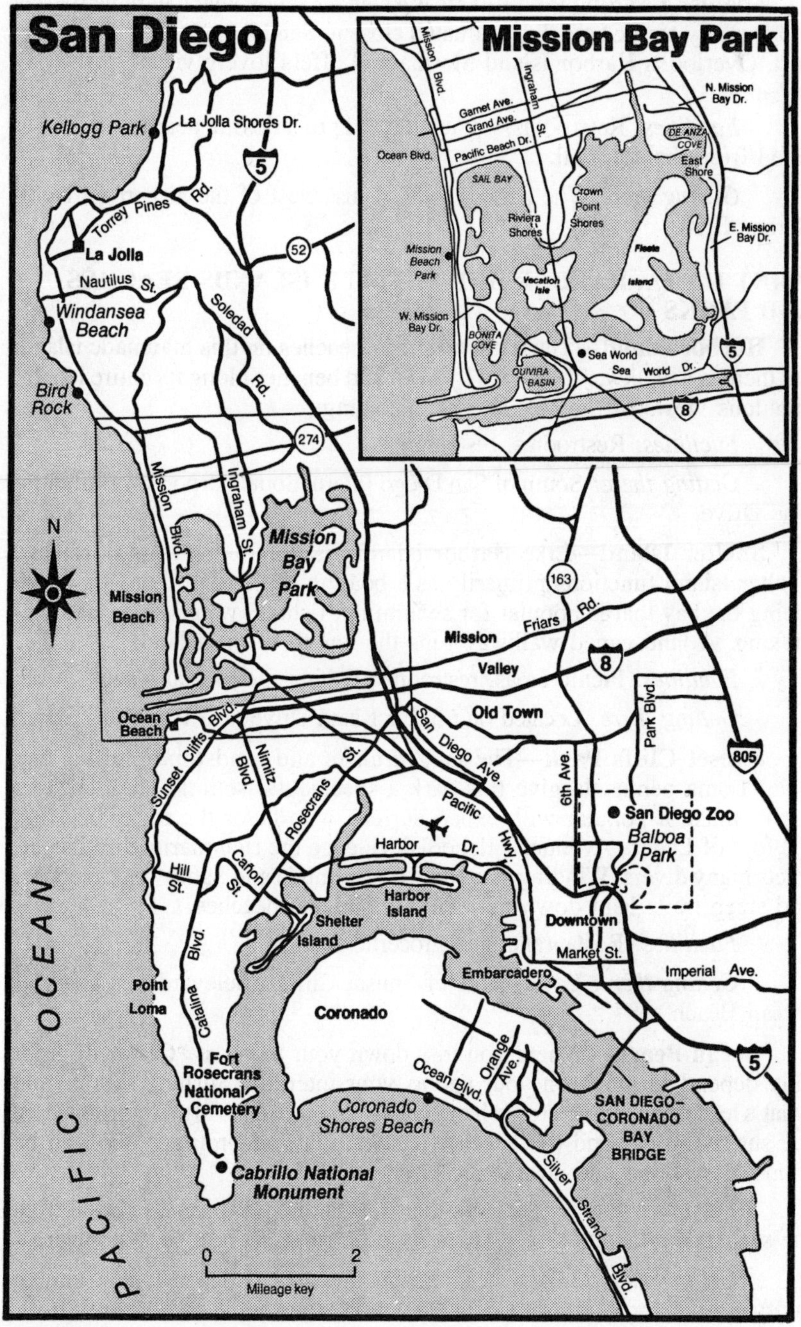

San Diego
Mission Bay Park
Mission Blvd.
Ingraham St.
Garnet Ave.
Grand Ave.
Pacific Beach Dr.
Ocean Blvd.
N. Mission Bay Dr.
DE ANZA COVE
East Shore
SAIL BAY
Crown Point Shores
Riviera Shores
E. Mission Bay Dr.
Mission Beach Park
Fiesta Island
Vacation Isle
W. Mission Bay Dr.
BONITA COVE
Sea World
Sea World Dr.
QUIVIRA BASIN
Kellogg Park
La Jolla Shores Dr.
Torrey Pines Rd.
La Jolla
Nautilus St.
Windansea Beach
Soledad Rd.
Bird Rock
Mission Blvd.
Ingraham St.
Mission Bay Park
Mission Beach
Mission
Friars Rd.
Valley
Old Town
Ocean Beach
Sunset Cliffs Blvd.
Nimitz Blvd.
Rosecrans St.
San Diego Ave.
Pacific Hwy.
6th Ave.
Park Blvd.
San Diego Zoo
Balboa Park
Harbor Dr.
Harbor Island
Hill St.
Cañon St.
Shelter Island
Downtown
Market St.
Imperial Ave.
Embarcadero
Point Loma
Catalina Blvd.
Coronado
Orange Ave.
Ocean Blvd.
Fort Rosecrans National Cemetery
Coronado Shores Beach
SAN DIEGO–CORONADO BAY BRIDGE
Silver Strand Blvd.
Cabrillo National Monument
PACIFIC OCEAN
N
0
2
Mileage key
5
52
274
163
8
805

Spanish Landing Park—This is a slender sandy beach with walkways and a grassy picnic area that's situated close to San Diego International Airport. Overlooks Harbor Island Marina and offers lovely views of the bay and city.

Facilities: Restrooms; restaurants and groceries are nearby. *Fishing:* Good from the sea wall.

Getting there: The park is located just west of the airport on North Harbor Drive.

POINT LOMA, HARBOR AND SHELTER ISLANDS BEACHES AND PARKS

Harbor Island—There are no sandy beaches on this manmade island, but there is a walkway bordered by lawn and benches along its entire length. Fabulous views of the city and great fishing.

Facilities: Restrooms, restaurants.

Getting there: South of San Diego International Airport on Harbor Island Drive.

Shelter Island—Like Harbor Island, its neighbor to the northeast, Shelter Island functions primarily as a boating center, but there's a beach facing the bay that is popular for swimming, fishing, waterskiing, and picnicking. A landscaped walkway runs the length of the island.

Facilities: Picnic areas, restrooms, fishing pier, restaurants.

Getting there: Located on Shelter Island Drive near Rosecrans Street.

Sunset Cliffs Park—The jagged cliffs and sandstone bluffs along Point Loma peninsula give this park a spectacular setting. High-cresting waves make it popular with expert surfers, who favor the rocky beach at the foot of Ladera Avenue. Tidepools evidence the rich marine life that attracts many divers. Winding staircases (at Bermuda and Santa Cruz avenues) and steep trails lead down to some nice pocket beaches.

Facilities: Restaurants and groceries nearby.

Getting there: Located off of Sunset Cliffs Boulevard just south of Ocean Beach.

Ocean Beach—Where you toss down your towel at "OB" will probably depend as much on your age as your interests. Surfers, sailors, and what's left of the hippie crowd hang out around the pier; farther north, where the surf is milder and the beach wider, families and retired folks can be found sunbathing and strolling.

Facilities: Picnic areas, restrooms, restaurants. *Fishing:* Good from the surf or the fishing pier. *Swimming:* Good. *Surfing:* Very popular.

Getting there: Take Ocean Beach Freeway (Route 8) west until it ends; turn left onto Sunset Cliffs Boulevard, then right on Voltaire Street.

SOUTH SAN DIEGO COUNTY BEACHES AND PARKS

Silver Strand State Beach—This two-mile strip of fluffy white sand fronts a narrow isthmus separating the Pacific Ocean and San Diego Bay. It was named for tiny silver sea shells found in abundance along the shore. The water is shallow and fairly calm on the ocean side, making it a good swimming beach. Things are even calmer and the water much warmer on the bay shore. The park also is popular for surf-fishing, clamming, and shell hunting.

Facilities: Picnic areas, restrooms, lifeguards, showers, equipment rentals; restaurants and groceries are several miles away in Imperial Beach; information, 619-435-5184. *Camping:* Permitted for RVs and trailers only.

Getting there: Located on Route 75 (Silver Strand Boulevard) and Coronado Caves Boulevard between Imperial Beach and Coronado.

Imperial Beach—A wide, sandy beach, popular at the south end with surfers; boogie-boarders and swimmers ply the waters between the two jetties farther north, just past the renovated fishing pier. The crowd is mostly young with many military personnel. Each July Imperial Beach hosts the annual U.S. Open Sandcastle Competition, attracting huge crowds.

Facilities: Restrooms, lifeguards; deli nearby. *Surfing:* Very popular on both sides of the pier and rock jetties.

Getting there: Take Palm Avenue exit west off Route 5 all the way to the water.

Border Field State Park—True to its name, this oceanfront park actually borders on Mexico. It features a two-mile-long stretch of sandy beach, backed by dunes and salt marshes studded with daisies and chaparral. Equestrian and hiking trails crisscross this unsullied wetlands area which adjoins a federal wildlife refuge at the mouth of the Tijuana River. Sounds idyllic except for the constant racket from Border Patrol helicopters and the ever-present threat of untreated sewage drifting north from Mexico.

Facilities: Restrooms; restaurants and groceries are several miles away in San Ysidro or Imperial Beach; information, 619-428-3034. *Fishing:* Not recommended because of pollution. *Swimming:* Not recommended because of pollution.

Getting there: Take the Dairy Mart Road exit off Route 5 and go west. The name changes to Monument Road about a mile before reaching the park entrance.

INLAND SAN DIEGO COUNTY PARKS

Cleveland National Forest—A major mountain preserve, this sprawling retreat is divided into three districts, two of which encompass more than 400,000 acres in San Diego County. Northernmost is the Palomar District, covering 189,000 acres around the famous observatory and stretching south beyond Lake Henshaw. Its main feature is the rugged Agua Tibia Wilderness

Area, with several excellent trails. Farther south, the 216,000-acre Descanso District adjoins Cuyamaca Rancho State Park. Here the Mount Laguna Recreation Area offers camping, picnicking, and hiking.

Facilities: Picnic areas, restrooms; information: Palomar District, 619-788-0250; Descanso District, 619-445-6235. *Camping:* Permitted.

Getting there: Access to the Palomar District is via Routes 79, S6, and S7; the Descanso District and the Mount Laguna Recreation Area are located on Route S1 (Sunrise Highway) a few miles north of Route 8.

Palomar Mountain State Park—Thick forests of pine, fur, and cedar combine with rambling mountain meadows to create a Sierra Nevada-like atmosphere. The average elevation here on the side of Mount Palomar is 5500 feet, so the evenings are cool and heavy snow is common in the winter. Doane Pond is stocked with trout for year-round angling.

Facilities: Picnic areas, restrooms, showers; restaurant and groceries are nearby at Palomar General Store; information, 619-742-3462. *Camping:* Permitted.

Getting there: Located on Route S7 on top of Mount Palomar.

William Heise Park—Beautifully situated in a forest of pines and oaks, this preserve rests at 4200-foot elevation in the Laguna Mountains near Julian. The park is largely undeveloped and provides more than 900 acres of hiking and riding trails. It's also one of the few county parks where the snowfall is sufficient for winter recreation.

Facilities: Picnic areas, restrooms, showers; groceries and restaurants are about five miles away in Julian; information, 619-565-3600. *Camping:* Permitted.

Getting there: From Route 79 (one mile west of Julian) go south on Pine Hills Road for two miles, then east on Frisius Road for two more miles.

Cuyamaca Rancho State Park—Broad meadows, forests of pine and oak, and numerous streams make the Cuyamaca Peninsular Range one of Southern California's most beautiful areas. Encompassing 25,000 acres (including 13,000 acres of wilderness), the park provides a habitat for deer, coyote, fox, bobcat, and mountain lion, as well as over 100 species of birds.

Facilities: Museum, picnic areas, restrooms, showers; restaurants and groceries are nearby in Descanso and Julian; information, 619-765-0755. *Camping:* Permitted.

Getting there: The park is located on Route 79 about ten miles south of Julian.

Lake Morena Park—As its name suggests, the highlight of this hideaway is a 1000-acre lake renowned for its bass, crappie, bluegill, and catfish. Located near the Mexican border, the park covers a total of 3250 acres, which range from flat terrain to low hills covered with oak and scrub.

Facilities: Picnic areas, restrooms, showers; fishing facilities and boat rentals; groceries are nearby; information, 619-565-3600.

Getting there: Located off Route 8 (Buckman Springs Road) in the southeast corner of San Diego County.

Los Peñasquitos Canyon Preserve—This 2200-acre parcel, a canyonland wilderness several miles from the coast, features narrow rock gorges, mesa plateaus, and streamside woodlands. There are hiking trails as well as historic adobe houses to explore.

Facilities: Restrooms.

Getting there: Located off Black Mountain Road near Mira Mesa.

Hiking

Most of the San Diego County coastline is developed for either residential or commercial purposes, limiting the hiking possibilities. There are some protected areas set aside to preserve remnants of the county's unique coastal chaparral communities and tidelands. These reserves offer short hiking trails. Inland San Diego County, particularly in the Palomar and Laguna mountains, also provides backpacking opportunities.

Serious hikers might also consider taking on the San Diego section of the **California Coastal Trail**. It follows the shoreline, as much as possible, from the Mexican border all the way to San Onofre State Beach.

TORREY PINES STATE RESERVE TRAILS

Without a doubt, this 1750-acre sanctuary offers the county's best hiking. It was named for the world's rarest pine tree *(Pinus torreyana)* which the reserve was established to protect. An estimated 6000 of the gnarled and twisted trees cling to rugged cliffs and ravines, some growing as tall as 60 feet.

Several major trails offer hikers a variety of challenges and natural attractions. Most are easily walked loops through groves of pines, such as the **Parry Grove Trail** (.5 mile), which passes stands of manzanita, yucca, and other shrubs; and **Guy Fleming Trail** (.6 mile), which scans the coast at South Overlook. There are more strenuous treks such as **Broken Hill Trail** (1.3 mile), zigzagging to the coast past chamiso and scrub oak; and **Razor Point Trail** (.6 mile), which follows the Canyon of the Palisades and takes in eroded cliffs and ocean vistas.

Del Mar Beach Trail (3 miles) leads from the Del Mar Amtrak Station along the beach past flatrock tidepools and up to the bluffs of Torrey Pines State Reserve.

OTHER COASTAL TRAILS

Three Lagoons Trail (5 miles) originates on the beach in Leucadia and heads north along the sand past three saltwater lagoons, ending in Carlsbad. Best place to begin is at the beach parking lot at Grandview Street in Leucadia.

La Jolla Coastal Walk (1 mile), a dirt path atop La Jolla Bluffs, affords some of the most spectacular views anywhere on the San Diego County coastline. It begins on Coast Boulevard just up the hill from La Jolla Cove and continues past a sea cave accessible from the trail.

SILVER STRAND STATE BEACH TRAILS

Silver Strand Beach Walk (3 miles) follows a lengthy sandspit en route from the Hotel del Coronado to Silver Strand State Beach. It passes the Navy Amphibious Base as well as some pretty beachfronts.

CABRILLO NATIONAL MONUMENT TRAILS

Bayside Trail (1 mile) begins at the Old Point Loma Lighthouse, beautifully restored to its original 1855 condition, and meanders through the heart of a scenic coastal chaparral community. A wide variety of native plants including prickly pear cactus, yucca, buckwheat, and Indian paintbrush grow along the path. In addition to stunning views of San Diego, there are remnants of the coastal defense system built here during World Wars I and II.

BORDER FIELD STATE PARK TRAILS

Hiking trails crisscross the dunes and marshes of this largely undeveloped park, which forms the coastal border between the United States and Mexico. Trails lead through dunes anchored by salt grass, pickleweed, and sand verbena. The marshy areas, especially those in an adjacent federal wildlife refuge around the Tijuana River estuary, provide feeding and nesting grounds for several hundred species of native and migratory birds, including hawks, pelicans, plovers, terns, and ducks.

Border Field to Tijuana River Trail (1.5 miles) is a level beach walk past sand dunes and the Tijuana River Estuary.

Border Field to Imperial Beach Trail (3 miles) covers the same ground, then continues past houses and low bluffs.

INLAND SAN DIEGO COUNTY TRAILS

Rising along San Diego County's northern border, the Palomar Mountain Range provides a number of demanding trails. Well-protected and maintained within Cleveland National Forest, they offer hikers a prime wilderness experience.

Observatory Trail (4 miles) is one of the area's easiest treks and rewards the hiker with a view of that famous silver hemisphere, the Mount Palomar Observatory.

The Agua Tibia Wilderness Area in the northwest corner of Cleveland National Forest is the setting for rugged **Dripping Springs Trail** (13 miles). Ascending the side of Agua Tibia Mountain, the trail leads through precipitous canyons to vista points with views of the Pacific, more than 40 miles away.

Scott's Cabin Trail (3.5 miles) loops through varied terrain in Palomar State Park. The trail passes the remains of a homesteader's cabin, descends into a fir forest, and climbs to a lookout tower.

Cuyamaca Rancho State Park, located further south in the Laguna Mountains, offers nearly a dozen trails covering more than 100 miles. **Cuyamaca Peak Trail** (7 miles) ascends a 6512-foot mountain, traversing forests of oak, pine, and fir. The views from the top extend from the Pacific to Mexico.

Stonewall Peak Trail (4 miles) takes you to the summit of 5730-foot Stonewall Peak, with views of an 1870-era mine site along the way. Nearby **Azelea Glen Trail** (3 miles) loops through open meadows as well as forests of oak and pine. **Paso Nature Trail** (.8 mile) is a self-guided loop designed to introduce visitors to the local flora.

Travelers' Tracks

Sightseeing

Thanks to its illustrious history, splendid natural setting, equable climate, and quality visitor attractions, the once-sleepy seaside town of San Diego has blossomed into one of California's most popular year-round vacation destinations. The city itself is water-oriented, owing much of its beauty and appeal to a vast natural harbor that has been attracting enthusiastic visitors since the Spanish landed in 1542.

Intelligent city planning, evident since the boom years of the 1880s, has left San Diego a legacy of important, well-preserved historic sites and some fine parks, ranging from the cultured environs of Balboa Park to the aquatic excitement of Mission Bay Park. And, of course, there's the world famous zoo.

Up the coast are gemlike seaside villages, fronted by sandstone cliffs, grassy bluffs, and some of California's widest and sandiest beaches. Across the border lies the foreign fascination of Mexico. And to the east stretches a lengthy cordillera, rising to elevations of over 6000 feet and separating San Diego from the desert.

NORTH SAN DIEGO COUNTY

The best way to see North County's fine beaches is to cruise along Old Route 101, which preceded Route 5 as the north–south coastal route. It changes names in each beach town along the way, but once you're on it you won't be easily sidetracked.

Your first sightseeing opportunity in San Diego County is at **San Onofre State Beach**, about 16 miles north of Oceanside. Unique in that it's actually two beaches, North and South, this certainly is one of the county's most scenic beach parks. Its eroded sandstone bluffs hide a variety of secluded sandy coves and pocket beaches. But all this beauty is broken by an eerie and ungainly structure rising from the shoreline. Dividing the park's twin beaches is a mammoth facility, potent and ominous, the San Onofre nuclear power plant.

Old Route 101 leads next into **Oceanside**, gateway to Camp Pendleton Marine Base. San Diego county's second largest city is busy renovating its beachfront and image. The refurbished fishing pier is a lengthy one, stretching almost 2000 feet into the Pacific.

Farther south, **Carlsbad** is a friendly, sunny beachfront town that has been entirely redeveloped, complete with cobblestone streets and quaint shops. Originally the place established its reputation around the similarity of its mineral waters to the springs of the original Karlsbad in Czechoslovakia. But don't waste your time looking for the fountain of youth, the spring has long since dried up. Go to the beach instead.

Encinitas is popularly known as the "Flower Capital of the World" and the hillsides east of the beach are a riot of colors. A quick call to the friendly folks at the local **Chamber of Commerce** (619-753-6041) will net you information concerning the area.

Yogis, as well as those of us still residing on terra firma, might want to make a stop at Paramahansa Yogananda's **Self Realization Fellowship Center** (215 K Street, Encinitas; 619-753-2888). The gold-domed towers of this monastic retreat were built by an Indian religious sect in the 1930s and are still used as a retreat. Yogananda's house and the gardens inside the compound are beautifully maintained and open to the public on Sundays. The views, overlooking the famous "Swami's" surfing beach, are spectacular.

Although **Del Mar** is inundated every summer by "beautiful people" who flock here for the horse racing, the town itself has retained a casual, small-town identity. Its trim, Tudor-style village center and luxurious oceanfront homes reflect the town's subtle efforts to "keep up with the Joneses" next door (i.e., La Jolla).

While seasonal, the **Del Mar Race Track** (Route 5 and Via de la Valle; 619-755-1141; admission) and companion **Fairgrounds** are the main attractions here. The track was financed in the 1930s by such stars as Bing Crosby, Pat O'Brien, and Jimmy Durante to bring thoroughbred racing to the fairgrounds. It was no coincidence that Del Mar, "where the turf meets the surf," became a second home for these and many other top Hollywood stars.

On the east side of Route 5, about five miles inland on either Via de la Valle or Lomas Santa Fe Drive, is **Rancho Santa Fe**. If La Jolla is a jewel, then this stylish enclave is the crown itself. Residing in hillside mansions and horse ranches parceled out from an old Spanish land grant are some of America's wealthiest folks. Rancho Santa Fe is like Beverly Hills gone country. The area became popular as a retreat for rich industrialists and movie stars in the 1920s when Douglas Fairbanks and Mary Pickford built their sprawling **Fairbanks Ranch**. To make a looping tour of this affluent community, drive in on Via de la Valle, then return to Route 5 via Linea del Cielo and Lomas Santa Fe Drive.

LA JOLLA

A certain fascination centers around the origins of the name La Jolla. It means "jewel" in Spanish, but according to Indian legend it means "hole" or "caves." Both are fairly apt interpretations: this Mediterranean-style enclave perched on a bluff above the Pacific is indeed a jewel; and its dramatic coves and cliffs are pocked with sea caves. Choose your favorite interpretation but for goodness sake don't pronounce the name phonetically—it's "La Hoya."

La Jolla is a community within the city of San Diego, though it considers itself something more on the order of a principality—like Monaco. Locals call it "The Village" and boast that it's an ideal walking town, which is another way of saying La Jolla is a frustrating place to drive around. Narrow, curvy 1930-era streets are jammed with traffic and hard to follow. A parking place in The Village is truly a jewel within the jewel.

The beauty of its seven miles of cliff-lined sea coast is La Jolla's *raison d'être*. Spectacular homes, posh hotels, chic boutiques, and gourmet restaurants crowd shoulder to shoulder for a better view of the ocean. Each of the area's many beaches has its own particular character and flock of local devotees. Though most beaches are narrow, rocky, and not really suitable for swimming or sunbathing, they are the best in the county for surfing and skindiving.

To get the lay of the land, wind your way up **Mount Soledad** (east on Nautilus Street from La Jolla Boulevard), where the view extends across the city skyline and out over the ocean. That large white cross at the summit is a memorial to the war dead and the setting for sunrise services every Easter Sunday.

Ah, but exploring The Village is the reason you're here, so head back down Nautilus Street, go right on La Jolla Boulevard, and continue until it leads into **Prospect Street**. This is La Jolla's hottest thoroughfare and where it intersects **Girard Avenue**, the town's traditional "main street," is the town epicenter. Here, in the heart of La Jolla, you are surrounded by the elite and elegant.

Although Girard Avenue features as wide a selection of shops as anyplace in San Diego, Prospect Street is much more interesting and stylish. By all means, walk Prospect's curving mile from the cottage shops and galleries on the north to the **Museum of Contemporary Art** (700 Prospect Street; 619-454-3541; admission) on the south. The museum, by the way, is a piece of art in itself. Its modern lines belie the fact it was designed as a private villa back in 1915, one of many striking contemporary structures in La Jolla by noted architect Irving Gill. The museum's highly regarded collection focuses on minimal, California, pop, and other avant-garde developments in painting, sculpture, and photography.

During this stroll along Prospect Street, also visit the lovely **La Valencia Hotel** (1132 Prospect Street; 619-454-0771), a very pink, very prominent resting place nicknamed "La V." This pink lady is a La Jolla landmark and a local institution, serving as both village pub and town meeting hall. You can feel the charm and sense the rich tradition of the place the moment you enter. While "La V" has always been a haven for the gods and goddesses of Hollywood, the Gregory Peck, Mel Ferrer, and Olivia de Haviland gang of old has been replaced by a client roster of current stars like Liza Minelli and Dustin Hoffman.

Another center of interest lies at the northern end of La Jolla. The best beaches are here, stretching from the ritzy La Jolla Shores to the scientific sands at Scripps Beach. The latter strand fronts Scripps Institute of Oceanography, the oldest institution in the nation devoted to oceanography and the home of the **Scripps Museum** (8602 La Jolla Shores Drive; 619-534-6933; admission). Here you'll find two dozen marine life tanks, a manmade tidepool, breathtaking exhibits of coastal underwater habitats, and displays illustrating recent advances in oceanographic research.

Another research center, **The Salk Institute** (at the crest of North Torrey Pines Road just north of the University of California–San Diego campus), created by the man whose vaccine helped vanquish polio, is renowned not only for its research but its architecture as well. The surrealistic concrete structure was designed by Louis Kahn in 1960 to be an environment that would stimulate original thinking. It is a stunning site, perched on the lip of a high canyon overlooking the Pacific. For information on tours call 619-453-4100, ext. 200.

Next to the institute is the **Torrey Pines Glider Port** (2800 Torrey Pines Scenic Drive) where you can watch hang-gliding masters soar over the waves from atop a 360-foot cliff. Trails leading down to the notorious

Black's Beach begin here. Black's is San Diego's unofficial, illegal, ever-loving nude beach. And a beautiful strip of natural landscape it is.

Bordering Black's on the north is **Torrey Pines State Beach and Reserve** (west of North Torrey Pines Road, two miles north of Genesee Avenue), whose 1750-acre preserve was established to protect the world's rarest pine tree, the Torrey Pine. The tree itself is a gnarled and twisted specimen. Centuries ago these pines covered the southern coast of California; today they are indigenous only to Santa Rosa Island, off the coast of Santa Barbara, and to the reserve. A network of trails through this blufftop reserve makes hiking sheer pleasure. Among the rewards are the views, extending along the cliffs and ocean, and the chance to walk quietly among La Jolla's rare treasures.

MISSION BAY AND THE BEACHES

Dredged from a shallow, mosquito-infested tidal bay, 4600-acre **Mission Bay Park** is the largest municipal aquatic park in the world. For San Diego's athletic set it is Mecca, a recreational paradise dotted with islands and lagoons and ringed by 27 miles of sandy beaches.

Here, visitors join with residents to enjoy swimming, sailing, windsurfing, waterskiing, fishing, jogging, cycling, golf, and tennis. Or perhaps a relaxing day of kite flying and sunbathing.

More than just a playground, Mission Bay Park features a shopping complex, resort hotels, restaurants, and the popular marine park, **Sea World** (Sea World Drive; 619-226-3901; admission). This 150-acre park-within-a-park has rapidly developed into the world's largest oceanarium, known for its killer whale shows and Penguin Encounter, an icy habitat for the largest colony of penguins north of Antarctica. Also be sure to take in the "Forbidden Reef," home to dozens of bat rays and over 100 moray eels.

The trained killer whales perform in a flashy stadium; world-class high divers execute both daring and comical stunts; singers, dancers, and street entertainers perform; there is an aerial tram and a Sky Tower ride that lifts visitors in a capsule 320 feet above Mission Bay. It's quality material, but much of it is wasted on me. I prefer simply to watch the penguins waddling about on a simulated iceberg and zipping around after fish in their glass-contained ocean. Or to peer in at the fearsome makos at the shark exhibit. The park's magnificent marine creatures are all the entertainment I need.

Down along the oceanfront, **Mission Beach** is strung out along a narrow jetty of sand protecting Mission Bay from the sea. Mission Boulevard threads its way through this eclectic, wall-to-wall mix of shingled beach shanties, condominiums, and luxury homes.

The historic 1925 "Giant Dipper" has come back to life after years of neglect at the all new **Belmont Park** (on the beach at Mission Boulevard and West Mission Bay Drive; 619-488-0668). One of only two West Coast seaside coasters, this beauty is not all the park has to offer. There's also a carousel, video arcade, indoor swimming pool, and a host of shops and eateries along the beach and boardwalk.

Pacific Beach, which picks up at the northern edge of the bay, is the liveliest of the city beaches, an area packed with high school and college students. Designer shorts, a garish Hawaiian shirt, strapped-on sunglasses, and a skate board are all you need to fit in perfectly along the frenetic boardwalk at "PB." Stop and see the 1920s **Crystal Pier** (end of Garnet Avenue) with its tiny motel built out over the waves. Or take a stroll along the boardwalk, checking out the sunbathers, skaters, joggers, and cyclists.

SAN DIEGO HARBOR

San Diego's beautiful harbor is a notable exception to the rule that big-city waterfronts lack appeal. Here, the city embraces its bay and presents its finest profile along the water.

The best way to see it all is on a harbor tour. A variety of vessels dock near Harbor Drive at the foot of Broadway. **San Diego Harbor Excursion** (1050 North Harbor Drive; 619-234-4111) provides leisurely trips around the 22-square-mile harbor, which is colorfully backdropped by commercial and naval vessels as well as the dramatic cityscape. My favorite sunset harbor cruises are aboard the 151-foot schooner *Invader* (619-234-8687; admission).

All along the cityside of the harbor from the Coast Guard Station opposite Lindbergh Field to Seaport Village is a lovely landscaped boardwalk called the **Embarcadero**. It offers parks where you can stroll and play, a floating maritime museum, and a thriving assortment of waterfront diversions.

The **Maritime Museum of San Diego** (1306 North Harbor Drive; 619-234-9153; admission) is composed of three vintage ships: most familiar is the 1863 *Star of India*, the nation's oldest iron-hulled merchant ship still afloat. Visitors go aboard for a hint of what life was like on the high seas more than a century ago. You can also visit the 1898 ferry *Berkeley*, which helped in the evacuation of San Francisco during the 1906 earthquake, and the 1904 steam yacht *Medea*.

Nautical buffs or anyone concerned about American naval power will be interested in the huge **U.S. Navy** presence in San Diego harbor. As headquarters of the 11th Naval District, San Diego hosts one of the world's largest fleets of fighting ships—from aircraft carriers to nuclear submarines. Naval docks and yards are off-limits but you'll see the sprawling facilities and plenty of those distinctive gray-hulled ships during a harbor cruise. Naval vessels moored at the Broadway Pier hold open house on weekends.

Both Navy and Marine centers present colorful **military reviews** every Friday. Marching ceremonies begin at exactly 1 p.m. at the Naval Training Center (619-524-1152) and at 9:45 a.m. at the Marine Corps Recruiting

Depot (619-524-1772). Both centers are reached from downtown by going north on Pacific Highway to Barnett Avenue, then left to Gate 1.

Near the south end of the Embarcadero sits the popular shopping and entertainment complex known as **Seaport Village** (Pacific Highway and Harbor Drive). Designed to replicate an Early California seaport, it comprises 14 acres of bayfront parks and promenades, shops, and galleries. On the south side, overlooking the water, is the 45-foot-high Mulkilto Lighthouse, official symbol of the village, a recreation of a famous lighthouse in Washington state. Nearby is the Broadway Flying Horses Carousel, a hand-carved, turn-of-the-century model that originally whirled around Coney Island.

One of the latest additions to the city skyline, the **San Diego Convention Center** (111 West Harbor Drive; 619-525-5115) looks like an erector set gone mad. An uncontained congeries of flying buttresses, giant tents, and curved glass, it is fashioned in the form of a ship, seemingly poised to set sail across San Diego Harbor. This architectural exclamation mark is certainly worth a drive by or a quick tour.

DOWNTOWN SAN DIEGO

At one time downtown San Diego was a collection of porn shops, tattoo parlors, and strip-tease bars. Billions of dollars invested in a stunning array of new buildings and in the restoration of many old ones have changed all that.

Within the compact city center there's Horton Plaza, an exciting experiment in avant-garde urban architecture, and the adjacent Gaslamp Quarter, which reveals how San Diego looked at the peak of its Victorian-era boom in the 1880s.

Horton Plaza (bounded by Broadway and G Street and 1st and 4th avenues) is totally unlike any other shopping center or urban redevelopment project. It has transcended its genre in a whimsical, multilevel, open-air, pastel-hued concoction of ramps, escalators, rambling paths, bridges, towers, piazzas, sculptures, fountains, and live greenery. Mimes, minstrels, and fortune tellers meander about the six-block complex performing for patrons.

Horton Plaza was inspired by European shopping streets and districts such as the Plaka of Athens, the Ramblas of Barcelona, and Portobello Road in London. In all, 14 different styles, ranging from Renaissance to Post Modern, are employed in the design.

The **Gaslamp Quarter** is one of America's largest national historic districts, covering a 16-block strip along 4th, 5th, and 6th avenues from Broadway to the waterfront. Architecturally, the Quarter reveals some of the finest Victorian-style commercial buildings constructed in San Diego during the 50 years between the Civil War and World War I. It was this area, along 5th Avenue, that became San Diego's first main street. The city's core began on the bay where Alonzo Horton first built a wharf in 1869.

It was this same area that later fell into disrepute as the heart of the business district moved north beyond Broadway. By the 1890s, prostitution and gambling were rampant. Offices above the street level were converted into bordellos and opium dens. The area south of Market Street became known as the "Stingaree," an unflattering reference coined by the many who were stung by card sharks, con men, and of course, con ladies.

Rescued by the city and a dedicated group of preservationists, the area not only survived but played a major role in the massive redevelopment of downtown San Diego. The city has added wide brick sidewalks, period street lamps, trees, and benches. In all, more than 100 grand old Victorian buildings have been restored to their original splendor.

History buffs and lovers of antique buildings should promptly don their walking shoes for a tour of the Gaslamp Quarter. One way to do this is to join a walking tour (see the "Transportation" section in this chapter). Or head out on your own, accompanied by a map available at the **William Heath Davis House** (410 Island Avenue; 619-233-5227; admission).

The Quarter includes 153 buildings so I couldn't hope to describe them all, but let me take you on a mini-tour of the most important structures. Begin at the aforementioned William Heath Davis House, a well-preserved example of a pre-fabricated "salt box" family home, dating to about 1850. Framed on the East Coast, it was shipped to San Diego by boat around Cape Horn and represents the oldest structure in the Quarter.

Just across the street is the **Royal Pie Bakery** (554 4th Avenue). Almost unbelievably, a bakery has been on this site since 1875. Around the turn of the century the bakery found itself in the middle of a red-light district. It never stopped turning out cakes and pies, though a notorious bordello operated on the second floor.

Go back down Island Avenue to 5th Avenue and turn left. Not only was this block part of the Stingaree, as hinted by the old 1887 hotel by the same name on your left, at 542 5th Avenue, but it was San Diego's Chinatown. **Wong's Nanking Café** (467 5th Avenue) was built in 1921 and retains the atmosphere of the past.

The nearby **Timken Building** (5th Avenue and Market Street), notable for its fancy arched brick facade, was erected in 1894. Across the street is the **Backesto Building** a beautifully restored late-19th-century structure.

The tall, Romanesque Revival **Keating Building** (5th Avenue and F Street) was one of the most prestigious office buildings in San Diego during the 1890s, complete with such modern conveniences as steam heat and an elevator. Next door is the **Ingersoll-Tutton Building** (832 5th Avenue). When this 90-foot-long structure was built in 1894 for $20,000 it was considered the most expensive building on the block!

Most of the block on the other side of 5th Avenue, from F up to E streets, represents the most architecturally significant row in the Gaslamp

Quarter. From south to north, there's the **Marston Building** on the corner of F Street. Built in 1881, it was downtown San Diego's leading department store. Next is the 1887 **Hubbell Building**, originally a dry goods establishment. The **Nesmith-Greeley Building** next door is another example of the then-fashionable Romanesque Revival style with its ornamental brick coursing. With twin towers and intricate Baroque Revival architecture, the 1888 **Louis Bank of Commerce** is probably the most beautiful building in the Quarter. It originally housed a ground-floor oyster bar that was a favorite haunt of Wyatt Earp. The famous Western lawman-cum-real-estate speculator resided in San Diego from 1886 to 1893. Be sure to go to the fourth floor to see the beautiful skylight.

Though it's situated a few blocks east of the Gaslamp Quarter, make a point to visit **Villa Montezuma** (1925 K Street; 619-239-2211; admission). This ornate, Queen Anne-style Victorian mansion, magnificently restored, was constructed by a wealthy group of San Diegans in 1887 as a gift to a visiting musician. Culture-hungry civic leaders actually "imported" world-famous troubadour Jesse Shepard to live in the opulent dwelling as something of a court musician to the city's upper crust. Shepard stayed only two years but decorated his villa to the hilt with dozens of stained-glass windows and elaborate hand-carved wood trim and decorations.

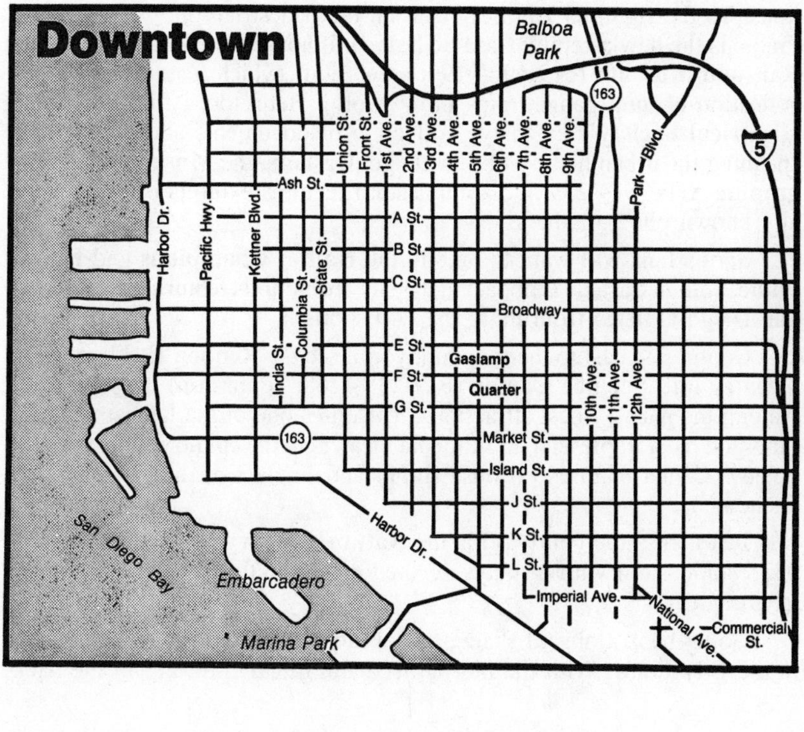

BALBOA PARK AND THE SAN DIEGO ZOO

History is unclear as to whether it was intelligent foresight or unbridled optimism that prompted the establishment of **Balboa Park**. Certain that a fine neighborhood would flourish around it, city fathers in 1868 set aside 1400 acres of rattlesnake-infested hillside above "New Town" as a public park. The park's eventual development, and most of its lovely Spanish Baroque buildings, came as the result of two world's fairs—The Panama-California Exposition of 1915–16 and the California-Pacific International Exposition of 1935–36.

Today Balboa Park ranks among the largest and finest of America's city parks. Wide avenues and walkways curve through luxurious subtropical foliage leading to nine major museums, three art galleries, four theaters, picnic groves, the world's largest zoo, a golf course, and countless other recreation facilities. Its verdant grounds teem with cyclists, joggers, skaters, picnickers, weekend artists, and museum mavens.

The main entrance is from 6th Avenue onto Laurel Street, which becomes El Prado as you cross Cabrillo Bridge. Begin your visit at the **House of Hospitality** at the southeast corner of Plaza de Panama. It houses the **Park Information Center** (619-239-0512) which has free pamphlets and maps on the park.

From here you can stroll about, taking in Balboa Park's main attractions. To the right, as you head east on the pedestrian-only section of El Prado, is the newly rebuilt Casa de Balboa. It houses the **San Diego Model Railroad Museum** (619-696-0199; admission), which features the largest collection of mini-gauge trains in the world. Here, too, is the **San Diego Historical Society's** extensive collection of documents and photographs spanning the urban history of San Diego. Upstairs, the **Museum of Photographic Arts** (619-239-5262; admission) features exhibits of internationally known photographers.

Sports fans will want to take in the **Hall of Champions** and **Hall of Fame**, both in Casa de Balboa. On display are exhibits featuring world-class San Diego athletes from more than 40 sports.

Continuing east to the fountain, you'll see the **Reuben H. Fleet Space Theater and Science Center** (619-238-1168; admission) on your right. Among the park's finest attractions, it features one of the largest planetariums and most impressive multimedia theaters in the country. The hands-on Science Center features various exhibits and displays dealing with modern phenomena.

Just across the courtyard is the **Natural History Museum** (619-232-3821; admission) with displays devoted mostly to the Southern California environment.

Going back along El Prado, take a moment to admire your reflection in the **Lily Pond**. With the old, latticed **Botanical Building** in the background, the scene is a favorite among photographers. The fern collection inside is equally as striking.

Next is the **Timken Museum of Art** (619-239-5548), considered to have one of the West Coast's finest collections of European and Early American paintings. The displays include works by Rembrandt and Cézanne, as well as an amazing collection of Russian icons.

Right next door on the plaza is the **San Diego Museum of Art** (619-232-7931; admission), with an entrance facade patterned after the University of Salamanca in Spain. The museum treasures a permanent collection of Italian Renaissance, Dutch, and Spanish Baroque paintings and sculpture, a display of Asian art, a gallery of Impressionist paintings, contemporary California art, and a contemporary American collection.

The grandest of all Balboa Park structures, built as the centerpiece for the 1915 Panama–California Exposition, is the 200-foot Spanish Renaissance **California Tower**. The **Museum of Man** (619-239-2001; admission), at the base of the tower, is a must for anthropology buffs and those interested in Native American cultures.

Another museum not to be missed is the **Aerospace Museum and Hall of Fame** (619-234-8291; admission), several blocks south of the plaza. It contains a replica of Charles Lindbergh's famous *Spirit of St. Louis*, the original of which was built in San Diego. En route you'll pass the **Spreckels Organ Pavilion**. Those 4416 pipes make it the world's largest outdoor instrument of its kind.

You'll want to attend a play at the **Old Globe Theatre** (619-239-2255; admission) to absorb the full greatness of this Tony Award-winning stage, but for starters you can stroll around the 581-seat theater, famed for its Shakespearean presentations. Located in a grove on the north side of California Tower, the Old Globe is part of the trio of theaters that includes the **Cassius Carter Centre Stage** and the outdoor **Festival Stage**.

North of the Balboa Park museum and theater complex is **San Diego Zoo** (619-234-3153; admission), which needs no introduction. It quite simply is the world's top-rated zoo. The numbers alone are mind-boggling: 3900 animals, representing 900 species, spread out over 125 acres. Most of these wild animals live in surroundings as natural as man can make them. Rather than cages there are many moated enclosures where lions roam free on grassy islands and exotic birds fly about in a tropical rain forest. All around is a manmade jungle forest overgrown with countless species of rare and exotic plants.

Best of the best is the zoo's state-of-the-art primate exhibit. Some of the world's rarest and most interesting primates can be viewed here. In the "Sun Bear Forest," an equatorial rain forest, you'll encounter sun bears and lion-tailed macaques. For a bird's-eye view of the entire zoo, you can take the "Skyfari" aerial tramway.

Incidentally, the San Diego Zoo has a large collection of those cuddly koalas from Australia. You can pet one at the **Children's Zoo**. Don't let the name mislead you! There are as many adults in this enclosure as kids. There's even a hatchery where you can watch baby chicks peck out of their shells.

Balboa Park's museums charge an admission fee but selected ones can be visited free on the first Tuesday of the month.

CORONADO

Once known as the "Nickel Snatcher," the Coronado Ferry for years crossed the waters of San Diego Harbor between the Embarcadero and Coronado. All for five cents each way.

That's history, of course, but the 1940-vintage, double-deck *Silvergate* still plies the waters. The **San Diego Bay Ferry** (619-234-4111) leaves from the Bay Café on North Harbor Drive at the foot of Broadway on the hour and docks 15 minutes later at the Old Ferry landing on the Coronado side.

The **Harbor Hopper** (619-229-8294), a bay water taxi service that can be arranged by appointment or on the spot, leaves from San Diego and docks at the Old Ferry Landing. From there the **Coronado Trolley Line** (619-437-1861), operating on the hour, will take you on a 20-minute sightseeing tour and drop you at the Hotel del Coronado.

An isolated and exclusive community in San Diego Bay, Coronado is almost an island, connected to the mainland only by the graceful San Diego-Coronado Bay Bridge and by a long, narrow sandspit called the Silver Strand.

The town's main attraction is the **Hotel del Coronado** (1500 Orange Avenue; 619-435-6611), a red-roofed, Victorian-style, wooden wonder, a century-old National Historic Landmark. Explore the old palace and its manicured grounds, discovering the intricate corridors and cavernous public rooms. It was Elisha Babcock's dream, when he purchased 4100-acres of barren, wind-blown peninsula in 1888, to build a hotel that would be the "talk of the Western world." Realizing Babcock's dream from the beginning, it attracted such famous guests as Thomas Edison, Robert Todd Lincoln, Henry Ford, and a dozen United States presidents.

Although shadowed by its noted neighbor, the **Glorietta Bay Inn** (1630 Glorietta Boulevard; 619-435-3101) is a worthy landmark in its own right. It was built in 1908 as the private mansion of sugar scion John D. Spreckels. From here you can cruise the quiet neighborhood streets that radiate off Orange Avenue between the bay and the ocean, enjoying the town's handsome blend of cottages and historic homes.

POINT LOMA, SHELTER AND HARBOR ISLANDS

The Point Loma peninsula forms a high promontory that shelters San Diego Bay from the Pacific. It also provided Juan Rodríguez Cabrillo an excellent place from which to contemplate his 16th-century discovery of

California. Naturally, **Cabrillo National Monument** (1800 Cabrillo Memorial Drive; 619-557-5450; admission), featuring a statue of the navigator, stands facing his landing site at Ballast Point. The sculpture itself, a gift from Cabrillo's native Portugal, isn't very impressive but the view is outstanding. With the bay and city spread below, you can often see all the way from Mexico to the La Jolla mesa.

The visitor's center includes a small museum. The nearby **Old Point Loma Lighthouse** guided shipping from 1855 to 1891.

On the ocean side of the peninsula is **Whale Watch Lookout Point** where, during winter months, you can observe the southward migration of California gray whales. Close by is a superb network of tidepools where rangers lead daily tours during low tide periods. Call 619-557-5450 for schedules and information.

To reach Point Loma from San Diego, go southwest on Rosecrans Street and follow the signs. You'll enter the monument through the U.S. Navy's Fort Rosecrans, home to a variety of sophisticated military facilities and the haunting **Fort Rosecrans National Cemetery**. Here, thousands of trim, white markers march down a grassy hillside in mute testimony to San Diego's fallen troops and deep military roots.

When you leave the monument, follow Catalina Boulevard to Hill Street and go left. At water's edge turn right onto Sunset Cliffs Boulevard and enjoy one of San Diego County's most dramatic coastlines. Continue north a bit to **Ocean Beach**, whose reputation as a haven for hippie holdouts is not entirely undeserved.

OLD TOWN AND MISSION VALLEY

Back in 1769, Spanish explorer Gaspar de Portolá selected a hilltop site overlooking the bay for a mission that would begin the European settlement of California. A town soon spread out at the foot of the hill, complete with plaza, church, school, and the tile-roofed adobe casas of California's first families. Through the years, Spanish, Mexican, and American settlements thrived until an 1872 fire destroyed much of the town, prompting developers to relocate the commercial district nearer the bay.

Some of the buildings and relics of the early era survived, however, and have been brought back to life at **Old Town San Diego State Historic Park** (park headquarters, 4002 Wallace Street; 619-237-6770). Lined with adobe restorations and brightened with colorful shops, the six blocks of Old Town provide a lively and interesting opportunity for visitors to stroll, shop, and sightsee.

The park sponsors a free walking tour at 2 p.m. daily, or you can easily do it on your own by picking up a map at park headquarters or the **Old Town Information Center** (2422 San Diego Avenue; 619-291-4903). You can also hop aboard the **Old Town Trolley** (4040 Twiggs Street, 619-298-

8687; admission) for a delightful two-hour narrated tour of Old Town and a variety of other highlights in San Diego and Coronado.

As it has for over a century, everything focuses on **Old Town Plaza** (sometimes called Washington Square). This was the social and recreational center of the town: political meetings, barbecues, dances, shootouts, and bullfights all happened here.

Casa de Estudillo, at the Mason Street corner of the plaza, is the finest of the original adobe buildings. It was a mansion in its time, built in 1827 for the commander of the Mexican Presidio.

Casa de Bandini (Mason and Calhoun streets) was built in 1829 as a one-story adobe but gained a second level when it became a stagecoach station in the 1860s. **Seeley Stables** next door is a replica of the barns and stables of Albert Seeley, who operated the stage line. Nowadays it houses a collection of horse-drawn vehicles and Western memorabilia.

Casa de Altamirano (San Diego Avenue and Twiggs Street) was Old Town's first frame building and the site where the *San Diego Union* was first printed in 1868. It has been restored as a 19th-century printing office. Adjacent to the old newspaper office is **Squibob Square**, a collection of shops finished with Old West-style falsefronts.

Shoppers seem to gravitate in large numbers toward the north side of the plaza to browse the unusual shops comprising **Bazaar del Mundo**. Built in circular fashion around a tropical courtyard, this complex also houses several restaurants.

On the outskirts of Old Town lies **Heritage Park** (Juan and Harney streets), an area dedicated to the preservation of the city's Victorian past. Seven historic 1880-era houses and an old Jewish temple have been moved to the hillside site and beautifully restored.

The original mission and Spanish Presidio once stood high on a hill behind Old Town. This site of California's birthplace now houses **Serra Museum** (2727 Presidio Drive; 619-297-3258), a handsome Spanish Colonial structure containing an excellent collection of Native American and Spanish artifacts from the state's pioneer days.

Within five years after Father Serra dedicated the first of California's 21 missions, the site had become much too small for the growing numbers it served. So **Mission San Diego de Alcala** (10818 San Diego Mission Road; 619-281-8449; admission) was moved from Presidio Hill six miles east into Mission Valley. Surrounded now by shopping centers and suburban homes, the "Mother of Missions" retains its simple but striking white adobe facade topped by a graceful campanile. There's a museum containing mission records in Junípero Serra's handwriting and a lovely courtyard with gnarled olive trees.

SOUTH SAN DIEGO COUNTY

Border Field State Park (619-428-3034) and the adjoining **Tijuana Slough National Wildlife Refuge** comprise the county's largest and most pristine estuarine sanctuary. For nature lovers, this haven of salt marsh and sand dunes is a must-see diversion. Trails lead to the beach and wildlife refuge at this fascinating wetland (see the "Beaches and Parks" and "Hiking" sections of this chapter for more information).

INLAND SAN DIEGO COUNTY

Sightseeing San Diego County's rugged backcountry means wandering through a landscape filled with rambling hills, flowering meadows, and rocky peaks. There are old missions and gold mines en route, as well as farms and ranches. More than anything else, exploring this region means driving over miles of silent country road.

Beginning in the county's northwest corner, Route 76 will carry you to **Mission San Luis Rey** (619-757-3651). Known as the "King of the Missions," this beautifully restored complex was originally constructed in 1789 and represents the largest California mission. Today you can visit the museum chapel and cemetery while walking these historic grounds.

Guajome Park (Guajome Lake Road about seven miles east of Route 5; 619-565-3600), a 569-acre playground, offers a variety of natural, historical, and recreational opportunities. The park is centered around Guajome Adobe, considered one of the region's best examples of early Spanish architecture. Just steps away is a 25-acre fishing lake. Hiking trails thread the property and there are picnic areas and a playground.

Farther inland lies **Mission San Antonio de Pala** (Pala; 619-742-3317). An *asistencia*, or branch of the larger mission, it has been conducting mass since it was built in 1816. The original chapel and bell tower have been faithfully restored, and the long, low walls of the church interior are still decorated with primitive Indian frescoes. Located on the Pala Indian Reservation, it is the only mission primarily serving Indians.

Rockhounds will be interested in **Gems of Pala** (Route 76 and Magee Road, Pala; 619-742-1356), which has exhibits and retail displays of some of the world's finest tourmaline. These pink gems are extracted from the nearby Stewart Mine.

There's no finer wildlife sanctuary in the country than the San Diego Zoo's remarkable **Wild Animal Park** (15500 San Pasqual Valley Road, Escondido; 619-234-6541; admission). This 1800-acre spread, skillfully landscaped to resemble Asian and African habitats, houses over 2500 animals. Among them are several endangered species not found in zoos elsewhere. Many of the animals roam free while you view them from monorails and elevated walkways. After visiting the fearsome lions and gorillas, you can follow that line of children to the "Petting Krall," where the kids can fluff up a lamb or tug on a friendly billy goat.

(Text continued on page 318.)

South of the Border

Tijuana, a favorite day-trip destination for San Diego visitors, has been amazingly transformed in recent years from a bawdy border-town to a modern, bustling city of almost two million people. Gone, or very well hidden, are the borderline attractions which once lured sailors and marines. In their place is a colorful center of tourism suitable for the entire family.

A major revitalization effort brought highrise buildings, broad boulevards, huge shopping centers, and classy shops and restaurants. But don't get the idea Tijuana has become completely Americanized. It still retains much of its traditional Mexican flavor and offers visitors an exciting outing and some surprising cultural experiences.

Perhaps the most impressive attraction, ideal for learning about Mexico, is the **Centro Cultural Tijuana** (Paseo de los Héroes and Calle Mina; 84-11-11). Here the striking 85-foot-high Omnimax Space Theater is a silvery sphere held up by a stylized hand that symbolizes the earth housing a world of culture. Inside, the giant 180° screen carries viewers on a journey through Mexico. The complex, designed by Pedro Ramírez Váquez, architect of Mexico City's famous Anthropological Museum, houses four exhibit halls and a multilevel cultural and historical museum.

Spectator sports are an exciting and popular pastime for Tijuana visitors, including thoroughbred and greyhound racing at **Caliente Race Track** (Boulevard Agua Caliente; 81-78-11 in Tijuana; 619-231-1919 from San Diego); and colorful bullfights in two separate rings, **El Toreo** (Boulevard Agua Caliente) and **Plaza Monumental** (six miles west via Highway 1D). Call Mexicoach for tickets and information, 619-232-5049.

Jai alai fans crowd the newly refurbished **Frontón Palacio** (Avenida Revolución and Calle 7a; 85-16-12) for the fastest moving sport in the world (the ball travels at speeds in excess of 160 miles per hour). Call the **Tijuana and Baja Visitors Bureau** at 619-298-4105 for information about all events.

No doubt a major reason to visit "TJ" is to shop. The central shopping district is downtown, along Avenida Revolución, where arcades, stalls, and hawkers line the boulevard promoting the usual selection of tourist trinkets, piñatas, colorful flowers, serapes, pottery, and lace. There are numerous shops featuring quality merchandise such as leather goods, designer clothes, perfumes, artwork, and jewelry at incredible savings. **Sara's Imports** (Avenida Revolución No. 635 at Calle 4a; 85-76-85) has ladies designer fashions and perfumes; **Jorge Espinoza Designers** (Avenida Revolución No. 918; 85-68-85) features a beautiful selection of custom jewelry; and **Tolan-Arte de México** (Avenida Revolución No. 1111; 88-36-37; 706-688-3637) offers authentic Mexican folk art and fashions.

American currency is accepted everywhere but small bills are recommended since getting change can sometimes be a problem. U.S. residents receive a duty and federal tax exemption on the first $400 in personal goods purchased in Mexico. One liter of alcoholic beverage is allowed for those 21 years and older.

Tijuana has some exceptional restaurants. **Perin's** (Avenida Revolución No. 1115; 85-40-52) serves succulent seafood in a quiet, comfortable atmosphere. **Fiesta Mexicana** (Calle 7a No. 1942; 85-07-44) has an interesting and enticing menu of nouvelle and Mexican cuisine. **Tía Juana Tilly's** (Avenida Revolución, No. 601 and Calle 7a; 85-60-24; 706-681-6024) is a great spot to sit on the patio, sip margaritas, munch on tacos, and listen to mariachis.

Should you decide to stay longer than a day, enjoy Tijuana's stylish hotel, **Fiesta Americana Tijuana** (Boulevard Agua Caliente No. 4500; 81-70-00, 706-681-7000 in Tijuana; 619-298-4105 in San Diego). This 422-room luxury complex boasts dramatic city views from its 32-story glass towers and offers four restaurants, three bars, a disco, a gallery of shops, tennis courts, and a health club.

Just a little further south of Tijuana, along the coast, the small towns of Rosarito Beach and Ensenada provide a less commercial glimpse of Mexico. A modern highway makes the trip easy and comfortable.

Two miles east of the park is **San Pasqual Battlefield State Historic Park** (15808 San Pasqual Valley Road, Escondido; 619-238-3380), where an interpretive center tells the story of a strange and little-known battle. It seems that during the Mexican War in 1846 about 100 U.S. Dragoons, including the famous scout Kit Carson, suffered an embarrassing defeat at the hands of the California Mexicans. Today a small monument marks the battle site.

On a more modern note, **Lawrence Welk Village** (8860 Lawrence Welk Drive, Escondido; 619-749-3000), an elaborate resort complex, contains a museum featuring the famous "one-ana-two" entertainer's memorabilia. High camp at its most bizarre.

One of the fastest growing places in California, Escondido is also home to almost half of the state's 26,000 acres of avocados. Planted in neat rows, they climb the hillsides north and east of town.

Progress continues to intrude upon this once-rustic region, but you can still chat with the folks at **Ferrara Winery** (1120 West 15th Avenue, Escondido; 619-745-7632) and stroll around the vineyards. A small family enterprise, the winery has been producing vintages for three generations.

Among other Escondido vintners are **Bernardo Winery** (13330 Paseo del Verano Norte; 619-487-1866), the oldest operating winery in the county, and **Deer Park Escondido Winetasting** (29013 Champagne Boulevard; 619-749-1666), which offers tastings of wines from its Napa vineyards as well as a fine collection of vintage automobiles.

From Escondido, you can drive northeast along scenic Route S6 to Pauma Valley, and then pick up Route 76, which will carry you from a verdant region of citrus groves up into the pine-rimmed high country of Cleveland National Forest.

A spiraling road leads to that great silver dome in the sky, **Mount Palomar Observatory** (619-742-2119). With a clear shot heavenward from its 6100-foot-high perch, one of the world's largest reflecting telescopes scans the night skies for celestial secrets. Staffed by scientists and astronomers from the California Institute of Technology, this is an active research facility and, only reluctantly, a tourist attraction. You can glimpse the 200-inch Hale Telescope from the visitor's gallery, view a movie on how research is conducted, and look at photos in the museum, but there's little else to see or do. Unless of course you have the time and the legs to hike around the mountain (see the "Hiking" section in this chapter).

Southeast of Mount Palomar, Route 76 ends at Route 79, which then courses through backcountry to the tiny town of Santa Ysabel. **Mission Asistencia de Santa Ysabel** (619-765-0810), where a 20th-century church stands on the site of an 18th-century branch mission, lacks the appeal of its sister missions.

Most of the pilgrims in these parts are bound not for the chapel but for **Dudley's Bakery** (Routes 78 and 79, Santa Ysabel; 619-765-0488), where dozens of kinds of bread, including a delicious jalapeño loaf, come steaming from the oven.

Down the road in **Julian** you'll come upon the belle of Southern California mountain mining towns. During the 1890s, the local mines employed 2000 miners, who hauled up $15 million in gold ore. Today the region produces red apples rather than gold nuggets and Julian, with its dusty aura of the Old West, has become a major tourist attraction.

Some of the falsefront stores along **Main Street** are 19th-century originals. Have a look, for instance, at the 1897 **Julian Hotel**, and don't miss the **Julian Drug Store**, an old-style soda fountain serving sparkling sarsaparilla and conjuring images of boys in buckskin and girls in bonnets. The white clapboard **Town Hall** still stands, and over at the **Julian Museum** (619-765-0227), the townsfolk have turned an old brewery into a charming hodgepodge of local collectibles.

The first hard rock mine in Julian, today a state historic site, **Washington Mine** (northeast end of C Street; 619-765-0174) is open daily. Although the tunnels have long since collapsed, the Julian Historical Society displays mining memorabilia depicting the mining era.

Operations closed in 1942, but the **Eagle and High Peak Mines** (end of C Street; 619-765-0036; admission) still offer tours of the tunnels and an opportunity to pan for gold. What seems certain to be a "tourist trap" actually pans out as an interesting and educational experience.

But remember, these days apples are actually the main business in Julian and dozens of orchards drape the hillsides below town. The countryside all around is quilted with pear and peach orchards as well, and there are Appaloosa ranches and roadside stands selling fruits and jams.

Route 79 points south from Julian along a densely forested ridge of the Laguna Mountains to **Cuyamaca Rancho State Park**. Isolated Indian country that was turned into a Spanish rancho in the 19th-century, this alpine sanctuary rests amid rugged mountain terrain. The vistas reach from desert to ocean and the park is rich in wildlife.

After exploring the shores of lovely Lake Cuyamaca, take in the Indian museum at **park headquarters** (619-765-0755). Exhibits here portray the tragic clash between Westerners and indigenous Diegueño tribes. The **Stonewall Mine** site, representing a later era, consists of old building foundations and rusting mine equipment.

Near Lake Cuyamaca, Route S1 (Sunrise Highway), leads southeast to **Mount Laguna**, a region rich in recreational areas and desert views. You can continue your backcountry adventure by following the highway (which becomes Buckman Springs Road) south toward the Mexican border. This is rough, arid, scrub country, but you'll find an oasis at **Lake Morena**, where an oak-shaded park borders a fishing lake. Further south lies the high desert outpost of **Campo**, with its sun-baked streets and 19th-century ruins. From here you can head south across the border or west toward the seaside metropolis of San Diego.

Shopping

To explore San Diego County's shopping opportunities is to embrace the particular personality of each town and city within the region. In San Diego proper, there's Horton **Plaza**, with its multilevel mélange of shops, and Old Town's colorful Mexican bazaars. Sporty beach-town boutiques contrast with the sophisticated salons and galleries of La Jolla and Rancho Santa Fe.

NORTH SAN DIEGO COUNTY SHOPPING

Carlsbad has blossomed with a variety of trendy shops. You'll see many beach-and-surf-type shops, as well as a variety of specialty gift shops like those tucked away in the arcade of **Old World Center** (Roosevelt Street and Grand Avenue; 619-434-4557). **Alt Karlsbad Hanse Gift Shop** (2802 Carlsbad Boulevard; 619-729-6912), ensconced in a German-style stone house, sells European art and collectibles, including steins, Hummels, and crystal pieces.

Conveniently situated in Encinitas on the east side of Route 101 between I and E streets, **The Lumberyard** is an attractive woodframe shopping village on the former site of an old lumber mill.

Detouring, as every sophisticated shopper must, to Rancho Santa Fe, you'll find an assortment of chic shops and galleries along Paseo Delicias. My favorites are **Marilyn Mulloy Estate Jewelers** (6020 Paseo Delicias; 619-756-4010), with its stunning collection of old and new pieces, and **The Two Goats** (6012 Paseo Delicias; 619-756-1996), featuring designer fashions and exclusive gifts. There are lots of millionaires per acre here, but bargains can still be found: **Carolyn's** (6033-J Paseo Delicias; 619-756-2765) is a consignment shop boasting designer fashions from the closets of the community's best-dressed women. Another place where the rich like to rummage is **Country Friends** (6030 El Tordo; 619-756-1192), a charity-operated repository of antique furniture, silver, glass, and china priced well below local antique shops.

If little else, Solana Beach harbors an enclave of good antique stores. One of the best is the **Antique Warehouse** (212 South Cedros Avenue; 619-755-5156), with its collection of 101 small shops.

A seacoast village atmosphere prevails along Del Mar's half-mile-long strip of shops. Tudor-style **Stratford Square**, the focal point, houses a number of shops in what once was a grand turn-of-the-century resort hotel. The most intriguing enterprises here are the adjoining **Ocean Song** (1438

Camino del Mar; 619-755-7664) and **Earth Song Books** (1440 Camino del Mar; 619-755-4254), which offer unique gifts, cards, musical items, and books.

The stylized **Del Mar Plaza** (1555 Camino del Mar, Del Mar; 619-792-1555) is a welcome addition. Home to over 35 retail shops, this tri-level mall sells everything from sportswear to upscale Scandinavian fashions and has a host of eateries.

Flower Hill Mall (2710 Via de la Valle, Del Mar; 619-481-7131), a rustic mall, has the usual fashion and specialty shops. But the real draw here is the **Bookworks** (619-755-3735) and an adjoining coffeehouse called **Pannikin Café** (619-481-8007). Together they're perfect for a relaxed bit of book browsing and a spot of tea.

LA JOLLA SHOPPING

Once a secluded seaside village, La Jolla has emerged as a world-famous resort community that offers style and substance. The shopping focuses on Girard Avenue (from Torrey Pines Road to Prospect Street) and along Prospect Street. Both are lined with designer boutiques, alluring specialty shops, and fabulous art galleries.

In La Jolla's many galleries, traditional art blends with contemporary paintings, and rare Oriental antiques complement 20th-century bronze sculpture. **Simic Galleries** (7925 Girard Avenue; 619-454-0225) offers a fine selection of seascapes and master Impressionist work.

The **Landmark Gallery** (955 Prospect Street; 619-456-8078) hangs the paintings of a variety of artists like Erté, Frederick Hart, Chinese artist Jiange, and popular contemporaries like Neiman. **Hanson Art Galleries** (1227 Prospect Street; 619-454-9799) features unique contemporary art exhibitions representing new graphic works and rare selections from important 20th-century artists.

Housed as it is in a landmark 1903 cottage covered with wisteria, **John Cole's Book Shop** (780 Prospect Street; 619-454-4766) provides a refuge from these slick, chic La Jolla shops. Its nooks and crannies are lined with books ranging from best sellers to rare editions.

Located some distance south of the village center, **Capriccio** (6919 La Jolla Boulevard; 619-459-4189) has made its mark in the world of women's fashions, having been numbered by *Women's Wear Daily* among the top three fashion stores in America.

One of the oldest and most unusual shops in La Jolla guards the entrance to a sea cave and can actually be entered from land or sea. Dating to 1903, the **La Jolla Cave and Shell Shop** (1325 Coast Boulevard; 619-454-6080) displays every kind of shell imaginable along with a variety of nautical gifts and tourist baubles. From inside the shop, 141 steps lead down a tunnel to the main chamber of Sunny Jim Cave.

MISSION BAY AND THE BEACHES SHOPPING

Commercial enterprises in the beach communities cater primarily to sun worshipers. Beachie boutiques and rental shops are everywhere. A new shopping center on the beach, **Belmont Park** (3190 Mission Boulevard; 619-488-0668) has a host of shops and restaurants.

The Promenade at Pacific Beach (Mission Boulevard between Pacific Beach Drive and Reed Street; 619-490-9097), a modern, Mediterranean-style shopping complex, houses around 30 smartly decorated specialty shops.

DOWNTOWN SAN DIEGO SHOPPING

No other shopping center in the county is quite like **Horton Plaza** (between Broadway and G Street, 5th and 4th avenues; 619-239-8180). More than 140 individually designed stores are situated here. Anchored by four department stores, a flood of specialty and one-of-a-kind shops complete the picture. Along the tiled boulevard are shops and vendors offering whimsical items—everything from saltwater taffy to psychic readings.

Clever designs distinguish many of the shops, such as **Adventure 16** (619-234-1751), where a split-log cabin facade invites you in to shop for outdoor and adventure travel apparel, books, and accessories. Nearby on the same level is **Banana Republic** (619-238-0080), a popular emporium for clothes, baggage, footwear, hats, and travel accessories. There are men's apparel shops, shoe stores, jewelry shops, art galleries, and women's haute couture boutiques, dozens of stores in all. Worth a special visit is **Horton Plaza Farmers' Market** (619-696-7766), where 30,000 square feet of fresh produce and specialty food products are beautifully displayed.

The **Gaslamp Quarter** (along 5th Avenue) is a charming 16-square-block assemblage of shops, galleries, and sidewalk cafés in the downtown center. Faithfully replicated in the quarter are Victorian-era street lamps, red-brick sidewalks, and window displays thematic of turn-of-the-century San Diego. Stroll down the **G Street Arts Corrido** to the **Java Coffee-house-Gallery** (837 G Street; 619-235-4012), where you can relax, browse, and enjoy a cup of fine-blend coffee. The gallery presents a constantly changing selection of contemporary art with a focus on works by Southern Californians.

A favorite spot for antique lovers is **The Olde Cracker Factory** (448 West Market Street; 619-233-1669), which offers a 20-store selection in the restored 1913 Bishop Cracker Factory. Legend has it that a resident ghost named "Crunch" shuffles through mounds of broken crackers here searching for a small brass cookie cutter.

A perfect place to stock up for a picnic is the **Farmers Bazaar** (245 7th Avenue; 619-233-0281), a down-to-earth produce market.

Seaport Village (foot of Pacific Highway and Harbor Drive) was designed to capture the look and feel of an Early California waterfront setting.

Its 65 shops dot a 14-acre village and include the usual mix of boutiques, galleries, clothing stores, and gift shops.

Thursday through Sunday, **Kobey's Swap Meet** (Sports Arena Boulevard; 619-226-0650; admission) converts the parking lot of the San Diego Sports Arena into a giant flea market where over 1000 sellers hawk new and used wares.

Hillcrest, the center of San Diego's gay community, is also a center for nostalgia seekers. Shops around Park Boulevard and University Avenue are rich in antiques and turn-of-the-century bric-a-bric.

CORONADO SHOPPING

Coronado's fancy Orange Avenue in the village center harbors six blocks of unusual shops and two mini-malls, **Coronado Plaza** (1330 Orange Avenue; 619-435-4620) and in the **El Cordova Hotel** (1351 Orange Avenue; 619-435-4131).

The **Old Ferry Landing** (619-435-8895) has been renovated to include a modern shopping area complete with boutiques, specialty shops, galleries, and eateries.

The **Hotel del Coronado** (1500 Orange Avenue) is a city within a city and home to many intriguing specialty shops, such as the **British Importing Company** (619-435-6611), where you can locate your family's crest or coat of arms. Crests, plain or gold-plated, are available for purchase.

OLD TOWN AND MISSION VALLEY SHOPPING

Historic Old Town is blessed with several exciting bazaars and shopping squares. By far the grandest is the **Bazaar del Mundo** (Calhoun Street between Twigg and Juan streets; 619-296-3161), Old Town's version of the famous marketplaces of Spain and Mexico. Adobe casitas house a variety of international shops. Here **Fabrics and Finery** unfurls cloth, beads, and craft accessories from around the world, and **Ariana** (619-296-4989) features wearable art.

Walk down San Diego Avenue and take a gander at **Squibob Square** (2611 San Diego Avenue). The cactus-lined courtyard and bougainvillea-laced cottages lend an authentic feel of yesteryear to the souvenir shops.

A haven for art lovers is **Spanish Village Center** (1770 Village Plaza, near the San Diego Zoo entrance; 619-233-9050). Over 40 studios are staffed by artists displaying their work. For sale are original paintings, sculpture, photographs, ceramics, jewelry, and gems.

SOUTH SAN DIEGO COUNTY SHOPPING

Plaza Bonita (3030 Plaza Bonita Road; 619-267-2851) in National City is a modern mall with four department stores and a range of smaller outlets.

Chula Vista's newly renovated downtown is highlighted by **Park Plaza in the Village Shopping Plaza** (310 3rd Avenue; 619-282-6814). Here 20 stores, including fashion and specialty shops, cluster around a central court. In addition, the shopping district on 3rd Avenue between E and H streets is a charming mix of long-standing family businesses and quality shops.

INLAND SAN DIEGO COUNTY SHOPPING

Jewelry is a high art form at **The Collector** (912 South Live Oak Park Road, Fallbrook; 619-728-9121), where every piece is crafted by hand. The owners go right to the source for the best gems—Colombia for emeralds, Sri Lanka for rubies, and Africa for diamonds.

Mega-malls are popping up all around San Diego these days, but few match Escondido's **North County Fair** (Via Rancho Parkway and Route 15; 619-489-2344). This 83-acre complex has a half-dozen major department stores and a host of independent shops.

Collectibles are a way of life at **Family Affair** (13330 Paseo del Verano Norte, Rancho Bernardo; 619-485-5850). The plates, lithographs, figurines, and ornaments assembled here from around the world are hand-numbered, limited-edition items.

Even if you're not in the market for nuts, dried fruit, or candy, a visit to **Bates Nut Farm** (15954 Woods Valley Road, Valley Center; 619-749-3334) is mandatory. Name the nut and they have it—walnuts, cashews, pistachios, pecans, almonds, and peanuts—attractively displayed with an equally amazing variety of dried and glazed fruits, jellies, honey, and candy.

Main Street in Julian is lined with dozens of antique, gift, clothing, and curio shops. Among the more intriguing ones are the **Antique Boutique** (2626 Main Street; 619-765-0541), with an especially nice selection of furniture and collectibles; **Julian's Toy Chest** (2116 Main Street; 619-765-2262), featuring unusual educational toys and children's books; and **Quinn Knives** (2116 Main Street; 619-765-2230), where you can buy anything from a sword to a Swiss Army knife. Nearby is **Applewood & Company** (2804 Washington Street; 619-765-1185), a popular emporium for antiques, home accessories, and quilts.

Harvest Ranch Market (759 Jamacha Road, El Cajon; 619-442-0355) is an epicure's delight. Deli items, farm-fresh produce, international gourmet foods, picnic supplies, and rack after rack of fine wines are available at this pleasant country store.

La Mesa Boulevard, the center of La Mesa's revitalized downtown, looks like an all-American hometown business district circa 1930. Old storefronts have been refurbished and filled with specialty shops, making it a great street to stroll and shop.

Nightlife

NORTH SAN DIEGO COUNTY NIGHTLIFE

There's an ocean view from the upstairs bar at **Fisherman's Restaurant** (1 Oceanside Pier; 619-722-2314). If you'd prefer a harbor view, cast an eye toward **Monterey Bay Canners** (1325 Harbor Drive North, Oceanside; 619-722-3474).

Comedy Nite (2216 El Camino Real, Oceanside; 619-757-2177) hosts professional comedians, many nationally known, Tuesday through Sunday. Cover.

Ireland's Own (656 1st Street, Encinitas; 619-944-0233) is an Irish pub complete with shamrocks, Guinness on tap, genuine Irish whiskey, and traditional Irish folk music every Thursday, Friday, and Saturday.

You can watch deejays spinning platters, live rock on weekends, blues on Sunday afternoons, and stand-up comedians working the crowd at the Spanish-style **Full Moon Nightclub** (485 1st Street, Encinitas; 619-436-7397). Cover for live shows.

Pastels (2591 North Route 101, Cardiff; 619-942-1487) is a real find, a fashionable club that hosts national and local jazz bands nightly.

Solana Beach's low-profile daytime image shifts gears at night when the-little-town-that-could spotlights two of North County's hottest clubs. **Surfside Diego's** (635 South Route 101; 619-755-8247) is an opulent nightclub, while the **Belly Up Tavern** (143 South Cedros Avenue; 619-481-9022) is a converted quonset hut that now houses a concert club and often draws big-name rock and blues stars. Cover.

An energetic crowd packs the Spanish-style **Full Moon Nightclub** (485 1st Street, Encinitas; 619-436-7397) in pursuit of live rock music and stand-up comedy. Cover for live shows.

Tucked away in the Flower Hill Mall, the **Bookworks-Pannikin Coffeehouse** (2670 Via de la Valle, Del Mar; 619-481-8007) brings a true taste of culture in the form of live jazz, classical guitarists, and poetry readings.

LA JOLLA NIGHTLIFE

The dark-paneled **Whaling Bar** (La Valencia Hotel, 1132 Prospect Street; 619-454-0771) attracts lots of La Jolla's big fish. A fine place to relax, listen to piano music, and nibble gourmet hors d'oeuvres.

Among the most romantic restaurants in town, **Top O' The Cove** (1216 Prospect Street; 619-454-7779) features an equally romantic piano bar. A panoramic view of the ocean makes **Elarios** (Summer House Inn, 7955 La Jolla Shores Drive; 619-459-0541) the perfect place to enjoy a mix of local and national jazz acts nightly. Cover on weekends.

The Comedy Store (916 Pearl Street; 619-454-9176) features comedians exclusively, many with national reputations. Cover plus minimum.

San Diego finally got its own **Hard Rock Café** (909 Prospect Street; 619-456-5456), where crowds line the streets nightly just to get in. The main attraction here is the collection of rock-and-roll memorabilia; even the bar is modeled after Pete Townshend's guitar.

Hidden inside a nondescript building, **D. G. Wills Books and Coffee-house** (7527 La Jolla Boulevard; 619-456-1800) is a tiny literary haven featuring lectures and poetry readings and serving desserts and coffees.

The **La Jolla Chamber Music Society** (619-459-3724) hosts summer and fall performances by such notables as the Isaac Stern, Yo-Yo Ma, and the Stuttgart Chamber Orchestra. The prestigious **La Jolla Playhouse** (619-534-6760), located on the University of California's San Diego campus, produces innovative dramas and musicals and spotlights famous actors.

MISSION BAY AND THE BEACHES NIGHTLIFE

Blind Melons (710 Garnet Avenue; 619-483-7844), on Crystal Pier, is best described as a Chicago beach bar featuring live blues music every night. Cover.

The **Cannibal Bar** (Catamaran Hotel, 3999 Mission Boulevard; 619-488-1081) features live jazz bands every Wednesday, and rock and oldies bands during the rest of the week. Cover on weekends.

The undisputed king of beach area nightlife is **Club Diego's** (860 Garnet Avenue; 619-272-1241). Modeled after the high-tech video discos of New York and London, it features black tile dancefloors and video screens monitoring the "beautiful people" who pack the place to capacity nightly. Cover.

Diego's Loft is located above Club Diego's but instead of disco serves up live jazz Thursday through Saturday with Sunday jam sessions. Cover.

Just next door, the **Improv Comedy Club and Restaurant** (832 Garnet Avenue; 619-483-4521), a 1930s-style cabaret, showcases many local and East Coast comedians. Cover.

Standing-room-only crowds are attracted to the **Old Pacific Beach Café** (4287 Mission Boulevard; 619-270-7522), where blues and reggae bands perform all week. Cover.

Moose McGillycuddy's (1165 Garnet Avenue; 619-274-2323) is a popular nightclub where recorded music keeps the crowd active.

The Pennent (2893 Mission Boulevard; 619-488-1671) is a Mission Beach landmark where local writers and beachies congregate en masse on the deck to get rowdy and watch the sunset. The entertainment here is the clientele.

Texas Teahouse (4970 Voltaire Street; 619-222-6895) should be listed under "Dives" in the yellow pages. This musty, Ocean Beach hole-in-the-wall is the home of Tom "Cat" Courtney, a real-life legend who's been singing and playing the blues every Thursday night here for some 17 years. He's strummed guitar with the likes of T-Bone Walker, Lightnin' Hopkins, and Freddie King. More blues bands play on weekends. Cover.

DOWNTOWN SAN DIEGO NIGHTLIFE

The sun is certainly the main attraction in San Diego, but the city also features a rich and varied nightlife, offering the night owl everything from traditional folk music to high-energy discos. There are piano bars, singles bars, a few gay bars, and a growing number of jazz clubs.

If you're a culture vulture with a limited pocketbook, try **ArtTix** (619-238-3810), a 24-hour recorded announcement listing half-priced theater, music, and dance tickets. Call **COMBO** (Combined Arts and Education Council; 619-231-6979) for its monthly arts calendar and information about inexpensive events. KIFM Radio (98.1 FM) hosts the 24-hour **Lights Out Jazz Hotline** (619-458-9898), which provides the latest in jazz happenings.

THE BEST BARS

An elegant Old World setting of marble, brass, and leather makes **Grant Grill Lounge** (U.S. Grant Hotel, 326 Broadway; 619-232-3121) *the* place for the elite to meet. Pianists play a mix of contemporary tunes, popular standards, and jazz.

Johnny M's (801 4th Avenue; 619-233-1131) is in the Gaslamp Quarter is a favored place to bend an elbow. There is often jazz on weekends.

For a good-time pub try **Reidy O'Neils Irish Bar** (939 4th Avenue; 619-231-8500). This beautifully appointed mahogany-and-glass bar, accented by green shamrock carpets. O'Neils draws the after-work crowd and is enlivened on weekends with a three-piece Irish band.

At **Croce's** (802 5th Avenue; 619-233-4355) fans of the immortal Jim Croce will love the bar built as a memorial to the late singer-songwriter by his wife, Ingrid. Family mementos line the walls in tribute to a talented recording artist. Just next door, **Croce's Top Hat** (818 5th Avenue; 619-233-6945) is a snazzy New Orleans-style club featuring live rhythm-and-blues. Cover on weekends.

There's no hotel at **Cabo Cabo Hotel Bar** (203 5th Avenue; 619-232-2272), but there is a grand 50-foot-long bar. This hot spot carries its Mexican theme to the hilt with decorative exotica such as piñatas, stuffed wildcats, and a giant Chihuahua beer bottle chandelier.

Karl Strass' Old Columbia Brewery (1157 Columbia Avenue at B Street; 619-234-2739) may well have the best beer in town. This newcomer in the old Gaslamp Quarter has been well-greeted by San Diegans.

It's easy to spot the shocking pink, neon-lit facade of **Fat City** (2137 Pacific Highway; 619-232-0686). Art deco styling marks the exterior, but the bar features an authentic Victorian decor. It's not a meat market, but Fat City is a favorite among friendly young singles and hosts a variety of musical styles Friday and Saturday.

Plaza Bar (1055 2nd Avenue; 619-238-1818), at the distinctive Westgate Hotel, is a graceful period French lounge where prominent locals and visitors enjoy classy piano entertainment nightly.

Mr. A's (2550 5th Avenue; 619-239-1377) is the critics' choice for "best drinking with a view." The atmosphere at this piano bar is one of monied luxury, and gentlemen are expected to wear jackets.

If it's '50s fun you're seeking, go to the **Corvette Diner, Bar and Grill** (3946 5th Avenue; 619-542-1001). Great oldies keep this joint jumpin'.

There's a wonderful view of San Diego Bay from the Seaport Village restaurant, **Papagayo** (861 West Harbor Drive; 619-232-7581), where a tropical setting creates a relaxed atmosphere.

Featuring views of San Diego Bay and one of the largest dancefloors in town, **Harbor House** (831 West Harbor Drive, Seaport Village; 619-232-1141) is a good spot for a relaxed drink.

THEATER

The **Simon Edison Theatre Centre for the Performing Arts** (Balboa Park; 619-239-2255) presents classic and contemporary plays in three Balboa Park theatres.

The **Gaslamp Quarter Theater Company** (619-234-9583) offers productions of classical and contemporary works.

In addition to performances of the San Diego Opera, the **San Diego Civic Theater** (202 C Street; 619-236-6510) presents a variety of entertainment ranging from pop artists to plays to dance performances.

The **San Diego Repertory Theatre** (79 Horton Plaza; 619-235-8025), performs dramas, comedies, and musicals.

Just north of the downtown theater district, the **Blackfriars Theatre** (1057 1st Avenue; 619-232-4088) stages contemporary and often controversial theater. Many works are original and/or San Diego premieres of powerful national plays.

The Marquis Theatre (3717 India Street; 619-295-5654) is noted for its original scripts, improvisation, experimental productions, and music.

OPERA, SYMPHONY, AND DANCE

The **San Diego Opera** (202 C Street; 619-232-7636) presents such international stars as Luciano Pavarotti, Joan Sutherland, and Kiri Te Kanawa. The season runs from January through May, with some additional recitals in the spring and fall.

Performing in the historic 1929 Spanish Renaissance-style Copley Symphony Hall (1245 7th Avenue), the **San Diego Symphony Orchestra** (619-699-4205) offers an array of guest conductors and artists. During the summer, the symphony presents outdoor performances at the Embarcadero Marina Park South (5th Street and Harbor Boulevard).

California Ballet Center (619-560-5676) presents a diverse repertoire of contemporary and traditional ballets.

THE GAY SCENE

Club West Coast (2028 Hancock Street; 619-295-3724) is a high-energy gay club featuring deejay disco dancing nightly and special events. Four large bars, a game room, and a patio are housed in this artfully decorated, extravagant spot. Located near Old Town. Cover on weekends.

Bourbon Street (4612 Park Boulevard; 619-291-0173) is a comfortable piano bar that features an outdoor patio.

There is dancing to deejay-selected videos at the **Brass Rail** (3796 5th Avenue; 619-298-2233). On Monday and Tuesday night they feature a female impersonator show and on Wednesdays there is a lip sync contest.

The order of the day (or night) at the **Chee Chee Club** (929 Broadway; 619-234-4404), a local cruise bar, revolves around listening to video music, shooting pool, and playing pinball.

Similarly, **The Loft** (3610 5th Avenue; 619-296-6407) offers jukebox music and pool playing.

Touted as "San Diego's hottest women's bar," **The Flame** (3780 Park Boulevard; 619-295-4163) features a dancefloor, pool tables, and a video bar. There is live entertainment (and a corresponding cover charge) on weekends.

Shooter's (3815 30th Street; 619-574-0744), a popular sports bar, boasts three large-screen televisions, seven pool tables, pinball, video games, and a video juke box.

While most of the gay bars are located in the Hillcrest neighborhood, there is one place down by the beach. **Matador** (4633 Mission Boulevard; 619-483-6943), one block from Mission Beach, features taped music, a pool table, and video games.

CORONADO NIGHTLIFE

If you're out Coronado way, stop for a cocktail in the famed Hotel del Coronado's **Ocean Terrace Lounge** (1550 Orange Avenue; 619-435-6611). The Del's latest addition is the **Palm Court**, offering live piano music in a palm-studded lounge.

Mexican Village (120 Orange Avenue; 619-435-1822) is a Mexican-theme nightclub, but the music isn't Mexican at all. Solo performers play classics and contemporaries on the piano from Sunday through Thursday, then disco dancing charges up the weekends.

SHELTER AND HARBOR ISLANDS NIGHTLIFE

For the mellow crowd interested in enjoying cocktails, yummy appetizers, and conversation while overlooking a picturesque marina, there's **Hurricanes** (2051 Shelter Island Drive; 619-223-2572).

Even musicians head outdoors during San Diego summers. **Humphrey's** (2241 Shelter Island Drive; 619-224-3577) hosts the city's most ambitious series of jazz and mellow rock shows, which include an impressive lineup of name artists in a beautiful bayside lawn setting.

Aside from being a popular restaurant and lounge, **Tom Ham's Lighthouse** (2150 Harbor Island Drive; 619-291-9110) is a real lighthouse and the official Coast Guard-sanctioned beacon of Harbor Island. This scrimshaw-filled nautical lounge is a great place to relax while taking in the view and listening to jazz.

OLD TOWN AND MISSION VALLEY NIGHTLIFE

The prevailing culture in Old Town is Mexican, as in mariachis and margaritas. The **Old Town Mexican Café y Cantina** (2489 San Diego Avenue; 619-297-4330), a festive, friendly establishment, has a patio bar.

O'Hungry's (2547 San Diego Avenue; 619-298-0133), a nearby folk club, features folk singers and guitarists Tuesday through Sunday.

If you want to dance disco, **Confetti's** (5373 Mission Center Road; 619-291-8635) has a multilevel dancefloor and, of course, confetti spewing from the ceilings. All three bars are packed nightly.

SOUTH SAN DIEGO COUNTY NIGHTLIFE

If you're looking for nighttime entertainment in these areas, you'll probably want to consider a trip to the city. Otherwise be content with scattered restaurant bars and local pubs. There's one notable exception: **J. J.'s Hot Rock** (1862 Palm Avenue, Imperial Beach; 619-429-1161). Advertised as San Diego's largest nightclub, it houses two dance clubs. A pair of live bands appears on weekends. Cover.

INLAND SAN DIEGO COUNTY NIGHTLIFE

J. P.'s Lounge (2001 South Route 395, Fallbrook; 619-728-5881), a classy and contemporary watering hole at Pala Mesa Resort, is one of the region's top nightclubs. You can count on a sophisticated crowd and frequent live entertainment.

Built in 1912 as a training camp for Jack Dempsey, **Pine Hills Lodge** (2960 La Posada Way, Julian; 619-765-1100) uses the champ's old ring as a dinner theater stage. And it looks as though they've scored a knockout. A dedicated and talented local company performs light plays and musicals. Friday and Saturday only.

Deep in the mountains south of Julian, you'll come upon **Sunrise Inn** (28940 Old Route 80, Pine Valley; 619-473-8727), a country lodge with an open-beam ceiling and an *après* ski atmosphere. It's quiet and cozy during the week, but they raise the rafters on weekends with live rock-and-roll.

The **East County Performing Arts Center** (210 East Main Street, El Cajon; 619-440-2277) is the cultural flagship of the region, offering everything from chamber music to Mel Torme. The cultural calendar here includes orchestras, dance companies, and repertory theater groups.

El Cajon's Southwest-style **Bull and Bear** (690 North 2nd Street; 619-479-3663) fills up nightly with locals dancing to live Top-40 music.

The **Circle D Corral** (1013 Broadway, El Cajon; 619-444-7443), a hot Western club, cooks up a live batch of country-and-western music five nights a week. Cover.

For jazz, folk, and easy listening music, slip over to the **Boathouse** (5500 Grossmont Center Drive, La Mesa; 619-589-5353). This restaurant lounge keeps the crowds intrigued playing satellite trivia games.

The **Lamplighter Community Theatre** (8053 University Avenue, La Mesa; 619-464-4598) presents a year-round series of stage plays by a local theater group.

CENTRAL COAST

CHAPTER SIX
Central Coast

To call any one section of the California Coast the most alluring is to embark upon uncertain waters. Surely the Central Coast, that 200-mile swath from Ventura to San Simeon, is a region of rare beauty. Stretching across Ventura, Santa Barbara, and San Luis Obispo counties, it embraces many of the West's finest beaches.

Five of California's 21 missions—in Ventura, Santa Barbara, Lompoc, San Luis Obispo, and further inland in Solvang—lie along this stretch. Chosen by the Spanish in the 1780s for their fertile pastures, natural harbors, and placid surroundings, they are an historic testimonial to the varied richness of the landscape.

The towns that grew up around these missions, evocative of old Spanish traditions, are emblems of California's singular culture. Santa Barbara, perhaps the state's prettiest town, is a warren of whitewashed buildings and red tile roofs, backdropped by rocky peaks and bounded by a five-mile palm-fringed beach.

Ventura and San Luis Obispo represent two of California's most underrated towns. In addition to a wealthy heritage, Ventura possesses beautiful beaches and San Luis Obispo is set amid velvet hills and rich agricultural areas. Both are less expensive than elsewhere and offer many of the same features without the pretensions.

Offshore are the Channel Islands, a 25-million-year-old chain and vital wildlife preserve. Sandblasted by fierce storms, pristine in their magnificence, they are a China shop of endangered species and unique life forms. While the nearby reefs are headstones for the many ships that have crashed here, the surrounding waters are crowded with sea life.

Together with the rest of the coast, the islands were discovered by Juan Rodríguez Cabrillo in 1542. The noted explorer found them inhabited by Chumash Indians, a collection of tribes occupying the coast from Malibu to Morro Bay. Hunters and gatherers, the Chumash were master mariners who built woodplank canoes called *tomols*, capable of carrying ten people across treacherous waters to the Channel Islands. They in turn were preceded by the Oak Grove Tribes, which inhabited the region from 7000 to 3000 B.C.

Once Gaspar de Portolá opened the coast to Spanish colonialists with his 1769 explorations, few Indians from any California tribes survived. Forced into servitude and religious conversion by the padres, the Chumash revolted at Santa Barbara Mission and Mission de la Purísima Concepción in 1824. They held Purísima for a month before troops from Monterey overwhelmed them. By 1910 the Westerners who had come to save them had so decimated the Indians that their 30,000 population dwindled to 1250.

By the mid 1800s these lately arrived white men set out in pursuit of any sea mammal whose pelt would fetch a price. The Central Coast was a prime whale-hunting ground. Harpooners by the hundreds speared leviathans, seals, and sea lions, hunting them practically to extinction. Earlier in the century American merchants, immortalized in Richard Henry Dana's *Two Years Before the Mast*, had combed the coast trading for cattle hides.

The land that bore witness to this colonial carnage endured. Today the Central Coast and its offshore islands abound in sea lions, harbor seals, Northern fur seals, and elephant seals. Whales inhabit the deeper waters and gamefish are plentiful. The only threats remaining are those from developers and the oil industry, whose offshore drilling resulted in the disastrous 1969 Santa Barbara spill.

The Central Coast traveler finds a Mediterranean climate, dry and hot in the summer, tempered by morning fog and winds off the ocean, then cool and rainy during winter months. Two highways, Routes 1 and 101, lead through this salubrious environment. The former hugs the coast much of the way, traveling inland to Lompoc and San Luis Obispo, and the latter, at times joining with Route 1 to form a single roadway, eventually diverges into the interior valleys.

Almost as much as the ocean, mountains play a vital part in the life of the coast. Along the southern stretches are the Santa Monica Mountains, which give way further north to the Santa Ynez Mountains. Below them, stretching along the coastal plain, are the towns of Oxnard, Ventura, Santa Barbara, and Goleta.

Both mountain systems are part of the unique Transverse Range, which unlike most North American mountains, travels from east to west rather than north and south. They are California's Great Divide, a point of demarcation between the chic, polished regions near Santa Barbara and the rough, wild territory around San Luis Obispo.

Arriving at the ocean around Point Conception, the Transverse Range separates the curving pocket beaches of the south and the endless sand dunes

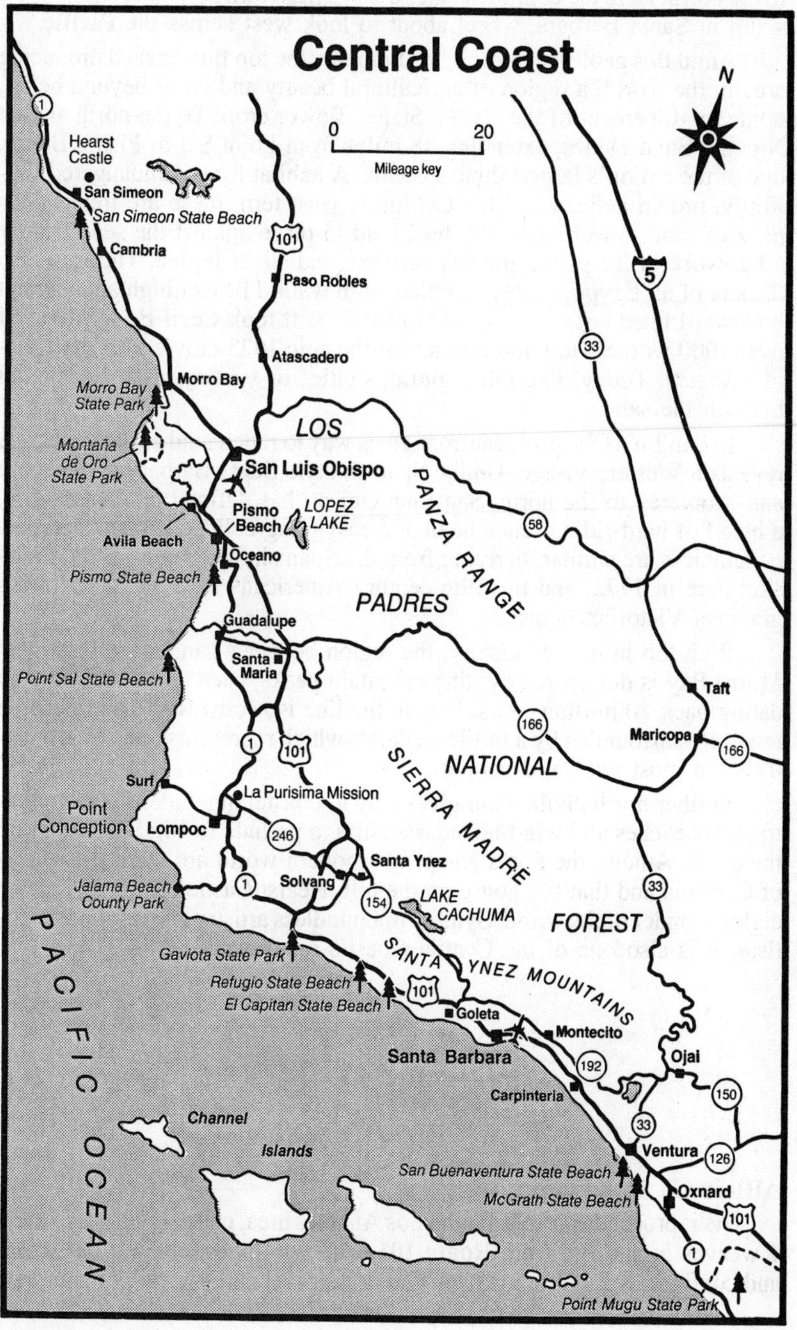
Central Coast
N
0
20
Mileage key
1
Hearst Castle
San Simeon
San Simeon State Beach
Cambria
101
Paso Robles
5
33
Atascadero
Morro Bay
Morro Bay State Park
Montaña de Oro State Park
LOS
San Luis Obispo
PANZA RANGE
Pismo Beach
LOPEZ LAKE
58
Avila Beach
Oceano
Pismo State Beach
PADRES
Guadalupe
Santa Maria
Point Sal State Beach
Taft
166
Maricopa
166
1
101
SIERRA MADRE
NATIONAL
Surf
La Purisima Mission
Point Conception
Lompoc
246
Santa Ynez
Jalama Beach County Park
1
Solvang
154
LAKE CACHUMA
33
FOREST
PACIFIC OCEAN
Gaviota State Park
SANTA YNEZ MOUNTAINS
Refugio State Beach
101
El Capitan State Beach
Goleta
Montecito
Santa Barbara
192
Ojai
Carpinteria
150
Channel
Islands
33
Ventura
126
San Buenaventura State Beach
Oxnard
McGrath State Beach
101
1
Point Mugu State Park

to the north. Here the continent takes a sharp right turn as the beaches, facing south in Santa Barbara, wheel about to look west across the Pacific.

Amid this geologic turmoil lies Lompoc, the top flower seed producing area in the world, a region of agricultural beauty and color beyond belief, home to 40 percent of the United States' flower crop. To the north are the Nipomo Sand Dunes, extending 18 miles from Point Sal to Pismo Beach, one of the nation's largest dune systems. A habitat for the endangered California brown pelican and the California least tern, these are tremendous piles of sand, towering to 450 feet, held in place against the sea wind by a lacework of ice plant, grasses, verbena, and silver lupine. They are also the site of an Egyptian city, complete with walls 110 feet high and a grand boulevard lined with sphinxes and pharaohs. It took Cecil B. deMille and over 1000 workers to build this set for the epic 1923 movie *The Ten Commandments*. Today, like other glorious cities of yesteryear, it lies buried beneath the sand.

In San Luis Obispo oceanfront gives way to ranch land as the landscape reveals a Western visage. Unlike Spanish-style Santa Barbara to the south and Monterey to the north, San Luis Obispo has defined its own culture, a blend of hard-riding ranch hand and easygoing college student. Its roots nonetheless are similar, deriving from the Spanish, who founded their mission here in 1772, and the 19th-century Americans who built the town's gracious Victorian homes.

Rich too in natural history, the region between San Luis Obispo and Morro Bay is dominated by nine mountain peaks, each an extinct volcano dating back 20 million years. Last in the line is Morro Rock, an imposing monolith surrounded by a fertile wetlands which represents one of the country's ten most vital bird habitats.

Further north civilization gives way to coastal quietude. There are untracked beaches and wind-honed sea cliffs, a prelude to Big Sur further up the coast. Among the few signs of the modern world are the artist colony of Cambria and that big house on the hill, Hearst Castle, California's own eighth wonder of the world. Symbol of boundless artistry and unbridled egotism, it is also one of the Central Coast's many wonders.

Easy Living

Transportation

ARRIVAL

As it proceeds north from the Los Angeles area, coastal highway **Route 1** weaves in and out from **Route 101**. The two highways join in Oxnard and continue as a single roadway until a point 30 miles north of Santa Barbara. Here they diverge, Route 1 heading toward the coast while Route 101 takes an inland route. The highways merge again near Pismo Beach and continue north to San Luis Obispo. Here Route 1 leaves Route 101 and begins its long, beautiful course up the coast past Morro Bay and San Simeon.

BY AIR

Santa Barbara and San Luis Obispo have small airports serving the Central Coast. Several airlines stop at the **Santa Barbara Municipal Airport**, including American Airlines, United Airlines, and Sky West Airlines. The **Santa Barbara Airbus** (805-964-7759) meets all scheduled arrivals and transports folks to Carpinteria, Isla Vista, and Goleta as well as downtown Santa Barbara and Los Angeles International Airport. There are also a number of taxi companies available. For the disabled, call **Easy Lift Transportation** (805-568-5114).

San Luis Obispo Municipal Airport is serviced by West Air, Wings West, and Sky West Airlines. Ground transportation is provided by **Yellow Cab** (805-568-5114) and **Yellow Cab of Five Cities** (805-489-1155).

BY TRAIN

For those who want spectacular views of the coastline, try **Amtrak**'s "Coast Starlight." This train hugs the shoreline, providing rare views of the Central Coast's cliffs, headlands, and untracked beaches. Amtrak (800-872-7245) stops in Oxnard, Santa Barbara, and San Luis Obispo on its way north to Oakland and Seattle.

BY BUS

Greyhound/Trailways Bus Lines has continual service along the Central Coast from Los Angeles or San Francisco. Terminals are located in Ventura (291 East Thompson Boulevard; 805-653-0164), Santa Barbara (Carrillo and Chapala streets; 805-965-3971), and San Luis Obispo (150 South Street; 805-543-2123).

For a funky alternative "trip" by bus, book reservations with **Green Tortoise** (805-569-1884). This New Age company has once-a-week service from Los Angeles or San Francisco.

CAR RENTALS

The larger towns in the Central Coast have car rental agencies; check the yellow pages to find the best bargains. To pick up a car in the Oxnard-Ventura area, try **Avis Rent A Car** (805-652-2275), **Budget Rent A Car** (805-647-3536), **Hertz Rent A Car** (805-985-0911), **National Car Rental** (805-985-6100), and **Thrifty Car Rental** (805-654-0101). For second-hand cars try **America Rent A Car** (805-485-0475).

At the airport in Santa Barbara try **Avis Rent A Car** (805-964-4848), **Budget Rent A Car** (805-964-6791), **Hertz Rent A Car** (805-967-0411), or **National Car Rental** (805-967-1202). Agencies located outside the airport with free pick-up include **Dollar Rent A Car** (805-683-1468) and **Enterprise Rent A Car** (805-569-3636).

In San Luis Obispo, car rental agencies at the airport include **Avis Rent A Car** (805-544-0630), **Budget Rent A Car** (805-541-2722), **Hertz Rent A Car** (805-543-8843), and **Thrifty Car Rental** (805-544-3777). Among those with free pickup service, try **Enterprise Rent A Car** (805-541-4811).

PUBLIC TRANSPORTATION

Public transportation in the Central Coast is fairly limited. In the Ventura area you'll find **South Coast Area Transit** (805-487-4222), or SCAT, which serves Oxnard, Port Hueneme, Ojai, and Ventura.

In the Santa Barbara area, the **Santa Barbara Metropolitan Transit** (Carrillo and Chapala streets; 805-683-3702) stops in Summerland, Carpinteria, Santa Barbara, Goleta, and Isla Vista.

The San Luis Obispo area has **San Luis Obispo Transit** (805-541-2877), or SLO, which operates on weekdays during daylight hours and even less frequently on weekends.

Hotels

Lodging facilities all along the Central Coast run the gamut from budget to ultra-deluxe. Most are concentrated in Ventura, Santa Barbara, and San Luis Obispo, as well as the Pismo Beach and Morro Bay area. Room prices here fluctuate more than elsewhere along the California Coast and are often considerably cheaper during the winter and on weekdays.

VENTURA AREA HOTELS

For something spacious, plush, and formal consider the **Bella Maggiore Inn** (67 South California Street, Ventura; 805-652-0277). Set in downtown Ventura, this 32-room hostelry follows the tradition of an Italian inn. There are European appointments and antique chandeliers in the lobby and a Roman-style fountain in the courtyard. The accommodations I saw were painted in soft hues and decorated with pastel prints. The furniture was a mixture of cane, washed pine, and antiques. Moderate to deluxe.

Up the hill, overlooking Ventura and the ocean, sits **La Mer European Bed & Breakfast** (411 Poli Street, Ventura; 805-643-3600). The flags decorating the facade of this 1890 house illustrate the inn's international theme. Each of the five guest rooms is decorated after the fashion of a European country—England, Austria, Norway, Germany, and France. All with private baths and entrances, they vary from the Norwegian "Captain's Cove," decorated nautically, to the French "Madame Pompadour," with its bay window. Deluxe to ultra-deluxe.

OJAI AREA HOTELS

The premier mountain resort hereabouts is **Ojai Valley Inn** (Country Club Drive, Ojai; 805-646-5511), a 200-acre retreat with tennis courts, pool, and 18-hole golf course. Set on a ridge top with spectacular mountain vistas, the complex has been refurbished and modernized. Rooms are on a full European plan and rent in the ultra-deluxe category. They are quite spacious, imaginatively decorated, and share the resort's oh-so-incredible views. There is an ample lobby for lounging plus such amenities as a croquet court, putting green, hiking trails, and dining room.

For moderate-to-deluxe-priced accommodations consider **Ojai Rancho Motel** (615 West Ojai Avenue, Ojai; 805-646-1434). It's a 17-unit affair with large, attractive rooms, paneled entirely in knotty pine and carpeted wall-to-wall. Some rooms are equipped with kitchenettes.

For bed and breakfast accommodations try **Ojai Manor Hotel** (210 East Matilija Street, Ojai; 805-646-0961), set in a vintage 1874 schoolhouse. The six-room facility has rentals in the moderate-to-deluxe range. A typical guest room is small but attractively decorated with throw rugs across the softwood floor and a wrought-iron bed. Guests share bathrooms and can use the living room, porch, and side yard.

Because of its surrounding mountains Ojai is extremely popular with the health conscious. One of the region's leading resorts, **The Oaks at Ojai** (122 East Ojai Avenue, Ojai; 805-646-5573), caters to this interest. It provides a full menu of physical activity including aerobic exercise, weight training, yoga classes, body conditioning, and massage. Guests take all their meals—low-calorie vegetarian plates—at the resort. The accommodations include comfortable, spacious rooms in the lodge and in multiunit cottages. Included in the tab are three meals, fitness classes, and use of the pool, saunas, jacuzzi, and other health facilities. Ultra-deluxe.

SANTA BARBARA AREA HOTELS

South of Santa Barbara in Carpinteria, the **Eugenia Motel** (5277 Carpinteria Avenue, Carpinteria; 805-684-4416) has ten rooms (four with kitchens) renting in the budget range. Each is small, carpeted, and clean. The furniture is comfortable though nicked. The baths have stall showers.

Because of its excellent beach Carpinteria is very popular with families. Many spend their entire vacation here, so most facilities rent by the week or month. Among the less expensive spots for overnighters is **La Casa del Sol Motel** (5585 Carpinteria Avenue, Carpinteria; 805-684-4307). This multiunit complex has rooms available at budget prices (including eight with kitchens). The one I saw was paneled in knotty pine and trimly furnished. Small pool.

Because of its excellent beach Carpinteria is very popular with families. Many spend their entire vacation here, so most facilities rent by the week or month. Among the less expensive spots for overnighters is **La Casa del Sol Motel** (5585 Carpinteria Avenue, Carpinteria; 805-684-4307). This multiunit complex has rooms available at budget prices (including eight with kitchens). The one I saw was paneled in knotty pine and trimly furnished. Small pool.

To provide an idea of the full range of accommodations available in the Santa Barbara area there are two centralized reservation agencies in town. **Accommodations in Santa Barbara** (3344 State Street; 805-687-9191) and **Santa Barbara Hotspots** (36 State Street; 805-564-1637) can give information on prices and availability. Since room rates in Santa Barbara fluctuate by season and day of the week, it's advisable to check.

For modest-priced accommodations within a block or two of the beach, check out **Cabrillo Boulevard**. This artery skirts the shoreline for several miles. Establishments lining the boulevard are usually a little higher in price. But along the side streets leading from Cabrillo are numerous generic motels.

From these you can generally expect rooms which are small but tidy and clean. The wall-to-wall carpeting is industrial grade, the furniture consists of naugahyde chairs and formica tables, and the artworks make you appreciate minimalism. There's usually a swimming pool and surrounding terrace, plus a wall of ice machines and soda dispensers. One such place, **Pacific Crest Motel** (433 Corona del Mar Drive; 805-966-3103) has 26 units renting at budget-to-moderate prices during summer months, budget in winter. Next door, that generic facility, **Motel 6** (443 Corona del Mar Drive; 805-564-1392), has budget-priced rooms. Both are a block from Santa Barbara's best all-around beach.

Over in the West Beach area, **Beach House Motel** (320 West Yanonali Street; 805-966-1126) has 12 units located two blocks from the beach. Rooms here are larger than usual and most have kitchens, but there's no pool. Moderate to deluxe in summer; budget to moderate during the rest of the year. **L-Rancho Motel** (316 West Montecito Street; 805-962-0181), a block further away, has 23 units. Ask for a room with a kitchen. No pool. Budget to moderate in summer; budget during the rest of the year. The **Tides Motel** (116 Castillo Street; 805-963-9772), one block from the water, has 24 units and a jacuzzi but no pool. Rates are moderate, with or without a kitchen, except on weekends when they jump into the deluxe range.

The **Miramar Hotel-Resort** (1555 South Jameson Lane, Montecito; 805-969-2203) is billed as "the only hotel right on the beach" in the Santa Barbara area. Indeed there is 500 feet of beautiful beachfront. It also is right on noisy Route 101. Not to worry—the Miramar is still the best bargain around. Where else will you find dining facilities, room service, two swimming pools, tennis courts, health spa, and shuffleboard at moderate to deluxe prices? Granted that will place you in a plainly appointed room closer to motor city than the beach, but you can be oceanfront for a deluxe price. Wherever you choose, you'll be in a lovely 15-acre resort inhabited by blue-roofed cottages and tropical foliage.

For chic surroundings there is **Villa Rosa** (15 Chapala Street; 805-966-0851). Built during the 1930s in Spanish palazzo fashion, it was originally an apartment house. Today it is an 18-room inn with raw wood furnishings, pastel walls, and private baths. There's a pool and spa in the courtyard. Guests commingle over continental breakfast and afternoon wine-and-cheese, then settle into plump armchairs around a tile fireplace with port and sherry in the evening. The spacious rooms, some with fireplaces, are pleasantly understated and located half a block from the beach. Deluxe to ultra-deluxe.

The **California Hotel** (35 State Street; 805-966-7153) has one thing going for it—location. It sits on the main street in Santa Barbara just a block from the beach. The hotel is in a blocky, four-story building with a restaurant and lounge downstairs. Popular with Europeans; the rooms are trimly appointed. If you can get an oceanside room on the fourth floor it could be worth it, otherwise keep on reading. Moderate.

The Eagle Inn (232 Natoma Avenue; 805-965-3586) is an attractive Mediterranean-style apartment house converted into a 17-room hotel. Just two blocks from the beach, most of the rooms are studio units with living rooms, some with kitchens. Prices fluctuate but are generally pegged in the moderate-to-deluxe range.

Small and intimate as bed and breakfasts tend to be, the **Simpson House Inn** (121 East Arrellaga Street; 805-963-7067) is even more so. Close to downtown, it resides along a quiet tree-lined block. The century-old Victorian inn features six guest rooms set on one acre of sculptured English gardens. Each room is individually furnished with antiques, Oriental rugs and English lace; some have private decks and one, bay windows. Guests meet in the elaborate dining room for breakfast and enjoy wine and hors d'oeuvres in the library later. Bicycles and croquet complete the package. Deluxe to ultra-deluxe.

The Old Yacht Club Inn (431 Corona del Mar Drive; 805-962-1277) is two inns in one. The main facility is a 1912 California Craftsman-style house with five rooms priced in the moderate to deluxe range. There's a parlor with piano downstairs and a decorative motif throughout that brings back cheery memories of grandmother's house. Next door, in a 1927-vintage stucco, are four rooms with private baths tabbed deluxe. Each has been decorated by a different family and features their personal photographs and other heirlooms. The inn is just one block from East Beach, serves a full breakfast and provides bicycles, beach chairs, and towels to guests. Three Saturdays a month, owner Nancy Donaldson offers an elegantly prepared five-course gourmet dinner to guests. The Inn books far in advance on these nights, but it's well worth the wait.

The Glenborough Inn (1327 Bath Street; 805-966-0589) is laid out in similar fashion. The main house is a 1906 California Crafts man design with moderate-priced rooms sharing baths. An ultra-deluxe suite is decorated in turn-of-the-century nouveau style with a fireplace, private entrance, garden, patio, and bath. The second house is an 1880-era cottage with rooms and suites priced deluxe and enjoying private baths. The theme in both abodes is romance. The rooms are beautifully fashioned with embroidered curtains, inlaid French furniture, rocking chairs, canopied beds, crocheted coverlets, and needlepoint pieces. There's a garden and hot tub at the main house and a patio beside the cottage. Guests enjoy a gourmet breakfast in bed and afternoon hors d'oeuvres; they also share a cozy living room with tile fireplace.

Down the road at the **Bath Street Inn** (1720 Bath Street; 805-682-9680) you'll encounter a Queen Anne Victorian constructed in 1873. It's an attractive house with an equally charming hostess, Susan Brown. Enter along a garden walkway into a warm living room with marble-trimmed fireplace. The patio in back is set in another garden. Rooms on the second floor feature the hardwood floors and patterned wallpaper which are the hallmarks of California bed and breakfasts. The third floor has a cozy sloped-roof and a television lounge for guests. Rooms price in the deluxe category and include private baths, breakfast, evening refreshments, and use of the inn's bicycles.

Personally, I prefer the **Upham Hotel** (1404 De la Vina Street; 805-962-0058) to the nearby bed and breakfasts. Established in 1871, it shares a sense of history with the country inns, but enjoys the lobby and restaurant amenities of a hotel. Victorian in style, the two-story clapboard is marked by sweeping verandas and a cupola. While not as personalized as the bed and breakfast guest rooms, the accommodations are nicely appointed with hardwood furnishings and period furnishings. Prices are in the deluxe range and include continental breakfast and afternoon wine and cheese. Not a bad price for a stay at "the oldest cosmopolitan hotel in continuous operation in Southern California." Around the landscaped grounds are garden cottages, some with private patios and fireplaces, and a carriage house with five Victorian-style rooms in the ultra-deluxe category.

Santa Barbara's two finest hotels dominate the town's two geographic locales, the ocean and the mountains. **Four Seasons Biltmore Hotel** (1260 Channel Drive; 805-969-2261) is a grand old Spanish-style hotel set on spacious grounds beside the beach. It's the kind of place where guests play croquet or practice putting on manicured lawns, then meander over to the hotel's Coral Casino Beach and Cabaña Club. There are several dining rooms as well as tennis courts, swimming pools, and a complete spa. The refinished rooms are quite large and have an airy feel heightened by white plantation shutters, light wood furnishings, and full marble baths. Many are located in multiplex cottages and are spotted around the magnificent grounds which have made the Biltmore one of California's most famous hotels since it opened back in 1927. Ultra-deluxe.

El Encanto (1900 Lasuen Road; 805-687-5000) sits back in the Santa Barbara hills and is a favorite hideaway among Hollywood stars. The hotel's 83 rooms are set in cottages and villas which dot this ten-acre retreat. The grounds are beautifully landscaped and feature a lily pond, tennis court, and swimming pool. The ocean views are simply spectacular. Rooms are very spacious with attached sitting rooms, plus extra features like room service, refrigerator, and terrycloth bathrobes. Many have private patios. The decor is French country with a lot of brass and etched-glass fixtures. Deluxe to ultra-deluxe.

In the Santa Ynez foothills above Montecito sits another retreat where the rich and powerful mix with the merely talented. **San Ysidro Ranch** (900 San Ysidro Lane, Montecito; 805-969-5046) sprawls across 540 acres, most of which is wilderness traversed by hiking and horse trails. There are tennis courts, pool, bocci ball court, riding stables, and a nearby hot spring. The grounds vie with the Santa Barbara Botanical Gardens in the variety of plant life: there are meadows, mountain forests, and an orange grove. The Stonehouse Restaurant serves gourmet dishes and the complex also features sitting rooms and lounges. Privacy is the password: all these features are shared by guests occupying just 45 units. The accommodations are dotted around the property in cottages and small multiplexes. Rooms are ultra-deluxe in price. They vary in decor, but even the simplest are trimly appointed and spacious with hardwood furnishings and woodburning fireplaces.

SANTA YNEZ VALLEY HOTELS

Up in the Santa Ynez Valley, tucked between the Santa Ynez and San Rafael mountains, lies **Alisal Guest Ranch** (1054 Alisal Road, Solvang; 805-688-6411). A 10,000-acre working cattle ranch, Alisal represents one of the original Spanish land grants. Part of the ranch is an exclusive resort featuring 73 units, a golf course, swimming pool, spa, tennis courts, and dining room. Guests ride horseback through the property and fish and sail on a mile-long lake. Square dances, hay rides, and summer barbecue dinners add to the entertainment. Breakfast and dinner are included in the rate, which is ultra-deluxe.

Inexpensive lodging in the Santa Ynez Valley usually means finding a place in Solvang. This Danish town has numerous motels, many of which line Route 246. One I recommend is **Solvang Gaard Lodge** (293 Alisal Road; 805-688-4404). Designed in old Danish style, it's a standard motel with basic facilities and rooms in the budget range. If they are booked solid, try the **Denmark Motel** (279 Alisal Road; 805-688-6813) next door. At either place be sure to reserve in advance; they fill up fast, particularly in summer and on weekends.

SAN LUIS OBISPO AREA HOTELS

Lodging in the Pismo Beach–Shell Beach–Avila Beach area generally means finding a motel. None of these seaside towns has expanded more than a few blocks from the waterfront, so wherever you book a room will be walking distance from the beach.

For budget-to-moderate-tabbed accommodations there's **Cypress Motel** (541 Cypress Street, Pismo Beach; 805-773-5505), a small seven-unit establishment. The furniture and decoration is standard motel style, but each room has a kitchenette. **Adams Motel** (1000 Dolliver Street, Pismo Beach; 805-773-2065) is a 20-unit hostelry (12 with kitchenettes) priced similarly.

It's a step up and a lot nearer the water at **Seawall Motel** (170 Main Street, Pismo Beach; 805-773-4706). This place is right above the beach (hence the name) and each of its 22 units has an ocean view. Moderate (deluxe for room with a kitchenette). **Surfside Motel & Apartments** (256 Front Street, Avila Beach; 805-595-2300) is directly across the street from lovely Avila Beach. Here rooms with or without kitchenette are budget to moderate in price.

If it's panoramic Pacific Coast views you are after, try **The Best Western Shore Cliff Lodge** (2555 Price Street, Pismo Beach; 805-773-4671). Perched on the cliffs just off Route 101, the hotel offers spacious, although conventional, rooms with private balconies and expected amenities. There is a restaurant, lounge, pool, spa, sauna, and tennis courts. Rooms rate in the deluxe to ultra-deluxe range, but what a view!

Sycamore Mineral Springs Resort (1215 Avila Beach Drive, San Luis Obispo; 805-595-7302) reposes on a hillside one mile inland from Avila Beach. Situated in a stand of oak and sycamore trees are 27 motel-style rooms. Each has a private spa and patio; there are also redwood hot tubs scattered about in the surrounding forest; swimming pool. The rooms are decorated in contemporary style and rent for deluxe prices.

Heritage Inn Bed & Breakfast (978 Olive Street, San Luis Obispo; 805-544-7440) is a San Luis Obispo anomaly. There aren't many country inns in town and this one is not even representative of the species. It sits in a neighborhood surrounded by motels and a nearby freeway. What's more, the house was moved—lock, stock, and bay windows—to this odd location. Once inside, you'll be quite pleased. There's a warm, comfortable sitting parlor and nine guest rooms, all furnished with antiques. The beds are brass or oak; and some accommodations include window seats and terraces. All but three of the rooms in this 1902 home share baths. Moderate.

The motels that keep the Heritage Inn company are strung out along Monterey Street. This buzzing strip is the center for drive-in-and-sleep establishments; they line both sides of the street. But why stop at just anyplace when you can spend the night snoring in an historic building? The **Motel**

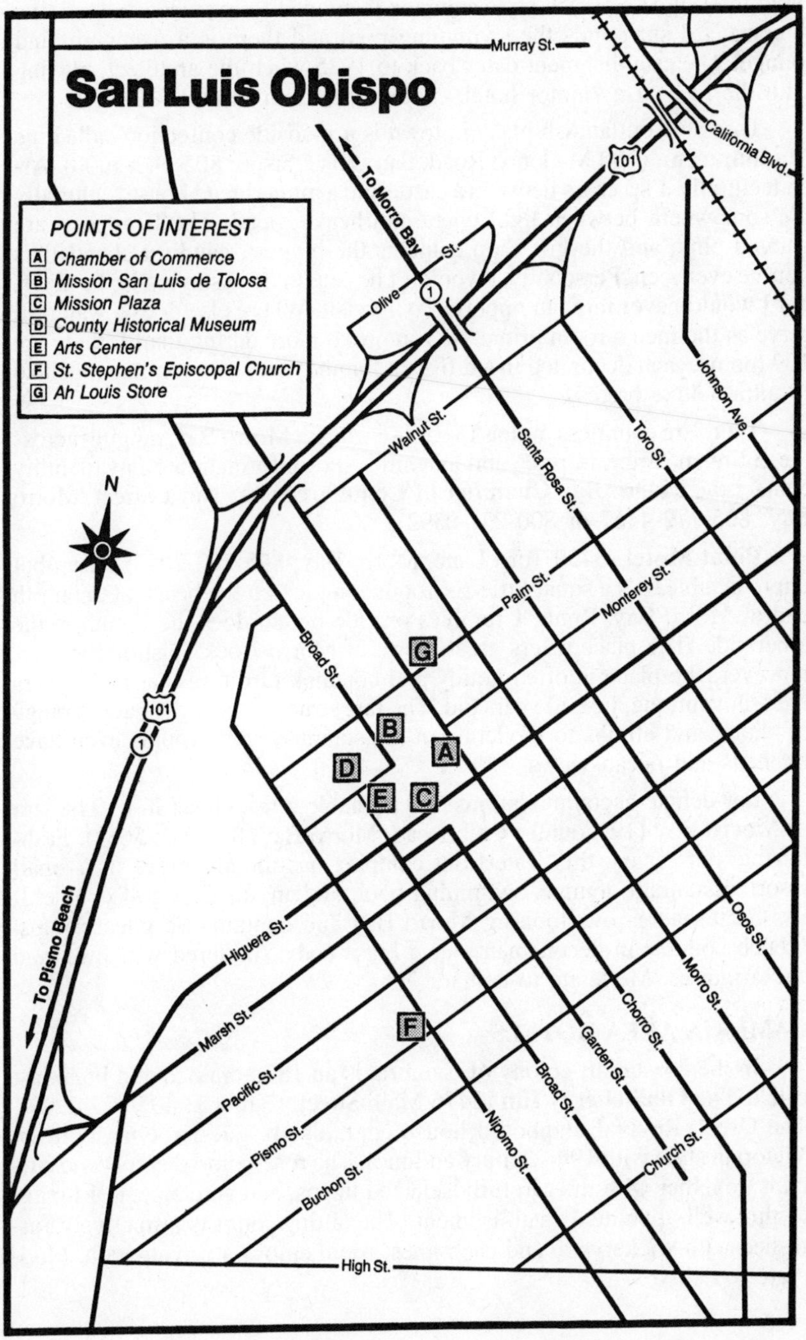

San Luis Obispo
POINTS OF INTEREST
A Chamber of Commerce
B Mission San Luis de Tolosa
C Mission Plaza
D County Historical Museum
E Arts Center
F St. Stephen's Episcopal Church
G Ah Louis Store
Murray St.
To Morro Bay
California Blvd.
101
1
Olive
St.
Johnson Ave.
Walnut St.
Santa Rosa St.
Toro St.
Palm St.
Monterey St.
Broad St.
Higuera St.
Marsh St.
Pacific St.
Pismo St.
Buchon St.
Nipomo St.
Broad St.
Garden St.
Chorro St.
Morro St.
Osos St.
Church St.
High St.
To Pismo Beach
N

Inn (2223 Monterey Street, San Luis Obispo; 805-543-4000) is the world's first motel. It's a Spanish-style complex fashioned from stucco and red tile. A courtyard surrounds the swimming pool and there is a restaurant and lounge. The establishment dates back to 1925 when the architect, playing with the idea of a "motor hotel," coined the term "motel." Budget.

The most outlandish place in town is a roadside confection called the **Madonna Inn** (100 Madonna Road, San Luis Obispo; 805-543-3000). Architecturally it's a cross between a castle and a gingerbread house, culturally it's somewhere between light opera and heavy metal. The lampposts are painted pink, and the gift shop contains the biggest, gaudiest chandeliers you've ever seen. Personally, I wouldn't be caught dead staying in the place, but I would never miss an opportunity to visit. Where else does a waterfall serve as the men's room urinal? If you prove more daring than I, there are 109 rooms, each decorated in a different flamboyant style, renting at deluxe to ultra-deluxe prices.

There are countless motels to choose from in Morro Bay, ranging across the entire spectrum in price and amenities. For information on availability contact the **Morro Bay Chamber of Commerce** (895 Napa Street, Morro Bay; 805-772-4467 or 800-231-0592).

Point Motel (3450 Toro Lane, Morro Bay; 805-772-2053) cheap but unpredictable. It's a squat little six-room complex on the beach at the north end of Morro Bay. Route 1 rumbles outside but so does the ocean on the other side. The place offers great views of Morro Rock. Visitors beware, however; the place is often untidy and contains furniture that is 40 years old—not antique, just 40 years old. The rate structure is in the budget range in winter and climbs to moderate in the summer; some rooms even have kitchens and ocean views.

For deluxe accommodations at reasonable rates, check in to **The Inn at Morro Bay** (19 Country Club Road, Morro Bay; 805-772-5651). Fashionable but casual, this waterfront complex has the amenities of a small resort: restaurant, lounge, swimming pool, and an adjacent golf course. It sits on ten acres overlooking Morro Bay and contains 96 guest rooms. French country in decor, many have brass beds, shuttered windows, and oak armoires. Moderate to deluxe.

CAMBRIA AREA HOTELS

In the coastal art colony of Cambria is an 1870-era bed and breakfast called **The Olallieberry Inn** (2476 Main Street, Cambria; 805-927-3222). The Greek Revival clapboard house contains six guest rooms, done in Victorian style with 19th-century antiques. The rose-colored carpet and curtains, together with the carefully selected linens, add an element of luxury to this well-appointed establishment. The sitting room is attractively furnished with wickerware and each guest room enjoys a private bath. Moderate to deluxe.

A Small Hotel by the Sea (2601 Main Street, Cambria; 805-927-4305) has five cottages renting at budget-to-moderate prices. These are quaint, tidy units, some with kitchens.

If you would prefer a more rustic atmosphere, head up to **Cambria Pines Lodge** (2905 Burton Drive, Cambria; 805-927-4200). Set amid 25 acres of Monterey pines, are rambling split-rail lodges with additional cabins dotted about the property. The main building offers a spacious lobby with stone fireplace plus a restaurant and lounge; other amenities include a swimming pool and jacuzzi. Moderate to deluxe.

North of Hearst Castle, where Route 1 becomes an isolated coastal road with few signs of civilization, are two hostelries. **Piedras Blancas Motel** (Route 1, seven miles north of Hearst Castle; 805-927-4202) has 14 standard motel-type rooms renting at moderate rates (budget in the winter). Most have ocean views.

Further along, on a ridge poised between the highway and ocean, sits the more appealing **Ragged Point Inn** (Route 1, 15 miles north of Hearst Castle; 805-927-4502). This 19-unit facility has attractive rooms furnished with contemporary hardwood furniture. Another compelling reason to stay is the beautiful ocean view from this clifftop abode. Despite the inn's proximity to the road, it is peaceful and quiet here; fox and raccoon wander near the rooms and sea sounds fill the air. A steep trail leads down to a rock-and-sand beach. Moderate to deluxe.

Restaurants

VENTURA AREA RESTAURANTS

For a budget-priced meal near the beach there's **Neptune's Net Seafood** (42505 Route 1, Malibu; 805-488-1302). Located across the highway from County Line Beach (at the Los Angeles–Ventura county border), it's a breezy café frequented by surfers. There are egg dishes for breakfast; during the rest of the day they serve sandwiches, burgers, clam chowder, as well as shrimp, oyster, clam, and scallop baskets. Ocean views at beach bum prices.

Up at the Fisherman's Wharf complex in Oxnard you'll find another budget eatery, the **Captain's Galley** (3900 West Channel Islands Boulevard; 805-985-7754), which offers breakfast dishes as well as hamburgers, sandwiches, and salads.

For an elegant meal, head up the coast to the **Seafood and Beverage Co.** (211 East Santa Clara Street, Ventura; 805-643-3264) where the dinner entrées include Alaskan King crab legs, Australian lobster tails, seafood brochette, chicken, and New York steak. Housed in a 1914-vintage home, this comfortable dining place is painted in pastel shades and adorned with leaded-glass windows. Open for lunch and dinner, it features mesquite-broiled dishes. Prices are moderate, but there's a limited early-bird menu from 4 to 6:30 p.m. with dinners tabbed in the budget range.

Or try **Eric Ericsson's Fish Company** (1140 South Seaward Avenue, Ventura; 805-643-4783), a small snuggery done in casual California style. At lunch they could be serving fish chowder, seafood pasta, poached shrimp, or fresh fish tacos. Then for dinner they might charbroil mahimahi, salmon, swordfish, or sea bass, depending on the season. Located near the beach this understated restaurant is a good place for fresh fish. Moderate to deluxe.

Franky's Restaurant (456 East Main Street, Ventura; 805-648-6282) is a trip. The place resembles a mini-art gallery, decorated with paintings, mobiles, and statuary. All the artwork is for sale, so the decorative scheme is ever-changing. The interior is liable to be adorned with marble busts and Modernist canvases. Moving from palette to palate, the lunch menu contains omelettes and salads, plus pita bread sandwiches and croissants stuffed with chicken salad, shrimp, or tuna. Budget to moderate.

OJAI AREA RESTAURANTS

Everyone's favorite Ojai restaurant is the **Ranch House** (South Lomita Avenue; 805-646-2360). Little wonder since this dining terrace rests in a tranquil garden surrounded by ferns, bamboo, and rose bushes. A flowering hedge shelters one side while a statue of Buddha gazes out from the other. Nearby, a graceful footbridge curves across a koi pond. Open Wednesday through Sunday for dinner (two seatings on Saturday, four on Sunday). Dinner includes Indonesian-style beef, Boston scrod, flaked crab, and veal in cream sauce. Desserts come from the restaurant's bakery, as do the three varieties of bread served with each meal. At lunch they feature those same delicious baked goods, plus Greek dolmas, spanakopita, and chicken in coconut milk. A must. Sunday brunch; deluxe to ultra-deluxe.

For fine French dining **L'Auberge** (314 El Paseo Road, Ojai; 805-646-2288), a venerable old house replete with brick fireplace and chandeliers, sets the tone. You can also dine on the terrace, choosing from a menu that includes scampi, frogs' legs, poached sole, tournedos, pepper steak, sweetbreads, and duckling in orange sauce. Lunch is on weekends only and features almost a dozen different crêpes. Moderate to deluxe.

Healthful dishes at moderate prices could well be the slogan at **Roger Keller's Restaurant** (331 East Ojai Avenue; 805-646-7266). Here you can dine on fresh soups, salads, a fish of the day selection, pasta dishes, and fresh-baked bread. Or if you'd prefer to let your culinary desires run wild they also feature hamburgers, espresso, and a host of other sinful offerings. Moderate.

If Ojai is a mountain hideaway then **The Restaurant at Wheeler Hot Springs** (Route 33, six miles north of Ojai; 805-646-8131) is a retreat from a retreat. Set creekside in the mountains above town, the century-old lodge features a stone fireplace surrounded by blond wood furniture and potted palms. The California-cuisine menu changes seasonally. Dinner in this intimate environment might start with appetizers such as spinach pasta filled with lobster, include smoked gouda cheese and tomato salad, then move on to lamb loin stuffed with sun-dried tomatoes, roasted in a mustard crust, and served with a garlic-rosemary butter. The health motif carries over to brunch on Saturday and Sunday; no breakfast or lunch; moderate to deluxe; meal-and-hot-tub packages available.

SANTA BARBARA AREA RESTAURANTS

At **The Palms** (701 Linden Avenue, Carpinteria; 805-684-3811) you cook your own steak or halibut dinner, or have them prepare a shrimp or scallop meal. A family-style restaurant with oak chairs and pseudo-Tiffany lamps, it hosts a salad bar and adjoining lounge. Not bad at all for the budget to moderate price; lunch and dinner.

A step upscale at **Clementine's Steak House** (4631 Carpinteria Avenue, Carpinteria; 805-684-5119) they feature filet mignon, fresh fish dishes, vegetarian casserole, steak teriyaki, and Danish-style liver. It's dinner only here, but the meal—which includes soup, salad, vegetable, starch dish, homemade bread, and pie—could hold you well into the next day. The interior has a beamed ceiling and patterned wallpaper. Lean back in a captain's chair and enjoy some home-style cooking. Prices are moderate to deluxe.

For a scent of Santa Barbara salt air with your lunch or dinner, **Brophy Brothers Restaurant & Clam Bar** (119 Harbor Way; 805-966-4418) is the spot. Located out on the Breakwater, overlooking the marina, mountains, and open sea, it features a small dining room and patio. If you love seafood, it's heaven; if not, then fate has cast you in the wrong direction. The clam bar serves all manner of clam and oyster concoctions and the restaurant is so committed to fresh fish they print a new menu daily to tell you what the boats brought in. When I was there the daily fare included fresh snapper, shark, scampi, salmon, sea bass, halibut, mahimahi, redfish, and butterfish. No breakfast; moderate.

Best of Santa Barbara's budget restaurants is **La Tolteca** (614 East Haley Street; 805-963-0847). This tortilla factory contains an informal, self-order café serving delicious Mexican food. Almost everything is fresh, making it *the* place for tacos, tostadas, burritos, and enchiladas. You can sit at one of the few tables inside or out near the sidewalk.

Santa Barbara natives have been eating at **Joe's Café** (536 State Street; 805-966-4638) for sixty years. Crowds line the coal-black bar, pile into the booths, and fill the tables. They come for a moderately priced, meat-and-potatoes lunch and dinner menu that stars prime rib. This is where you go for pork chops, lamb, rainbow trout, and steak. The walls are loaded with mementos and faded photographs; softball trophies, deer antlers, and a buffalo head decorate the place; and the noise level is the same as the Indy 500. Paradise for slummers.

Santa Barbara Shellfish Company (230 Stearns Wharf; 805-963-4415) ain't fancy: just a take-out stand with a few picnic tables. But they serve fresh crab and shrimp cocktails, chowder, crab Louie, and hot seafood platters at budget-to-moderate prices. Even better, they're located way out on Stearns Wharf where you can enjoy the open waterfront. Lunch and early dinner only.

Downey's (1305 State Street; 805-966-5006), a small, understated dining room, numbers among Santa Barbara's premiere restaurants. The dozen tables here are set amid white washed walls lined with local artwork. The food is renowned: specializing in California cuisine, Downey's has a menu which changes daily. A typical evening's entrées are salmon with forest mushrooms, lamb loin with grilled eggplant and chiles, sea bass with artichokes, duck with fresh papaya chutney, and scallops with tomato salsa. There is a good wine list featuring California vintages. Lunch and dinner; deluxe. Very highly recommended.

The graphics on the wall tell a story about the cuisine at **The Palace Café** (8 East Cota Street; 805-966-3133). Portrayed are jazz musicians, catfish, redfish, and scenes from New Orleans. The message is Cajun and Creole, and this informal bistro is very good at delivering it. Serving dinner only, the moderate-to-deluxe-priced restaurant prepares soft-shelled crab, blackened filet mignon, crawfish *étouffée*, and jambalaya. For dessert, honey, we have key lime pie and bread pudding with pecan sauce.

If you prefer your bistros French, there's an excellent place a few doors up called **Mousse Odile** (18 East Cota Street; 805-962-5393). Plaid tablecloths and folk art create an easy lunch ambience here. For dinner, out come the white and pink linens. Menu selections includes couscous, mushrooms on pastry shell, and veal in basil cream; lunch features *ficelles*, those foot-long Parisian sandwiches, as well as quiche and stuffed croissants. Even the breakfasts have a French flair. Modest but well managed, Mousse Odile is quite popular with local residents. Moderate to deluxe.

If your mother is Italian you'll know what to expect at **Mom's Italian Village** (421 East Cota Street; 805-965-5588). If not you'll still feel at home. This friendly, familiar eatery is a local institution. Mom has been cooking for more than 50 years, preparing the North Italian dishes that fill the lunch and dinner menus. Lasagna is a house specialty, but there's also chicken cacciatore, beef *spezzatini*, breaded veal cutlet, and a kitchenful of pasta dishes. Moderate.

Hanging out in coffeehouses is my favorite avocation. There's no better spot in Santa Barbara than **Sojourner Coffeehouse** (134 East Cañon Perdido; 805-965-7922). Not only do they serve espresso and cappuccino, but lunch and dinner as well. Everyone seems to know everyone else in this easygoing café. They come to kibitz and enjoy the tostadas, rice-and-vegetable plates, and stuffed baked potatoes. The accent is vegetarian so expect daily specials like Szechuan peanut pasta or spanakopita, Greek spinach and egg pastry. They also serve fresh fish and chicken dishes like African-style chicken with couscous. Budget.

Café del Sol (30 Los Patos Way; 805-969-0448) is the rarest of creatures, an upscale "Santa Barbara-style" restaurant. Enter this Cabo San Lucas-style eatery, where you'll find a tortilla deli/bar. Here you can sample tapas, Mexican appetizers like seafood fajitas and margaritas. A large bank of windows allows dining room guests a view of the Andree Clark Bird Refuge while they dine on a menu varying from lamb shanks to enchiladas. Deluxe in price.

Dining at **El Encanto** (1900 Lasuen Road; 805-687-5000) is pleasurable not only for the fine California and French cuisine but the sweeping vistas as well. The restaurant resides in a hillside resort overlooking Santa Barbara. There's a luxurious dining room and a terrace for dining outdoors. Dinner prepared by chef James Sly, who trained in Europe, is a gourmet experience. Changing daily according to harvest and catch, the menu could include steamed filet of salmon with dijon mustard crème, grilled veal chops with a medley of mushrooms, or breast of Muscovy duck in a *daube* (French stew) with red wine. The appetizers and desserts are equally outrageous, as are the breakfast and lunch courses. Deluxe to ultra-deluxe.

The **Stonehouse Restaurant** (900 San Ysidro Lane, Montecito; 805-969-5046), located at the legendary San Ysidro Ranch, serves lunch, dinner, and Sunday brunch with a classic American flavor. You can begin with poblano peppers, then indulge in the salmon or aged New York steak. Top off the meal with some bourbon pecan pie. Ultra-deluxe.

Located outside town, on the beach at Arroyo Burro Country Park, is the **Brown Pelican** (2981½ Cliff Drive; 805-687-4550). It's a good restaurant with ocean views—what more need be said? They serve sandwiches, salads, hamburgers, and several fresh seafood and pasta dinners. Trimly appointed and fitted with a wall of plate glass, it looks out upon a sandy beach and tawny bluffs. A moderate-to-deluxe-priced answer to waterfront tourist traps (with an espresso bar to boot!).

SANTA YNEZ VALLEY RESTAURANTS

A vestige of the Old West, **Cold Spring Tavern** (5995 Stagecoach Road off Route 154; 805-967-0066) is a former stagecoach stop dating back to the 19th century. The floors tilt, the bar is wood plank, and the walls are stained with a century of use; a cow head with antlers decorates the stone fireplace. Dinner in this roughhewn time capsule features marinated rabbit, steak, pork back ribs, and swordfish. The evening special might be elk or buffalo. At lunch you can order a venison steak sandwich, *chile verde*, or a buffalo burger. Make a point of stopping by. Prices are in the moderate to deluxe range.

There's another stagecoach-stop-turned-restaurant in the Santa Ynez Valley. **Mattei's Tavern** (Route 154, Los Olivos; 805-688-4820) is a mammoth old building that served as an inn back in the 1880s. Today it's a multiroom complex where you can dine in a rustically decorated room or out on the patio. Dinner features steaks, prime rib, and fresh seafood dishes. For a sense of history and a good meal, it's a safe bet. Moderate to deluxe in price.

Finger foods are part of the fun in dining around Solvang. Stop by **The Front Yard** (475 1st Street; 805-688-7674) for sandwiches or hot pretzels smothered in cheddar cheese. This Danish town is also famous for its bakeries. **Solvang Bakery** (460 Alisal Drive; 805-688-5713) has excellent Danish pastries and other Scandinavian treats.

For more substantial fare, the **Continental Inn** (1645 Copenhagen Drive; 805-688-5410) serves an elaborate smorgasbord. This traditional Danish meal includes soup, salad, red cabbage, Danish meatballs, and a variety of other Scandinavian dishes. Open for all meals, they also offer wienerschnitzel, pork cordon bleu, Danish roast duck, and German *rouladen*. Moderate in price.

You'll find similar menus in more upscale surroundings at **The Danish Inn** (1547 Mission Drive; 805-688-4813). This white-tablecloth dining room has stuffed cabbage leaves, steak with sautéed onions, smorgasbord, and other Scandinavian specialties. Moderate to deluxe.

SAN LUIS OBISPO AREA RESTAURANTS

For breakfast and lunch in Pismo Beach try the **All American Café** (1053 Price Street, Pismo Beach; 805-773-2764). The wallhangings make it look like we're still fighting World War II. But if you can handle the chauvinism, there's a good breakfast menu with over a dozen egg and omelette dishes. At lunch they have the usual assortment of sandwiches and salads. Budget.

At **The Old Custom House Restaurant** (324 Front Street, Avila Beach; 805-595-7555) ask for a table out on the patio. It's a garden arrangement with umbrellas shading the tables. Quite nice, and besides, the indoor dining area is just a counter and a series of plain formica tables. Serving three meals daily, they specialize in seafood (what else?) and steak. Dinners are prepared on an oak pit barbecue; breakfast features 20 different omelettes. Moderate.

If you missed the swinging doors in the saloon you'll get the idea from the moose head trophies and branding irons. "Taste the Great American West" is the motto for **F. McLintock's Saloon & Dining House** (750 Mattie Road, Shell Beach; 805-773-1892). This is the place where on Sundays you can get an 18-ounce steak for breakfast. At lunch there are buffalo burgers. And every evening, when the oak pit barbecue really gets going, there are a dozen kinds of steak and ribs, Cornish game hen, pan-fried rainbow trout, grilled veal liver, and scampi. If popularity means anything, this place is tops. It's always mobbed. So dust off the Stetson and prepare to chow down. Deluxe. Early supper at reduced rates.

Sick of seafood by now? Tired of saloons serving cowboy-sized steaks? Happily, San Luis Obispo has several ethnic restaurants. Two are located in The Creamery, a turn-of-the-century dairy plant that has been transformed into a shopping mall.

Tsurugi Japanese Restaurant (570 Higuera Street, San Luis Obispo; 805-543-8942) features a sushi bar and dining area decorated with Oriental screens and wallhangings. At lunch and dinner there are shrimp tempura, chicken teriyaki, *nigiri*, and other Asian specialties. The atmosphere is placid and the food quite good; moderate. Next door at **Tortilla Flats** (1051 Nipomo Street, San Luis Obispo; 805-544-7575) they have fashioned an attractive restaurant from the brick walls, bare ducts, and exposed rafters of the old creamery. It's lunch, dinner, and Sunday brunch at this Mexican eatery where the bar serves margaritas by the pitcherful; budget to moderate in price.

If you can get past the garish red and yellow sign at **Golden China Restaurant** (675 Higuera Street, San Luis Obispo; 805-543-7576), there's an array of standard Chinese dishes printed on a menu that continues for pages. Budget to moderate.

Italy enters the picture with **Café Roma** (1819 Osos Street, San Luis Obispo; 805-541-6800), a delightful restaurant decorated in country inn style. Copper pots as well as portraits from the old country decorate the walls. Lunch and dinner include Italian sausage, veal marsala, steak *fiorentina*, and several daily specials. There are also assorted pasta and antipasto dishes, an extensive Italian wine list, and homemade ice cream for dessert. Run by an Italian family, it serves excellent food; highly recommended; moderate to deluxe.

For a budget-priced meal in a white-tablecloth restaurant with views of the surrounding hills, beat a path to the California Polytechnic campus. **Vista Grande Restaurant** (Grand Avenue, San Luis Obispo; 805-756-1204) serves Cal Poly students as well as the public in a comfortable plate-glass dining room. Open for lunch, dinner, and Sunday brunch, it features veal parmesan, teriyaki chicken, and fish and chips. There are also several different salads and a host of sandwiches.

Outside town there's a particularly good Western-style restaurant. (You didn't think I'd let you off scott free, did you?). **This Old House** (740 West Foothill Boulevard, San Luis Obispo; one and one-half miles west of Route 1; 805-543-2690) is another oak pit grill serving steak and ribs, plus lobster, sweetbreads, barbecued chicken, and fresh halibut. The decor is early Western with oxen yokes, cowboy boots, and branding irons on the wall. With its unique barbecue sauce and rib-sticking meals, This Old House merits a visit. Moderate to deluxe.

You needn't cast far in Morro Bay to find a seafood restaurant. Sometimes they seem as frequent as fishing boats. One of the most venerable is **Dorn's Original Breakers Café** (801 Market Street, Morro Bay; 805-772-4415). It's a bright, airy place with a postcard view of the waterfront. While they serve all three meals, in the evening you better want seafood because there are about two dozen fish dishes and only a couple steak platters. Moderate to deluxe.

For inexpensive American fare at breakfast and lunch, there is ye olde reliable **Coffee Pot Restaurant** (1001 Front Street; 805-772-3176). Possessing the easy ambience of a roadside café, it offers a full array of all of mom's favorite dishes. Besides that, it is conveniently located. Who could ask for more? Breakfast and lunch only.

Fine California cuisine is the order of the day at **The Inn at Morro Bay** (19 Country Club Drive, Morro Bay; 805-772-5651). Situated in a waterfront resort, the dining room looks out over Morro Bay. In addition to great views and commodious surroundings, it features an enticing list of local and French entrées. All three meals are served, but the highlight is dinner. The menu might include home-smoked salmon with crème fraîche caviar, roast duckling, and fresh fish in a mustard-chive butter. Moderate to deluxe.

CAMBRIA AREA RESTAURANTS

Farther north, ethnic and vegetarian food lovers will fare well at **Robin's** (4095 Burton Drive, Cambria; 805-927-5007). Set in a 1930s Mexican-style house, it serves homemade lunches and dinners. Selections range from burritos to sweet-and-sour prawns to stir-fried tofu. It's an eclectic blend with the accent on Italian and Asian cuisine. Patio seating is available. Moderate in price.

For fine California cuisine try **Ian's Restaurant** (2150 Center Street, Cambria; 805-927-8649). The decor is contemporary, featuring floral prints on pastel-shaded walls, blond wood furniture, and upholstered banquettes. The menu draws upon local fresh produce, herbs, and seafood. Also among the specialties are duck, rabbit, and lamb. The fare also includes abalone, fresh lobster, prawns in garlic and cream, and beef dishes. Dinner only; moderate to deluxe.

The Great Outdoors

The Sporting Life

SPORTFISHING

Albacore, barracuda, bonito, bass, halibut, yellowtail, and marlin are just some of the fish that ply the waters off the Central Coast and the Channel Islands. If you're interested in a fishing cruise, contact one of the following companies: **Cisco's Sportfishing** (Captain Jack's Landing, 4151 South Victoria Avenue, Oxnard; 805-985-8511), **Captain Don's** (Stearns Wharf, Santa Barbara; 805-969-5217), **Sea Landing Aquatic Center** (The Breakwater, Santa Barbara; 805-963-3564), **Virg's Fish'n** (1215 Embarcadero, Morro Bay; 805-772-1222), or **Paradise Sportfishing** (Pier 3, Avila Beach; 805-595-7200).

WHALE WATCHING

If you're in the mood for a whale-watching excursion during the annual migration, contact **Cisco's Sportfishing** (Captain Jack's Landing, 4151 South Victoria Avenue, Oxnard; 805-985-8511), **Captain Don's** (Stearns Wharf, Santa Barbara; 805-969-5217), **Sea Landing Aquatic Center** (The Breakwater, Santa Barbara; 805-963-3564), **Virg's Fish'n** (1215 Embarcadero, Morro Bay; 805-772-1222), or **Paradise Sportfishing** (Pier 3, Avila Beach; 805-595-7200).

SEA KAYAKING

A unique way to explore the "aquatic garden" of Morro Bay is by kayak. **Good Clean Fun** (136 Ocean Front, Cayucos; 805-995-1993) and **Kayaks of Morrow Bay** (Morro Bay 805-772-1119) provide exciting tours that let you hobnob with seals and local birds.

SCUBA DIVING

For those more interested in watching fish, several outfits in the Central Coast area sponsor dive boats and also offer skindiving rentals and lessons. In the Ventura area try **Ventura Dive and Sport** (1559 Spinnaker Drive #108, Ventura; 805-656-0167).

In Santa Barbara call **Divers Den** (22 Anacapa Street, Santa Barbara; 805-963-8917) or **Sea Landing Aquatic Center** (The Breakwater, Santa Barbara; 805-963-3564).

Bill's Sporting Goods (Cayucos Pier, Cayucos; 805-995-1703) and **Sea Wink** (750 Price Street, Pismo Beach; 805-773-4794) serve the San Luis Obispo area.

SURFING AND WINDSURFING

Hang ten or catch the wind with board rentals from the following enterprises: **Pipe Line Surf Shop** (1124 South Seaward Avenue, Ventura; 805-

652-1418; surfing only), **Sundance Ocean Sports** (2036 Cliff Drive, Santa Barbara; 805-966-4400), **Good Clean Fun** (136 Ocean Front, Cayucos; 805-995-1993), or **Wavelengths Surf Shop** (998 Embarcadero, Morro Bay; 805-772-3904; surfing only).

GOLF

Golf enthusiasts will enjoy the weather as well as the courses along the Central Coast. In the Oxnard-Ventura area try **River Ridge** (2401 West Vineyard Avenue, Oxnard; 805-983-4653), **Olivas Park** (3750 Olivas Park Drive, Ventura; 805-642-4303), or **San Buenaventura** (5882 Olivas Park Drive, Ventura; 805-485-3050).

In the Santa Barbara area try **Santa Barbara Golf Club** (Las Positas Road and McCaw Avenue, Santa Barbara; 805-687-7087), **Twin Lakes Golf Course** (6034 Hollister Avenue, Goleta; 805-964-1414), **Sand-piper Golf Course** (7925 Hollister Avenue, Goleta; 805-968-1541), or **Ocean Meadows Golf Course** (6925 Whittier Drive, Goleta; 805-968-6814).

The San Luis Obispo area has **Pismo State Beach Golf Course** (25 Grand Avenue, Grover City; 805-481-5215), **Laguna Lake Golf Course** (11175 Los Osos Valley Road, San Luis Obispo; 805-781-7309), **San Luis Bay Golf Course** (Avila Beach Road, Avila Beach; 805-595-2307), **Morro Bay Golf Course** (State Park Road, Morro Bay; 805-772-4560), and **Sea Pines Golf Course** (250 Howard Avenue, Los Osos; 805-528-1788).

TENNIS

Tennis anyone? Courts are available at the following sites: **Moranda Park** (200 Moranda Parkway, Port Hueneme; 805-986-6584), **Santa Barbara Municipal Courts** (contact the Santa Barbara Recreation Department; 805-564-5418), **Cuesta College** (Route 1, San Luis Obispo; 805-546-3207), and **Sinsheimer Park** (900 Southwood Drive, San Luis Obispo; 805-781-7300). Additional courts are on Price Street near Shore Cliff Lodge and at Shell Beach and Florin roads.

HORSEBACK RIDING

A variety of riding opportunities are available in the Central Coast. **Circle Bar B Stables** (1800 Refugio Road, Goleta; 805-968-3901), **The Livery Stable** (1207 Silverspur Place, Oceano; 805-489-8100), or **The Rocking D** (555 Avila Drive, San Luis Obispo; 805-595-7407).

SAILING

To sail the Pacific or visit the Channel Islands, contact **Sailing Center of Santa Barbara** (The Breakwater, Santa Barbara; 805-962-2826) for boat rentals. **Sea Landing Aquatic Center** (The Breakwater, Santa Barbara; 805-963-3564) offers coastal cruises and charters.

BICYCLING

Bicycling the Central Coast can be a rewarding experience. The coastal route, however, presents problems in populated areas during rush hour.

The town of **Ventura** offers an interesting bicycle tour through the historical section of town with a visit to the county historical museum and mission. Another bike tour of note, off of Harbor Boulevard, leads to the Channel Islands National Monument and Wildlife Refuge Visitor Center.

Santa Barbara is chock-full of beautiful bicycle paths. There are also several bike trails around the area: two notable beach excursions are the **Atascadero Recreation Trail**, which starts at the corner of Encore Drive and Modoc Road and ends over seven miles later at Goleta Beach, and **Cabrillo bikeway**, which takes you from Andree Clark Bird Refuge to Leadbetter Beach. The **Goleta Valley bikeway** travels from Santa Barbara to Goleta along Cathedral Oaks Road. Also, the **University of California-Santa Barbara** has many bike paths through the campus grounds and into Isla Vista.

Exploring the shores of Morro Bay is popular with cyclists. For the hardy biker a ride up **Black Mountain** leads to sweeping views of the Pacific Ocean.

BIKE RENTALS For bicycles in Ventura and Santa Barbara try **Beach Rentals** (901 San Pedro Drive, Ventura, 805-641-1932; and 8 Cabrillo Boulevard, Santa Barbara, 805-963-2524, which offers tandem and mountain bikes.

Kites Galore (1108 Front Street; 805-772-8322) rents tandems, four-wheeled surreys, and traditional bikes in Morro Bay.

Beaches and Parks

VENTURA AREA BEACHES AND PARKS

Point Mugu State Park—This outstanding facility extends along four miles of beachfront and reaches back six miles into the Santa Monica Mountains. The beaches—which include **Sycamore Cove Beach, Thornhill Broome**, and **Point Mugu Beach**—are wide and sandy, with rocky outcroppings and a spectacular sand dune. To the interior the park rises to 1266-foot Mugu Peak and to Tri-Peaks, 3010 feet in elevation. There are two large canyons as well as wide, forested valleys. Over 70 miles of hiking trails lace this diverse park.

Facilities: Picnic areas, restrooms, lifeguards; restaurants and groceries within a few miles; information center at Sycamore Cove, 805-987-3303. *Camping:* Permitted inland at Sycamore Canyon (showers and flush toilets) and at Thornhill Broome Beach (primitive facilities). There are hike-in campsites in La Jolla Valley. *Swimming:* Good; also a prime spot for bodysurfing; but watch for rip currents. *Surfing:* Good a few miles south of the park at **County Line Beach**.

Getting there: Located on Route 1 about ten miles south of Oxnard.

McGrath State Beach—This long, narrow park extends for two miles along the water. The beach is broad and bounded by dunes. A lake and wildlife area attract over 200 bird species. The Santa Clara River, on the northern boundary, is home to tortoises, squirrels, muskrats, weasels, and other wildlife. Together the lake and preserve make it a great spot for camping or daytripping at the beach.

Facilities: Restrooms, showers, lifeguards; restaurants and groceries are nearby in Ventura; information, 805-654-4611. *Camping:* Permitted. *Swimming:* Strong swimmers only; watch for rip currents. *Surfing:* Good.

Getting there: Located at 2211 Harbor Boulevard in Oxnard.

San Buenaventura State Beach—In the world of urban parks this 114-acre facility ranks high. The broad sandy beach, bordered by dunes, extends for two miles to the Ventura pier. Since the pier is a short stroll from the city center, the beach provides a perfect escape hatch after you have toured the town.

Facilities: Picnic areas, restrooms, showers, dressing rooms, snack bar, lifeguards; groceries and restaurants nearby in Ventura; information, 805-654-4611. *Camping:* Not permitted. *Swimming:* The breakwaters here provide excellent swimming. *Surfing:* Good at **Surfer's Point Park,** foot of Figueroa Street; and at **Peninsula Beach**, at the north end of Spinnaker Drive. *Fishing:* From the 1700-foot pier anglers catch bass, shark, surf perch, corbina, and halibut. The nearby rock jetties are a haven for crabs and mussels.

Getting there: Located along Harbor Boulevard southeast of the Ventura Pier in Ventura.

Emma Wood State Beach—Sandwiched between the ocean and the Southern Pacific railroad tracks, this slender park measures only 116 acres. The beach consists almost entirely of rocks, making it undesirable for swimmers and sunbathers. There is a marsh at one end inhabited by songbirds and small mammals. Considering the fabulous beaches hereabouts, I rank this one pretty low.

Facilities: Restrooms; restaurants and groceries nearby in Ventura; information, 805-654-4611. *Camping:* There is camping at nearby **Emma Wood County Park, Faria County Park,** and **Hobson County Park**; information, 805-654-3951. These are small, rocky beaches north of Emma Wood State Beach on the Old Pacific Coast Highway. *Fishing:* Cabezon, perch, bass, and corbina are caught here.

Getting there: Located on the northwest boundary of Ventura just off Route 101.

OJAI AREA PARKS

Lake Casitas Recreation Area—This is a 6200-acre park surrounded by forested slopes and featuring a many-fingered lake. No swimming is permitted since Casitas is a reservoir, but fishing and boating are encouraged. Outlying mountains and the proximity of Ojai make it a particularly popular locale.

Facilities: Picnic areas, restrooms, shower, snack bar, bait and tackle shop, grocery store; boat rental for rowboats and motorboats, 805-649-2043; information center, 805-649-2233. *Camping:* Permitted. *Fishing:* Bass, trout, and channel catfish are caught in these waters.

Getting there: Located at 11311 Santa Ana Road about ten miles north of Ventura.

SANTA BARBARA AREA BEACHES AND PARKS

Rincon Beach County Park—Wildly popular with nudists and surfers, this is a pretty white sand beach backed by bluffs. At the bottom of the wooden stairway leading down to the beach, take a right along the strand and head over to the seawall. There will often be a bevy of nude sunbathers snuggled here between the hillside and the ocean in an area known as **Bates Beach**. Surfers, on the other hand, turn left and paddle out to Rincon Point, one of the most popular surfing spots along the entire California coast.

Facilities: Picnic area, restrooms; restaurants and groceries are two miles away in Carpinteria. *Swimming:* Good. *Surfing:* Excellent.

Getting there: Located two miles southeast of Carpinteria; from Route 101 take the Bates Road exit.

Carpinteria State Beach—This ribbon-shaped park extends for nearly a mile along the coast. Bordered to the east by dunes and along the west by a bluff, the beach has an offshore shelf which shelters it from the surf. As a result, Carpinteria provides exceptionally good swimming and is nicknamed "the world's safest beach." Wildlife here consists of small mammals and reptiles as well as many seabirds. It's a good spot for tidepooling; there is also a lagoon here. The Santa Ynez Mountains rise in the background.

Facilities: Picnic areas, restrooms, dressing rooms, showers, lifeguards; restaurants and groceries nearby in Carpinteria; information, 805-684-2811. *Swimming:* Excellent. *Skindiving:* Good along the breakwater reef, a habitat for abalone and lobsters. *Surfing:* Very good in the "tar pits" area near the east end of the park. *Fishing:* Cabezon, corbina, and barred perch are caught here.

Getting there: Located at the end of Palm Avenue in Carpinteria.

(Text continued on page 362.)

The Channel Islands

Gaze out from the Ventura or Santa Barbara shoreline and you will spy a fleet of islands moored offshore. At times fringed with mist, on other occasions standing a hand's reach away in the crystal air, they are the Channel Islands, a group of eight volcanic islands.

Situated in the Santa Barbara Channel 11 to 40 miles from the coast, they are a place apart, a wild and storm-blown region of sharp cliffs, rocky coves, and curving grasslands. Five of the islands—Anacapa, Santa Cruz, Santa Rosa, San Miguel, and Santa Barbara—comprise Channel Islands National Park while the surrounding waters are a marine sanctuary.

Nicknamed "America's Galapagos," the chain teems with every imaginable form of life. Sea lions and harbor seals frequent the caves, blowholes, and offshore pillars. Brown pelicans and black oystercatchers roost on the sea arches and sandy beaches. There are tidepools crowded with brilliant purple hydrocorals and white-plumed sea anemones. Like the Galapagos, this isolated archipelago has given rise to many unique life forms, including 40 endemic plant species and the island fox, which grows only to the size of a house cat.

The northern islands were created about 14 million years ago by volcanic activity. Archaeological discoveries indicate that they could be among the oldest sites of human habitation in the Americas. When explorer Juan Cabrillo revealed them to the West in 1542 they were populated with thousands of Chumash Indians.

Today, long since the Chumash were removed and the islands given over to hunters, ranchers, and settlers, the Channel Islands are largely uninhabited. Several, however, are open to hikers and campers. At the mainland-based **Channel Islands National Park Visitor Cen-**

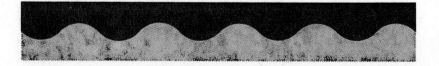

ter (1901 Spinnaker Drive, Ventura; 805-658-5730) there are contemporary museum displays and an excellent 25-minute movie to familiarize you with the park.

Next door at **Island Packers** (1867 Spinnaker Drive, Ventura, CA 93001; 805-642-1393) you can arrange transportation to the islands. This outfit schedules regular daytrips by boat to Anacapa, Santa Barbara, Santa Cruz, Santa Rosa, and San Miguel islands. They can arrange camping trips on four of the five islands or will book you into a room at the 19th-century Scorpion Ranch on Santa Cruz Island.

The Nature Conservancy (213 Stearns Wharf, Santa Barbara; 805-962-9111) also leads seasonal tours of Santa Cruz, the largest and most diverse of the islands. Here you will find an island just 24 miles long which supports 600 species of plants, 130 types of land birds, and several unique plant species. There are Indian middens, earthquake faults, and two mountain ranges to explore. To the center lies a pastoral valley while the shoreline is a rugged region of cliffs, tidepools, and offshore rocks.

Anacapa Island, the island closest to shore, is a series of three islets parked 11 miles southwest of Oxnard. There are tidepools here, a nature trail, and a 19th-century grounded steamer. Like the other islands, it is a prime whale-watching spot and is surrounded by the giant kelp forests which make the Channel Islands one of the nation's richest marine environments.

Whether you are a sailor, swimmer, daytripper, hiker, archaeologist, birdwatcher, camper, tidepooler, scuba diver, seal lover, or simply an interested observer, you'll find this amazing island chain a place of singular beauty and serenity.

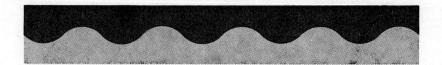

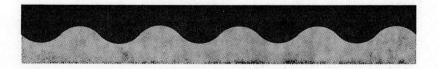

Summerland Beach—This narrow strip of white sand is a popular nude beach. It's backed by low-lying hills, which afford privacy from the nearby freeway and railroad tracks. The favored skinny-dipping spot is on the east end between two protective rock piles. Gay men congregate further down the beach at Loon Point.

Facilities: None here, but nearby **Lookout Park** (805-969-1720) has picnic areas, restrooms, lifeguards, and playground; restaurants and groceries nearby in Summerland. *Swimming:* Good. *Surfing:* Good bodysurfing.

Getting there: Located in Summerland six miles east of Santa Barbara. Take the Summerland exit off Route 101 and get on Wallace Avenue, the frontage road between the freeway and ocean. Follow it east for three-tenths of a mile to Finney Road and the beach.

East Beach—Everyone's favorite Santa Barbara beach, this broad beauty stretches more than a mile from Montecito to Stearns Wharf. In addition to a fluffy sand corridor there are grassy areas, palm trees, and a wealth of service facilities. Beyond Stearns Wharf the strand continues as **West Beach**. A nude beach lies at the far east end.

Facilities: Restrooms, showers, lifeguards, playground, and volleyball courts. **Cabrillo Pavilion Bathhouse** (1118 East Cabrillo Boulevard, Santa Barbara; 805-965-0509) provides lockers, showers, and a weight room for a small daily fee; restaurant next door. Other facilities are at Stearns Wharf. *Swimming:* Very good. *Fishing:* Good.

Getting there: Located in Santa Barbara along East Cabrillo Boulevard between the Andree Clark Bird Refuge and Stearns Wharf. The nude beach can be reached by following East Cabrillo Boulevard east past the Cabrillo Pavilion Bathhouse until the road turns inland. From this juncture continue along the beach on foot. The clothing-optional area is just beyond the Clark Mansion.

Leadbetter Beach—A crescent of white sand, this beach rests along a shallow cove. While it is quite pretty here, with a headland bordering one end of the strand, it simply doesn't compare to nearby East Beach.

Facilities: Picnic areas, restrooms, lifeguards, snack bar; restaurants and groceries nearby. *Swimming:* Good. *Surfing:* Good west of the breakwater.

Getting there: Located along the 800 block of Shoreline Drive in Santa Barbara.

Shoreline Park—The attraction here is not the park but the beach that lies below it. The park rests at the edge of a high bluff; at the bottom, secluded from view, is a narrow, curving length of white sand. It's a great spot to escape the Santa Barbara crowds while enjoying a pretty beach. Stairs from the park lead down to the shore.

Facilities: Topside in the park are picnic areas, restrooms, and a playground. Restaurants and groceries are within a mile in Santa Barbara.

Getting there: Located in Santa Barbara along Shoreline Drive.

Mesa Lane Beach or **Hendry's Beach** (★)—This is the spot Santa Barbarans head when they want to escape the crowds at the better-known beaches. It's a meandering ribbon of sand backed by steep bluffs. You can walk long distances along this secluded strand.

Facilities: None. Restaurants and groceries several miles away in Santa Barbara. *Surfing:* Good.

Getting there: There's a stairway to the beach at the end of Mesa Lane, off Cliff Drive in Santa Barbara.

Arroyo Burro County Park—This six-acre facility is a little gem. The sandy beach and surrounding hills are packed with locals on summer days. If you can arrive at an uncrowded time you'll find beautiful scenery along this lengthy strand.

Facilities: Picnic areas, restrooms, lifeguards, restaurant, snack bar; information, 805-687-3714. *Swimming:* Good. *Surfing:* Excellent west of the breakwater. *Fishing:* Good.

Getting there: Located at 2981 Cliff Drive in Santa Barbara.

More Mesa (★)—According to nude beach aficionado Dave Patrick, this is the region's favorite bare-buns rendezvous. Thousands of sunbathers gather at this remote site on a single afternoon. "On a hot day," Patrick reports, "the beach almost takes on a carnival atmosphere, with jugglers, surfers, world-class frisbee experts, musicians, dancers, joggers, horseback riders, and volleyball champs." A scene that should not be missed.

Facilities: None.

Getting there: That's the trick. It's located between Hope Ranch and Goleta, three miles from Route 101. Take the Turnpike Road exit from Route 101; follow it south to Hollister Avenue, then go left; from Hollister turn right on Puente Drive, right again on Vieja Drive, then left on Mockingbird Lane. At the end of Mockingbird Lane a path leads about three-quarters of a mile to the beach.

NORTH OF SANTA BARBARA

El Capitan State Beach—Another of Southern California's sparkling beaches, it stretches along three miles of oceanfront. The park is 168 acres and features a nature trail, tidepools, and wonderful opportunities for hiking along the beach. El Capitan Creek, fringed by oak and sycamore trees, traverses the area. Seals and sea lions often romp offshore and in winter gray whales cruise by.

Facilities: Picnic areas, restrooms, showers, store, lifeguard; information center, 805-968-1033. *Camping:* Permitted in the park near the beach.

There is also a private campground, **El Capitan Ranch Park** (11560 Calle Real, Goleta; 805-685-3887), about one-half mile inland. It is a sprawling 100-acre complex with picnic areas, restrooms, showers, store, pool, playground, game areas, and outdoor theater. *Swimming:* Good. *Surfing:* Good off El Capitan Point. *Fishing:* Good. Also a good place to catch grunion.

Getting there: Located in Goleta off Route 101 about 20 miles north of Santa Barbara.

Refugio State Beach—This is a 39-acre park with over a mile of ocean frontage. You can bask on a sandy beach, lie under palm trees on the greensward, and hike or bicycle along the two-and-a-half-mile path that connects this park with El Capitan. There are also interesting tidepools.

Facilities: Picnic areas, restrooms, showers, lifeguard, store; information, 805-968-1033. *Camping:* Permitted by reservation. *Swimming:* Good. *Surfing:* Good. *Fishing:* Good.

Getting there: Located on Refugio Road in Goleta, off Route 101 about 23 miles north of Santa Barbara.

San Onofre Beach (★)—This nude beach is a rare find indeed. Frequented by few people, it is a pretty white sand beach that winds along rocky headlands. There's not much here except beautiful views, shore plant life, and savvy sun bathers. Wander for miles past cliffs and coves.

Facilities: None. Restaurants and groceries located about two miles away in Gaviota.

Getting there: Located off Route 101 about 30 miles north of Santa Barbara and two miles south of Gaviota. Driving north on Route 101 make a U-turn on Vista del Mar Road; drive south on Route 101 for seven-tenths of a mile to a dirt parking area. Cross the railroad tracks; a path next to the railroad light signal leads to the beach.

Gaviota State Park—This mammoth 2776-acre facility stretches along both sides of Route 101. The beach rests in a sandy cove guarded on either side by dramatic sedimentary rock formations. A railroad trestle traverses the beach and a fishing pier extends offshore. On the inland side a hiking trail leads up to **Gaviota Hot Springs** and into Los Padres National Forest.

Facilities: Picnic areas, restrooms, showers, store, lifeguard, fishing pier; information, 805-968-1033. *Camping:* Permitted at the beach. *Swimming:* Good. *Fishing:* Good off the pier.

Getting there: The beach is located off Route 101 about 33 miles north of Santa Barbara. To get to the hot springs take Route 101 north from the beach park; get off at Route 1 exit; at the end of the exit ramp turn right; turn right on the frontage road and follow it a short distance to the parking lot. The trail from the parking lot leads several hundred yards to the hot springs.

Jalama Beach County Park—This remote park sits at the far end of a 15-mile long country road. Nevertheless, in summer there are likely to be many campers here. They come because the broad sandy beach is fringed by coastal bluffs and undulating hills. Jalama Creek cuts through the park, creating a wetland frequented by the endangered California brown pelican. Point Conception lies a few miles to the south, and the area all around is undeveloped and quite pretty (though Vandenberg Air Force Base is situated north of the beach). A good area for beachcombing as well as rock-hounding for chert, agate, travertine, and fossils.

Facilities: Picnic areas, restrooms, store, snack bar, playground; information, 805-736-6316. *Camping:* Permitted. *Swimming:* Dangerous rip currents. *Surfing:* Good at Tarantula Point about one-half mile south of the park. *Fishing:* You can surf fish for perch or fish from the rocky points for cabezon and rock fish.

Getting there: From Lompoc take Route 1 south for five miles; turn onto Jalama Beach Road and follow it 15 miles to the end.

Point Sal State Beach (★)—This is one of the most secluded and beautiful beaches along the entire Central Coast. Access is over a nine-mile country road, part of which is unpaved and impassable in wet weather. When you get to the end of this steep, serpentine monster there are no services available. But the scenery is magnificent. A long crescent beach curves out toward Point Sal, a bold headland with a rock island offshore. The Casmalia Hills rise sharply from the ocean, creating a natural amphitheater. Sea birds roost nearby and the beach is a habitat for harbor seals.

Facilities: None; information, 805-733-3713. *Fishing:* There's surf fishing from the beach and rocks.

Getting there: From Route 1 three miles south of Guadalupe turn west on Brown Road, then pick up Point Sal Road. Together they travel nine miles to a blufftop overlook. Steep paths lead to the beach.

SANTA YNEZ VALLEY PARKS

Lake Cachuma County Park—Surrounded by the 4000-foot Santa Ynez Mountains and 6000-foot San Rafael Mountains, this is one of the prettiest lakes along the entire Central Coast. Oak forests and fields of tall grass border much of the shoreline. There are full facilities for camping, boating, bicycling, and hiking. A great place for families and people exploring the backcountry above Santa Barbara.

Facilities: Picnic areas, restrooms, swimming pools, snack bar, store, boat rental, bicycle rental, par course, game field, hiking trails; information, 800-822-2267. *Camping:* Permitted. *Swimming:* Not permitted in lake, but there are pools here. *Fishing:* Trout, perch, bass, bluegill, crappie, and catfish are among the fish caught.

Getting there: Located on Route 154 north of Santa Barbara.

SAN LUIS OBISPO AREA BEACHES AND PARKS

Guadalupe Dunes Beach—The Sahara Desert has nothing on this place. The sand dunes throughout the area are spectacular, especially 450-foot Mussel Rock, the highest dune on the West Coast. The dunes provide a habitat for California brown pelicans, California least terns, and other endangered birds and plants. The Santa Maria River, which empties here, forms a pretty wetland area.

Facilities: None; restaurants and groceries are five miles away in Guadalupe; information, 805-937-1302. *Fishing:* Very good.

Getting there: From Route 1 in Guadalupe, follow Main Street west for five miles to the beach. Windblown sand sometimes closes the road, so call beforehand.

Pismo State Beach—This spectacular beach runs for six miles from Pismo Beach south to the Santa Maria River. Along its oceanfront are some of the finest sand dunes in California, fluffy hills inhabited by shorebirds and tenacious plants. Also home to the pismo clam, it's a wonderful place to hike and explore.

Facilities: Picnic areas, restrooms at one campground; restaurants and groceries nearby in Pismo Beach; information, 805-489-2684. *Camping:* Permitted in two campgrounds near the beach. There is also camping at **Oceano Memorial County Park** (near Mendel Drive and Pier Avenue, Oceano; 805-549-5219). *Fishing:* Good from the **Pismo Beach Pier** (end of Winds Avenue, Pismo Beach) for cod and red snapper. You can also dig for pismo clams along the beach (check local restrictions).

Getting there: The park parallels Route 1 in Pismo Beach.

Pirate's Cove or **Mallagh Landing (★)**—This crescent-shaped nude beach is a beauty. Protected by 100-foot cliffs, it curves for a half mile along a placid cove. At one end is a rocky headland pockmarked by caves.

Facilities: None. Restaurants and groceries are about a mile away in Avila Beach. *Swimming:* Very good. The beach is in a sheltered area and the water is shallow. *Skindiving:* Very good.

Getting there: Located ten miles south of San Luis Obispo in Avila Beach. From Route 101 take Avila Beach Drive west for two miles; turn left on Cave Landing Road (the road travels immediately uphill); go six-tenths of a mile to a dirt parking lot; crude stairs lead down to the beach.

Montaña de Oro State Park—This 9000-acre facility is one of the finest parks along the entire Central Coast. It stretches over a mile along the shore, past a sandspit, tidepools, and sharp cliffs. There are remote coves for viewing seals, sea otters, and migrating whales and for sunbathing on hidden beaches. Monarch butterflies roost in the eucalyptus-filled canyons and a hiking trail leads to Valencia Peak, with views scanning almost 100 miles of coastline. Wildlife is abundant along 50 miles of hiking trails.

Chaparral, Bishop pine, and Coast Live oak cover the hillsides; in spring wildflowers riot, giving the park its name, "Mountain of Gold."

Facilities: Picnic areas, restrooms; restaurants and groceries are several miles away in Los Osos; information, 805-528-0513. *Camping:* Permitted above the beach and in several primitive sites. *Fishing:* Good. There's also clamming here. *Surfing:* Good around Hazard Canyon.

Getting there: Located on Pecho Valley Road about ten miles south of Morro Bay.

Morro Bay State Park—Located amid one of the biggest marshlands along the California coast, this 2435-acre domain is like an outdoor museum. The tidal basin attracts over 250 species of sea, land, and shore birds. Great blue herons roost in the eucalyptus trees. There's a marina where you can rent canoes to explore the salt marsh and nearby sandspit, and a natural history museum with environmental displays. Camping is in an elevated area trimmed with pine and other trees. Since the park fronts the wetlands, there is no beach here; but you can reach the beach at **Morro Bay State Park Sand Spit** by private boat (see the "Sightseeing" section in this chapter).

Facilities: Picnic areas, restrooms, showers; restaurants and groceries are one mile away in Morro Bay; information, 805-772-7434. *Camping:* Permitted. *Fishing:* Good.

Getting there: Located on State Park Road in Morro Bay.

Morro Strand State Beach—Another of the Central Coast's long, skinny parks, this sandy beach stretches almost two miles along Morro Bay. Private homes border one side, but in the other direction there are great views of Morro Rock. It's a good place for beachcombing and clamming.

Facilities: Restrooms; restaurants and groceries nearby in Morro Bay; information, 805-772-2560 or 805-528-0513. *Camping:* Permitted. *Fishing:* Good.

Getting there: Located parallel to Route 1 north of Morro Bay; park entrance is along Yerba Buena Street.

Los Padres National Forest—The southern section of this mammoth park parallels the coast from Ventura to San Luis Obispo. Rising from sea level to almost 9000 feet, it contains the Sierra Madre, San Rafael, Santa Ynez, and La Panza mountains. Characterized by sharp slopes and a dry climate, only one third of the preserve is forested. But there are Coast redwoods, ancient bristlecone pines, and amazingly diverse plant life. Los Padres was formerly home to the rare California condor, which with its nine-foot wingspan is the largest land bird in North America. Among the animals still remaining are golden eagles, quail, owls, woodpeckers, wild pig, mule deer, black bear, and desert bighorn sheep.

Facilities: The northern and southern sectors of the national forest contain over 1700 miles of hiking trails, almost 500 miles of streams, a ski trail on Mt. Pinos, and 88 campgrounds. For information and permits contact forest headquarters at 6144 Calle Real, Goleta, CA 93117; 805-683-6711. *Camping:* Permitted.

Getting there: Route 33 cuts through the heart of Los Padres. Route 101 provides numerous access points.

CAMBRIA AREA BEACHES AND PARKS

San Simeon State Park—This wide sand corridor reaches for about two miles from San Simeon Creek to Santa Rosa Creek. It's a wonderful place to wander and the streams, with their abundant wildlife, add to the enjoyment. Unfortunately, Route 1 divides the beach from the camping area and disturbs the quietude. Other parts of the park are very peaceful, especially the **Moonstone Beach** section opposite Cambria, known for its moonstone agates and otters.

Facilities: Picnic areas, restrooms; restaurants and groceries nearby in Cambria.

Getting there: Located on Route 1 in Cambria.

William R. Hearst Memorial State Beach—Located directly below Hearst Castle, this is a placid crescent-shaped beach. The facility measures only two acres, including a grassy area on a rise above the beach. There is a 1000-foot long fishing pier. Scenic San Simeon Point curves out from the shoreline, creating a pretty cove and protecting the beach from surf.

Facilities: Picnic areas and restrooms; restaurants and groceries nearby in San Simeon town; information, 805-927-2035. *Swimming:* Very good. *Fishing:* Good. Also, charter boats leave from San Simeon Landing.

Getting there: Located on Route 1 opposite Hearst Castle.

Hiking

With its endless beaches and mountain backdrop, the Central Coast is wide open for exploration. Shoreline paths and mountain trails crisscross the entire region.

First among equals in this hiker's dreamland is the **California Coastal Trail**, the 600-mile route that runs the entire length of the state. Here it begins at Point Mugu and travels along state beaches from Ventura County to Santa Barbara. In Santa Barbara the trail turns inland toward the Santa Ynez Mountains and Los Padres National Forest. It returns to the coast at Point Sal, then parallels sand dunes, passes the hot springs at Avila Beach, and continues up the coast to San Simeon.

VENTURA AREA TRAILS

Bounded by the Santa Monica and Santa Ynez mountains and bordered by 43 miles of shoreline, Ventura County offers a variety of hiking opportunities.

Sycamore Canyon Loop Trail (10 miles) starts at the Big Sycamore Canyon entrance to Point Mugu State Park and leads through a wooded canyon, dropping down sharply to Deer Camp Junction. The trail continues beside a stream lined with sycamores.

La Jolla Valley Loop Trail (4 miles) begins at a Route 1 turnoff north of Big Sycamore Canyon and heads up the steep right side of the canyon. En route to Mugu Peak, La Jolla Valley walk-in camp is a good spot for a picnic. From Mugu Peak an alternative trail leads back down through oak copses and open grassland. There are wonderful views of the ocean and Channel Islands along the way.

Ventura River Trail (3 miles) is a lovely shoreline hike from the Emma Wood State Beach to Seaside Wilderness Park; popular with birdwatchers.

OJAI AREA TRAILS

Nine miles east of Ojai, **Santa Paula Canyon Trail** (3.5 miles) provides an easy hike to Santa Paula Creek. The path leads to waterfalls and a camp situated in a lovely area.

In Matilija Canyon the **Middle Matilija Trail** (3.1 miles) offers a moderately difficult backpacking hike in a stunning oak-filled area.

Near Ojai, the **Murietta Trail** (1 mile) is a good place to bring the kids for an easy trek.

SANTA BARBARA AREA TRAILS

What distinguishes Santa Barbara from most California coastal communities is the magnificent Santa Ynez mountain range, which forms a backdrop to the city and provides excellent hiking terrain.

A red steel gate marks the beginning of **Romero Canyon Trail** (5.75 miles) on Bella Vista Road in Santa Barbara. After joining a fire road at the 2350 foot elevation, the trail follows a stream shaded by oak, sycamore, and bay trees. From here you can keep climbing or return via the right fork, a fire road which offers an easier but longer return trip.

San Ysidro Trail (4.5 miles), beginning at Park Lane and Mountain Drive in Santa Barbara, follows a stream dotted with pools and waterfalls, then climbs to the top of Camino Cielo ridge. For a different loop back, it's only a short walk to Cold Springs Trail.

Cold Springs Trail, East Fork (4.5 miles) heads east from Mountain Drive in Santa Barbara. The trail takes you through a canyon covered with alder and along a creek punctuated by pools and waterfalls. It continues up into Hot Springs Canyon and crosses the flank of Montecito Peak.

Cold Springs Trail, West Fork (2 miles) leads off the better known East Fork. It climbs and descends along the left side of a lushly vegetated canyon before arriving at an open valley.

Tunnel Trail (4 miles) is named for the turn-of-the-century tunnel through the mountains which brought fresh water to Santa Barbara. The trail begins at the end of Tunnel Road in Santa Barbara and passes through various sandstone formations and crosses a creek before arriving at Mission Falls.

San Antonio Creek Trail (3.5 miles), an easy hike along a creek bed, starts from the far end of Tucker's Grove County Park in Goleta. In the morning or late afternoon you'll often catch glimpses of deer foraging in the woods.

Thirty-five miles of coastline stretches from Stearns Wharf in Santa Barbara to Gaviota State Beach. There are hiking opportunities galore along the entire span.

The **Summerland Trail** (2.5 miles), starting at Lookout Park in Summerland, takes you along Summerland Beach, past tiny coves, then along Montecito's coastline to the beach fronting the Biltmore Hotel.

Goleta Beach Trail (3.5 miles) begins at Goleta Beach County Park in Goleta and curves past tidepools and sand dunes en route to Goleta Point. Beyond the dunes is Devereux Slough, a reserve populated by egrets, herons, plovers, and sandpipers. The hike also passes the Ellwood Oil Field where a Japanese submarine fired shots at the mainland United States during World War II.

Gaviota Hot Springs and Peak Trail (2.5 miles) begins in Gaviota State Park. The first stop on this trek is the mineral pools at Gaviota Hot Springs (about a half mile from the trailhead). After a leisurely dip you can continue on a somewhat strenuous route into Los Padres National Forest, climbing to Gaviota Peak for a marvelous view of ranch land and the Pacific.

The **Point Sal Trail** (6 miles) offers an excellent opportunity to hike in a forgotten spot along the coast. (But beware, it's not for inexperienced hikers or those afraid of heights.) Alternating between cliffs and seashore, the trail takes you past tidepools, pelicans, cormorants, and basking seals. An excellent whale-watching area, the trail ends near the mouth of the Santa Maria River.

SANTA BARBARA MOUNTAIN TRAILS

Santa Barbara's backcountry offers an inexhaustible number of hiking opportunities ranging from day hikes to week-long treks.

A favorite hiking spot among college students is the **Sespe Hot Springs Trail** (17.5 miles). This steep trail follows a river bed to a hot springs favored by nude bathers. This trip is a two- to three-day trek.

Southern Wilderness Loop (64.5 miles) is a seven- to ten-day backpacker's delight. This strenuous hike leads along creeks and through pine forests, canyons, and chaparral country. Overnight stopovers can be made at any of several camps.

For those interested in a less arduous trek, try **Reyes Peak to Piedra Blanca Trail** (14.5 miles), a two-day trek down Reyes Peak along Piedra Blanca Creek Road. Three Mile Camp and Lion Campground offer inviting overnight respites.

An easy hike for backpackers is the **Blue Canyon Trail** (7.7 miles), located on the far side of the Santa Ynez Mountains from Santa Barbara. This serene canyon country is ideal for exploration.

Also located in the Santa Ynez Mountains is **Rattlesnake Canyon Trail** (3 miles). Beginning near Skofield Park, the trail follows Mission Creek, along which an aqueduct was built in the early nineteenth century. Portions of the waterway can still be seen. A pleasant hike, the trail offers shaded pools and meadows.

SAN LUIS OBISPO AREA TRAILS

The San Luis Obispo area, rich in wildlife, offers hikers everything from seaside strolls to mountain treks. Many of the trails in this area are in the Los Padres National Forest (for information, call 805-925-9538).

Nipomo Dunes Trail (4 miles) is especially rewarding for dune lovers. There's a multitude of dune flowers like magenta and yellow sand verbena, daisies, asters, and coreopsis. The trail begins at Oso Flaco Lake (in the dunes south of Oceano) and wends its way to the mouth of the Santa Maria River. This wetland area is a habitat for many endangered birds.

The golden mustard plants and poppies along the way give **Montaña de Oro Bluffs Trail** (2 miles) its name ("Mountain of Gold"). This coastal trail takes you past Spooner's Cove (a mooring place for bootleggers during Prohibition). You'll pass clear tidepools, sea caves, basking seals, otters, and ocean bluffs.

For an interesting hike along the sandspit which separates Morro Bay from Estero Bay, try the **Morro Bay Sandspit Trail** (4 miles). The trail leads past sand dunes and ancient Chumash shell mounds. Stay on the ocean side of the sandspit if you want to avoid the muck.

LOPEZ LAKE TRAILS

Several trails in the vicinity of Lopez Lake Recreational Area (805-489-8019) offer opportunities to see the region's flora and fauna. Deer, raccoon, fox, and wood-rats predominate, along with a variety of birds species (not to mention rattlesnakes and poison oak.)

At the entrance to the park, **Turkey Ridge Trail** (1.1 miles) climbs steeply through oak and chaparral and offers splendid views of the lake and the Santa Lucia Mountains.

Two Waters Trail (1.5 miles) connects the Lopez and Wittenberg arms of Lopez Lake. It offers marvelous views. The trailheads are located at Encinal or Miller's Cove.

Blackberry Spring Trail (1 mile) commences at upper Squirrel campground and passes many plant species used by the Chumash Indians. This is a moderate hike with a 260-foot climb which connects with High Ridge Trail.

Little Falls Creek Trail (2.75 miles) begins along Lopez Canyon Road and ascends 1350 feet up the canyon past a spectacular waterfall. Views of the Santa Lucia wilderness await you at the top of the mountain.

Travelers' Tracks

Sightseeing

VENTURA AREA

The serpentine highway and magnificent ocean views that have made Malibu famous continue as Route 1 wends north from Los Angeles into Ventura County. Backdropped by the Santa Monica Mountains, the road sweeps past a string of fluffy white beaches.

At **Point Mugu**, a talus-covered outcropping, a vista point overlooks miles of beaches to the south and a wildlife sanctuary to the north. Then, as nature gives way to civilization, Route 1 plunges through **Oxnard**, a fast-developing beach town, and continues into Ventura.

Situated 60 miles northwest of Los Angeles and 30 miles to the southeast of Santa Barbara, **Ventura** has generally been overlooked by travelers. History has not been so remiss. Long known to the Chumash Indians, who inhabited a nearby village named Shisholop, the place was revealed to Europeans in 1542 by the Portuguese explorer Juan Rodríguez Cabrillo. Father Junípero Serra founded a mission here in 1782 and the region soon became renowned for its fruit orchards.

Today the city preserves its heritage in a number of historic sites. Stop by the **Visitor and Convention Bureau** (89-C South California Street; 805-648-2075) for brochures and maps.

The highlight of a stroll through Ventura is **San Buenaventura Mission** (211 East Main Street; 805-643-4318; admission), a whitewash and red tile church flanked by a flowering garden. The dark, deep chapel is lined with Stations of the Cross paintings and features a Romanesque altar adorned with statues and pilasters. My favorite spot is the adjacent garden with its tile fountain and stately Norfolk pines.

Just down the street, the **Ventura County Museum of History and Art** (100 East Main Street; 805-653-0323) traces the region's secular history with displays of Chumash Indian artifacts and a farm implement collection.

The art gallery features revolving exhibits of local painters and photographers. There's a collection of 20,000 photos depicting Ventura County from its origin to the present.

Then stroll across to the **Albinger Archaeological Museum** (113 East Main Street; 805-648-5823) and view an archaeological dig that dates back 3500 years. A small museum displays the arrowheads, shell beads, crucifixes, and pottery uncovered here. At the dig site itself you'll see the foundation of an 18th-century mission church, an ancient earth oven, and a remnant of the Spanish padres' elaborate aqueduct system.

Further along sits the **Ortega Adobe** (215 West Main Street; 805-648-5823), a small, squat home built in 1857. With its woodplank furniture and bare interior it provides a strong example of how hard and rudimentary life was in that early era.

Backtrack to San Buenaventura Mission and wander down **Figueroa Plaza**, a broad promenade decorated with tile fountains and flowerbeds. This is the site of the town's old Chinatown section, long since passed into myth and memory.

Figueroa Street continues to the waterfront, where a **promenade** parallels the beach. This is a prime area for water sports, and countless surfers, with their blond hair and black wetsuits, will be waiting offshore, poised for the perfect wave. Along the far end of the esplanade, at the **Ventura Pier**, you'll encounter one more Southern California species, the surf fisherman.

Another local wonder is the **Ventura County Courthouse** (501 Poli Street), a sprawling structure designed in Neo-Classical style. The place is a mélange of Doric columns, bronze fixtures, and Roman flourishes. But forget the marble entranceway and grand staircase, what makes it memorable is the row of friars' heads adorning the facade. Where else but in Southern California would a dozen baroque priests stare out at you from the hall of justice?

By contrast, the **Olivas Adobe** (4200 Olivas Park Drive; 805-644-4346) is a spacious hacienda surrounded by flowering gardens. This two-story gem, with balconies running the full length of the upper floor, is a study in the Monterey-style architecture of 19th-century California. The rooms are furnished in period pieces and there is a museum adjacent to the house, providing a window on the world of California's prosperous Spanish settlers. Open daily, tours are available on the weekends.

Outside Ventura in the suburban town of Simi Valley lies the **Ronald Reagan Presidential Library** (40 Presidential Drive; 805-522-8444; admission). Here you'll find a visual history of Reagan's 1980s-era presidency in the form of film clips, videos, artifacts, and photos. There's a piece of the Berlin Wall, a replica of the Oval Office; and, re-creating Reagan's earlier years, memorabilia from his boyhood and Hollywood career.

OJAI AREA

To Chumash Indians the word "ojai" signified "the nest." And to the generations of mystics, health aficionados, artists, and admirers who have settled here, the place is indeed a secluded abode. Geographically it resembles its Chumash namesake, nestling in a moon-shaped valley girded by the Topa and Sulphur Mountains.

A town of 7900 souls, Ojai is an artist colony crowded with galleries and studios. The site is also a haven for the health conscious, with spas and hot springs. To the metaphysically minded it is a center for several esoteric sects.

Ever since the 1870s, when author Charles Nordhoff publicized the place as a tourist spot, it has been popular with all sorts of visitors. The cultural life of the town focuses around an annual music festival. For sport there is nearby Lake Casitas, Los Padres National Forest, 4500-foot mountains, and a network of hiking trails extending over 400 miles.

Inland just 14 miles from Ventura, Ojai is a valley so extraordinary it was used as the setting for Shangri-La in the movie *Lost Horizon* (1937). Sun-bronzed mountains rise in all directions, fields of wildflowers run to the verge of forested slopes, and everywhere there is tranquility, making it clear why the region is a magnet for mystics.

Set on top of a hill overlooking Ojai Valley is the **Krotona Institute of Theosophy** (Krotona Hill; 805-646-2653). This 118-acre forested estate is a center for "students of Theosophy and the ancient wisdom." A spiritual-philosophical movement which developed early in the 20th century, Theosophy combines science with religion and draws from the classic philosopher Pythagoras. Visitors can tour the library and enjoy the grounds, which are beautifully landscaped.

Another sect, the **Krishnamurti Foundation**, has an equally secluded library (1130 McAndrew Road; 805-646-4948) in the hills on the other side of town. At nearby **Meditation Mount** (10340 Reeves Road; 805-646-5508), meditative sessions celebrate the full moon.

Before venturing to these etherial heights, stop off at the **Ojai Valley Chamber of Commerce** (338 East Ojai Avenue; 805-646-8126), which has maps and brochures of the area. The 1917 Mission Revival **Post Office** (201 East Ojai Avenue) and the Spanish-style **City Hall** (401 South Ventura Street; 805-646-5581) are also downtown.

To capture the spirit of Ojai, hike, bicycle, or drive the back roads and mountain lanes. **Grand Avenue loop** will carry you past orange orchards and horse ranches to the foot of the mountains. It leads along thick stone walls built by Chinese laborers during the 19th century. (Take Ojai Avenue, Route 150, east from town; turn left on Reeves Road, left again on McAndrew Road, left on Thatcher Road, and left on Carne Road. This returns to Route 150, completing the ten-mile loop).

East End drive follows Route 150 east past palm trees and farmhouses. Three miles from town, on a promontory with a stone bench inscribed "The Ojai Valley," is the overlook from which actor Ronald Colman gazed down on Shangri-La in *Lost Horizon.* With deep green orchards below and sharp gold mountains above, it truly evokes that fictional utopia.

(Near Ojai, especially along Route 150 east of town and off Route 33 around Oakview, are farms where visitors can pick fresh fruits and vegetables—oranges, melons, pumpkins, nuts, grapefruit, lemons, peaches, and a host of other products.)

The path to the mountains surrounding town lies along Route 33. Leading north it passes rows of orchards and cuts into a narrow canyon before arriving at the luxurious spa at **Wheeler Hot Springs** (Route 33, six miles from Ojai; 805-646-8131). The private rooms here are pine-paneled affairs with skylights and hot and cold tubs. There are massage rooms, a spring-fed swimming pool, and a lodge housing a fine restaurant.

The highway winds higher into the sun-scorched mountains past forests of pine and oak. Paralleling the Sespe River, Route 33 bisects rocky defiles and skirts 7500-foot Reyes Peak. For sixty miles the road tracks through the mountains until it meets Route 166, where the alternatives are heading east to the Central Valley or west toward the coast.

Another Ojai sightseeing jaunt follows Route 150 west as it snakes down from the hills. The valleys are covered with scrub growth and small farms and the heights support lofty forests. The road skirts **Lake Casitas,** whose 60-mile shoreline is a labyrinth of coves and inlets. Ten miles from Ojai it joins Route 192, which leads to Santa Barbara. This meandering country road, in the hills above Carpinteria, traverses pretty pastureland. All around lies a quiltwork of orchards, fields, and tilled plots. Shade trees overhang the road and horses graze in the distance.

SANTA BARBARA AREA

From Ventura, Route 101 speeds north and west to Santa Barbara. For a slow-paced tour of the shoreline, take the **Old Pacific Coast Highway** instead. Paralleling the freeway and the Southern Pacific Railroad tracks, it rests on a narrow shelf between sharply rising hills and the ocean. The road glides for miles along sandy beaches and rocky shoreline, passing the woodframe communities of Solimar Beach and Seacliff Beach.

Past this last enclave the old road ends as you join Route 101 once more. With the Santa Ynez Mountains looming on one side and the Pacific extending along the other, you'll pass the resort town of Carpinteria. The temperature might be 80° with a blazing sun overhead and a soft breeze off the ocean. Certainly the furthest thing from your mind is the North Pole, but there it is, just past Carpinteria—the turnoff for Santa Claus Lane.

Santa Claus Lane? It's a block-long stretch of trinket shops and toy stores with a single theme. A giant rooftop Santa Claus with a waistline measuring maybe 30 feet oversees the New England-style village. It's one of those places that's so tacky you feel like you've missed something if you pass it by. If nothing else, you can mail an early Christmas card. Just drop it in the mailbox at **Toyland** (3821 Santa Claus Lane, Carpinteria; 805-684-3515) and it will be postmarked (ready for this?) "Santa Claus, California."

Tucked between a curving bay and the Santa Ynez Mountains lies one of the prettiest places in all California. It's little wonder that the Spanish who settled **Santa Barbara**, establishing a presidio in 1782 and a mission several years later, called it *la tierra adorada*, the beloved land.

Discovered by a Portuguese navigator in 1542, it was an important center of Spanish culture until the Americans seized California in the 19th century. The town these Anglo interlopers built was a post-Victorian style community. But a monstrous earthquake leveled the downtown area in 1925 and created a *tabla rasa* for architects and city planners.

Faced with rebuilding Santa Barbara, they returned the place to its historic roots, combining Spanish and Mission architecture to create a Mediterranean metropolis. The result is modern day Santa Barbara with its adobe walls, red tile roofs, rounded archways, and palm-lined boulevards.

Sightseeing Santa Barbara is as simple as it is rewarding. First stop at the **Santa Barbara Visitors' Center** (1 Santa Barbara Street; 805-965-3021). The myriad materials here include more pamphlets, books, and booklets than you ever want to see. The most important piece is a brochure entitled "Santa Barbara" which outlines a "Red Tile Tour" for walkers as well as a lengthier "Scenic Drive." Together they form two concentric circles along whose perimeter lie nearly all the city's points of interest.

RED TILE TOUR

The 14-block **Red Tile Tour** begins at the **Santa Barbara County Courthouse** (1100 Block of Anacapa Street; 805-962-6464), the city's grandest building. This U-shaped Spanish-Moorish "palace" covers almost three sides of a city block. The interior is a masterwork of beamed ceilings, arched corridors, and palacio tile floors. On the second floor of this 1929 courthouse are murals depicting California history. The highlight of every visit is the sweeping view of Santa Barbara at the top of the clock tower. From the Santa Ynez Mountains down to the ocean all that meets the eye are palm trees and red tile roofs.

Two blocks down, the **Hill Carrillo Adobe** (11 East Carrillo Street) is an 1826-vintage home built by a Massachusetts settler for his Spanish bride. Today the house is furnished with period pieces.

Along State Street, the heart of Santa Barbara's shopping district, many stores occupy antique buildings. **El Paseo** (814 State Street) represents one of the most unique malls in the entire country. It is a labyrinthine shopping arcade comprised of several complexes. Incorporated into the architectural

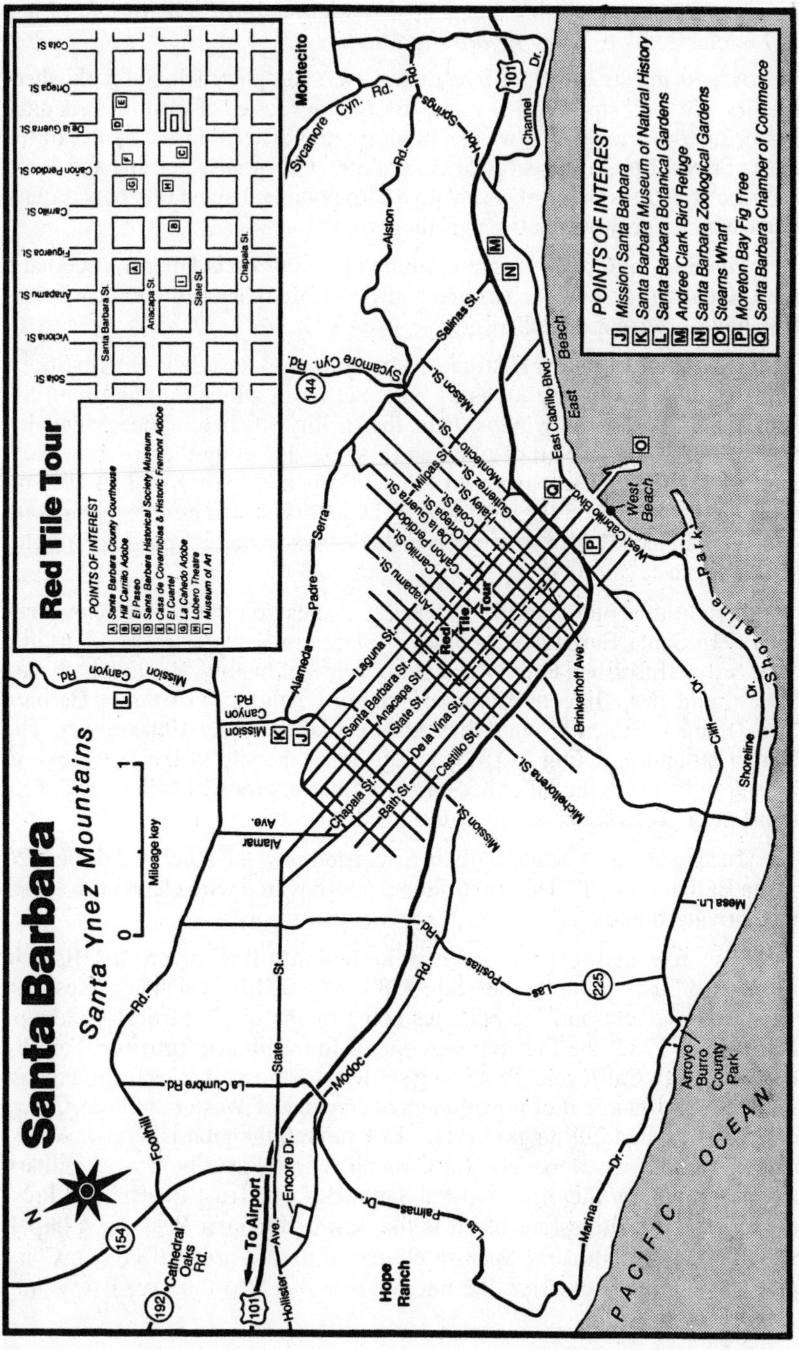

Santa Barbara
Santa Ynez Mountains
Mileage key
0
1
Red Tile Tour
POINTS OF INTEREST
A Santa Barbara County Courthouse
B Hill Carrillo Adobe
C El Paseo
D Santa Barbara Historical Society Museum
E Casa de Covarrubias & Historic Fremont Adobe
F El Cuartel
G La Cañedo Adobe
H Lobero Theatre
I Museum of Art
POINTS OF INTEREST
J Mission Santa Barbara
K Santa Barbara Museum of Natural History
L Santa Barbara Botanical Gardens
M Andree Clark Bird Refuge
N Santa Barbara Zoological Gardens
O Stearns Wharf
P Moreton Bay Fig Tree
Q Santa Barbara Chamber of Commerce
Montecito
PACIFIC OCEAN
Hope Ranch
Arroyo Burro County Park
To Airport
West Beach
East Beach
Red Tile Tour
Sycamore Cyn. Rd.
Hot Springs Rd.
Channel Dr.
Alston Rd.
Salinas St.
Mason St.
East Cabrillo Blvd.
West Cabrillo Blvd.
Shoreline Park
Shoreline Dr.
Cliff Dr.
Mesa Ln.
Las Positas Rd.
Marina Dr.
Las Palmas Dr.
Modoc Rd.
Encore Dr.
Hollister Ave.
Cathedral Oaks Rd.
Foothill Rd.
La Cumbre Rd.
State St.
Alamar Ave.
Mission Canyon Rd.
Alameda Padre Serra
Laguna St.
Santa Barbara St.
Anacapa St.
De La Vina St.
Castillo St.
Bath St.
Chapala St.
Mission St.
Micheltorena St.
Brinkerhoff Ave.
Milpas St.
Montecito St.
Gutierrez St.
Haley St.
Cota St.
Ortega St.
De la Guerra St.
Cañon Perdido St.
Carrillo St.
Anapamu St.
Figueroa St.
Victoria St.
Sola St.
154
192
101
144
225

motif is **Casa de la Guerra**, a splendid house built in 1827 for the commander of the Santa Barbara presidio and described by Richard Henry Dana in his classic *Two Years Before the Mast.*

Across the street rests **Plaza de la Guerra**, a palm-fringed park where the first city hall stood in 1875. Nearby, another series of historic structures has been converted into a warren of shops and offices. In the center of the mall is **Presidio Gardens** (de la Guerra Street between Anacapa and Santa Barbara streets), a tranquil park with a carp pond and elephant-shaped fountains which spray water through their trunks.

The **Santiago de la Guerra Adobe** (110 East de la Guerra Street) and the **Lugo Adobe**, set in a charming courtyard, are other 19th-century homes that have been converted to private use.

The **Santa Barbara Historical Museum** (136 East de la Guerra Street; 805-966-1601) certainly looks its part. Set in an adobe building with tile roof and wrought-iron window bars, the facility sits behind heavy wooden doors. Within are fine art displays and a series depicting the Spanish, Mexican, and early American periods of Santa Barbara's history, including memorabilia from author Richard Henry Dana's visits. There is a pleasant courtyard in back with a fountain and shade trees, a perfect place for a sightseer's siesta.

A right turn on Santa Barbara Street carries you to **Casa de Covarrubias** (715 Santa Barbara Street). Most places in Santa Barbara are a little too neatly refurbished to provide a dusty sense of history. But this L-shaped house, and the adjacent **Historic Fremont Adobe** (715 Santa Barbara Street), are sufficiently wind-blasted to evoke the early 19th century. The former structure, dating to 1817, is said to be the site of the last Mexican assembly in 1846; the latter became headquarters for Colonel John C. Fremont after Americans captured the town later that year.

Turn back along Santa Barbara Street and pass the **Rochin Adobe** (820 Santa Barbara Street). This 1856 adobe, now covered with clapboard siding, is a private home.

It's a few steps over to **El Presidio de Santa Barbara State Historic Park** (123 East Cañon Perdido Street; 805-966-9719), which occupies both sides of the street and incorporates some of the city's earliest buildings. Founded in 1782, the Presidio was one of four military fortresses built by the Spanish in California. Protecting settlers and missionaries from Indians, it also served as a seat of government and center of Western culture. Today only two original buildings survive. **El Cuartel**, the guards' house, served as the soldiers' quarters. The **La Caneda Adobe**, also built as a military residence, is now the offices of the Santa Barbara Trust for Historic Preservation. Most interesting of all is the **Santa Barbara Presidio Chapel,** which re-creates an early Spanish church in its full array of colors. Compared to the plain exterior, the interior is a shock to the eye. Everything is done in red and yellow ochre and dark blue. The altar is painted to simulate a great cathedral. Drapes and columns, difficult to obtain during Spanish days, have been drawn onto the walls. Even the altar railing is painted to imitate colored marble.

The last stop on this walking tour will carry you a step closer to the present. The **Lobero Theatre** (33 East Cañon Perdido Street; 805-963-0761) was constructed in 1925. It is a three-tiered design which ascends to a 70-foot high stage house. The original Lobero dates back to 1872, Santa Barbara's first theater.

After exploring Santa Barbara, kids appreciate a visit to the **Children's Museum of Santa Barbara** (La Cumbre Plaza Mall, 110 South Hope Avenue; 805-682-0845; admission). Here they will discover a Chumash village, fire station, laser exhibits, and doctor's office.

SCENIC DRIVE

The **Scenic Drive** around Santa Barbara, a 30-mile circle tour, incorporates several of the sites covered along the Red Tile Tour. To avoid repetition begin at the **Santa Barbara Museum of Art** (1130 State Street; 805-963-4364; admission) with its collection of American paintings, Asian art, and classical sculpture.

Then head up to **Mission Santa Barbara** (2201 Laguna Street; 805-682-4713; admission), which sits on a knoll overlooking the city. Founded in 1786 and restored in 1820, this twin-tower beauty follows a design from an ancient Roman architecture book. The interior courtyard is a colonnaded affair with a central fountain and graceful flower garden. The chapel itself is quite impressive with a row of wrought-iron chandeliers leading to a multicolored altar. There are also museum displays representing the original Indian population, early 19th-century mission artifacts, and examples of crafts works. Also visit the Mission Cemetery, a placid and pretty spot where frontier families and about 4000 Chumash Indians are buried in the shade of a Moreton Bay fig tree.

Further uphill at the **Santa Barbara Museum of Natural History** (2559 Puesta del Sol Road; 805-682-4711; admission) are successive rooms devoted to marine, plant, vertebrate, and insect life. Excellent for kids, it also features small exhibits of Indian tribes from throughout the United States.

Nearby Mission Canyon Road continues into the hills for close-up views of the rocky Santa Ynez Mountains and a tour of **Santa Barbara Botanic Gardens** (1212 Mission Canyon Road; 805-682-4726; admission). The five and one-half miles of trails here wind past a desert section carpeted with cactus and a meadow filled with wildflowers. Near the top of the park, beyond the ancient Indian trail, where the forest edges down from the mountains, is a stand of cool, lofty redwood trees.

Backtrack to Alameda Padre Serra and cruise this elite roadway past million-dollar homes with million-dollar views. From this thoroughfare a series of side roads leads through the exclusive bedroom community of **Montecito**. Here a variety of architectural styles combine to create a luxurious neighborhood. After exploring the town's shady groves and manicured lawns, you can pick up **Channel Drive**, a spectacular street which skirts beaches and bluffs as it loops back toward Santa Barbara.

From this curving roadway you'll spy oddly shaped structures offshore. Looking like a line of battleships ready to attack Santa Barbara, they are in fact **oil derricks**. Despite protests from environmentalists and a disastrous 1969 oil spill, these coastal waters have been the site of drilling operations for decades. Those hazy humps further out past the wells are the **Channel Islands**.

The **Andree Clark Bird Refuge** (1400 East Cabrillo Boulevard) is a placid lagoon filled with ducks, geese, and other freshwater fowl. There's a tree-tufted island in the center and a trail around the park. Upstaging all this is the adjacent **Santa Barbara Zoological Gardens** (500 Niños Drive; 805-962-6310; admission) with its miniature train ride and population of monkeys, lions, elephants, giraffes, and exotic birds.

Cabrillo Boulevard hugs the shore as it tracks past **East Beach**, Santa Barbara's longest, prettiest strand. With its rows of palm trees, grassy acres, and sunbathing crowds, it's an enchanting spot.

For a taste of sea air and salt spray walk out along **Stearns Wharf** (foot of State Street). From the end of this wooden pier you can gaze back at Santa Barbara, realizing how aptly author Richard Henry Dana described the place: "The town is finely situated, with a bay in front, and an amphitheater of hills behind." Favored by local anglers, the wharf is also noted for the **Sea Center** (211 Stearns Wharf; 805-962-0885; admission), a marine museum with an aquarium, underwater photographs, computerized learning center, a 37-foot replica of a gray whale and calf, and a touch tank filled with local marine life.

If you tire of walking, remember that Stearns Wharf is the departure point for the **Santa Barbara Trolley**, an old-fashioned vehicle which carries visitors along the waterfront, through the downtown area, and out to the mission.

The **Moreton Bay Fig Tree** (Chapala and Moreton streets), another local landmark, is a century-old giant with branches that spread 160 feet. This magnificent specimen stands as the largest tree of its kind in the United States.

Back along the waterfront, Cabrillo Boulevard continues to the **Yacht Harbor** (West Cabrillo Boulevard and Castillo Street) where 1200 pleasure boats, some worth more than homes, lie moored. The walkway leads past yawls, ketches, sloops, and fishing boats to a breakwater. From here you can survey the fleet and take in the surrounding mountains and ocean.

To continue this seafront excursion, follow Shoreline, Cliff, and Marina drives as they parallel the Pacific, past headlands and beaches, en route to **Hope Ranch**. Santa Barbara is flanked by two posh communities: Montecito in the east and this elite enclave to the west. It's a world of country clubs and cocktail parties, where money and nature meet to create forested estates.

SANTA YNEZ VALLEY

The mountain road from Santa Barbara, Route 154, curves up into the Santa Ynez Mountains past forests of evergreen and oak. All along the roadside are rocky promontories with broad views back toward the city and out over the ocean.

Turn off onto Stagecoach Road, head downhill a mile and rein in at **Cold Spring Tavern** (5995 Stagecoach Road; 805-967-0066). Back in the 1880s this squat wood structure served as a rest stop for stagecoaches coming through San Marcos Pass. Next door is a split-log cabin with stone fireplace.

Beyond the mountain pass, amid striated hills and rolling ranch country, lies **Lake Cachuma** (805-688-4658). Fed by creeks from Los Padres National Forest, this eight-mile long lake is a jewel to the eye. Boating and fishing facilities lie nearby and hiking trails lead into the encroaching wilderness.

Thirty miles from Santa Barbara the mountains open onto the Santa Ynez Valley. Here a string of sleepy towns creates a Western-style counterpoint to California's chic coastline. **Santa Ynez** is a falsefront town complete with a white-steeple church that dates to 1897. Downtown **Ballard** is one block long; the town was settled in 1880 and features the **Ballard School** (2425 School Street), a little red schoolhouse that was constructed a few years later. Nearby **Los Olivos** is home to **Mattei's Tavern** (Route 154; 805-688-4820). This former stagecoach inn, constructed in 1886, is a fine old woodframe building with a trellised porch.

The valley's other town, the most famous of all, does not resemble any of the others. It doesn't really resemble anything in California. **Solvang** is a town that looks like it was designed by Walt Disney. The place is a Danish village complete with cobblestone walks, gaslights, and stained-glass windows. Steep-pitched roofs with high dormers create an Old World atmosphere here. Stores and homes reveal the tall, narrow architecture of Scandinavia and windmills dominate the view. What saves the place from being a theme park is that Solvang actually is a Danish town. Emigrants from Denmark established a village and school here in 1911.

For visitors, wandering around town means catching a ride on a horse-drawn **Danish streetcar**, then popping into a **Scandinavian bakery** for hot pretzels or *aebleskiver*, a tasty Danish pastry.

Bethania Lutheran Church (Atterdag Road and Laurel Avenue) illustrates Danish provincial architecture. The model of a fully rigged ship hanging from the ceiling is traditional to Scandinavian churches.

To further confuse things, the centerpiece of Solvang in no way fits the architecture of the town. **Mission Santa Inés** (Mission Drive) does, however, meet the building style of the rest of California. Founded in 1804, the mission church follows the long, narrow rectangular shape traditional in Spanish California. The altar is painted brilliant colors and the colonnaded courtyard is ablaze with flowers. A small museum displays 18th-century bibles and song books and one chapel contains a 17th-century statue of polychromed wood.

To escape the bustle of Solvang, take a ride out Alisal Road. After six miles this rustic road arrives at **Nojoqui Falls**. There's a picnic park here and a short hiking trail up to hillside cascades.

The Santa Ynez Valley is horse country. Stud farms and working ranches dot the countryside and thoroughbreds graze in the meadows.

It's also a prime winegrowing region with several dozen wineries scattered around the valley on picturesque back roads. The **Santa Ynez Valley Winery** (343 North Refugio Road, Santa Ynez; 805-688-8381), housed in an old dairy building, is a 110-acre spread growing sauvignon blanc, chardonnay, gewürztraminer, and other grapes. With vines dating to 1969, it claims to be the oldest commercial vineyard in the valley, indicating just how recent winegrowing is to the area.

For a long country ride, travel out Zaca Station and Foxen Canyon roads in Los Olivos. A string of wineries begins with the most elegant. **Firestone Vineyard** (5017 Zaca Station Road; 805-688-3940) is set in stone-trimmed buildings and features a courtyard with fountain and picnic tables. The largest winery in the valley, it offers several estate-grown varietal wines.

Zaca Mesa Winery (6905 Foxen Canyon Road; 805-688-3310) sits about nine miles from Route 101. Set in a modern woodframe building with an attractive tasting room, it's a beautiful winery with vineyards lining Foxen Canyon Road. Other wineries lie further along the road and elsewhere throughout the valley.

NORTH OF SANTA BARBARA

Route 101 streams northwest past a series of suburban communities, including Goleta and Isla Vista, where the **University of California–Santa Barbara** is located. Cutting a swath between mountains and ocean, the road passes a series of attractive beach parks, then turns inland toward the mountains and interior valleys.

About 35 miles from Santa Barbara Routes 101 and 1 diverge. For a rural drive past white barns and meandering creeks, follow **Route 1**. En route to Lompoc it passes farmlands, pastures, and rolling hills. About five miles south of Lompoc, you can follow **Jalama Road** (★), a country lane which cuts through sharp canyons and graceful valleys on a winding 15-mile course to the ocean, ending at a beach park.

This journey becomes a pilgrimage when Route 1 approaches **La Purísima Mission** (2295 Purisima Road, Lompoc; 805-733-3713; admission). The best restored of all 21 California missions, this historic site has an eerie way of projecting you back to Spanish days. There's the mayordomo's abode with the table set and a pan on the oven, or the mission store, its barrels overflowing with corn and beans. The entire mission complex, from the sanctified church to the tallow vats where slaughtered cattle were rendered into soap, is re-created. Founded nearby in 1787, the mission was re-established at this site in 1813. Today you can tour the living quarters of priests and soldiers, the workshops where weaving, leathermaking, and carpentry were practiced, and the mission's original water system.

In spring and summer the hills around **Lompoc** dazzle with thousands of acres of flowers. The countryside is a rainbow of color throughout the season. Then in fall fields of poppies, nasturtiums, and larkspurs bloom.

SAN LUIS OBISPO AREA

PISMO BEACH

After its lengthy inland course through Lompoc and Guadalupe, Route 1 rejoins Route 101 and returns to the coast at **Pismo Beach**. An unattractive congeries of mobile homes and beach rental stands, this nondescript town has one saving grace—its dunes. They are sand castles in the air, curving, rolling, ever-changing hills of sand. Wave after wave of them parallel the beach, like a crystalline continuation of the ocean.

In fact they comprise the most extensive coastal dunes in California. From Pismo Beach the sand hills run six miles south where they meet the 450-foot-high **Guadalupe dunes** (see the "Beaches and Parks" section of this chapter), forming a unique habitat for wildflowers and shorebirds.

Back in the 1930s and 1940s a group of bohemians, the "Dunites," occupied this wild terrain. Comprised of nudists, artists, and mystics, the movement believed that the dunes were a center of cosmic energy. Today the area is filled with beachcombers, sunbathers, and off-highway vehicles.

Stop by the **Pismo Beach Chamber of Commerce** (581 Dolliver Street, Pismo Beach; 805-773-2055) for brochures and maps of the San Luis Bay region. Of the three seaside communities lining this harbor—Pismo Beach, Shell Beach, and Avila Beach—the prettiest of all is **Avila Beach**. Here you can comb a white sand beach or walk out along three fishing piers. At the far end of town a dramatic headland curves out from the shoreline, creating a crescent-shaped harbor where sailboats bob at their moorings.

There are hot springs in the hills around Avila Beach. **Sycamore Mineral Springs Resort** (1215 Avila Beach Drive, Avila Beach; 805-595-7302; admission) has tapped these local waters and created a lovely spa. There are hotel units, volleyball courts, and a swimming pool here, but the real attractions are the redwood hot tubs. Very private, they are dotted about on a hillside and shaded by oak and sycamore.

From the Pismo Beach–Avila Beach strip, you can buzz into San Luis Obispo on Route 101 or take a quiet country drive into town via **See Canyon Road** (★). The latter begins in Avila Beach and corkscrews up into the hills past apple orchards and horse farms. Along its 13-mile length, half unpaved, you'll encounter mountain meadows and ridgetop vistas. During the fall harvest season you can pick apples at farms along the way.

SAN LUIS OBISPO

San Luis Obispo, a pretty jewel of a town, lies 12 miles from the ocean in the center of an expansive agricultural region. Backdropped by the Santa Lucia Mountains, the town focuses around an old Spanish mission. Cowboys from outlying ranches and students from the nearby campus add to the cultural mix, creating a vital atmosphere that has energized San Luis Obispo's rapid growth.

For a sense of the region's roots, pick up information at the **San Luis Obispo Chamber of Commerce** (1039 Chorro Street; 805-543-1323). A self-guided tour of this historic town logically begins at **Mission San Luis de Tolosa** (Chorro and Monterey streets; 805-543-6850). Dating to 1772, the old Spanish outpost has been nicely reconstructed, though the complex is not as extensive as La Purísima Mission in Lompoc. There's a museum re-creating the Native American, Spanish, and Mexican eras as well as a pretty church. Mission Plaza, fronting the chapel, is a well-landscaped park.

The **County Historical Museum** (696 Monterey Street; 805-543-0638) continues the historic overview with displays from the pre-Hispanic, Spanish, and American periods. Across the street at the **San Luis Obispo Art Center** (1010 Broad Street; 805-543-8562) are exhibits of works by local artists.

St. Stephen's Episcopal Church (Nipomo and Pismo streets) is a narrow, lofty, and strikingly attractive chapel. Built in 1867, it was one of California's first Episcopal churches. The **Dallidet Adobe** (Toro Street between Pismo and Pacific streets), constructed by a French vintner in 1853, is another local architectural landmark. A block away and about a century later Frank Lloyd Wright designed the **Kundert Medical Building** (Pacific and Santa Rosa streets).

The **Ah Louis Store** (800 Palm Street) symbolizes the Chinese presence here. A sturdy brick building with wrought-iron shutters and balcony, it dates to 1874 and once served the 2000 Chinese coolies who worked on nearby railroad tunnels.

Around the corner, the **Sauer-Adams Adobe** (964 Chorro Street), covered in clapboard, is an 1860-era house with a second-story balcony. By the turn of the century, Victorian-style homes had become the vogue. Many of San Luis Obispo's finest Victorians are located in the blocks adjacent to where Broad Street intersects with Pismo and Buchon streets.

Those with young ones in tow can stop by the **San Luis Obispo Children's Museum** (1010 Nipomo Street; 805-544-5437; admission). In this imaginative environment kids can race to a fire engine, visit a planetarium, learn the principles of photography, and discover a Chumash Indian cave.

If you're in town on a Thursday evening, be sure to stop by the **Farmers' Market** (Higuera Street between Osos and Nipomo streets). Farmers from the surrounding area turn out to sell fresh fruits and vegetables. They barbecue ribs, cook sweet corn and fresh fish, then serve them on paper plates to the throngs that turn out weekly. Puppeteers and street dancers perform as the celebration assumes a carnival atmosphere.

To pick your own produce, ask at the Chamber of Commerce about the **farm trails** program. They'll provide information on where to go around town and throughout San Luis Obispo County to gather ripe strawberries, apples, avocados, tomatoes, and dozens of other fruits and vegetables.

MORRO BAY

As Route 1 angles north and west from San Luis Obispo toward the ocean, separating again from Route 101, you'll encounter a procession of nine volcanic peaks. Last in this geologic parade is a 576-foot plug dome called **Morro Rock**. The pride of Morro Bay, it stands like a little Gibraltar, connected to the mainland by a sand isthmus. You can drive out and inspect the brute. Years ago, before conservationists and common sense prevailed, the site was a rock quarry. Today it's a nesting area for peregrine falcons.

All around Morro Bay you'll encounter the same contradiction. The town combines unique natural resources with ugly manmade features. The waterfront is a study in blue-collar architecture with bait-and-tackle shops, plywood restaurants, and slapdash stores everywhere; and dominating the skyline, vying with the great rock itself, are three monstrous concrete smokestacks.

Turn your back on this travesty and you are in a bird sanctuary. Extending for miles out toward Morro Rock is a dramatic **sandspit**, a teeming region of sand dunes and sea life. From town there's a funky **sandspit shuttle** (699 Embarcadero; 805-772-8085) to boat you across to the dunes (the shuttle runs from May to November). For something more formal, **Tiger's Folly** (1205 Embarcadero, at the Harbor Hut Restaurant; 805-772-2257) sponsors cruises of the harbor in an old-fashioned paddlewheeler.

Back on terra firma, visit the **Morro Bay State Park Museum** (Morro Bay State Park; 805-772-2694; admission) with its displays of local history and wildlife. The museum itself is unimpressive, but it is located at White Point, a rock outcropping in which Indian mortar holes are still evident. From this height there are views of the sandspit, Morro Bay, and Morro

Rock. The nearby lagoon, a habitat for 250 migratory and resident bird species, is one of the largest salt marshes in California.

CAMBRIA AREA

North from Morro Bay, Route 1 passes the antique village of **Harmony** (population 18), then continues to the seaside town of **Cambria**. Originally settled in the 1860s, Cambria later expanded into a major seaport and whaling center. As the railroad replaced coastal shipping, Cambria declined, only to be resurrected during the past few decades as an artist colony and tourist center. There's even a **Cambria Chamber of Commerce** office (767 Main Street; 805-927-3624).

It's a pretty place, with ridgetop homes, sandy beaches, and rocky coves. But like many of California's small creative communities, Cambria has begun peering too long in the mirror. The architecture along Main Street has assumed a cutesy mock-Tudor look and the place is taking on an air of unreality.

Still, there are many fine artists and several exceptional galleries here. It's a choice place to shop and seek out gourmet food. While you're at it, head up to **Nit Wit Ridge** (Hillcrest Drive just above Cornwall Street). That hodgepodge house on the left, the one decorated with every type of bric-a-brac, is the home of Art Beal, a.k.a. Captain Nit Wit. He has worked on this folk-art estate, listed in the National Register of Historic Landmarks, since 1928. Then take a ride along **Moonstone Beach Drive**, a lovely oceanfront corridor with vista points and tidepools. It's a marvelous place for beachcombers and daydreamers.

Funny thing about travel, you often end up visiting places in spite of themselves. You realize that as soon as you get back home friends are going to ask if you saw this or that, so your itinerary becomes a combination of the locales you've always longed to experience and the places everyone else says you "must see."

The world-renowned **Hearst Castle** (Route 1, San Simeon; 805-927-2000; admission) is one of the latter. Built by newspaper magnate William Randolph Hearst and designed by architect Julia Morgan, the Hearst San Simeon State Historical Monument includes a main house that sports 37 bedrooms, three guest houses, and part of the old Hearst ranch, which once stretched 40 miles along the coast.

The entire complex took 27 years to build. Back in the 1930s and 1940s, when Hearst resided here and film stars like Charlie Chaplin, Mary Pickford, Clark Gable, and Cary Grant frequented the place, the grounds contained the largest private zoo in the world. Ninety species of wild animals —including lions, tigers, yaks, and camels—roamed about.

An insatiable art collector, Hearst stuffed every building with priceless works. La Casa Grande, the main house, is fronted by two cathedral towers and filled with Renaissance art. To see it is overwhelming. There is no place for the eye to rest. The main sitting room is covered everywhere with tapestries, bas-relief works, 16th-century paintings, Roman columns, and a carved wood ceiling. The walls are fashioned from 500-year-old choir pews, the French fireplace dates back 400 years; there are handcarved tables and silver candelabra, (I am still describing the same room), overstuffed furniture, and antique statuary. It is the most lavish mismatch in history.

Hearst Castle crosses the line from visual art to visual assault. The parts are exquisite, the whole a travesty. And yet, as I said, you must see the place. It's so huge that four different two-hour tours are scheduled daily to various parts of the property. Since over one million people a year visit, the guided tours are often booked solid. I recommend that you reserve in advance and plan on taking Tour 1, which covers the ground floor of La Casa Grande, a guest house, the pools, and the gardens. Reservations are made through MISTIX; in California call 800-444-7275; outside the state, 619-452-1950.

Ultimately you'll find that in spite of the pomp and grandiosity, there is a magic about the place. In the early morning, when tour shuttles begin climbing from sea level to the 1600-foot-elevation residence, fog feathers through the surrounding valleys, obscuring everything but the spiked peaks of the Santa Lucia Mountains and the lofty towers of the castle. The entire complex, overbearing as it is, evokes a simpler, more glamorous era, before the Depression and World War II turned the nation's thoughts inward, when without blinking a man could build an outlandish testimonial to himself.

Beyond Hearst Castle Route 1 winds north past tidepools and pocket beaches. There are pretty coves and surf-washed rocks offshore. To leeward the hills give way to mountains as the highway ascends toward the dramatic Big Sur coastline. Over two hundred miles further north sits the city which Hearst made the center of his publishing empire, an oceanfront metropolis called San Francisco.

Shopping

OJAI AREA SHOPPING

The center of the shopping scene in the mountain resort town of Ojai is **Arcade Plaza**, a promenade between Ojai Avenue and Matilija Street that extends from Montgomery Street to Signal Street. Within this tile-roofed warren and along surrounding blocks are crafts stores and galleries. Many are operated by the community of artisans which has grown over the years in Ojai.

The Artist and the Outlaw Gallery (321 East Ojai Avenue; 805-646-5735) has an outstanding collection of contemporary work by local artists. There are batik on silk pieces, carved walking sticks, evocative oil paintings, and soft watercolors. Most impressive are the porcelain pieces which combine the craft of pottery with the art of sculpture.

An even more extensive collection of pottery is on display at the **Human Arts Gallery** (310 East Ojai Avenue; 805-646-1525). In addition to ceramics there are wallhangings, handblown glass pieces, and hand-wrought jewelry items.

For women's fashions consider **Flash 'n' Trash** (320 East Ojai Avenue; 805-646-9782), specializing in Beverly Hills styles. For stylish fashions, visit the **Barbara Bowman** shops (125 and 133 East Ojai Avenue; 805-646-2970) owned by the well-known designer.

Quite a collection it is at **The Antique Collection** (236 West Ojai Avenue; 805-646-6688): it seems that a number of dealers gathered together, formed a collective, and combined their stock, filling an entire warehouse with room after room of heirlooms.

An important gathering place for the spiritual movement in Ojai is the **Heart of Light Bookstore** (451 East Ojai Avenue; 805-646-3812) with its collection of mystical works, crystals, and religious paraphernalia. But the bookstore of bookstores is a place called **Bart's Books** (302 West Matilija Street; 805-646-3755), which is almost entirely outdoors. Here browsers can soak up the sun, enjoy mountain breezes, and wander through a maze of used books.

For fine traditional pottery, head east from town to **The Pottery** (971 McAndrew Road, Ojai; 805-646-3393). Vivika and Otto Heino, a husband and wife team, have been working together in porcelain and stoneware for 35 years. After browsing the showroom visitors can wander the landscaped grounds viewing the carp pond, cactus garden, and peacocks.

Further outside town, in a hilltop estate flanked by gardens, is the **Beatrice Wood Studio** (8560 Route 150, Ojai), a place that you absolutely must visit. Beatrice Wood, whose autobiography is entitled *I Shock Myself*, is a regional institution. Tremendously talented, she has been a potter for six decades. Her work is more like sculpture than pottery. Pieces are wrought as figurines of people and animals: vases feature forms in bas-relief; pitchers are shaped as people, their arms pouring spouts; couples are cast in bed or standing forlornly.

SANTA BARBARA AREA SHOPPING

Since Santa Barbara's shops are clustered together, you can easily uncover the town's hottest items and best bargains by concentrating on a few key areas. The prime shopping center lies along State Street, particularly between the 600 and 1300 blocks.

Piccadilly Square (813 State Street) is a warehouse-type mall with shops arranged contiguously, separated only by open spaces and low railings. There are boutiques galore here as well as an artisans' loft selling various crafts items.

El Paseo (814 State Street; 805-963-8741), a famous promenade, is one of the most imaginative malls I've ever seen. It consists of an historic adobe house and surrounding buildings, combined and converted into a succession of stores. This is a middle- and high-ticket complex: the art galleries, jewelry stores, and designer dress stores number among the best, but there are also curio shops and toy stores.

Pier 1 Imports (928 State Street; 805-965-0118) looks like a Hong Kong warehouse. It's stuffed to the rafters with wickerware, glassware, scented candles, wood carvings, ethnic rugs, ceramics, and cotton fabrics.

La Arcada Court (1114 State Street; 805-966-6634) is another spiffy mall done in Spanish style. The shops here, along the upper lengths of State Street, are more chic and contemporary than elsewhere. **Ghurka HQ.** (1114 State Street; 805-966-1669) sells luggage, belts, handbags, and wallets.

A favorite Santa Barbara bookstore is **Earthling Bookshop** (1137 State Street; 805-965-0926), a spacious store with a friendly staff and tasteful selection of hardbacks and paperbacks.

On the lower end of State Street, **Pacific Travellers Supply** (529 State Street; 805-963-4438) carries a complete stock of guidebooks. They also have luggage and travel paraphernalia.

Antiques in Santa Barbara are spelled Brinkerhoff Avenue. This block-long residential street conceals a half-dozen antique shops. Set amid simple clapboard houses is **Sally's Alley** (502 Brinkerhoff Avenue; 805-966-9454), a general store specializing in china, glass, and jewelery. Around the corner at **Redwood Inn Antiques** (124 West Cota Street; 805-965-2175) you'll find jewelry and furniture. My favorite, **Carl Hightower Galerie** (528 Brinkerhoff Avenue; 805-965-5687), is crowded with jewelry, ceramics, and everything else imaginable.

The corner of State and Ortega streets marks the center for vintage clothing. **Yellowstone Clothing** (619-A State Street; 805-963-9609) features Hawaiian shirts and other old-time favorites. Also try **Pure Gold** (718 State Street; 805-962-4613), which has everything from early exotic to late lamented.

For over twenty years Santa Barbara County artists and craftspeople have turned out for the **Arts & Crafts Show**. Every Sunday and holiday from 10 a.m. until dusk they line East Cabrillo Boulevard. The original artwork for sale includes paintings, graphics, sculptures, and drawings. Among the crafts are macrame, stained glass, woodwork, textiles, weaving, and jewelry. If you are in town on a Sunday make it a point to stop by.

SANTA YNEZ VALLEY SHOPPING

The Danish town of Solvang is a choice spot to shop for imported products from Northern Europe. Walk the brick-paved streets and you'll encounter everything from cuckoo clocks to lace curtains. Many of the shops line **Copenhagen Drive**.

There are Danish handknit sweaters, music boxes, tiles, and pewter items. The toy stores are designed to resemble doll houses and shops throughout town feature the tile roofs and high gables of Scandinavian stores.

In the nearby town of **Los Olivos** several art galleries and antique shops will help round out your shopping spree.

SAN LUIS OBISPO AREA SHOPPING

In this old Spanish town the best stores are located along the blocks surrounding Mission Plaza. Stroll the two blocks along Monterey Street between Osos and Chorro streets, then browse the five-block stretch on Higuera Street from Osos Street to Nipomo Street. These two arteries and the side streets between form the heart of downtown.

The Natural Selection (1111 Morro Street; 805-541-6755) is a unique shop dedicated to nature and science. The posters, books, toys, and greeting cards all follow a similar theme. So if you've been searching everywhere for that moon map, rain gauge, or *Tyrannosaurus rex* T-shirt, look no further.

The Network Mall (778 Higuera Street) is a collection of crafts shops and small stores. Also consider **The Creamery** (Higuera and Nipomo streets; 805-543-1011), an old dairy plant converted into an ingenious arcade.

CAMBRIA AREA SHOPPING

Located a few miles south of Hearst Castle, this seaside enclave has developed into an artist colony and become an important arts-and-crafts center, with numerous galleries and specialty shops. Several antique shops are also located here; like the crafts stores, they cluster along Main Street and Burton Drive.

Among the foremost galleries is **Seekers Collection & Gallery** (4090 Burton Drive; 805-927-8626). It's a glass menagerie inhabited by contemporary, one-of-a-kind vases, goblets, and sculptures.

The Soldier Factory (789 Main Street; 805-927-3804) is a journey back to childhood. Part toy store and part museum, it serves as headquarters for thousands of hand-painted toy soldiers. These antiques are deployed in battle formation, re-enacting clashes from the Civil War and other engagements. Many of the pewter pieces are made in the adjacent "factory." This unique shop has been featured in the *Wall Street Journal*.

For a journey into another world visit **Victoriana** (Arlington Street near Main Street; 805-927-3833). This diminutive store sells miniatures of Victorian house furnishings.

Nightlife

VENTURA AREA NIGHTLIFE

Bombay Bar & Grill (143 South California Street; 805-643-4404) offers live entertainment nightly with a musical medley that changes frequently. The South Seas-style bar, with overhead fans and oak-and-mirror decor, features piano plunkers, while the room in back hosts live dance bands nightly. Cover on weekends.

Over at **Club Soda** (317 East Main Street; 805-652-0100) they painted the walls to resemble a psychedelic nightmare. Then they gave each night a different theme. Maybe you'll walk in on "Get Tea'd on Tuesday," or "Hollywood Strip Wednesday." The video music is strictly deejay format. Cover.

Scene of scenes in the seaside community of Ventura is the **Ventura Theatre** (26 South Chestnut Street; 805-648-1936), a refurbished movie house. With its intricate gold fixtures, stained-glass windows, and ornamental molding, this 1928 structure has been redone in grand style and converted into a restaurant/concert hall. The club frequently draws top-name entertainers and offers a cultural mix that includes jazz, rock, reggae, and blues. Cover.

Or perhaps you just wanted a comfortable place overlooking the water. That would be **Charlie's Seaside Café & Restaurant** (362 California Street; 805-648-6688), where you can enjoy a quiet drink out on the patio or hear local rock or rhythm-and-blues ensembles inside nightly. Cover on the weekend.

The Wild Goose (2485 East Main Street; 805-653-9194) draws a mixed crowd of gay men and women. There's a cover charge on weekends when the deejay revs up; pool tables, video games, and dancing all week.

OJAI AREA NIGHTLIFE

Up at the posh **Ojai Valley Inn** (Country Club Drive, Ojai; 805-646-5511) you can order a drink, relax, and enjoy a mountain view from The Club.

Deer Lodge Tavern & Restaurant (2261 Route 33, Ojai; 805-646-4256), a jukebox-and-pool-table bar, has dancing to rhythm-and-blues and rock bands every Friday and Saturday.

SANTA BARBARA AREA NIGHTLIFE

The Palms (701 Linden Avenue, Carpinteria; 805-684-3811) features local rock and country-and-western bands every Thursday, Friday, and Saturday night. There's a small dancefloor here for footloose revelers.

The State Street strip in downtown Santa Barbara offers several party places. **Zelo** (630 State Street; 805-966-5792), a video nightclub, features dancing to deejay music and a live band on Wednesday. Cover.

Up at **Acapulco Restaurant** (1114 State Street; 805-963-3469), in La Arcada Court, you can sip a margarita next to an antique wooden bar or out on the patio. No entertainment, but it's a pretty place to drink.

If for no other reason than the view, **Harbor Restaurant** (210 Stearns Wharf; 805-963-3311) is a prime place for the evening. A plate-glass establishment, it sits out on a pier with the city skyline on one side and open ocean on the other. The bar upstairs features surf videos.

For sunset views, nothing quite compares to **El Encanto Lounge** (1900 Lasuen Road; 805-687-5000). Located in a posh hotel high in the Santa Barbara hills, it features a split-level terrace overlooking the city and ocean. In the evening there's a piano bar Wednesday through Saturday.

You can also consider the **Lobero Theatre** (33 East Cañon Perdido Street; 805-963-0761), which presents a full schedule of dance, drama, concerts, and lectures. Or head into the mountains about 25 miles outside Santa Barbara and catch a show at the **Circle Bar B Dinner Theater** (1800 Refugio Road; 805-965-9652). This well-known facility offers a menu of comedies, musicals, and light dramas.

Part of the gay scene in Santa Barbara is represented by **Gold Coast** (30 West Cota Street; 805-965-6701), which features a small dancefloor and on weekends a deejay.

Another gay gathering place is **The Pub** ((224 Helena Avenue; 805-962-3911). With dancing on weekends and a piano bar during the week, it features an outdoor patio.

SANTA YNEZ VALLEY NIGHTLIFE

Carousing at **Cold Spring Tavern** (5995 Stagecoach Road, off Route 154; 805-967-0066), a log cabin set high in the mountains outside Santa Barbara, is like being in an old Western movie. Every Friday through Sunday you can pull up a stool and listen to the rock, country-and-western, and rhythm-and-blues bands that ride through.

AJ Spurs (350 Route 246, Buellton; 805-686-1655) hosts live bands every Friday and Saturday night. This is an elegant Western saloon with log walls, stone fireplace, and frontier artifacts.

And don't forget the **Solvang Theaterfest** (805-922-8313), one of the West's oldest repertory groups. Performing during summer months in an open-air theater, they present musicals and dramas.

SAN LUIS OBISPO AREA NIGHTLIFE

Ready for a Western saloon? Stone fireplace, antlers on the wall, etc.? It's called **F. McLintock's Saloon & Dining House** (750 Mattie Road, Shell Beach; 805-773-1892). Unlike its rowdier counterparts, this lounge is low key. The music, seven nights a week, is by solo guitarists playing soft rock and country-and-western.

There's a posh piano bar at **The Inn at Morro Bay** (19 Country Club Drive, Morro Bay; 805-772-5651). Appointed with bentwood furniture and pastel paneling, it's a beautiful bar. The most striking feature of all is the view, which extends out across the water to Morro Rock.

Camozzi's Saloon (2262 Main Street, Cambria; 805-927-8941) is a century-old bar with longhorns over the bar, wagon wheels on the wall, and a floor that leans worse than a midnight drunk. The place is famous. Besides that, it has a rock band every Friday and Saturday.

LOW DESERT

CHAPTER SEVEN
Low Desert

East of metropolitan Los Angeles lies a land of brilliant greens and dusty browns, scorched flats and snow-thatched mountains. The Colorado Desert, the hottest, driest desert in the country, covers a broad swath of California's southeastern quarter. Here winter, with daily highs in the 70s and 80s, attracts sun worshippers, while summer brings withering heat waves.

It's a place where visitors can swim and ski in the same day. Little wonder that its entertainment capital, Palm Springs, has become a celebrity playground. Ever since 1930, when silent film stars Ralph Bellamy and Charlie Farrell began buying up desert land at $30 an acre, Hollywood has been vacationing in Palm Springs. The racquet club that Bellamy and Farrell initiated soon attracted Humphrey Bogart, Ginger Rogers, and Clark Gable. Latter-day luminaries like Bob Hope, Frank Sinatra, and Kirk Douglas continue to strengthen the spot's celebrity cachet.

Only 400 feet above sea level, the town nestles beneath mountains two miles high. Today Palm Springs is the golf capital of the world, sponsoring over 100 tournaments every year. In addition to dozens of golf courses, the region boasts hundreds of tennis courts and a swimming pool for every five residents. Together with satellite towns like Rancho Mirage and Palm Desert, it has become an opulent enclave in which billboards are prohibited, buildings are limited to heights of 30 feet, and manicured lawns are more common than cactus plants.

It was the Agua Caliente Indians who inhabited the area originally and discovered the desert's hot mineral baths. These Native Americans hunted and gathered in the surrounding mountains and attributed magical healing powers to the natural springs. Eventually the United States government divided the entire territory into alternating squares of real estate, giving the odd-numbered sections to the Southern Pacific Railroad and deeding the rest to the Agua Calientes.

Today much of this valuable Indian property is leased to tourist resorts. Located just 100 miles from Los Angeles, the desert has become a major travel destination. Visitors arrive not only to soak in the sun and spas of Palm Springs, but also to tour the palm groves of Indio. The date-growing center of the country, this bland agricultural town is a date palm oasis, with gardens reaching from road's edge to the fringe of the mountains. Little Indio's day in the sun arrives every February when it hosts the National Date Festival, a gala celebration complete with ostrich and camel races, Arabian Nights pageantry, and booths displaying over 100 varieties of dates.

Farther south lies the Salton Sea, California's largest lake, a briny trough which sits astride the notorious San Andreas Fault. Nearby Anza-Borrego Desert State Park stretches across parts of three counties and encompasses a half-million acres of gem-like springs, rock promontories, and sandstone chasms. Created about 150 million years ago by an earthquake fault system, the region includes the Jacumba Mountains, a granite jumble filled with eerie rock formations. Named for Juan Bautista de Anza, the Spanish explorer who trekked through in 1774, and *borrego*, the desert sheep which inhabits its hillsides, Anza-Borrego was a vital route for 1850-era stagecoaches and mail wagons.

Joshua Tree National Monument, the area's other major park, lies astride the Low and High deserts, rising from the scorching Colorado Desert to the cooler climes and higher elevations of the Mojave. Noted for its cactus gardens and stands of Joshua trees, this vast preserve was formerly home to the Chemehuevi Indians. Miners entered the territory following the Civil War, striking gold in 1873. Within a few years, cattle ranchers also arrived, creating vast ranges and driving the Indians from the land.

Rising between Los Angeles and Palm Springs, creating a gateway to the Low Desert, is a rapidly developing region known as the Inland Empire. Bounded to the north by the San Bernardino Mountains, which rise over 11,000 feet and embrace the popular resort areas of Lake Arrowhead and Big Bear Lake, it is bordered on the east by the San Jacinto Mountains.

A Spanish explorer named Pedro Fage uncovered the Inland Empire during a 1772 expedition and in the 1830s missionaries began colonizing the region. By the next decade powerful Spanish families had transformed the territory into sprawling cattle and horse ranches.

Then in 1851 a party of Mormons settled here, staying for only six years but leaving an indelible legacy. They planted wheat, harvested lumber, and founded the city of San Bernardino.

Located at the foot of Cajon Pass along a vital route between Los Angeles and the East Coast, the area expanded in importance. The railroad arrived in 1875; and during the same decade Luther and Eliza Tibbetts planted three orange saplings shipped across the country from Washington, D.C., giving birth to the Inland Empire's vaunted citrus industry.

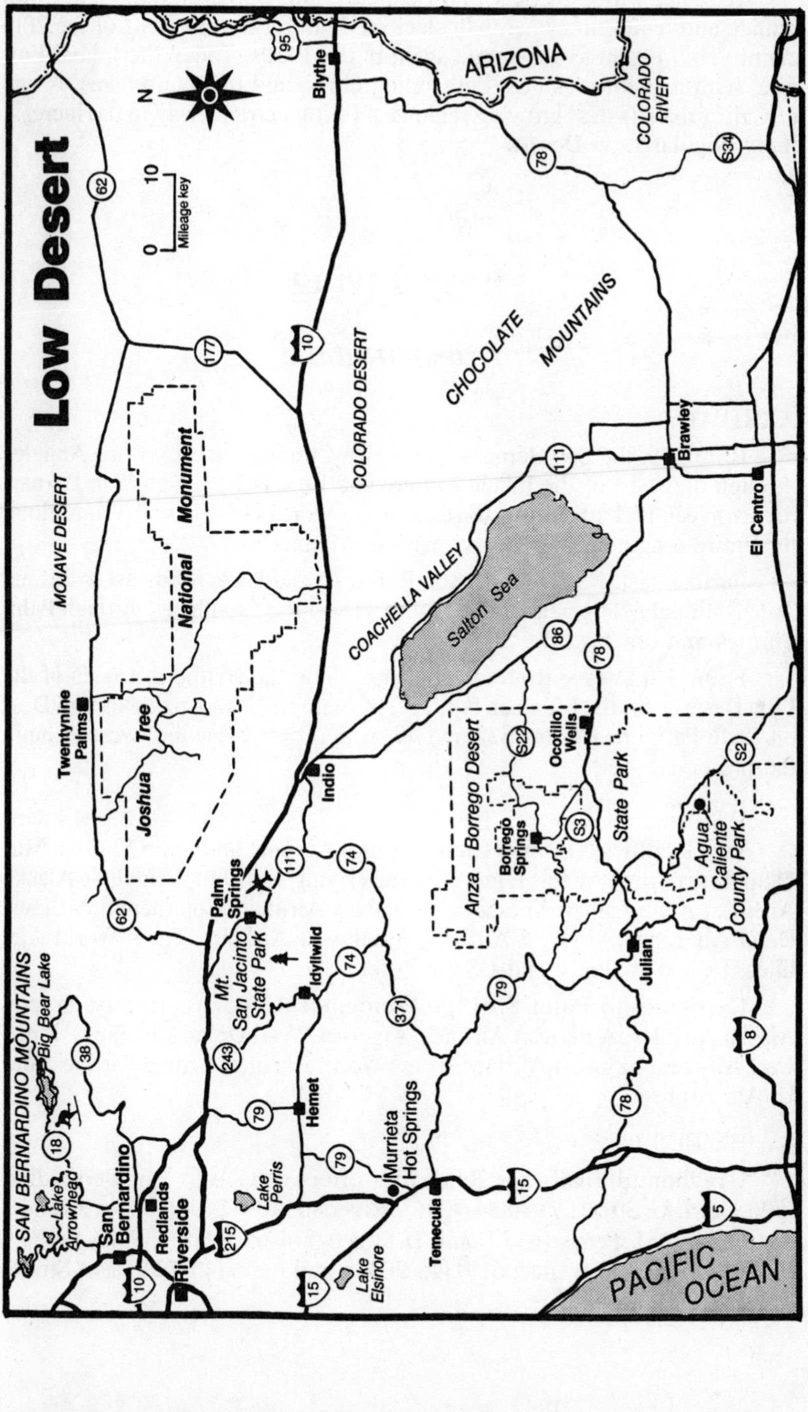
Low Desert
Mileage key
0
10
N
MOJAVE DESERT
Joshua Tree National Monument
Twentynine Palms
COLORADO DESERT
CHOCOLATE MOUNTAINS
COACHELLA VALLEY
Salton Sea
ARIZONA
COLORADO RIVER
Blythe
Indio
Palm Springs
Mt. San Jacinto State Park
Idyllwild
Hemet
Murrieta Hot Springs
Temecula
Lake Elsinore
Lake Perris
Riverside
Redlands
San Bernardino
SAN BERNARDINO MOUNTAINS
Big Bear Lake
Lake Arrowhead
Anza – Borrego Desert State Park
Borrego Springs
Ocotillo Wells
Julian
Agua Caliente County Park
Brawley
El Centro
PACIFIC OCEAN
10
15
215
5
8
95
62
177
111
74
371
243
79
38
18
86
78
S22
S3
S2
S34

Together with Riverside and Redlands, San Bernardino sprouted with orange and lemon trees. Growth slackened during the first half of the 20th century, but began to accelerate again in the 1950s. Today the Inland Empire, with its trim orchards, burgeoning cities, and mountain lakes, is one of California's fastest growing regions, a fitting entranceway to the increasingly popular Low Desert.

Easy Living

Transportation

ARRIVAL

Route 10, the San Bernardino Freeway, travels east from Los Angeles through the heart of the Inland Empire and Low Desert. Near San Bernardino you can pick up **Route 18** (Rim of the World Drive), which runs along the entire length of the San Bernardino Mountains.

Further east, **Route 62** departs Route 10 and leads northeast to Joshua Tree National Monument, while **Route 111** courses southeast through Palm Springs and down to the Salton Sea.

From San Diego, **Route 8** goes east along the southern fringes of the Low Desert near the Mexican border. The main roads in Anza-Borrego Desert State Park are **Routes S22** and **78**, which travel east and west through the preserve.

BY AIR

Two facilities, **Ontario International Airport** and Palm Springs Municipal Airport, serve this region. Carriers flying into Ontario include Alaska Airlines, American Airlines, America West Airlines, Continental Airlines, Delta Air Lines, Skywest Airlines, Southwest Airlines, Trans World Airlines, United Airlines, and USAir.

Carriers into **Palm Springs Municipal Airport** currently include Alaska Airlines, American Airlines, America West, Delta Air Lines, Northwest Airlines, Skywest Airlines, Trans World Airlines, United Airlines, and USAir Express.

BY BUS

Greyhound/Trailways Bus Lines offers service to San Bernardino (596 North G Street; 714-884-4796), Riverside (3911 University Avenue; 714-686-2345), Perris (637 South D Street; 714-657-7813), Palm Springs (311 North Indian Avenue; 619-325-2053), and Indio (45-524 Oasis Street; 619-347-3020).

BY TRAIN

All aboard. **Amtrak** (800-872-7245) has two passenger trains to San Bernardino (1170 West Third Street; 714-884-1307), the "Desert Wind" and "Southwest Chief." Another train, the "Sunset," stops at the railroad platform on Jackson Street in Indio. From here Greyhound/Trailways Bus Lines connects to Palm Springs.

CAR RENTALS

Located at Ontario International Airport are the following rental agencies: **Avis Rent A Car** (714-983-3689), **Budget Rent A Car** (714-983-9691), **Dollar Rent A Car** (714-467-3600), and **Hertz Rent A Car** (714-986-2024). Less expensive car rentals include **Alamo Rent A Car** (714-983-2733), **Allstar Rent A Car** (714-983-2211), **Holiday Payless Rent A Car** (714-984-5551), **National Car Rental** (714-988-7444), and **Thrifty Car Rental** (714-988-8581). These agencies are located outside the airport but most provide pickup service.

Several agencies are located at the Palm Springs terminal: **Avis Rent A Car** (619-327-1353), **Budget Rent A Car** (619-327-1404), **Dollar Rent A Car** (619-325-7333), **Hertz Rent A Car** (619-778-5100), and **National Car Rental** (619-327-1438). Near the airport, a less expensive agency offering free airport pickup is **A-Best Rent A Car** (619-324-3825). For used cars try **A-Best Rent A Car** (619-324-3825) or **Foxy Wheels Rent A Car** (619-320-8299). There are four-wheel drives galore at **California Jeep Rentals** (Indian Canyon Way and Vista Chino, Palm Springs; 619-322-9799).

PUBLIC TRANSPORTATION

For local bus service in San Bernardino, Redlands and points in between call **OmniTrans** (714-825-8341). Riverside is served by the **Riverside Transit Agency** (714-682-1234).

In the Palm Springs area, **Sun Bus** (619-343-3451) carries passengers to destinations throughout the Coachella Valley. From Palm Springs, **Desert Stage Lines** (619-367-3581) provides transportation to Twentynine Palms.

From inland San Diego county, **Northeast Rural Bus System** (619-765-0145) takes passengers to Borrego Springs.

TAXIS

To hail a cab in Palm Springs, call **Caravan Cab** (619-346-2981) or **Desert Cab** (619-324-8233).

Hotels

Since the California desert is extremely popular with local residents, hotels are often quite crowded on weekends. Room rates tend to be less during the week and substantially lower in the torrid summer months.

INLAND EMPIRE HOTELS

SAN BERNARDINO MOUNTAINS

Saddleback Inn (300 South Route 173, Lake Arrowhead; 714-336-3571) beautifully plays the role of mountain lodge. A vintage 1917 structure—complete with steep-pitched roof, gables, and stone chimney—it's a 34-unit bed and breakfast. The architecture is a mix of formal and country styles and the location is just a few blocks from Lake Arrowhead. A restaurant and lounge round out the amenities in the main building, but the true attraction is the cluster of cottages dotting the property. Similar to the lodge rooms, they feature washed pine furniture, Laura Ashley designs, fireplaces, and tile baths with jacuzzi tubs. Deluxe to ultra-deluxe.

For moderate-priced accommodations, head uphill about a mile from the lake. **Arrowhead Tree Top Lodge** (27992 Rainbow Drive, Lake Arrowhead; 714-337-2311), an attractive woodframe motel, has 20 units available. Paneled in knotty pine, they are carpeted wall to wall and equipped with veneer furniture. There are also suites with kitchens at deluxe cost. Pool.

A rare find indeed, **Holiday Haven** (Route 18, Big Bear Lake; 714-866-2340) is a group of six log cabins set amid a ponderosa pine grove. Cramped but cozy, each house has a living room with fireplace, bedroom, and kitchen. The interior is done in knotty pine (which seems obligatory among these old-time cabins) and furnished with an eclectic assortment of scuffed tables and upholstered armchairs. The bathrooms are little bigger than closets and have stall showers rather than tubs. But for these budget rates (moderate in winter) most people are willing to bathe standing up.

For a location right on Big Bear Lake, you need look no further than **Shore Acres Lodge** (40090 Lakeview Drive; 714-866-8200). Here 11 woodframe cabins rest in the shade of a pine grove. Each is a full-facility unit with living room, bedroom, and kitchen; several feature two bedrooms and can easily sleep a family. The interiors are bland but quite trim and contemporary. Located away from the main road, Shore Acres is a quiet, private enclave with a pool, jacuzzi, dock, and swings. Moderate to deluxe.

The **Knickerbocker Mansion** (869 South Knickerbocker Road, Big Bear Lake; 714-866-8221), a three-story log cabin built in 1920, represents the perfect mountain retreat. Resting amid two acres of piney woods and bordering a national forest, the historic house is still within walking distance of Big Bear Lake and a major commercial district. With ten guest rooms, the Knickerbocker Mansion and an adjacent carriage house convey a feeling of comfortable rusticity. A double-sided stone fireplace, split-log staircase, and two-story veranda add to the architectural sophistication. They're complemented in the guest rooms by antique furnishings and patchwork quilts. Accommodations with shared or private baths are deluxe to ultra-deluxe.

REDLANDS-RIVERSIDE

Other than being the second largest city in the Inland Empire, San Bernardino has little to recommend it. Since the intersection of Routes 10 and 215 lies along the edge of town, many desert travelers use San Bernardino as a jumping off point, though few remain more than one night. One of the most convenient motel strips is Hospitality Lane, a frontage road adjacent to Route 10. **La Quinta Motor Inn** (205 East Hospitality Lane; 714-888-7571), a representative sample, has 153 units at moderate prices.

In neighboring Redlands, the **Morey Mansion Bed & Breakfast Inn** (190 Terracina Boulevard; 714-793-7970), with its French mansard roof and onion dome, is nothing short of spectacular. An 1890-era Victorian, the inn is garnished with Italianate balustrades, Gothic arched windows, beveled glass from Belgium and France, and hand-carved oak. The sitting rooms are museum quality examples of the age of Victorian architecture and the five upstairs bedrooms are embellished with rare fixtures and antique furnishings. Accommodations in this big, old, marvelous house are priced deluxe to ultra-deluxe.

The **Mission Inn** (3649 7th Street, Riverside; 714-784-0300), the region's most luxurious hotel and one of the most famous hostelries in the country, is slated to re-open in late 1992. Originally constructed in the 19th century, the hotel has been completely renovated to preserve its elegant and original design. A veritable palace, the Mission Inn features an arched entranceway that extends a full city block, Oriental gardens, and a cloister complete with music room and museum. The rotunda curves upward to a galeria where there are now meeting rooms and office space. There is also a chapel with Tiffany windows and a 19th-century gold-leaf altar from Mexico. When the hotel finally opens again, following several years of work, it undoubtedly will be the cynosure of the entire Inland Empire.

SOUTHERN INLAND EMPIRE

The **Virginia Lee Bed & Breakfast Hotel** (248 East Main Street, San Jacinto; 714-654-2270) occupies an 1884 clapboard building and offers 12 rooms at budget to moderate prices. Highlights of this historic hotel are the parlor, with its bonnet collection, and the yard, a pretty garden with shade trees and fountain. The accommodations are small but comfortable and feature either shared or private baths. In some cases the furniture is antique, in other instances it's simply old. Generally, however, the place conveys a sense of ease and tradition.

Murrieta Hot Springs (39405 Murrieta Hot Springs Road, Murrieta; 714-677-7451), an historic health spa, has rooms available at moderate to deluxe prices. These include use of the resort's mineral bath facilities. For further information, consult the "Sightseeing" section in this chapter.

At long last there's a proper bed and breakfast in the scenic Temecula Valley wine country. **Loma Vista Bed and Breakfast** (33350 La Serena Way, Temecula; 714-676-7047) is a classy, Mission-style hilltop home overlooking vineyards. It offers a choice of six spacious designer rooms, each done in a different decorative motif. Guests share a lovely living room with a fireplace and take breakfast family-style in a formal dining room. Deluxe.

Strawberry Creek Inn (26370 Route 243; 714-659-3202) is a rambling old mountain home nestled among the pines and oaks of the San Jacinto Mountains. Country-decorated and carefully maintained, it offers a cozy, cabin-in-the-woods atmosphere within walking distance from Idyllwild's busy village center. Guests can choose from several original rooms in the main house or newer ones in an added wing at the rear. A full gourmet breakfast is served in a bright, cheery wraparound dining porch. Moderate to deluxe.

A place with a name like **Knotty Pine Cabins** (54340 Pine Crest Drive, Idyllwild; 714-659-2933) could easily devolve into a self-parody. But there they are, eight woodframe cabins nestled in a conifer grove. Nicely secluded yet still within walking distance of town, the units feature fireplaces, homespun decorations, and knotty-pine walls. Most offer a living room, bedroom, and kitchen, and price in the moderate to deluxe range; one cabin, the "Sleepy Pine," is a single room without kitchen at a budget price. You can also rent houses and cabins in Idyllwild through a local agency, **Associated Idyllwild Rentals** (P.O. Box 43, Idyllwild, CA 92349).

LOW DESERT HOTELS

PALM SPRINGS AREA

The Abbey West (772 Prescott Drive; 619-325-0229) is a flashback to the old days in Palm Springs, when movie stars and starlets slipped away from Hollywood for some private sun time in the desert. Sixteen handsome rooms form a low-rise horseshoe around a landscaped pool and outdoor spa. Custom-designed furniture, whimsical framed artwork, private patios, and kitchenettes make these ultra-deluxe-priced accommodations comfortable for a week-long stay.

Travelers interested in rubbing elbows with show-biz types should consider the elegant little **Ingleside Inn** (200 West Ramon Road; 619-325-0046). Garbo slept here, they say, and Sinatra, Schwarzenneger and Shields. And why not? The double rooms, villas, and minisuites are cozy, charming, and laden with unusual antiques. Extras include fireplaces, private steambaths, and terraces, but everyone gets the same old-fashioned (i.e., attentive) service at this ultra-deluxe-priced inn.

The **Mira Loma Hotel** (1420 North Indian Canyon Drive; 619-320-1178), a conservatively styled complex, has 14 rooms surrounding a pool.

The interior patio is lined with flagstones and planted with citrus trees, creating an attractive desert environment. Laid out in the fashion of a motel, Mira Loma's guest rooms are moderate to deluxe in price and very spacious; most have dressing areas and some are equipped with kitchens.

Located in a quiet residential neighborhood, the **Tuscany Manor** (350 Chino Canyon Road; 619-325-2349) is only a few blocks from the foothills of the San Jacintos. All 24 units are one- and two-bedroom apartments complete with full kitchen facilities. The furniture is undistinguished and out-of-date, though generally acceptable. The true attraction is the courtyard, a beautifully landscaped plot with pool, jacuzzi, and shuffleboard. Rates start in the deluxe range during winter and are moderate the rest of the year.

The ultra-deluxe-priced private villas at **La Mancha Private Villas and Court Club** (444 Avenida Caballeros; 619-323-1773) are the last word in romantic escapism. Spanish-Moroccan architecture, high arched windows, and massive ceiling beams give the 54 accommodations an almost castlelike ambience. All the villas have private courtyards; many, private pools. Spa and in-room dining are among the amenities.

Out on the southern edge of Palm Springs, **Tiki Spa Hotel** (1910 South Camino Real; 619-327-1349) is a 28-unit facility occupying almost two acres. Polynesian in style, it offers jacuzzis, saunas, swimming pool, game room, and a restaurant. The accommodations vary from hotel rooms to apartment units, with the latter featuring kitchens and private patios. Deluxe in winter, moderate the rest of the year.

Guests at any of the 240-plus accommodations at the **Ritz-Carlton Rancho Mirage** (68-9000 Frank Sinatra Drive, Rancho Mirage; 619-321-8282) have only to open the french doors to their patio or balcony to enjoy a commanding view of the entire Palm Springs area. Located on a 650-foot-high plateau in the Santa Rosa Mountain foothills, this is a 24-acre hotel and tennis resort. Fine artwork, custom fabrics, antiques, crown moldings, and luxury-level amenities are standard in the rooms; the suites are truly elegant. Ultra-deluxe.

La Serena Cottages/Sequoia Bungalows (344 South Cahuilla Road; 619-325-3216) is one of those places people come back to year after year. A colony of semi-detached houses, it offers guests a home-like atmosphere with yards, flowerbeds, and two swimming pools. While some units resemble standard hotel rooms, others are one-bedroom apartments with kitchens and patios. Located in a residential neighborhood, La Serena, true to its claim, is "clean, quaint, and quiet." Cottages begin in the moderate range; larger units are deluxe.

Mountain View Inn (200 South Cahuilla Road; 619-325-5281), one block away, rests within shouting distance of the San Jacintos. Another small, personalized hotel, its 11 guest rooms are situated around two swimming pools. Each room is slightly different in decor and all have kitchens.

The grounds are tenderly maintained, with flower gardens, palm trees, and poolside umbrellas. Moderate to deluxe.

With its overweening wealth, Palm Springs inevitably possesses numerous luxury resorts. Unlike many, **Villa Royale Inn** (1620 South Indian Trail; 619-327-2314) displays its richness in an understated, personalized fashion. The owners spent six years buying antiques in Europe and shipping them home to furnish their sumptuous bed and breakfast inn. Every room of this walled-in complex follows an individual theme, reflecting the art and culture of a different European country. Many have kitchens, fireplaces, and private patios. Covering more than three acres, the grounds are a series of interior courtyards framed by pillars and planted in bougainvillea. Amid brick footpaths and asymmetrical gardens are two swimming pools, jacuzzis, and a restaurant. Room tabs here in Eden are moderate to deluxe for standard rooms and ultra-deluxe for larger rooms with private outdoor patio spas and suites.

The hot mineral pools which the Agua Caliente Indians originally discovered are today part of the **Spa Hotel and Mineral Springs** (100 North Indian Avenue; 619-325-1461). Bubbling from the ground at 106° and containing 32 trace minerals, the waters made Palm Springs famous. They have also made the Spa Hotel a unique resort. On the grounds are two Roman-style tubs, an outsize swimming pool, a rooftop solarium and spa facilities including inhalation rooms, dry saunas and mineral baths, all free to guests. For an extra charge, lodgers can enjoy herbal wraps and massages or join in exercise classes in the gymnasium. The entire hotel is lavishly decorated with pastel-hued carpets, upholstered armchairs, and contemporary oil paintings. Guest rooms, pegged in the deluxe and ultra-deluxe categories, are equally as fashionable.

If you listen to their publicity agents, many resorts are destinations unto themselves, providing everything a traveler could possibly desire. **Two Bunch Palms** (67-425 Two Bunch Palms Trail, Desert Hot Springs; 619-329-8791) is an entire oasis unto itself, a world of hot mineral baths surrounded by ancient palm trees. This exclusive 28-acre retreat, with its guarded entrance, serves as a hideaway for Hollywood celebrities.

They've been visiting since the 1930s, when mobster Al Capone reputedly built the place. According to local lore, Capone turned an oasis into a fortress, constructing a stone house with a lookout turret and secret escape tunnel. The gangster's gambling casino has given way to a gourmet restaurant and his ultra-secure hideout has become an informal resort. Guests soak in two hot mineral pools, utilize a spa facility with saunas and massage therapists, and wander an estate which includes lawns, tennis courts, swimming pool, nude sunbathing areas, and a koi pond. Deluxe to ultra-deluxe.

Desert Hot Springs also offers lower-priced facilities, many of which are parked along Hacienda Drive. **Linda Vista Lodge** (67-200 Hacienda

Drive; 619-329-6401) is a motel-style establishment with 42 rooms clustered around two hot mineral pools. There are also saunas and jacuzzis; budget.

GAY HOTELS With almost 30 resorts and hotels serving a gay clientele, Palm Springs is a major vacation destination for both gay men and women. Lodgings range from small six-unit bed and breakfast inns to deluxe resorts and serve singles, couples, or a mix of both.

Alexander Resort (598 Grenfall Road; 619-327-6911) offers eight garden apartments, five of which are equipped with kitchenettes. Tastefully appointed and featuring individual patios, these moderately priced guesthouses are surrounded by landscaped grounds, a spa, and swimming pool. The resort affords complete privacy and allows nude sunbathing. Men only.

Harlow Club Hotel (175 East El Alameda; 619-323-3977) bills itself as "a civilized Eden." Surrounded by tropical gardens, it features Spanish-style 1930s-era bungalows. Guest rooms, designed in award-winning style, include fireplaces and private patios. There's also a gymnasium, spa, and rooftop sun deck for guests. Men only. Deluxe.

The **Desert Knight Hotel** (435 Avenida Olancha; 619-325-5456) is a moderate-priced establishment that plays host to both gay men and women. Each of the eight studio units comes with a kitchen and private patio and there is a swimming pool in a garden setting.

Spread across two acres, **Hacienda En Sueño** (586 Warm Sands Drive; 619-327-8111) is an upscale retreat with seven one-bedroom apartments. There are gardens, trees, and grassy areas at this refined, ultra-deluxe-priced getaway. All men.

A women-only establishment, **Smoke Tree Villa Hotel** (1586 East Palm Canyon Drive; 619-323-2231) offers rooms and a suite with kitchen facilities. This bed-and-breakfast facility is open year round.

JOSHUA TREE AND ANZA-BORREGO

A desert traveler could not ask for more than a rustic, family inn in a palm oasis. Located in a natural setting within eyeshot of Joshua Tree National Monument headquarters, **29 Palms Inn** (73950 Inn Avenue, Twentynine Palms; 619-367-3505) has 12 adobe cottages and three renovated, old-frame cottages. With fireplaces, country decor, and sturdy old furniture, they bear personalized names like "Ghost Flower" and "Fiddle Neck." This marvelous inn, encompassing 70 acres, was founded in 1928 and has been in the same family for three generations. Pool, restaurant, lounge; moderate.

Anza-Borrego's premier hostelry is **La Casa del Zorro** (Borrego Springs and Yaqui Pass roads, Borrego Springs; 619-767-5323), a desert hideaway in a garden setting. Spread across several acres, the resort is a collection of Spanish-style buildings positioned around several swimming pools and jacuzzis. There are tennis courts, a restaurant, and a cozy lounge. The Southwestern-theme lobby contains spacious sitting rooms finished with washed pine. Guest rooms vary from small traditional motel rooms at deluxe prices in high season to lavish suites and casitas with fireplaces, private patios, and desert accouterments (ultra-deluxe).

The **Oasis Motel** (366 Palm Canyon Drive [West Route S22], Borrego Springs; 619-767-5409) is a small seven-unit establishment. Set amid palm trees and offering views of the mountains, it has rooms with or without kitchens available at moderate cost.

Restaurants

INLAND EMPIRE RESTAURANTS

SAN BERNARDINO MOUNTAINS

At nearby **Cedar Glen Inn** (28942 Hook Creek Road, Cedar Glen; 714-337-8999), a simple, wood-paneled café, they serve breakfast until 3 p.m. at budget rates. There is a sandwich lunch menu and they serve dinner as well, but the bargain here is eggs, eggs, eggs.

Praised by critics far and wide as Big Bear Lake's finest restaurant, the **Iron Squirrel** (646 Pine Knot Boulevard; 714-866-9121) is a class act indeed. It's quite a delight to find escargots, duckling in orange sauce, and cherries jubilee at a restaurant deep in the mountains. But here it is, a fine French country dining room. Dinner and Sunday brunch only; deluxe.

In English the name is "gingerbread house," so you won't have any trouble spotting **George & Sigi's Knusperhauschen** (829 West Big Bear Boulevard, Big Bear Lake; 714-585-8640). Looking more like a prop from "Snow White" than a fine restaurant, Knusperhauschen will further surprise you with both the quantity and quality of its European-style cuisine. Sauerbraten, Hungarian goulash, Polish sausage, stuffed cabbage, and seven kinds of schnitzel are among the specialties. Dinner only; moderate to deluxe.

REDLANDS-RIVERSIDE

In San Bernardino, check out **GuadalaHarry's** (280 East Hospitality Lane; 714-824-6903), a hacienda-style Mexican restaurant. With its brilliantly colored walls, interior balcony, and serape decor, the place evokes a sense of the high life in Old Mexico. Despite the ironwork and handcarved beams, this multichambered establishment is budget-priced. The menu presents a medley of burrito, *chimichanga*, and taco dishes as well as *favoritos Mexicanos* like fajitas, flautas, and chili. Lunch and dinner.

Griswold's Smorgasbord (Route 10 at Ford Street offramp, Redlands; 714-793-2158) is one of those common-denominator, all-you-can-eat places that draw crowds with bargain basement prices. You're liable to find one or two dozen different salads, scores of pies, a half-dozen hot entrées, and many, many other items at this endless buffet. Budget.

SOUTHERN INLAND EMPIRE

Ask for a table in the vault at **The Bank** (28645 Front Street, Temecula; 714-676-6160) and withdraw your favorite Mexican dishes at budget prices. Housed in the 1913 First National Bank of Temecula building, this is the town's most unusual restaurant. The enchiladas, quesadillas, fajitas, and tacos, served at lunch and dinner, make it the area's favorite Mexican eatery.

Café Champagne (32575 Rancho California Road, Temecula; 714-699-0088) is ideally located overlooking the vineyards at the John Culbertson Winery. The elegant California-style decor makes this the perfect spot to sip champagne or wine. Entrée choices vary but typically include angelhair primavera and a mixed seafood grill. They even serve a gourmet burger for lunch and dinner. Moderate to deluxe.

The local gathering place up in the mile-high town of Idyllwild is **Jan's Red Kettle** (54220 North Circle Drive; 714-659-4063). Homey as a log cabin, it's a knotty-pine café with lace curtains. Breakfast items fill about half the menu and include *huevos rancheros*, "old-fashioned oatmeal," omelettes, and biscuits with gravy. Completing the daily offerings are soups, salads, hamburgers, and sandwiches. No dinner; moderate.

Among Idyllwild's finest restaurants is **Gastrognome** (54381 Ridgeview Drive; 714-659-5055), a pretty woodframe place with a stone fireplace and beam ceiling. The selections are diverse, portions plentiful, and the food delicious. Beef tournedos, Australian lobster, and rack of lamb head the menu; also included are calamari, chicken Kiev, and a variety of seafood pasta dishes and fresh fish. Dinner and Sunday brunch; moderate to deluxe.

Italian food in these parts is spelled **Michelli's** (Route 243, Idyllwild; 714-659-3919). This traditional dining room features four different parmigiana dishes—veal, eggplant, chicken, and zucchini. Open for dinner nightly, they also have seafood entrées, lasagna, fettucine, and canneloni at moderate prices. Or if you prefer pizza . . .

LOW DESERT RESTAURANTS

PALM SPRINGS AREA

Everybody's favorite lunch counter is **Louise's Pantry** (124 South Palm Canyon Drive; 619-325-5124), a landmark café so popular with the local gentry that people are inevitably lined up outside the door. A plastic-and-formica eatery painted sickly yellow, it provides standard American fare at budget to moderate prices. Settle into a booth or pull up a counter stool and dine on meat loaf, pork chops, or jumbo shrimp.

A spacious hacienda with murals, fountains, and inlaid tile, **Las Casuelas Terraza** (222 South Palm Canyon Drive; 619-325-2794) is a classic Hispanic dining room. Pass through the archways and you'll discover hanging plants and exquisite wrought-iron decorations throughout. A step above other Mexican restaurants, the establishment serves *pollo asado* (marinated chicken), *pescado greco* (fish filet in garlic and wine), and *camarones florencio* (shrimp in salsa), as well as standard south-of-the-border fare. Lunch and dinner; moderate.

Perrina's (340 North Palm Canyon Drive; 619-325-6544) features an old-time San Francisco-style bar and an excellent little restaurant. Photos of athletes are parked on the walls and the place projects an air of being unpretentious but ever-popular. You're liable to find the bar open anytime, but the kitchen works only in the evening. That's when the chef prepares scampi, veal *saltimbocca*, prime beef, and numerous pasta dishes. Moderate to deluxe.

If you do nothing but admire the stained glass at **Lyon's English Grille** (233 East Palm Canyon Drive; 619-327-1551), it will prove worth the price of admission. This grand British dining room displays a museum-quality collection of plates, Toby jugs, and art pieces from Olde England. The bill of fare at this enchanting establishment includes steak-and-kidney pie, braised lamb shank, roast duckling, prime rib, calf's liver, and fresh seafood. Dinner only; moderate to deluxe.

For entertainment with your dinner, make reservations at **Moody's Supper Club** (123 North Palm Canyon Drive; 619-323-1806). You'll dine in an intimate lounge on a sumptuous variety of chicken, steak, fish, and pasta dishes. An ensemble with four vocalists and a pianist will perform songs from Broadway musicals; and at the conclusion of this festive but relaxed evening, the waiter will present you with a deluxe dinner tab.

Melvyn's (200 West Ramon Road, in the Ingleside Inn; 619-325-2323) is one of those famous establishments with as many awards on the wall as items on the menu. Among the toniest addresses in town, it's a classic continental restaurant complete with mirrors, crystal chandeliers, and upholstered armchairs. Celebrities have frequented the place for years. Among its other attributes is an inventory of entrées that features Norwegian salmon hollandaise, Milanese shrimp scampi, châteaubriand, filet dijonnaise, and rack of lamb. Lunch and dinner; deluxe to ultra-deluxe.

Le Vallauris (385 West Tahquitz Canyon Way; 619-325-5059) is an enclave of country French cuisine and decor just off the main drag. A piano bar sets the tone in this converted private residence for rich dishes such as duck and foie gras and New Zealand venison. Velvet armchairs and a garden of ficus trees and blooming cyclamen warm up this attractive two-room restaurant. Deluxe to ultra-deluxe.

In a town noted for celebrities, it's logical that the top must-see restaurant in Palm Springs is **Bono** (1700 North Indian Canyon Way; 619-322-6200), formerly owned by entertainer-turned-mayor Sonny Bono. The Northern-Italian and American menu may include homemade pastas, fresh seafood or steaks. Moderate to deluxe.

Kam Lum (66610 8th Street, Desert Hot Springs; 619-251-1244), a small café set in a mini-mall, serves Cantonese dishes at budget prices. Open for lunch and dinner, they offer chow mein, chop suey, egg foo yung, and a dozen specialty dishes.

El Gallito Café (68-820 Grove Street, Cathedral City; 619-328-7794) is a cheap, funky, bare-bones Mexican restaurant with good food at even better prices. There are piñatas and hokey paintings on the walls and some talented people back in the kitchen. The crowd is local, the menu solid and predictable. Budget.

Tucked away in a highway-side shopping center, **Cattails** (69-369 Route 111, Cathedral City; 619-324-8263) rewards its patrons with a romantic candlelit setting with background classical music. Their changing menu features classical French cuisine with a southwestern flavor, each dish beautifully presented and tabbed at deluxe prices.

Seafood provides a welcome change of pace in the landlocked desert. **Scoma's of San Francisco** (69-620 Route 111, Rancho Mirage; 619-328-9000) specializes in shrimp, prawns, crab, scallops, and fish much like its namesake restaurant up on Fisherman's Wharf. Every entrée is served with a dish of pasta and fresh vegetables in this peach-and-Celadon green restaurant, nicely lit from upturned seashell fixtures. Moderate to deluxe.

Cedar Creek Inn (73-445 El Paseo, Palm Desert; 619-340-1236) is a little old-fashioned, which might be the reason it's so popular with local residents. White walls, flowery curtains, and oak booths are a trademark here. The cuisine, accordingly, is American, with such entrées as fresh salmon, New York steak, beef *médaillons*, and rack of lamb. Lunch and dinner; moderate to deluxe.

JOSHUA TREE AND ANZA-BORREGO

Near the northern entrance to Joshua Tree National Monument, **29 Palms Inn** (73950 Inn Avenue, Twentynine Palms; 619-367-3505) is a homespun restaurant with a friendly staff and family photos on the walls. Situated in a rustic hotel, it serves American cuisine at lunch and dinner. There's grilled halibut, steak, lobster, steamed vegetables, and several daily specials. Moderate.

With whitewashed walls, *viga* ceilings, and candle sconces, the dining room at **La Casa del Zorro** (Borrego Springs and Yaqui Pass roads, Borrego Springs; 619-767-5323) is Southwestern in atmosphere. Part of a lavish resort complex, the restaurant serves three meals daily, offering guests a traditional selection of dishes. Among the entrées are scampi, Alaskan salmon, chicken cordon bleu, veal chops, prime rib, and rack of lamb. Deluxe.

Never let it be said that the seclusion of the desert prevents local folks from enjoying a hearty Mexican meal. **El Mexicali Café** (on Route S22 in Borrego Springs; 619-767-4365) is nothing to write back to civilization about, but they serve a passable dinner at budget prices.

Out toward the eastern border of Anza-Borrego Desert State Park, **Burro Bend Restaurant** (Route 78 near Ocotillo Wells; 619-767-5970) provides café-type meals at budget cost. You've seen the place in a thousand locales—ham and eggs in the morning, hamburgers for lunch, and steak and seafood at dinner.

The Great Outdoors

The Sporting Life

FISHING

Lakes in the Inland Empire and Low Desert areas offer a variety of fishing opportunities. Alpine Trout Lakes, Silverwood Lake State Recreation Area, Lake Perris State Recreation Area, Lake Arrowhead, Big Bear Lake, and the Salton Sea are stocked with an assortment of fish, including trout, bass, catfish, bluegill, corbina, croaker, sargo, and tilapia.

For fishing boat and equipment rentals contact **Silverwood Lake State Recreation Area Marina** (619-389-2320), **Big Bear Marina** (Lakeview Drive, Big Bear; 714-866-3218), **Pleasure Point Landing** (603 Landlock Landing Road, South Shore, Big Bear Lake; 714-866-2455), **Gray's Landing** (North Shore, Big Bear Lake; 714-866-2443), **Bob's Playa Riviera** (10565 Route 111, North Shore, Salton Sea; 619-345-1835), and **Bombay Marina** (Route 111, Bombay Beach, Salton Sea; 619-348-1694).

BOATING, CANOEING, WATERSKIING

For boating and canoeing expeditions on mountain lakes and the Salton Sea, contact **Pine Knot Landing** (439 Pine Knot Avenue, Big Bear Lake; 714-866-2628), and for rentals **Pleasure Point Landing** (603 Landlock Landing Road, South Shore, Big Bear Lake; 714-866-2455).

GOLF

Golfers in the San Bernardino Mountains can try **El Rancho Verde Country Club** (Country Club Drive, Rialto; 714-875-5346) or **Shandin Hills Golf Club** (3380 North Little Mountain Drive, San Bernardino; 714-886-0669). Around Big Bear Lake you'll have to settle for the nine-hole **Bear Mountain Golf Course** (43100 Clubview Drive, Moonridge; 714-585-8002).

Palm Springs golfers, on the other hand, will think they have died and gone to heaven. This desert oasis is chockablock with courses open to the public, including **Palm Springs Municipal Golf Course** (1885 Golf Club Drive, Palm Springs; 619-328-1005), **Canyon South Golf Course** (1097 Murray Canyon Drive, Palm Springs; 619-327-2019), **Mesquite Country Club** (2700 East Mesquite Avenue, Palm Springs; 619-323-1502), **Desert**

Falls Country Club (1111 Desert Falls Parkway, Palm Desert; 619-341-4020), **Oasis Country Club** (42-300 Casbah Way, Palm Desert; 619-345-2715), **Palm Desert Resort Country Club** (77-333 Country Club Drive, Palm Desert; 619-345-2791), and **De Anza–Palm Springs Country Club** (36-200 Date Palm Drive, Cathedral City; 619-328-1315).

In Indio, try **Indio Municipal Golf Course** (83-040 Avenue 42; 619-347-9156).

TENNIS

For the tennis set, there are a few public courts around Big Bear Lake. Contact the local park district at 714-866-3652 for locations.

In Palm Springs, public courts are located at **Demuth Park** (4365 Mesquite Avenue; 619-323-8272), **Palm Springs Tennis Center** (1300 Baristo Road; 619-320-0020) and **Ruth Hardy Park** (Tamarisk Road and Avenida Caballeros). In Desert Hot Springs, try **Wardman Park** (66150 8th Street). Courts in Indio are available at **South Jackson Park** (Jackson Street and Date Avenue; 619-347-3484) and **Miles Avenue Park** (Miles Avenue).

Also, check local papers for information on weekly events and activities sponsored by private clubs.

HORSEBACK RIDING AND WAGON TOURS

In Palm Springs, **Smoke Tree Stables** (2500 Toledo Avenue; 619-327-1372) offers guided rides through stunning desert terrain. **Covered Wagon Tours** (La Quinta; 619-347-2161) hosts pioneer-style desert tours.

BALLOONING

You can soar through the desert skies in a balloon manned by **American Balloon Society** (Palm Springs; 619-568-6700), **Desert Balloon Charters** (Palm Desert; 619-346-8575), or **Sunrise Balloons** (800-548-9912; in Palm Springs, Borrego Springs, and Temecula).

BICYCLING

Cycling is popular throughout the Inland Empire and Low Desert. There's mountain riding in the San Bernardino Mountains, desert cycling around Palm Springs, Joshua Tree, and Anza-Borrego, and recreational riding in the regional park areas.

Many of the regional and national parks listed in the "Beaches and Parks" section of this chapter have miles of bicycle trails, including **Silverwood Lake State Recreation Area** and **Lake Perris State Recreation Area**. Riding in **Anza-Borrego** and **Joshua Tree** is also very good.

Mountain riding is popular around **Lake Arrowhead** and **Big Bear Lake**, especially on forest service roads. The north shore of Big Bear Lake is a popular route, as is **Skyline Drive** (Route 2N10), a graded road which travels past Snow Summit to the Goldmine Ski area. Another graded thoroughfare, **Sand Canyon Road** (Route 2N27) in the Moonridge district, is also a lovely ride.

Thirty-five miles of bike trails encircle **Palm Springs**. Popular riding spots include the luxurious residential neighborhoods, the Mesquite Country Club area, the Indian Canyons, and around the local parks. A notable trail is the ten-mile long **White Water Wash** which begins in Palm Springs and extends into Palm Desert. Check with bike rental shops for more tour information.

BIKE RENTALS For bike rentals, contact **Sports Country Limited** (222 North G Street, San Bernardino, 714-884-1273), **Skyline Ski and Sports** (653 Pine Knot Boulevard, Big Bear Lake; 714-866-3501), **Mac's Bike Rental** (70155 Route 111, Rancho Mirage; 619-327-5721), **Burnett's Bicycle Barn** (429 South Sunrise Way, Palm Springs; 619-325-7844), and **Canyon Bicycle Rentals and Tours** (305 East Arenas, Palm Springs; 619-327-7688).

Beaches and Parks

INLAND EMPIRE BEACHES AND PARKS

San Bernardino National Forest—The most popular national forest in the country, this 633,000-acre park encompasses Lake Arrowhead, Big Bear Lake, and a half-dozen ski areas. It's divided into two sections, one covering the San Bernardino Mountains and eastern section of the San Gabriel Mountains, the other extending across the San Jacinto Mountains. Topographically, the preserve reaches from desert to mountains, Joshua trees to Jeffrey pines. There are six peaks over 10,000 feet high, three wilderness areas, and 470 miles of hiking trails (as well as a 200-mile section of the Pacific Crest Trail). Skiers, anglers, and boaters will also find complete amenities.

Facilities: Picnic areas, restrooms, showers; restaurants and groceries are in nearby towns; information, 714-383-5588. *Camping:* Permitted in 50 campgrounds. *Fishing:* The park's 110 miles of streams teem with trout, crappie, bluegill, and smallmouth bass.

Getting there: Route 18 north of San Bernardino is the main highway through the national forest's northern section. Routes 74 and 243, between Hemet and Palm Springs, lead through the southern portion.

Silverwood Lake State Recreation Area—A 976-acre lake and 13 miles of hiking trails make this park a prime destination. It's located at 3355 feet elevation in the San Bernardino Mountains. Except for the recreation area and marina, Silverwood remains undeveloped, a great place to swim and fish. Almost 130 species of birds have been spotted here; coyotes, bobcats, and ring-tailed cats range the forested slopes that encircle the lake.

Facilities: Restrooms, picnic areas, snack bar, store, boat rental, lifeguards; information, 619-389-2303. *Camping:* Permitted. *Fishing:* Trout, bass, bluegill, and other fish inhabit the lake.

Getting there: Located on Route 138 about 30 miles north of San Bernardino.

Glen Helen Regional Park—There are 500 acres of shady groves and chaparral-coated hills here at the foot of the San Bernardino Mountains. Two lakes stocked with trout and catfish, a one-mile nature trail through a marsh, and ample playground and picnic areas are among the features.

Facilities: Restrooms, showers, boat rentals, waterslide and other swimming equipment; restaurants and groceries are nearby in Devore; information, 714-880-2522. *Camping:* Only group camping is permitted here, but there is individual overnighting at **Yucaipa Regional Park** (33900 Oak Glen Road, Yucaipa; 714-790-3120).

Getting there: Located at 2555 Devore Road in Devore (near the intersection of Routes 15 and 215).

Lake Perris State Recreation Area—Another of the Inland Empire's attractive lakes, Perris is bounded by the Russell Mountains and Bernasconi Hills. It features rock-climbing areas, a sandy beach for swimming, boat rentals, and a nine-mile bike trail around the lake. More than 100 bird species have been spotted here, including ducks and geese, and the eastern shore is open seasonally to hunters. Everything from lizards to mule deer inhabits the surrounding sage scrub countryside.

Facilities: Picnic areas, restrooms, showers, lifeguards, marina, waterslide; information, 714-657-0676. *Camping:* Permitted. *Fishing:* Try for bass, trout, catfish, and bluegill.

Getting there: Located at 17801 Lake Perris Drive in Perris.

Lake Elsinore State Park—Bounded by a large lake on one side and lofty mountains on another, this popular park is inevitably filled with anglers, boaters, and aquatic enthusiasts of all stripes. Far from idyllic, the recreation area consists of a sprawling parking lot fringed with palm trees and campsites.

Facilities: Picnic area, restrooms, showers, playground, snack bar, boat rentals; restaurants and groceries are nearby; information, 714-674-3177. *Camping:* Permitted. *Fishing:* Good, when water level is high.

Getting there: Located on Route 74 two miles southwest of the intersection with Route 15.

Mount San Jacinto State Park—Extending from Idyllwild in the west to Palm Springs in the east, this magnificent preserve encompasses a broad swath of the San Jacinto Mountains. It features mountain meadows and subalpine forests as well as granite peaks 10,000 feet high. The park itself cov-

(Text continued on page 416.)

The Salton Sea

One of California's strangest formations lies deep in the southern section of the state, just 30 miles from the Mexican border. The Salton Sea, a vast inland waterway 36 miles long and 15 miles wide, may be the biggest engineering blunder in history.

Situated 234 feet below sea level, directly atop the San Andreas Fault, the area has been periodically flooded by the Colorado River for eons. From six million until two million years ago forests covered the hillsides and local hollows were filled with lakes and streams. But as the region became increasingly arid, the lakes dried up, and for two million years the basin was desert.

Then in 1905 the irrigation system for the Imperial Valley went amok, the Colorado River overflowed its banks, and a flood two years in duration inundated the land. The Salton Sea was reborn. Because of present-day evaporation as well as minerals left by earlier seas, the water is ten percent saltier than the Pacific.

California's largest lake, it continues even today to grow from agricultural runoff. As you approach it from the north, this vast sea, ringed by palms and seeming to extend endlessly, resembles the ocean itself. Lying at the confluence of the Imperial and Coachella valleys, one of the lushest agricultural regions in the world, the Salton Sea possesses rare beauty. Along its northwest shore on Route 86, rows of date palms run to the water's edge and citrus orchards create a brilliant green landscape backdropped by chocolate-brown mountains. Other sections of shore, given over to trailer parks, mud flats, and alkali deposits, are astonishingly ugly.

The best place to fish and enjoy sandy beaches is at the **Salton Sea State Recreation Area** (619-393-3052) on Route 111. Long and narrow, this amazing park extends for 18 miles along the northeast shore. Since the lake represents California's richest inland fishery, there are great opportunities to fish for sargo, tilapia, and gulf croaker. Swimming is popular at each of the park's five campgrounds, but is best at Mecca Beach.

The Salton Sea supports 350 bird species, so birdwatchers also flock here in significant numbers. The best places to birdwatch are at Sneaker Beach, the marshes around Salt Creek Campground, and between the campgrounds at park headquarters and Mecca Beach.

Marinas and boat rentals are nearby, and at **North Shore Resort** (99115 Sea View Road, North Shore; 619-393-3071) you'll find a 48-unit motel nicely situated next to a marina and sandy beach. Offering standard rooms at budget prices, it has a lawn, pool, and shuffleboard court out back.

Restaurants are rather rare around the Salton Sea. So even a small family-owned-and-operated café like **The Sea Hut** (99241 Access Road, off Route 111; 619-393-3977) looks good. Serving American and Mexican cuisine, it sits about a block from the waterfront.

Further south lies the **Salton Sea National Wildlife Refuge** (entrances from Sinclair Road west of Calipatria and Vendel Road north of Westmorland; 619-348-5278). This preserve is a prime avian habitat as some 371 bird species have been sighted here, including stilts, pintails, green-winged teal, and the endangered Yuma clapper rail. The heightening of sea level has diminished the park's land area from 35,000 to 2000 acres, but you're still liable to see great blue herons wading along the shore and snow geese arriving for the winter.

ers about 3500 acres and an adjacent wilderness area extends across 10,000 acres.

Facilities: Picnic areas, restrooms, showers; information, 714-659-2607. *Camping:* Permitted in several campgrounds and hike-in camps. There is also camping at **Idyllwild County Park** (Idyllwild; 714-684-0196 for reservations or 714-659-2656 for information).

Getting there: Located on Route 243 in Idyllwild; the park can also be reached via the aerial tramway in Palm Springs.

LOW DESERT BEACHES AND PARKS

Lake Cahuilla County Park—Stark is the word for this place. It's a manmade lake with dirt banks, very little vegetation, and bald mountains looming in every direction. One section of the park has been landscaped with lawns and palm trees; the rest is as dusty as the surrounding desert. Since the lake is stocked with trout and catfish, most people come to fish, swim, or to camp.

Facilities: Picnic areas, restrooms, showers, lifeguards, playground; restaurants and groceries are several miles away in Indio; information, 619-564-4712. *Camping:* Permitted, with RV hookups and primitive sites. This park is locked at 10 p.m., so campers cannot go in or out until 6 a.m.

Getting there: Located at 58-075 Jefferson Street in Thermal.

Joshua Tree National Monument—Covering 850 square miles, most of it wilderness, this famous preserve lies on the border of California's High and Low deserts. It possesses characteristics of both the Mojave and Colorado deserts, ranging from Joshua tree forests at 4000 feet to ocotillo and cholla cactus at lower elevations. The preserve's granite hills offer sport for rock climbers, while its miles of hiking trails attract day-hikers and wilderness enthusiasts alike. The desert life includes tarantulas, roadrunners, sidewinders, golden eagles, and coyotes, but it is the desert plants that make the sanctuary truly special.

Facilities: Picnic areas, restrooms, museums; restaurants and groceries are located in towns outside the park; three information centers, 619-367-7511. *Camping:* Permitted in nine campgrounds; wilderness camping is also allowed with a permit.

Getting there: Entrances are off Route 62 in Joshua Tree and Twentynine Palms and off Route 10 east of Indio.

Anza-Borrego Desert State Park—Spreading across 600,000 acres of the Colorado Desert, this dusty behemoth is the largest state park in the contiguous United States. It's a tumbling region of jagged mountains, hidden springs, and deep sandstone canyons. The tree life ranges from palms at sea level to pines at 5000 feet; over 150 bird species have been sighted here. Hiking trails lead along the desert floor, through multihued valleys, and up into the mountains.

Facilities: Picnic areas, restrooms, showers; restaurants, groceries, and hotels are nearby in Borrego Springs; visitor center and museum; information, (619-767-5311). *Camping:* Permitted in two developed campgrounds and several primitive sites.

Getting there: Routes 78 and S22 lead into the park from both the east and west.

Agua Caliente County Park—Surrounded by Anza-Borrego Desert State Park, this scenic desert reserve measures 910 acres. It's located at 1300 feet elevation on the eastern slope of the Tierra Blanca Mountains. The greatest attraction here is the system of natural waters—four springs, one cool and pure, the others warm and sulfurous, percolate to the surface. As a result, the park has two pools—an outdoor wading area and an indoor pool with jacuzzi jets.

Facilities: Picnic areas, restrooms, store, hiking trails; information, 619-694-3049. *Camping:* Permitted here and at **Vallecito County Park** (619-565-3600).

Getting there: Located on Route S2, 23 miles south of Scissors Crossing; Vallecito Park is four miles north of Agua Caliente.

Hiking

SAN BERNARDINO MOUNTAINS TRAILS

Hikers will delight in the San Bernardino Mountains trails, with their sweeping views of valleys and surrounding peaks.

Pacific Crest Trail covers the entire length of the chain. It passes through pine forests, overlooks Big Bear Lake, and continues on to Lake Arrowhead before turning north toward Deep Creek.

Just above Mount Baldy Village, **Icehouse Canyon to Cucamonga Peak via Icehouse Saddle Trail** (6 miles) is an arduous hike through subalpine wilderness to an 8859-foot summit. The views are worth the struggle.

Another ascent, **San Bernardino Peak Trail** (4.7 miles) leads up the jagged slope of its 10,624-foot namesake, providing breathtaking vistas.

Serious hikers should not miss **Mt. San Gorgonio Trail** (8 miles). The highest peak in this range, 11,499-foot Mt. San Gorgonio presents an extraordinary challenge. The trail leads through meadows and past lakes to a summit high above the world.

The strenuous **Siberia Creek Trail** (7 miles) passes the largest known lodgepole pine, Champion Lodgepole, then continues through coniferous forest to the edge of a picturesque meadow. Here the route crosses Siberia Creek and descends Lookout Mountain to Siberia Creek Group Camp.

Near Lake Arrowhead, **Arboretum Trail** (.8 mile) offers a fascinating loop tour through deciduous and coniferous forests.

SAN JACINTO MOUNTAINS TRAILS

Rising high above the desert, the 10,000-foot San Jacinto Mountains present endless alpine hiking opportunities.

From Idyllwild County Park Visitor Center, **Deer Springs Trail** (3.8 miles) ascends Marion Ridge, past oak and pine forests to Suicide Rock (7510 feet), a granite monolith which offers spectacular views.

From Mountain Station at the top of the Palm Springs Aerial Tramway, there's an exhilarating hike along **Mt. San Jacinto Trail** (6.3 miles) to the 10,804-foot summit. A shorter, two-and-a-half mile trek leads through pine and white fir forest to Round Valley.

PALM SPRINGS AREA TRAILS

For those uninterested in playing golf or lolling about in swimming pools, the desert environs of Palm Springs offer numerous hiking adventures.

In Palm Springs, the **Museum Trail** (1 mile) ascends the mountain behind the Palm Springs Desert Museum. Markers along this nature trail describe the plant life and other features of the terrain.

For a splendid view of Palm Springs and the Coachella Valley, climb the **Shannon Trail** (3.5 miles), a steep hike which ascends 1522-foot Smoke Tree Mountain.

At the eastern end of the Living Desert Reserve sits **Eisenhower Mountain Trail** (3 miles). The path carries across a wash and up the mountain slope for sweeping views of the Coachella Valley.

Bear Creek Canyon Trail (2 miles), located near La Quinta, also probes a desert valley. In the spring this lovely area is alive with golden poppies and a bubbling creek.

Another vantage point is reached via **Edom Hill Trail** (3 miles). Located at the center of the Coachella Valley, this 1610-foot promontory offers views of Mt. San Jacinto, Mt. San Gorgonio, and the Salton Sea.

In Mecca Hills, **Painted Canyon Trail** (3 miles) explores a beautifully sculpted canyon.

JOSHUA TREE NATIONAL MONUMENT TRAILS

Joshua Tree National Monument is an area where the High Desert meets the Low Desert, providing marvelous hikes through both environments.

Ryan Mountain Trail (1.5 miles) is a prime place to view both the Joshua trees and granite outcroppings for which the park is renowned. This difficult trail, which leads to the top of Mt. Ryan (5470 feet), also offers views of several valleys.

Another sweeping vista is reached along **Mastodon Peak Trail** (2 miles). Atop the 3371-foot promontory, the Hexie Mountains, Pinto Basin, and the Salton Sea extend before you.

Hidden Valley Trail (1 mile), beginning near Hidden Valley Campground, is a twisting loop through boulder-strewn desert to a legendary cattle rustler's hideout.

From Canyon Road, **Fortynine Palms Oasis Trail** (1.5 miles) is a moderate hike to a refreshing desert oasis. Near Cottonwood Visitor Center, **Lost Palms Oasis Trail** (4 miles) leads through a canyon to another oasis, which sports the largest group of fan palms in the park.

Lost Horse Mine Trail (2 miles) takes you to an old gold mine. It's a moderately strenuous hike which should be avoided in hot weather— there is no shade or water en route. A less taxing trip for anyone intent on exploring abandoned diggings is the **Desert Queen Mine Trail** (.8 mile), located off Geology Tour Road (four-wheel drive only).

The **Cottonwood to Morton Mill Trail** (.5 mile) leads to a gold-refining mill.

For the hearty hiker, **Scout Trail** (7.8 miles) leaves from Indian Cove and traverses the western edge of Wonderland of Rocks.

Ideal for families, **Arch Rock Nature Trail** (.5 mile) in White Tank Campground wanders through intriguing rock formations while interpreting the geology of the region.

ANZA-BORREGO DESERT STATE PARK TRAILS

An arid landscape filled with desert wonders awaits hikers in Anza-Borrego. As with all desert hiking, you'll need plenty of water, protection from the sun, and a map of the area.

The most popular trail in Anza-Borrego Desert State Park is the **Borrego Palm Canyon Nature Trail** (1.5 miles). This short route leads to a palm grove and cool stream. If you're in good shape, you can continue up the canyon on **Borrego Palm Canyon Trail** (3 miles). There's a lot of boulder hopping, but the rewards are a palm-studded and colorful route.

In the Split Mountain area, rare elephant trees are the highlight of **Elephant Trees Discovery Loop Trail** (1 mile).

A steep climb along **Marshal South Home Trail** (1 mile) leads to ruins of a writer's home on top of Ghost Mountain. The trailhead is in the Blair Valley area.

Also in Blair Valley, **Morteros Trail** (.2 mile) leads to a field of large granite boulders used by Indians as bedrock mortars.

Nearby **Pictograph Trail** (1 mile) guides you to rocks painted by Diegueño Indians, then continues to a vista point above Vallecito Valley.

California Riding and Hiking Trail (6 miles) courses down a chaparral-covered mountain to the desert below. Lovely views of the Borrego Desert are seen from the ridge between Hellhole and Dry canyons. The trailhead is in the Culp Valley camp area.

From the Bow Willow area, **Mountain Palm Springs Canyon, North Fork** (1.3 miles) leads to a natural bowl ringed with more than 100 palm trees. **Mountain Palm Springs Canyon, South Fork** (1.5 miles) explores a pygmy palm grove and stand of elephant trees.

Travelers' Tracks

Sightseeing

INLAND EMPIRE

Extending south from the San Bernardino Mountains, California's Inland Empire encompasses the cities of San Bernardino, Redlands, and Riverside. Once a cattle-ranching region and later a prime citrus-growing area, this interior belt is presently being developed at a mind-boggling rate. For travelers it provides several possibilities: you can tour the San Bernardino Mountains, seek out sites in Riverside and Redlands, or continue further south to the Murrieta Hot Springs and the pine forests of Mt. San Jacinto.

SAN BERNARDINO MOUNTAINS

One of the highest ranges in California, the San Bernardino Mountains rise to over 11,000 feet elevation. Together with the San Gabriels to the west, they provide a pine-rimmed barrier between the Los Angeles Basin and Mojave Desert. A popular winter and water sports area, the mountains are encompassed within San Bernardino National Forest and offer a string of alpine lakes and lofty peaks.

During the 1860s prospectors combed the area in search of gold. After their luck petered out, loggers and cattle ranchers took over the territory. Later in the century, as dams created the mountain lakes, herds of tourists began roaming the landscape.

Today a single highway, Route 18, nicknamed "Rim of the World Drive," courses through the entire region. Beginning in Crestline, north of San Bernardino, it winds east to Big Bear Lake, offering postcard vistas of the San Bernardino region.

Before departing on this mountaintop cruise, follow Route 138 from Crestline out to **Silverwood Lake**, the least developed of these mountain pools. Here a state recreation area provides opportunities to fish, boat, swim, and explore the secluded fringes of the lake (see the "Beaches and Parks" section in this chapter). **Lake Gregory**, a smaller lake near Crestline, is fully developed and offers numerous facilities.

The prettiest and most precious of these alpine gems is **Lake Arrowhead**, a socially exclusive enclave encircled by private homes. Popular with Hollywood notables and Los Angeles business executives, the lake has public facilities along the south shore. The closest most people come to the remaining shoreline is aboard the **Arrowhead Queen** (Lake Arrowhead Village; 714-336-6992; admission), a 60-passenger paddlewheeler that tours the lake.

About the only thing you'll encounter on Route 18 between Lake Arrowhead and Big Bear Lake, except for panoramic views, is **Santa's Village** (714-337-2481; admission). A theme park for little ones, this mock-Northpole outpost features a puppet theater, petting zoo, pony ride, and other attractions. (It's advisable to call ahead to confirm that the village is open.)

A short distance further east lies the **Heaps Park Arboretum**. Here a three-quarter-mile loop trail meanders past ponderosa pines, cypresses, ferns, quaking aspens, and young sequoia trees. The views from this ridge sweep south toward San Bernardino and north across the Mojave Desert.

Larger, friendlier, and less formal than Lake Arrowhead, **Big Bear Lake** stretches for seven miles at a 7000-foot altitude. Lined with resort facilities, it is generally less expensive and less private than its counterpart to the west. Created in the 1880s by a single arch dam, Big Bear is a popular ski area in winter. During summer months it offers a full array of aquatic amenities.

To tour the lake, you can climb aboard the **Big Bear Queen** (Big Bear Marina, Big Bear Lake; 714-866-3218; admission). While on board, the most unusual place you'll pass will be that stark white dome on the north shore. Called the **Big Bear Solar Observatory**, the telescope is a research station for scientists from Cal Tech.

Miners nicknamed part of this territory "Starvation Flats," but a few of them struck it rich in **Holcomb Valley** (★). During the 1860s this conifer-studded region boasted a boom town that rivaled Los Angeles in size. Today rough dirt roads lead to the last vestiges of those golden days. From Fawn-skin on the north shore of Big Bear Lake, you can pick up Poligue Canyon Road and other well-marked roads, which bump for five miles past Wilber's Grave, the log remains of Two-Gun Bill's Saloon, Hangman's Tree, and an old log cabin.

Another favored destination for children is **Moonridge Animal Park** (Moonridge Road two miles south of Route 18, Big Bear Lake; 714-585-3656). Featuring animals indigenous to the San Bernardino Mountains, the zoo contains bobcats, mountain lions, timber wolves, and black bears.

REDLANDS–RIVERSIDE AREA

Blessed with water from Big Bear Lake, the town of Redlands became a prime citrus-growing region during the 1880s. By the turn of the century wealthy Easterners seeking mild winters began building mansions amid the orange groves. Today the town numbers about 350 period homes, from tiny California-style bungalows to gaudy Victorian estates.

Among the most spectacular is **Kimberly Crest** (1325 Prospect Drive, Redlands; 714-792-2111), constructed in 1897. An overweening assemblage of turrets, gables, arches, and fountains, this hilltop château is surrounded by five acres of Italian gardens. The grounds are open daily and there are tours of the house every Thursday through Sunday from 1 to 4 p.m.

Redlands also takes pride in its public buildings. Several brick stores line Orange Street (just north of Redlands Boulevard), a commercial strip highlighted by the Grecian-style **Santa Fe Railroad Station**.

The **A. K. Smiley Public Library** (125 West Vine Street, Redlands; 714-798-7565) is a Moorish structure dramatized by carved sandstone friezes, stained-glass windows, and elaborate woodwork. Behind this 1898 edifice stands the **Lincoln Memorial Shrine**, a small but noteworthy museum devoted to Abraham Lincoln. Built of polished limestone in 1932, the octagonal building displays marvelous WPA-type murals.

San Bernardino County Museum (2024 Orange Tree Lane, Redlands; 714-798-8570), one of the region's major historical facilities, has three floors of changing exhibits. There's an anthropology hall with Indian artifacts and covered wagons, plus an excellent mineral collection. It also features the largest bird egg collection in southern California. Around the grounds you'll find orange groves and antique mining equipment as well as odds and ends from the golden age of the railroad.

Whitewashed adobe buildings surround a tranquil courtyard at **Asistencia Misión de San Gabriel** (26930 Barton Road, Redlands; 714-793-5402). Built in 1830 as an outpost of the San Gabriel Mission, the chapel was used during later years as a rancho. The tree-shaded plaza is a wonderful place to sit and ponder; to divert your attention, there are two small museums re-creating the era of padres and pioneers.

The **Yucaipa Adobe** (32183 Kentucky Street; 714-795-3485) in neighboring Yucaipa dates to 1859. As the oldest standing two-story adobe in San Bernardino County, the house is a showcase of antiques from the era. With overhanging trees and rusting farm implements, the surrounding yard is another throwback to California's colonial era.

A **country drive** (★) out Oak Glen Road will carry you past orange groves and into apple country. Orchards, blossoming each spring and heavy with fruit in autumn, blanket the landscape. Between Yucaipa and Cherry Valley the road winds through foothills, passing cider mills and roadside stands.

En route are two small county museums, unique but often overlooked. The **Mousley Museum of Natural History** (35350 Panorama Drive, Yucaipa; 714-790-3163) claims to have the largest sea shell collection west of the Mississippi. This appealing little showroom also displays fossils, minerals, and glowing rocks. Open Thursday through Sunday only.

Equally imaginative is the **Edward-Dean Museum of Decorative Arts** (9401 Oak Glen Road, Cherry Valley; 714-845-2626; admission), with a rare selection of fine furniture, porcelain, and crystal. The museum has gathered one of the country's best collections of Far Eastern bronzes. The beautifully landscaped grounds are also a pleasure to visit.

Two cities, San Bernardino and Riverside, dominate the Inland Empire. While the former has few noteworthy attractions, the latter provides visitors with several opportunities. Riverside's chief landmark is 1337-foot **Mount Rubidoux**, a rocky prominence on the west side of town. Capped by a memorial cross and peace tower, the cactus-coated hill affords a full-circle vista of the Inland Valley. A narrow thoroughfare, Mount Rubidoux Drive, corkscrews to the summit.

Pride of the city is the **Riverside County Court House** (4050 Main Street), a Beaux-Arts beauty built in 1903. The community also boasts several museums. The **Riverside Art Museum** (3425 7th Street; 714-684-7111), set in a 1929 Mediterranean-style building designed by Julia Morgan, hosts changing exhibits and special events.

At the nearby **Riverside Municipal Museum** (3720 Orange Street; 714-782-5273), housed in the equally inviting 1912 Post Office building, cultural exhibits portray Native American crafts and trace the history of citrus growing in the region. Among the natural history displays are fossils, minerals, and dioramas illustrating local animal life in its native habitat.

Riverside's most historic museum was undergoing a $45 million facelift as this book went to press. The **Mission Inn** (3649 7th Street; 714-784-0300), one of California's most famous hotels, dates to the 1880s when Frank Miller began expanding his family's adobe house to accommodate guests. The home eventually became a palace with room keys, sprawling across an entire city block and entertaining eight United States presidents. Built in Mission Revival fashion, with Moorish and Oriental elements, Miller's dream became a labyrinth of alcoves and art galleries, balconies and terraces, and patios. This magnificent hotel, complete with an art and history museum, will hopefully re-open late in 1992.

If you tour the campus of the University of California–Riverside (west end of University Avenue), be sure to take in the **Botanic Gardens** (714-787-4650). Extending across 39 acres of rugged terrain, it contains cactus, rose, and iris gardens as well as a fruit orchard. The preserve specializes in plants from California, Australia, and southern Africa.

SOUTHERN INLAND EMPIRE

Down in Perris, a town better known as a center for hot-air ballooning, the **Orange Empire Railway Museum** (2201 South A Street; 714-657-2605; admission for rides) displays freight and passenger cars, cabooses, and trolleys. A kind of junkyard for trains, this outdoor museum also contains steam engines, a station house, and several antique buildings. The facility is rather disorganized, however, with exhibits scattered across a sprawling railyard. On weekends and minor holidays, when they muster enough volunteers, the museum provides train and trolley rides.

The century-old town of **San Jacinto**, rapidly developing in all directions, preserves its heritage along Main Street, where falsefront buildings line several blocks. Nearby Hemet is home to the Ramona Pageant, an annual re-enactment of Helen Hunt Jackson's fabled love story of an Indian maiden. The **Ramona Bowl** (Ramona Bowl Road; 714-658-3111), a natural amphitheater where the play is presented, is set in the foothills of Mt. San Jacinto and utilizes the rocky terrain as its stage.

The Native Americans portrayed in the Ramona extravaganza once occupied the entire area. An outstanding example of their artistry is evident at the **Maze Stone (★)** outside Hemet. This large, perfectly preserved pictograph, carved into a hillside boulder, presents a detailed labyrinth. To get there, take Route 74 about five miles west from Hemet; turn north on California Avenue; turn left on Tres Cerritos Avenue and follow for two and two-tenths miles; then turn right on Reinhardt Canyon Road.

Numerous manmade lakes dot the Inland Empire, including **Lake Elsinore** (near the intersection of Routes 15 and 74), a resort destination bordering Cleveland National Forest. While the lake offers a full array of water sports, the town of Lake Elsinore provides all the amenities needed for boating, fishing, and swimming. Among its historic buildings are hotels, restaurants, and shops.

A geologic hot spot, the Inland Empire contains some of California's finest spas. **Murrieta Hot Springs** (39405 Murrieta Hot Springs Road, Murrieta; 714-677-7451; admission), a 46-acre resort, sits atop the Elsinore fault. Built at the turn of the century, its warm springs and mineral baths have been soothing weary bones since the days of the Temecula Indians.

The complex is beautifully landscaped with ponds, fountains, and gardens. You can stretch out in the shade of a palm tree, relax on the lawn, or utilize the resort's ample facilities. There are saunas, mud baths, mineral pools, jacuzzis, tennis courts, and a golf course as well as a complement of classes, lectures, and exercise programs. Open to day visitors and overnight guests alike.

Smaller and lacking the hotel facilities of Murrieta, **Glen Ivy Hot Springs** (25000 Glen Ivy Road, Corona; 714-277-3529; admission) is also less formal than its health-conscious counterpart. Here at "Club Mud" you can down a platter of nachos from the snack bar while relaxing in a jacuzzi, sauna, or mineral pool. The favorite spot, one for which Glen Ivy has gained its nickname, is the red clay mud bath. Guests plop down into this caramel-colored ooze, smear it across their ever-loving bodies, then bask in the sun till it hardens. Human mud pies.

Like many towns in transition throughout the Inland Empire, **Temecula** is an Old West community that is simply exploding with development. Falsefront stores still line Front and Main streets, with wooden sidewalks leading to local antique stores. And the **Old Town Temecula Museum**

(41950 Main Street; 714-676-0021), located within eyeshot of shopping complexes and housing developments, preserves the village's early history.

The Temecula Valley is a prime winegrowing region. Travel east from Temecula along Rancho California Road and you'll discover nearly a dozen vineyards. **Callaway Vineyard & Winery** (32720 Rancho California Road; 714-676-4001), largest of the lot, produces premium white wines from its 720-acre spread. At **Mount Palomar Winery** (33820 Rancho California Road; 714-676-5047) there are shady picnic areas amid 100 acres of vineyards. **Maurice Carrie Vineyard and Winery** (34225 Rancho California Road; 714-676-1711), with 113 acres and a contemporary tasting room. These and most other local vineyards offer free tours and tastings.

John Culbertson Winery (32575 Rancho California Road; 714-699-0099), in addition to the winery tour, offers a champagne bar, where for a fee, you can sample a variety of champagnes, fresh baked breads and goat cheese inside or on a patio overlooking its 20 acres of vineyards.

Bordering the Inland Empire to the east are the San Jacinto Mountains, a spectacular chain of 10,000-foot peaks dividing the region from Palm Springs and the Low Desert. Routes 243 and 74 climb into this alpine environment from the north and west respectively.

At the center of the chain sits the mile-high town of **Idyllwild**. Tucked beneath bald granite peaks, this pine-tufted community is surrounded by San Bernardino National Forest. Once inhabited by Cahuilla Indians, the area now is a major tourist destination. In addition to restaurants and shops, Idyllwild has a host of secluded cabins for rent. For information on trails and campgrounds throughout the region, stop by the **Idyllwild County Park Visitor Center** (54000 Route 243; 714-659-3850).

LOW DESERT

PALM SPRINGS AREA

Take a desert landscape thatched with palm trees, add a 10,000-foot mountain to shade it from the sun, then place an ancient mineral spring deep beneath the ground. What you have is a recipe for Palm Springs. It's a spot where the average daily temperature swings from an invigorating 55° to a toasty 85°.

Little wonder that the town represents the nation's desert showplace, one of the few Western locales where winter brings the best weather. A fashionable health spa and celebrity playground, Palm Springs is the ultimate destination for sunning, swimming, and slumming. Many attractions close or have limited hours during the hot summer months. It's advisable to call in advance.

To direct you, divert you, and help you determine an itinerary for touring the town, there are two local agencies—**Desert Resorts** (Antrium Building, Route 111, Rancho Mirage; 619-770-9000) and the **Palm Springs**

Chamber of Commerce (190 West Amado Road; 619-325-1577). Both dispense printed information and friendly advice.

They'll inevitably point you toward the **Palm Springs Desert Museum** (101 Museum Drive; 619-325-7186; admission), one of California's great regional art centers. Contained in a dynamic and contemporary structure with stone facade, the museum combines desert art, culture, and natural history. There are dioramas illustrating local animal life, a wing devoted to Death Valley, exhibits of basketry by indigenous Cahuilla Indians, and stark black-and-white photos of the American West. Backed against the mountains in an exclusive section of Palm Springs, the complex includes works of contemporary art as well as a section devoted to Western American art. The most appealing places of all are the sculpture gardens—lovely, restful plots with splashing fountains and native palms.

If it's local history you're after, the **Village Green Heritage Center** (221 South Palm Canyon Drive; 619-323-8297; admission) will do quite nicely. Incongruously located amid a row of luxury shops are three antique buildings. Each seems to have been restored a bit too efficiently, making this downtown attraction look more like a mock-antique mall than a museum.

The interiors, however, encapsulate the entire sweep of local history. In the **McCallum Adobe** you'll find tools, clothes, paintings, and books from Palm Springs' early years. Constructed in 1884, the town's oldest building, it's also filled with photos of Hollywood stars, including one of Groucho Marx without his trademark moustache.

Neighboring on the old McCallum place is **Cornelia White's House**, the 1893 home of a pioneer woman. Fabricated from railroad ties, it displays turn-of-the-century appurtenances, including a wrought-iron wood stove and Palm Springs' first telephone.

Had Cornelia lived longer, she could have patronized **Ruddy's General Store** (619-327-2156). A re-creation of a 1930-era general store, this marvelous museum is literally lined with tins of Chase & Sanborn coffee, boxes of Rinso Detergent, and an entire wall of apothecary jars. One of the most complete collections of its kind, it contains an inventory of over 6000 items, almost all filled with their original contents. Ruddy's has penny gumball machines, nickel candy bars, and yes, Prince Albert in a can.

One of the most luxuriant labyrinths you will ever traverse is a place called **Moorten's Botanical Garden** (1701 South Palm Canyon Drive; 619-327-6555; admission). The result of a 50-year effort by the Moorten family, this living monument to the desert displays over 3000 varieties of desert plants. There are prickly pears, agaves, and a cactarium with a desert's worth of cacti in a single greenhouse. It's an enchanted garden, inhabited by birds and turtles, dotted with petrified trees, and filled with dinosaur fossils.

Renowned as a retreat for millionaires and movie stars, Palm Springs for centuries was the private domain of the Agua Caliente Indians. A band of the Cahuilla Indian group, the Agua Calientes roamed the territory, seeking out the cool canyons of the San Jacinto Mountains in summer, then descending during winter months to the warmth and healing mineral springs of the desert floor.

Among the most scenic parcels are the **Indian Canyons** (four miles south of Palm Springs, off South Palm Canyon Road; 619-325-5673), a string of four lush mountain valleys that reach from desert bottomlands deep into the San Jacinto Mountains. For an admission fee visitors can spend the day hiking, exploring, and picnicking in these preserves:

Andreas Canyon, a spectacular mountain gorge, contains Indian rock art as well as mortar holes left by Indian women pounding beans and acorns into meal. A stream tumbles through the valley, cutting the canyon walls and watering the 150 plant species that parallel its course. From here a three-mile trail leads to **Murray Canyon,** where more than 750 palm trees cluster around deep pools and small waterfalls. Mountain sheep and wild ponies roam this remote chasm.

Palm Canyon stretches for 15 miles and contains more than 3000 Washingtonia palm trees, some as old as 2000 years. An island of palms in a desert sea, it displays exotic rock formations and mountain pools. **Tahquitz Canyon,** where many of the scenes for *Lost Horizon* (1937) were shot, is currently closed to the public. All canyons close from late June to early September.

If hiking 14 miles up Palm Canyon is really a bit much, you can soar into the San Jacinto Mountains on the **Palm Springs Aerial Tramway** (Tramway Road; 619-325-1391). Climbing at a teeth-clattering 50° angle and ascending more than a mile to 8516 feet elevation, this mountain shuttle makes Mr. Toad's wild ride seem like a cakewalk.

The reward for those white knuckles is a view of the Coachella Valley from Joshua Tree to the Salton Sea. On a clear day you might not see forever, but you will spot a mountain peak near Las Vegas, 175 miles away.

In addition to the usual snack bar/souvenir shop amenities, there are several trails at the top, including a three-quarter-mile nature loop. The nearby **ranger station** (619-327-0222), which serves this section of Mount San Jacinto State Park, has information on longer hikes. You can also take a 20-minute **mule ride** around the slopes before descending on the tram. From mid-November to mid-April, snow permitting, the **Nordic Ski Center** is open for cross-country skiing.

Cabot's Old Indian Pueblo (67-616 East Desert View Avenue, Desert Hot Springs; 619-329-7610; admission), the home of a feisty desert pioneer, is a four-story adobe built in the fashion of the Hopi Indians. With 35 rooms, 150 windows, and walls two feet thick, this maze-like building is a testament to the strange vision of a single individual. Cabot Yerxa, who arrived in the desert in 1913, spent more than 20 years building his house. A personal museum, it is filled with pioneer relics, Indian artifacts, and turn-of-the-century photographs of the great tribes. Today the carefully preserved pueblo is open to anyone with an interest in this pioneer spirit.

South of Palm Springs lie **Rancho Mirage** and **Palm Desert**, two extraordinarily wealthy bedroom communities. Parked in the middle of the desert, these havens for the rich and retired display so many country clubs, palm trees, and landscaped estates as to create a kind of release from reality. They name streets after people like Bob Hope and Frank Sinatra and use water everywhere—for fountains, cascades, golf greens—in a splendid display of excess.

The ultimate expression of this profligacy is **Marriott's Desert Springs Resort and Spa** (74-855 Country Club Drive, Palm Desert; 619-341-2211), a 400-acre resort with hanging gardens, five-tiered waterfalls, and a lagoon with motorboats. Here white desert sands slope down to crystalline lakes and one of the swimming pools is a 12,000-square-foot extravaganza. To combine such unrestrained decadence with so much water, the Romans would have had to conquer Venice.

Aptly named indeed is **The Living Desert** (47-900 Portola Avenue, Palm Desert; 619-346-5694; admission), a 1200-acre nature park that presents a raw and realistic picture of desert life. This grand outdoor zoo contains bighorn sheep, gazelles, and Arabian oryx from the deserts of Africa. Bats, rattlesnakes, and screech owls inhabit a special display which simulates the desert at night; and a walk-through aviary houses finches, green herons, and hermit thrushes.

There are also botanical gardens planted with vegetation from eight of the world's deserts, and hiking trails that wind for more than six miles into nearby foothills. Ponds re-create the life of desert oases and special lizard and tortoise exhibits present some of the region's most familiar creatures. Culturally speaking, this exceptional park is an oasis in itself.

For an overview of the entire area, head up Route 74 on the **Palms to Pines Tour**, which will carry high into the Santa Rosa Mountains. Desert ironwood trees and creosote bushes front the road, giving way at higher elevations to manzanita and mountain mahogany. As the highway climbs to lofty heights, dramatic vistas of the Coachella Valley open to view. If you're ambitious, it's possible to connect with Routes 243, 10, and 111 on a 130-mile loop trip through the San Jacinto Mountains and back to Palm Springs.

Indio may be flat, dry, and barren, but it has one home-grown product that puts the place on everyone's map—dates. The only region in the United States where the fruit is grown, Indio boasts 3000 acres of date palms. Tall, stately trees with fan-shaped fronds, they transform a bland agricultural town into an attractive oasis.

At **Shield's Date Gardens** (80-225 Route 111, Indio; 619-347-0996) they serve date shakes and date ice cream. Unfortunately, the best thing about their slide show, "The Romance and Sex Life of the Date," is the title. Here or at **Jensen's Date & Citrus Garden** (80-653 Route 111, Indio; 619-347-3897) you can wander through a date orchard.

If you still haven't had your fill, the **Coachella Valley Museum and Cultural Center** (82-616 Miles Avenue, Indio; 619-342-6651; admission) features displays on local agriculture. This small regional showplace also contains an Indian room with artifacts from the Cahuilla tribe and a collection of heirlooms donated by local residents.

JOSHUA TREE NATIONAL MONUMENT AREA

No, that's not a hallucination on Route 10 west of Palm Springs, those really are dinosaurs at the **Dinosaur Gardens** (5800 Seminole Drive, Cabazon; 714-849-8309; admission) looming above the highway. Or dinosaur replicas anyway: a *Brontosaurus* 45 feet high and 150 feet long, and his companion, a *Tyrannosaurus rex* that stands 65 feet high. Each weighs more than 40 tons and has interior viewing platforms. The *Brontosaurus* even contains a museum with fossils and Indian artifacts.

Bridging the gap between the High and Low desert areas is **Big Morongo Wildlife Reserve** (East Drive, Morongo Valley; 619-363-7190), a 3900-acre facility managed by the Nature Conservancy. This oasis, with several springs and one of the region's few year-round streams, features several nature trails. Bobcat and bighorn sheep inhabit the area, which is also prime birdwatching territory. The bird population here is about 100 times as plentiful as elsewhere in the desert. Varying from a cottonwood-rimmed stream to desert washes, the canyon is also a place of rare beauty.

Fiction, it seems, has become reality in **Pioneertown** (four miles northwest of Yucca Valley on Pioneertown Road). This unusual hamlet was built in 1947 as a film set for Westerns. Somehow the producers never managed to start the cameras rolling and the place became an ersatz ghost town. Then people began moving in, converting falsefront buildings into a general store, post office, private homes, and even a bowling alley. Today several of the old raw wood structures survive and you can tour the neighborhood, exploring a fictional ghost town that returned to life.

In addition to dramatic rock formations, the town of Yucca Valley, a stopover on the way to Joshua Tree, possesses two points of interest. **Anto Martin Park** (north end of Mohawk Trail), created by one man during the last nine years of his life, portrays several biblical scenes. Among the outsize sculptures are a 16-ton statue of Christ and a tableau of the Last Supper. The town's **Hi-Desert Nature Museum** (57117 Twentynine Palms Highway; 619-228-5452) exhibits fossils, rocks and minerals, Indian artifacts, and arts and crafts. They also have a small zoo with desert animals and reptiles.

One of the great inland destinations, **Joshua Tree National Monument** is an awesome 850-square-mile sanctuary straddling California's High and Low deserts. Its northern region, of greater interest to visitors, rests at about

4000 feet elevation in the Mojave. To the south, where Joshua trees give way to scrub vegetation, lies the arid Colorado Desert.

The main entrance to the park, off Route 62 in Twentynine Palms, leads to the **Oasis Visitors Center** (619-367-7511), a full-facility stop with a museum and ranger station. The best place to chart a course through the preserve, it rests in the Oasis of Mara, a grove of palms once used by Indians and prospectors. **Black Rock Canyon Visitors Center** (619-365-9585), with a ranger station and small exhibit, lies approximately 30 miles farther west.

As you proceed south and west into the heart of the park, weathered granite, smoothed by the elements, rises in fields of massive boulders. In the foreground, Joshua trees, their branches like arms raised heavenward, stand forth against a cobalt sky. Many of the rocks are carved and hollowed to create skulls, arches, and whatever shapes the imagination can conjure.

The Joshua trees that complement this eerie landscape are giant yucca plants, members of the agave family, which grow to heights of almost 50 feet. They were named in the 1850s by Mormon pioneers, who saw in the stark, angular trees the figure of the prophet Joshua pointing them further westward.

West of Jumbo Rocks Campground, **Geology Tour Road**, a dirt track, leads for nine miles past unusual rock sculptures, alluvial fans, and desert washes. **Squaw Tank**, an ancient Indian campsite, contains Indian bedrock mortars and a concrete dam built by ranchers early in the century. A pamphlet available from the information centers will also help locate petroglyphs, mine shafts, and magnificent mountain vistas.

A paved route from the main roadway deadends at **Keys View**. The finest panorama in the park, it sweeps from 11,485-foot Mt. San Gorgonio across the San Jacinto Mountains to the Salton Sea, and takes in Palm Springs, the Colorado River Aqueduct, and Indio. The full sweep of the Coachella Valley lies before you, a dusty brown basin painted green with golf courses and palm groves.

Desert Queen Ranch, one of the few outposts of civilization in Joshua Tree, is accessible only by ranger-led tours (provided on weekends only). Built early in the century by William F. Keys—a former sheriff, prospector, and Rough Rider—it's a ghost village complete with ranch house, school, corral, and barn.

The unique transition zone between the Mojave and Colorado deserts becomes evident when you proceed toward the southern gateway to the park. As the elevation descends and temperatures rise, plant life becomes sparser.

Yet here, too, the inherent beauty of the park is overwhelming. **Cholla Cactus Garden**, a forest of cactus that is a pure delight to walk through, is one of Joshua Tree's prettiest places. With their soft, bristly branches, these Bigelow cactus live in a region that rarely receives more than four inches of rain a year.

Beyond this natural garden the road passes through a landscape of long, lithe ocotillo plants. Then you'll journey past the parched, dust-blown Pinto Basin to the **Cottonwood Visitors Center**, the southern gateway to Joshua Tree National Monument.

ANZA-BORREGO DESERT STATE PARK

The largest state facility in the United States, Anza-Borrego Desert State Park extends across a broad swath of the Colorado Desert, reaching almost to the Mexican frontier. Within its borders lie desert sinks, sculpted rocks, and multicolored badlands. Bighorn sheep roam the mountains and desert life abounds in the lowlands.

Borrego Springs, the only sizeable town in the entire preserve, contains an excellent **visitors center** (end of West Palm Canyon Drive; 619-767-5311). Here are nature trails, a cactus garden, and a small museum with displays, and a slide show.

For a **vantage point** overlooking this magnificent territory, follow Route S22 west toward Culp Valley. Sharply ascending into the mountains, the road looks out across the Borrego Badlands to the Salton Sea. To the north rise the Santa Rosa Mountains and in the south, deep brown against the blue sky, are the Vallecito Mountains.

Font's Point, one of the park's most popular vistas, will provide a close-up view of the Borrego Badlands. A truly spectacular spot, it overlooks rock formations painted brilliant colors and chiseled by wind and water. This heavily eroded area reveals remnants of the prehistoric Colorado River delta. To reach Font's Point, follow Route S22 for about 12 miles east from Borrego Springs, then turn south for four miles onto a marked road. This rough, sandy track lies at the bottom of a wash, so take care not to become mired in the sand.

The entire stretch of Route S22 from Borrego Springs east to the Salton Sea is nicknamed **Erosion Road**. Along its 30-mile length are countless sandstone hills, brilliant red in color and carved into myriad shapes. Many are banded with sedimentary layers containing marine fossils.

Perhaps one even contains the lost gold mine of "Pegleg" Smith. Thomas Long "Pegleg" Smith, it seems, was a prospector with a talent for tall tales. The nickname, he claimed, resulted from an 1827 Indian battle from which he emerged missing one leg. A few years later Pegleg passed through California, discovering a small amount of gold, which in the alembic of his imagination was eventually transformed into an entire mine.

Even a prospector needs a public relations man. Pegleg's publicity agent came along a century later when Harry Oliver, a Hollywood director, created the **Pegleg Monument** (Route S22 and Henderson Canyon Road, eight miles east of Borrego Springs). Drawing a circle on the ground, Oliver urged everyone hoping to discover Pegleg's lost gold mine to fill the area with rocks. Today the monument is a huge pile of stones to which you are obliged to contribute. Good luck!

Along the eastern border of the park, near Ocotillo Wells, lie the **Split Mountain/Fish Creek** (★). Sculpted by water, these heights have been transformed into a variety of textures and compositions. Each level presents a different color, as if the hills had been deposited layer by layer from on high. To get there, follow Split Mountain Road south from Route 78 for 12 miles; turn right on the road to Fish Creek campground and follow it about two-and-one-half miles (until it becomes impassable). When the road is in good condition, you can drive right into the gap in the mountain created by geologic forces.

South of Borrego Springs, Route S3 traverses Yaqui Pass. From the roadside (near the 2.0 mile sign), a quarter-mile trail leads to **Kenyon Overlook,** with views of Sunset Mountain and surrounding canyons.

Further south in the park, Route S2 parallels the historic Southern Emigrant Trail. At **Box Canyon Monument** (nine miles south of Scissors Crossing), a path leads to a point overlooking the old trail. It was here in 1847 that the Mormon Battalion hewed a track wide enough for wagons. Ten years later the first transcontinental mail service passed through this region and soon afterwards the Butterfield Overland Stage Line began transporting passengers.

The **Vallecito Stage Station** (Route S2, 19 miles south of Scissors Crossing), built in 1852, served the Butterfield and other lines for years. Today an adobe reconstruction of the building stands in Vallecito County Park. With its plentiful water supply, this site was also an important campground for the gold prospectors coming overland to Northern California mines in 1849.

For a dramatic idea of the terrain confronting these pioneers, continue to **Carrizo Badlands Overlook** (Route S2, 36 miles south of Scissors Crossing). In all directions from this windswept plateau, the landscape is an inhospitable mix of mountain peaks and sandy washes. Heavy erosion has worked its magic here, creating stone sculptures and hills banded with color.

Shopping

INLAND EMPIRE SHOPPING

Lake Arrowhead Village (Route 189), a mock mountain chalet shopping complex, contains dozens of shops. Located directly on Lake Arrowhead, the mall includes boutiques, galleries, sporting goods stores, and sundries shops.

At **Big Bear Lake** the stores are concentrated along Pine Knot Avenue and Big Bear Boulevard (Route 18). Here you'll find crafts shops and knickknack stores. My favorite is a must-see destination called **Sugarloaf Cord-**

wood Co. (42193 Big Bear Boulevard; 714-866-2220). The chain saw carvings of bears and Indians are as big as totem poles and the shop is cluttered with thousands of ingenious carvings.

Idyllwild, a mountain hamlet deep in the San Jacintos, offers numerous arts and crafts shops. Several country roads near the village center are dotted with cabins converted into small stores.

Maggie's Attic (54380 North Circle Drive, Idyllwild; 714-659-4479) typifies the homespun theme pervading most of these shops. Here you'll find quilts, decorative wreaths, stitchery, and sweaters. **Epicurean** (54791 North Circle Drive; 714-659-5251), by contrast, demonstrates the elite influence Palm Springs is exercising in this remote mountain town. Among its offerings are rare wines, gourmet specialties, and sleek decorative accessories.

LOW DESERT SHOPPING

Palm Canyon Drive, the Main Street of Palm Springs, contains the region's greatest concentration of shops. There are almost as many signature stores as palm trees along this swank boulevard. The center within the center is **Desert Fashion Plaza** (between Tahquitz Way and Amado Road; 619-320-8282), a stone-floor-and-splashing-fountain labyrinth which wends past jewelers, designer boutiques, and department stores.

Adagio Galleries (193 South Palm Canyon Drive; 619-320-2230) down the street has a fine collection of Southwestern art. The inventory not only includes colorful oil paintings but Native American ceramics as well.

Across the street at **B. Lewin Galleries** (210 South Palm Canyon Drive; 619-322-2525), you'll find what is reputedly the world's largest collection of paintings by Mexican masters. Some of the works here are little short of magnificent.

Cathedral City has several shops that will delight any budget-minded shopper. **Pier 1 Imports** (Route 111 and Cathedral Canyon Drive; 619-321-6622) stocks a full range of decorative items and clothing styles. At **Little Baja** (34-750 Date Palm Drive; 619-328-3708) you'll find Mexican pottery, wall masks, statuary, and pre-Columbian idols.

Consumer central in Palm Desert is the **Palm Desert Town Center** (72-840 Route 111 at Route 74; 619-346-2121), a mammoth mall offering several department stores and a host of small shops.

The region's more elegant stores line **El Paseo**, a multiblock extravaganza which runs through the heart of Palm Desert. Among the galleries lining this well-heeled boulevard are the **A. Albert Allen Fine Art Gallery** (73-200 El Paseo; 619-341-8655), with Indian rugs and Southwestern art, and next door a gallery of the same name features a more traditional collection of fine art. **Crock-R-Box** (73-425 El Paseo; 619-568-6688) features crafts fashioned from wood, metal, and glass.

Also stop by **The Tortoise Shelf** (47-900 Portola Avenue, Palm Desert; 619-346-5694), the gift shop at the Living Desert Reserve. They have an excellent collection of books, prints, jewelry, and gift items, all relating to the desert.

Nightlife

INLAND EMPIRE NIGHTLIFE

The Milky Way will provide most of your evening entertainment in the San Bernardino Mountains. There are a few lounges around Lake Arrowhead and Big Bear Lake, particularly at the **Lake Arrowhead Hilton Lodge** (714-336-1511), but most are little more than pool-table bars.

Country-and-western describes the music and the setting at **Winchester Inn** (28314 Winchester Road, Winchester; 714-926-2690). This cowboy bar kicks up live entertainment seven nights a week.

PALM SPRINGS AREA NIGHTLIFE

The center of action in downtown Palm Springs is **Zelda's** (169 North Indian Avenue; 619-325-2375), a rocking disco with video screens, two dancefloors, and eight bars. Contests and fashion shows punctuate sets of deejay music. Cover.

Over at the **Comedy Haven** (109 South Palm Canyon Drive; 619-320-7855) you'll be entertained by stand-up comedians, improv groups, comedy, and magic; or you can dance to live Top-40 tunes in the lounge. Cover for live shows.

The place to view and be viewed in this celebrity-conscious town is **Melvyn's** (200 West Ramon Road; 619-325-0046). The lounge at this fashionable French restaurant features piano bar music and a small dancefloor.

The **Pompeii Nightclub** (67-399 Route 111; 328-5800) goes all out Thursday through Saturday when they feature comedy acts and a jazz duo as well as a disco. During the week only the discotheque is on tap. Cover.

Over at the Wyndham Palm Springs Hotel, **The Lobby Bar** (888 East Tahquitz Way; 619-322-6000) is a pleasant spot for a quiet drink.

The **Cactus Corral** (67501 Route 111, Cathedral City; 619-321-8558) features live country music and will even teach you to dance Western-style. Cover.

State-of-the-art and ultra-fashionable, the **McCallum Theatre for the Performing Arts** (73-000 Fred Waring Drive, in the Bob Hope Cultural Center, Palm Desert; 619-340-2787) represents the desert showplace for symphonies, dramas, and concerts. This 1140-seat theater is the cultural capital of the Palm Springs area.

Around Borrego Springs, in the heart of Anza-Borrego Desert State Park, you'll find the **Las Palmas Bar and Grill** (221 Palm Canyon Drive;

619-767-5341). This comfortable Western-style lounge has oak furniture and stained-glass windows.

Among the many gay nightspots in the area is **CC Construction Co.** (68-449 Perez Road, Cathedral City; 619-324-4241). This sprawling club boasts three bars—a dance bar, country-and-western, and a levis-and-leather cruise bar. Cover.

Also catering to gay men is **Daddy Warbuck's** (68-981 East Palm Canyon Drive, Cathedral City; 619-324-1022), with a dancefloor, piano, pool tables, and a host of shows ranging from live music to comedy burlesque to whipped cream wrestling. Cover.

More low-key and appealing to both gay men and women is **Gloria's** (2330 North Palm Canyon Drive, Palm Springs; 619-322-3224), a cozy piano bar.

HIGH DESERT

CHAPTER EIGHT
High Desert

Picture an endless expanse of basin and range, desert and mountain, a realm guarded by the sharp teeth of the Sierra Nevada and the gaping maw of Death Valley. California may be known for glittering cities and postcard beaches, but along its southeastern shoulder the Golden State unveils a different face entirely. Here the Mojave Desert reaches from Los Angeles County across an awesome swath of territory to Arizona and Nevada.

The sky in these parts is so immense as to swallow the land, and the landscape is so broad that mountains are like islands on its surface. The Mojave is a region of ancient lakebeds and crystalline sinks, ghost towns and deserted mines. When Jedediah Smith, one of the West's great explorers, trekked through in 1826, he declared the desert "a country of starvation."

Even today it seems desolate and unyielding. Winters are cold here, the summers hot. Rainfall, which dwindles from six inches in the western Mojave to less than two inches around Death Valley, comes only during winter. But plants proliferate and the area is alive with reptiles and small mammals.

Home to the NASA space shuttle and Edwards Air Force Base, the Mojave is a strategic aerospace center. Indeed its western reaches around Antelope Valley are rapidly filling with people spilling over from the Los Angeles Basin.

Foreign and unforgiving though it might be, the Mojave Desert has always possessed particular importance in the history of California. In 1774, Yuma Indians guided Juan Bautista de Anza and other Spanish explorers through this wasteland. By 1831 the vital Santa Fe Trail was open from Santa Fe to Los Angeles. Later in the century the U.S. Army converted other Indian paths into roads, opening them to wagon trains and stage coaches.

The land Jedediah Smith labeled "a complete barrens" proved rich in minerals. For four decades beginning in the 1870s, the Mojave was a major thoroughfare for 20-mule teams laden with borax and miners weighted down with gold, silver, zinc, and tungsten. The towns of Mojave and Barstow became important railroad centers; even now they remain essential crossroads, oases with amenities.

At the northern edge of the Mojave, in a land the Indians knew as "Tomesha" or "ground on fire," lies Death Valley. Measuring 120 miles long and varying in width from four to sixteen miles, it is among the hottest places on earth, second only to the Sahara. During summer the *average* daily high temperature is 116°.

A museum without air conditioning, Death Valley is a giant geology lab displaying salt beds, sand dunes, and an 11,000-foot elevation climb. Its multitiered hills contain layers that are windows on the history of the earth. One level holds Indian arrowheads, another Ice Age fish, and beneath these deposits lies Precambrian rock.

At the end of the Pleistocene, when warming temperatures melted glaciers atop the Sierra Nevada, this desiccated domain was covered by a vast inland sea. Today mud playas and the shadows of ancient shorelines are all that remain. Instead of water, the lowlands are filling with rock debris from the neighboring Black and Panamint mountains.

One of the most hauntingly beautiful places in the world, Death Valley received its ominous name in 1849 when a party of pioneers, intent on following a shortcut to the gold fields, crossed the wasteland, barely escaping with their lives. Later, prospectors stayed to work the territory, discovering rich borax deposits during the 1880s and providing the region with a home industry.

Testament to the diversity of the High Desert, Death Valley contains the lowest spot in the contiguous United States (Badwater, 282 feet below sea level), yet rests within 60 miles of the highest place (Mount Whitney, 14,495 feet above sea level). Its snow-rimmed neighbor, the Sierra Nevada, is the largest single mountain range in the country, a solitary block of earth 430 miles long and 80 miles wide. A mere child in the long count of geologic history, the Sierra Nevada rose from the earth's surface a few million years back and did not reach its present form until 750,000 years ago. During the Pleistocene epoch, glaciers spread across the land, grinding and cutting at the mountains. They carved river valleys and deep canyons, and sculpted bald domes, fluted cliffs, and stone towers.

The glaciers left a landscape dominated by ragged peaks where streams number in the thousands and canyons plunge 5000 feet. There are cliffs sheer as glass that compete with the sky for dominance. It is, as an early pioneer described it, a "land of fire and ice."

On the western flank of this massive range lie Sequoia and Kings Canyon national parks. Within eyeshot of the brine pools and scrub growth of Death Valley, they contain more than 1000 glacial lakes and boast rich stands of giant sequoia trees, the largest living things on earth.

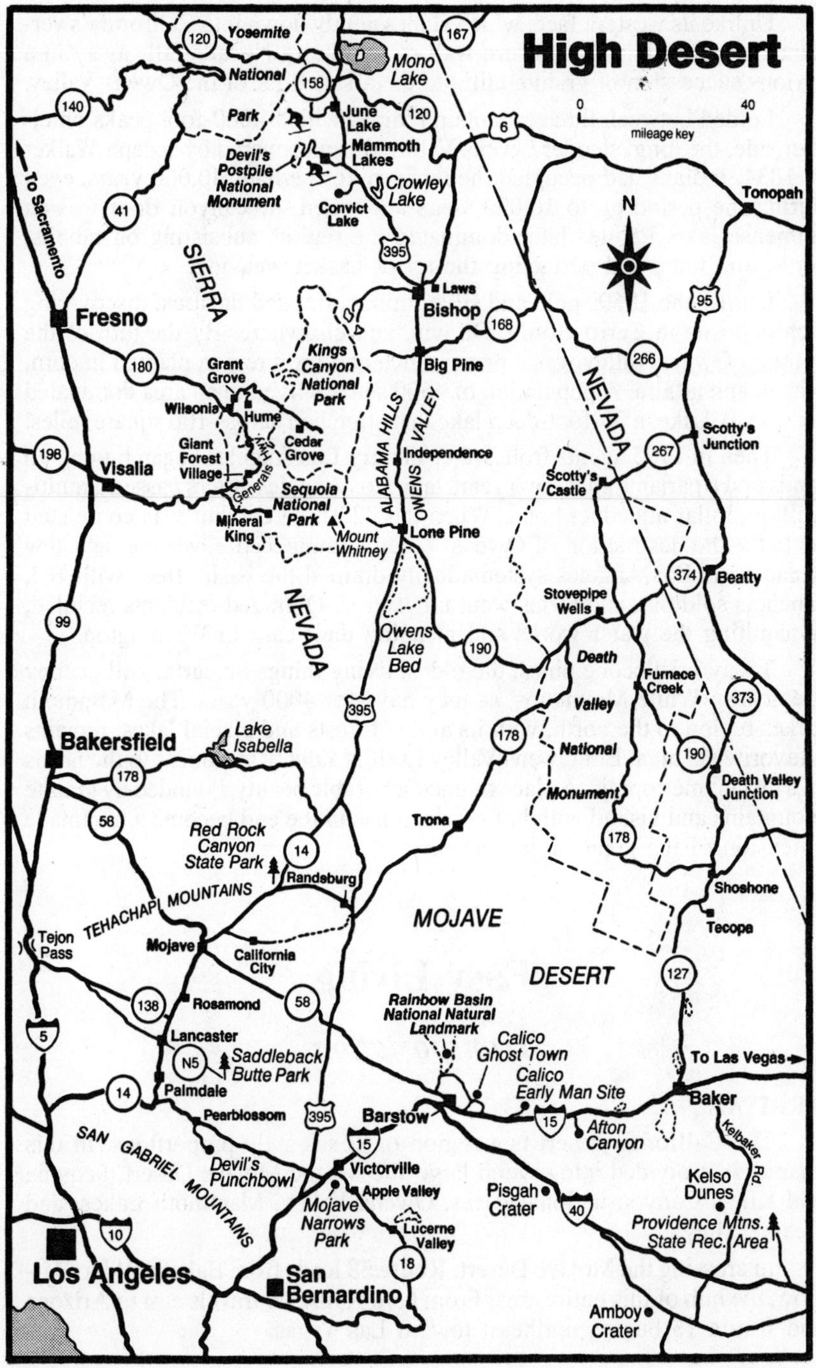

High Desert
0
40
mileage key
N
Yosemite
National
Park
Mono Lake
June Lake
Mammoth Lakes
Devil's Postpile National Monument
Crowley Lake
Convict Lake
To Sacramento
SIERRA
NEVADA
Fresno
Laws
Bishop
Big Pine
Tonopah
Grant Grove
Kings Canyon National Park
Wilsonia
Hume
Giant Forest Village
Cedar Grove
Generals Hwy
Visalia
Sequoia National Park
Mineral King
Mount Whitney
ALABAMA HILLS
OWENS VALLEY
Independence
Lone Pine
Owens Lake Bed
NEVADA
Scotty's Junction
Scotty's Castle
Beatty
Stovepipe Wells
Death Valley National Monument
Furnace Creek
Death Valley Junction
Bakersfield
Lake Isabella
Red Rock Canyon State Park
Randsburg
Trona
Shoshone
Tecopa
TEHACHAPI MOUNTAINS
Tejon Pass
Mojave
California City
MOJAVE
DESERT
Rosamond
Rainbow Basin National Natural Landmark
Calico Ghost Town
Calico Early Man Site
To Las Vegas
Lancaster
Saddleback Butte Park
Palmdale
Pearblossom
Barstow
Baker
Afton Canyon
Kelbaker Rd.
SAN GABRIEL MOUNTAINS
Devil's Punchbowl
Victorville
Apple Valley
Pisgah Crater
Kelso Dunes
Mojave Narrows Park
Lucerne Valley
Providence Mtns. State Rec. Area
Los Angeles
San Bernardino
Amboy Crater
120
167
158
140
120
6
41
395
95
168
180
266
198
267
374
99
190
373
395
178
190
178
178
58
14
127
138
58
5
N5
14
395
15
15
40
10
18

Unlike its western face, which slopes gently down into California's verdant Central Valley, the eastern wall of the Sierra Nevada falls away in a furious succession of granite cliffs to the alkali floor of the Owens Valley.

Folded between three mountain ranges, with 14,000-foot peaks on either side, the long, slender Owens Valley was discovered by Joseph Walker in 1834. Indians had occupied the territory for perhaps 40,000 years, even during the period up to 10,000 years ago when the canyon floor was an immense lake. Paiutes later dominated the region, subsisting on rabbits, birds, and nuts, and perfecting the art of basket weaving.

During the 1860s gold and silver miners flooded the area, discovering rich deposits in Cerro Gordo, Darwin, and elsewhere. By the turn of the century, Owens Valley was a prime ranch and farm region planted in corn, wheat, and alfalfa. A population of 4500 settlers lived in an area dominated by Owens Lake, a 30-foot-deep lake that stretched across 100 square miles.

Then in 1905 agents from water-hungry Los Angeles began buying up lands and riparian rights. Two years later Los Angeles voters passed a multimillion-dollar aqueduct bond. When the 223-mile conduit was completed in 1913, the destruction of Owens Valley commenced. Over the next few decades, as Los Angeles systematically drained the basin, trees withered, ranchers sold out, and farms went unwatered. Outraged residents rebelled, dynamiting the water works and pleading their case in Washington.

Today bristlecone pines, the oldest living things on earth, still occupy the nearby White Mountains, as they have for 4000 years. The Mammoth Lakes region to the north, with its alpine forests and glacial lakes, remains a favorite ski area. But Owens Valley itself is a dusty testament to the needs of a distant metropolis. A place of unconquerable beauty, bounded by granite mountains and visited with hot winds, it has in the end become a manmade extension of the great Mojave Desert.

Easy Living

Transportation

ARRIVAL

The California desert is a region of Texas-style proportions. In this chapter it is divided into several large slices—the Mojave Desert, Sequoia and Kings Canyon national parks, Owens Valley, Mammoth Lakes, and Death Valley.

In crossing the Mojave Desert, **Route 58** leads from Bakersfield to Barstow, the hub of this entire area. From here **Route 40** travels east to Arizona and **Route 15** buzzes northeast toward Las Vegas.

Two highways lead into Sequoia and Kings Canyon national parks, which are located on the western slopes of the Sierra Nevada: **Route 198** from Visalia and **Route 180** from Fresno. The **Generals Highway**, generally closed in winter, connects the parks.

From Route 15, **Route 127** proceeds north and links with **Route 178** and **Route 190**, which wind through Death Valley National Monument.

Route 395, the desert's major north–south thoroughfare, runs the entire length of the Owens Valley, then continues north to Mammoth Lakes.

There are several important points to remember when driving in the desert. Stay on the main roads unless you have inquired about the conditions of side roads. Turn back if a road becomes too difficult to navigate. Be sure to keep your radiator and gas tank filled and make sure the cooling system is in good condition. Also, carry spare water, food, and gas in your vehicle. If stranded in the summer heat, do not leave the shade of your car. Happy trails!

BY AIR

Airports in these areas are rare and regularly scheduled flights are even scarcer. A few small airlines provide flights from various California locations. For air travel to Sequoia and Kings Canyon national parks you'll have to fly into Fresno, then pick up ground transportation.

In the Mammoth Lakes area try **Alpha Air** (800-421-9353), which flies into Mammoth–June Lakes Airport. For information about charter service, contact **Mammoth Airport Information** (619-934-3825).

Death Valley visitors usually fly to Las Vegas, then drive from there.

BY BUS

Bus service in these areas is almost as scarce as air transportation. To visit Owens Valley and the Mammoth Lakes region, try **Greyhound/Trailways Bus Lines**, which stops in Lone Pine (107 North Main Street; 619-876-5300) and Mammoth Lakes (Mammoth Tavern Road).

BY TRAIN

The nearest **Amtrak** (800-872-7245) station servicing Sequoia and Kings Canyon is in Fresno, 55 miles east of the parks. From here you'll have to hike, hitch, or rent a car.

For service to Death Valley, the closest stops are Barstow and Las Vegas. Two trains, the "Desert Wind" and the "Southwest Chief," arrive in Barstow. The "Desert Wind" also stops in Las Vegas. Both towns offer car rental agencies.

CAR RENTALS

In Barstow, call **Avis Rent A Car** (619-256-8614) or **Budget Rent A Car** (619-256-8906). There's an **Auto Rental** (619-872-1730) in Bishop. Around Mammoth Lakes, try **Auto Rental** (619-935-4471) or **Mammoth Car Rental** (619-934-8111).

Hotels

MOJAVE DESERT HOTELS

Towns in the Mojave Desert are little more than corridors for cars. Lined with neon, they resound with the shudder and drone of passing trucks. The larger communities have standard motel accommodations, catering to truck drivers, desert rats, and itinerant salesmen. Bed and breakfast inns, it seems, are rare as rain out here.

Lancaster, located at the western fringe of the desert in Antelope Valley, has numerous resting places. **EZ-8 Motel** (43530 17th Street West; 805-945-9477) is a clean, trim facility with carpeted, neatly furnished rooms. Offering a pool and jacuzzi, it's a good deal considering the budget rates. There are similar motels crowded along Routes 58 and 14 in the town of Mojave.

The crossroads town of Barstow, where Routes 58, 14, and 40 converge, is another neon mecca. Here the sleeper's strip lies along Main Street, where you'll find the **Sunset Inn** (1350 West Main Street; 619-256-8921). Sporting a pool, jacuzzi, and cluster of adequately appointed rooms, it is budget-priced.

The nicest place in town is **Barstow Station Inn** (1511 East Main Street; 619-256-5673), a 148-unit hotel with adjoining restaurant, pool, and jacuzzi. Ultramodern in design, it's clean to the point of being sterile. Guest rooms are finished in blond woods and nicely appointed. They are fairly spacious, well carpeted, and include room service. The ample lobby area is decorated with fabric paintings and furnished with plump, irresistible armchairs. Moderate.

SEQUOIA AND KINGS CANYON HOTELS

Accommodations in both Sequoia and Kings Canyon national parks fall into several categories. There are "rustic cabins," available only in summer, which lack bathrooms and decoration, utilize oil or wood stoves, often have canvas roofs, and price in the budget range. The "cabins," on the other hand, are trim woodframe structures with pine furniture, private baths, decorative posters, and thermostat heaters. These are moderately priced and quite comfortable.

Both parks also offer "motel rooms." Tabbed in the moderate category, they are roadside-style accommodations with veneer furniture, wall-to-wall carpeting, decorative appointments, and private baths. The central number for reservations to all facilities is 209-561-3314. Remember, large sections of the parks are closed in winter.

A variety of good low-cost accommodations and restaurants can be found in Three Rivers, located three miles from the southern entrance to Sequoia National Park.

The main complex in Sequoia National Park is **Giant Forest Lodge** (209-561-3314). Located along Generals Highway, it is part of a village layout that includes a restaurant, cafeteria, market, and lounge. Accommodations include rustic cabins, cabins, and motel rooms.

Stony Creek (209-561-3314), located on Generals Highway between Sequoia and Kings Canyon, features a lodge with motel-type accommodations. There's a dining room, gift shop and market here as well as a lobby with stone fireplace.

Grant Grove Lodge (209-561-3314), the central facility in Kings Canyon National Park, sits in a village that features a restaurant, grocery, gift shop, and information center. Facilities at Grant Grove include rustic cabins and cabins.

Cedar Grove (209-561-3314), located on Route 180 deep within Kings Canyon, is a mountain lodge idyllically set in a grove of tall trees beside a river. There are motel rooms here, as well as a snack bar, market, and gift shop.

Sequoia National Park's **Bearpaw Meadow Backcountry Camp** offers rustic cabins. Extremely popular, this mountain hideaway lies at the end of an 11-mile trail along which guests hike in. The accommodations include breakfast and dinner.

For a full-facility mountain resort, you'll be hard pressed to find anything quite like **Montecito Sequoia Lodge** (209-565-3388). Located at 7500 feet elevation along Generals Highway between Sequoia and Kings Canyon national parks, it's a family vacation camp with rustic cabins and a lodge. The complex rests next to a lake on 38 acres, and offers a swimming pool, tennis courts, basketball, volleyball, canoeing, waterskiing, archery, horseback riding and cross-country skiing in winter months. There's a dining room with a stone fireplace, an ample recreation room, and a bar. Guest rooms in the lodge are priced moderately and include breakfast (deluxe price with dinner included). The cabins, for which you must provide towels and bedding, rent in the deluxe range but include all meals. They are available only in summer; lodge rooms are open year-round.

On the road down into Kings Canyon, surrounded by roughhewn mountains, lies **Kings Canyon Lodge** (67751 Route 180; 209-335-2405). This way station, with its homemade café and gravity-feed gas pumps, contains a cluster of simple woodframe cottages. They are basic accommodations, with knotty-pine walls and uninspired furnishings. Located just off the highway, some have kitchen facilities; moderate.

Also serving the national parks are several motels in the nearby town of Three Rivers. Located along Route 198 within a few miles of Sequoia National Park is the **Lazy J Ranch Motel** (39625 Sierra Drive; 209-561-4449), a 16-unit facility with plain rooms at budget prices and rooms with kitchens at moderate cost. Nearby, **The River Inn** (45176 Sierra Drive; 209-561-4367) has standard rooms at moderate prices.

OWENS VALLEY HOTELS

The neon strip along Route 395 serves as motel row in Lone Pine. Several resting places line the highway, each providing adequate accommodations. The **Dow Villa Hotel and Motel** (310 South Main Street; 619-876-5521) features a modern motel attached to a 1920s-era hotel. The complex includes a lobby, pool, and spa. Rooms in the hotel are time-worn but tidy and rent at budget prices; the motel rooms, more modern and very comfortable, are tabbed budget to moderate.

But who wants a busy motel with seclusion so near at hand? **Cuffe Guest Ranch** (★) (Whitney Portal Road about four miles west of Route 395, Lone Pine; 619-876-4161), set on 160 rustic acres in the Alabama Hills, is an extraordinary (though poorly maintained) getaway. With its rugged hills, meandering creek, and old wagon wheels, the place looks so much like the Old West that movie makers have frequently used it as a location. With Mount Whitney rising in the distance, the views of basin and range are extraordinary.

The housekeeping cabins here are pretty basic—bare bulbs, even barer furnishings, and kitchens equipped with hot plates and small refrigerators. But there's an orchard outside your door and picnic tables yonder under the cottonwood trees. Rooms in the main house are attractively decorated and appointed with antiques and share a stately living room with stone fireplace. One of my favorite locales in the Eastern Sierra. Moderate.

Another important find is **Winnedumah Country Inn** (619-878-2040), an imposing two-story edifice across the street from the Inyo County Court House on Route 395 in Independence. Built in 1927, its spacious lobby greets guests with a stone fireplace, beam ceiling, and cozy armchairs. The accommodations are bright, friendly rooms with quilts and antique furnishings. Budget.

Bishop also has its share of roadside motels, strung like lights along Route 395. **High Sierra Lodge** (1000 North Route 395; 619-873-8426) is a two-story complex with a pool and spa. Among the 52 units are rooms with or without kitchens; each is spacious, carpeted, and well maintained; rents are budget to moderate.

That pretty place at the edge of town, the historic house with lace curtains and porches on both floors, is a bed and breakfast. **The Matlick House** (two miles north of Bishop on Route 395; 619-873-3133), with its handmade quilts and beveled-mirror armoires, is known for miles around. Each of the four guest rooms has been decorated with a flourish: there are overhead fans, iron beds, turn-of-the-century settees, Victorian love seats, and other antiques. Guests enjoy a full breakfast and evening hors d'oeuvres. Moderate to deluxe.

Up at 8500 feet elevation, socked in by mountains and graced with a stream and natural pool, is **Cardinal Village Resort** (Route 168 about 18 miles west of Bishop; 619-873-4789). Part of an old mining claim, this retreat consists of a cluster of cabins dating to 1906. Attractive houses, they combine such old-fashioned amenities as wooden counters with newfangled conveniences like tile baths. Blended into the nearby aspen grove are the general store and café as well as a lodge complete with stone fireplace and library. All 11 units contain kitchens and rent at moderate rates.

MAMMOTH LAKES HOTELS

Convict Lake Resort (Convict Lake Road about two miles west of Route 395; 619-934-3800), located near one of the region's prettiest lakes, features a colony of cabins bounded by an aspen grove. Built of pine, they are plain mountain lodgings with wall heaters and full kitchens. Set at 7500 feet, the resort includes a restaurant, store, and marina. Prices are in the moderate range.

Mammoth Mountain Inn (Minaret Road outside Mammoth Lakes; 619-934-2581) is a modern hotel with a distinct Swiss atmosphere. Located across the road from Mammoth/June Lakes Ski Resort, the inn is primarily a ski lodge, but its easy proximity to Devil's Postpile and other natural features makes it popular year-round. There are restaurants, lounges, spas, and shops here as well as a wood-and-stone lobby. Hotel rooms during spring and summer are moderate; in fall and winter they hold the moderate line during the week, then jump to deluxe on weekends. Condominiums, with kitchen facilities, start in the moderate range in the off-season, then rise to deluxe and ultra-deluxe during peak periods.

One of the prettiest and most secluded spots in Mammoth Lakes is **Tamarack Lodge Resort** (Tamarack Lodge Road; 619-934-2442). A classic mountain lodge with split log walls and stone fireplace, it sits on Twin Lakes in the shadow of the mountains. The lobby is a cheery alpine room inevitably filled with guests warming themselves by a roaring fire. There are small rooms (with shared and private baths) in the lodge, sentimentally decorated and paneled in knotty pine. More than 25 cabins, ranging from studios to four-bedroom extravaganzas, also dot the six-acre grounds. While these are traditional woodframe structures, the interiors of many are modern in design with wall-to-wall carpeting, stall showers, and contemporary kitchens. Most offer partial views of the lake. Located at 8600 feet, the resort is in a major nordic ski area, with trails radiating in all directions. It also features a restaurant. Rates on lodge rooms with shared baths are budget from mid-June to mid-September, moderate during the rest of the year; cabins begin in the moderate or deluxe ranges, also depending on the season.

Laurel Lodge (103 Lake Mary Road; 619-934-2525), a small mountain motel on the outskirts of Mammoth Lakes, features standard rooms as well as accommodations with kitchens. The place is located on a main road but is set amid trees and offers partial mountain views. Many of the rooms are furnished in knotty pine and have carpets and wall prints. Very economical during warm months when they are budget-priced, the accommodations jump to the moderate range in winter. One- and two-bedroom facilities with kitchens rise from moderate to deluxe between seasons.

For assistance booking reservations in the Mammoth Lakes region, contact **Mammoth Lakes Resort Association** (619-934-2522) or **Minaret Reservation Service** (619-934-9423).

Over in the June Lake area, **Big Rock Resort** (1 Big Rock Road, June Lake; 619-648-7717) has eight cabin units. These are attractive duplexes with kitchens and knotty-pine interiors. Some have fireplaces. Nicely situated on the lake, the complex includes a tackle shop and marina. It's a convenient locale if you want to fish, swim, boat, or gaze out at the mountains. Moderate.

DEATH VALLEY HOTELS

Near the southwest corner of Death Valley, in the postage-stamp town of Shoshone, the **Shoshone Inn** (619-852-4335) has standard motel rooms. There is a tree-shaded courtyard, nearby swimming pool, restaurant and bar, and the Shoshone is conveniently placed for exploring the southern stretches of Death Valley. Budget.

Furnace Creek, the main village in Death Valley, features two facilities. **Furnace Creek Ranch** (619-786-2345) is a 124-unit resort sprawling across several acres. In addition to three restaurants, a saloon, and general store, the ranch contains a swimming pool, tennis courts, and playground. Guest accommodations include duplex "cabins" (moderate), fully furnished but lacking extra amenities, and standard rooms (deluxe), which are plusher, more spacious, and feature televisions and refrigerators.

The poshest place for many miles is **Furnace Creek Inn** (619-786-2345), a 70-room hotel set on a hillside overlooking Death Valley. This Spanish-Moorish-style building, built of stone and adobe, is surrounded by flowering gardens. Palm trees shade the grounds and a stream feeds three koi ponds. There are two restaurants, a swank lobby, tennis courts, jacuzzi, and a spring-fed swimming pool. Guest rooms are trimly appointed and quite comfortably furnished. They offer such features as tile baths with brass fittings; most have fireplaces. The price tag is ultra-deluxe but includes breakfast and dinner.

Stove Pipe Wells Village (Stovepipe Wells; 619-786-2387) is an attractive 82-unit motel about 25 miles up the road. With a pool, lounge, restaurant, general store and gas station, it's as well-equipped as you could expect. If your heroes have always been cowboys, you'll sleep well here; some of the rooms are decorated Western-style with oxen yokes attached to the headboards and steer heads carved into the light fixtures. Budget.

Restaurants

MOJAVE DESERT RESTAURANTS

Chain restaurants and fast-food outlets proliferate throughout Antelope Valley. In Lancaster, the largest town in this western Mojave region, you'll encounter **Marie Callender's** (1649 West Avenue K; 805-945-6958), a sterile brass-and-hardwood-style restaurant known more for its homemade pies than gourmet dinners. The menu, comfortably priced in the budget to moderate league, includes numerous fresh pasta dishes as well as vegetable casserole, meat loaf, hamburgers, and chicken dishes.

For Mexican fare consider **Casa de Miguel** (44245 North Sierra Highway, Lancaster; 805-948-0793), a contemporary hacienda-style restaurant with hand-painted walls, high-back chairs, and outsize metal chandeliers. The raw wood, tilework, and fountain make the place appealing, if slightly overdone. The menu is equally elaborate, offering the standard medley of Mexican dishes plus specialties like red snapper, sirloin tips, New York steak, and broiled chicken. Lunch, dinner, and Sunday brunch. Prices are in the moderate range.

Idle Spurs Steak House (29557 West Route 58; 619-256-8888) is Barstow's gathering place, a common denominator destination for locals and outlanders alike. A Texas-size establishment with dance lounge and two dining rooms, it's Western in style. The menu is a moderately priced steak-and-seafood affair with prime rib, pork ribs, sautéed chicken, scallops, lobster, and halibut. Lunch and dinner are served weekdays, dinner only on the weekends.

The year-round Christmas lights add to the local color at **Peggy Sue's Nifty 50's Diner** (Yermo and Ghost Town roads, Yermo; 619-254-3370), a juke-box and soda-fountain joint that serves hamburgers, sandwiches, and all-American lunches and dinners. Meat loaf, honey-dipped chicken, roast beef, and chicken-fried steak are specialties. For decor there are photos of '50s celebrities as well as period pieces from the early era of rock-and-roll. Budget.

When in doubt, cover all bases: that seems to be the motto at **Canton Restaurant** (1300 West Main Street, Barstow; 619-256-9565). Ostensibly a Chinese restaurant, it offers egg rolls, sweet and sour pork, *chow yuk*, and other Asian standards. But the switch-hitting eatery also serves breakfast all day and prepares sandwiches, steaks, rainbow trout, fried scallops, and fried chicken on toast. On toast? Budget.

SEQUOIA AND KINGS CANYON RESTAURANTS

You can scale granite cliffs in Sequoia and Kings Canyon, shoot whitewater rapids, and return unscathed. What will kill you is the food. Nowhere is the "good enough for government work" philosophy more closely followed than in the kitchens of these national parks.

Adding inconvenience to insult, there aren't very many places to eat, and most are open only in summer. Probably the nicest is Sequoia National Park's **Lodge Dining Room** (Giant Forest Village; 209-565-3393). Overlooking a mountain meadow and stands of sequoia, it's an attractive dining room serving standard breakfast dishes. Dinner features chicken Veronique, New York steak, rainbow trout, prime rib and chicken fettucine; moderate. The nearby **Village Cafeteria** (209-565-3393) ladles out steam-tray food for all three meals at budget prices. At **Lodge Pole** (209-656-3301) a deli serves up barbecued ribs, fried chicken and an assortment of sandwiches, burgers and hot dogs.

The **Grant Grove Coffee Shop** (209-335-2314) is located at Grant Grove Inn, park headquarters, adjacent to the information center. A simple mountain eatery, the coffee shop offers a menu of soups, salads, and sandwiches at lunch and dinner. Daily specials feature such entrées as ravioli, fettucine, fish and chips, and steak. Budget.

The decor consists of stuffed game animals and wilderness photos. The bar is hewn from pine, and the dining room is filled with oilcloth tables. Otherwise **Kings Canyon Lodge** (67751 Route 180; 209-335-2405), set deep in the mountains, is just your average backcountry café. The menu features standard breakfast fare and sandwiches and hamburgers for lunch and dinner. Budget.

OWENS VALLEY RESTAURANTS

Dining on the other side of the Sierra Nevada is as grand a gourmet experience as in Sequoia and Kings Canyon. Somehow the love of the good life in this area has never been translated to the dinner table. All the towns along Route 395 are lined with restaurants, but most are cafés unworthy of note.

Beef, barbecued beef, and more beef are the order of the day at restaurants here in mountain country. **The Sportsman** (206 South Main Street, Lone Pine; 619-876-5454) serves several kinds of steak as well as beef ribs and prime rib. Even the pork and chicken dishes are barbecued. If you're otherwise inclined, they offer a few fish entrées plus a salad bar. For decor there are marvelous old stills from Western movies. Prices range from budget to moderate.

Over at **Margie's Merry Go-Round** (212 South Main Street, Lone Pine; 619-876-4115) they specialize in steaks, pork chops, and barbecue dishes. This small, friendly restaurant offers a children's menu and attracts a local crowd. Moderate.

If local crowds are any indication, **Bishop Grill** (281 North Route 395; 619-873-3911) is the best place in Bishop to eat. It's certainly the cheapest: the low budget prices at this café are vintage 1960s. The cuisine is straight Americana from the ham dinners to the pork chops to the breaded trout. Meat and potato entrées extend to steak, veal, and sausage. The breakfast and lunch menus can be derived by deduction.

Then there's the place that offers the world's strangest Sunday champagne brunch special—all the Chinese food you can eat. Hopefully you won't be stopping at **Imperial Gourmet Chinese Restaurant** (785 North Route 395, Bishop; 619-872-1144) on your way to church. Instead I recommend lunch and dinner, when you'll find enough Asian atmosphere and a variety of Chinese dishes for an enjoyable meal. Moderate.

MAMMOTH LAKES RESTAURANTS

One of the area's prime dining rooms is not on Mammoth Lakes at all, but a few miles south near a neighboring lake. **The Restaurant at Convict Lake** (Convict Lake Road about two miles west of Route 395; 619-934-3803) is a plush but rustic place. A fireplace with copper hood dominates the main room and the adjoining lounge has a woodburning stove. But the menu is the true drawing card at this gourmet establishment. Serving dinner only, the chef prepares a California-cuisine-style menu of rack of lamb, beef wellington, duck breast sauté, crab cakes, garlic chicken, and a nightly fresh fish special like salmon. Critically acclaimed, it is priced deluxe.

Shogun Japanese Restaurant (Sierra Centre Mall, Old Mammoth Road, Mammoth Lakes; 619-934-3970) may be parked in a shopping mall, but it still provides marvelous views of the mountains. Equipped with a sushi bar and adjoining lounge, the restaurant has sukiyaki, *tonkatsu*, tempura, and teriyaki dishes at moderate prices.

Matsu Restaurant (Route 203, Mammoth Lakes; 619-934-8277), a small wood-paneled place, offers an Asian grab bag. Dinner covers a lot of geography, ranging from Filipino-style *pansit* (shrimp and pork sautéed with onions and noodles) to teriyaki dishes from Japan to Chinese courses like sweet and sour chicken. Open for lunch and dinner weekdays, dinner only on weekends; moderate.

Pine plank walls and hand-stitched decorations make **La Sierra's Mexican Restaurant and Cantina** (3789 Route 203, Mammoth Lakes; 619-934-8083) worth the budget to moderate price of admission. They prepare a full array of dishes from south of the border. The restaurant serves all three meals, with a champagne brunch on Sundays.

With its Swiss alpine atmosphere, the **Matterhorn Restaurant** (Minaret Road; 619-934-3369) is one of Mammoth Lakes' most congenial dining places. The continental dinner menu begins with pâté, smoked salmon, escargots, and onion soup. Among the entrées are more than a dozen dishes—champagne-poached salmon, rainbow trout, rack of lamb with basil, pepper steak, scampi, grilled chicken, wienerschnitzel, duckling, and veal *médaillons*. Add a wine list plus dessert tray and you have an excellent opportunity to feast. Moderate to deluxe.

Informal, inexpensive café dining is the specialty of the house at **Blondie's Kitchen** (Sierra Centre Mall, Old Mammoth Road, Mammoth Lakes; 619-934-4048). Famous for its squaw bread and homemade specialties, this unassuming spot is favored by a local crowd. Breakfast, served all day, includes granola and oatmeal, omelettes, *machacas* (shredded beef and eggs), and blueberry pancakes. Lunch features cheeseburgers, a "veggie" sandwich with cream cheese, avocado, and sprouts, plus burritos and homemade soup. Budget; no dinner.

It's a far stretch from the sea, but **Ocean Harvest Restaurant** (64 Old Mammoth Road; 619-934-8539) has an impressive selection of broiled seafood dishes. This moderate-priced establishment also offers steaks, chicken dishes, and baby back ribs in a comfortable setting.

The **Sierra Inn Restaurant** (619-648-7774), near the center of town in June Lake, performs double duty. Part of the complex is a coffee shop serving standard breakfast, lunch and dinner items. In the evening the dining room opens, providing fresh seafood dishes as well as steaks, lasagna, and chicken dinners. With a high-beamed ceiling and full lounge, the dining room overlooks June Lake. Moderate.

Who would have guessed that a place called **Carson Peak Inn** (two miles west of June Lake on Route 158; 619-648-7575) would be right there at the base of Carson Peak offering spectacular views of the mountain. In addition to plate-glass vistas this moderate-to-deluxe-priced restaurant serves up steaks and seafood as well as pork ribs and vegetarian dishes.

DEATH VALLEY RESTAURANTS

Not far from the southern entrance to Death Valley, there's a café where water is served in mason jars and red-checkered curtains cover every window. The **Red Buggy** (Shoshone; 619-852-9908) offers sandwiches, Mexican dishes, and standards such as steak, pork chops, fried chicken and trout filet. Open from October through May. Budget.

Eat heartily because the next facilities are 72 miles away in Furnace Creek. Here you'll find five restaurants, all of which can be reached at 619-786-2345.

The least expensive food in all Death Valley, except for dishes you cook around your campfire, is in the **Cafeteria** at Furnace Creek Ranch. Open for breakfast and lunch, this steam-tray emporium serves fried chicken, beef stroganoff, hamburgers, and sandwiches. Atmosphere is nonexistent and the food has invariably been warming for hours before it hits your plate, but oh, those budget prices! In the evening, the Cafeteria becomes the **Wrangler Steak House**, serving moderate-to-deluxe-priced steak, chicken, and seafood entrées.

The **49er Coffee Shop** next door has omelettes, hot sandwiches, burgers and a selection of dinners ranging from pork chops and steak to calf's liver and fried trout. With woodplank walls and ranch atmosphere, it's a good place for a moderately priced meal.

The **Mexican Restaurant** serves traditional Mexican cuisine inside, and pizzas outside on the patio. Cozy and informal, the place consists of an unassuming room decorated with Mexican rugs. Prices range from moderate to deluxe.

The fine dining places are up at Furnace Creek Inn. At **L'Ottimos** you can feast on shrimp scampi, veal scallopine and pasta primavera. Dinner only; jackets required; deluxe.

Upstairs at the **Inn Dining Room**, candlelight and a beamed ceiling create a more formal atmosphere. Gentlemen are requested to wear jackets during dinner, and the menu is a fixed price. The ultra-deluxe price tag allows you to choose from among nearly 40 entrées including sole Oscar and medallions of beef. Breakfast and lunch menus are standard.

In Stovepipe Wells you'll find a spacious **Dining Room** (619-786-2387) embellished with Indian rugs and paintings of the Old West. The cuisine matches the ambience, an all-American menu featuring filet mignon, fried chicken, rainbow trout, steak, prawns, and halibut. Moderate.

The Great Outdoors

The Sporting Life

FISHING AND BOATING

The Kern and Kings rivers in Sequoia and Kings Canyon national parks offer trout fishing. The Mammoth Lakes area is also an angler's delight.

For fishing gear rentals, tackle, and friendly information, contact **Ernie's Tackle and Ski Shop** (June Lake; 619-648-7756). If you'd like to try fly fishing, **Western Waters Fly Fishing** (Mammoth Lakes; 619-934-4897) offers instruction.

A few places rent fishing boats, including **Kaweah Marina** (35597 Sierra Drive, Lemon Cove; 209-597-2526), **June Lake Marina** (June Lake; 619-648-7726), and **Lake Sabrina Boat Landing** (Bishop Creek, Bishop; 619-873-7425).

HORSEBACK RIDING AND PACK TOURS

Out here in the High Desert you can saddle up and ride into the American past. To rent horses around Victorville try **Mojave Narrows Riding Stables** (619-244-1644); in the Barstow area contact **Dan McCue Ranch Stables** (619-254-2184). In Sequoia and Kings Canyon national parks there are stables located at **Wolverton Pack Station** (209-565-3445), **Grant Grove** (209-335-2374), **Cedar Grove** (209-565-3464), and **Mineral King** (209-561-3404).

Pack trips in the Sierra Nevada often combine horseback riding with fishing expeditions. If you prefer something less adventurous, most outfits offer full-day or half-day excursions as well as longer treks. For details contact **Schober Pack Station** (Bishop; 619-873-4785), **Red's Meadow Resort Pack Train** (Mammoth Lakes; 619-934-2345 in summer; 619-873-3928 in winter), **Frontier Pack Station** (June Lake; 619-648-7701), **Mineral King Pack Station** (Three Rivers; 209-561-4142), or **Cedar Grove Pack Station** (Three Rivers; 209-565-3464).

In Death Valley, **Furnace Creek Ranch** (619-786-2345) rents horses and offers wagon and carriage rides (winter only).

WINDSURFING, WATERSKIING, AND SAILING

Water sports are nearly as popular as skiing in Mammoth Lakes. Windsurfing, waterskiing, and sailing are available through **Alpine Adventures** (Mammoth Lake; 619-934-7188). There is no waterskiing on June Lake, but windsurfing is permitted.

KAYAKING AND WHITEWATER RAFTING

Shooting the rapids on the Kern and Kings rivers is great sport. Several California tour companies offer exciting adventures on rubber rafts, and some offer kayaking. Among them are **Sierra South** (Kernville; 619-376-3745), **Spirit Whitewater** (1001 Rose Avenue, Penngrove; 707-795-7305), **Zephyr River Expeditions** (P.O. Box 510, Columbia; 209-532-6249), and **Whitewater Voyages** (El Sobrante; 415-222-5994).

GOLF

The desert may be one huge sand trap, but you won't find many greens in these parts. Among the exceptions are the **Victorville Municipal Golf Course** (14144 Green Tree Boulevard, Victorville; 619-245-4860), **Camelot Golf Course** (Camelot Boulevard, Mojave; 805-824-4107), **Three Rivers Golf Course** (41117 Sierra Drive, Three Rivers; 209-561-3133), **Mount Whitney Golf Course** (Route 395, south of Lone Pine; 619-876-9885), **Bishop Country Club** (South Highway 395, Bishop; 619-873-5828), and **Furnace Creek Golf Course** (Highway 190, Death Valley; 619-786-2301).

BALLOONING AND GLIDING

Soaring in a hot air balloon is all part of a day's work at **Balloon Adventure** (Lancaster; 818-888-0576), **High Sierra Ballooning and Alpine Adventures** (Mammoth Lakes; 619-934-7188), or **L.A. Balloon Port** (42222 50th Street West, Quartz Hill; 805-943-7676).

Another way to sail through the air is in a glider: contact **Aronson's Air Service** (40th Street West, Rosamond; 805-256-2200) or **Crystal Soaring** (32810 165th Street East, Llano; 805-944-3341).

BICYCLING

The Eastern Sierra is a prime place for mountain riding. In Mammoth Lakes, the **Mammoth Scenic Loop** (off of Minaret Road) offers a lovely, though hilly, overview of this majestic area. Another picturesque ride is the **June Lake Loop** (Route 158), an easy 16-mile route around the base of the mountains and along the lake shore. For experienced bike riders, the road from **Tom's Place to Rock Creek Winter Lake** is nine miles of uphill pedaling through a stunning canyon. Think of the fun you'll have coming back.

Death Valley may seem like the last place to ride a bicycle, but it's actually quite pleasant from October to April. The main road in the park is paved and there's little traffic. The side roads to some of the sights are gravel, however, and require a mountain bike.

Furnace Creek is a good starting point: it's an easy ride from here to Badwater and Artists Drive, though the latter destination requires uphill pedaling. For an even more challenging ride you can venture up, up, uphill to Dante's View; plan on an all-day effort and bring provisions (especially water!).

BIKE RENTALS Up around Mammoth Lakes try **Mammoth Sporting Goods** (Old Mammoth Road; 619-934-3239) or **Footloose** (619-934-2400) for mountain bikes.

Beaches and Parks

MOJAVE DESERT AND DEATH VALLEY PARKS

Saddleback Butte State Park—Sprinkled with Joshua trees and backdropped by its 3651-foot namesake, this desert facility gazes out toward distant mountains. Roadrunners, desert tortoises, kit fox, and rattlesnakes inhabit these 2875 acres. Trails lead up the granite butte and through the state park.

Facilities: Picnic areas, restroom; restaurants and groceries are four miles away in Lake Los Angeles or 17 miles to Lancaster; information center, 805-942-0662. *Camping:* Permitted.

Getting there: Located on East Avenue J, 17 miles east of Lancaster.

Red Rock Canyon State Park—This 10,000-acre facility, situated amid sculpted cliffs, is a major sightseeing destination. Its deposits of red sandstone, white clay, lava, and pink tuff have been uplifted and then eroded to create a dramatic landscape. Joshua trees, desert holly, and creosote bushes abound and wildlife is plentiful.

Facilities: There is a small store in Cantel, about eight miles away, restaurants and groceries about 20 miles away in Mojave; information, 805-942-0662. *Camping:* Permitted.

Getting there: Located on Route 14 about 20 miles north of Mojave.

Mojave Narrows Regional Park—Sitting astride an old riverbed, this 860-acre park boasts two lakes and an intaglio of waterways. There are broad meadows and stately stands of willow and cottonwood. Renowned for its fishing (permits required and can be obtained at park), the park also offers riding stables and hiking trails.

Facilities: Restrooms, picnic areas, snack bar, bait shop; restaurants and groceries are nearby in Victorville; information, 619-245-2226. *Camping:* Permitted.

Getting there: Located at 18000 Yates Road in Victorville.

Providence Mountains State Recreation Area—This 5900-acre park, set on a mountain slope overlooking a vast desert panorama, is remarkably beautiful. Hiking trails lead into the hills; and Mitchell Caverns, a series of spectacular limestone formations, provide sightseeing opportunities. Bighorn sheep, wild burros, coyotes, and bobcats traverse the area while yucca and cacti cover the hillsides.

Facilities: Information center (no phone), restrooms, picnic area; restaurants and groceries are dozens of miles away. See the "Sightseeing" section in this chapter for further details. *Camping:* Permitted in six sites on a first-come, first-served basis.

Getting there: From Barstow go east on Route 40 for 100 miles; then northwest on Essex Road for 16 miles.

Afton Canyon—One of the rare places in the Mojave Desert to have year-round running water, this valley has been carved for millennia by the Mojave River. The result is a remarkable series of eroded cliffs, brilliantly colored and reminiscent of the Grand Canyon. There are remote gorges to explore and ancient Indian trails nearby. The railroad runs through the center of this scenic wonder, with a steel trestle crossing one span. The place is also popular with off-road vehicles, so you have to weigh the beauty against the bother.

Facilities: Restrooms, picnic areas; restaurants and groceries are about 35 miles away in Barstow. *Camping:* Permitted.

Getting there: From Barstow take Route 15 east for 33 miles, then go south for three miles on Afton Road.

Death Valley National Monument—Extending across more than two million acres and rising from below sea level to over 11,000 feet, this park is a land unto itself, varied and full of possibility. It contains 200 square miles of salt flats, 14 square miles of sand dunes, and several mountain ranges. Death Valley itself covers only a small part of the facility.

In addition to standard sightseeing spots there are hiking trails and 100 miles of jeep tracks leading to obscure high desert locales. Over 350 bird species are found here, together with desert tortoises, rattlesnakes, mountain lions, bobcats, mule deer, and bighorn sheep. For complete information see the "Sightseeing" and other sections in this chapter.

Facilities: Information center and museum, 619-786-2331; hotels, restaurants, picnic areas, restrooms, groceries. *Camping:* Permitted in nine campgrounds; Furnace Creek is open year-round; three low-elevation facilities are open from October to April; and three high-elevation campgrounds are available from April to October. No advance reservations.

Getting there: Located in the northern Mojave Desert along Routes 178 and 190.

SIERRA NEVADA PARKS

Sequoia National Forest—Located at the southern edge of the Sierra Nevada, this facility boasts more than 30 sequoia groves. It also includes several resort spots like Kern Canyon, popular with weekend refugees from Los Angeles. Climbing from 1000 to 12,000 feet, the preserve contains three wilderness areas.

Facilities: Information, 209-784-1500. *Camping:* Permitted in 48 campgrounds. *Fishing:* About 1200 miles of streams and several dozen high-country lakes offer ample opportunities.

Getting there: Access is via Routes 178, 155, and 190.

Sequoia and Kings Canyon National Parks—These adjoining facilities, together covering more than 850,000 acres, are discussed at length elsewhere in this chapter. For wilderness enthusiasts they offer 800 miles of trails, 14,000-foot peaks, and opportunities for horseback riding and cross-country skiing.

Facilities: Restrooms, picnic areas, restaurants, cabins, museums. Information: Sequoia and Kings Canyon, 209-565-3341, or Kings Canyon Visitors Center, 209-335-2315. *Camping:* Permitted in 13 campgrounds, most of which are closed in winter. Reservations are required for Lodgepole Campground (the largest of the sites at 225 spaces) at MYSTIX outlets. All others are available on a first-come, first-served basis. Wilderness camping is very popular. For permit information, call 209-565-3307. *Fishing:* There are streams and lakes throughout both parks, with many good trout pools.

Getting there: Route 198 leads into Sequoia from the southwest and Route 180 (General's Highway) connects the two parks.

(Text continued on page 458.)

Ski the Southland

As a travel destination, Southern California offers everything. Even during winter, when rain spatters the coast and fog invades the valleys, the Southland has one more treat in its bottomless bag—snow.

No sooner has the white powder settled than skiers from around the world beeline to the region's high altitude resort areas. They come to schuss through fir forests in the San Gabriel Mountains, challenge the runs above San Bernardino, and breathe the beauty of Mammoth Lakes at Christmas.

The season begins in late fall and sometimes lasts until May. During those frosty months dozens of alpine areas offer both downhill and cross-country skiing.

Within Los Angeles County itself, Angeles National Forest features both **Kratka Ridge** (818-449-1749) and **Mt. Waterman** (818-790-2002) ski areas plus five nordic ski trails. For further information, contact the local ranger station at 818-790-1151. One of Southern California's most popular ski areas is **Mt. Baldy** (714-981-3344), a 10,064-foot peak just 45 minutes from the city. With a vertical drop of 2140 feet, the facility provides 24 runs, four lifts, a lodge, and a ski school.

The neighboring San Bernardino Mountains, which rise to over 11,000 feet, offer several alpine ski areas. Located along Route 18 between Lake Arrowhead and Big Bear Lake, these resorts include **Snow Valley** (714-867-2751), **Snow Summit** (714-866-5766), and **Bear Mountain Ski Resort** (714-585-2519).

Even Palm Springs, California's vaunted warm-weather hideaway, gives spa-goers a chance to challenge the surrounding slopes. The Palm Springs Aerial Tramway carries desert dwellers to over 8000 feet elevation in **Mount San Jacinto State Park** (619-327-0222), where a nordic center rents cross-country gear, and two loop trails circle through backcountry wilderness. Permit required and obtainable at the station.

This more demanding nordic-style skiing is gaining increased popularity around the state. It's the adventurer's way to explore the slopes—fill a daypack, strap on skis, and take off across the mountains. In the pack are extra clothes, food, water, flashlight, knife, map, compass, blanket, matches, equipment repair tools, and a first-aid kit.

Unrestricted by ski lifts and marked runs, cross-country skiers venture everywhere that geography and gravity permit. Their sport is tantamount to hiking on skis, with the entire expanse of the mountain range their domain. Some skiers disappear into the wilderness for days on end, emerging only when supplies run low.

If you prefer a base of operations from which to experience the wild, several nordic ski centers operate in Sequoia and Kings Canyon national parks. The Giant Forest and Lodgepole/Wolverton sections of Sequoia, for instance, feature 35 miles of trails and offer rentals, lessons, and other recreational activities. Giant Forest Village contains restaurants and motel accommodations; nearby **Sequoia Ski Touring** (209-565-3435) assists skiers in making arrangements.

Grant Grove in Kings Canyon National Park has five marked trails, varying in difficulty, and offers lessons and rentals through **Grant Grove Ski Touring** (209-335-2348). Like Sequoia National Park, Kings Canyon sits amid a network of High Sierra cross-country trails. Miles of these alpine paths extend in every direction, leading through forests of giant sequoia trees. There are frozen lakes to explore, extraordinary mountain vistas, and secluded warming huts.

Many resorts, on the other hand, focus on downhill and alpine-style skiing and provide complete facilities for their athletic guests. Some, like those around Mammoth Lakes in the eastern Sierra, are self-contained villages with every amenity imaginable. Such resorts often have boutiques, galleries, pools, tennis courts, groceries, restaurants, and *après*-ski spots. There are instructors for beginners and intermediate skiers alike, snow schools for children, and enough diversions to keep even a non-skier content.

For Angelenos, the Mammoth/June Lakes region represents skier heaven. Located high in the Sierra Nevada chain, about 300 miles from the streets of Los Angeles, **Mammoth Mountain** (619-934-2571) is one of the largest ski areas in the United States. A major center for both alpine and nordic skiers, it boasts mountain lodges, crag.,y peaks, and enough white powder to create an aura of the Alps right here in sun-drenched Southern California.

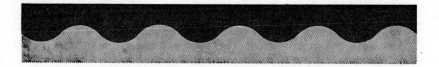

Sierra National Forest—Tucked between Kings Canyon and Yosemite national parks, this 1,300,000-acre preserve climbs from 1000 to 14,000 feet elevation and ranges from rolling chaparral country to bald peaks. There are two groves of sequoias and 1100 miles of trails. More than one-quarter of the forest is wilderness.

Facilities: Information, 209-487-5155. *Camping:* Permitted in 61 campgrounds, most of which are closed in winter. *Fishing:* About 1200 miles of streams and more than 1000 lakes (including Bass Lake) provide excellent opportunities for trout, bass, and kokanee salmon.

Getting there: Access is via Routes 168 and 41.

Inyo National Forest—This sprawling giant, divided into two sections by Owens Valley, contains within its domain the Ansel Adams Wilderness (formerly Minarets Wilderness), Mammoth Lakes, the John Muir Wilderness, Devils Postpile, the White Mountains, and Mount Whitney. Numbering 500 lakes and 100 streams, it is traversed by 1150 miles of trails, including the John Muir Trail.

Facilities: Information, 619-873-5841. *Camping:* Permitted in 67 campgrounds, most of which are closed in winter. *Fishing:* Excellent trout streams and well-stocked lakes.

Getting there: Access points are generally located off Route 395 in the Owens Valley and Mammoth Lakes areas.

Hiking

SEQUOIA AND KINGS CANYON TRAILS

Sequoia and Kings Canyon national parks offer miles of serene trails amid towering sequoia trees and tumbling waterfalls.

Mist Falls Trail (4 miles), near Zumwalt Meadow, leads north past a massive stone face called The Sphinx, then continues on toward its namesake, a cascade so light it resembles mist.

A strenuous hike along **Sugarbowl–Redwood Canyon–Hart Tree Loop Trail** (10 miles) takes you through some of the most beautiful country in Kings Canyon. Beginning on Sugarbowl Trail, then connecting with Redwood Canyon Trail and Hart Tree Trail, the loop passes the 209-foot Hart Tree. The trailhead is located at Redwood Saddle. (Check ahead with the ranger, the area is sometimes closed.)

For a 360° view of the Sierra Crest, Kings Canyon, and the sequoias of Redwood Canyon, hike **Buena Vista Peak** (1 mile), the highest point west of Generals Highway. (The trailhead is south of Kings Canyon Overlook.)

Another majestic view lies along **Little Baldy Trail** (1.7 miles). From here on a clear day you can see the San Joaquin Valley. Begin this trail at Little Baldy Saddle, 11 miles north of Giant Forest Village on Generals Highway.

Ever-popular **Muir Grove Trail** (2 miles), which begins near Dorst campground contains magnificent sequoias in a lovely setting.

An easy hike along the **Tokopah Falls Trail** (1.7 miles) leads through Tokopah Valley, where the Marble Fork of the Kaweah River flows between soaring granite cliffs. The trailhead is located at Lodgepole campground.

From the same campground, **Pear Lake Trail** (6.7 miles), a moderate climb, carries past Emerald Lake and through an area rich in wildlife and wildflowers to Pear Lake. The trail ends in a granite-bound basin amid a dozen tiny lakes and crystal creeks.

Of the many trails crossing Mineral King, several offer day-excursions. **Tar Gap Trail** (4 miles), rising quickly from Cold Spring campground, crosses several creeks and provides views of Sawtooth Peak, Empire Mountain, and Timber Gap.

Timber Gap Trail (4 miles), which begins near the end of the road in Mineral King, passes through a red fir forest, crosses a summit, then descends into the flower-strewn meadows of Timber Gap Creek.

Sawtooth Pass Trail (3 miles), beginning at the same trailhead as Timber Gap, follows Monarch Creek upward through manzanita cover to Groundhog Meadow. Here Monarch Lakes Trail continues across the creek and zigzags up through open pine and fir stands to Monarch Lakes.

From the road's end in Mineral King, **Eagle Lake Trail** (3.4 miles) follows Eagle Creek through fragrant sagebrush and colorful wildflowers. The path ascends 2000 feet before reaching Eagle Lake, which nestles below White Chief Peak in a granite bowl.

OWENS VALLEY TRAILS

The Sierra Nevada offer the finest hiking in California, attracting adventurers from all over the world. Along Route 395 in the Owens Valley, roads leading to major trailheads branch off in nearly every town.

Sparkling lakes, wildflowers, cascades, and encircling peaks await when you climb the **Kearsarge Pass to Flower Lake Trail** (2.5 miles). The trailhead is at the end of Onion Valley Road, outside Independence.

East of Bishop, Lake Sabrina and South Lake are important trailheads for serious backpackers. Backdropped by glacier-bearing peaks, **South Lake to Treasure Lakes Trail** (5 miles) climbs 1000 feet through mixed coniferous forest to the south fork of Bishop Creek.

Lake Sabrina to Dingleberry Lake Trail (4.5 miles) ascends 1500 feet to an alpine lake and presents a panorama of lakes, forests, and lofty Sierra crests.

The most famous climb in the Sierra is along **Mount Whitney Trail** (10.7 miles) to the 14,495-summit. The lure of ascending the highest peak in the "lower 48" is irresistible to many. Camping is permitted at Outpost Camp (3.5 miles) and Trail Camp (6 miles). Camping permits good from March 1 to May 31 are available from Mount Whitney Ranger District, P.O. Box 8, Lone Pine, CA 93545; 619-876-5542. There is a quota, so applications are picked by lottery. Day-use permits are available at the trailhead.

MAMMOTH AND JUNE LAKES TRAILS

The Mammoth and June lakes region is a key entranceway to the Ansel Adams (formerly Minarets) and John Muir wilderness areas. From here there is easy access to the **Pacific Crest** and **John Muir trails**. The John Muir Trail, which extends from Lake Tahoe to Mount Whitney, is a 200-mile-long portion of the Pacific Crest Trail. (Permits are required for these wilderness areas and should be obtained well in advance.) A special note: as tempting as mountains waters look, don't drink from them unless you have brought water-purification equipment: the intestinal parasite *Giardia* is wide-spread in this area. Also, when possible, avoid trails used by pack trains.

Day-hikes up Coldwater Creek and Mammoth Creek from Lake Mary offer great outings. Try **Mammoth Creek to Duck Lake Trail** (5.5 miles) with its many lakes, vistas, and flowering meadows. Duck Lake is an ideal trout-fishing spot.

An easy hike along **Mammoth Rock Trail** (3 miles) leads east past its namesake, a fossil-embedded marble and limestone monolith. The trail, which begins from Old Mammoth Road, also skirts the largest Jeffrey pine forest in the world.

It's a beautiful hike along the **Sherwin Creek Canyon Trail** (3 miles) to the five small Sherwin Lakes. Switchbacks ease the 800 foot climb. Once here, you can ascend further along **Valentine Lake Trail** (4.5 miles) to a forest-fringed lake squeezed into a glaciated cirque. Sherwin Creek Canyon trailhead is located one mile west of Sherwin Creek campground.

Lake George to Crystal Lake Trail (1 mile) treks through mountain hemlock to a serene lake at the base of Crystal Crag. For sweeping views, continue up to the top on **Mammoth Crest Trail** (2 miles).

You'll experience a touch of wilderness with little effort along **Lake George–Lake Barrett–T.J. Loop Trail** (1.5 miles). It starts at Lake George campground and follows the lake shore before veering uphill through flowering meadows and stands of alder and pine.

From the June Lake Loop, **Agnew Lake Trail** (2 miles) departs near Silver Lake and rises 1300 feet to a picnic area and cold mountain lake.

Another hike leaving the Silver Lake area is **Fern Creek Trail** (1.5 miles), which climbs nearly 2000 feet en route to Fern Lake. A branch trail travels another three miles to Yost Lake.

Convict Creek Trail (10 miles) is a long but rewarding trek from Convict Lake past three alpine lakes, well-stocked with fish, over a 10,000-foot ridge. The trail then switchbacks down to Laurel Canyon Road.

Horseshoe Lake to Reds Meadow Trail (6.5 miles) passes through pine-hemlock forest, skirts McCloud Lake, and crosses the Sierra Crest. The trail then descends to the old John Muir Trail where a side trip leads to Red Cones, a formation of geologically young cinder cones. The main trail continues through red-fir forests to Reds Meadow campground with its refreshing hot springs.

DEATH VALLEY TRAILS

Rugged hiking in the desert and mountains is a favorite sport around Death Valley. Special precautions, however, must be taken throughout this area: be sure to carry plenty of water; watch for rattlesnakes; do not enter mine shafts and tunnels; and avoid desert hiking between May and October. Maps of more than 20 hiking trails are available at the ranger station.

The **Salt Creek Interpretive Trail** (.5 mile), near the sand dunes at Stove Pipe Well, provides a glimpse of the salt-tolerant grasses and rare pupfish of Salt Creek. Arriving at dawn you will see the tracks left by numerous nocturnal animals.

One mile west of Stovepipe Wells Village, a short dirt road heads south to **Mosaic Canyon Trail** (2 miles). Formed by a fault zone, the canyon's walls are polished by wind and water. The multicolored rock debris deposited here gives the canyon its name.

For a view from the highest peak for miles around, park your car at Mahogany Flat and climb **Telescope Peak Trail** (7 miles). Spring and fall are the best seasons for this moderate ascent. Once atop this 11,049-foot peak you can gaze east across Death Valley and west to the Sierra Nevada.

A less ambitious trip is up **Wildrose Peak Trail** (4 miles) from Charcoal Kilns. Here you'll find wide vistas and a variety of animals and plants, including bristlecone pines.

Traveler's Tracks

Sightseeing

THE MOJAVE DESERT

Stretching from Los Angeles County all the way to Arizona and Nevada, the Mojave Desert is a region of daunting distance. Sightseeing this open range means driving hundreds of miles between points of interest. As a result, the descriptions below are organized by geographic region, some covering extremely extensive areas.

Bakersfield actually lies west of the Mojave but incorporates much of its history and culture. Antelope Valley sits in the desert's western corner just south of the town of Mojave. The "Barstow area" extends south from the town of Barstow for 35 miles and east for over 100 miles. Death Valley, actually part of the Mojave Desert, is treated as a separate destination.

BAKERSFIELD AREA

Up in Grapevine Canyon, where Tejon Pass cuts a notch in the Tehachapi Mountains, the U.S. Army built an outpost in 1854 to keep Native American tribes on their reservations. At **Fort Tejon State Historic Park** (Route 5, Lebec; 805-248-6692; admission), a few adobe structures survive, set against a backdrop of curving mountains. Once headquarters for the First Dragoons and Camel Corps, the fort used camels to carry its provisions. Today there is little to see here, though mock Civil War battles and re-enactments of 1850s military life are staged on the third Saturday of each month, April through October.

Pride of Bakersfield is the **Kern County Museum's Pioneer Village** (3801 Chester Avenue; 805-861-2132; admission), a reconstructed town dating to the late-19th century. Dotted across the 16-acre grounds are about five dozen Western structures, each depicting life on the early frontier. There are watchmaker and dressmaker shops, a split-wood corral, and a log cabin complete with photographs of Abe Lincoln over the fireplace. You can step up to the Fellows Hotel, visit old Mr. Pinckney's house, and tour the railway station. An excellent outdoor museum, the town contains everything from caboose to calaboose and features an adjacent museum which re-creates the history of the region's vital farm industry.

ANTELOPE VALLEY

For Angelenos, the Mojave Desert begins in **Antelope Valley** on the far side of the San Gabriel Mountains. Here urbanization has sprawled over the hills to create Palmdale and Lancaster, towns long on aerospace and short on soul.

Backed against the mountains are several natural attractions which make this western corner of the Mojave a dramatic introduction to the desert. The first is a scenic drive into the **Juniper Hills** (★) (go south from Pearblossom along 106th Street East and Juniper Road). Climbing to 4600 feet, this loop trades the Joshua trees of the valley floor for higher-elevation piñon and juniper trees and provides endless views across a multihued desert.

Connect with Route N6 and you'll arrive at **Devil's Punchbowl County Natural Area** (28000 Devil's Punchbowl Road, Pearblossom; 805-944-2743). This wedge-shaped canyon, paralleled on two fronts by earthquake faults, has been crushed between opposing geologic forces. On either side sedimentary rocks have been thrust upward to create vertical walls that are folding in upon each other like the pages of a closing book. Hiking trails lead through these angular sandstone slabs, passing stands of juniper, piñon, and manzanita.

Unique is too timid a term to describe the **Antelope Valley Indian Museum** (15701 East Avenue M, Lancaster; 805-942-0662; admission). With displays of bone tools, arrowheads, Kachina dolls, and basketry, the museum offers a cross section of Native American life in California. But the truly impressive element is the museum building itself. Built directly into the rocks that backdrop the complex, it's a chalet-style house with two gabled turrets and seven different roof levels. Constructed in the 1930s as a private home, the facility contains walls of wood and natural bedrock. One room has a rock floor with huge boulders rising in the center. These natural formations combine with brilliant murals and colorfully painted ceilings to create a striking desert setting. Call for tour reservations; open on the weekend only.

On the other side of Lancaster's sprawling metropolis, more than 20 miles away, lies the **Antelope Valley California Poppy Reserve** (15101 West Lancaster Road; 805-724-1180). From March until May, when California's state flower blooms, these slopes are transformed into a wildflower wonderland. In addition to the bright-hued countryside, there is an architecturally noteworthy visitor center, with three sides built into the earth for insulation against desert extremes.

To determine whether the poppies are blooming and for general information on the Antelope Valley area, contact the **Lancaster Chamber of Commerce** (44335 Lowtree Avenue, Lancaster; 805-948-4518).

Most of the gold mines which once flowered in Antelope Valley have long since died. **Burton's Tropico Gold Mine**, shut down and closed to the public, can still be seen from afar in its hillside setting. Amid slag heaps and the detritus of a bygone era stand the mining buildings. Formerly one of Southern California's richest strikes, it is now a cluster of tin structures and woodframe houses ravaged by desert wind. (To get there from Route 14 in Rosamond, take Rosamond Boulevard west four miles, then turn right on Mojave Tropico Road for one mile.)

MOJAVE AREA

One of nature's most impressive desert displays is **Red Rock Canyon State Park** (Route 14 about 20 miles north of Mojave; 805-942-0662), a photogenic badlands which resembles a miniature Grand Canyon. As you enter through the sheer-wall gorge that leads into the valley, the landscape opens into a succession of accordion-pleated cliffs. Eroded by water, the rockfaces are carved into minarets, spires, and crenelated towers. Nearby walls of white clay have been formed by weather to create columnar structures resembling stalagmites.

This 4000-acre park rests in a biologic transition zone between the Mojave and the Sierra Nevada and is alive with flora and fauna from both areas. The canyon also sits on a geologic cusp between the Mojave and the Great Basin, making it a kind of outdoor museum. Little wonder that everyone from early Native Americans to modern-day movie makers has been attracted to the region.

Desert Tortoise Natural Area (619-375-7125), a unique habitat housing the largest known concentration of desert tortoises, lies about three miles northeast of California City along Randsburg-Mojave Road (graded). This 16,000-acre preserve serves as sanctuary for a reptile that can live up to 100 years. Measuring only 15 inches, the desert tortoise digs communal burrows which are often 20 feet long. Since they hibernate in winter and stay underground to avoid summer heat, the best time to see them is from March to June in the morning and late afternoon.

The "living ghost town" of **Randsburg**, as well as neighboring **Johannesburg** and **Red Mountain**, is rich in minerals and history. Together these frontier communities formed a mining district that boomed first from gold deposits, then tungsten and silver. Of course that was a century ago, but today Randsburg still retains an aura of the 1890s. Many of the houses in town are stripped of paint and seem ready to fall to the next desert wind; others are restored and occupied. There's a gravity-feed gas pump, wooden sidewalk, and an outhouse with a crescent moon carved in the door. You'll pass a white-steepled church and a succession of tin-roof stores whose signs have long since faded into indecipherable blurs.

The **Randsburg General Store** (35 Butte Avenue, Randsburg; 619-374-2418) still has its antique soda fountain and grizzled clientele. And over at the **Desert Museum** (Butte Avenue) you can view such mining-era artifacts as a miniature five-ton steam locomotive (which seems more like a toy train for big kids than a real machine). Open weekends.

BARSTOW AREA

Crossroads of the Mojave is the sun-baked community of Barstow. An important railroad town, Barstow is the converging point for the Union Pacific and Santa Fe railways. It's also the intersection of Routes 58, 15, and 40, which together cover much of the California desert.

Communications central for this region is the **California Desert Information Center** (831 Barstow Road, Barstow; 619-256-8313). This hilltop museum features displays reflecting the area's flora, fauna, and history. There are also pamphlets, maps, and an information desk.

The nearby **Mojave River Valley Museum** (270 East Virginia Way, Barstow; 619-256-5452) has a more complete collection of artifacts and memorabilia. Dedicated to the preservation of local history and culture, it contains discoveries from the Calico Early Man Site and specimens of desert minerals and gems. Other displays re-create the era of Spanish explorers and the recent advent of the space industry.

Surprisingly, just a few miles from the drab streets of Barstow you'll discover folded and faulted mountains that are layer cakes of color. Drive out to **Rainbow Basin National Natural Landmark** and encounter a deep canyon surrounded by striped cliffs of sedimentary rock. Rich in fossil deposits, the hills were created over eons and contain the remains of mastodons, rhinos, and camel-type creatures.

Even more impressive is the bald beauty of the place. These are hills the color of dawn built in a myriad of shapes that change character with the light. The three-mile road that loops through this rock preserve passes zebra-striped buttes, boulders formed into fists, and tortuously twisted formations. To explore the basin from Barstow follow Fort Irwin Road north for five and a half miles from Route 58, then turn left on Fossil Bed Road for three miles to the loop drive.

The commercial outlets are as numerous as the memories at **Calico Ghost Town San Bernardino Regional Park** (Ghost Town Road, ten miles northeast of Barstow; 619-254-2122; admission). This old mining center has been transformed into a kind of windblown theme park complete with narrow-gauge railroad rides, a hall of illusions, and a hokey Western playhouse. Native charm endures despite it all. There are stone houses built into the surrounding mountain and woodframe stores bent with time. Mining paraphernalia lies scattered everywhere; and the town's cemetery and open mines remain prime exploring sites. Camping is permitted.

It was 1881 when prospectors struck it rich and Calico boomed to life with over 20 saloons, a temperance society, and its own Chinatown. More than $86 million in gold, silver, and other minerals was mined from the multihued "calico" mountains before the town went bust. Eventually Walter Knott, of Knott's Berry Farm fame, restored the ramshackle town and turned it over to the local government.

Perhaps 200,000 years before Calico Ghost Town was even conceived, hunters roamed the **Calico Early Man Archaeological Site**. Back in those Pleistocene times the landscape was lush with junipers, live oaks, and pines. The climate was temperate and a large body of water, Lake Manix, attracted mammoths, sloths, and saber-toothed cats.

This scientifically important site was a tool factory where early man rendered local deposits of chert and chalcedony into choppers, picks, and scrapers. Directed for several years by Dr. Louis S. B. Leakey, famed discoverer of Africa's Olduvai Gorge, the site is so ancient it upset earlier theories that man was in the New World for only 10,000 or 20,000 years. In fact Calico Early Man might not have been a *Homo sapiens* at all, but a now-extinct species such as *Homo erectus* or *Homo sapiens neandertalensis*.

Today, either on a guided or self-guided tour, you can view the archaeological pits, see early stone tools, and wander back in your mind to an age of ice when the desert was in bloom. To get your body to the place from which your mind can wander, take Route 15 for about 15 miles east from Barstow, get off at the Minneola exit, and go north three miles. Closed Monday and Tuesday; for information contact the San Bernardino County Museum, 714-798-8570.

North of the San Bernardino Mountains, where the hills descend to meet the Mojave Desert, lie the Lucerne and Apple valleys. Characterized by dry lake beds and granite heights, the region is 35 miles south of Barstow.

Victorville, the chief town hereabouts, is known primarily as a stop along Route 15, the golden road that whisks Angelenos to the promised land of Las Vegas. This unassuming crossroads is also a point of pilgrimage for buckaroos everywhere, home to the **Roy Rogers–Dale Evans Museum** (15650 Seneca Road; 619-243-4547; admission). You'll thrill to the diorama of Roy and Dale as well as the photos of Roy's mom and dad and of the cowboy as a lad back in Duck Run, Ohio. Roy's African safari heads are here, as well as Dale's dining room table and Roy's decorative saddles. There are awards galore and an entire section filled with religious mementoes (Christian, of course). Climax to it all is Roy's faithful horse Trigger, stuffed, in a display case, fully saddled and ready to ride. (Don't forget to stop at the Happy Trails Gift Shop on the way out.)

Two long, lonesome highways, Routes 40 and 15, travel east from Barstow deeper into the desert. Along Route 40, which tracks due east toward Arizona and New Mexico, chocolate brown mountains crowd the horizon in every direction.

About 35 miles from town **Pisgah Crater**, a 250-foot cinder cone, rises to the south. Another young volcano, **Amboy Crater**, lies along old Route 66 (National Trails Highway), which diverts from Route 40 in Ludlow. A curving black figure against a mountain backdrop, the volcano is surrounded by a vast lava field. To the southeast this lava flow gives way to **Bristol Dry Lake**, an ancient freshwater lake that now supports an extensive chloride works.

One of the region's most remarkable features is the 600-foot-high mountain of sand created by the **Kelso Dunes** (★). Tallest dunes in the California desert, they are like a giant's sand box. An intriguing phenomenon here results from the wind, which shifts around the dunes in circular fashion, causing the tall grasses to etch round tracks in the sand with their tips. If you hike the dunes, watch for these telltale marks and for the lizards inhabiting this forlorn but beautiful spot. To get there from Route 40, travel 80 miles east of Barstow, then go north 15 miles on Kelbaker Road (which alternates between paved and unpaved sections); turn left onto a marked road (just past the power line). This rough dirt road leads three miles to a parking lot.

If you think this place is remote, consider **Providence Mountains State Recreation Area.** Located at a famous address—the middle of nowhere—it rests sidesaddle on the slopes of a rugged mountain. From the visitor center, perched at 4300 feet, you can gaze across 300 square miles of desert to mountains 125 miles away in Arizona. Buttes, dunes, broad *bajadas*, and desert valleys extend along a 180° panorama.

The park's most remarkable feature, however, lies not upon the earth but within it. Carved deep into the Providence Mountains are the **Mitchell Caverns** (619-389-2281), limestone caves filled with elaborate rock formations. Touring El Pakiva and Tecopa caves, you'll see delicate stalactites and monstrous stalagmites in a natural cathedral. The bones of a Pleistocene ground sloth were uncovered here and for about 500 years the Chemehuevi Indians used the caves, blackening the walls with campfires. To reach the park take Route 40 east from Barstow for 100 miles, then go 16 miles northwest on Essex Road. There is no phone; cavern tours are scheduled weekdays at 1:30 p.m. and on weekends and holidays at 10 a.m., 1:30 p.m., and 3 p.m.; no tours in summer; plan accordingly.

SEQUOIA AND KINGS CANYON NATIONAL PARKS

Two of California's finest parks, Sequoia and Kings Canyon, lie next to each other along the western slopes of the Sierra Nevada range. Encompassing 14,000-foot peaks, alpine lakes, and stands of giant sequoia trees, they provide a lush counterpoint to the flat, dry Mojave.

SEQUOIA NATIONAL PARK

Prelude to the park is the drive to Mineral King, a remote mountain hamlet that boomed as a silver mining center during the 1870s and quickly went bust. The 25-mile Mineral King Road, branching from Route 198 a few miles before the park entrance, leads to a remote and particularly pretty section of Sequoia National Park.

Though paved along most stretches, the road winds through the mountains in maddening fashion, tracing the random course of the Kaweah River. En route are sharp canyons, switchbacks that jackknife above sheer cliffs, and a lone arched bridge.

Mule deer and black bear inhabit the region. Along the precipitous slopes sequoia give way to white fir and incense cedar, ponderosa pine and quaking aspen. At **Atwell Mill**, a late-19th-century logging center, there are Indian bedrock mortars as well as an old steam engine. Here you'll also see the ever-present sequoia stumps that are a legacy of the logging era. Further along lies **Cold Springs**, a mountain village studded with numerous log cabins, each braced against the winter wind by the chimney stem of a woodburning stove.

At **Mineral King** (★) there's a campground, ranger station, a cluster of cozy cottages, and a lovely subalpine meadow. All around are the mountains, rock-ribbed ranges that leap up and outward from the town, leaving far behind on their shoulders waterfalls, talus slides, and rivers that are silver pennants fluttering down the canyons. And everywhere there are hiking trails, which radiate from Mineral King like spokes from a hub.

Generals Highway, the road through Sequoia and Kings Canyon, is a continuation of Route 198, which enters the park at Ash Mountain. The nearby **visitors' center** (209-565-3134) provides maps and information, but your symbolic entrance into this world of granite mountains and giant trees comes a few miles further as you pass beneath **Tunnel Rock**. The roadway here has been cut from a monstrous boulder which serves as a stone portal.

At **Hospital Rock**, a granite outcropping near the turnoff to Buckeye Flats, there are pictographs from an early tribe of Indians. These painted designs, red stains against gray rock, were a vital element in local Native American culture. Of a more practical nature are the nearby mortar holes, ground into the resistant bedrock by Indian women pounding acorns into meal.

Generals Highway is menacingly steep, ascending 4700 feet in 16 miles between Ash Mountain and Giant Forest, and numbering in its serpentine course some 230 curves. Each switchback reveals a succession of ridges folded against one another. Domes and spires of granite dominate the horizon; from the valleys stands of conifers run along the hillsides, vaulting upward and then falling back just short of the peaks. As you ascend into the heart of the park, this mix of scrub vegetation and tall pine surrenders to stately groves of sequoia.

Giant Forest Village, a mountain complex complete with lodge and cafeteria, lies at the center of Sequoia National Park. **Round Meadow**, located just below the lodge, is a flowering glade with a one-mile loop trail that passes regal stands of sequoia.

A short distance from the village, Crescent Meadow Road curves through the woods past several points of interest. **Auto Log**, a giant tree which fell in 1917, has been dug out to form a driveway. If for some unspeakable reason you long to wheel your car onto a sequoia, this is your only chance. The **Parker Group**, a pretty grove of sequoias, lies further up the road, as does **Tunnel Log**, a felled sequoia under which you can drive (having already driven *over* another of the brutes).

From here, noble explorers, it's on to **Crescent Meadow**, an overgrown marsh surrounded by sequoias and filled (in spring and summer) with wildflowers. Continue four-fifths of a mile along the meadow trail and you'll arrive at **Tharp's Log**, a hollow sequoia which was converted into a log cabin (in the literal sense of the term).

A fork from Crescent Meadow Road runs past **Hanging Rock**, a granite boulder poised uneasily above a deep chasm, and **Moro Rock**, where a steep quarter-mile staircase ascends a magnificent dome. The views from this 6725-foot summit reach along the Great Western Divide, a chain of 12,000-foot peaks. In the dizzying depths 4000 feet below, the Middle Fork of the Kaweah River carves a stone channel en route to the San Joaquin Valley.

During summer months one-hour tours of **Crystal Caves** are available. The hike down to these beautiful caverns is steep and requires sturdy shoes. Once beneath the earth you'll encounter temperatures of 48°, so bring along extra clothing.

Next, you can follow Generals Highway up to the central attraction of the entire park. Surrounded by conifers that appear little more than children, stands the **General Sherman Tree**. The largest living thing on earth, this leviathan weighs 1385 tons, measures 102 feet around, and rises 275 feet high. About 2500 years old, the tree is as tall as a 27-story building. Even statistics so overwhelming fall short in conveying the magnificence of this colossus.

To truly appreciate the General Sherman Tree, stand for a few minutes in his lengthy shadow and then explore the adjacent **Congress Trail**. This two-mile loop passes several awesome stands of sequoias, including one grove named for the United States Senate and another honoring the House of Representatives.

Generals Highway climbs and weaves from Sequoia to Kings Canyon. There are groves of the big trees along the way, as well as broad vistas of the Sierra Nevada mountains. At **Lodgepole Visitor Center** (Generals Highway several miles north of Giant Forest Village; 209-565-3782) you can gain your bearings at the information desk, tour a mini-museum, and watch a slide show on the region.

KINGS CANYON NATIONAL PARK

Near the park entrance, **Big Stump Trail**, a one-mile nature loop, demonstrates some of the natural and manmade disasters that can befall giant trees. Within its narrow ambit the path crosses a sequoia scarred by lightning, another shattered into unusable pieces by clumsy loggers, and a third sequoia that was reduced to sawdust piles big as giant anthills. The most striking specimen is the Mark Twain Stump, a 24-foot-wide behemoth felled as a display piece for the American Museum of Natural History in New York City.

Headquarters in Kings Canyon National Park for sightseers, rangers, hikers, and assorted others is Grant Grove. This mountain village, a few miles from the park entrance, offers a small grocery, restaurant, lodge, and gift shop. The **Grant Grove Visitor Center** (209-335-2315) provides information, maps, books, and wilderness permits. There is also a small museum dedicated to the sequoia tree.

Pride of the park is the **General Grant Grove**, a forest of giants dating back more than 2000 years. Here a short loop leads past a **twin sister sequoia** (on the left at the end of the parking lot), formed when two trunks grew from a single base. Nearby lies the **Fallen Monarch**, the proverbial tree that crashed in the forest when there was no one around to record its demise. A 120-foot-long hollow log, it has served as a loggers' shelter, saloon, and stable. Today this natural tunnel makes a unique corridor for inquisitive hikers.

The Civil War is still being fought here in Grant Grove. Among these sentinel-straight sequoias is the **Robert E. Lee Tree**, rising 254 feet above the forest floor. The **General Grant Tree** is a gnarly giant tattooed with woodpecker holes and adorned with thick, stubby branches that twist upward. Proclaimed the Nation's Christmas Tree, it is the site of special services every year. Needless to say, the General Grant outstrips its Confederate counterpart, topping out at 267 feet and boasting a diameter (40 feet) greater than any other sequoia.

In the shadow of this leviathan sits the **Gamlin Cabin**, a log house built in 1872 by an early settler. Looking as sturdy as the trees around it, the structure was used at one time by U.S. Cavalry patrols.

From Grant Grove a mountain road corkscrews up to **Panoramic Point**. Situated at 7520 feet, this lookout could as soon be at sea level considering the peaks that rise above it. Stretched along the horizon in a kind of granite amphitheater is a line of bald domes, cresting at 13,000- and 14,000-foot heights. Each bears a name resonant of the simple poetry of stone—Kettle Dome, Marble Mountain, Eagle Peaks, and Thunder Mountain. Cradled beneath them, an aquamarine glint in a forest of green, is Hume Lake.

Follow Route 180 from Grant Grove down into Kings Canyon itself. Along this 35-mile mountain road, which twists and curves as it descends the canyon walls, are countless vista points. You can peer down sharp rockfaces, gaze out at massive ridges, and take in the rivers which rumble into the San Joaquin Valley.

A side road diverges to **Hume Lake**, a small mountain lake which reflects in its glassy surface the faces of surrounding peaks. Then Route 180 descends through lofty mountains that break the sunlight into shafts and splinters. As you spiral further and further into this shadowy canyon, the granite walls edge closer and climb more steeply. Eventually the landscape narrows to a sharp defile and then reopens to reveal a tumbling river strewn with boulders, the South Fork of the Kings River.

Here, where road meets river, sits **Boyden Cavern** (209-736-2708; admission). Formed over a 300,000-year period, this limestone cave descends past rock pools, massive stalagmites, cave pearls, and ornate stalactites. Among these marvelous underground formations are sights named Upside Down City, Layer Cake, Christmas Tree Room and the Drapery Room.

Route 180 continues along the river past **Cedar Grove,** where civilization rises in the form of a lodge with grocery store and snack bar. Just beyond this oasis lies **Roaring River Falls,** a cascade that rolls down from the mountains, crashes through a granite chasm, and debouches into an emerald pool.

Nearby **Zumwalt Meadow** is awash with color in spring when the wildflowers bloom. For an even more intimate view of the natural surroundings, drive or hike the **Motor Nature Trail,** which bumps for three miles along a dirt road, paralleling the river and passing rich marshland.

Here, deep in the canyon, you will find the river loud in your ears. Sounds echo off the surrounding walls, ricocheting upward along flinty rockfaces and vertiginous cliffs. Vying with Yosemite in grandeur, the valley is more than 8000 feet beneath the surrounding mountains, the deepest canyon in the United States.

OWENS VALLEY

The backbone of the Eastern Sierra is Route 395, which runs north past black lava hills, red cinder cones, and other volcanic outcroppings. The land all about is a morass of sand divided in random fashion by arroyos, a dust bowl with a rim of mountains. This is the **Owens Valley,** bled dry by Los Angeles, which has diverted its once plentiful water. Today only the mountains remain—to the east the Inyos, Panamints, and Whites, in the west the Sierra Nevada. From them the valley, victimized by a metropolis hundreds of miles away, derives its identity and maintains its dignity.

At **Fossil Falls,** 20,000-year-old lava flows have solidified to create dramatic cascades of black rock. (To get there take Route 395 for 3 miles north of Little Lake; go east one-half mile on Cinder Road; turn right on the dirt road and proceed three-quarters of a mile to a parking lot; hike one-quarter mile to the falls; a second set of falls lies several hundred yards further south.)

Route 395 continues past miles of sage brush in a landscape that is broken only occasionally by a solitary and spindly cactus. **Owens Lake Bed,** once part of a rich string of intermountain lakes, stretches for miles to the west—a dry, salt-caked expanse.

To understand the allure of Owens Valley, stop by the **Eastern Sierra InterAgency Visitors' Center** (Route 395 one mile south of Lone Pine; 619-876-4252). A valuable resource, the information center has a good selection of maps and pamphlets and an excellent collection of books on California's mountain and desert regions.

In the neon town of Lone Pine you can pick up Whitney Portal Road (one of America's greatest byways), which climbs from 4000 to 8300 feet elevation in its 13-mile course. Passing streams shaded by cottonwood trees, it cuts through the **Alabama Hills**, a unique formation of weathered granite whose reddish colors contrast brilliantly with the gray backdrop of the Sierra Nevada.

If all this seems a bit too familiar, little wonder: the Alabama Hills have served as the setting for countless Westerns. At one time they were almost as important to the movie industry as the Hollywood Hills. Hopalong Cassidy, Gene Autry, and the Lone Ranger all rode this range.

For a close-up of cowboy country, turn right on Movie Road (off Whitney Portal Road three miles from Route 395). A network of dirt roads leads past **Movie Flat** (★), where many sequences were shot, then continues into this badlands of humpbacked boulders.

Then Whitney Portal Road rides out of this rolling range land, trading the soft contours of the Alabamas for the cold granite world of the Sierra Nevada. These latter mountains are young (geologically) and roughhewn, with adze-like slopes that lift away from the road in vertical lunges. Far from embracing admirers, the surrounding heights seem to dare people to ascend them. Even the pine trees, which grow in crowded groves along the early slopes, quit the climb half way up.

When the road itself quits at **Whitney Portal**, base camp for climbers, you find above you Mount Whitney, at 14,495 feet the tallest mountain in the contiguous United States. In the giant's shadow stand six other peaks, all topping 14,000 feet. It is a scene of unpronounceable beauty, fashioned from dark chasms and stone minarets, almost two miles above the floor of Owens Valley.

On the slopes of a 9000-foot peak outside Lone Pine lie the rusting remains of **Cerro Gordo** (★). One of the High Desert's best-preserved ghost towns, its story begins in 1865 when rich silver deposits were discovered. Within a few years almost 2000 miners had arrived, hauling out as much as 5300 tons of bullion each year. Among the ruins is a store, two-story house, and other tumbledown buildings constructed in 1871. Later structures, dating to 1916, are dotted around the property. Cerro Gordo is now privately owned, but the public is welcome. The owner asks that you check in with them at their home to sign a liability waiver before entering. (To get there, pick up Route 136 just south of Lone Pine and follow it 12.6 miles; turn left on Cerro Gordo Road and proceed for five miles along this graded but *very* steep road.)

Proceeding north along Route 395 from Lone Pine (particularly in early morning and late afternoon), pull over about four miles outside town and gaze eastward toward the river bottom. A herd of **tule elk,** whose ancestors once inhabited California's Central Valley, roams the area.

Farther outside town, with the Sierra Nevada looming in the background like an impenetrable wall, stands **Manzanar**. In 1942, when panic over Pearl Harbor pervaded the country, 10,000 Americans of Japanese ancestry were interned here. Perceived as potential spies and saboteurs, they were uprooted from their West Coast homes and "relocated" to concentration camps like Manzanar. Today little remains to commemorate their tragedy other than two guard stations, fashioned, almost insultingly, like pagodas. There is also a plaque imploring that "the injustices and humiliation suffered here as a result of hysteria, racism, and economic exploitation never emerge again."

Even more overwhelming in its moral ramifications is the **Manzanar cemetery (★)**, where internees were buried. The place inspires sadness and remorse, and also a sense of terror. It is not so much the stark white monument set against the unyielding Sierra Nevada that evokes this final response, but the cemetery itself. Running in a double line around the burial ground, dividing it dramatically from the countryside, indeed from the country itself, is a barbed wire fence. (To get there, continue on Route 395 north for four-fifths of a mile, turn left on the dirt road; when it forks after one mile, bear left to the cemetery.)

The **Eastern California Museum** (155 Grant Street; 619-878-2010) in nearby Independence contains photographs and news clips retracing the story of Manzanar. There are snapshots of the tarpaper barracks and wooden sentry towers as well as personal belongings of the internees. This excellent regional facility also contains such Indian artifacts as arrowheads, baskets, and beadwork. Tools of the trade from cowboy days include branding irons, a mule pack canteen, leather chaps, and even a spittoon. The handwoven quilts, antique telephones, and accordion cameras of the region's more genteel set are also presented. Out back, many of the town's original buildings—weather-beaten, woodframe structures—still stand.

The **Mount Whitney Fish Hatchery** (off Route 395 about two miles north of Independence) raises fingerling trout for stocking backcountry streams (making this area one of the most popular freshwater fishing regions in the state). Breeding rainbow, brook, brown, and golden trout, the facility offers an opportunity to watch gamefish hatching and to glimpse fat but spirited adult fish. The building alone, a stone structure with Tudor flourishes and a red tile roof, built in 1916, makes the visit worthwhile.

In the little town of Big Pine, Route 168 connects with a side road which leads up into the White Mountains. Climb this backcountry byway and a dazzling 180° **mountain panorama** of the Sierra Nevada and Inyos will open to view. The mountains seem to wrap around you, forming an amphitheater of stone and snow. Within this ring of 13,000-foot peaks rests **Palisade Glacier**, the southernmost glacier in North America.

Then the road ascends to over 10,000 feet elevation and—in a kind of high altitude riddle—enters a territory where the living reside next to the dead and the dead are often half alive. The denizens of this mysterious locale are over 4000 years old, the world's most ancient living things, dating back to the days of the Egyptian pyramids.

The site is an **Ancient Bristlecone Pine Forest**, where short, squat trees with needles like fox tails grow on an icy, windblown landscape. Sculpted by the elements, they resemble living driftwood; many of the trees are partially dead, sustained by a narrow vein of living tissue.

In the park's Schulman Grove, where the oldest trees survive, you can follow a one-mile loop trail past Pine Alpha, a 4300-year-old tree. From here a sometimes impassable dirt road continues for 12 miles along the lip of the world, through a lunar landscape, and past ever-thinning forest to The Patriarch Grove, a second stand of bristlecones located at 11,000 feet.

Bishop is one of those towns that exist not in and for themselves but for what is around them. The **Bishop Chamber of Commerce** (690 North Main Street; 619-873-8405) serves as the local information center, a good place to plan an exploration of the area.

Dedicated to Native American traditions, the town's **Paiute Shoshone Indian Cultural Center** (2301 West Line Street; 619-873-4478) has outstanding displays of basketry, leathercrafts, and beadwork. There are also showcases filled with petroglyphs and arrowheads. Centerpiece of the showroom is a circular house of straw, replicating the traditional homes of Owens Valley tribes.

Route 168 buzzes west from Bishop for about 20 miles into the high country of the Sierra Nevada. Here **Lake Sabrina** and **South Lake**, favored fishing holes, are like crystal inlaid in a setting of granite.

Directly north of Bishop, the **Volcanic Tablelands** rise above the valley floor, ascending to 7912-foot Casa Diablo Mountain. Built from a series of lava flows, this sparse plateau is cut by sharp, narrow canyons. Gleaming red against the gray walls of the Sierra Nevada and White Mountains, it's a desolate but enchanting region, particularly pretty around dawn and dusk. (To get there, pick up Five Bridges Road at the north end of Bishop and take it to the end, where it continues as Casa Diablo Road, a dirt road that climbs all the way to Casa Diablo Mountain).

The nearby town of Laws, a major railroad stop during the 1880s, is re-created at the **Laws Railroad Museum and Historical Site** (Route 6 about four miles northeast of Bishop; 619-873-5950). Combining the town's original buildings with antique structures relocated from other parts of the valley, it conveys an atmosphere of the Old West.

The general store is here with its lard buckets and spice canisters; tumblers still turn in the mailbox locks at the post office; and the surgical tools in the doctor's office look as threatening as they did back when. In addition, the original Bishop Catholic Church has been converted into a library, museum and art gallery and the Wells Fargo office now displays rock crystals and Indian artifacts.

But the centerpiece of the exhibit is still the railroad yard. Here the station, with its waiting room, telegraph office, and loading dock, has been nicely preserved. Resting just down the track is old Southern Pacific Engine Number Nine, with a line of freight cars and a bell whose clangs still echo across the valley.

Artifacts of a much earlier era, **Indian petroglyphs (★)**, lie off the beaten track north of Laws. Etched into volcanic rocks, these ancient drawings portray people, deer, snakes, and insects. Possibly left by ancestors of local Paiutes, the figures carry significant symbolic meaning. Since they occur along old deer trails, one theory holds they were intended to bring the blessing of good hunting. For maps and directions to the petroglyphs, contact the Bureau of Land Management (787 Route 395, Suite P, Bishop; 619-872-4881).

MAMMOTH LAKES

Sharp contrast to the dust-blown basin of Owens Valley is the alpine ski area known as Mammoth Lakes. Here on the eastern face of the Sierra Nevada, volcanoes and earthquakes have wracked the region, leaving a legacy of lakes. Among the most lovely is **Convict Lake** (Convict Lake Road about two miles west of Route 395), a mountain jewel formed by receding glaciers. Bounded by precipitous cliffs and multihued rocks, the lake was the scene of a famous 1871 gun battle between a sheriff's posse and a band of fugitives.

Hot Creek (★), a beautiful stream set deep in a rock-rimmed canyon, is one of Mammoth Lakes most deceptive and alluring spots. One section, peaceful as a babbling brook, is popular with fly fishermen. Further downstream, there are hot springs which warm the water to perfect spa temperatures. Then, within a 100 yards of this popular bathing pool, the creek erupts in low geysers and dramatic steam vents. Vapors percolate from gray mud holes and pungent bubbles rise out of the depths. (Hot Creek is located six miles south of Mammoth Lakes. From Route 395 turn east on the road next to Mammoth–June Lakes Airport and follow it three and one-half miles to the parking lot; then hike down to the creek.)

The facts and figures concerning Mammoth Lakes are found at two locations. The **Mammoth Visitor Center** (Route 203 just outside Mammoth Lakes; 619-934-2505) offers information on hiking, camping, and other outdoor activities. At **Mammoth Lakes Resort Association** (Village Center Mall along Route 203, Mammoth Lakes; 619-934-2712) they provide details on local hotels, restaurants, and other amenities; this facility will also help with reservations.

A thumbnail introduction to the history of this former mining region awaits along Old Mammoth Road. Back in 1878, after gold and silver were uncovered, Mammoth City developed into a boom town with 22 saloons, two breweries, 13 stores, and two newspapers. The place went bust within a year, but a few artifacts from the glory days remain.

During summer months the **Mammoth Museum**, housed in a log cabin, traces the region's story from the days of mining and ranching to the current era. About a mile from the top of Old Mammoth Road, the grave of one Mrs. J. E. Townsend, deceased 1882, rests in a shaded grove. Further along, across from a state historical marker, are the remains of a log cabin and the ill-fated mine.

Lake Mary Road climbs past a chain of beautiful glacial lakes. **Twin Lakes**, a wasp-waisted body of water which was once two separate lakes, sits in a granite bowl. Just beyond here a half-mile trail leads to **Panorama Dome**, a volcanic rock with outstanding views of the surrounding lakes and the White Mountains.

The loop around **Lake Mary**, largest of this glacial group, diverts to **Lake George**, a crystal pool dominated by a single granite shaft. During early summer, meadows along the nearby hiking trails are lush with flowers.

Spilling down from **Lake Mamie** are the **Twin Falls**, which cascade 300 feet along a granite bed into Twin Lakes. **Horseshoe Lake**, the only lake where swimming is permitted, sits near the top of the road at 8950 feet elevation. To explore the alpine waters that rest beyond Horseshoe Lake, you'll have to don hiking boots.

A number of sights lie along Minaret Road (Route 203), which ascends from the town of Mammoth Lakes into the mountains. Unsettling evidence of Mammoth Lakes' dramatic geology lies along the sharp walls of the **earthquake fault**. A nature trail wends along the sides of this fracture, where the earth has opened to create a deep fissure. The rocks on either side fit perfectly into their counterparts, providing a graphic illustration of how an earthquake can split the globe like a ripe fruit. At Mammoth/June Lakes Ski Resort farther uphill, you can take a **gondola ride** (619-934-2571; admission) to the 11,053-foot summit of Mammoth Mountain. Of course if it's winter and the area has been graced with the white powder for which locals pray, you can ski back down.

Minaret Vista, with its views of the Ansel Adams Wilderness, is otherworldly. The San Joaquin River winds through the deep canyon below; and the stark peaks of the Ritter Range loom above, a setting in which the top of the world seems to have been ripped away, leaving a jagged line of needle-point peaks and razor-edge ridges.

At **Rainbow Falls** (off Minaret Road and along a 1.3 mile trail) the San Joaquin River plunges 100 feet over volcanic rock to an alpine pool, creating multihued patterns in the mist. This spot is particularly pretty in the afternoon.

But enough mere beauty, at **Devils Postpile National Monument,** where Minaret Road (Route 203) reveals its final surprise, physical beauty is combined with the magic of geology. Here layer on layer of angular shafts, some vertical, others twisted into curving forms, create a 60-foot-high cliff with smooth-sided columns.

Volcanic forces molded this rare formation when surface cracks appeared during the cooling of molten lava. The surface breaks extended vertically through the rock, creating the polygonal posts. Then glaciers flowed over the fractured mass 10,000 years ago, polishing the tops of the posts and leaving a geometric surface resembling a tile floor (which can be viewed from atop Devils Postpile).

Along the trail at the bottom you can gaze at this unique wall of pillars, some of which curve toward the mountain, seeming to support the posts behind, while others lean free and appear about to collapse. Directly below them, like splinters from a magnificent sculpture, lie piles of fallen columns.

Mammoth Scenic Loop, branching from Minaret Road one mile outside Mammoth Lakes, contains within its ambit several points of interest. **Inyo Craters** (one mile down a dirt side road and one-quarter mile up a trail) is a string of three volcanic cavities created by violent eruptions. Part of the volcanic ridge that runs between Mammoth Mountain and Mono Lake, these craters and their lakes are mere babies in geologic terms, dating back perhaps 1500 years.

En route to June Lake, another string of glacial lakes, the local geology shows another of its many faces. **Obsidian Dome** (follow Route 395 about 11 miles north of Mammoth Lakes, then turn west for one and one-half miles on Glass Flow Road) is a glass mountain composed entirely of obsidian. This black volcanic glass, created during the cooling of molten lava, was used by local Indians to fashion arrowheads.

June Lake Loop (Route 158), a mountain road 15 miles north of Mammoth Lakes, curves past June Lake and three other pools. Each is an alpine beauty, a shimmering blue lake bounded by forest and lofty peaks. Popular for fishing, camping, and hiking, the region is also crowded with skiers in winter. June Mountain, situated at the head of the horseshoe-shaped loop, has a **gondola ride** (619-648-7733; admission) open to sightseers and skiers.

As the loop closes upon Route 395, with Mono Lake in the distance, a series of volcanic mountains rise in the east. These are the **Mono Craters,** which reach elevations of about 2700 feet. Built of pumice, the craters contain rich deposits of obsidian along their flanks.

DEATH VALLEY AREA

BAKER TO DEATH VALLEY AREA

A fitting prelude to dusty, desiccated Death Valley lies along the southern gateway to this fabled destination. Here, stretching north along Route 127 from the town of Baker, is a chain of **dry lakes**. Once part of Lake Mojave, an ancient body of water which drained over 3500 square miles, they are now flat expanses baked white in the sun. Silver Dry Lake, which appears to the west four miles outside Baker, was an Indian habitat over 10,000 years ago.

To the east rise the Silurian Hills, backdropped by the Kingston Range. If there is a snow-domed mountain in the far distance, it's probably 11,918-foot Charleston Peak, 60 miles away in Nevada. Those pretty white hills with the soft curves are the Dumont Dunes, 30 miles north of Baker.

Beyond Ibex Pass, as the road descends into another ancient lake bed, you'll pass **Tecopa Lake Badlands**, where erosion has carved fascinating formations from soft sedimentary rock.

A side road leads several miles to **Tecopa Hot Springs** (619-852-4264), a series of rich mineral baths once used by Paiute Indians. Today this natural resource has been transformed into a bizarre tourist attraction.

If there is a last outpost before the world ends, this will be the place. A white mineral patina covers the ground everywhere, as though salt had been shaken across the entire desert. Water sits in stagnant pools. Wherever you look—backgrounded by rugged, stark, glorious mountains—there are trailers. Hundreds of trailers, metal refuges against the Mojave sun, painted white like the earth and equipped with satellite dishes. In a kind of desert monopoly game, if you collect enough mobile homes you can hang a sign out front and call it a motel.

The species that inhabits these tin domiciles is on permanent vacation. This is, after all, a health resort; people walk about clad in bathrobes. They wander from the private baths at the trailer parks and "motels" to the public baths, which, in the single saving grace to this surreal enclave, are free.

DEATH VALLEY NATIONAL MONUMENT

Better times lie ahead. Picking up Route 178 as it leads into Death Valley National Monument, and maintaining a steady composure despite the raw landscape and signs that threaten "No Roadside Services Next 72 Miles," you will enter the most famous desert in the United States. Set between the lofty Black and Panamint ranges, it is a place renowned for exquisite but merciless terrain. A region of vast distances (the national park is half again as large as Delaware) and plentiful plant life (over 900 plant species subsist here, 22 of them growing only in this area), Death Valley holds a magician's bag of surprises.

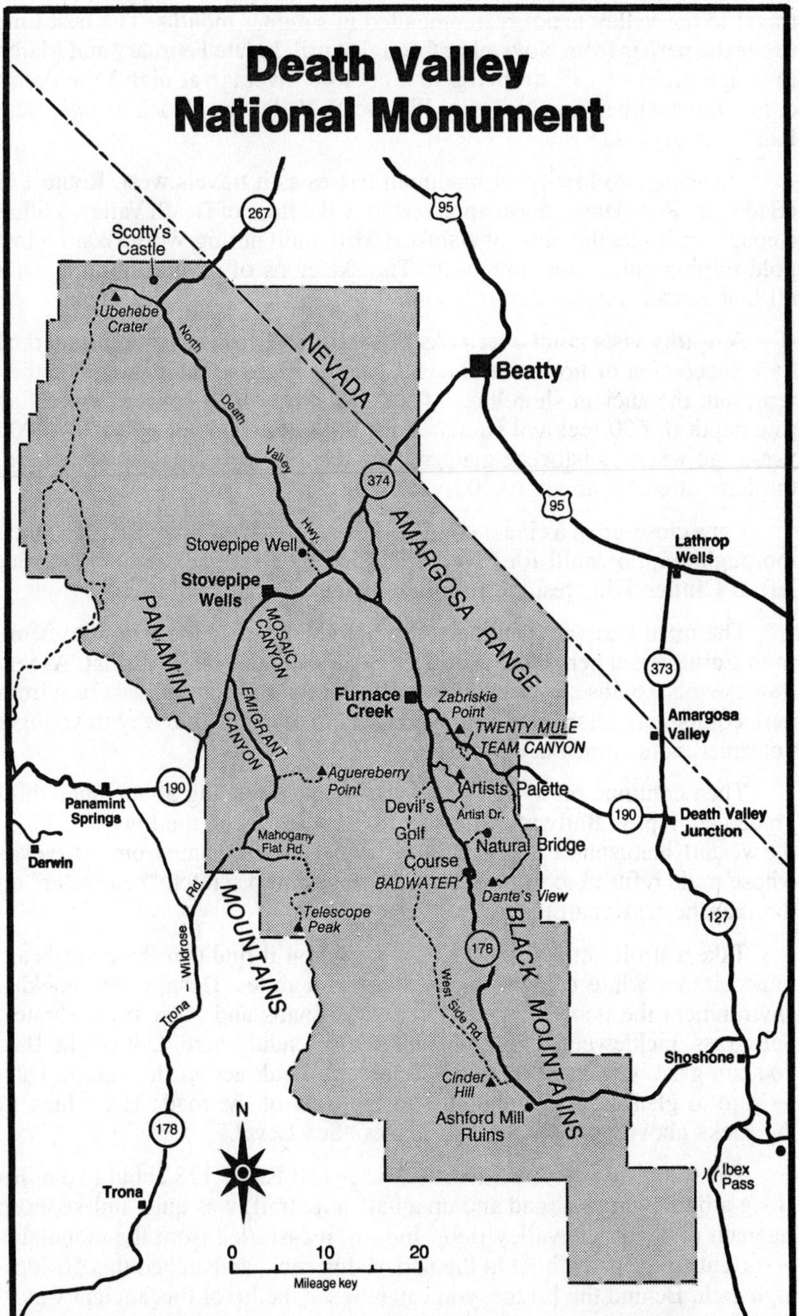
Death Valley
National Monument
267
95
Scotty's Castle
Ubehebe Crater
North Death Valley Hwy.
NEVADA
Beatty
374
95
AMARGOSA RANGE
Stovepipe Well
Stovepipe Wells
Lathrop Wells
PANAMINT
MOSAIC CANYON
373
Furnace Creek
Zabriskie Point
EMIGRANT CANYON
TWENTY MULE TEAM CANYON
Amargosa Valley
Aguereberry Point
190
Panamint Springs
Artists Palette
Devil's Golf Course
Artist Dr.
190
Death Valley Junction
Natural Bridge
Darwin
Mahogany Flat Rd.
BADWATER
Dante's View
MOUNTAINS
BLACK MOUNTAINS
Telescope Peak
127
Trona – Wildrose Rd.
178
West Side Rd.
Shoshone
Cinder Hill
Ashford Mill Ruins
N
178
Ibex Pass
Trona
0
10
20
Mileage key

Due to the extreme summer temperatures (average July highs of 116°!), travel to the valley is not recommended in summer months. The best time to see the park is from November through April. In late February and March (average highs of 73°, dropping to a cool 46° average at night) the desert comes alive with spring blossoms like Death Valley sage, rock *mimulus* and Panamint daisies.

Crossing two low-lying mountain passes as it travels west, Route 178 (Badwater Road) turns north upon reaching the floor of Death Valley. Within a couple miles lie the ruins of **Ashford Mill,** built during World War I when gold mining enjoyed a comeback. The skeletons of several buildings are all that remain of that early dream.

A nearby vista point overlooks **Shoreline Butte,** a curving hill marked by a succession of horizontal lines. Clearly visible to the naked eye, they represent the ancient shorelines of Lake Manly, which covered the valley to a depth of 600 feet and stretched for 90 miles. Formed perhaps 75,000 years ago when Pleistocene glaciers atop the Sierra Nevada began melting, the lake dried up about 10,000 years ago.

For a close-up of a cinder cone, follow nearby West Side Road, a graded thoroughfare, downhill for two miles. That reddish-black mound on your left is **Cinder Hill,** residue from an ancient volcano.

The main highway continues through the heart of the region to **Mormon Point.** From here northward Death Valley is one huge salt flat. As you traverse this expanse, notice how the Black Mountains to the east turn from dark colors to reddish hues as gray Precambrian rocks give way to younger volcanic and sedimentary deposits.

Then continue on to that place you've been reading about since third grade geography, **Badwater,** 282 feet below sea level, the lowest point in the western hemisphere. Legend has it the place got its name from a surveyor whose mule refused to drink here, inspiring him to scratch "bad water" on the map he was charting.

Take a stroll out onto the salt flats and you'll find that the crystals are joined into a white carpet which extends for miles. Despite the brackish environment the pool itself supports water snails and other invertebrates. Salt grass, pickleweed, and desert holly also endure here. Out on the flats you can gaze west at 11,049-foot **Telescope Peak** across the valley. Then be sure to glance back at the cliff to the west of the road. There high in the rocks above you a lone sign marks "Sea Level."

The water that carved **Natural Bridge** (off Route 178 about two miles along a bumpy gravel road and up a half-mile trail) was quite unlike those stagnant pools on the valley floor. Indeed, it cascaded from the mountains in torrents, punched a hole in the underlying rock, and etched this 50-foot-high arch. Behind the bridge, you can still see the lip of this ancient waterfall. Also notice the formations along the canyon walls that were left by evaporating water and bear a startling resemblance to dripping wax.

Another dirt side road travels one mile to the **Devil's Golf Course.** Rather than a sand hazard, this flat expanse is one huge salt trap, complete with salt towers, pinnacles, and brine pools. The sodium chloride here is 95 percent pure, comparable to table salt, and the salt deposits are three to five feet thick. They were formed by a small lake that evaporated perhaps 2000 years ago; below them earlier deposits from larger lakes reach over 1000 feet beneath the surface.

Artist Drive, a nine-mile route through the Black Mountains, is one of Southern California's most magnificent roads. The hills all around are splashed with color—soft pastels, striking reds, creamy browns—and rise to sharp cliffs. En route at **Artists Palette,** the hills are colored so vividly they seem to pulsate. It's a spot admired by photographers from around the world, a place where the rainbow meets the badlands.

If you'd like a scientific explanation for all this beauty—the artistic medium is oxidation: chloride deposits create the green hues, manganese oxides form the blacks, and the reds, yellows, and oranges are shades of iron oxide. These contrasting colors are most spectacular during late afternoon.

Mushroom Rock, the sculptor's answer to Artists Palette, rises on the right several hundred yards after you regain Route 178. A boulder of basalt lava, it was carved by windblown sand.

Up in **Golden Canyon,** erosion has chiseled chasms into the bright yellow walls of a narrow gorge. Climb the three-quarter-mile trail here and you arrive in a natural amphitheater, named for the iridescent quality of the canyon walls, which are the embodiment of sunlight.

In this entire wasteland of wonders the only major center of civilization is **Furnace Creek,** where a gas station, campground, restaurants, and two hotels create a welcome oasis. The **Death Valley National Monument Visitor Center** (619-786-2331) is a good resource for maps and information. It houses a museum re-creating the history of Native Americans and early prospectors. There are also mineral displays and an oversize relief map of the valley.

The nearby **Borax Museum** features the oldest house in Death Valley, a sturdy 1883 structure built by a borax miner. There's also a wonderful collection of stage coaches as well as a huge Rube Goldberg contraption once used to extract gold deposits from rock.

While the yellow metal symbolizes the romance of desert prospecting, the lowly borax mineral proved of much greater value to Death Valley miners. Important as a cleaning agent, the white crystal was first discovered in 1881. Eventually it inspired its own romantic images, with 20-mule teams hauling 36-ton wagonloads across 180 miles of desert to the railhead in Mojave.

A two-and-one-half-mile trail climbs from Golden Canyon to **Zabriskie Point**, but most folks follow Route 190, which leads southeast from Furnace Creek. In any case, everyone inevitably arrives at this place, as though it were a point of pilgrimage for paying homage to nature.

What else can a mortal do, confronted with beauty of this magnitude? In the east amber-hued hills roll like waves toward the horizon. To the west lies a badlands, burnished by blown sand to fierce reds and soft pastels. All around, the landscape resembles a sea gone mad, waves of sand breaking in every direction, with a stone tsunami, Manly Beacon, high above the combers, poised to crash into Death Valley.

Prosaic though it sounds, these mustard-colored hills are dry mud, lakebed sediments deposited two to 12 million years ago, then uplifted to their present height. In the early morning and late afternoon, when the place is suffused with color, Zabriskie Point demonstrates that humble origins are of little consequence.

For a close-up view of those mud hills, follow the nearby dirt road through **Twenty Mule Team Canyon**. It winds almost three miles through a former borax-mining region.

Then to get above it all, venture on to **Dante's View**, a 5475-foot perch with a 360° vista. From this coign of vantage the salt flats and trapped pools of Death Valley are like a bleak watercolor. Though the Panamint Mountains wall off the western horizon, a steep half-mile trail (up the knoll north of the parking lot) leads to a point where you can gaze beyond them to the snow-thatched Sierra Nevada. Here in a single glance you can see Badwater and Mount Whitney, the lowest and highest points in the contiguous United States.

Backtracking to Furnace Creek, Route 190 proceeds north toward the upper end of Death Valley. The history of the region's most valuable mineral is further revealed at the **Harmony Borax Works**. Surrounded by the ruins of Death Valley's most successful borax plant is an original 20-mule team rig.

At the very end of Death Valley, when you've gone as far north as you can without bumping fenders with the Nevada border, you'll find the strangest feature in the entire park—a castle in the desert. It's a place called **Scotty's Castle** (admission), though Scotty never owned it. In fact Scotty swindled the fellow who did own it, then became his lifelong friend. Sound preposterous? Perhaps.

It seems that one Walter "Death Valley Scotty" Scott, a former trick rider in Buffalo Bill's Wild West Show, once convinced a Chicago millionaire, one Albert Johnson, to invest in a nonexistent gold mine. Johnson traveled west to see the mine, discovered that the dry desert clime helped his fragile health, forgave Scotty, and decided during the 1920s to build a mansion in the sand.

The result was a $2 million Moorish castle, a wonderfully ridiculous building with wrought-iron detailing, inlaid tile, carved-beam ceilings, expensive antiques, and nothing for miles around. Scotty, the greatest story teller in Death Valley history, told everyone it was his castle. Hence the name. Somehow it reminds me of Hearst Castle in San Simeon, a place too gaudy to appreciate but too outrageous to ignore.

Ubehebe Crater, eight miles from Scotty's lair, is another of the park's natural wonders. One-half mile in diameter and reaching a depth of 450 feet, this magnificent landmark was created by a single explosion The force of the volcanic steam scattered debris over a six-square-mile area and blew the crater walls so clean that one side retains its original sedimentary colors. Whether the crater dates back 10,000 years or is only a few hundred years old is currently being debated by geologists. They do agree that other nearby craters have been formed in the last few centuries.

From the crater a winding gravel road leads 27 miles to **The Racetrack** (★), another of nature's magic acts. This two-mile mud playa, set at the bottom of a dry lake, is oval shaped like a racecourse. In fact an outcropping at the north end of the valley is dubbed The Grandstand. The racers, oddly enough, are rocks, ranging in size from pebbles to boulders. Pushed by heavy winds across the mud-slick surface, they leave long, faint tracks that reveal the distances they have "raced."

Stovepipe Wells, Death Valley's other village, is even smaller than Furnace Creek. A motel, restaurant, store, gas station, and campground comprise the entire town. It was here at **Burned Wagons Point** (historic marker) that a desperate party of '49ers killed their oxen and dried the meat by burning their wagons.

Six miles east of the village a graded road departs Route 190 and travels four miles past **sand dunes** before joining North Death Valley Highway, the road to Scotty's Castle. Alive with greenery, these undulating dunes support numerous plant species, including creosote bushes, mesquite, and pickleweed. Coyotes hunt prey in the sandhills and there are kit fox, lizards, and kangaroo rats.

Further along rests the old **Stovepipe Well** from which the village derived its name. Used by prospectors crossing Death Valley, the well was fitted with a tall stovepipe so travelers could see it even when sand blanketed the area.

One person found neither well nor stovepipe. **Val Nolan's grave**, a simple resting place within crawling distance of the well, consists of a pile of stones and a wooden marker. Carved into the grave is an epitaph that graphically reveals Val Nolan's last days: "A Victim of the Elements."

DEATH VALLEY TO TRONA AREA

Stovepipe Wells marks the northern gateway to Death Valley. From here Route 190 travels out of the valley southwest through a pass in the Panamint Mountains. Once beyond the valley, follow Trona–Wildrose Road south through Emigrant Canyon. This route, leading to Trona, passes several intriguing spots.

Aguereberry Point, a 6433-foot overlook, lies at the end of a six-mile-long side road. From atop this crag you gaze back at Death Valley and enjoy a circular view of the Black Mountains and the Sierra Nevada. (Despite a sign advising 4-wheel drive, the road is graded and usually passable by 2-wheel-drive vehicles.)

Another detour onto Mahogany Flat Road (partially paved) leads seven miles to a startling site. As you round a bend, ten beehives, 25 feet high, line the road. At least they look like beehives; in fact these stone-sided cones are **Charcoal Kilns**, used to create fuel for nearby silver smelters.

Meanwhile Trona–Wildrose Road descends into the Panamint Valley, a sun-parched plain bounded by the Panamint and Argus ranges. Here another side road cuts east for four miles to **Ballarat** (★), a ghost town dating to 1897. The wood and adobe ruins are remnants of a mining supply center which flourished until 1905. In its heyday this desolate spot boasted a stagecoach stop, three general stores, a school, Wells Fargo office, and hotel.

Shopping

Somehow the desert seems an unlikely place to find fine art and con temporary fashions. There are stores in Mojave and Barstow, but most serve the local populace. You'll also find souvenir shops in Sequoia and Kings Canyon national parks and in the Furnace Creek section of Death Valley.

Calico Ghost Town, a kind of antique theme park in the mountains ten miles northeast of Barstow, has several shops. These are located in the town's 1880-era buildings and include a confectionery, spice shop, antique store, and rock shop. The Old West town also features the obligatory general store, which in this case generally sells tourist items.

Nightlife

The prospects for evening entertainment are about as promising as those for shopping.

Out in the railroad town of Barstow, the **Idle Spurs Steak House** (29557 West Route 58; 619-256-8888) has live entertainment every Friday and Saturday. This lounge also features a dancefloor.

The Fireside Room (Giant Forest Village; 209-565-3381) in Sequoia National Park is a down-home bar with a mountain atmosphere. There's a stone fireplace as well as a pool table, jukebox, and (hopefully) a lively crowd.

In Mammoth Lakes, where the ski crowd livens up the territory, there are several nightspots worthy of note. During summer and winter, the bar at **Slocums Italian American Grill** (Route 203; 619-934-7647) is a popular watering hole.

During winter months there's dancing to live bands Tuesday through Sunday at **La Sierra's Mexican Restaurant and Cantina** (3789 Route 203; 619-934-8083). This club has one of the largest dancefloors in town.

Nevados (Minaret Road and Main Street; 619-934-4466) features a spiffy, modern-style lounge complete with metallic silver bar and Southwestern atmosphere. There are sports on the screen and contemporary sounds in the air.

For a quiet drink and a view of June Lake, try the lounge at **Sierra Inn Restaurant** (619-648-7774) near the center of town in June Lake.

In Death Valley, the Furnace Creek Inn includes the **Oasis Lounge** (Furnace Creek; 619-786-2345) among its elegant facilities. Featuring live entertainment nightly, it's a lovely spot to enjoy a quiet evening.

The Badwater Saloon (619-786-2387) in Stovepipe Wells also hosts juke-box dancing. With Western-style decor and a dancefloor, it's a night owl's oasis.

The finest entertainment for many miles is at the **Amargosa Opera House** (Death Valley Junction; 619-852-4316). This amazing one-woman show is the creation of Marta Becket, who performs dance pantomimes in a theater which she personally decorated with colorful murals. Her performances run every Friday, Saturday, and Monday from November to April and every Saturday in October and May. Locally renowned, she's extremely popular, so call for reservations.

Index

Abbreviations used for chapter areas of Southern California are: (CC) Central Coast, (HD) High Desert, (LA) Los Angeles, (LAC) Los Angeles Coast, (LD) Low Desert, (OC) Orange Coast, and (SD) San Diego.

Abbreviations have been used for parks, beaches, sightseeing attractions, and most natural features, but generally not for towns or cities. Hotel and restaurant names have not been indexed here, unless cited as a sightseeing or historical attraction. Trail names have also been excluded.

Also Available From Ulysses Press

HIDDEN SAN FRANCISCO AND NORTHERN CALIFORNIA
A major resource for travelers exploring the Bay Area and beyond. 444 pages. $14.95

HIDDEN HAWAII
A classic in its field, this top-selling guide captures the spirit of the islands. Winner of the Lowell Thomas Award and the Hawaii Visitors' Bureau Award for Best Guidebook. 384 pages. $13.95

HIDDEN MEXICO
Covers the entire 6000-mile Mexican coastline in the most comprehensive fashion ever. 444 pages. $13.95

HIDDEN NEW ENGLAND
A perfect companion for exploring America's birthplace from Massachusetts colonial villages to the fog-shrouded coast of Maine. 564 pages. $14.95

HIDDEN BOSTON AND CAPE COD
This compact guide ventures to historic Boston and the windswept Massachusetts coastline. 228 pages. $7.95

DISNEY WORLD AND BEYOND
The Ultimate Family Guidebook
Unique and comprehensive, this handbook to Orlando's theme parks and outlying areas is a must for family travelers. 300 pages. $9.95

DISNEY WORLD AND BEYOND
Family Fun Cards
This innovative "guidebook you can shuffle" covers Orlando's major theme parks with a deck of 90 cards, each describing a different ride. $7.95

About the Author

Ray Riegert is the author of seven travel books, including *Hidden San Francisco and Northern California*. His most popular work, *Hidden Hawaii*, won the coveted Lowell Thomas Travel Journalism Award for Best Guidebook. In addition to his role as publisher of Ulysses Press, he has written for the *Chicago Tribune*, *Saturday Evening Post*, *San Francisco Examiner & Chronicle* and *Travel & Leisure*. A member of the Society of American Travel Writers, he lives in the San Francisco Bay Area with his wife, travel publisher Leslie Henriques, and their son Keith and daughter Alice.

About the Illustrator

Timothy Carroll worked as a graphic designer before turning his talents to illustration. He has illustrated several other Ulysses Press guidebooks, including *Hidden Florida* and *Hidden New England*. His artwork has also appeared in *Esquire*, *GQ*, the *Boston Globe*, *San Francisco Focus*, *Premiere* and the *Washington Post*.